AS COMPUTER SCIENCE FOR AQA UNITS 1 & 2

KEVIN R BOND

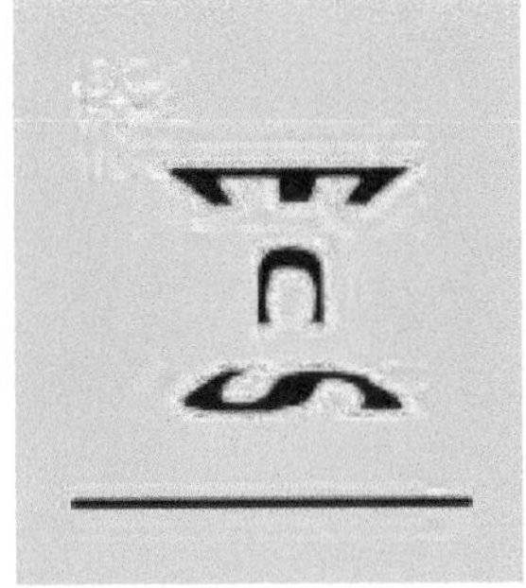

Educational Computing Services Ltd

Structure of the book

The structure of this book follows closely the structure of AQA's AS Computer Science specification for first teaching from September 2015. The content of the book has been constructed with the aim of promoting good teaching and learning, so where relevant practical activities have been suggested and questions posed for the student to answer. The book includes stimulus material to promote discussion and deeper thinking about the subject. Additional material to support teaching and learning will be available from the publisher's website.

About the author

Dr Kevin R Bond is an experienced author. Kevin has 24 years of examining experience. He also has many more years of experience teaching AS and A Level Computing and Computer Science. Before becoming a computer science teacher, he worked in industry as a senior development engineer and systems analyst designing both hardware and software systems.

Published in 2016 by
Educational Computing Services Ltd
42 Mellstock Road
Aylesbury
Bucks
HP21 7NU
United Kingdom
Tel: 01296 433004
e-mail: mail@educational-computing.co.uk

First published in 2016

ISBN 978-0-9927536-3-4

Approval message from AQA

This textbook has been approved by AQA for use with our qualification. This means that we have checked that it broadly covers the specification and we are satisfied with the overall quality. Full details of our approval process can be found on our website.

We approve textbooks because we know how important it is for teachers and students to have the right resources to support their teaching and learning. However, the publisher is ultimately responsible for the editorial control and quality of this book.

Please note that when teaching the AS (7516) course, you must refer to AQA's specification as your definitive source of information. While this book has been written to match the specification, it cannot provide complete coverage of every aspect of the course.

A wide range of other useful resources can be found on the relevant subject pages of our website: aqa.org.uk

Acknowledgements

The author and publisher are grateful to the following for permission to reproduce images, clipart and other copyright material in this book under licence or otherwise:

Chapter 1.1.3

Figure 1.1.3.2 Capstan Shutterstock / 381034510.

Chapter 1.1.8

Figure 1.1.8.1 Rolling dice Shutterstock / 329817896.

Chapter 1.2.1

Figure 1.2.1.2 Head silhouette Shutterstock / 152509136.

Chapter 4.1.2

Figure 4.1.2.1 Ball of wool Shutterstock / 59259781.

Figure 4.1.2.1 Woollen pullover Shutterstock / 85713035.

Table 4.1.2.1 Music stave Shutterstock / 85713035.

Figure 4.1.2.2 Capstan Sutterstock / 381034510.

Task 1 - based on an exercise from CSInside Algorithm Development, CS department, Glasgow university

Chapter 4.1.3

Figure 4.1.3.2 London underground map Reg. User No 16/E/3021/P Pulse Creative Ltd.

Figure 4.1.3.5 Solar panels Shutterstock / 293938154.

Figure 4.1.3.7 Shutterstock / 236943415 / 269590388 / 403734298 / 49052899.

Chapter 4.1.7

Figure 4.1.7.1 ATM Queue Shutterstock / 276171293.

Figure 4.1.7.2 Queue of people in silhouette Shutterstock / 253319245.

Figure 4.1.7.8 Stack of books Shutterstock / 976714136.

Chapter 4.1.8

Figure 4.1.8.3 © Crown copyright 2016 OS 100057707 and courtesy of Anquet Technology Ltd.

Chapter 4.1.10

Figure 4.1.10.1 Lego bricks Shutterstock / 197086964.

Chapter 5.1.1

Figure 1.1.1 "Late Babylonian clay tablet: table of numerals representing lunar longitudes", image ID 00851897001, British Museum.

Pages 1, 2: Clip art
www.123rf.com: green apple: 123rf / 14199537; red apple: 123rf / 1419906; banana: 123rf / 39056131; orange: 123rf / 38547844; purse: 123rf / 27347756.

Chapter 5.1.2

Page 4: Thermometer - "Thermometre froid a plat" Fotolia / 11368653 © Albachiara

Page 5: Cake - 123rf / 33382329 (www.123rf.com).

Chapter 5.1.4

Page 12: Greek character - 123rf / 32698394 (www.123rf.com).

Chapter 5.1.5

Page 14: Road going off into the desert - www.canstockphoto / csp9388362.

Chapter 5.1.7

Page 20: Dreaming sheep - Shutterstock / 110338271; Page 20: Ruler - Shutterstock / 198850166.

Chapter 5.2.1

Figure 2.1.1 Microsoft® Windows® 7 Calculator screenshot used with permission from Microsoft, Microsoft and Windows are either registered trademarks or trademarks of Microsoft Corporation in the United States and/or other countries; Figure 2.1.4 Microsoft® Windows® 7 Device Manager version 6.1.7600.16385 screenshot used with permission from Microsoft.

Chapter 5.3.1

Page 34: Penguins - Shutterstock / 114208987; Page 34: Peacock - 123rf / 36970936 (www.123rf.com).

Page 34/35: Highway code signs used in question 2, and page 35 are based on Highway Code signs, © Crown copyright 2007, and are reproduced under Open Government Licence v3.0.

Page 35: Tree rings - Shutterstock / 97674011; Figure 3.1.4 red apples - 123rf / 1419906 (www.123rf.com).

Page 36: pound coin showing head - 123rf / 20150613_ml (www.123rf.com).

Page 36: pound coin showing tail - 123rf / 35831780 (www.123rf.com).

Chapter 5.3.2

Figure 3.2.2 Microsoft® Windows 7 command line window screenshot used with permission from Microsoft.

Page 41: Apple® MacBookPro® and OS X® are trademarks of Apple Inc., registered in the U.S. and other countries.

Chapter 5.4.3

Page 52: CPU - Shutterstock / 222009121.

Chapter 5.5

Figure 5.5.1 Shutterstock / 157001045; Figure 5.5.2 Shutterstock / 1226401; Figure 5.5.3 Shutterstock / 185237537; Figure 5.5.5 123rf / 31206024 (www.123rf.com); Figure 5.5.6 123rf / 32168839 (www.123rf.com)

Chapter 5.6.2

Figure 5.6.2.2 adapted with permission of Engineering Toolbox from www.engineeringtoolbox.com/air-altitude-pressure-d462.html with kind permission of the editor.

Chapter 5.6.8

Figure 5.6.8.14 "A one-time pad" - reproduced with kind permission of Paul Reuvers, Crypto Museum (www.cryptomuseum.com).

Figure 5.6.8.16 (a) "Image generated from random numbers generated by the PHP rand() function on Microsoft Windows." idea for this courtesy of Bo Allen, http://boallen.com/ who kindly provided permission to use his PHP script to generate this image.

Figure 5.6.8.17 "Gilbert Vernam" - image in public domain.

Figure 5.6.8.19(a) "Plaintext image to be encrypted using a one-time pad." - Mathematician & computer scientist Claude Shannon, Getty Image library, image 5337874

Chapter 8.1

Page 258 "Information Technology alone has this capacity to both automate and reflect information (informate)" - Professor Shoshana Zuboff, Charles Edward Wilson Professor of Business Administration at the Harvard Business School.

Page 261 Memories for life: Page 99 "The Spy in the Coffee Machine" © Kieron O'Hara and Nigel Shadbolt 2008, reproduced with permission of the publishers Oneworld Publications.

Page 260 Case study: "From Forbes.com, 16/02/2012 © 2012 Forbes LLC. All rights reserved. Used by permission and protected by the Copyright Laws of the United States. The printing, copying, redistribution, or retransmission of this Content without express written permission is prohibited." http://www.forbes.com/sites/kashmirhill/2012/02/16/how-target-figured-out-a-teen-girl-was-pregnant-before-her-father-did/

Contents

How to use this book

The structure and content of this textbook maps to sections 3.1 to 3.9 of AQA's AS Computer Science specification (7516). For example, the chapter number 5.1.1 corresponds to specification section 3.5.1.1. The chapter title is **Number systems: Natural numbers**. The chapters in the book do not use the leading 3 as this designates **Subject content – AS** in the specification.

Flipped classroom

This textbook has been written with the flipped classroom approach very much in mind. This approach reverses the conventional classroom lesson and homework model of teaching. Instead, chapters in this textbook should be used to prepare for a lesson so that classroom-time can be devoted to exercises, projects, and discussions.

The features in this book include:

Learning objectives

Learning objectives linked to the requirements of the specification are specified at the beginning of each chapter.

Key concept — Concepts that you will need to understand and to be able to define or explain are highlighted in blue and emboldened, e.g. **Integers**. The same concepts appear in the glossary for ease of reference.

Key principle — Principles that you will need to understand and to be able to define or explain are highlighted in blue and emboldened, e.g. **Abstraction**. The same principles appear in the glossary for ease of reference.

Key fact **Key point** **Key term**

Facts, points and terms that are useful to know because they aid in understanding concepts and principles are highlighted in blue and emboldened, e.g. **Whole number:** Whole number is another name for an integer number.

Information **Background**

References information that has the potential to assist and contribute to a student's learning, e.g. Read Unit 1 section 4.2.2 for more background on sets and set comprehension. Background knowledge that could also contribute to a student's learning.

Did you know? **Extension Material**

"Did you know?" - interesting facts to enliven learning. "Extension Material" - content that lies beyond the specification.

Task — Activity to deepen understanding and reinforce learning.

Programming tasks — Practical activity involving the use of a programming language to deepen understanding and reinforce learning of concepts and principles.

Questions — Short questions that probe and develop your understanding of concepts and principles as well as creating opportunities to apply and reinforce your knowledge and skills.

Web links for this book

The URLs of all websites referenced in this book are recorded at www.educational-computing.co.uk/aqacs/aslevelcs.html

Educational Computing Services are not responsible for third party content online, there may be some changes to this content that are outside our control. If you find that a Web link doesn't work please email webadmin@educational-computing.co.uk with the details and we will endeavour to fix the problem or to provide an alternative.

Introduction

If you are reading this book then you will already have chosen to be a part of an exciting future, for Computer Science is at the heart of an information processing revolution. This revolution applies not just to seeking patterns of meaning in data accumulated on an unprecedented scale by the huge growth in connected computing devices but also the realisation that all forms of life are controlled by genetic codes. Genetic codes are instructions in a procedural information sense which together with the environment that they inhabit control and guide the development of organisms.

Computer scientists concern themselves with

- representations of information in patterns of symbols, known as data or data representations,
- the most appropriate representation for this data
- the procedures in the form of instructions that can transform this data into new forms of information.

The procedures themselves are also a form of information of an instructional kind.

The key process in Computer Science is **abstraction** which means building models which represent aspects of behaviour in the real-world which are of interest. For example, if we wanted to build an automated recommendation system for an online book store, we might choose to record the types of book and number of each type purchased as well as details that identify the respective customer.

Computer Science is not alone in building abstractions, mathematics and the natural sciences also build abstractions but their models only serve to describe and explain whereas Computer Science must, in addition, perform actions on and with the data that has been modelled if it is to solve problems. These actions are described by **algorithms** or step-by-step instructions which form what is called the **automation** stage of problem solving. Whilst it is true that automation of tasks existed before Computer Science, their nature involved concrete, real-world objects, e.g. the Jacquard loom, not informational abstractions such as an online book recommendation system.

So far it has not been necessary to mention digital computers. Digital computers are just the current means by which algorithms can be implemented to execute on data. Both algorithms and the models on which they act need to be **implemented** in the form of code or instructions that a digital computer can understand, i.e. a computer program. The first part of this book is largely about the fundamentals of programming, data structures, software development and theory of computation.

The second part covers how data is represented and communicated between devices, the logic gate circuits that enable computing devices to perform operations and to store information. It covers the fundamentals of computer organisation and architecture, the structure and role of the processor, the language of the machine, binary (machine code) and how it is used to program the hardware directly. This leads on to external hardware devices and then the fundamentals of networking.

It is right that having journeyed through the fundamentals, the a student should have an opportunity to discuss, using hypotheticals and case studies, what kind of philosophy of information is appropriate for any advanced information society. This is explored in the section Consequences of uses of computing where guiding principles of behaviour are explored.

1 Fundamentals of programming

1.1 Programming

Learning objectives:

- *Understand the concept of a data type*
- *Understand and use the following appropriately:*
  - *real/float*
  - *Boolean*
  - *character*
  - *string*
  - *date/time*
  - *records (or equivalent)*
  - *arrays (or equivalent)*
- *Define and use user-defined data types based on language-defined (built-in) data types*

Information

A bit is a binary digit which is either 0 or 1.

A bit pattern is just a sequence of bits, e.g. 0100100001101001.

The bit pattern

0100100001101001

in memory box 1 can be interpreted as representing an unsigned integer with decimal value 18537.

The bit pattern

0110100001101111

in memory box 2 can be interpreted as representing an unsigned integer with decimal value 26735.

The bit pattern in memory box 3 in Figure 1.1.2

1011000011011000

can be interpreted as representing an unsigned integer with decimal value 45272.

1.1.1 Data types

Introduction to programming

Any system that computes can be described as executing sequences of actions, with an action being any relevant change in the state of the system.

For example, the following orders or commands change the states of register boxes labelled 1, 2 and memory box labelled 3:

Action 1: FETCH the number in memory box 1 and place in register box 1

Action 2: FETCH the number in memory box 2 and place in register box 2

Action 3: ADD contents of register box 1 to contents of register box 2

Action 4: STORE the answer in memory box 3.

Figure 1.1.1 shows the starting state and the impending actions. *Figure 1.1.2* shows the final state after the above actions have been carried out. See the information panel for help in interpreting the bit patterns as unsigned integers.

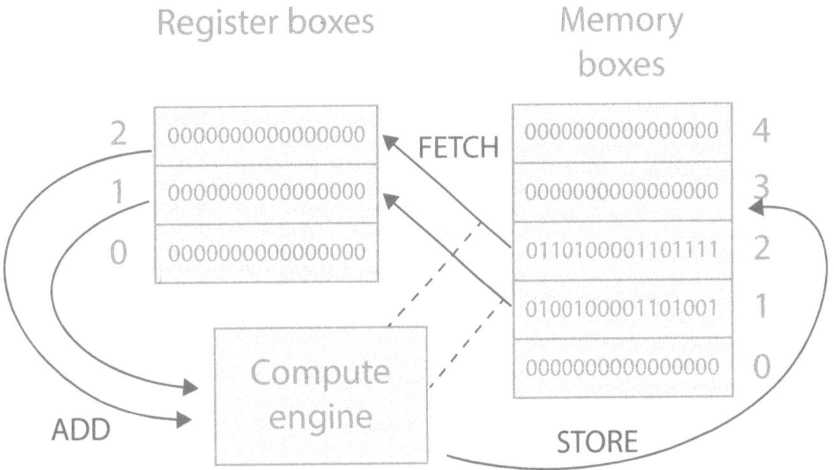

Figure 1.1.1 Starting state of the machine

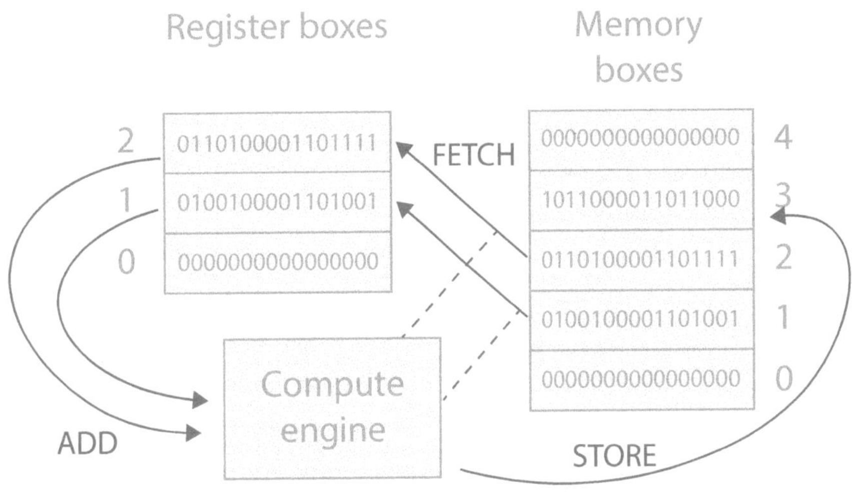

Figure 1.1.2 Final state of the machine

Information

Programming languages which enforce data typing - a typed language - are employed because they can prevent an expression from being used which will lead to a data type error when the program is executed, e.g. 4 + 'D'. Data type errors may be detected at compile time or runtime.

Data types

What is a data type?

Note that in *Figure 1.1.1* and *Figure 1.1.2*, the register and memory boxes contain bit patterns consisting of zeros and ones.

The arithmetic operation ADD performed by the compute engine treats these bit patterns as numbers. The bit patterns have been **data typed** with the meaning number, specifically the number type (positive) **integer**. We say that the **data type** of these bit patterns is (positive) integer.

This isn't the only possible interpretation that can be placed on these bit patterns:

> The text "Hi" and the integer number 18537 can both be represented with the same zeros and ones in a digital computer (0100100001101001).
> One interpretation of this bit pattern is a **string** "Hi" consisting of two characters 'H' and 'i', and another is a **16-bit integer**. See *Chapter 5.5* for the ASCII coding scheme for characters such as 'H'.

Questions

1 What data type do you think the following values belong to
(a) "Have a nice day" (b) 45

Key term

Sequence:
A sequence is simply an ordered collection of things, e.g. a b c ... or the sequence of digits in a telephone number, 433004.

What do the bits mean?

This is one role performed by a **data type**: to establish what the bits mean.

Unless we know the meaning the only things that we see in a computer is a datum, i.e. 0s and 1s.

A bit pattern is referred to as a datum.

Formally, a **datum** is a finite sequence of 0s and 1s, e.g. 0100100001101001.

Key point

Meaning of datum:
A datum is a finite sequence of 0s and 1s, e.g. 0100100001101001.

Computations operate on values and produce other values as results,

e.g. 5 + 6 = 11.

The meaning of **value** is a **datum** together with its **meaning** or **interpretation**. Therefore, every value must have a **data type** - datum + meaning.

Key point

Meaning of value:
The meaning of value is a datum together with its interpretation.

For example, the data type of *whole number* values such as 5, 6 and 11 is integer.

The following data types are associated with the given example values shown below

- integer, e.g. value 18537
- real number, e.g. value 3.142
- character, e.g. value 'H'
- string, e.g. value "Hi"
- Boolean, e.g. value True

Specifically, a data type is a correspondence between a mathematical entity such as integer (see Chapter 5.1.2) and a set of datums, e.g. all datums of length 16 bits (0000000000000000 to 1111111111111111 in binary or 0 to 65535 in decimal).

Questions

 Give two possible interpretations of the bit pattern 0100100001101001

What operations can be performed with the data type?

Computations within a digital computer are carried out on data in the form of bit patterns consisting of 0s and 1s.

Another role of data type is to define which computations/operations may be carried out on the bit patterns.

For example, if the interpretation of a datum is number then the arithmetic operations ADD, SUBTRACT, MULTIPLY, DIVIDE applied to number values make sense but if the interpretation of a datum is string of characters then arithmetic operations ADD, SUBTRACT, MULTIPLY and DIVIDE don't make sense. ADD would have to be redefined as a string operation called concatenation.

For example, adding one string "Hi" to another "ho" produces the single string "Hiho" which is the bit pattern for "Hi" followed by the bit pattern for "ho." But what does "Hi" divided by "ho" mean?

If the operation is an arithmetic one then adding the number 18537 (0100100001101001), which has the same bit pattern as "Hi", to the number 26735 (0110100001101111), which has the same bit pattern as "ho", produces the expected result: number 45272 (1011000011011000) if we interpret the bit patterns as numbers.

However, the result of adding the number 18537 to the string "ho" is not defined and therefore should be reported as an error.

Enforcing data typing enables outcomes which are undefined to be detected and prevented from occurring.

Questions

 Is the following addition of two values a valid operation

"two" + 3?

How many bits are allocated to a data type?

When a bit pattern is interpreted as an integer we are mapping this machine integer onto a subset of mathematical integers. A machine integer is a datum whose data type represents some finite subset of the mathematical integers. Mathematical integers are positive and negative whole numbers and zero. However, the set of mathematical integers is infinite but a machine's ability to

Key point

Data type:

A data type is a correspondence between a mathematical entity such as integer (see Unit 2 - Chapter 5.1.2) and a set of datums, e.g. all datums of length 16 bits (0000000000000000 to 1111111111111111 in binary or 0 to 65535 in decimal).

A bit pattern (datum) interpreted as an integer is a mapping from a (digital) machine integer onto a subset of mathematical integers.

Key term

Set:

A set is an unordered collection of different things, e.g. the set of all students in my computer science class: John Smith, Mary Brown, Kamal Patel, Sui Ling, ...

Key concept

Data type:

A data type

1. is a method of interpreting a bit pattern
2. defines which computations / operations may be carried out on the bit patterns
3. specifies the number of bits allocated to each datum.

store bit patterns is not. All computing machines have a finite memory. This means that we must specify a finite number of bits for machine integers.

This is the third role of a data type: specifying the number of bits allocated to each datum. A fixed number of bits is therefore allocated to each datum of a data type, e.g. 32 bits.

Questions

 4 What is meant by data type?

Integer data type

Signed 32-bit (4-byte) integers range in value from -2,147,483,648 through 2,147,483,647. Values in this range represent mathematical integers exactly. The range is clearly a subset of the range of mathematical integers. Mathematical integers outside this range cannot be represented.

Questions

 5 Is $2^{2^{100}}$ in the integer range 0 to 2,147,483,647?

Floating point numbers (real/float data type)

Most computers store and manipulate real numbers such as 3.142 using the IEEE 754 floating point standard.

IEEE floating point numbers can be very large or very small on a scale from the size of galaxies to the size of sub-atomic particles.

Floating-point numbers are little more than scientific notation encoded as bits. Any real number N that can be put in scientific notation can also be put in the form

$$N = s \times m \times 10^{e}$$

where s is −1 or 1, m is a natural number, and e is an integer.

For example, -1.543×10^{-10} represents a real number in scientific form. To put this in the above form, the decimal point is moved 3 places to the right, and 3 is subtracted from the e to get $-1 \times 1543 \times 10^{-13}$.

A number N's significant digits are represented by m either exactly or approximately. Significant digits define the precision of a number.

Digital computers operate with powers of two rather than powers of ten so floating-point numbers that represent real numbers are put in the form

$$N = s \times m \times 2^{e}$$

Key term

Integer data type:
A machine integer is a datum whose data type represents some finite subset of the mathematical integers.
A fixed number of bits are allocated to the datum, e.g. 32 bits.
Signed 32-bit (4-byte) integers range in value from
-2,147,483,648 through
2,147,483,647.
The integer data type is free of rounding errors. Mathematical integers are represented exactly. However, this type has a limited range.

Did you know?

Integer data type:
When the range is exceeded integer types wrap around, e.g. when 1 is added to the integer value 2,147,483,647 it becomes -2,147,483,648 if the data type is signed 32-bit integer.

Key term

Floating point data type:
Computers store and manipulate real numbers such as 3.142 using the IEEE 754 floating point standard (knowledge of its detail is not required for AS or A Level).
Floating-point numbers are little more than scientific notation encoded as bits.
Floating-point numbers that represent real numbers are put in the form

$$N = s \times m \times 2^{e}$$

where s is −1 or 1, m is a natural number, and e is an integer.
A number's significant digits are represented by m either exactly or approximately.
IEEE floating point numbers can be very large or very small on a scale from the size of galaxies to the size of sub-atomic particles.

Floating-point numbers represent the real numbers of mathematics. However, floating-point numbers are an approximate representation of these mathematical real numbers because there is

- an infinite number of numbers between any two numbers on the real number line.
- a finite number of values in any floating point data type because we are limited to a finite number of bits for each datum.

Some of the levels of precision (number of bits for each datum[1]) present in IEEE 754 floating point standard are as follows

- 16-bit: Half - half precision
- 32-bit: Single - single precision
- 64-bit: Double - double precision

If single precision (32 bits) is used the

- minimum positive value is $2^{-126} \approx 1.18 \times 10^{-38}$
- maximum positive value is $(1 - 2^{-24}) \times 2^{128} \approx 3.402823 \times 10^{38}$.

All integers with six or fewer significant decimal digits can be converted to a single precision IEEE 754 floating point value without loss of precision. Some integers up to nine significant decimal digits can be converted without loss of precision, but no more than nine significant decimal digits can be stored.

The name real or the name float is typically used as the data type name for values expressed in floating point form.

Key fact

Significant digits:

123456, 123456000, 0.00123456 all have the same number of significant decimal digits. Significant digits define the precision of a number.

Key term

Real/float:

The name *real* or the name *float* are typically used for the data type name for values expressed in floating point form.

Questions

6 (a) Calculate $(x - y) \times (x + y)$ rounded off to 6 significant digits where x = 293452 and y = 153761 using Windows Calculator or similar.

(b) Calculate x^2 rounded off to 6 significant digits where x = 293452.

(c) Calculate y^2 rounded off to 6 significant digits where y = 153761.

(d) Calculate $x^2 - y^2$ rounded off to 6 significant digits.

If the calculations were done by representing each integer value with a single precision IEEE 754 floating point number, why would the first calculation $(x - y) \times (x + y)$ differ from the second $x^2 - y^2$ even though algebraically $x^2 - y^2 = (x - y) \times (x + y)$?

7 Data types integer (32-bit) and float (32-bit single precision IEEE 754) are available. State which data type could be used for each of the following decimal values without loss of precision and explain why

(a) 45 (b) -2,147,483,648 (c) 3, 124, 560, 000

8 Data types integer (32-bit) and float (32-bit single precision IEEE 754) are available. State which data type could be used for each of the following decimal values and explain why

(a) 3.142 (b) 1.18×10^{-36} (c) 2.46215×10^{38}

---

1 Precision is determined by how many datum bits are reserved for significant digits, m. One bit is reserved for the sign and several bits are reserved for the exponent, e.

Key term

Boolean data type:
Two values only belong to the data type Boolean:

- the truth value True
- the truth value False.

Boolean data type

The statement "It is raining" is either true or false.
Two values only belong to the data type Boolean:

- the truth value True
- the truth value False.

Only one bit is needed to represent a Boolean truth value but in practice multiple bits are normally used.
Typically, the datum or bit pattern 1111111111111111 is used to represent the truth value True in 16 bits (32 1's in 32 bits, 64 1's in 64 bits and so on).
Typically, the datum or bit pattern 0000000000000000 is used to represent the truth value False in 16 bits (32 1's in 32 bits, 64 1's in 64 bits and so on).

Questions

9 What is the data type of the result of evaluating the following expressions
(a) 5 > 6 (b) 5 < 6 (c) 7 = 7?

Character data type

A character is a letter of the alphabet (upper or lower case) or the digits 0 to 9, or punctuation symbols or some special symbols, e.g. / .

Information

Extended-ASCII:
Extended-ASCII uses 8 bits to encode characters.

A digital machine can only understand sequences of 1's and 0's. Therefore, to denote or represent a character value, e.g. A, inside a computer we must use a bit pattern. One method of allocating bit patterns to characters is the ASCII code system, another is Unicode. ASCII uses seven bits whilst Unicode uses either 16 bits (UTF-16), 32 bits (UTF-32) or one to four bytes (UTF-8) where a byte is eight bits - see Chapter 5.5.

The meaning of datum 1000001 is character A if the data type of the datum is character (7-bit ASCII). Straight single or double quotation marks are used to indicate a character value, e.g. 'A' or "A".

Questions

10 Shown below are some 7-bit bit patterns along with their decimal equivalents. Use the ASCII look-up table Table 5.5.1 in Chapter 5.5 to look up the corresponding character value, i.e. the human readable form.
(a) 1011001 (89) (b) 1001000 (72) (c) 1001100 (76)
(d) 1111001 (121)

11 You may use the ASCII look-up table Table 5.5.1 in Chapter 5.5 to help you answer this question.
Do you think that each of the following expressions could be valid, i.e. evaluated successfully? Give your reason for each of your answers.
(a) 'B' > 'A' (b) '5' < '7' (c) '6' = '6'

String data type

Figure 1.1.3 shows beads on a string with each bead labelled with a character value (the space character value corresponds to the unlabelled bead).

Figure 1.1.4 shows beads on a string with each bead labelled with the corresponding character datum (7-bit ASCII), e.g. 1110011 is datum with value 's'.

Borrowing from the beads on a string analogy, a string is just a sequence of characters, e.g. "A string". Straight double or single quotation marks are used to indicate a string value. The corresponding sequence of bit patterns or datum for the string value "A string" is

1000001 0100000 1110011 1110100 1110010 1101001 1101110 1100111

if each character of this string is represented in 7-bit ASCII.

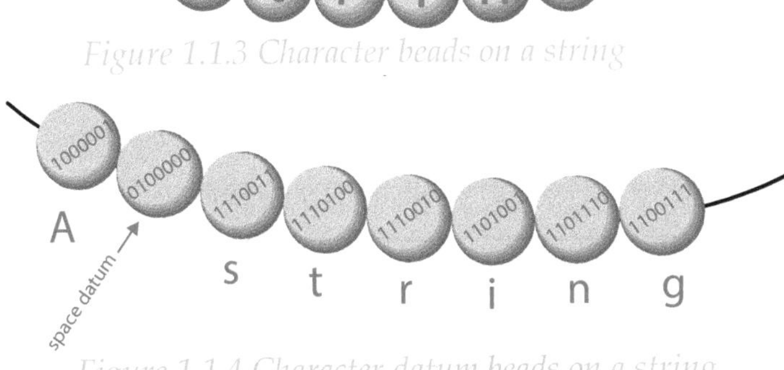

Figure 1.1.3 Character beads on a string

Figure 1.1.4 Character datum beads on a string

Key point

Meaning of value:
Value = datum + its meaning

Datum:
A datum is a finite sequence of 0s and 1s, e.g. 0100100001101001.

Questions

12 Why might a string data type be useful?

Data types Integer, Real/float, Boolean, Character, and String for various programming languages

At the lowest level, as far as computer science is concerned, all data (plural of datum) in digital computers is represented by bits packaged into bytes (8 bits) and words (multiples of 8 bits).

A bit (0 or 1) is a convenient notation that represents which of two observable physical states holds. For example, bit value 1 might mean that the observable output of an electrical circuit making up an element of the computer's memory is 5 volts, and bit value 0 might mean that it is 0 volts. The physical state of this element of the computer's memory is thus either 5 volts or 0 volts.

Information that is stored in a computer system is represented by physical states.

Time and energy are needed to sense (read) or alter (write) these physical states.

This means that a bit is not capable of an existence which can be manipulated until it is recorded in a physical medium where a machine can get at it.

The bits become real objects when recorded in a computer's various memories.

However, any real digital computer has a limited or finite amount of memory in which to record these bits, i.e. it has a finite number of physical states to choose from (the physical states of all memory bits combined). This is the point at which computing deviates from classical mathematics which has no such limitation.

The computer programs that you write in this course will control physical processes involving matter and energy at the level of atoms and electrons but you will rely upon computing abstractions to hide much of this from you (until you hear the fan that keeps a CPU cool switch on).

Programming languages provide abstractions to make life easier for you as a programmer. You have now studied one such abstraction, data typing.

Each programming language that supports explicit data typing has its own names for its built-in data types.

For example, C# has a data type with the name int which represents a subset of the mathematical integers.

This data type int covers the range of integer values from -2,147,483,648 to 2,147,483,647 with each datum in this range represented by 32 bits (physically represented by different energy states of about 10^{24} atoms).
Pascal has a data type with the appropriate name real which represents a subset of real numbers (formed from the union of the set of rational numbers and the set of irrational numbers) from mathematics. Python, Java and C# use the name float which reflects in the name how real numbers are stored in a digital computer, i.e. as floating point numbers.
Table 1.1.1 shows the names for some of the data types that represent integers, real numbers, truth values, characters and strings in the given languages.

Language	Integer	Real/float	Boolean	Character	String
C#	**int**: 32-bit signed two's complement integer	**float**: 32-bit IEEE 754 floating point **double:** 64-bit IEEE 754 floating point	**bool**: true/false	**char**	**string**
Java	**int**: 32-bit signed two's complement integer	**float**: single-precision 32-bit IEEE 754 floating point **double:** 64-bit IEEE 754 floating point	**boolean**: true/false	**char**: single 16-bit Unicode character	**String**
Pascal	**Integer**	**Real**	**Boolean**: True/False	**Char**	**String**
Delphi	**Integer:** 32-bit two's complement integer -2147483648 to 2147483647	**Double**: 64-bit IEEE 754 floating point supporting approximately 15 decimal digits of precision in a range from 2.23×10^{-308} to 1.79×10^{308} (Real available as well)	**Boolean**: True/False	**Char**: holds a single character in 8 bits. **AnsiChar:** character type guaranteed to be 8 bits in size	**String**
Python	**int**: 32-bit signed two's complement integer	**float**: double-precision 64-bit IEEE 754 floating point	**bool**: True/False	**unicode**	**str**
VB.Net	**Integer**: 32-bit signed two's complement integer	**Double**	**Boolean**: True/False	**Char**: 2 bytes	**String:** 0 to approximately 2 billion Unicode characters (but depends on platform)

Table 1.1.1 Integer, Real/float, Boolean, Character, String data types for the given programming languages

Date/time

Values may be dates, e.g. 28/05/2016, or a time of day, e.g. 15:35:16. Internally, these are just bit patterns. For these bit patterns to have the meaning date or the meaning time of day, the bit patterns must be data typed. This requires a data type date and a data type time or a combination of the two, a data type datetime.

Table 1.1.2 shows the names of these data types[2] in the programming languages, C#, Java, Pascal, Delphi, Python, VB.Net.

Language	
C#	**DateTime:** eight bytes — two four-byte integers. The DateTime value type represents dates and times with values ranging from 00:00:00 (midnight), January 1, 0001 Anno Domini (Common Era) through 11:59:59 P.M., December 31, 9999 A.D. (C.E.) in the Gregorian calendar. Four bytes are allocated to date and four bytes to time. Time values are measured in 100-nanosecond units called ticks, and a particular date is the number of ticks since 12:00 midnight, January 1, 0001 A.D. (C.E.) in the Gregorian Calendar (excluding ticks that would be added by leap seconds).
Java	Java SE8 package java.time **LocalDate, LocalTime, LocalDateTime:** represent date and time from the context of the observer, e.g. local calendar or clock
Pascal	**TDateTime:** data type double, with the date as the integral part, and time as fractional part. The date is stored as the number of days since 30 December 1899.
Delphi	**TDateTime:** data type double, with the date as the integral part, and time as fractional part. The date is stored as the number of days since 30 December 1899.
Python	**datetime.date:** An idealized naive (not aware of time zone and daylight saving time information) date, assuming the current Gregorian calendar always was, and always will be, in effect. Attributes: year, month, and day. **datetime.time:** An idealized time, independent of any particular day, assuming that every day has exactly 24*60*60 seconds (there is no notion of "leap seconds"). Attributes: hour, minute, second, microsecond, and tzinfo.
VB.Net	See C#

Table 1.1.2 Date and Time data types for the given programming languages

Questions

13 What data type could be used for the value of a student's date of birth?

2 C#, VB.Net, Python, Java datetime, date and time data types are actually classes but this requires an understanding of object-oriented programming (OOP) to explain. AS Computer Science does not cover OOP.

Records

Figure 1.1.5 shows a card index consisting of cards on which information has been recorded. Each card contains a record of something. In *Figure 1.1.5*, it is a **record** of a person's name, address, latitude, longitude, no of rooms in their dwelling, whether the dwelling has loft insulation or not, and Council Tax band. It is intended that the card shown will be filed in the section of the card index labelled 'B'. We can say that the card index contains a file of records ordered by initial letter of surname. Notice that the information on the card in *Figure 1.1.5* is subdivided into an area for the surname, an area for the forename, and so on. Each area is called a **field of the record**. Each **field has a name**, e.g. surname, and a value, e.g. BOND.

We have learned that every value has a data type. The data type of each value recorded in the given record is as follows

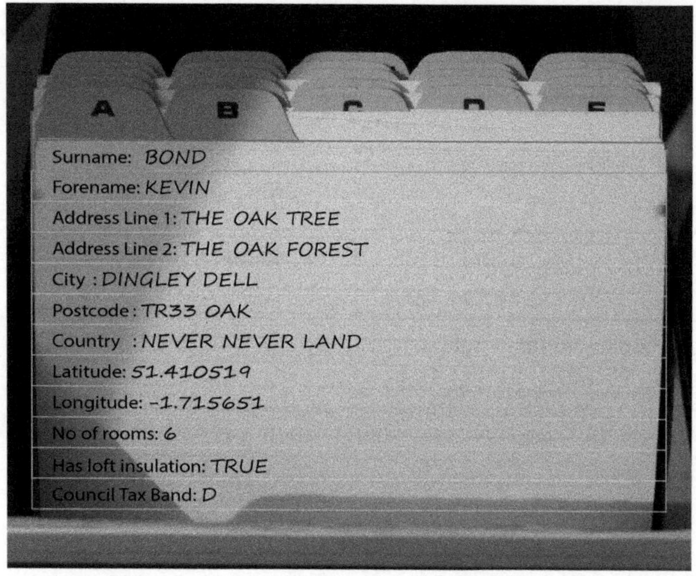

Figure 1.1.5 Card index showing one record

BOND *String*
KEVIN *String*
THE OAK TREE *String*
THE OAK FOREST *String*
DINGLEY DELL *String*
TR33 OAK *String*
NEVER NEVER LAND *String*
51.410519 *Real*
-1.715651 *Real*
6 *Integer*
TRUE *Boolean*
D *Character*

To record the information about the person with surname BOND in a machine, the human readable values of the record are replaced with their data type equivalent bit patterns. At the machine level the information becomes a sequence of bits as follows

10000101001111100111010001001001011100010111011101001001100111 0. . .

SURNAME *FORENAME*

Key term

Record data type:
A record data type is a data type composed of related data of various data types.
A record data type is divided into named fields.

If we view the entire bit pattern for the person's record and use the "**method of interpreting a bit pattern definition of data type**", we now have a new data type which has **structure** consisting of **named fields** and their **corresponding data types**. This new data type is called a **record data type** - see *Figure 1.1.6*. This record data type consists of 12 fields.

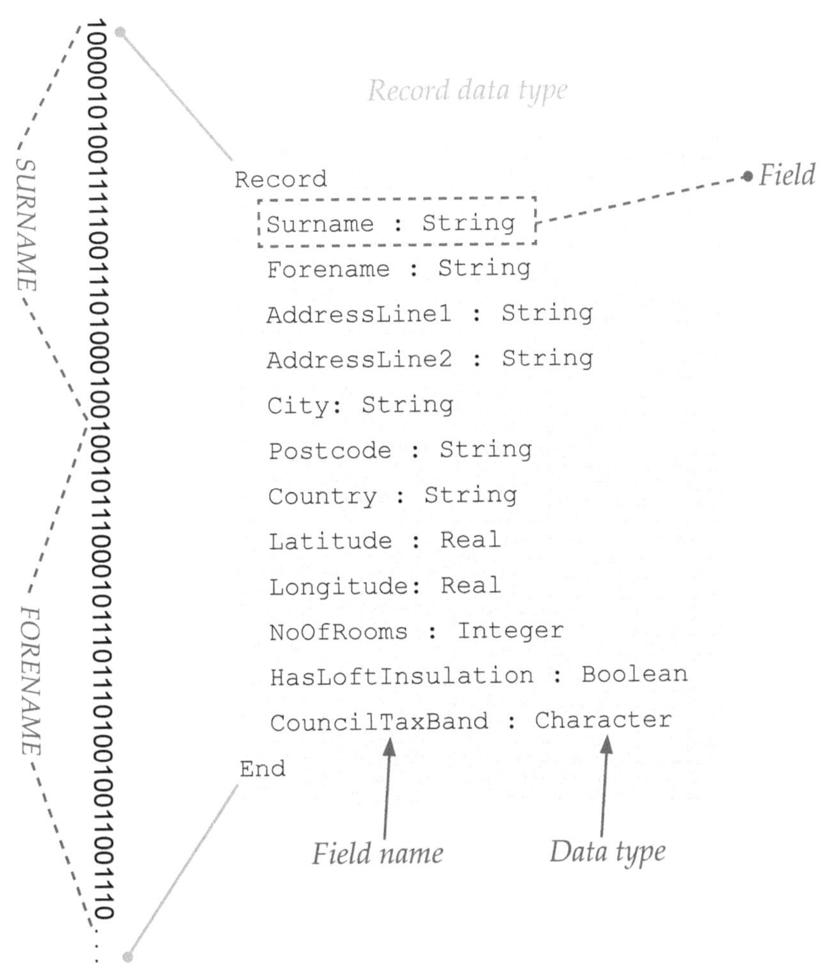

Record data type
Record
Surname : String
Forename : String
AddressLine1 : String
AddressLine2 : String
City: String
Postcode : String
Country : String
Latitude : Real
Longitude: Real
NoOfRooms : Integer
HasLoftInsulation : Boolean
CouncilTaxBand : Character
End
Field
Field name
Data type
SURNAME
FORENAME
1000010100111100111010001001001011100010111011101001001001110...

Figure 1.1.6 Record data type which imposes meaning to bit pattern consisting of values surname, forename, etc.

The record data type is a data type in which the constituent parts of a bit pattern may have different meanings, e.g. string, integer, real, etc.

The higher level view is:

> **a record data type is a data type composed of related data of various data types.**

Table 1.1.3 shows how record data types can be defined in the programming languages Pascal/Delphi, C#, Python, Java, and VB.Net.

Questions

14 Using the data types integer, real, character, Boolean, and string, define a record data type which will enable the following details of a book to be recorded:
Title, ISBN, whether in stock or not, number of pages, price, category which may be fiction (F) or nonfiction (N).

Pascal/Delphi	C#

`TExam = Record`
`        Name : String;`
`        ExamScore : Integer;`
`        ExamGrade : Char;`
`        Resit : Boolean;`
`        MeanGCSEScore : Real;`
`      End;`
	`struct Exam`
	`{`
	`  public string name;`
	`  public int ExamScore;`
	`  public char ExamGrade;`
	`  public bool Resit;`
	`  public float MeanGCSEScore;`
	`};`

Python	**Java**

`class exam(object):`
`  def __init__(name,examscore,examgrade,resit,meangcsescore)`
`    self.name = name`
`    self.examscore = examscore`
`    self.examgrade = examgrade`
`    self.resit = resit`
`    self.meangcsescore = meangcsescore`
	`class Exam {`
	`  String name;`
	`  int examScore;`
	`  char examGrade;`
	`  boolean resit;`
	`  float meanGCSEScore;`
	`}`

VB.Net	

`Structure exam`
`    Public name As String`
`    Public examScore As Integer`
`    Public examGrade As Char`
`    Public resit As Boolean`
`    Public meanGCSEScore As Double`
`End Structure`	

Table 1.1.3 Defining the record data type in various programming languages

Arrays

When a number of similar data items are put alongside each other and treated as a unit the result is an **array data structure**. For example, temperature readings recorded over a twelve hour period as shown in *Figure 1.1.7*.

Figure 1.1.7 Temperature readings gathered and recorded over a 12 hour period

The individual values shown in *Figure 1.1.7* are all the same data type **integer**. As a unit the data type is **array of integer**. The unit shown has 12 cells for 12 integer values, one per cell. The data type of the value in each cell is integer. An **array data type** is a (fixed-size if static) **sequential collection of elements** of the **same type**.

In Pascal/Delphi this data type could be defined as follows

```
TArrayOfTemperature = Array[0..11] Of Integer;
```

`Array[0..11]` means that the array has 12 cells labelled 0, 1, 2, 3, . . ., 9, 10, 11. Cell labelling is important because it is the mechanism by which the value in a particular cell is accessed. The name array index is used for a cell label.

The cell data type in the example is integer but cell data types can be any data type supported by the programming language. The only requirement is that every cell must be of the same data type.

Key term

Array data type:
An array data type is a (fixed-size if static) sequential collection of elements of the same type.

Table 1.1.4[3] shows examples of how an array is defined in Pascal/Delphi, C#, Python, Java, and VB.Net. The Python example uses a package called numpy. Numpy is a package used for scientific computing with Python.

Pascal/Delphi	C#
`TArrayOfTemperature = Array[0..11] Of Integer;` `ArrayOfTemperature : TArrayOfTemperature;`	`int [] arrayOfTemperature = new int[12];`
VB.Net	**Java**
`Dim ArrayOfTemperature(12) As Integer`	`int [12] arrayOfTemperature;`
Python	

`import numpy as np`
`>>> arrayoftemperature = np.linspace(0, 11, num=12, dtype=int)`
`>>> arrayoftemperature`
`array([0, 1, 2, 3, 4, 5, 6, 7, 8, 9, 10, 11])`	

Table 1.1.4 Defining an array in various programming languages

Questions

15 What is meant by an array data type?

16 Define an array data type that has 5 cells labelled 0, 1, 2, 3, 4 with cell data type Real. Use the syntax shown on page 341.

Built-in data types

Data types which are already predefined in the programming are called built-in data types.
For example, the following are the names of some built-in data types for the programming language Pascal:

Integer, Real, Boolean, Char, String.

User-defined data types

The built-in data types are often not enough to do what a programmer wants to do. Programming languages allow programmers to build their own data types. These are called user-defined data types.
For example, in Pascal/Delphi an integer subrange data type may be defined as follows

```
Type
  MyFirstSubRangeType = 0..9;
```

Values of this type are restricted to integers in the range 0 to 9.

3 In both Python and C# examples a variable of the desired array type is created

Programming languages that support user-defined data types can prevent expressions with such data typed values from being used if a value occurs outside the permitted range of values when the program is compiled/executed.

The record and array data types that have been covered already are also examples of user-defined data types.

Questions

 17 What is meant by a user-defined data type?

In this chapter you have covered:

- the concept of a data type
- the following data types:
  - real/float
  - Boolean
  - character
  - string
  - date/time
  - records (or equivalent)
  - arrays (or equivalent)
- user-defined data types based on language-defined (built-in) data types

1 Fundamentals of programming

1.1 Programming

Learning objectives:

- *Use, understand and know how the following statement types can be combined in programs:*
    - *variable declaration*
    - *constant declaration*
    - *assignment*
    - *iteration*
    - *selection*
    - *subroutine(procedure/function*
- *Use definite and indefinite iteration, including indefinite iteration with the condition at the start or end of the iterative structure. A theoretical understanding of condition(s) at either end of an iterative structure is required, regardless of whether they are supported by the language being used*
- *Use nested selection and nested iteration structures*
- *Use meaningful identifier names and know why it is important to use them.*

Key concept

Variable:
In programming, a variable can be thought of as a container for a value.
Like a physical container a variable may be empty, in which case we say that its value is undefined.

1.1.2 Programming concepts

Variable declaration

Variable

Data which are subject to change are modelled in a program by variables.
A variable is simply a container in which a value may be stored for subsequent manipulation within a program - *Figure 1.1.2.1*.

Figure 1.1.2.1 shows the value 6 about to be stored in variable x represented by the yellow container

The stored value may be changed by the program as it executes its instructions, hence the use of the term "variable" for the container.

Under the bonnet, the container is realised as one or more reserved memory locations in the RAM of the machine.

Variable declaration

A **variable declaration** is one way of causing a variable to be created.

For example, in Pascal/Delphi, an integer variable, x, may be declared as follows

```
Var
  x : Integer;
```

The amount of reserved memory allocated to a variable and what is allowed to be stored in this reserved memory depend upon its data type.

This declaration reserves a **named space** in memory (RAM) for a value of data type `Integer`. The space is named `x` and the amount of RAM is four bytes because that is what Pascal's `Integer` data type specifies[1].

By assigning different data types to each variable, *integers, numbers with a fractional part, characters, strings, arrays, records* and *other entities,* may be stored in these variables.

In some languages, e.g. Python, variables do not need an explicit declaration for memory space to be reserved. The declaration happens automatically when a value is assigned to a variable. Values in Python are strongly typed but variables are not.

---

1 It is implementation dependent but four bytes is typical.

Key concept

Variable declaration:
A variable declaration is one way of causing a variable to be created.

Key point

Modelling data by variables:
Data which are subject to change are modelled by variables.

Key concept

Constant:
In programming, data which never change are modelled in a program by constants. This means stating their values explicitly.
To make a program easier to read, understand and maintain, a constant is given a symbolic name which can be used throughout the program whenever the value of the constant is required.

Questions

1. What is a variable?
2. What is a variable declaration?
3. What is a constant declaration?

Initialising variables

It is common practice to initialise a variable when it is declared.
For example, in Pascal/Delphi

```
Var
  x : Integer = 6;
```

In C#, an integer variable, x, may be declared and initialised as follows

```
int x = 6;
```

In Java, an integer variable, x, may be declared and initialised as follows

```
int x = 6;
```

In VB.Net, an integer variable, x, may be declared and initialised as follows

```
Dim x As Integer = 6
```

Constant declaration

Some of the data used in programs never change. For example, the ratio of the circumference of a circle to its diameter which is approximately 3.142.

Data which never change are modelled in a program by constants.

This means stating their values explicitly. To make a program easier to read, understand and change, a constant is given a **symbolic name** which can be used throughout the program whenever the value of the constant is required.

For example, in Pascal/Delphi a constant for the value 3.142 can be defined using the language keyword `Const` as follows

Language keyword ⟶ `Const`

```
Pi = 3.1.42;
```

Symbolic name for constant

In C# the symbolic name by convention is in uppercase and can use underscores for spaces, e.g. `NO_OF_DAYS_IN_WEEK`. The following is an example of a constant definition in C#

```
(public/private) const float PI = 3.142f;
```

or

```
(public/private) const double PI = 3.142;
```

The data type `double` is a double-precision 64-bit IEEE 754 floating point number. The data type `float` is a single-precision 32-bit IEEE 754 floating point number. In the case of `float` the letter `f` must be appended to the value.

In Java the symbolic name by convention is in uppercase and can use underscores for spaces. The following is an example of a constant definition in Java

```
(public/private)static final float PI = 3.142f;
```

or

```
(public/private) static final double PI = 3.142;
```

The data type `double` is a double-precision 64-bit IEEE 754 floating point number. The data type `float` is a single-precision 32-bit IEEE 754 floating point number. In the case of `float` the letter `f` must be appended to the value.

In VB.Net

```
Const pi As Double = 3.142
```

Python has no way to declare constants. Variables with symbolic names written in uppercase letters and with underscores for spaces signify that their values will be used as constants but the language cannot prevent the values from being changed. It is only a convention.

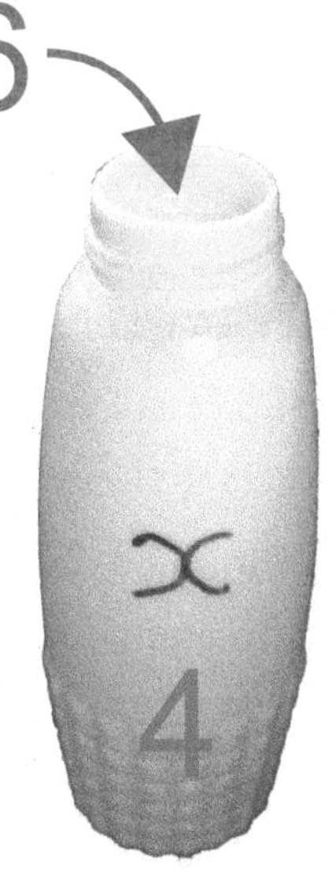

Figure 1.1.2.2 shows the value 6 about to be stored in variable x which currently contains the value 4

Questions

 The calculation 2 x 3.141592654 x radius is made in several places in a program. Give **two** reasons why replacing 3.141592654 by the named constant `pi` could improve this program?

Assignment

An instruction which alters the value of a variable is called an assignment statement and the operation is called assignment. A value is copied into a variable when a computer executes an assignment statement. The action replaces the currently stored value in the variable as illustrated in Figures 1.1.2.2 and 1.1.2.3 for a variable `x`.

For example, in Pascal/Delphi an assignment statement that assigns the value 6 to variable `x` is written as follows

```
x := 6;
```

The operand, `x`, to the left of the `:=` operator is the name of the variable and the operand, 6, to the right of the `:=` operator is the value that will be stored in the variable when assignment is carried out. The value in `x` before assignment occurs is overwritten by the assignment operation. This is shown by example in Figure 1.1.2.3 where the value 4 is overwritten by the value 6.

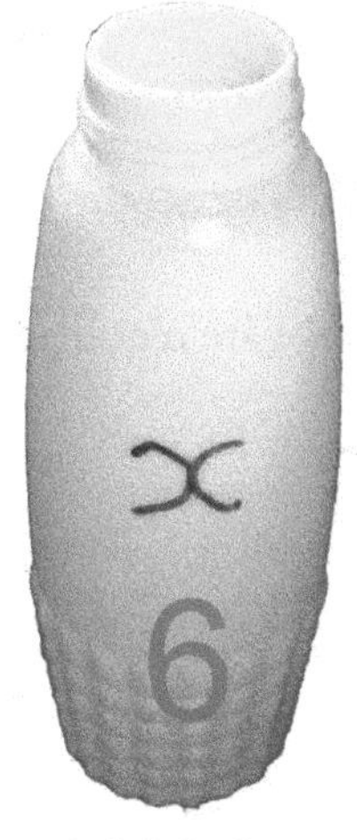

Figure 1.1.2.3 shows that value 4 has been replaced by value 6

The `:=` operator is called the assignment operator. In pseudo-code, a left-pointing arrow ← is used to represent the assignment operator.

The term "statement" is used universally for historical reasons. It would have been better to have adopted the term "command" or "instruction". Examples of assignment statements and assignment operators in other programming languages and in pseudo-code are shown below.

In C#,	`x = 6;`
In Java,	`x = 6;`
In Python,	`x = 6`
In VB.Net,	`x = 6`
In pseudo-code,	`x ← 6`

Key term

Assignment statement:
An instruction which alters the value of a variable is called an assignment statement.
The operation is known as assignment.

Questions

 What is assignment ?

Pseudo-code

Pseudo-code is a programming-like language which is employed to communicate a solution to a problem in a manner which is independent of any particular production programming language such as Pascal, Delphi, C#, Java, Python or VB.Net. The given pseudo-code solution may then be recast in any one of these programming languages, if necessary.

You have seen that Pascal/Delphi uses := for the language construct known as the assignment operator whilst = is used in C#, Java, Python and VB.Net. Pseudo-code provides a common way of expressing programming language constructs, e.g. the assignment operator, which are independent of any actual programming language.

However, it is not usually possible to execute pseudo-code in a machine. If it were, it would become a fully-fledged programming language.

Instead, pseudo-code is executed by hand which means reading it and processing it statement-by-statement in your head. The process is called a trace or hand-trace execution.

Which authority defines pseudo-code?

You can design and use your own pseudo-code.

AQA uses pseudo-code for its AS and A level Computer Science examinations.

Generally speaking, one person's pseudo-code may differ in some respects from another's but usually the differences are not sufficient to make reading and understanding difficult.

> **Information**
>
> **Pseudo-code:**
> Pseudo-code is a programming-like language which is employed to communicate a solution to a problem in a manner which is independent of any particular production programming language.

Iteration

Suppose we are required to sum the first 10 natural numbers, i.e.

1 + 2 + 3 + 4 + 5 + 6 + 7 + 8 + 9 + 10

One way that this could be done is to **repeat** the addition of each natural number in turn to a running total, initialised to 0, **until** all 10 natural numbers have been added together.

In pseudo-code this might be expressed as shown in Table 1.1.2.1.

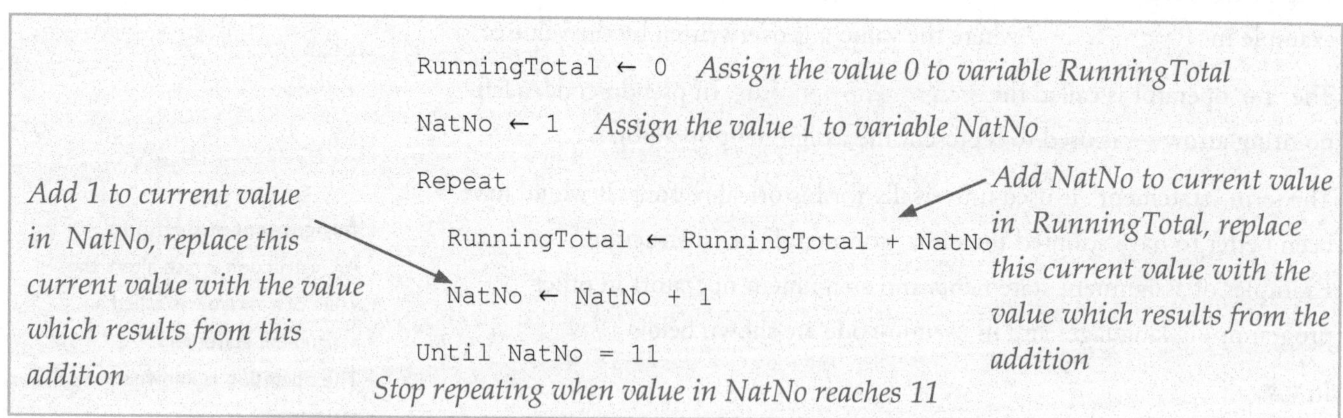

Table 1.1.2.1 Pseudo-code example which adds the first 10 natural numbers

Figures 1.1.2.4 and 1.1.2.5 show the execution of the assignment statement

```
NatNo ← NatNo + 1
```

split over two stages. `NatNo` contains the value 6 just before this statement is executed and afterwards it contains the value 7.

The pseudo-code in Table 1.1.2.1 illustrates repetition or **iteration**. The general form of such iteration is

```
Repeat
  instructions
Until condition
```

which means that the instructions between the words `Repeat` and `Until` are executed repeatedly until the condition specified in `Until condition` is met.

The instructions between `Repeat` and `Until` are known as the **loop body**. The iteration performed by `Repeat Until` is called a **loop** because execution loops back and forth between `Repeat` and `Until`.
The condition occurring in `Until condition` is called the **terminating condition** of the loop.

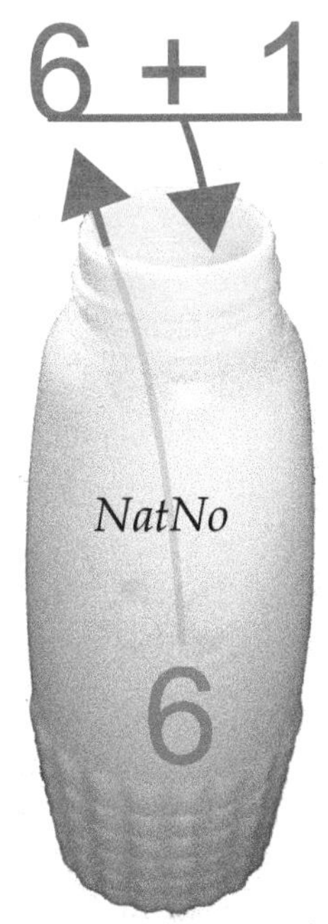

Figure 1.1.2.4 shows the value 6 stored in variable NatNo, being copied then added to 1 and the result 7 about to be stored

Figure 1.1.2.5 shows the value 7 stored in variable NatNo

Questions

6. Trace the execution of the pseudo-code shown in Table 1.1.2.1. Record in Table 1.1.2.2 the value of `NatNo` and `RunningTotal` as they change during the execution. The first value of each variable has been recorded for you in the table.

NatNo	RunningTotal
1	0

Table 1.1.2.2 Trace table for Count and RunningTotal

The final value of `RunningTotal` should be 55.

7. How would you change the pseudo-code in Table 1.1.2.1 so that when executed, it adds the first 15 natural numbers?
Check that your change is correct by hand-tracing the resulting pseudo-code. The final value of `RunningTotal` should be 120.

Key term

Iteration statements:
Instructions are executed repeatedly until the terminating condition is met.

Table 1.1.2.3 shows another way to add the first 10 natural numbers.

```
RunningTotal ← 0
NatNo ← 1
While NatNo < 11        Stop repeating when value in NatNo reaches 11
  RunningTotal ← RunningTotal + NatNo
  NatNo ← NatNo + 1
EndWhile
```

Table 1.1.2.3 Pseudo-code example which adds the first 10 natural numbers

Questions

8 Trace the execution of the pseudo-code shown in Table 1.1.2.3. Record in Table 1.1.2.4 the value of `NatNo` and `RunningTotal` as they change during the execution. The first value of each variable has been recorded for you in the table.

NatNo	RunningTotal
1	0

Table 1.1.2.4 Trace table for NatNo and RunningTotal

9 How would you change the pseudo-code in Table 1.1.2.3 so that when executed it adds the first 15 natural numbers?

Check that your change is correct by hand-tracing the resulting pseudo-code. The final value of `RunningTotal` should be 120.

10 What is the final value of `RunningTotal` when the following pseudo-code is executed by hand if x in `RunningTotal x Choice` is the multiplication operator?

```
RunningTotal ← 1
Count ← 2
Repeat
  RunningTotal ← RunningTotal x Count
  Count ← Count + 1
Until Count = 11
```

Sequence

The following two instructions (assignment statements) of the pseudo-code in Table 1.1.2.3 are executed one after the other

```
RunningTotal ← RunningTotal + NatNo

NatNo ← NatNo + 1
```

They form a sequence of steps governed by the following rules

1. The steps are executed one at a time
2. The order in which the steps are written is the order in which they are executed
3. Each step is executed exactly once.

We say that this part of the solution to the problem of adding the first 10 natural numbers is constructed using a program design principle called sequence.

Key term

Sequence statements:
Statements are executed one at a time, one after another in the order in which they are written with each executed exactly once.

Questions

11 A variable x contains the value 7 and a variable y the value 3.
Using only sequence, write assignment statements that swap the values contained in x and y. You may use Temp, a third variable.

Selection

If statement

If solutions to problems consist only of steps in sequence then there is no possibility of solving problems which need to deviate from the given sequence of execution if circumstances require this.

For example, suppose instead of summing the first 10 natural numbers we are required to sum only the even numbers amongst the first 10 natural numbers, using the pseudo-code in Table 1.1.2.3. The solution must test to see if the next natural number is even. Only if it is even will it then be added it to the running total.

The revised sequence section of the pseudo-code solution in Table1.1.2.3 will take the form

```
If NatNo is even                                     ← condition
  Then RunningTotal ← RunningTotal + NatNo           ← step
EndIf
NatNo ← NatNo + 1
```

The conditional part of this pseudo-code fits the general form

```
If condition
  Then step
```

where *condition* specifies the circumstance under which the *step* is to be executed. If *condition* is true then *step* is executed; otherwise it is not.

`If condition Then step` is a statement known as selection.

Suppose instead of summing the first 10 natural numbers we are required to sum the even numbers in one running total and the odd numbers in a different running total. We now have two alternative steps to be executed.

The revised sequence section of the pseudo-code solution in Table 1.1.2.3 will take the form

```
If NatNo is even                                        ← condition
  Then EvenRunningTotal ← EvenRunningTotal + NatNo      ← step 1
  Else OddRunningTotal ← OddRunningTotal + NatNo        ← step 2
EndIf
NatNo ← NatNo + 1
```

The general form of selection in which selection is between one of two alternative steps is

```
If condition
  Then step 1
  Else step 2
```

where `condition` determines whether `step 1` is executed or `step 2` is executed. We thus have two forms of `If` selection statement:

```
If condition
  Then step
```

```
If condition
  Then step 1
  Else step 2
```

Key term

Selection:

A selection statement takes one of two possible forms:

```
If condition
  Then step
```

or

```
If condition
  Then step 1
  Else step 2
```

The condition determines whether or not `step` is executed, `step1` or `step2` is executed.

Questions

12 Rewrite the following If statements as a single If Then Else statement

```
If Age < 37 Then AgeCategory ← 'A'
If Age >=37 Then AgeCategory ← 'B'
```

13 The pseudocode in *Table 1.1.2.5* finds the largest of two numbers, `No1`, `No2`.

The value of the largest of the two numbers is stored in variable `Largest`.

(a) If `No1` stores the value 6, `No2` the value 3 which branch of the selection statement is executed, `Then` or `Else`? Explain your answer.

(b) If `No1` stores the value 6, `No2` the value 7 which branch of the selection statement is executed, `Then` or `Else`? Explain your answer.

Key fact

Combining principles:

The three combining principles (sequence, iteration/repetition and selection/choice) are basic to all imperative programming languages.

```
If No1 > No2
  Then Largest ← No1
  Else Largest ← No2
EndIf
```

Table 1.1.2.5 Pseudo-code to find the largest of two numbers

Case/Switch statement

The **Case/Switch statement** is used to select one of several alternatives. In *Table 1.1.2.6* if x is in the range `0..9` then the statement `Output 'Single digit number'` is executed and the remaining statements in the *Case* statement are skipped. If x is in the range `10..99` then the statement `Output 'Double digit number'` is executed and the other statements in the *Case* statement are skipped. The *Case* statement tries to match the value of x with *Case* list `0..9`, `10..99`, `100..999`. If it fails then it executes the statement selected by `Else`, i.e. `Output 'Not a single/double/triple digit number'`. The variable x is known as the **case selector**.

```
Case x Of
  0..9 : Output 'Single digit number'
  10..99 : Output 'Double digit number'
  100..999 : Output 'Triple digit number'
  Else Output 'Not a single/double/triple digit number'
EndCase
```

Table 1.1.2.6 Pseudo-code Case statement

The Case/Switch statement is shown in Figures 1.1.2.6 to 1.1.2.9 for Delphi/Pascal, C#, Java and VB.NET.

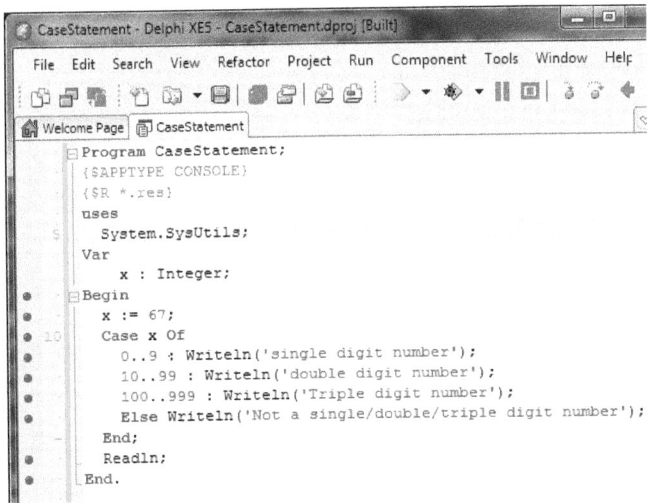

```
Program CaseStatement;
{$APPTYPE CONSOLE}
{$R *.res}
uses
  System.SysUtils;
Var
     x : Integer;
Begin
  x := 67;
  Case x Of
    0..9 : Writeln('single digit number');
    10..99 : Writeln('double digit number');
    100..999 : Writeln('Triple digit number');
    Else Writeln('Not a single/double/triple digit number');
  End;
  Readln;
End.
```

```
Program CaseStatement;
Var
    x : Integer;
Begin
  x := 67;
  Case x Of
    0..9 : Writeln('single digit number');
    10..99 : Writeln('double digit number');
    100..999 : Writeln('Triple digit number');
    Else Writeln('Not a single/double/triple digit number');
  End;
  Readln;
End.
```

Figure 1.1.2.6 Case statement in Delphi and Lazarus Pascal

```
/**
 * @(#)JavaCaseStatement.java
 *
 * JavaCaseStatement application
 *
 * @author
 * @version 1.00 2016/7/22
 */

public class JavaCaseStatement {

    public static void main(String[] args) {
        int x = 1;
        switch (x) {
          case 0:
            System.out.println("0");
            break;
          case 1:
             System.out.println("1");
             break;
          case 2:
             System.out.println("2");
             break;
          default:
             System.out.println("Not in range 0 to 2");
        }
    }
}
```

Figure 1.1.2.7 Switch Case statement in Java

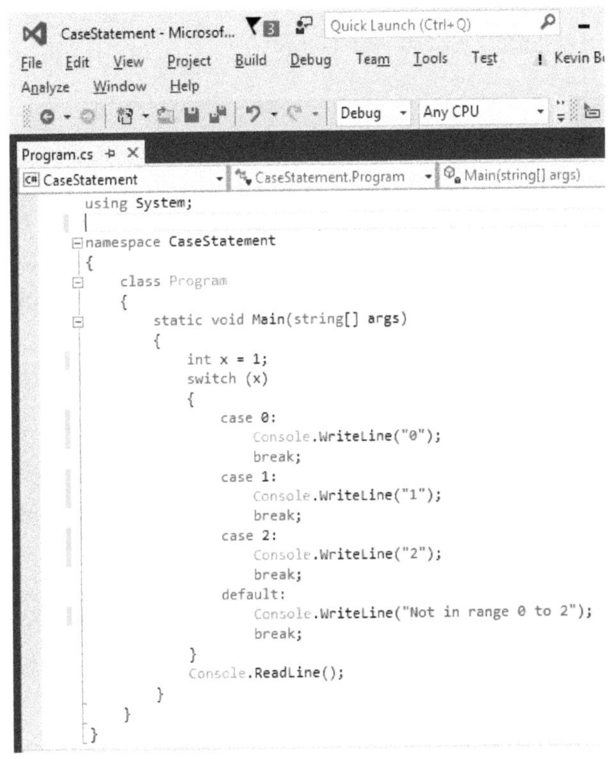

```
using System;

namespace CaseStatement
{
    class Program
    {
        static void Main(string[] args)
        {
            int x = 1;
            switch (x)
            {
                case 0:
                    Console.WriteLine("0");
                    break;
                case 1:
                    Console.WriteLine("1");
                    break;
                case 2:
                    Console.WriteLine("2");
                    break;
                default:
                    Console.WriteLine("Not in range 0 to 2");
                    break;
            }
            Console.ReadLine();
        }
    }
}
```

Figure 1.1.2.8 Switch Case statement in C#

```
Module Module1

    Sub Main()
        Dim x As Integer = 67
        Select Case x
            Case 0 To 9
                Console.WriteLine("single digit number")
            Case 10 To 99
                Console.WriteLine("Double digit number")
            Case 100 To 999
                Console.WriteLine("Triple digit number")
            Case Else
                Console.WriteLine("Not a single/double/triple digit number")
        End Select
        Console.ReadLine()
    End Sub

End Module
```

Figure 1.1.2.9 Select Case statement in VB.NET

Java and C# do not support ranges in their Switch Case statement alternatives. The chosen value for x in the Java and C# examples is different from the other languages for this reason.

There is no Case/Switch statement in Python so a combination of *if* and *elifs* have to be used instead.

Subroutine

A subroutine is a **named self-contained block of instructions**, e.g. `drawsquare`.

By encapsulating and naming a block of instructions in a program it becomes possible to call the block from other parts of the program. This is very useful in situations where the same block of instructions or action or calculation needs to be repeated in multiple places in a program.

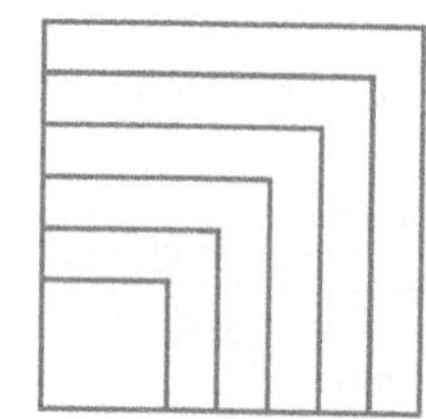

Figure 1.1.2.10 Pattern of squares

Suppose that we wish to draw the pattern containing six squares shown in *Figure 1.1.2.10*. The size (side-length) of the squares increases by the same fixed amount. One way of drawing a square with length of side, `size`, is to use a pen-carrying turtle moving under the guidance of the sequence of instructions or commands shown in *Figure 1.1.2.11*.

```
turtle.forward(size)
turtle.left(90)
turtle.forward(size)
turtle.left(90)
turtle.forward(size)
turtle.left(90)
turtle.forward(size)
turtle.left(90)
```

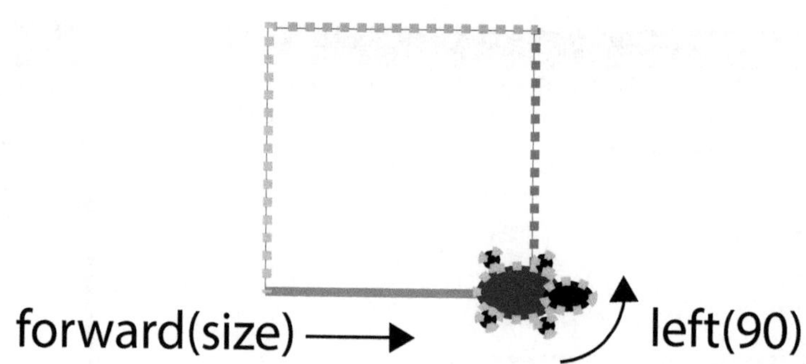
forward(size)
left(90)

Figure 1.1.2.11 Path followed by a turtle obeying the sequence of commands shown opposite

It is good practice to use active verbs for subroutine names, e.g. Read, Write, Add, DoSomething.

If this sequence of instructions in *Figure 1.1.2.11* is named `drawsquare` then a program could call upon this subroutine to draw a square of a specific size, say, 25, as follows: `drawsquare(25)`

A program that calls upon the subroutine `drawsquare` is said to **call the subroutine** `drawsquare`.

To draw a differently-sized square of size, say, 35, `drawsquare` would need to be called upon as follows

`drawsquare(35)`

The square-drawing turtle subroutine itself could be written as shown in *Table 1.1.2.7*.

The variable `size` is called the **formal parameter of the subroutine**: it is used in the **body of the subroutine** to define how big the square will be.

When the subroutine is called, the **actual parameter** 25 or 35, for example, provides a specific value for `size`, and thus determines how big the square will be in each call.

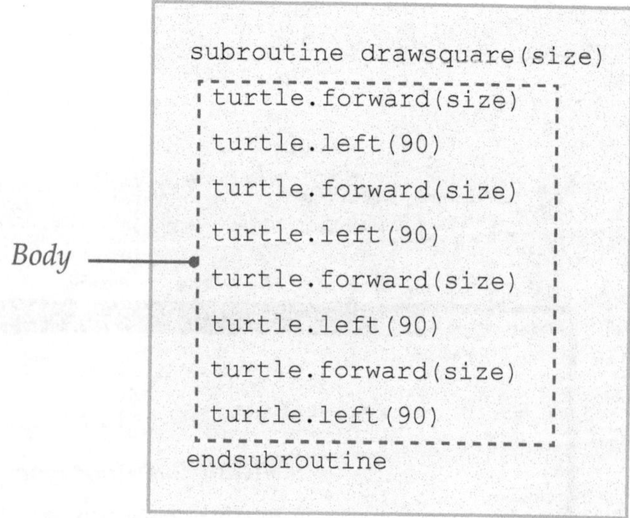
Body

```
subroutine drawsquare(size)
  turtle.forward(size)
  turtle.left(90)
  turtle.forward(size)
  turtle.left(90)
  turtle.forward(size)
  turtle.left(90)
  turtle.forward(size)
  turtle.left(90)
endsubroutine
```

Table 1.1.2.7 Subroutine drawsquare(size) defined

The subroutine `drawsquare` itself calls subroutines `turtle.forward` and `turtle.left`.

drawsquare(25)
drawsquare(35)
drawsquare(45)
drawsquare(55)
drawsquare(65)
drawsquare(75)

Table 1.1.2.8 Calling subroutine drawsquare(size) with different actual parameters

To draw the pattern of squares in *Figure 1.1.2.10* we need the sequence of calls to subroutine `drawsquare` shown in *Table 1.1.2.8*.

Figure 1.1.2.12 shows how the `drawsquare` subroutine could be defined in Python 3.4 and how it would be called to produce the pattern of squares shown in *Figure 1.1.2.10*.

A subroutine may also contain its own *variable*, *type*, *label*[2] and *const* declarations. In fact, it may also define other subroutines within its declaration section.

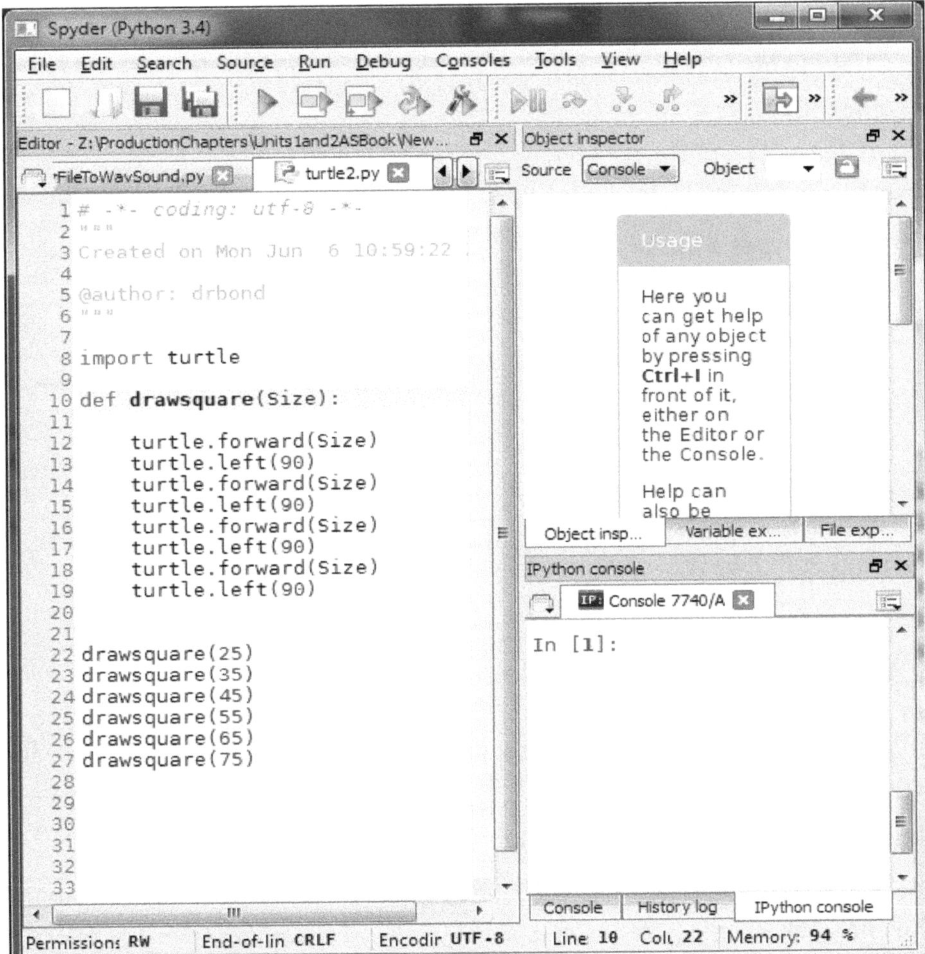

Figure 1.1.2.12 Python 3.4 program to draw a pattern of squares

Key term

Subroutine:

A subroutine is a named self-contained block of instructions, e.g. `drawsquare`, which may be called (i.e. executed) from anywhere within a program where its name appears.

Procedures and functions

There are two types of subroutines:

- Procedure
- Function

A procedure is a subroutine consisting of one or more statements or actions which may or may not return a result. If it returns a result it does so through output parameters in its interface - see page 115. The statements are referred to collectively by a name assigned to the procedure called the procedure name. The procedure must be declared/defined – its name must be stated and its statements listed. The procedure's statements are executed wherever its name is encountered in the executable part of a program - see *Figure 1.1.2.12*. This is called calling a procedure.

Key term

Procedure:

A procedure is a subroutine consisting of one or more statements or actions which may or may not return a result.

2 Not in AQA specification

In Pascal, a procedure is declared and used as follows:

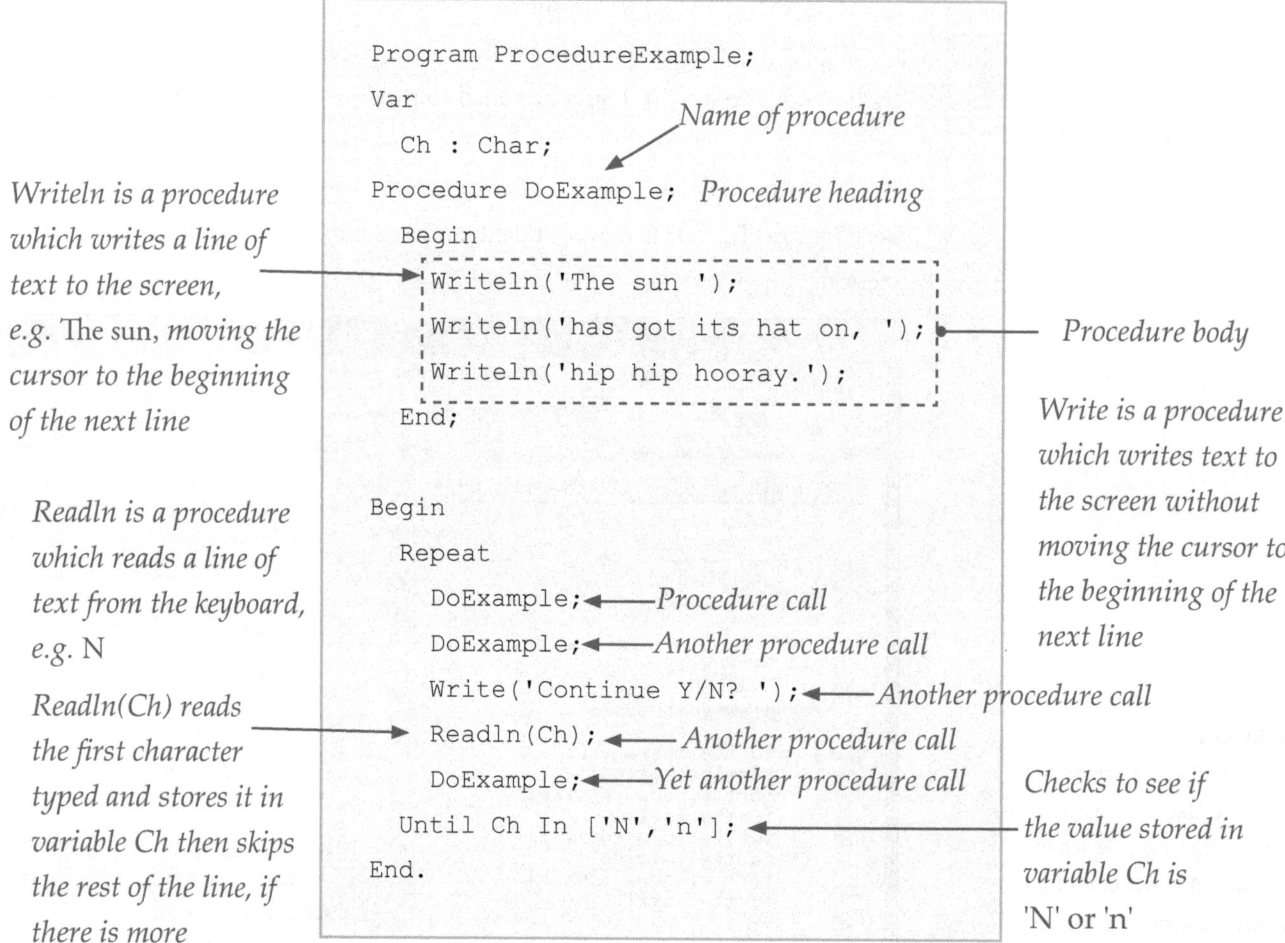

Program ProcedureExample;
Var
Ch : Char;
Name of procedure
Procedure DoExample; Procedure heading
Begin
Writeln('The sun ');
Writeln('has got its hat on, ');
Writeln('hip hip hooray.');
End;
Procedure body
Writeln is a procedure which writes a line of text to the screen, e.g. The sun, moving the cursor to the beginning of the next line
Write is a procedure which writes text to the screen without moving the cursor to the beginning of the next line
Begin
Repeat
DoExample; Procedure call
DoExample; Another procedure call
Write('Continue Y/N? '); Another procedure call
Readln(Ch); Another procedure call
DoExample; Yet another procedure call
Until Ch In ['N','n'];
End.
Readln is a procedure which reads a line of text from the keyboard, e.g. N
Readln(Ch) reads the first character typed and stores it in variable Ch then skips the rest of the line, if there is more
Checks to see if the value stored in variable Ch is 'N' or 'n'

Table 1.1.2.9 Pascal program containing calls to procedures DoExample, Writeln, Write, Readln

Table 1.1.2.10 shows a VB.Net program which declares a user-defined procedure called `DoExample`. The procedure `DoExample` is called three times when the program executes. `Main()` is called to run the program.

```
Module ProcedureExample
    Sub DoExample()
        Console.WriteLine("The sun has ")
        Console.WriteLine("got its hat on,  ")
        Console.WriteLine("hip hip hooray.")
    End Sub
    Sub Main()
        DoExample()
        DoExample()
        DoExample()
        Console.ReadLine()
    End Sub
End Module
```

Table 1.1.2.10 VB.Net program containing calls to a procedure DoExample

In VB.Net, `Main()` is a standard procedure name found in every executable module (Visual Studio supplies a module template containing `Main()`).

VB.Net doesn't use the keyword `Procedure` but instead surrounds the body of the procedure with the keywords `Sub` and `End Sub`.

Instead of the language keyword `Program` as in Pascal, VB.Net uses the keyword `Module`. It has a matching keyword `End Module` placed at the very end of the program.

Figure 1.1.2.13 shows one call to a Python 3.5 procedure with the name do_example which has been defined using Python's keyword `def`.

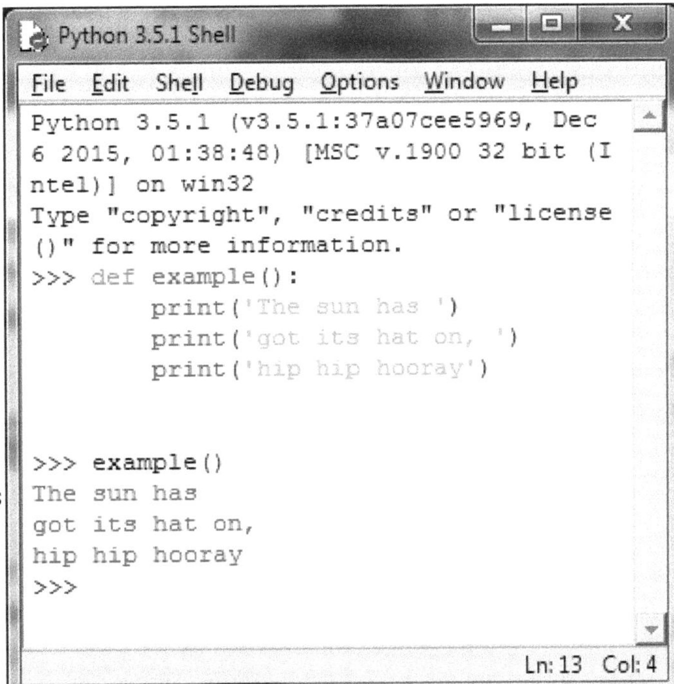

Figure 1.1.2.13 Shows one call to a Python 3.5 procedure with the name do_example which has been defined using Python's keyword `def`

Procedure interface

A procedure interface is a mechanism for passing data into and out of a procedure.

In Pascal, for example, `x` is known as a formal parameter as shown in Table 1.1.2.11. This is a variable used in the body of the procedure and which appears in the interface. When the procedure is called an actual parameter is supplied through the procedure's interface, e.g. `DoInterfaceExample(MyName)` where the variable `MyName` is the actual parameter. The value in `MyName` is copied into the variable `x` when the procedure is called by `DoInterfaceExample(MyName)`.

Suppose `MyName` stores the string 'Fred Bloggs', then the variable `x` in the body of the procedure will contain the string 'Fred Bloggs'.

Key concept

Procedure interface:
A procedure interface is a mechanism for passing data into and out of a procedure.

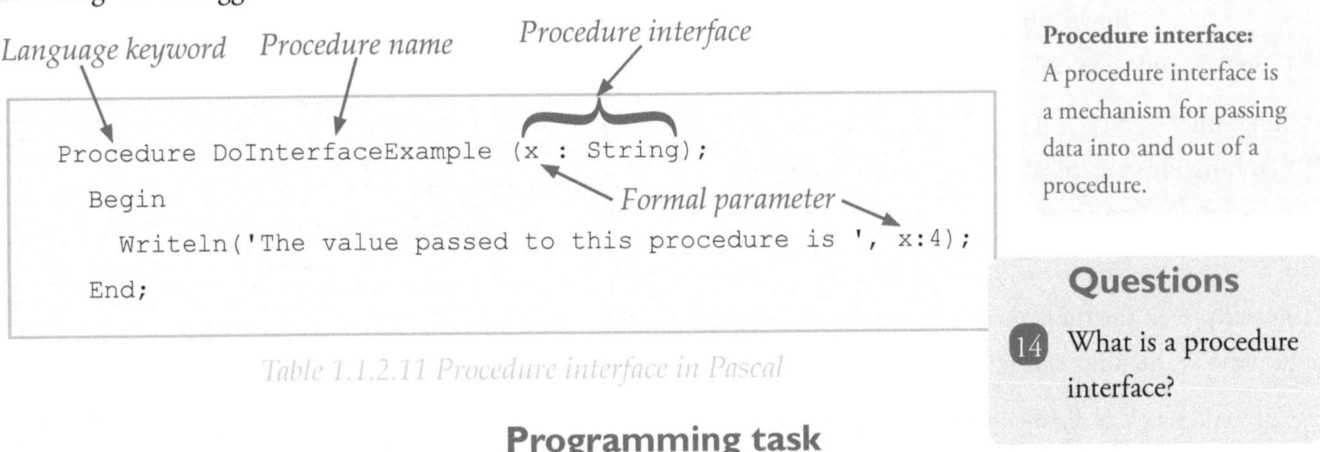

Table 1.1.2.11 Procedure interface in Pascal

Questions

14 What is a procedure interface?

Programming task

1 In a programming language with which you are familiar, write a program which defines a procedure that displays the message passed it through its interface.

Function

A function is a type of subroutine designed to always return a single result. The mechanism by which the result is returned is different from that used by a procedure.

Functions may appear in expressions such as `5 x cube(3)` where `cube` is a mathematical function.
This is possible because a function returns a value.
So `5 x cube(3)` evaluates to `5 x 27` which evaluates to `135`.

In the first evaluation step, `cube(3)` is replaced by `27`, the result returned from the execution of function `cube(3)`. Any attempt to use a procedure in this manner would fail.

This is a key difference between a function and a procedure.

Procedure calls do not support a mechanism by which a value is substituted for the procedure call when the latter completes and returns control. If the procedure did then it would be a function[3].

For example, the following does not make sense as an expression because `drawsquare` doesn't "evaluate" to a single value which can be multiplied by 5 to produce a numeric result, e.g. 127:

`5 x drawsquare(3)` where `drawsquare` is a procedure.

Because functions "evaluate" to a single value[4] they may appear on the right-hand side of an assignment statement.

Key term

Function:
A function is a type of subroutine designed to always return a single result. It may appear in expressions and on the right hand-side of an assignment statement unlike a procedure.

For example,

```
x ← cube(3)
```

After this statement is executed, the variable `x` contains/stores the value 27, because the result of calling `cube(3)` is 27.

Attempting the following would fail because `Writeln` is a procedure. It also would not make sense.

```
x := Writeln('The sun has got its hat on');
```

In Pascal, the code `Writeln('The sun has got its hat on')` is a command which writes the string `'The sun has got its hat on'` to the screen then moves the screen's cursor to the beginning of the next line.

Figure 1.1.2.14 shows a function `cube(n)` defined in Python 3.5, and then called with argument 3.

In function `cube(n)`, `n` is called the formal parameter. When functions are called we use a slightly different nomenclature. The actual parameter is now called the **argument**.

For example, in the function call `cube(3)`, 3 is the argument to the function.

Pascal makes a clear distinction between procedure and function by using different keywords for defining each. *Table 1.1.2.12* shows a function `Cube` being defined using the language keyword `Function`. As Pascal is a strongly typed language, the data type of the formal parameter and the data type of the returned value must be specified. It is `Integer` for both in this example.

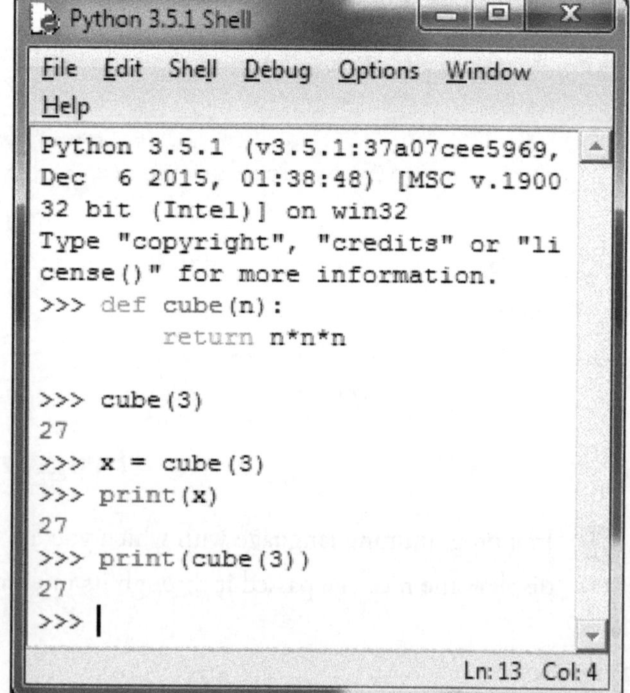

Figure 1.1.2.14 Function cube(n) defined and used in Python 3.5

Questions

15 State **one** key difference between a function and a procedure.

3 Impure functions in addition to returning a result, may have side effects which is the collective name for other things that the function may do as well.

4 In some programming languages functions are allowed to return a structured result i.e. a result with more than one value.

Pascal uses the name of the function to assign the value that is to be returned.

Alternatively, the keyword Result can be used in place of Cube.

```
Function Cube (n : Integer) : Integer;
  Begin
    Cube := n * n * n;
  End;
```

Table 1.1.2.12 Function Cube(n) defined in Pascal

C#

In C#, the approach to defining subroutines is different from Pascal. In C#, subroutines are called functions, whether in their behaviour they are procedures or functions. In C#, the subroutine heading takes the following form

<visibility> <modifier ><return type> <subroutine-name>(<parameters>)

The first part is the visibility, and is optional. If not specified then the function will be private.
The second part is the modifier, and is optional. If it is specified then the function belongs to the class otherwise it belongs to a specific object of the class[5]. The modifier is the keyword `static`.

The third part is the return type. If this is `void` then no result is returned via the function mechanism. In this case the subroutine behaves as a procedure. The term "`void`" is meant to indicate that the return value is empty or nonexistent.

If the return type is a valid data type, e.g. `int`, then a result is returned via the function mechanism. In this case the subroutine behaves as a function.

Figure 1.1.2.15 shows a Visual Studio 2015 C# program which defines a procedure `DoExample` which is called twice by `Main`. It is a procedure because the specified return type is `void`. The procedure belongs to the type `class Program` because the modifier is specified with the keyword `static`.

Figure 1.1.2.16 shows a Visual Studio 2015 C# program which defines a function `Add2Numbers` which is called by `Main`.

It is a function because the specified return type is `int`.

The function belongs to the class `Program` because the modifier of `Add2Numbers` is specified with the keyword `static`.

`Add2Numbers` is used as a function in `Main`.
It appears on the right-hand side of an assignment statement as follows

```
int answer = Add2Numbers(4, 8);
```

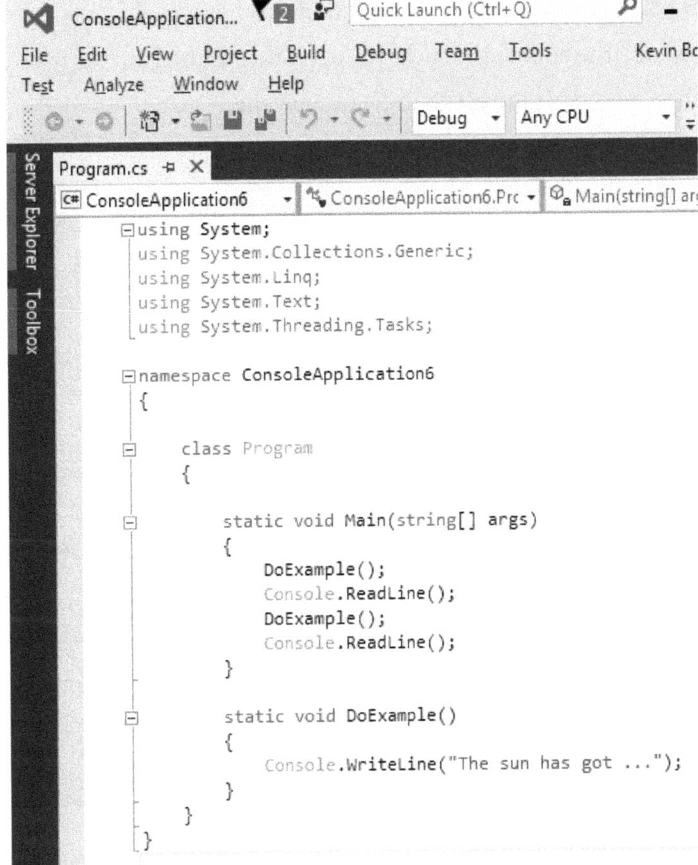

Figure 1.1.2.15 C# DoExample procedure

5 Object-oriented programming not in AS

Function `Add2Numbers` makes it possible to add two numbers from various places in a program, simply by calling this function instead of having to write the calculation code each time.

Java

In Java, the approach to defining subroutines is similar to C#'s approach.

```
<visibility> <modifier> <return-type>
<subroutine-name > ( <parameters >) {
      statements
}
```

The statements between the braces, { and }, in a subroutine definition make up the body of the subroutine.

The first part is the visibility, and is optional. If it isn't specified then the function will be private.

The second part is the modifier, and is optional. If it is specified then the function belongs to the class otherwise it belongs to a specific object of the class[6]. The modifier is the keyword `static`.

The third part is the return type. If this is `void` then no result is returned via the function mechanism. In this case the subroutine behaves as a procedure. The term "`void`" is meant to indicate that the return value is empty or nonexistent.

Figure 1.1.2.17 shows a Java program which defines a procedure `doExample` which is called twice by `Main`. It is a procedure because the specified return type is `void`. The procedure belongs to the class `Procedure` because the modifier of `doExample` is specified with the keyword `static`.

Figure 1.1.2.18 shows a Java program which defines a function `add2Numbers` which is called by `Main`.

It is a function because the specified return type is `int`.

The function belongs to the class `JavaAdd2Numbers` because the modifier of `add2Numbers` is specified with the keyword `static`.

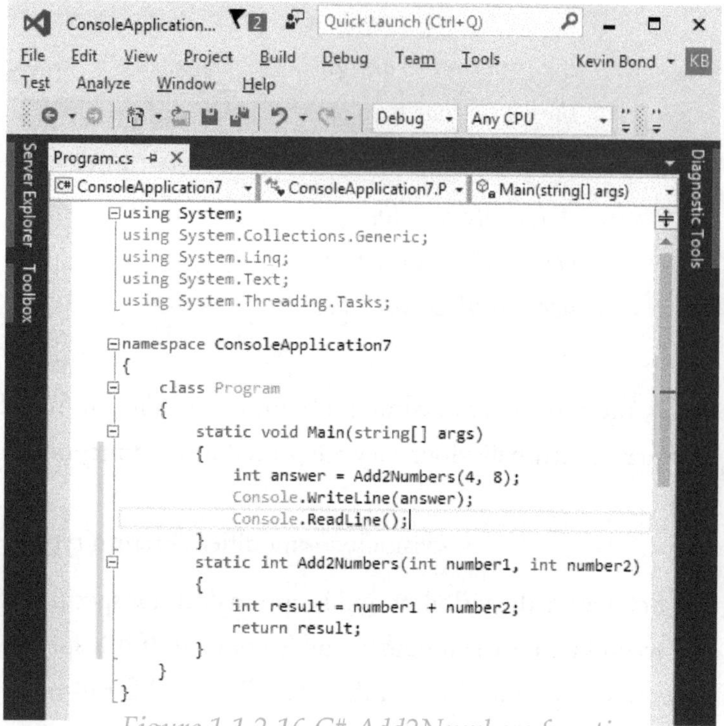

ConsoleApplication...
Quick Launch (Ctrl+Q)
File Edit View Project Build Debug Team Tools Kevin Bond
Test Analyze Window Help
Debug Any CPU
Program.cs
ConsoleApplication7
ConsoleApplication7.P
Main(string[] args)
Server Explorer Toolbox
Diagnostic Tools
using System;
using System.Collections.Generic;
using System.Linq;
using System.Text;
using System.Threading.Tasks;
namespace ConsoleApplication7
{
class Program
{
static void Main(string[] args)
{
int answer = Add2Numbers(4, 8);
Console.WriteLine(answer);
Console.ReadLine();
}
static int Add2Numbers(int number1, int number2)
{
int result = number1 + number2;
return result;
}
}
}

Figure 1.1.2.16 C# Add2Numbers function

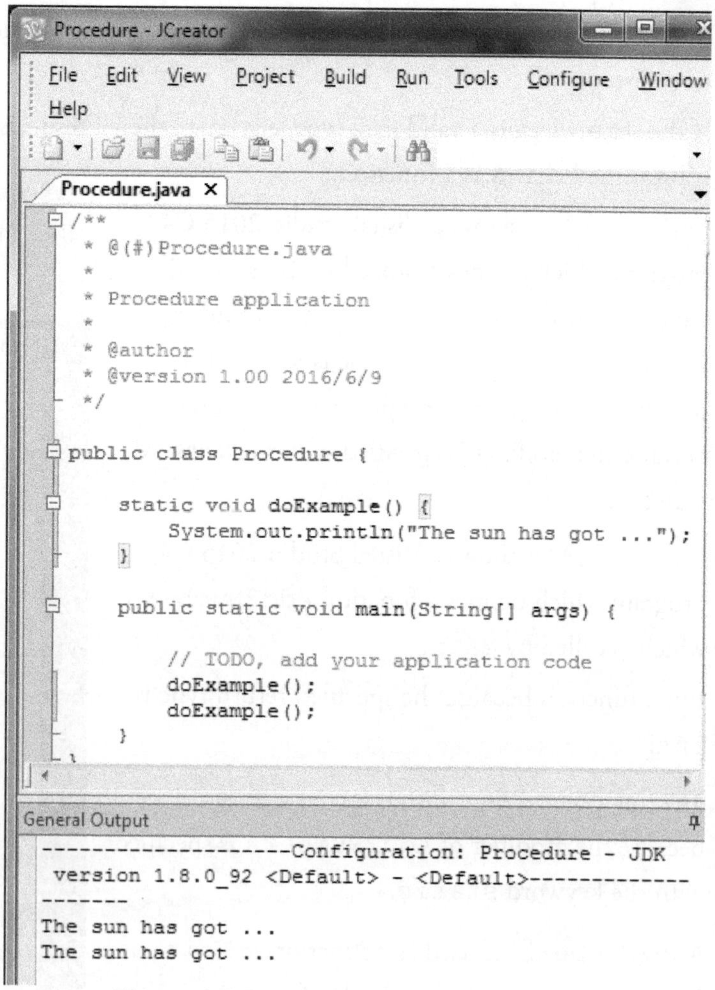

Procedure - JCreator
File Edit View Project Build Run Tools Configure Window
Help
Procedure.java
/**
* @(#)Procedure.java
*
* Procedure application
*
* @author
* @version 1.00 2016/6/9
*/
public class Procedure {
static void doExample() {
System.out.println("The sun has got ...");
}
public static void main(String[] args) {
// TODO, add your application code
doExample();
doExample();
}
General Output
--------------------Configuration: Procedure - JDK version 1.8.0_92 <Default> - <Default>--------------------
The sun has got ...
The sun has got ...

Figure 1.1.2.17 Java doExample procedure

`add2Numbers` is used as a function in `Main`. It appears on the right-hand side of an assignment statement as follows `int answer = add2Numbers(4, 8);`

6 Object-oriented programming is not covered in AS

VB.NET

In VB.Net, the approach to defining a function is as follows

```
<visibility> <modifier> Function <FunctionName>
(<parameters>) As <return type>
        <Statements>
End Function
```

The first part is the visibility, and is optional. If it isn't specified then the function will be private.

The second part is the modifier, and is optional. The third part is the return type, e.g. Integer.

Figure 1.1.2.19 shows a VB.NET program which defines a function `Add2Numbers` which is called by `Main` from two different places in `Main`.

The return type of this function is `Integer`.

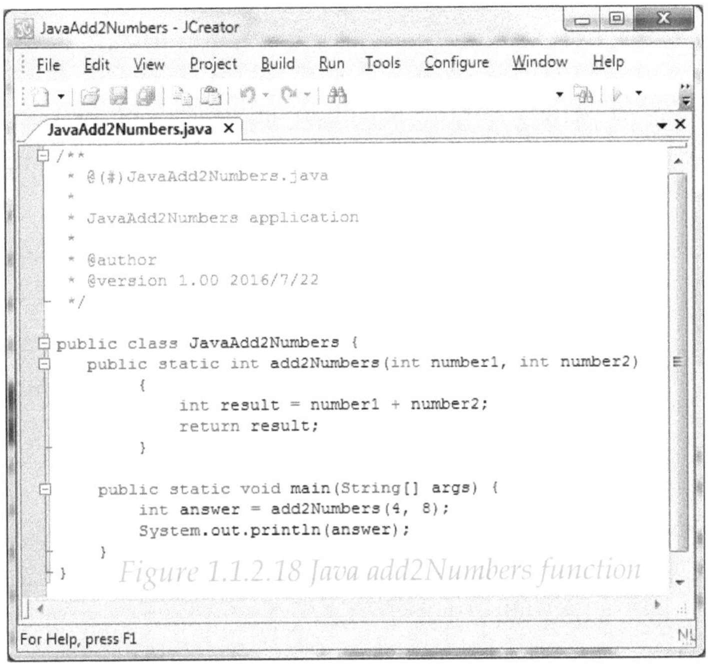

```
JavaAdd2Numbers - JCreator
File Edit View Project Build Run Tools Configure Window Help
JavaAdd2Numbers.java

/**
 * @(#)JavaAdd2Numbers.java
 *
 * JavaAdd2Numbers application
 *
 * @author
 * @version 1.00 2016/7/22
 */

public class JavaAdd2Numbers {
    public static int add2Numbers(int number1, int number2)
        {
            int result = number1 + number2;
            return result;
        }

     public static void main(String[] args) {
        int answer = add2Numbers(4, 8);
        System.out.println(answer);
     }
}

For Help, press F1
```

Figure 1.1.2.18 Java add2Numbers function

`Add2Numbers` is used as a function in `Main`. It appears on the right-hand side of an assignment statement as follows `answer = Add2Numbers(4, 8)`

It also appears in a second call as an actual parameter to the procedure `WriteLine` as follows

```
Console.WriteLine(Add2Numbers(6,9))
```

```
FunctionAdd2Numbers.vb
Module FunctionAdd2Numbers
    Function Add2Numbers(number1 As Integer, number2 As Integer) As Integer
        Return number1 + number2
    End Function
    Sub Main()
        Dim answer As Integer
        answer = Add2Numbers(4, 8)
        Console.WriteLine(answer)
        Console.ReadLine()
        Console.WriteLine(Add2Numbers(6, 9))
        Console.ReadLine()
    End Sub
End Module
```

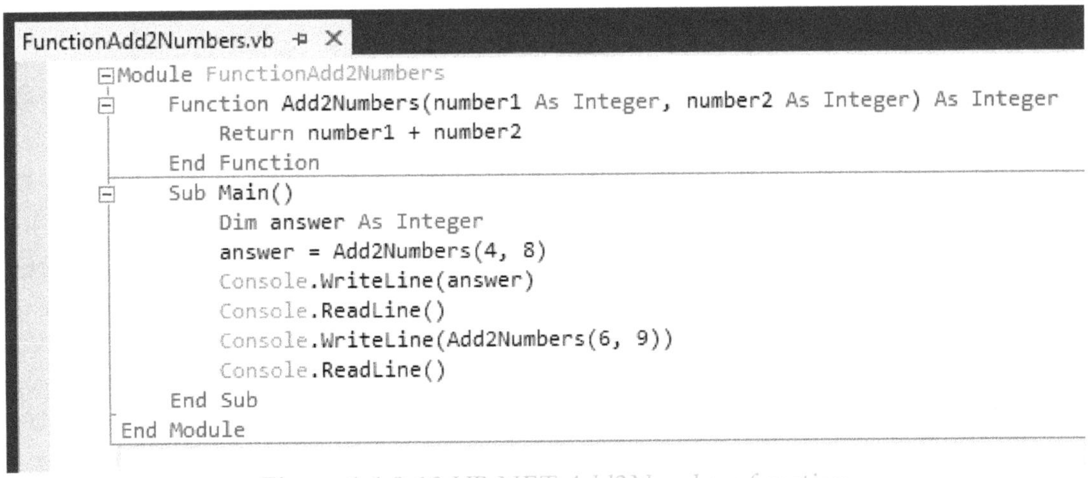

Figure 1.1.2.19 VB.NET Add2Numbers function

Programming task

2 In a programming language with which you are familiar:

(a) Write a program which defines a function that sums the first *n* natural numbers and returns this sum. The program should display this sum for a given *n*.

(b) Write a program which defines a function that sums the even numbers amongst the first *n* natural numbers and returns this sum. The program should display this sum for a given *n*.

(HINT: `If ((NatNo Mod 2) = 0) Then Even ← True Else Even ← False`)

(c) Write a program which defines a function that finds the largest of two given integers, *x* and *y*. The program should display the largest.

Definite and indefinite iteration

We introduced the concept of a loop in the section on iteration. In this section, we explore ways in which the number of iterations (i.e. repetitions of the body of the loop) is determined.

We have two cases to consider, definite and indefinite iteration:

- In definite iteration, the number of iterations is known before the execution of the body of the loop is started. For example, repeat 5 times writing the string "Hello World!" to the output device.
- In indefinite iteration, the number of iterations is not known before the execution of the body of the loop starts. The number of iterations depends on when a specific condition is met (and this depends on what happens in the body of the loop). For example, repeat printing the string "Hello World"until when asked the user declines to continue.

Definite iteration

Suppose that we wanted to output the value of a variable `i`, first when it is 1, next when it is 2, and so on until it is 5. We could do this with a *repeat until* loop or a *while* loop as shown by the pseudo-code examples in Table 1.1.2.13. The number of iterations of each loop is known in advance, it is five, so these are examples of definite iteration.

Note that a

- *repeat until <condition>* loop executes at least once
- a *while <condition>* executes zero or more times

Key term

Definite iteration: In definite iteration the number of iterations is known before the execution of the body of the loop is started.

```
i ← 0
Repeat
   i ← i + 1
   Output i
Until i = 5
```

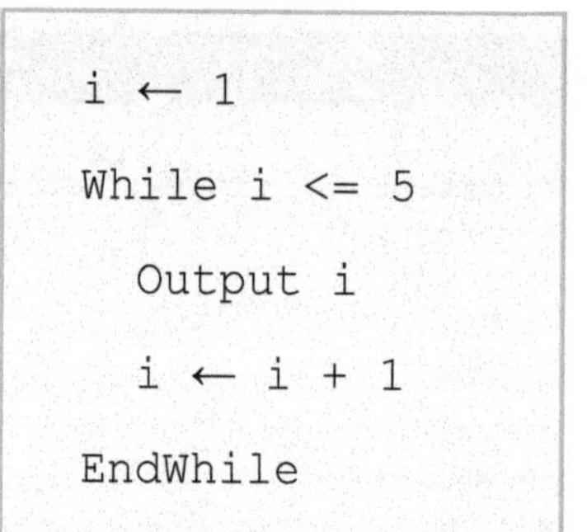

```
i ← 1
While i <= 5
   Output i
   i ← i + 1
EndWhile
```

Table 1.1.2.13 Definite iteration with repeat and while loops

Key term

Loop terminating condition: The condition which causes execution of the loop body to terminate is known as the terminating condition.

Loop terminating condition

In both *repeat* and *while* loops quite a lot of work has to be done by the programmer.

In the example, the variable `i` has to be initialised, with 0 for the repeat loop and with 1 for the while loop.

It has to be incremented (`i ← i + 1`), and it has to be tested with the test condition `i = 5` for the repeat loop and `i <= 5` for the while loop.

The *repeat until* loop terminates when its test condition is true.

The *while loop* terminates when its test condition is false.

In each case, the condition which causes execution of the loop body to terminate is known as the terminating condition.

In definite iteration, this terminating condition is met after a known and predictable number of iterations.

For loop

There is an easier way for the programmer to program definite iteration called the for loop.

This pseudo-code for the *for loop* shown in Table 1.1.2.14 is executed as follows

Step 1: The initial value of variable `i` is set to 1, "`i ← 1`". This step happens only once, regardless of how many times the loop repeats.

Step 2: The "`To 5`" part evaluates the condition (`i <= 5`) by comparing the value of `i` with 5.
If `i` is less than or equal to 5, the condition evaluates to true, and the statement "`Output i`" is executed. This sends the value of i to the output device, e.g. the VDU.
If `i` is greater than 5, the condition evaluates to false, and **the loop is exited**. The instruction immediately following `EndFor` is then executed next.

Step 3: The value of `i` is incremented by 1.

Step 4: The loop returns to *step* 2 to evaluate the condition again.

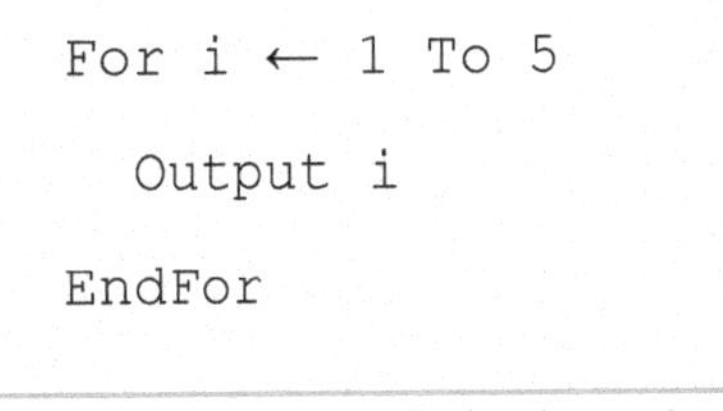

```
For i ← 1 To 5
  Output i
EndFor
```

Table 1.1.2.14 Definite iteration with a for loop

Note that if the initial value of `i` is greater than the 5 as shown in Table 1.1.2.15 the body of the loop should not be executed.

Variable `i` in this example is called the loop control variable.

A loop control variable must be an ordinal data type (see ordinal number Chapter 5.1.6 page 249). An ordinal data type is one that consists of an ORDERED set of things in which each member has a single value only, e.g. an integer data type.

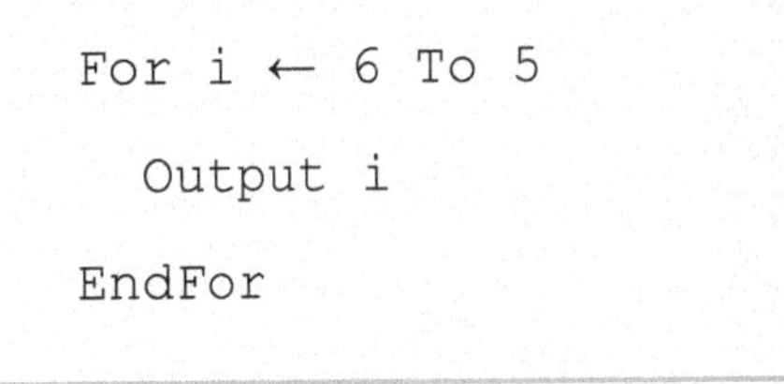

```
For i ← 6 To 5
  Output i
EndFor
```

Table 1.1.2.15 Definite iteration with a for loop

Questions

16 What is the output of the following pseudocode?

```
For i ← 1 To 5
  j ← 2 * i
  Output j
EndFor
```

17 What is the output of the following pseudocode?

```
For Ch ← 'A' To 'C'
  Output Ch
EndFor
```

18 How many times is the pseudo-code loop executed in Table 1.1.2.16?

```
For i ← 4 To 4
  j ← 2 * i
  Output j
EndFor
```

Table 1.1.2.16

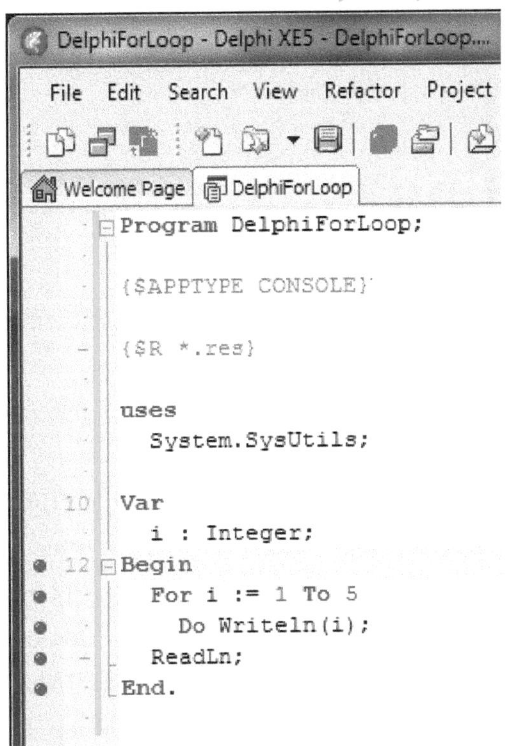

Figure 1.1.2.20 Delphi/Pascal For loop example

Figure 1.1.2.20 shows an example of a *for loop* in Delphi/Pascal.

Figure 1.1.2.21 shows an example of a *for loop* in VB.NET.

For loops in C# and Java take a different form from Delphi/Pascal and VB.NET. This form is as follows

```
for (initialiser; condition; iterator)
    body
```

Figure 1.1.2.22 shows a C# and Figure 1.1.2.23 a Java *for loop* example.

The *iterator* `i++` means increment `i` by 1. The *initialiser* `int i = 1` means create a loop control variable `i` and give it an initial value of 1.

The condition `i <= 5` evaluates to true if `i` is less than or equal to 5; false if `i` is greater than 5.

Python's *for loop* is different altogether from that of Delphi/Pascal, VB.Net, C# and Java.

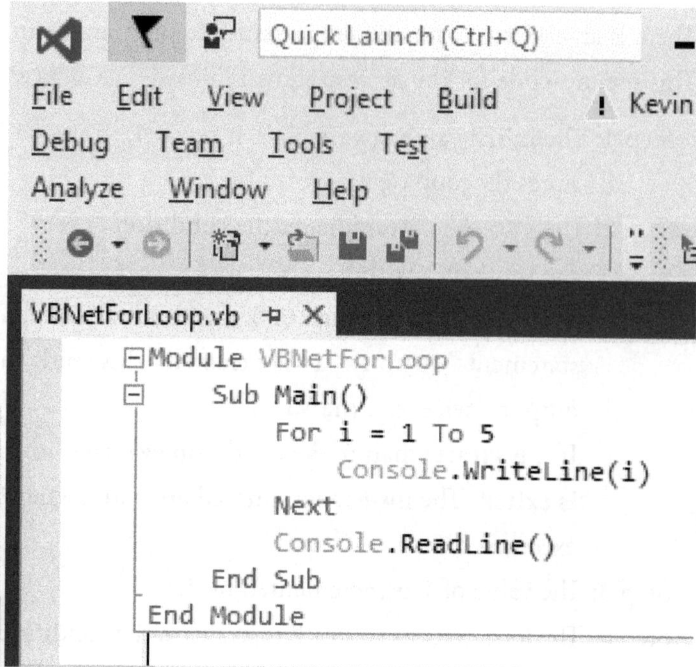

Figure 1.1.2.21 VB.NET For loop example

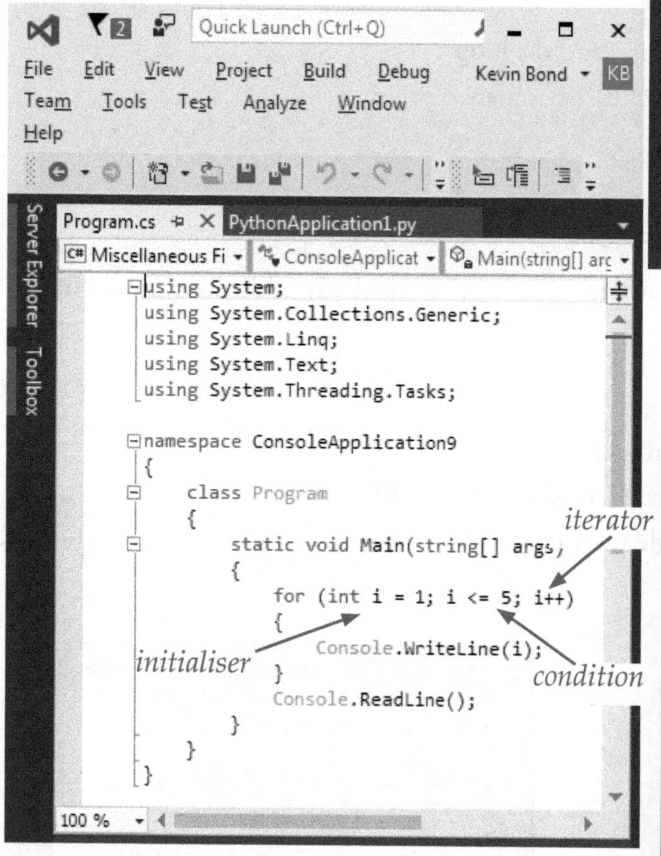

Figure 1.1.2.22 C# for loop example

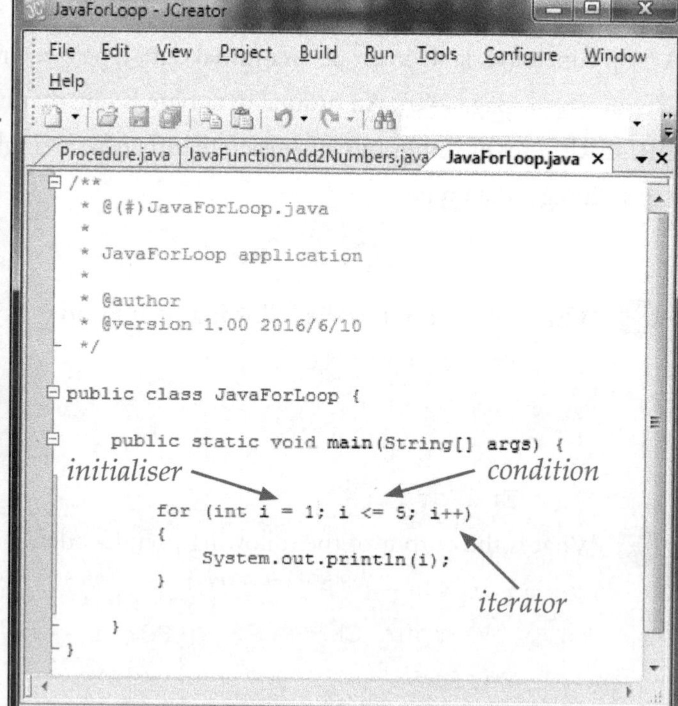

Figure 1.1.2.23 Java for loop example

Figure 1.1.2.24 shows a simple *for loop* example in Python 3.5.

The *range* function call `range(1,6)` generates the sequence of integers 1, 2, 3, 4, 5.

The last value generated is always one less then the upper bound value for the range, e.g. the last value is 5 if upper bound is 6.

Step 1: The loop control variable `i` is given the initial value 1, the first value in the range.

Step 2: The hidden condition (`i <= 5`) is evaluated by comparing the value of `i` with 5.

> If `i` is less than or equal to 5, the condition evaluates to true, and the statement `print(i)` is executed.
>
> If `i` is greater than 5, the condition evaluates to false, and the loop is exited. The instruction immediately following the body of the loop is then executed next, if one exists.

Step 3: The value of `i` is incremented by 1.

Step 4: The loop returns to the start of step 2 to evaluate the condition again.

Programming task

3 In a programming language with which you are familiar, write a program that codes the pseudo-code shown in Question 16.

Key term

Indefinite iteration:
In indefinite iteration, the number of iterations is not known before the execution of the body of the loop starts.

Key term

Infinite loop:
If the terminating condition cannot ever be met for some reason then the execution remains within the repeat or the while loop indefinitely. We then have a situation called an infinite loop.

```
for i in range(1,6):
    print(i)
```

Figure 1.1.2.24 Python 3.5 For loop example in Visual Studio 2015

Indefinite iteration

The two cases of indefinite iteration to consider are *repeat* and *while* loops. "*For loops*" do not support indefinite iteration only definite iteration.

In *Table 1.1.2.17* the value of i in both pseudo-code examples is changed inside the loop in a way that cannot be predicted because it is obtained from the user through the input device, e.g. a keyboard, when Input i executes.

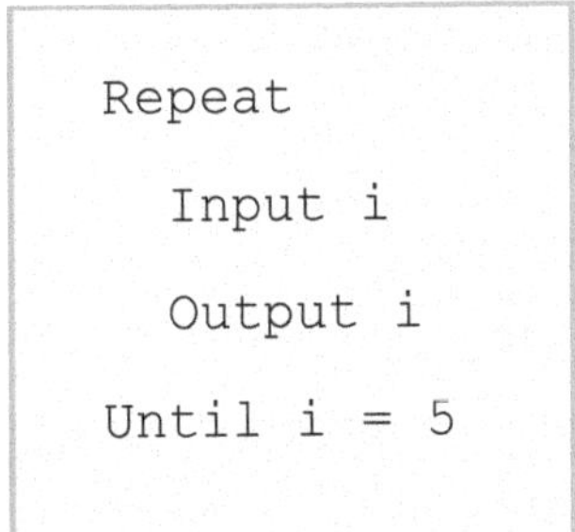

```
Repeat
   Input i
   Output i
Until i = 5
```

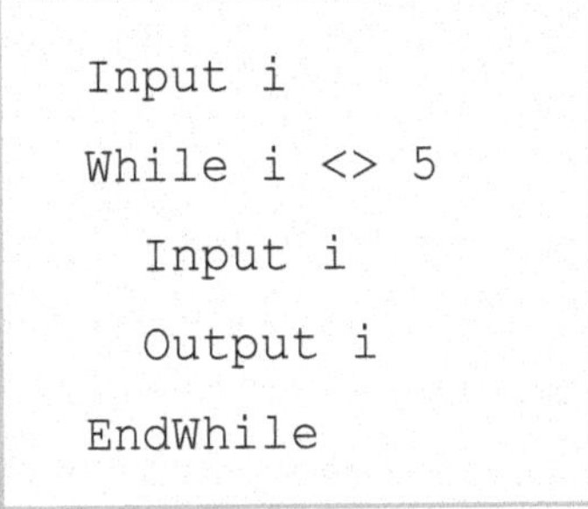

```
Input i
While i <> 5
   Input i
   Output i
EndWhile
```

Table 1.1.2.17 Indefinite iteration with repeat and while loops

The value of i before the *while loop* executes is only known at the time of execution when Input i executes.

It is therefore not possible to determine in advance the number of iterations of the body of each loop.

The number of iterations depends on when the terminating condition i = 5 becomes true for the *repeat loop* and when the terminating condition i <> 5 becomes false for the *while loop*.

If the terminating condition cannot ever be met for some reason then the execution remains within the *repeat* or the *while loop* indefinitely. We then have a situation called an **infinite loop**.

Table 1.1.2.18 shows how each loop could be written so that the iteration is indefinite.

Sometimes an infinite loop condition was not the intention but the loop's programmer has got it wrong. Exiting the loop then becomes impossible by ordinary means because the loop terminating condition can never be met.

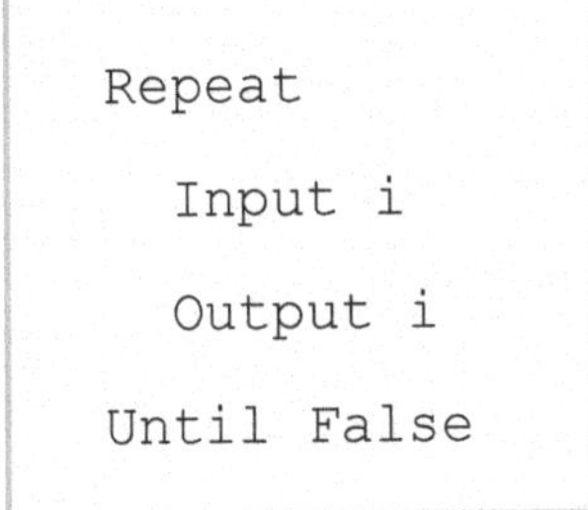

```
Repeat
   Input i
   Output i
Until False
```

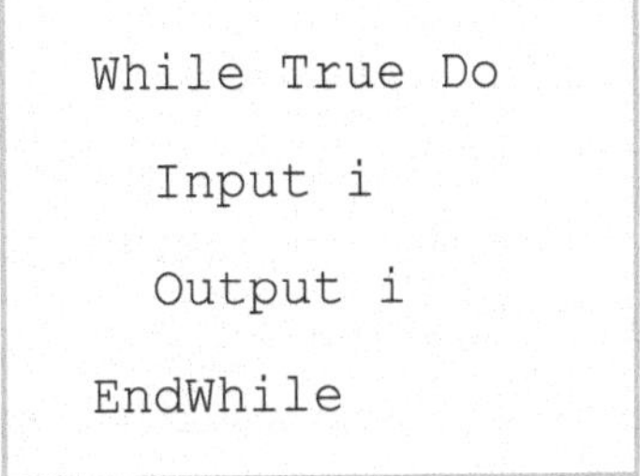

```
While True Do
   Input i
   Output i
EndWhile
```

Table 1.1.2.18 Indefinite iteration with repeat and while loops showing a situation called an infinite loop

Questions

19 What is the output of the following pseudo-code when the input is 1, 2, 3, 4, 0?

(a)
```
Sum ← 0
Repeat
  Input n
  Sum ← Sum + n
Until n = 0
Output Sum
```

(b)
```
Product ← 1
Input n
While n > 0 Do
  Product ← Product * n
  Input n
EndWhile
Output n
```

20 What is the output of the following pseudo-code?

(a)
```
j ← 4
Repeat
  j ← j - 1
  Output j
Until j < 1
```

(b)
```
j ← 4
Repeat
  j ← j + 1
  Output j
Until j > 6
```

(c)
```
j ← 4
While j < 5
  j ← j + 1
  Output j
EndWhile
```

21 What is the essential difference between *definite* and *indefinite iteration*?

22 What is the essential difference between a *repeat until* loop and a *while* loop?

23 What is meant by an *infinite loop*?

24 Write a loop in pseudo-code which demonstrates an *infinite loop*.

Indefinite iteration in Pascal, Delphi, VB.NET, C#, Java, Python

<> means not equal to in Pascal/Delphi

Figure 1.1.2.25 shows two simple examples which illustrate how a *repeat* and a *while* loop can be constructed in Pascal/Delphi. The *while loop* is the only indefinite loop supported in Python. An example is shown in Figure 1.1.2.26.

Figure 1.1.2.27 shows a simple example which illustrates how a *repeat loop* can be constructed in VB.NET. The syntax of the construct is actually of the form *Do Loop Until <condition>*. Figure 1.1.2.28 shows a simple example which illustrates how a *while loop* can be constructed in VB.NET using *Do While <condition> Loop*.

In C#, the *repeat loop* construct is implemented as a *do while loop* (Figure 1.1.2.29) and therefore the loop terminating condition is expressed as `(i != 5)`, the inverse of what it would be if *repeat until* could be used. "!=" means not equal to.

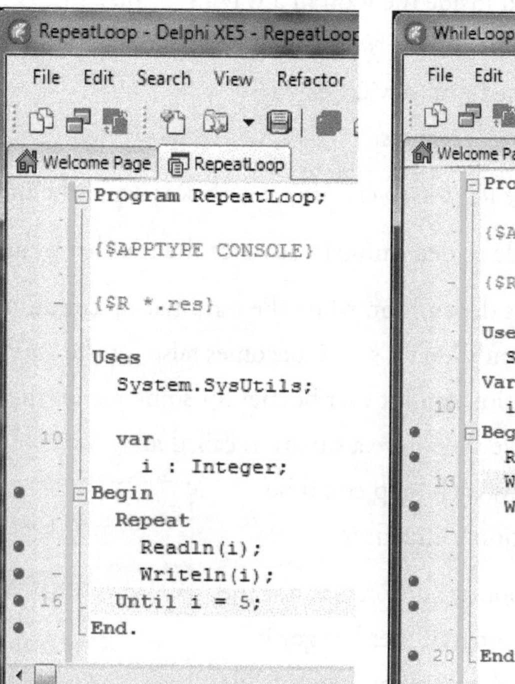

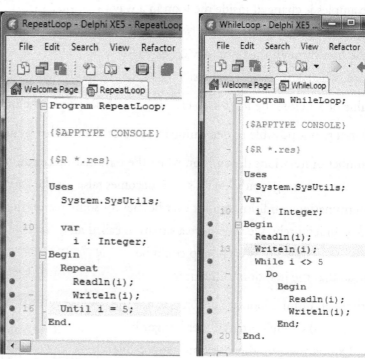

Figure 1.1.2.25 Repeat and while loops in Delphi

Figure 1.1.2.30 shows a simple example which illustrates how a *while loop* can be constructed in C#.

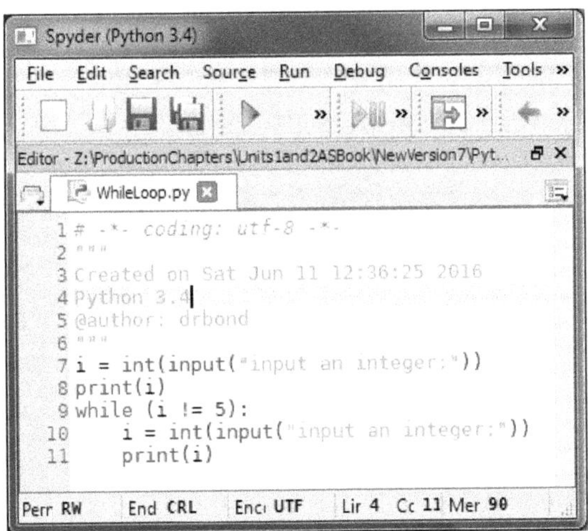

Figure 1.1.2.26 while loop in Python 3.4

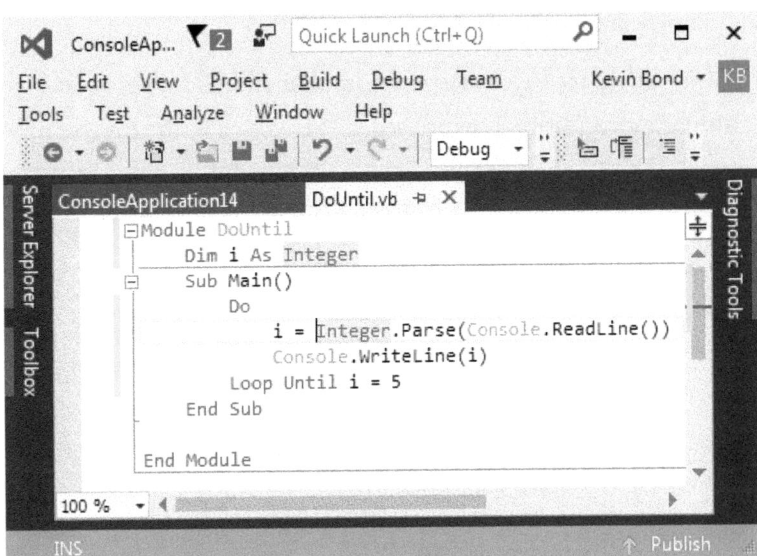

Figure 1.1.2.27 Repeat loop in VB.Net

!= means not equal to in Python

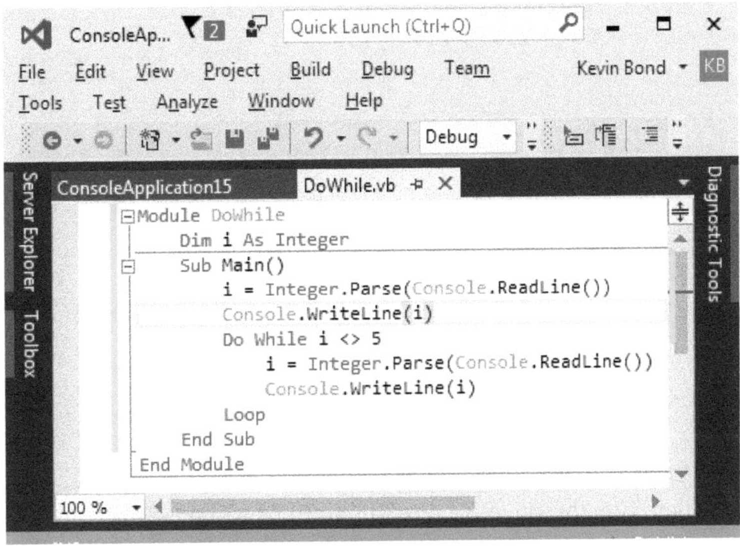

Figure 1.1.2.28 While loop in VB.Net

```
using System;
using System.Collections.Generic;
using System.Linq;
using System.Text;
using System.Threading.Tasks;

namespace ConsoleApplication13
{
    class Program
    {
        static void Main(string[] args)
        {
            int i;
            do
            {
                i = Int32.Parse(Console.ReadLine());
                Console.WriteLine(i);
            } while (i != 5);
        }
    }
}
```

Figure 1.1.2.29 Repeat loop in C# is implemented as a do while loop

```
using System;
using System.Collections.Generic;
using System.Linq;
using System.Text;
using System.Threading.Tasks;

namespace ConsoleApplication12
{
    class Program
    {
        static void Main(string[] args)
        {
            int i = Int32.Parse(Console.ReadLine());
            Console.WriteLine(i);
            while (i != 5)
            {
                i = Int32.Parse(Console.ReadLine());
                Console.WriteLine(i);
            }
        }
    }
}
```

Figure 1.1.2.30 while loop in C#

In Java, the *repeat loop* construct is implemented as a *do while loop* (Figure 1.1.2.31) and therefore the loop terminating condition is expressed as `(i != 5)`, the inverse of what it would be if *repeat until* could be used. Figure 1.1.2.32 shows a simple example which illustrates how a *while loop* can be constructed in Java.

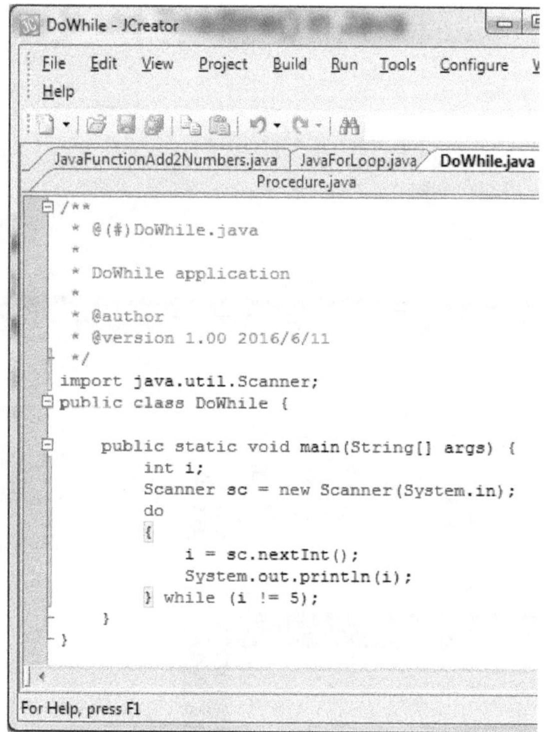

Figure 1.1.2.31 Repeat loop in Java is implemented as a Do While loop

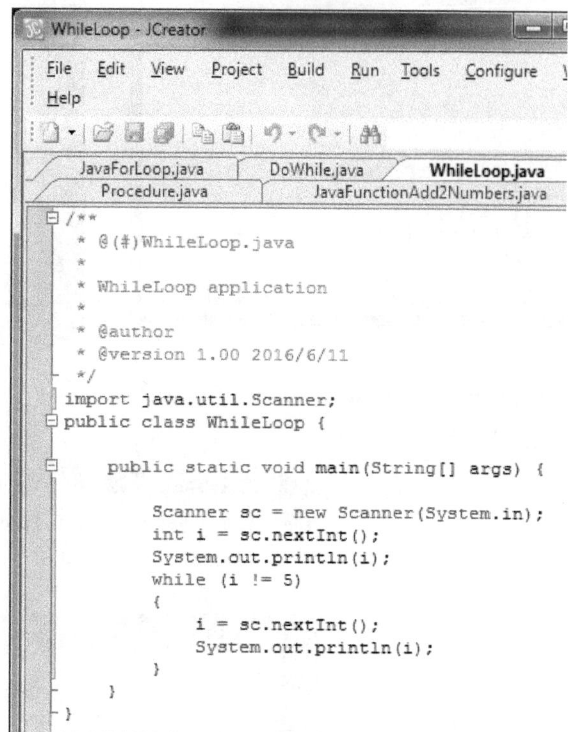

Figure 1.1.2.32 While loop in Java

Programming task

4 In a programming language with which you are familiar:

(a) Write programs that code the pseudo-code shown in Question 19(a) and 19(b).

(b) Write programs that code the pseudo-code shown in Question 20(a), 20(b) and 20(c).

Nested selection statements

The pseudo-code in Table 1.1.2.19 contains three occurrences of *selection*, one marked in **black**, one in red and one in blue. The red-marked *selection* and the blue-marked *selection statements* are each nested inside the **black**-marked *selection statement*. This pseudo-code finds the largest of three numbers. The value of the first number is stored in variable `No1`. The value of the second number is stored in variable `No2` and the third in `No3`.

The value of the largest of the three numbers is stored in variable `Largest`.

If `No1` stores the value 6, `No2` the value 3 and `No3` the value 8, the result of the comparison `If No1 > No2`

is true because 6 is greater than 3.

The `Then` block of the **black**-coloured *selection* is executed next.

```
If No1 > No2
  Then
    If No1 > No3
      Then Largest ← No1
      Else Largest ← No3
    EndIf
  Else
    If No2 > No3
      Then Largest ← No2
      Else Largest ← No3
    EndIf
EndIf
```

Table 1.1.2.19 Pseudocode to find the largest of three numbers

This block contains another `If Then Else` statement, the one marked in red.

The result of the comparison `If No1 > No3` is false because 6 is less than 8.

The `Else` coloured in red is executed next and the value stored in variable `No3` is assigned to variable `Largest`.

Questions

25 Using the pseudocode in Table 1.1.2.19

(a) If `No1` stores the value 6, `No2` the value 7 and `No3` the value 5 which selection statements are executed? Explain your answer.

(b) If `No1` stores the value 6, `No2` the value 6 and `No3` the value 5 which selection statements are executed? Explain your answer.

Programming task

5 Write a program which defines a function that finds the largest of three integers, *x*, *y*, and *z*. The program should display the largest.

Nested iteration statements

We may place a *for loop* inside a *for loop* as shown in Table 1.1.2.20 The inner *for loop* executes for each value of the loop control variable `i` of the outer *for loop*. The trace table, Table 1.1.2.21, shows the output and the values of `i` and `j`, the outer loop and inner loop control variables, respectively, for the first few values of the trace.

```
For i ← 1 To 5
  For j ← 1 To 4
    Output i
  EndFor
EndFor
```

Table 1.1.2.20 Nested for loop

i	j	Output
1	1	1
1	2	1
1	3	1
2	1	2
2	2	2
2	3	2

Table 1.1.2.21 Trace table

Questions

26 What is the output of the following pseudo-code?

(a)
```
For i ← 1 To 2
  For j ← 1 To 3
    Output j
  EndFor
EndFor
```

(b)
```
For i ← 1 To 3
  For j ← 1 To i
    Output j
  EndFor
EndFor
```

27 What is the output of the following pseudo-code?

(a)
```
For Ch1 ← 'A' To 'C'
  For Ch2 ← 'A' To Ch1
    Output Ch2
  EndFor
EndFor
```

(b)
```
For Ch1 ← 'a' To 'c'
  For Ch2 ← 'a' To 'c'
    For Ch3 ← 'a' To 'c'
      Output Ch1, Ch2, Ch3
    EndFor
  EndFor
EndFor
```

Questions

28 Write the following nested *for loop* as a single for loop

```
For i ← 1 To 4
  For j ← 3 To 5
    Output('*')
  EndFor
EndFor
```

29 Complete the trace table, Table 1.1.2.22, by hand tracing the following pseudo-code

```
For i ← 0 To 1
  For j ← 0 To 2
    Output j
  EndFor
EndFor
```

i	j	Output
0	0	

Table 1.1.2.22 Trace table

Programming tasks

6 In a programming language with which you are familiar,

(a) Write a program that codes the pseudo-code shown in Question 26(a).

(b) Write a program that codes the pseudo-code shown in Question 26(b).

Using meaningful identifier names

The names that have been used for variables, constants, subroutines such as `RunningTotal`, `NO_OF_DAYS_IN_WEEK`, `drawsquare`, `Cube` are all examples of identifiers. These identifiers describe what they represent, e.g. `RunningTotal`. **When an identifier is descriptive of what it represents or of its purpose, we say that it has a meaningful name.**

The following points are relevant to why programmers should use meaningful identifier names:

- Meaningful identifier names make it easier for the programmer to understand the source code because meaningfully-named identifiers describe what they represent or do
- Programmers spend far longer reading their source code than writing it so it is important that the source code is as descriptive of what it does as possible
- Programmers spend a lot of time reading other programmers' source code as well as their own and so it is important that the source code is as descriptive of what it does as possible
- Program source code needs to make sense when it is read, i.e. it should be possible to understand what the source code has been written to do, otherwise its intention will be unclear
- A programmer may wish/has to use source code that someone else has written. To do this successfully they need at least to understand the source code
- A programmer may be tasked to debug a program because it contains runtime/logical errors, e.g. it doesn't do what it is expected to do. The programmer will need to understand the source code in order to debug it

- A programmer may also be tasked to modify a program because what it is required to do has changed. The programmer will need to understand the source code to change it successfully.

Table 1.1.2.23 shows pseudo-code which sums the first 10 natural numbers.

```
x ← 0            // Initialise running total
y ← 1            // Initialise natural number
Repeat
  x ← x + y      // add natural number to running total
  y ← y + 1      // Increment natural number
Until y = 11     // Terminate loop when natural number is 11
```

Table 1.1.2.23 Pseudo-code to sum the first 10 natural numbers

Comments have been added to the pseudo-code which describe the purpose of each statement because the identifier names alone are not sufficient to make the purpose clear (this may be an oversimplified example but it is done to make a point).

Table 1.1.2.24 shows the pseudo-code rewritten with meaningful/self-describing identifier names.

Key term

Meaningful identifier name: When an identifier is descriptive of what it represents or of its purpose, we say that it has a meaningful name.

```
RunningTotal ← 0
NaturalNo ← 1
Repeat
  RunningTotal ← RunningTotal + NaturalNo
  NaturalNo ← NaturalNo + 1
Until NaturalNo = 11
```

Table 1.1.2.24 Pseudo-code to sum the first 10 natural numbers

The pseudo-code comments in Table 1.1.2.23 use 148 characters whilst the meaningful/self-describing identifiers in the pseudo-code in Table 1.1.2.24 use 61 characters.

We say that the pseudo-code in Table 1.1.2.24 is self-documenting and because of this comments are largely superfluous.

Questions

30 Why is it important to use meaningful identifier names?

Programming tasks

7 In a programming language with which you are familiar,

(a) Write a program to print a " 4 times table " in the form

```
1 x 4 =  4
2 x 4 =  8
3 x 4 = 12
etc.
```

(b) Write a program to read in any integer, represented by the letter *n* say, and print an 'n times table'.

8 Write a program to print all the multiples of 3, starting at 3 and finishing at 90.

Programming tasks

9 In a programming language with which you are familiar,

(a) Write a program to input 6 numbers and display how many of them are zero.

(b) Write a program to input 10 numbers and print the largest. (Hint: assume the first number is the largest, store it in Largest, compare each new number with Largest, store new number in Largest if new number is larger. Alternatively, set Largest to 0 at start of program, then compare each new number with Largest as before).

10 Write a program to determine if a given year is a leap year. A leap year is a year which is exactly divisible by 4 and not a century year unless the century year is exactly divisible by 400. (Hint: (Year Mod 4) = 0 tests for exact division by 4).

11 Write a program that will enable a user to input the day of the week on which a month begins and the number of days in the month. The program should produce as output a calendar for the given month in the format shown below

Sun	Mon	Tues	Wed	Thurs	Fri	Sat
		1	2	3	4	5
6	7	8	9	10	11	12
13	14	15	16	17	18	19
20	21	22	23	24	25	26
27	28	29	30	31		

The day on which the month begins should be entered as an integer where 1 corresponds to Sunday, 2 to Monday and so on.

In this chapter you have covered:

- The following statement types in sufficient depth to understand and be able to use them, and to know how they can be combined in programs:
  - variable declaration
  - constant declaration
  - assignment
  - iteration
  - selection
  - subroutine(procedure/function
- Use of definite and indefinite iteration, including indefinite iteration with the condition at the start or end of the iterative structure (a theoretical understanding of condition(s) at either end of an iterative structure is required, regardless of whether they are supported by the language being used)
- The use of nested selection and nested iteration structures
- Meaningful identifier names and why it is important to use them.

1 Fundamentals of programming

1.1 Programming

Learning objectives:

- *Be familiar with and be able to use:*
  - *addition*
  - *subtraction*
  - *multiplication*
  - *real/float division*
  - *integer division, including remainders*
  - *exponentiation*
  - *rounding*
  - *truncation*

1.1.3 Arithmetic operations in a programming language

Addition/Subtraction/Multiplication

Arithmetic expressions

5 + 2

is an example of an arithmetic expression.

This expression has two operands and one operator as shown in Figure 1.1.3.1.

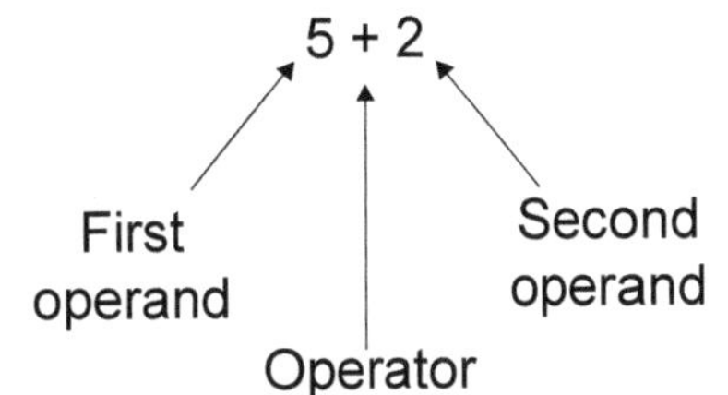

Figure 1.1.3.1 Arithmetic expression

Table 1.1.3.1 shows the arithmetic operators for the arithmetic operations addition, subtraction, multiplication and division in the programming languages C#, Java, Python, Pascal/Delphi and VB.NET.

Arithmetic Operator						
C#	Java	Python	Pascal/ Delphi	VB.NET	Operation	Example
+	+	+	+	+	Addition	3 + 5 is 8 3.0 + 2.0 is 5.0
-	-	-	-	-	Subtraction	6 – 3 is 3 6.0 – 3.0 is 3.0
*	*	*	*	*	Multiplication	3 * 2 is 6 3.0 * 2.0 is 6.0
/	/	/	/	/	Division	5.0 / 2.0 is 2.5

Table 1.1.3.1 Arithmetic operations in C#, Java, Python, Pascal/Delphi and VB.NET

Care needs to be taken with division because two kinds of division exist:

- Real number or float division
- Integer division

Real/floating point division

In real or floating point division, the quotient is a number with a fractional part, e.g. if 3 is divided by 2 the quotient is 1.5 in real/float division

3 / 2 = 1.5 (Floating point quotient)

whereas in integer division the quotient is integer, e.g.

3 / 2 = 1 (Integer quotient)

Questions

1. Express the following mathematical formulae in programming language form using the arithmetic operators from Table 1.1.3.1.

(a) $b^2 - 4ac$ (b) $\frac{1}{1 + x^2}$ (c) $\frac{1}{u} + \frac{1}{v}$

Programming task

1. Table 1.1.3.2 shows two simultaneous linear equations in two variables x and y. The coefficients are a, b, m, n. For example, if the two equations are 5x + 4y = 22 and 3x + 8y = 30 then a = 5, b = 4, c = 22, m = 3, n = 8 and d = 30. To solve for x and y we can use the following

$$x = \frac{(b*d - n*c)}{(m*b - a*n)} \qquad y = \frac{(a*d - m*c)}{(a*b - m*b)}$$

Write a program to solve for x and y given the coefficients a, b, m, n of two simultaneous linear equations. Test your program with a = 5, b = 4, c = 22, m = 3, n = 8 and d = 30.

a.x + b.y = c
m.x + n.y = d

Table 1.1.3.2

Programming languages differ in how they support the operations of real/float division and integer division. Table 1.1.3.3 shows examples of both real/float and integer division in C#, Java, Python 2.x, Python 3.x, Pascal/Delphi and VB.NET.

Language	Example	Output
C#	`Console.WriteLine("Integer quotient: {0}", 3/2);` `Console.WriteLine("Float quotient: {0}", 3.0/2);`	`Integer quotient: 1` `Float quotient: 1.5`
Java	`System.out.println("Integer quotient: " + 3/2);` `System.out.println("Float quotient: " + 3.0/2);`	`Integer quotient: 1` `Float quotient: 1.5`
Python 2.x	`print "Integer quotient: ", 3/2` `print "Float quotient: ", 3.0/2`	`Integer quotient: 1` `Float quotient: 1.5`
Python 3.x	`print("Integer quotient: ", 3//2)` `print("Float quotient: ", 3/2)`	`Integer quotient: 1` `Float quotient: 1.5`

Pascal/Delphi	`Writeln('Integer Quotient: ', 3 Div 2);`
	`Writeln('Real Quotient: ', 3/2);`
	`Writeln('Real Quotient: ', 3.0/2);`
		`Integer Quotient: 1`
		`Real Quotient: 1.5`
		`Real Quotient: 1.5`

VB.NET	`Console.WriteLine("Integer Quotient: {0}", 3\2)` `Console.WriteLine("Float Quotient: {0}", 3/2)`	`Integer Quotient: 1` `Float Quotient: 1.5`

Table 1.1.3.3 Comparison of real/float division and integer division in C#, Java, Python, Pascal/Delphi and VB.NET

Integer division

The operation of integer division computes the integral part of the result of dividing the first operand by the second. The integral part is the whole number of times the second operand (the divisor) goes into the first operand (the dividend).

Figure 1.1.3.2 shows a length of rope of integer length L round a capstan of integer circumference C. The number of times that the rope can be wound on the circumference of the capstan is L DIV C where DIV is the **integer division operator** applied to an integer dividend and an integer divisor.

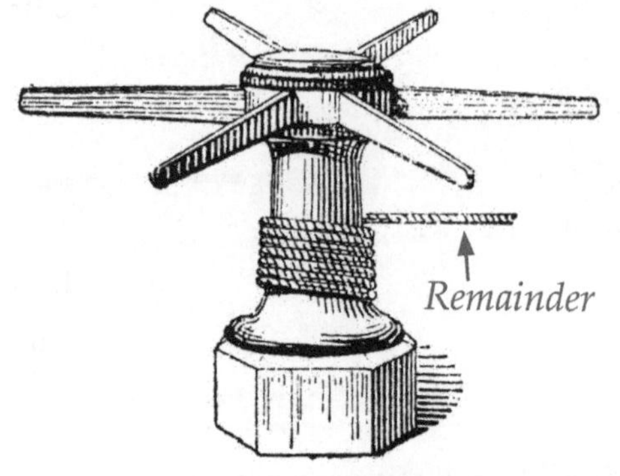

Figure 1.1.3.2 Rope wound round a capstan

The short length of rope left over is called the remainder because it is not long enough to fit the circumference. The remainder is given by *L* MOD *C* and is integral (a whole number).

Table 1.1.3.4 shows the integer division and integer remainder operators being used in C#, Java, Python, Pascal/Delphi and VB.NET.

Language	Example	Output
C#	`Console.WriteLine("Integer quotient: {0}", 5 / 2);` `Console.WriteLine("Integer remainder: {0}", 5 % 2);`	`Integer quotient: 2` `Integer remainder: 1`
Java	`System.out.println("Integer quotient: " + 5 / 2);` `System.out.println("Integer remainder: " + 5 % 2);`	`Integer quotient: 2` `Integer remainder: 1`
Python 3.x	`print("Integer quotient: ", 5 // 2)` `print("Integer remainder: ", 5 % 2)`	`Integer quotient: 2` `Integer remainder: 1`
Pascal/Delphi	`Writeln('Integer quotient: ', 5 Div 2);` `Writeln('Integer remainder: ', 5 Mod 2);`	`Integer quotient: 2` `Integer remainder: 1`
VB.NET	`Console.WriteLine("Integer quotient: {0}", 5 \ 2)` `Console.WriteLine("Integer remainder: {0}", 5 Mod 2)`	`Integer quotient: 2` `Integer remainder: 1`

Table 1.1.3.4 Integer division in C#, Java, Python, Pascal/Delphi and VB.NET

Questions

2 (a) How many times can a cotton thread of length 1655 cm be wound around a cotton reel of circumference 13 cm?

(b) How much cotton thread is left over?

3 Convert 4589 minutes into hours and minutes.

4 Explain how DIV and MOD can be used to obtain the number of hundreds, tens and units of a 3-digit integer, N.

5 Dividing an integer x by an integer y using integer division, we obtain quotient q and the remainder r.
The relationship between x, y, q and r is expressed in the following formula $x = y * q + r$
e.g. dividend x = 5, divisor y = 2, quotient q = 2, remainder r = 1, applying the formula 5 = 2 * 2 + 1.
Complete Table 1.1.3.5.

Dividend x	Divisor y	Quotient q	Remainder r
5	2	2	1
6	3	2	0
25	4	6	1
36	6		
121	7		
23	3		
1	3		
5	10		

Table 1.1.3.5

Programming task

2 Write a program to determine if a given year is a leap year.
A leap year is a year which is exactly divisible by 4 and not a century year unless the century year is exactly divisible by 400.

3 Write a program to produce a display of the time of day in the form

hours : mins : secs

given the time in seconds that have elapsed since 12:00 midnight (Hint: use DIV and MOD).

4 Write a program to display the number of hundreds, tens and units of a 3-digit integer number, N.

5 Write a program to display the digits, one per line, of an integer, N.

Programming task

6 Write a program to work out the day of the week on which a given date falls using the formula shown below

DayCode = ((13 * Month – 1) DIV 5 + Decade DIV 4 + Century DIV 4 + Decade + Day – 2 * Century) Mod 7

This calculates the day of the week on which any date after 1 January 1583 will fall or has fallen.

In this formula, the year is considered as consisting of two parts neither of which have their usual meaning:

- a century represented by the first two digits of its integer representation, e.g. 20 in 2010, and
- a decade represented by the last two digits, e.g. 10 in 2010.

The date for which the corresponding day of the week is required must be coded in the following way:

- The day of the month an integer between 1 and 31 inclusive
- The year is an integer, e.g. 1996 represents the year 1996.
- The month must be coded as an integer as follows:
    - March is coded 1, April as 2 and so on until December, which is coded as 10
    - January and February are coded as 11 and 12 respectively of the **previous year**. So, for example, 15 February 1996 would be represented as day 15, month 12 of year 1995.

The result of applying this formula is an integer in the range 0 – 6 inclusive.
The integer 0 represents Sunday, 1 represents Monday and so on.
Your program should use the days of the week in its output, i.e. Sunday, Monday, etc.

Questions

6 The following pseudo-code calculates the quotient q and remainder r when an integer x is divided by an integer y using integer division

```
r ← x
q ← 0
While r >= y
   r ← r - y
   q ← q + 1
EndWhile
```

Complete Table 1.1.3.6 by tracing this pseudo-code by hand.

Iteration	x	y	r	q	r > = y
0	7	2	7	0	True

Table 1.1.3.6 Trace table

Exponentiation

Exponentiation is the operation of raising one quantity to the power of another,

e.g. $6^7 = 6 \times 6 \times 6 \times 6 \times 6 \times 6 \times 6 = 279936$.

C#, Java, Python, Delphi, and Pascal provide library support for the exponentiation operation as follows:

- C# : Math.Pow(Quantity, PowerValue)
- Java : Math.pow(quantity, powerValue)
- Python: math.pow(quantity, power_value) and quantity**power_value
- Delphi: System.Math.Power(Quantity, PowerValue)
- Pascal: Math.Power(Quantity, PowerValue)
- VB.NET provides the ^ operator: Quantity ^ PowerValue and Math.Pow(Quantity, PowerValue).

Operator precedence	Highest
()	Highest (evaluated first)
Exponentiation	↓
*, /, DIV, MOD	
+, -	Lowest (evaluated last)

Table 1.1.3.7 Operator precedence

Table 1.1.3.8 shows exponentiation in use in C#, Java, Python, Delphi, Pascal and VB.NET.

Language	Example	Output
C#	`Console.WriteLine("6 raised to the power of 7: {0}", Math.Pow(6, 7));`	6 raised to the power of 7: 279936
Java	`System.out.println("6 raised to the power of 7: " + Math.pow(6, 7));`	6 raised to the power of 7: 279936.0

Python	`import math`
	`print("6 raised to the power 7: ", math.pow(6, 7))`
	`print(6**7)`
		6 raised to the power of 7: 279936.0

Delphi	`Program Exponentiation;`
	`Uses`
	`  System.Math;`
	`Begin`
	`  Writeln('6 raised to the power of 7: ', Power(6, 7): 8:1);`
	`  Readln;`
	`End.`
		6 raised to the power of 7: 279936.0

Pascal (Lazarus)	`Program Exponentiation;`
	`Uses`
	`  Math;`
	`Begin`
	`  Writeln('6 raised to the power of 7: ', Power(6, 7): 8:1);`
	`  Readln;`
	`End.`
		6 raised to the power of 7: 279936.0

VB.NET	`Console.WriteLine("6 raised to the power of 7: {0}", 6 ^ 7)` `Console.WriteLine("6 raised to the power of 7: {0}", Math.Pow(6,7))`	6 raised to the power of 7: 279936

Table 1.1.3.8 Exponentiation in C#, Java, Python, Pascal/Delphi and VB.NET

Programming task

7 The volume of a sphere is $\frac{4\pi R^3}{3}$ where R is the radius of the sphere.
Write a program which calculates and displays the volume of a sphere of a given radius R. Your program should use exponentiation.

8 Write a program which sums the following series and displays the result

$$\frac{1}{2^1} + \frac{1}{3^2} + \frac{1}{5^3} + \frac{1}{7^4} + \frac{1}{9^5} + \frac{1}{11^6}$$

Programming task

9 A mortgage (a loan to purchase a house) is repaid monthly over Y years at an annual rate of interest of R%. The amount borrowed is A. The monthly repayment P is given by the formula

$$P = \frac{A \times \frac{R}{1200} \times \left(1 + \frac{R}{1200}\right)^{12Y}}{\left(1 + \frac{R}{1200}\right)^{12Y} - 1}$$

Write a program to calculate the monthly payment P for a loan A which is repaid over Y years at an annual interest of R%. The program should prompt the user to enter values for A, Y and R.

Rounding

Rounding off

Numbers can be rounded in many ways. *Table 1.1.3.9* shows rounding in C#, Java, Python, Pascal/Delphi and VB.NET in which rounding takes place to the closest integer value to the argument (**rounding off**).
When the fractional component is halfway between two integers, one of which is even and the other odd, then the even number is returned in C#, Python, Pascal/Delphi, and VB.NET. Java is the exception to this.

Lang.	Example	Output
C#	`Console.WriteLine("Rounding a float: {0}", Math.Round(5.667));`	`Rounding a float: 6`
	`Console.WriteLine("Rounding a float: {0}", Math.Round(-5.667));`	`Rounding a float: -6`
	`Console.WriteLine("Rounding a float: {0}", Math.Round(5.5));`	`Rounding a float: 6`
	`Console.WriteLine("Rounding a float: {0}", Math.Round(-5.5));`	`Rounding a float: -6`
	`Console.WriteLine("Rounding a float: {0}", Math.Round(5.4));`	`Rounding a float: 5`
	`Console.WriteLine("Rounding a float: {0}", Math.Round(-5.4));`	`Rounding a float: -5`
	`Console.WriteLine("Rounding a float: {0}", Math.Round(4.5));`	`Rounding a float: 4`
	`Console.WriteLine("Rounding a float: {0}", Math.Round(-4.5));`	`Rounding a float: -4`
Java	`System.out.println("Rounding a float: " + Math.round(5.667));`	`Rounding a float: 6`
	`System.out.println("Rounding a float: " + Math.round(-5.667));`	`Rounding a float: -6`
	`System.out.println("Rounding a float: " + Math.round(5.5));`	`Rounding a float: 6`
	`System.out.println("Rounding a float: " + Math.round(-5.5));`	`Rounding a float: -5`
	`System.out.println("Rounding a float: " + Math.round(5.4));`	`Rounding a float: 5`
	`System.out.println("Rounding a float: " + Math.round(-5.4));`	`Rounding a float: -5`
	`System.out.println("Rounding a float: " + Math.round(4.5));`	`Rounding a float: 5`
	`System.out.println("Rounding a float: " + Math.round(-4.5));`	`Rounding a float: -4`
Python	`from math import round`	
	`print("Rounding a float: ", round(5.667));`	`Rounding a float: 6`
	`print("Rounding a float: ", round(-5.667));`	`Rounding a float: -6`
	`print("Rounding a float: ", round(5.5));`	`Rounding a float: 6`
	`print("Rounding a float: ", round(-5.5));`	`Rounding a float: -6`
	`print("Rounding a float: ", round(5.4));`	`Rounding a float: 5`
	`print("Rounding a float: ", round(-5.4));`	`Rounding a float: -5`
	`print("Rounding a float: ", round(4.5));`	`Rounding a float: 4`
	`print("Rounding a float: ", round(-4.5));`	`Rounding a float: -4`
Pascal/ Delphi	`Writeln('Rounding a real: ', Round(5.667));`	`Rounding a real: 6`
	`Writeln('Rounding a real: ', Round(-5.667));`	`Rounding a real: -6`
	`Writeln('Rounding a real: ', Round(5.5));`	`Rounding a real: 6`
	`Writeln('Rounding a real: ', Round(-5.5));`	`Rounding a real: -6`
	`Writeln('Rounding a real: ', Round(5.4));`	`Rounding a real: 5`
	`Writeln('Rounding a real: ', Round(-5.4));`	`Rounding a real: -5`
	`Writeln('Rounding a real: ', Round(4.5));`	`Rounding a real: 4`
	`Writeln('Rounding a real: ', Round(-4.5));`	`Rounding a real: -4`
VB.NET	`Console.WriteLine("Rounding a float: {0}", Math.Round(5.667))`	`Rounding a float: 6`
	`Console.WriteLine("Rounding a float: {0}", Math.Round(-5.667))`	`Rounding a float: -6`
	`Console.WriteLine("Rounding a float: {0}", Math.Round(5.5))`	`Rounding a float: 6`
	`Console.WriteLine("Rounding a float: {0}", Math.Round(-5.5))`	`Rounding a float: -6`
	`Console.WriteLine("Rounding a float: {0}", Math.Round(5.4))`	`Rounding a float: 5`
	`Console.WriteLine("Rounding a float: {0}", Math.Round(-5.4))`	`Rounding a float: -5`
	`Console.WriteLine("Rounding a float: {0}", Math.Round(4.5))`	`Rounding a float: 4`
	`Console.WriteLine("Rounding a float: {0}", Math.Round(-4.5))`	`Rounding a float: -4`

Table 1.1.3.9 Rounding off in C#, Java, Python, Pascal/Delphi and VB.NET

Rounding up and rounding down

The operation of rounding up returns the smallest integral value that is greater than or equal to the specified real or floating-point number. This kind of rounding is sometimes called rounding toward positive infinity.

The operation of rounding down returns the largest integer less than or equal to the specified real or floating-point number. This kind of rounding is sometimes called rounding toward negative infinity.

Table 1.1.3.10 shows the functions for rounding up and rounding down available in in C#, Java, Python, Pascal/Delphi and VB.NET.

Lang.	Example	Output
C#	`Console.WriteLine("Rounding up a float: {0}", Math.Ceiling(5.667));` `Console.WriteLine("Rounding down a float: {0}", Math.Floor(5.667));`	`Rounding up a float: 6` `Rounding down a float: 5`
Java	`System.out.println("Rounding up a float: " + (int)Math.ceil(5.667));` `System.out.println("Rounding down a float: " + (int)Math.floor(5.667));`	`Rounding up a float: 6` `Rounding down a float: 5`

Python	`from math import ceil, floor`
	`print("Rounding up a float:  ", ceil(5.667))`
	`print("Rounding down a float:  ", floor(5.667))`
		`Rounding up a float: 6`
		`Rounding down a float: 5`

Pascal/ Delphi	`Writeln('Rounding up a real: ', Ceil(5.667));` `Writeln('Rounding down a real: ', Floor(5.667));`	`Rounding up a real: 6` `Rounding down a real: 5`
VB.NET	`Console.WriteLine("Rounding up a float: {0}", Math.Ceiling(5.667))` `Console.WriteLine("Rounding down a float: {0}", Math.Floor(5.667))`	`Rounding up a float: 6` `Rounding down a float: 5`

Table 1.1.3.10 Rounding up and rounding down in C#, Java, Python, Pascal/Delphi and VB.NET

In the case of Java, because the integral part of the argument is returned as a float, it displays as a float. To avoid this, the returned value is converted to integer by a process called casting. To cast the float to integer `(int)` is placed in front of `Math.floor(5.667)`. C# and VB.NET also return the integral value as a float but `WriteLine` formats the output as integer.

Truncation

When a number with a fractional part is truncated the fractional part is removed, e.g. 5.667 becomes 5.

The operation of truncation returns the integral part of the number. Table 1.1.3.11 shows this operation applied to the argument 5.667 in C#, Java, Python, Pascal/Delphi and VB.NET.

The method `floor` in Java gives the largest integer that is less than or equal to the argument.

In the case of negative values this will give a more negative value than the argument, e.g. -5.667 becomes -6 after the operation `(int) Math.floor` is applied. The method `ceil` in Java gives the smallest integer that is greater than or equal to the argument.

In the case of negative values this will give a less negative value than the argument, e.g. -5.667 becomes -5 after the operation `(int) Math.ceil` is applied.

Lang.	Example	Output
C#	`Console.WriteLine("Truncating a float: {0}", Math.Truncate(5.667));` `Console.WriteLine("Truncating a float: {0}", Math.Truncate(-5.667));`	`Truncating a float: 5` `Truncating a float: -5`
Java	`System.out.println("Truncating a float: " + (int)Math.floor(5.667));` `System.out.println("Truncating a float: " + (int)Math.ceil(-5.667));`	`Truncating a float: 5` `Truncating a float: -5`

Python	`from math import trunc`
	`print("Truncating a float:  ", trunc(5.667))`
	`print("Truncating a float:  ", trunc(-5.667))`
		`Truncating a float: 5`
		`Truncating a float: -5`

Pascal/ Delphi	`Writeln('Truncating a real: ', Trunc(5.667));` `Writeln('Truncating a real: ', Trunc(-5.667));`	`Truncating a real: 5` `Truncating a real: -5`
VB.NET	`Console.WriteLine("Truncating a float: {0}", Math.Truncate(5.667))` `Console.WriteLine("Truncating a float: {0}", Math.Truncate(-5.667))`	`Truncating a float: 5` `Truncating a float: -5`

Table 1.1.3.11 Truncation in C#, Java, Python, Pascal/Delphi and VB.NET

Questions

7. Explain how to obtain the 3 most significant figures of the number 5.6676593, i.e. 5, 6, 6 by using a combination of truncation, subtraction and multiplication by 10.

8. Explain how to round 5.6676593 to 2 decimal places by using a combination of multiplication and division by 10 and a rounding operation which rounds to the closest integer value to the argument

In this chapter you have covered:

- Be familiar with and be able to use:
    - addition
    - subtraction
    - multiplication
    - real/float division
    - integer division, including remainders
    - exponentiation
    - rounding
    - truncation

1.1 Programming

Learning objectives:

- *Be familiar with and be able to use:*
  - *equal to*
  - *not equal to*
  - *less than*
  - *greater than*
  - *less than or equal to*
  - *greater than or equal to*

1.1.4 Relational operators in a programming language

Relational operators

Expressions involving the relational operators shown in Table 1.1.4.1 produce Boolean results. For example,

2 < 3	True
5 > 6	False

Therefore, such Boolean expressions may be assigned to any Boolean variable, e.g. `FlagIsTrue`.

The following pseudo-code outputs the value True because 2 < 3 evaluates to True :

```
FlagIsTrue ← 2 < 3
Output FlagIsTrue
```

The following pseudo-code outputs the value False because 5 < 6 evaluates to False:

```
FlagIsTrue ← 5 > 6
Output FlagIsTrue
```

Operator C#	Operator Java	Operator Python	Operator Pascal/Delphi	Operator VB.NET	Meaning	Example (Pascal)	Outcome
==	==	==	=	=	Equal To	6 = 6	True
<	<	<	<	<	Less Than	4 < 7	True
<=	<=	<=	<=	<=	Less Than Or Equal To	7 <= 3	False
>	>	>	>	>	Greater Than	34 > 12	True
>=	>=	>=	>=	>=	Greater Than Or Equal To	23 >= 23	True
!=	!=	!=	<>	<>	Not Equal To	6 <> 6	False

Table 1.1.4.1 Relational operators in C#, Java, Python, Pascal/Delphi and VB.NET

Relational operators are more commonly used in selection statements and loops.

For example,

```
If x >= 6
  Then Output "x is greater than or equal to 6"
  Else Output "x is not greater than or equal to 6"
EndIf

While x < 7
  x ← x + 2
  Output x
EndWhile
```

Questions

1 What is the outcome of evaluating each of the following expressions if `x` stores the value 5 and `y` the value 10?

(a) `x = y` (b) `2*x < y` (c) `2*x <= y` (d) `x > y` (e) `2*x > y` (f) `x <> y` (g) `10*x <> 5*y`

2 What value is output by the following pseudo-code if `Flag` is a Boolean variable?

```
Flag ← 6 > 8
Output Flag
```

3 What message is output by the following pseudo-code?

```
If  6 <> 6
  Then Output "Have a nice morning!"
  Else Output "Have a nice evening!"
```

In this chapter you have covered:

- Using and becoming familiar with:
  - equal to
  - not equal to
  - less than
  - greater than
  - less than or equal to
  - greater than or equal to

1 Fundamentals of programming

1.1 Programming

Learning objectives:

- *Be familiar with and be able to use:*
  - *NOT*
  - *AND*
  - *OR*
  - *XOR*

1.1.5 Boolean operations in a programming language

Boolean operators

Operators which act on Boolean operands or Boolean values and evaluate or return a Boolean value are called **Boolean operators**.

Boolean operands or values are those that are either True or False.

Most programming languages support the Boolean operators NOT, AND, OR and XOR so that a programming statement such as the following involving a Boolean operation can be written

```
If (x > 5) AND (y < 3) Then Output "A message"
```

Boolean operators are used to perform the **Boolean operations**

- `x AND y`
- `x OR y`
- `x XOR y`
- `Not x`

where `x` and `y` are Boolean variables or Boolean expressions.

For example if operand `x` is True and operand `y` is False then

- `x AND y` evaluates to False
- `x OR y` evaluates to True
- `x XOR y` evaluates to True
- `Not x` evaluates to False

Table 1.1.5.1 shows the symbols used for these Boolean operators in the programming languages, C#, Java, Python, Pascal/Delphi and VB.NET and their meaning.

Key term

Boolean operators:
Operators which act on Boolean operands or Boolean values and evaluate or return a Boolean value are called Boolean operators.

Most programming languages support the Boolean operators NOT, AND, OR and XOR.

Boolean Operator					Meaning	Example (Pascal)	Outcome
C#	Java	Python	Pascal/ Delphi	VB.NET			
!	!	not	NOT	Not	Evaluates to true, if operand false; Evaluates to false if operand is true	NOT True	False
&&	&	and	AND	And	Evaluates to true if both operands are true otherwise evaluates to false	True AND True	True
||	|	or	OR	Or	Evaluates to true if at least one operand is true otherwise false	True OR False	True
^	^	^	XOR	Xor	Evaluates to true if one and only one of the operands is true. Evaluates to false if both operands are true or if both operands are false.	True XOR True	False

Table 1.1.5.1 Boolean or Logical operators operators in C#, Java, Python, Pascal/Delphi and VB.NET

Operator precedence

Operator precedence refers to the order in which operators are applied to operands in an expression.

The NOT operator has the highest precedence, followed by the AND operator, then OR and XOR operators which are at the same level of operator precedence.

Table 1.1.5.2 summarises operator precedence.

Operator precedence	Precedence
NOT	Highest (evaluated first)
AND	
OR, XOR	Lowest (evaluated last)

Table 1.1.5.2 Operator precedence of Boolean operators

For example, in the following logical expression `NOT x` is evaluated first because NOT has a higher precedence than AND.

`NOT x AND y`

If Boolean variable `x` stores the value False,

`NOT False` evaluates to True because `x` is False.

Substituting True for `NOT x` in the expression

`NOT x AND y`

we obtain `True AND y`

If Boolean variable `y` stores the value True, we obtain

`True AND True`

which evaluates to True.

If the expression is `NOT (x AND y)`

then `x AND y` is evaluated first

The result of evaluating `x AND y` is False if `x` is False and `y` is True.

We now have `NOT (False)`

which evaluates to True.

Now consider the logical expression with Boolean variables, `x`, `y` and `z` shown below

`x AND y OR z`

The operator precedence of AND is higher than OR.

If `x` and `y` store the value False and `z` the value True the expression evaluates in the following order

1. `x AND y` evaluates to False
2. `False OR z` evaluates to True

To change the order of evaluation we need to bracket the term `y OR z` in the expression `x AND y OR z` as follows

`x AND (y OR z)`

If `x` and `y` store the value False and `z` the value True the expression evaluates in the following order

1. `y OR z` evaluates to True
2. `x AND True` evaluates to False

Operators at the same level of precedence evaluate left to right in an expression.

In the following expression, x is True, y is True and z is False

```
x XOR y OR z
```

The expression evaluates in the following order

1. x XOR y evaluates to False
2. False OR False evaluates to False

If the expression is

```
x OR y XOR z
```

and x is True, y is True and z is False, the expression evaluates in the following order

1. x OR y evaluates to True
2. True XOR False evaluates to True

Questions

1. What is the outcome of evaluating each of the following expressions if x stores the value True and y the value False

   (a) NOT x (b) x AND y (c) x AND NOT y (d) x OR y (e) NOT x OR y

   (f) x XOR y (g) NOT x XOR y?

2. What is the outcome of evaluating each of the following expressions if x stores the value True, y the value False and z the value False

   (a) x AND y AND z (b) x AND y OR z (c) x OR y AND z

   (d) (x OR y) AND z (e) x AND NOT y AND z (f) x AND NOT (y AND z)

   (g) x AND NOT(y XOR z)?

3. Integer variable s stores the value 9 and integer variable t stores the value 8.
   What is the output of the following pseudo-code?

```
If (s > 3) AND (t < 6)
   Then Output "Have a nice morning!"
   Else Output "Have a nice evening!"
```

In this chapter you have covered:

- Becoming familiar with and using:
  - NOT
  - AND
  - OR
  - XOR

1 Fundamentals of programming

1.1 Programming

Learning objectives:

- *Be able to explain the differences between a variable and a constant*
- *Be able to explain the advantages of using named constants*

1.1.6 Constants and variables in a programming language

The differences between a variable and a constant

Data which are subject to change are modelled in a program by variables. A variable is simply a container in which a value may be stored for subsequent manipulation within a program.

The stored value may be changed by the program as it executes its instructions, hence the use of the term "variable" for the container.

Some of the data used in programs never change. For example, the ratio of the circumference of a circle to its diameter which is approximately 3.142.

Data which never change are modelled in a program by constants.

This means stating their values explicitly. To make a program easier to read, understand and change, a constant is given a **symbolic name** which can be used throughout the program whenever the value of the constant is required.

The advantages of using named constants

Constants make programs easier to understand by replacing data of a fixed nature such as 3.142 with a name which makes the purpose clear, e.g. Pi.

Constants make it easier to debug programs because the purpose of a constant in an expression in the program is made clear by its name, e.g. to represent the value of π. The literal value will appear in only one place in the program, i.e. where it is associated with its constant identifier, e.g. `Const Pi = 3.142`. Checking that the desired literal value is being used is easier to check if it is specified in one place only.

Constants make programs easier to modify.

For example, suppose a program needs to change the value used for π to one with greater precision. Using a named constant Pi in the program for the value of π is a benefit because changing its value where Pi is defined, e.g. `Const Pi = 3.142` automatically changes its value wherever else Pi is referenced in the program.

Constants make it easier to avoid mistakes when writing programs.

For example, suppose a literal value of π is used in several places in a program. In the first place the programmer wrote the value of π as 3.142 but in the second place the digits were transposed and the programmer wrote 3.412. In a third place, it was written 3.144.

These errors could have been avoided by defining a constant Pi = 3.142 and then using the constant's name Pi throughout the program.

Programming task

1. Write a program which calculates the following for a given radius R, use a value of $\pi = 3.142$
   - circumference of a circle
   - area of a circle
   - volume of a sphere
   - surface area of a sphere.

   You should write your program so that the value of π in the source code can be easily changed to one of greater or lesser precision.

2. The acceleration due to gravity, g, at the surface of the earth is given by

$$g = \frac{G \times M}{R^2}$$

   where G is the gravitational constant, M is the mass of the earth and R is the radius of the earth, assuming a spherical earth.
   Write a program, using the values $G = 6.672 \times 10^{-11}$,
   $M = 5.98 \times 10^{24}$, R = 6371030, which calculates the value of g.
   You should write your program so that the value of M can be easily changed in the source code to a different value (e.g. to calculate g on the moon), and easily modified to calculate the value of g at a height h above the surface of the earth.

Questions

1. State **one** difference in between a variable and a constant in a programming language.
2. State **three** advantages of using named constants in programs.

In this chapter you have covered:

- The differences between a variable and a constant
- The advantages of using named constants

1 Fundamentals of programming

1.1 Programming

Learning objectives:

- *Be familiar with and be able to use:*
  - *length*
  - *position*
  - *substring*
  - *concatenation*
  - *character → character code*
  - *character code → character*
  - *string conversion routines*
    - *string to integer*
    - *string to float*
    - *integer to string*
    - *float to string*
    - *date/time to string*
    - *string to date/time*

1.1.7 String-handling operations

ASCII and ANSI

We introduced the string data type in Chapter 1.1.1 as a sequence of characters.

Long ago, before the Internet and the World Wide Web, the only characters that mattered were unaccented uppercase and lowercase English letters based on a 26 letter alphabet, digits, and a variety of punctuation.

We have learned that computers work with numbers in the form of bit patterns. **Therefore, to store letters and other characters we have to assign each one a number.**

An encoding scheme called ASCII does just this. It was invented to encode the limited set of characters mentioned above.

In this scheme, characters are encoded using a number between 32 and 127. For example, in the ASCII character set, space is 32, and the letter "A" is 65. Device-control characters such as line feed and carriage return were added to this set of characters and allocated numbers in the range 0 to 31.

In all, the entire character set is encoded using numbers in the range 0 to 127. To represent this number range in the language of the machine, binary, requires 7 bits.

At the time, most computers worked with 8 bits not 7. Using the eighth bit made it possible to encode a further 128 characters, represented by codes in the range 128 to 255. Different OEM[1] character sets were dreamed up, which all used the top 128 characters for their own purposes.

Eventually, the OEM free-for-all got codified in the ANSI standard.

In the ANSI standard, everybody agreed on what to do for numbers below 128, which was in effect to use ASCII, but there were lots of different ways to handle the characters from 128 to 255, depending on which region of the world the computers were being made for. These different systems were called code pages. There are more than 220 DOS[2] and Windows code pages.

However, logogram-based languages such as Chinese have characters that number in the tens of thousands. These characters will never fit an 8-bit encoding scheme. It is impossible, therefore, to represent a string such as 你好世界 in any of the 8-bit ANSI encoding schemes.

Information

Code page identifiers:
Each code page is assigned a numeric code page identifier - https://msdn.microsoft.com/en-us/library/windows/desktop/dd317756(v=vs.85).aspx

Information

Character:
The Unicode Glossary defines a character as:
The smallest component of written language that has semantic value.

1 Original Equipment Manufacturer

2 DOS is short for disk operating system and an acronym for several computer operating systems that are operated by using the command line

Key term

Unicode:

Unicode is a computing industry standard for the consistent encoding, representation, and handling of text expressed in most of the world's writing systems. Unicode provides a unique number for every character: no matter what the platform; no matter what the program; no matter what the language.

Information

Unicode code charts:
http://www.unicode.org/charts/

Information

The Unicode Standard Version 8.0 - Core Specification:
http://www.unicode.org/versions/Unicode8.0.0/ch02.pdf

Information

Characters and glyphs:

Characters are represented by code points that reside only in a memory representation as strings in memory, on disk, or in data transmission. For example U+0041 is Latin capital letter A. **The Unicode Standard deals only with character codes.**

Glyphs represent the shapes that characters can have when they are rendered or displayed, e.g. 𝒜 A A A A are all Unicode U+0041. In contrast to characters, glyphs appear on the screen or paper as particular representations of one or more characters. A repertoire of glyphs makes up a font. **Glyphs are not part of the Unicode Standard.**

Unicode

The answer to this problem is an encoding scheme called Unicode (www.unicode.org).

Unicode covers all of the characters in all of the world's writing systems, plus accents and other special marks and symbols, and control codes such as tab and carriage return, and assigns each one a standard number called a Unicode code point.

Unicode version 8 defines code points for over 120,000 characters in well over 100 languages and scripts but not Klingon, which was rejected in 2001 by the Unicode Technical Committee.

The Unicode Glossary defines a character as:

- The smallest component of written language that has semantic value
- The basic unit of encoding for Unicode character encoding
- The English name for the ideographic written elements of Chinese origin.

UTF-32 is the simplest Unicode encoding form.

Each Unicode code point is represented directly by a single 32-bit code unit. Because of this, UTF-32 has a one-to-one relationship between encoded character and code unit; it is a fixed-width character encoding form.
As for all of the Unicode encoding forms, UTF-32 is restricted to representation of code points in the range $0..10FFFF_{16}$ which is a 21-bit code space.
Whilst UTF-32 provides the simplest mapping, it uses much more space than is necessary - 4 bytes for every Unicode code point or character.

Most computer-readable text is in ASCII, which requires only 7 bits which can be accommodated in 1 byte. In fact, all the characters in widespread use still number fewer than 65,536, which can be coded in 16 bits or 2 bytes. This gave rise to two other Unicode encoding forms - UTF-16 and UTF-8.

Figure 1.1.7.1 shows the three Unicode encoding forms - UTF-32, UTF-16, UTF-8 and how they are related to Unicode code points.

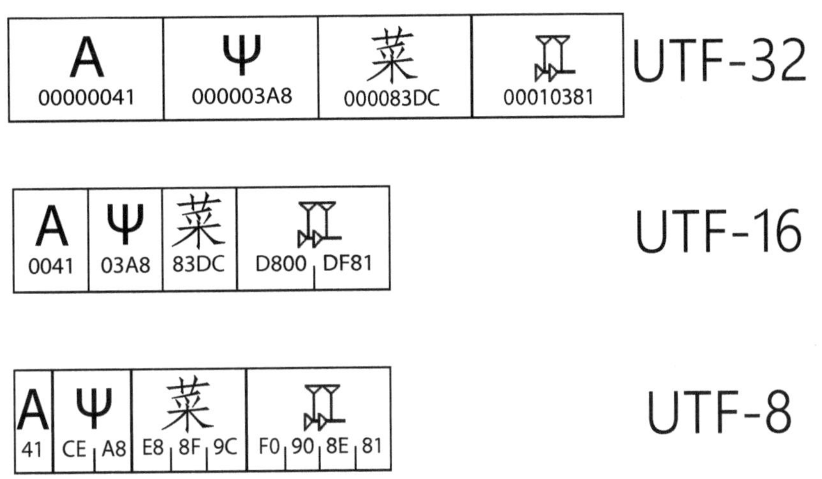

Figure 1.1.7.1 Unicode encoding forms

Note that for UTF-16 most characters can be expressed with one 16-bit code unit, whose value is the same as the code point for the character, but characters with high code points require a pair of 16-bit code units called surrogate units.

UTF-8 like UTF-16 is a variable-length encoding of Unicode code points.

UTF-8 uses between 1 and 4 bytes to represent a Unicode code point or character but only 1 byte for ASCII characters, and only 2 or 3 bytes for most characters in common use.

Information

Unicode code points:
Search Unicode code point and its corresponding character, UTF-32, UTF-16, UTF-8 encoding:
http://www.fileformat.info/info/unicode/char/search.htm

The high order bits of the first byte of the encoding indicate how many bytes follow. A high order 0 indicates 7-bit ASCII, where each character takes only 1 byte, so it is identical to conventional ASCII. A high order 110 indicates that each character takes 2 bytes; the second byte begins with 10. Larger code points are also encoded in a similar manner. Table 1.1.7.1 shows how the encoding indicates the number of bytes.

Key point

UTF:
Unicode offers multiple ways of representing the same code point (or Unicode character numerical value) in terms of actual storage, or of physical bytes.
UTF is an acronym for Unicode Transformation Format.
These are bidirectional, algorithmic mappings which map each code point (the absolute numeric representation of a character) to a unique sequence of bytes representing the given character.

Strings

A string is a sequence of zero or more characters.

				Code point range	
0xxxxxxx				0 - 127	ASCII
110xxxxx	10xxxxxx			128 - 2047	Values < 128 unused
1110xxxx	10xxxxxx	10xxxxxx		2048 - 65535	Values < 2028 unused
11110xxx	10xxxxxx	10xxxxxx	10xxxxxx	65536 - 0x10FFFF	Other values unused

Table 1.1.7.1 *Variable length encoding in UTF-8*

The encoding used for each character in a string could be ASCII (7-bits), ANSI (8 bits = ASCII/OEM), UTF-32, UTF-16, or UTF-8.
UTF-16 is effectively how characters are maintained internally in .NET[3]. Each character is encoded as a sequence of 2 bytes, other than surrogates which take 4 bytes. Surrogates are needed in those cases where the Unicode code point uses more than 16 bits, e.g. the white touch phone symbol has UTF-32 code point 1F57E. In UTF-16 it is the pair D83D, DD7E.
In UTF-16 the string 'ABC' will require 3 x 2 = 6 bytes of storage for its characters 'A', 'B' and 'C'.

Figure 1.1.7.2 shows the C# console program output for a UTF-16 encoded string '程序样例' consisting of four characters and a UTF-16 encoded string 'ABC', consisting of three characters. The program output also shows the code points in hexadecimal for each character. Note that characters, 'A', 'B' and 'C', each takes up 2 bytes but in each case, the leading byte hexadecimal value is not shown because it is zero.

In versions of Delphi from Delphi 2009 onwards, string characters are encoded in UTF-16. Figure 1.1.7.3 shows that the string '程序样例' consisting of four characters is encoded in 8 bytes with two bytes per character.

Key point

UTF-8:
UTF-8 transforms characters into a variable-length encoding of 1-4 bytes.
UTF-8 is used for HTML and similar protocols because it can be compact, most characters fall within the ASCII subset, e.g. HTML markers.
UTF-16:
In UTF-16 most characters can be expressed with one 16-bit code unit, whose value is the same as the code point for the character, but characters with high code points require a pair of 16-bit code units.
UTF-16 is popular in many operating systems and development environments such as Java and .NET. Most characters used in these scenarios fit in two bytes.
UTF-32:
In UTF-32 all code points encode to the same fixed length code (32 bits) but it is memory consuming and therefore has limited practical usage.

3 .NET Framework is a software framework developed by Microsoft

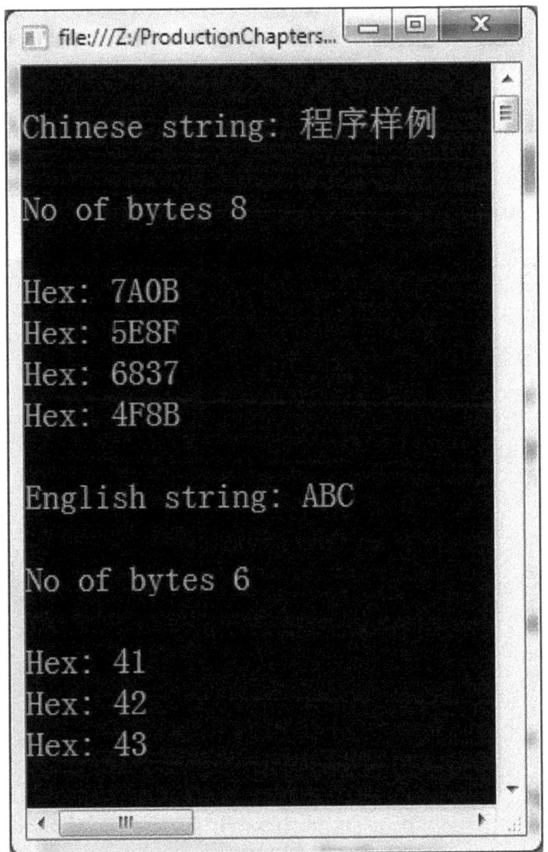

Figure 1.1.7.2 C# console program output for a UTF-16 encoded string '程序样例' *and a UTF-16 encoded string 'ABC'*

```
Z:\ProductionChapters\Units1and2ASBook\NewVersion7\DelphiCode\DelphiCo...

Hello World in Simplified Chinese: 程序样例
Code Page: 1200
String Element Size: 2
String Length: 4
String Size in bytes: 8
程   :   Hexadecimal:7A0B
序   :   Hexadecimal:5E8F
样   :   Hexadecimal:6837
例   :   Hexadecimal:4F8B
English ANSI: ABC
Code Page: 936
String Element Size: 1
String Length: 3
String Size in bytes: 3
A   :   Hexadecimal:41
B   :   Hexadecimal:42
C   :   Hexadecimal:43

Unicode UTF-16: ABC
Code Page: 1200
String Element Size: 2
String Length: 3
String Size in bytes: 6
A   :   Hexadecimal:41
B   :   Hexadecimal:42
C   :   Hexadecimal:43
```

Figure 1.1.7.3 Delphi XE5 console program output for a UTF-16 encoded string '程序样例' *and an ANSI string 'ABC'* and a UTF-16 string *'ABC'*

Information

UTF-16 and .NET:
UTF-16 is effectively how characters are maintained internally in .NET. Each character is encoded as a sequence of 2 bytes, other than surrogates which take 4 bytes.
Surrogates are needed in those cases where the Unicode code point uses more than 16 bits.

Key point

ASCII and Unicode:
ASCII *x* is the same character as Unicode *x* for all characters within ASCII.

Each character is a called a string element, e.g. 程. The string element size is 2 bytes because UTF-16 is used. However, the length of the string is 4 characters.

The code page identifier 1200 indicates that the encoding is UTF-16.

The program variable that contains the string 'ABC' was declared as an ANSI string (8 bits). The string element size is 1 byte and the string length 3 characters.

When the same string is encoded in UTF-16, the element size becomes 2 bytes and the string size in byes 6 bytes.

It does not make sense to have a string without knowing what encoding it uses.

For a string in memory, in a file, or in an email message, to be interpreted correctly or displayed to users correctly, its encoding must be known.

Questions

1. What is Unicode?
2. What problem was solved by Unicode?

String operations

Strings are used to store human-readable text. The literal string, 'Hello World!', consists of twelve characters placed between single quotes. Some programming languages use single quotes, some use double quotes and others allow the use of both, e.g. Python.

The literal string of twelve characters, 'Hello World!', is stored in a container with a capacity for more than twelve bytes because

- each character may need more than one byte, e.g. when UTF-16 is used
- some bytes must be used to store the count of characters or to indicate the end of the sequence of characters
- some bytes will be needed if the string is reference counted (the number of references made to the string may be more than one and the string must not be destroyed if the reference count is greater than zero)
- some bytes will be needed if the code page is stored.

For this and other reasons programming languages provide a library of routines and string operators for programmers to use when working with strings.

String indexing

To access individual characters of a string an indexing scheme is required. *Figure 1.1.7.4* shows a scheme that starts numbering string elements (characters) at 0. *Figure 1.1.7.5* shows a Delphi XE5 program and its output. The program creates a string container (variable) called `s` in a declaration. The program assigns the string value 'Hello World!' to variable `s`. It obtains the index number of the character 'H' when `s.IndexOf('H')` is evaluated. This number is 0 which is written to the console by `Writeln`. It then confirms that the index of 'H' is 0 with `Writeln(s[0])`.

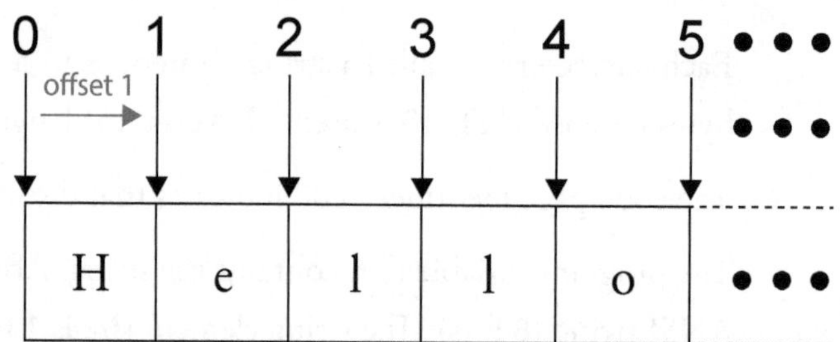

Figure 1.1.7.4 0-based numbering scheme for elements of a string

```
Program StringIndexingExample1;
{$APPTYPE CONSOLE}
{$ZEROBASEDSTRINGS ON}
{$R *.res}
Uses
  System.SysUtils;
Var s : String;
Begin
  s := 'Hello World!';
  Writeln(s.IndexOf('H'));
  Writeln(s[0]);
  Readln;
End.
```

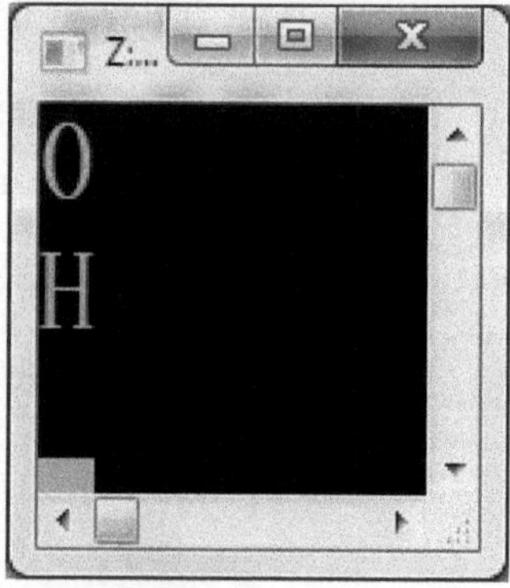

Figure 1.1.7.5 String indexing illustrated by a Delphi XE5 program and its output

The brackets `[]` are one mechanism by which individual characters of a string may be accessed.

In this example, the index is treated as an offset. If the offset is 0 then we stay on 'H'.

To test this, we try `s[1]` and `s[4]` - see Figure 1.1.7.6. The character one on from the beginning of the string is 'e', four on is 'o'.

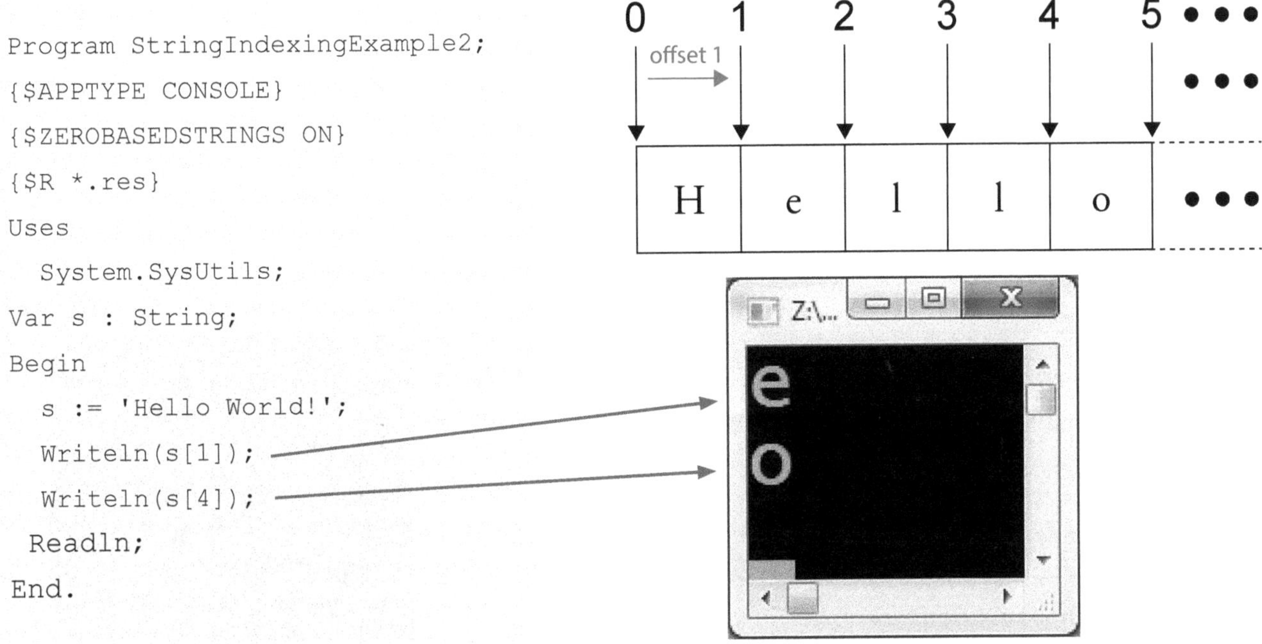
Program StringIndexingExample2;
{$APPTYPE CONSOLE}
{$ZEROBASEDSTRINGS ON}
{$R *.res}
Uses
System.SysUtils;
Var s : String;
Begin
s := 'Hello World!';
Writeln(s[1]);
Writeln(s[4]);
Readln;
End.
0
1
2
3
4
5
offset 1
H
e
l
l
o
Z:\...
e
o

Figure 1.1.7.6 String indexing illustrated by a Delphi XE5 program and its output, 'e' has index 1 because it is offset by 1 from beginning of string, 'o' has index 4 because it is offset by 4.

Figure 1.1.7.7 shows a VB.NET program which uses string indexing. In VB.NET the brackets `()` are used to access individual characters of a string. In this example, the index is treated as an offset. If the offset is 0 then we stay on 'H'.

```
Module StringIndexing
    Sub Main()
        Dim s As String
        s = "Hello World!"
        Console.WriteLine(s)
        Console.WriteLine(s.IndexOf("H"))
        Console.WriteLine(s(0))
        Console.WriteLine(s(1))
        Console.WriteLine(s(4))
        Console.ReadLine()
    End Sub
End Module
```

```
Hello World!
0
H
e
o
```

Figure 1.1.7.7 String indexing illustrated by a Visual Basic 2015 program and its output, the index of 'H' is 0, 'e' has index 1 because it is offset by 1 from beginning of string, 'o' has index 4 because it is offset by 4.

Figure 1.1.7.8 shows a C# program which uses string indexing. In C# the brackets `[]` are used to access individual characters of a string.

In this example, the index is treated as an **offset**. If the offset is `0` then we stay on 'H'.

```
using System;
namespace ConsoleStringIndexing
{
    class StringIndexing
    {
        static void Main(string[] args)
        {
            string s;
            s = "Hello World!";
            Console.WriteLine(s);
            Console.WriteLine(s.IndexOf('H'));
            Console.WriteLine(s[0]);
            Console.WriteLine(s[1]);
            Console.WriteLine(s[4]);
            Console.ReadLine();
        }
    }
}
```

```
Hello World!
0
H
e
o
```

Figure 1.1.7.8 String indexing illustrated by a Visual C# 2015 program and its output, the index of 'H' is 0, 'e' has index 1 because it is offset by 1 from beginning of string, 'o' has index 4 because it is offset by 4.

Figure 1.1.7.9 shows a Java program which uses string indexing. In Java, the function `charAt` is used to access individual characters of a string. In this example, the index is treated as an **offset**. If the offset is `0` then we stay on 'H'.

```
public class StringIndexing {
    public static void main(String[] args) {
        String s;
        s = "Hello World";
        System.out.println("Hello World!");
        System.out.println(s.indexOf("H"));
        System.out.println(s.charAt(0));
        System.out.println(s.charAt(1));
        System.out.println(s.charAt(4));
    }
}
```

```
M:\>java StringIndexing
Hello World!
0
H
e
o
```

Figure 1.1.7.9 String indexing illustrated by a Java program and its output, the index of 'H' is 0, 'e' has index 1 because it is offset by 1 from beginning of string, 'o' has index 4 because it is offset by 4.

Figure 1.1.7.10 shows string indexing in Interactive Python 3.4.

The brackets [ ] are used to access individual characters of the string "Hello World!".

In this example, the index is treated as an offset. If the offset is 0 then we stay on 'H'.

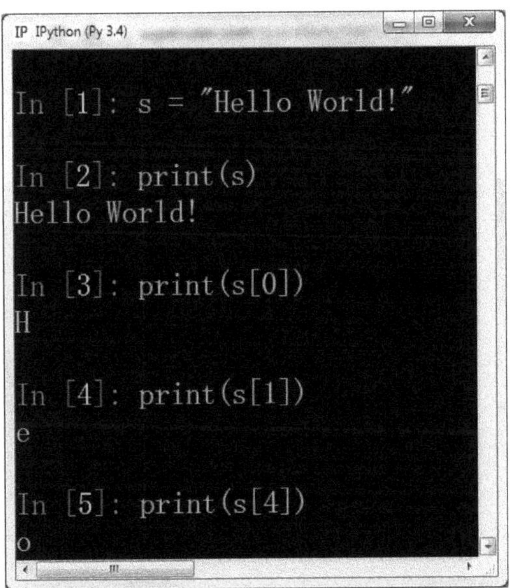
IPython (Py 3.4)
In [1]: s = "Hello World!"
In [2]: print(s)
Hello World!
In [3]: print(s[0])
H
In [4]: print(s[1])
e
In [5]: print(s[4])
o

Figure 1.1.7.10 String indexing illustrated in Interactive Python 3.4 and its output, the index of 'H' is 0, 'e' has index 1 because it is offset by 1 from beginning of string, 'o' has index 4 because it is offset by 4.

Information

In Delphi prior to XE2 string indexing is one-based as shown in *Figure 1.1.7.11*. Indexing is treated as an ordinal number not an offset. Delphi XE3 onwards requires the directive ZEROBASEDSTRINGS OFF for one-based string indexing.

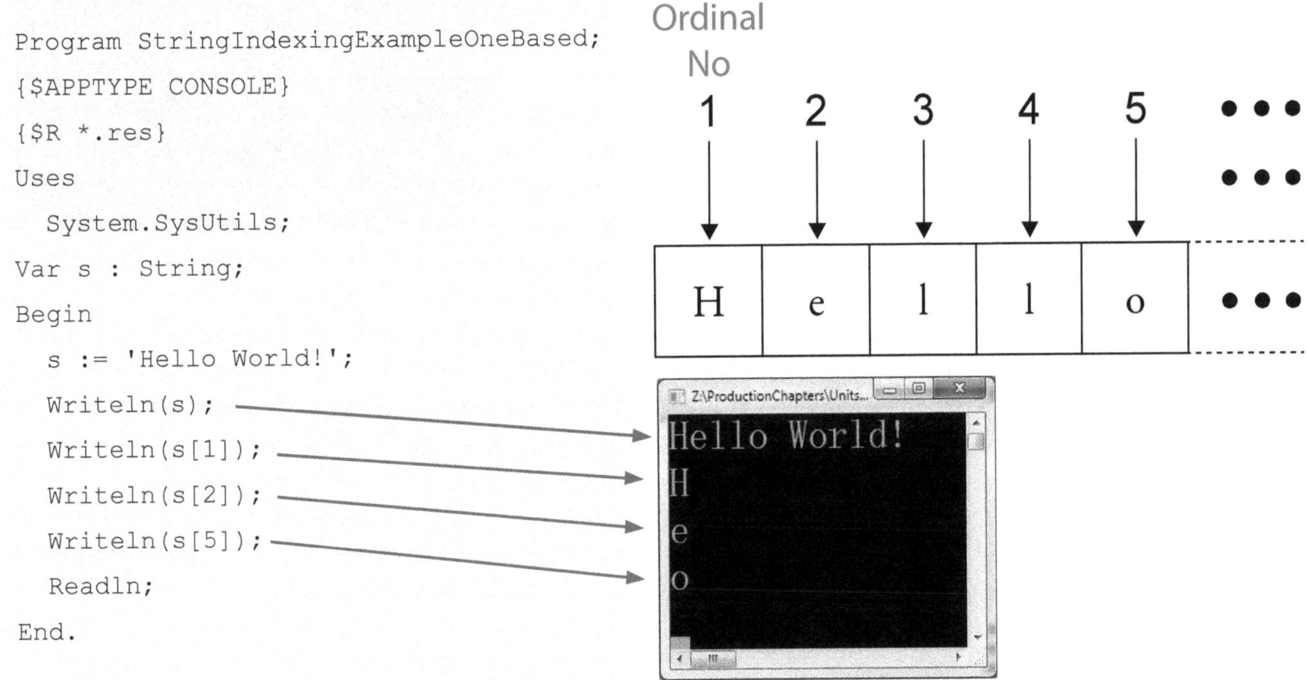
Program StringIndexingExampleOneBased;
{$APPTYPE CONSOLE}
{$R *.res}
Uses
System.SysUtils;
Var s : String;
Begin
s := 'Hello World!';
Writeln(s);
Writeln(s[1]);
Writeln(s[2]);
Writeln(s[5]);
Readln;
End.
Ordinal No
1
2
3
4
5
H
e
l
l
o
Z:\ProductionChapters\Units...
Hello World!
H
e
o

Figure 1.1.7.11 One-based string indexing illustrated by a Pascal/Delphi program and its output, the index of 'H' is 1, 'e' has index 2, 'o' has index 5.

Length of a string

In Pascal and Delphi the Length function returns the number of characters in a string.

Figure 1.1.7.12 shows the `Length` function returning 12 for the length of string `s` which contains string value 'Hello World!'. The *For loop* iterates from 0 to 11 (`Length(s) - 1`) to access each character of this zero-based-indexed string and `Writeln(s[i])` then sends a copy of the selected character to the console where it is displayed.

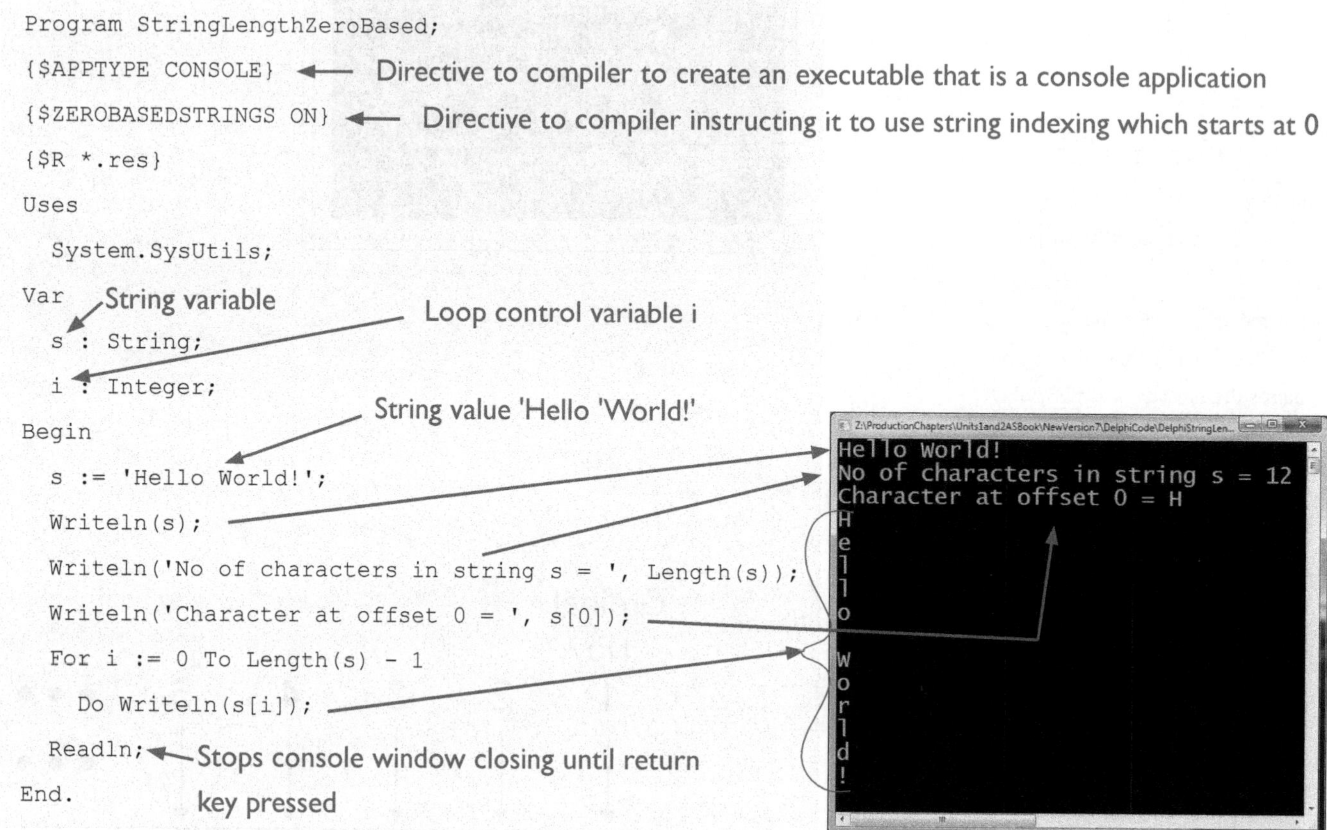

Program StringLengthZeroBased;
{$APPTYPE CONSOLE}
Directive to compiler to create an executable that is a console application
{$ZEROBASEDSTRINGS ON}
Directive to compiler instructing it to use string indexing which starts at 0
{$R *.res}
Uses
System.SysUtils;
Var
String variable
Loop control variable i
s : String;
i : Integer;
String value 'Hello 'World!'
Begin
s := 'Hello World!';
Writeln(s);
Writeln('No of characters in string s = ', Length(s));
Writeln('Character at offset 0 = ', s[0]);
For i := 0 To Length(s) - 1
Do Writeln(s[i]);
Readln;
Stops console window closing until return key pressed
End.
Hello World!
No of characters in string s = 12
Character at offset 0 = H
H
e
l
l
o
W
o
r
l
d
!

Figure 1.1.7.12 Using Pascal/Delphi's Length function to iterate through the characters of a zero-based string.

Figure 1.1.7.13 shows a C# program which uses the Length property of a C# string object. In C# a string is an object of type String whose value is a sequence of Char objects characters. The Length property of a string represents the number of Char objects it contains. The alias string is used in place of the class type String. Letter case is significant in C#.

String objects are immutable: they cannot be changed after they have been created. All of the String methods and C# operators that appear to modify a string actually return the results in a new string object.

In the following source code, string is an alias for the String class in the .NET framework:

```
string s = "Hello World!"
```

In the source code

```
Console.WriteLine("No of characters in string s = {0}", s.Length);
```

The expression `s.Length` evaluates to the length of the string that `s` contains.

In the literal string value `"No of characters in string s = {0}", s.Length);`

`{0}` is a place holder for the returned string length value 12.

```
using System;
namespace ConsoleStringLength
{
    class Program
    {
        static void Main(string[] args)
        {
            string s = "Hello World!";
            Console.WriteLine("No of characters in string s = {0}", s.Length);
            for (int i = 0; i < s.Length; i++)
            {
                Console.WriteLine(s[i]);
            }
            Console.ReadLine();
        }
    }
}
```

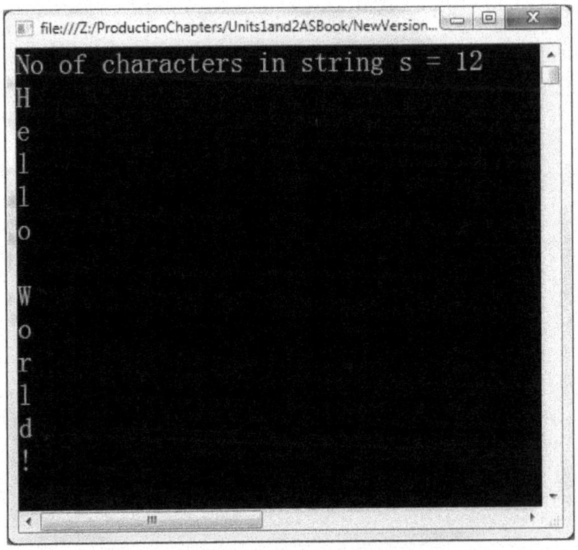

```
file:///Z:/ProductionChapters/Units1and2ASBook/NewVersion...
No of characters in string s = 12
H
e
l
l
o

W
o
r
l
d
!
```

Figure 1.1.7.13 Using C#'s Length property of a string object to iterate through the characters of a zero-based string.

Figure 1.1.7.14 shows a Java program which uses the **length** method of a Java string object. In Java, a string is an object of type **String** whose value is a sequence of characters of data type **char** - a single 16-bit Unicode character. The **length** method of a string object returns the number of characters it contains.

Enclosing a character string within double quotes automatically creates a new String object. String objects are immutable, which means that once created, their values cannot be changed.

```
C:\Windows\system32\cmd.exe
M:\>
M:\>java StringLength
No of characters in string s = 12
H
e
l
l
o

W
o
r
l
d
!

M:\>_
```

```
public class StringLength {
    public static void main(String[] args) {
        String s;
        s = "Hello World!";
        System.out.println("No of characters in string s = " + s.length());
        for (int i = 0; i < s.length(); i++){
            System.out.println(s.charAt(i));
        }
    }
}
```

Figure 1.1.7.14 Using Java's Length property of a string object to iterate through the characters of a zero-based string.

Figure 1.1.7.15 shows a VB.NET program which uses the **Length** property of a VB.NET string object. In VB.NET, a string is an object of type **String** whose value is a sequence of characters of data type **char** - a single 16-bit Unicode character. The **Length** property of a string object returns the number of characters it contains. Enclosing a character string within double quotes automatically creates a new String object. String objects are immutable, which means that once created, their values cannot be changed.

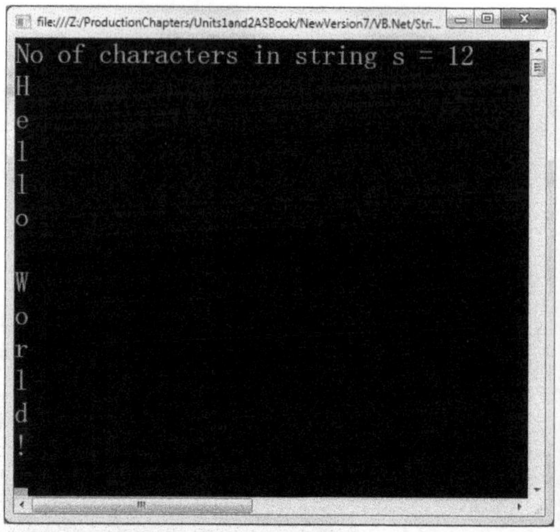

```
No of characters in string s = 12
H
e
l
l
o

W
o
r
l
d
!
```

```
Module StringLength
    Sub Main()
        Dim s As String = "Hello World!"
        Console.WriteLine("No of characters in string s = {0}", s.Length)
        For i As Integer = 0 To s.Length - 1
            Console.WriteLine(s(i))
        Next
        Console.ReadLine()
    End Sub
End Module
```

Figure 1.1.7.15 Using VB.NET's Length property of a string object to iterate through the characters of a zero-based string.

Figure 1.1.7.16 shows that the use of the Python `len` function applied to a string variable `s`, as follows: `len(s)`, returns the number of characters in the string value "Hello World!" which `s` contains.

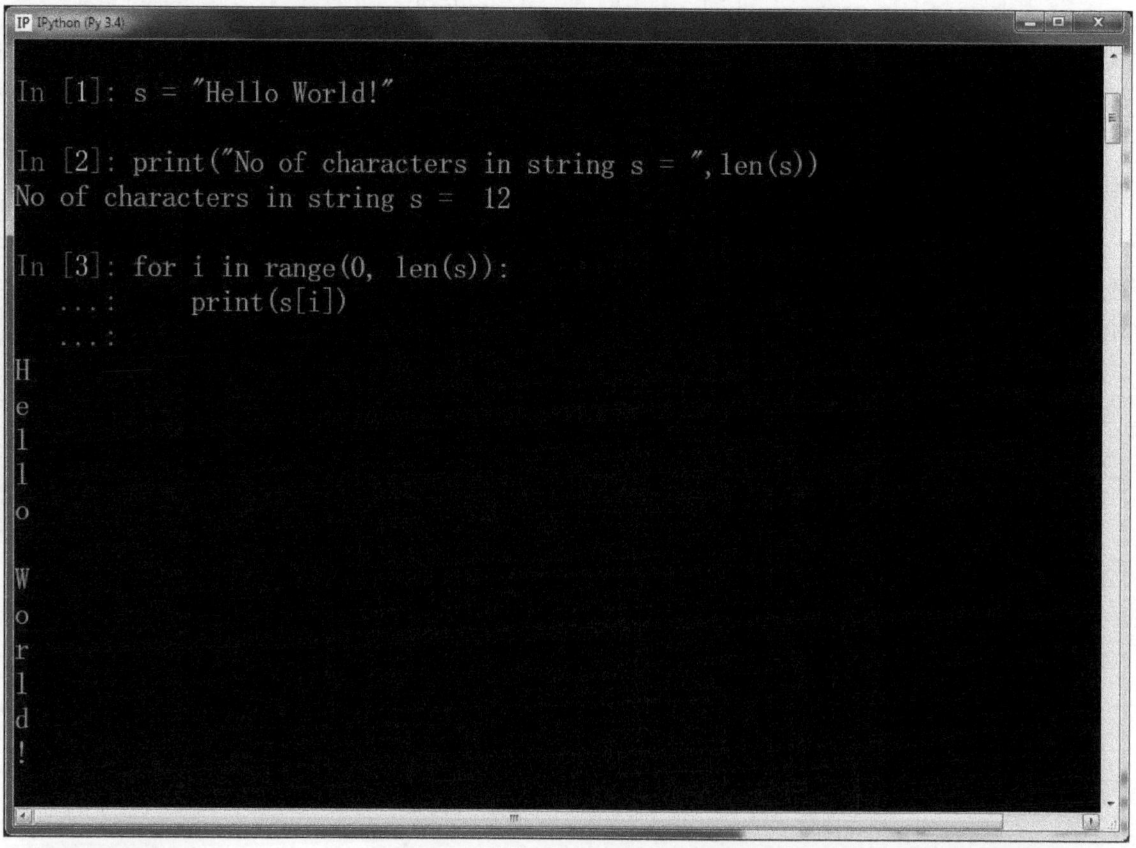

```
In [1]: s = "Hello World!"

In [2]: print("No of characters in string s = ",len(s))
No of characters in string s =  12

In [3]: for i in range(0, len(s)):
   ...:     print(s[i])
   ...:
H
e
l
l
o

W
o
r
l
d
!
```

Figure 1.1.7.16 Using Python's len function to obtain the length of a string, s, then iterate through the characters of this zero-based string.

Figure 1.1.7.17 shows that the use of the Pascal/Delphi `Length` function applied to a one-based string variable `s`, as follows: `Length(s)`, returns the number of characters in the string value "Hello World!" which variable `s` contains.

```
Program StringLengthOneBased;
{$APPTYPE CONSOLE}
{$R *.res}
Uses
  System.SysUtils;
Var
  s : String;
  i : Integer;
Begin
  s := 'Hello World!';
  Writeln(s);
  Writeln('No of characters in string s = ', Length(s));
  Writeln('Character at index 1 = ', s[1]);
  For i := 1 To Length(s)
    Do Writeln(s[i]);
  Readln;
End.
```

```
Z:\ProductionChapters\Units1and2ASBook\NewVersion7\DelphiCode\De...
Hello World!
No of characters in string s = 12
Character at index 1 = H
H
e
l
l
o

W
o
r
l
d
!
```

Figure 1.1.7.17 Using Pascal/Delphi's Length function to obtain the length of a string, s, then iterate through the characters of this one-based string.

Character → character code

Sometimes an operation needs to be carried out on a single character value, e.g. 'A', or a variable of character data type, e.g. `Ch`.

In Pascal and Delphi, the `Char` data type is used to create a single character variable and the `Ord` function converts a character value to its character code as shown in Figure 1.1.7.18.

```
Program CharacterExample;
{$APPTYPE CONSOLE}
{$R *.res}
Uses
  System.SysUtils;
Var
  Ch : Char;
Begin
  Ch := 'A';
  Writeln(Ch);
  Writeln(Ord(Ch));
  Readln;
End.
```

Figure 1.1.7.18 The Char data type and the Ord function in Pascal/Delphi which converts a character to its character code.

In VB.NET, a character variable is declared using the `Char` data type as shown in Figure 1.1.7.19. The `Asc` function returns the character code for a given character value.

```
Module CharacterExample
    Sub Main()
        Dim ch As Char = "A"
        Console.WriteLine(ch)
        Console.WriteLine(Asc(ch))
        Console.ReadLine()
    End Sub
End Module
```

Figure 1.1.7.19 The Char data type and the Asc function in VB.NET.

In Java, a character variable is declared using the `char` data type and to convert a character value to its character code in Java, data type casting is used as shown in *Figure 1.1.7.20* where `(int) ch` casts the value contained in `ch` to a value of type `int`.

```
public class CharacterExample {
    public static void main(String[] args) {
        char ch = 'A';
        System.out.println(ch);
        System.out.println((int) ch);
    }
```

causes data type cast from char to int

Figure 1.1.7.20 The char data type in Java and the use of data type casting, (int) to convert a character to its character code.

The `char` keyword is used in C# to declare an instance of the `System.Char` structure that the .NET Framework uses to represent a Unicode character. The value of a Char object is a 16-bit numeric (ordinal) value.

To convert a character to its character code in C#, data type casting is used as shown in *Figure 1.1.7.21*. *Figure 1.1.7.22* shows the use of the `ord` function in Python 3.4. to convert a character to its character code.

```
using System;
namespace CharExample
{
    class Program
    {
        static void Main(string[] args)
        {
            char ch = 'A';
            Console.WriteLine(ch);
            Console.WriteLine((int) ch);
            Console.ReadLine();
        }
    }
}
```

causes data type cast from char to int

Figure 1.1.7.21 The char data type in C# and the use of data type casting, (int) to convert a character to its character code.

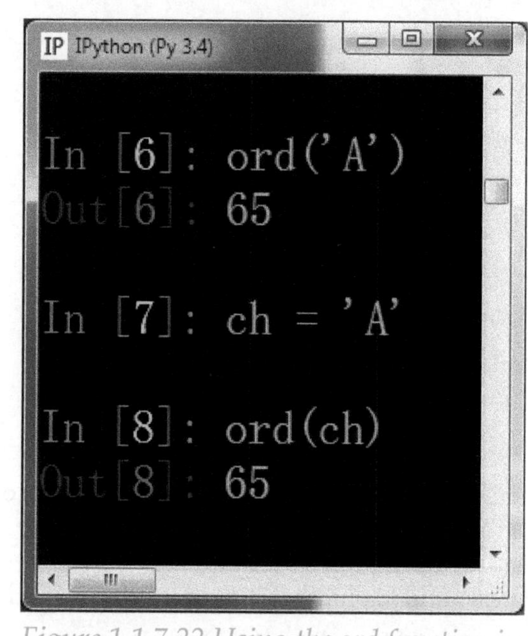
IPython (Py 3.4)
In [6]: ord('A')
Out[6]: 65
In [7]: ch = 'A'
In [8]: ord(ch)
Out[8]: 65

Figure 1.1.7.22 Using the ord function in Python 3.4 to convert a character to its character code.

Character code → character

Table 1.1.7.2 shows how to convert from character code to character in C#, Java, Pascal/Delphi, Python and VB.NET and display the result in the console window. C# and Java use data type casting whilst Pascal/Delphi and VB.NET use a function, `Chr`, and Python a function `chr`.

Language	Code
C#	`Console.WriteLine((char)65);`
Java	`System.out.println((char)65);`
Pascal/Delphi	`Writeln(Chr(65));`
Python	`print(chr(65))`
VB.Net	`Console.WriteLine(Chr(65))`

Table 1.1.7.2 Code to convert character code to character in C#, Java, Pascal/Delphi, Python and VB.NET and display the result in the console window.

String conversion operations

String to integer

C#

A string can be converted to a number using methods in the `Convert` class or by using the `TryParse` method found on the various numeric types (int, long, float, etc). `Convert.ToInt32` converts an integer written in string form, e.g. "-125" to a 32-bit integer value, e.g. `-125`.

```
Console.WriteLine("String -125 has integer value {0}",  Convert.ToInt32("-125"));
```

There are also other methods that may be used when converting a string representing a numeric value:

- `Parse`: If the string is not in a valid format, `Parse` throws an exception. `Int32.Parse("-125")` returns the 32-bit integer value -125. *Table 1.1.7.3* shows an example of this.
- `TryParse`: In the example in *Table 1.1.7.3*, `TryParse` returns true if the conversion succeeded, storing the result in `anotherNumber`, and false if it fails.

Both methods ignore *whitespace* at the beginning and at the end of the string, but all other characters must be characters that form the appropriate numeric type (int, long, ulong, float, decimal, etc). Any *whitespace* within the characters that form the number cause an error.

Java

The `Integer.parseInt(String s)` static method parses the string argument `s` as a signed decimal integer and returns an `int` value as shown in *Table 1.1.7.3*. The resulting value is not an instance of Java's Integer class but just a primitive `int` value.

The `Integer.valueOf(String s)` static method will return an `Integer` object holding the value of the specified `String s` argument.

VB.NET

A string can be converted to a number using methods in the `Convert` class or by using the `TryParse` method found on the various numeric types (int, long, float, etcetera). `Convert.ToInt32` converts an integer written in string form, e.g. "-125" to a 32-bit integer value, e.g. `-125`.

```
Console.WriteLine("String -125 has integer value {0}",  Convert.ToInt32("-125"))
```

There are also other methods that may be used when converting a string representing a numeric value:

- `Parse`: If the string is not in a valid format, `Parse` throws an exception. `Int32.Parse("-125")` returns the 32-bit integer value -125. *Table 1.1.7.3* shows an example of this.
- `TryParse`: In the example in *Table 1.1.7.3*, `TryParse` returns true if the conversion succeeded, storing the result in `anotherNumber`, and false if it fails.

Python

The Python standard built-in function `int()` converts a string into an integer value. It is called with an argument which is the string form of an integer. It returns the integer that corresponds to the string form of the integer.

Table 1.1.7.3 shows an example of the use of `int()`.

Pascal

The `StrToInt` function converts an Integer string such as '-125' to an integer as shown in *Table 1.1.7.3*.

Delphi

The `StrToInt` function converts an Integer string such as '-125' to an integer.

It is also possible to use `Parse` and `TryParse` as follows:

```
AnotherNumber := System.Int32.Parse('-125');
Writeln(AnotherNumber);
If System.Int32.TryParse('-125', YetAnotherNumber)
  Then Writeln(YetAnotherNumber)
  Else Writeln('String could not be parsed');
```

Table 1.1.7.3 shows examples of the use of each.

Language	Code

C#	`Console.WriteLine("String -125 has integer value {0}",`
	`                  Convert.ToInt32("-125"));`
	`int number = Int32.Parse("-125");`
	`Console.WriteLine(number);`
	`int anotherNumber;`
	`if (Int32.TryParse("-125", out anotherNumber))`
	`    Console.WriteLine(anotherNumber);`
	`else Console.WriteLine("String could not be parsed.");`

Java	`int number = Integer.parseInt("-125");`
	`System.out.println("The number is: " + number);`
	`int anotherNumber = Integer.valueOf("-125");`
	`System.out.println("The number is: " + anotherNumber);`

Pascal	`Number := StrToInt('-125');` `Writeln(Number);`

Delphi	`Var Result, YetAnotherNumber : Integer;`
	`...........`
	`Number := StrToInt('-125');`
	`Writeln(Number);`
	`AnotherNumber := System.Int32.Parse('-125');`
	`Writeln(AnotherNumber);`
	`If System.Int32.TryParse('-125', YetAnotherNumber)`
	`  Then Writeln(YetAnotherNumber)`
	`  Else Writeln('String could not be parsed');`

Python	`print(int("-125"))`

VB.NET	`Console.WriteLine("String -125 has integer value {0}",`
	`                  Convert.ToInt32("-125"))`
	`Dim number As Integer = Int32.Parse("-125")`
	`Console.WriteLine(number)`
	`Dim anotherNumber As Integer`
	`If Int32.TryParse("-125", anotherNumber) Then`
	`    Console.WriteLine(anotherNumber)`
	`Else Console.WriteLine("String could not be parsed")`
	`End If`

Table 1.1.7.3 Code examples in C#, Java, Pascal, Delphi, Python and VB.NET which demonstrate how to convert an integer in string form to an integer value

String to float

C#

A string can be converted to a number using methods in the `Convert` class or by using the `TryParse` method found on the various numeric types (int, long, float, etc). `Convert.ToSingle` converts a number written in string form, e.g. "-125.5" to a single precision floating point value, e.g. `-125.5`. See below and Table 1.1.7.4.

```
Console.WriteLine("String -125.5 has float value {0}", Convert.ToSingle("-125.5"));
```

The precision of a single floating point number is 7 decimal digits.

There are also other methods that may be used when converting a string representing a numeric value:

- `Parse:` If the string is not in a valid format, `Parse` throws an exception. `float.Parse("-125.5")` returns a single precision floating point value -125.5. Table 1.1.7.4 shows an example of this.
- `TryParse:` In the example in Table 1.1.7.4, `TryParse` returns true if the conversion succeeded, storing the result in `anotherNumber`, and false if it fails.

Both methods ignore *whitespace* at the beginning and at the end of the string, but all other characters must be characters that form the appropriate numeric type (int, long, ulong, float, decimal, etc). Any *whitespace* within the characters that form the number cause an error.

Java

The `Float.parseFloat(String s)` static method parses the string argument `s` as a signed number and returns a floating point value as shown in Table 1.1.7.4.

The `Float.valueOf(String s)` static method will returns a `Float` object holding the float value represented by the argument string `s`.

VB.NET

A string can be converted to a number using methods in the `Convert` class or by using the `TryParse` method found on the various numeric types (int, long, float, etcetera). `Convert.ToSingle` converts a number written in string form, e.g. "-125.5" to a single precision floating point value, e.g. `-125.5`. See below and Table 1.1.7.4.

```
Console.WriteLine("String -125.5 has float value {0}", Convert.ToSingle("-125.5"))
```

The precision of a single floating point number is 7 decimal digits.

There are also other methods that may be used when converting a string representing a numeric value:

- `Parse:` If the string is not in a valid format, `Parse` throws an exception. `float.Parse("-125.5")` returns a single precision floating point value -125.5. Table 1.1.7.4 shows an example of this.
- `TryParse:` In the example in Table 1.1.7.4, `TryParse` returns true if the conversion succeeded, storing the result in `anotherNumber`, and false if it fails.

Both methods ignore *whitespace* at the beginning and at the end of the string, but all other characters must be characters that form the appropriate numeric type (int, long, ulong, float, decimal, etc). Any *whitespace* within the characters that form the number cause an error.

<table>
<tr><th>Language</th><th>Code</th></tr>
<tr><td>C#</td><td><pre>Console.WriteLine("String -125.5 has float value {0}",
                   Convert.ToSingle("-125.5"));
float number = float.Parse("-125.5");
Console.WriteLine(number);
float anotherNumber;
if (float.TryParse("-125.5", out anotherNumber))
    Console.WriteLine(anotherNumber);
else Console.WriteLine("String could not be parsed.");</pre></td></tr>
<tr><td>Java</td><td><pre>float number = Float.parseFloat("-125.5");
System.out.println("The number is: " + number);
float anotherNumber = Float.valueOf("-125.5");
System.out.println("The number is: " + anotherNumber);</pre></td></tr>
<tr><td>Pascal</td><td><pre>Writeln(StrToFloat('-125.5'):8:2);</pre></td></tr>
<tr><td>Delphi</td><td><pre>Var Result, YetAnotherNumber : Single;
....
Writeln(StrToFloat('-125.5'):8:2);
AnotherNumber := System.Single.Parse('-125.5');
Writeln(AnotherNumber:8:2);
If System.Single.TryParse('-125.5', YetAnotherNumber)
  Then Writeln(YetAnotherNumber:8:2)
  Else Writeln('String could not be parsed');</pre></td></tr>
<tr><td>Python</td><td><pre>print(float("-125.5"))</pre></td></tr>
<tr><td>VB.NET</td><td><pre>Console.WriteLine("String -125.5 has float value {0}",
                   Convert.ToSingle("-125.5"))
Dim Number As Single = Single.Parse("-125.5")
Console.WriteLine(Number)
Dim AnotherNumber As Single
If (Single.TryParse("-125.5", AnotherNumber)) Then
    Console.WriteLine(AnotherNumber)
Else Console.WriteLine("String could not be parsed.")
End If</pre></td></tr>
</table>

Table 1.1.7.4 Code examples in C#, Java, Pascal, Delphi, Python and VB.NET which demonstrate how to convert a number in string form to a floating point value

Python

The Python standard built-in function `float()` converts a string into a floating point value. It is called with an argument which is the string form of a number It returns the floating point value that corresponds to the string form of the number.

Table 1.1.7.4 shows an example of the use of `float()`.

Pascal

The `StrToFloat` function converts a number string such as '-125.5' to a floating point value as shown in *Table 1.1.7.4*.

Delphi

The `StrToFloat` function converts a number string such as '-125.5' to a floating point value.

It is also possible to use `Parse` and `TryParse` as follows:

```
AnotherNumber := System.Single.Parse('-125.5');
Writeln(AnotherNumber);
If System.Single.TryParse('-125.5', YetAnotherNumber)
  Then Writeln(YetAnotherNumber)
  Else Writeln('String could not be parsed');
```

where `AnotherNumber` and `YetAnotherNumber` are single precision floating point variables declared as follows

```
Var
  AnotherNumber, YetAnotherNumber : Single;
```

Table 1.1.7.4 shows examples of the use of each. To use double precision substitute `Double` for `Single` in the code above.

Integer to string

C#

An integer can be converted to its equivalent string form using `Convert.ToString`, e.g. -125 to its string representation, e.g. "-125". See below and Table 1.1.7.5.

```
Console.WriteLine(Convert.ToString(-125));
```

Java

The Integer class has a static method that returns a `String` object representing the specified `int` parameter, e.g.

```
Integer.toString(-125));
```

as shown in Table 1.1.7.5.

VB.NET

An integer can be converted to its equivalent string form using `Convert.ToString`, e.g. -125 to " -125" as shown below and in Table 1.1.7.5.

```
Console.WriteLine(Convert.ToString(-125))
```

Python

The Python standard built-in function `str()` converts a number to its equivalent string form. It is called with a number argument, e.g. -125 and returns the equivalent string form "-125" as shown in Table 1.1.7.5.

Pascal/Delphi

The `IntToStr` function converts an integer such as -125. to its equivalent string form '-125' as shown in Table 1.1.7.5.

Language	Code
C#	`Console.WriteLine(Convert.ToString(-125));`

Java	`System.out.println(Integer.toString(-125));`
	`String numberString = String.valueOf(-125);`
	`System.out.println(numberString);`

Pascal/Delphi	`Var`
	` NumberString : String;`
	`......................`
	`NumberString := IntToStr(-125);`
	`Writeln(NumberString);`

Python	`print(str(-125))`
VB.NET	`Console.WriteLine(Convert.ToString(-125))`

Table 1.1.7.5 Code examples in C#, Java, Pascal, Delphi, Python and VB.NET which demonstrate how to convert an integer to an equivalent string form

Float to string

C#

A number stored in floating point form can be converted to its equivalent string form using `Convert.ToString`, e.g. -125.5 to its string representation, e.g. `"-125.5"`. See below and Table 1.1.7.6.

```
Console.WriteLine(Convert.ToString(-125.5));
```

Java

The `Float` and `Double` classes each have a static method that returns a `String` object representing the specified `Float` or `Double` parameter, e.g.

```
System.out.println(Float.toString(-125.5f));
System.out.println(Double.toString(-125.5));
```

as shown in Table 1.1.7.6.

Java has IEEE 754 single and double precision types supported by keywords:

```
float f = -125.5f; // 32 bit float, note f suffix
double d = -125.5d; // 64 bit float, suffix d is optional
```

Alternatively, we may use `String.valueOf(float f)`. If a float value, e.g. -125.5, is passed to this method as an argument, then the string representation of -125.5 is returned, i.e. "-125.5".

```
float number = -125.5f;
String numberString = String.valueOf(number);
```

VB.NET

A number stored in floating point form can be converted to its equivalent string form using `Convert.ToString`, e.g. -125.5 to " -125.5" as shown below and in Table 1.1.7.6.

```
Console.WriteLine(Convert.ToString(-125.5))
```

Python

The Python standard built-in function `str()` converts a number with a fractional part to its equivalent string form. It is called with a number argument, e.g. -125.5 and it returns the equivalent string form "-125.5" as shown in Table 1.1.7.6.

Pascal/Delphi

The `FloatToStr` function converts a number stored in floating point form such as -125.5 to its equivalent string form '-125.5' as shown in Table 1.1.7.6.

Language	Code
C#	`Console.WriteLine(Convert.ToString(-125.5));`

Java	`System.out.println(Float.toString(-125.5f));`
	`System.out.println(Double.toString(-125.5));`
	`float number1 = -125.5f;`
	`String numberString1 = String.valueOf(number1);`
	`System.out.println(numberString1);`
	`double number2 = -125.5;`
	`String numberString2 = String.valueOf(number2);`
	`System.out.println(numberString2);`

Pascal/Delphi	`Var`
	`  NumberString : String;`
	`......................`
	`NumberString := FloatToStr(-125.5);`
	`Writeln(NumberString);`

Python	`print(str(-125.5))`
VB.NET	`Console.WriteLine(Convert.ToString(-125.5))`

Table 1.1.7.6 Code examples in C#, Java, Pascal, Delphi, Python and VB.NET which demonstrate how to convert a floating point value to an equivalent string form

Date/time to string

Java

Java provides the `Date` class in the `java.util` package. This class encapsulates the current date and time. The `Date` class is imported with the statement

```
import java.util.Date;
```

An object, `date` of the `Date` class is constructed as follows

```
Date date = new Date();
```

and then used as follows with the Java `toString()` and `println` methods to display the current date and time

```
System.out.println(date.toString());
```

Alternatively, the `java.lang.String.format` method which returns a formatted string, using the specified format string and arguments, can be used, e.g.

```
String dateString = String.format("Current Date and time: %tc", date );
```

`%tc` is a place holder for the `date` argument. A two-letter format is used starting with `t` and ending in a letter that specifies the actual format. For example, the letter "`c`" means display *complete date and time.*

It is possible to invoke the method `printf` on the standard output pipe, `System.out`, to format the output according to a given format string and `date` object argument as follows

```
dateString = String.format("Current Time: %tT", date );
System.out.printf(dateString);
```

where `%tT` sets the format of the string output to be time in 24-hour format.

```
dateString = String.format("%1$tB %1$td, %1$tY", date);
System.out.printf(dateString);
```

In the format string, `"%1$tB %1$td, %1$tY"`, `%1` specifies which argument to insert, in this case, `date`. In the part of the format string, "`$tB $td, $tY`":

- uppercase "`B`" means use the long month name format, e.g. December.
- lowercase "`d`" means use a day number, e.g. 23
- "`,`" means insert a comma
- uppercase "Y" means use long year format, e.g. 2016.

C#

```
new DateTime(1550, 7, 21, 13, 31, 17)
```

initializes a new instance of the `DateTime` structure to the specified year, month, day, hour, minute, and second, e.g. year = 1550, month = 7, day = 21, hour of day = 13, minute of day = 31, second of day = 17.

The instance can be assigned to a variable `dateOld` of type DateTime as follows

```
DateTime dateOld = new DateTime(1550, 7, 21, 13, 31, 17);
```

The date part of this structure can be displayed using the `ToString` method and the format string argument `"d/M/yyyy"` as follows

```
Console.WriteLine(dateOld.ToString("d/M/yyyy"));
```

In the format string argument, `"d/M/yyyy"`,

- "`d`" means display day of the month, in numeric form, 1 through 31
- "`m`" means display month, in numeric form, 1 through 12
- "yyyy" means display the year as a four-digit number
- "/" means display /

Table 1.1.7.7 shows examples in the languages Java and C#.

Language	Code

Java	`Date date = new Date();`
	`System.out.println(date.toString());`
	`String dateString = String.format("Current Date and time: %tc", date );`
	`System.out.printf(dateString);`
	`System.out.println();`
	`dateString = String.format("Current Time: %tT", date );`
	`System.out.printf(dateString);`
	`System.out.println();`
	`dateString = String.format("%1$tB %1$td, %1$tY", date);`
	`System.out.printf(dateString);`

C#	`DateTime oldDateTime = new DateTime(1550, 7, 21, 13, 31, 17);`
	`Console.WriteLine(oldDateTime);`
	`Console.WriteLine(oldDateTime.ToString("d/M/yyyy"));`
	`Console.WriteLine(oldDateTime.ToString("H:m:s"));`
	`String oldDate = String.Format("{0:d/M/yyyy}", oldDateTime);`
	`String oldTime = String.Format("{0:H:m:s}", oldDateTime);`
	`Console.WriteLine(oldDate);`
	`Console.WriteLine(oldTime);`
	`DateTime localDateTime = DateTime.Now;`
	`Console.WriteLine(localDateTime.ToString("d/M/yyyy H:m:s"));`

Table 1.1.7.7 Code examples in Java and C# which demonstrate how to convert a date/time value to an equivalent string form

For example, if `DateTime(2016, 11, 3, 15, 21, 45)` is used then the date 3/11/2016 is displayed if the format string argument is `"d/M/yyyy"`.

The time part of this structure can be displayed using the format string argument `"H:m:s"` with the `ToString` method as follows

```
Console.WriteLine(dateOld.ToString("H:m:s"));
```

In the format string, `"H:m:s"`

- "H" means display the hour, using a 24-hour clock from 0 to 23.
- "m" means display the minute, in numeric form, 0 through 59.
- "s" means display the second, from 0 through 59
- ":" means display :

For example, if `DateTime(2016, 11, 3, 15, 21, 45)` is used then the time 15:21:45 is displayed if the format string argument is `"H:m:s"`.

There is another way to format string output which uses `String.Format` to convert the value of an object to a string based on the format specified, e.g. `"d/M/yyyy"`.

The following shows how a string of the desired format derived from `oldDateTime` may be assigned to variables `oldDate` and `oldTime` of type `String`:

```
String oldDate = String.Format("{0:d/M/yyyy}", oldDateTime);
String oldTime = String.Format("{0:H:m:s}", oldDateTime);
```

`0:` is the first argument and `0:d/M/yyyy` means apply format string `0:d/M/yyyy` to this argument, i.e. `oldDateTime`.

The two strings may then be displayed using

```
Console.WriteLine(oldDate);
Console.WriteLine(oldTime);
```

It is also possible to access the operating system for the current time and date.
For this a static property, `DateTime.Now`, of the `DateTime` structure may be used as follows

```
DateTime localDate = DateTime.Now;
```

and both date and time displayed as follows

```
Console.WriteLine(localDate.ToString("d/M/yyyy H:m:s"));
```

Static property means that no instance of an object needs to be created to use the property `DateTime.Now`, it is available globally because it is actually a property of an existing object called `System.Object`.

VB.NET

Table 1.1.7.8 shows examples for VB.NET which is similar to the C# examples because both C# and VB.NET rely on .NET classes.

Pascal/Delphi

Date and time processing in Pascal and Delphi depend on the `TDateTime` type. A variable of the `TDateTime` type can contain a date and time combination, e.g. `OldDateTime` as shown in *Table 1.1.7.8*.

A date and a time are encoded in a structure using `EncodeDateTime` and the specified year, month, day, hour, minute, second and miilisecond, e.g. year = `1550`, month = `7`, day = `21`, hour of day = `13`, minute of day = `31`, second of day = 17, millisecond of day = 0 as shown in *Table 1.1.7.8*.

The date part of this structure can be obtained and assigned using

```
OldDate := DateOf(OldDateTime);
```

The time part of this structure can be obtained and assigned using

```
OldTime :=  TimeOf(OldDateTime);
```

The string form of `OldDateTime`, `OldDate` and `OldTime` are obtained using `DateTimeToStr`, `DateToStr`, and `TimeToStr`, respectively.

To display the result on the console for each case, `Writeln` can be used as follows

```
Writeln(DateTimeToStr(OldDateTime));
Writeln(DateToStr(OldDate));
Writeln(TimeToStr(OldTime));
```

Formatted output can be achieved by applying the procedure `DateTimeToString` to a `TDateTime` variable, e.g. `OldDateTime`, and a format string, e.g. `'d/m/yyyy'`, as follows

```
DateTimeToString(OldDateString, 'd/m/yyyy', OldDateTime);
Writeln(OldDateString);
DateTimeToString(OldTimeString, 'h:n:s', OldDateTime);
Writeln(OldTimeString);
```

The procedure returns a formatted string in the variable in the first position in the parameter list, e.g. `OldDateString`.

It is also possible to access the operating system for the current time and date.
The function `Now` is used to obtain the current date and time as follows

```
LocalDateTime := Now;
Writeln(DateTimeToStr(LocalDateTime));
```

The `datetime` module in Python provides a number of types to deal with dates, times, and time intervals.
To use this module it needs to be imported as follows

```
import datetime
```

<table>
<tr><th>Language</th><th>Code</th></tr>
<tr><td>VB.NET</td><td><pre>Dim oldDateTime As DateTime = New DateTime(1550, 7, 21, 13, 31, 17)
Console.WriteLine(oldDateTime)
Console.WriteLine(oldDateTime.ToString("d/M/yyyy"))
Console.WriteLine(oldDateTime.ToString("H:m:s"))
Dim oldDate As String = String.Format("{0:d/M/yyyy}", oldDateTime)
Dim oldTime As String = String.Format("{0:H/m/s}", oldDateTime)
Console.WriteLine(oldDate)
Console.WriteLine(oldTime)
Dim localDateTime As DateTime = DateTime.Now
Console.WriteLine(localDateTime.ToString("d/M/yyyy H:m:s"))</pre></td></tr>
<tr><td>Pascal/
Delphi</td><td><pre>Var
  OldDateTime, LocalDateTime : TDateTime;
  OldDate : TDate;
  OldTime : TTime;
  OldDateString, OldTimeString : String;
Begin
  OldDateTime := EncodeDateTime(1550, 7, 21, 13, 31, 17, 0);
  Writeln(DateTimeToStr(OldDateTime));
  OldDate := DateOf(OldDateTime);
  Writeln(DateToStr(OldDate));
  OldTime := TimeOf(OldDateTime);
  Writeln(TimeToStr(OldTime));
  DateTimeToString(OldDateString, 'd/m/yyyy', OldDateTime);
  Writeln(OldDateString);
  DateTimeToString(OldTimeString, 'h:n:s', OldDateTime);
  Writeln(OldTimeString);
  LocalDateTime := Now;
  Writeln(DateTimeToStr(LocalDateTime));
  Readln;
End.</pre></td></tr>
<tr><td>Python</td><td><pre>import datetime
olddatetime = datetime.datetime(1550, 7, 21, 13, 31, 17)
olddate = olddatetime.date()
oldtime = olddatetime.time()
print(olddatetime)
print(olddate)
print(oldtime)
print(olddatetime.ctime())
print(olddate.strftime("%d/%m/%Y"))
print(oldtime.strftime("%H:%M:%S"))
localdatetime = datetime.datetime.now()</pre></td></tr>
</table>

Table 1.1.7.8 Code examples in VB.NET, Pascal/Delphi, and Python which demonstrate how to convert a date/time value to an equivalent string form

Python

In Python a `datetime` object is a single object containing all the information from a `date` object and a `time` object. As objects are not strings they need to be converted to strings. This can be done with the Python function `str`.

Python's `print` procedure (Python calls it a function) automatically converts `datetime`, `date` and `time` objects to strings before printing to the console window.

The following code creates, initialises and assigns a `datetime` object

```
olddatetime = datetime.datetime(1550, 7, 21, 13, 31, 17)
```

for the specified year, month, day, hour, minute, second, e.g. year = `1550,` month = `7,` day = `21,` hour of day = `13,` minute of day = `31,` second of day = `17`.

The following code extracts and assigns the `date` object within the `datetime` object

```
olddate = olddatetime.date()
```

and the following code extracts and assigns the `date` object within the `datetime` object

```
oldtime = olddatetime.time()
```

These may be displayed on a console using the following code

```
print(olddatetime)
print(olddate)
print(oldtime)
```

The `strftime` method can be used in the following manner to format `olddate` and `oldtime` when these are printed

```
print(olddate.strftime("%d/%m/%Y"))
print(oldtime.strftime("%H:%M:%S"))
```

It is also possible to access the operating system for the current time and date.
The `now` method is used as follows to obtain the current date and time

```
localdatetime = datetime.datetime.now()
```

String to date/time

Table 1.1.7.9 shows how to convert a date and a time in string form to an equivalent date/time type form in Java and C#.

<table>
<tr><th>Language</th><th>Code</th></tr>
<tr><td>Java</td><td><pre>import java.text.DateFormat;
import java.text.SimpleDateFormat;
import java.util.Date;
public class StringToDateConversion {
    public static void main(String[] args) {
      String dateString = "14/09/2016";
      DateFormat df = new SimpleDateFormat("dd/MM/yyyy");
      Date equivalentDate;
      try
        {equivalentDate = df.parse(dateString);
         System.out.println("Formatted date: " + equivalentDate);
        }
      catch (Exception e)
        {System.out.println("Something has gone wrong: " + e);}
    }
}
----
import java.text.DateFormat;
import java.text.SimpleDateFormat;
import java.util.Date;
public class StringToTimeConversion {
    public static void main(String[] args) {
      String timeString = "12:30:45 am";
      DateFormat tf = new SimpleDateFormat("hh:mm:ss a");
      try
        {Date equivalentTime = tf.parse(timeString);
         System.out.println("Formatted time: " + equivalentTime);
        }
      catch (Exception e)
        {System.out.println("Something has gone wrong: " + e);}
    }
}</pre></td></tr>
<tr><td>C#</td><td><pre>string date = "14/08/2016";
DateTime d = Convert.ToDateTime(date);
Console.WriteLine("Day: {0}, Month: {1}, Year: {2}", d.Day, d.Month, d.Year);
string dateTime = "14/08/2016 12:30:45.15";
DateTime dt = Convert.ToDateTime(dateTime);
Console.WriteLine("Day: {0}, Month: {1}, Year: {2}, Hour: {3}, Minute: {4},
Second: {5}, Millisecond: {6}",dt.Day, dt.Month, dt.Year, dt.Hour, dt.Minute,
dt.Second, dt.Millisecond);</pre></td></tr>
</table>

Table 1.1.7.9 Code examples in Java and C# which demonstrate how to convert a date/time in string form into an equivalent date/time form

Table 1.1.7.10 shows how to convert a date and a time in string form to an equivalent date/time type form in VB.NET, Pascal/Delphi and Python.

Language	Code

VB.NET

```
Module Module1
  Sub Main()
    Dim aDate As DateTime = DateTime.Parse("14/08/2016")
    Console.WriteLine(aDate)
    aDate = DateTime.Parse("Sunday, August 14, 2016")
    Console.WriteLine(aDate)
    Dim aDateAndTime = DateTime.Parse("Sun, 14 Aug 2016 15:06:35 GMT")
    Console.WriteLine(aDateAndTime)
    aDateAndTime = DateTime.Parse("14/08/2016 15:06:35")
    Console.WriteLine(aDateAndTime)
    Console.ReadLine()
  End Sub
End Module
```

```
file:///Z:/ProductionChap...
14/08/2016 00:00:00
14/08/2016 00:00:00
14/08/2016 16:06:35
14/08/2016 15:06:35
```

Pascal/ Delphi

```
Program StringToDateExample;
Uses Sysutils;
Var
  DateString : String;
  DateFromString : TDateTIme;
Begin
  DateString := '14/08/2016';
  DateFromString := StrToDate(DateString);
  Writeln(FormatDateTime('DD MM YYYY', DateFromString));
  Readln;
End.
-------------------------------------------------------------------------------
Program StringToTimeExample;
Uses Sysutils;
Var
  TimeString : String;
  TimeFromString : TDateTIme;
Begin
  TimeString := '15:45:23';
  TimeFromString := StrToTime(TimeString);
  Writeln(FormatDateTime('hh:nn:ss', TimeFromString));
  Readln;
End.
```

Python

```
import datetime
a_date = datetime.datetime.strptime('14/08/2016', '%d/%m/%Y')
a_time = datetime.datetime.strptime('17:15:50', '%H:%M:%S')
print(a_date)
print(a_time)
```

Table 1.1.7.10 Code examples in VB.NET, Pascal/Delphi, and Python which demonstrate how to convert a string representing a date/time into an equivalent date/time data type form

Substring

A substring is a subset of a string between one index and another. For example, the substring 'mit' is a subset of the string 'smith'.

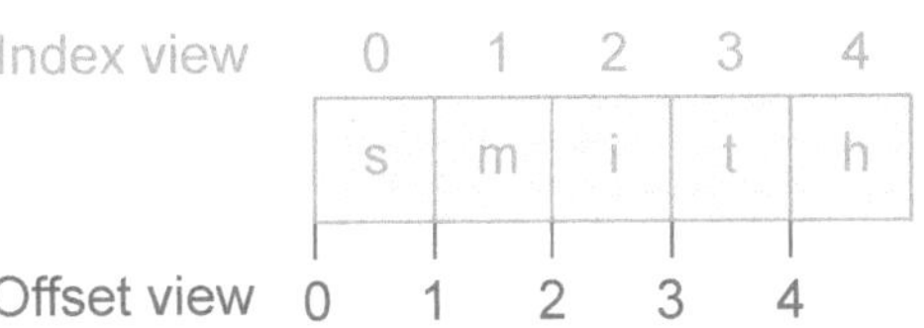

Figure 1.1.7.23 The string 'smith' and two ways to identify a substring of the string, by Index or by Offset

Figure 1.1.7.23 shows two ways to identify a substring of the string by

- Index
- Offset

Suppose a subroutine called `Substring` returns a substring of a given string, `s`.

It is called with arguments `s`, `StartIndex` and `EndIndex` as shown in Table 1.1.7.11 and the substring returned is assigned to another string variable, `SubOfs`.

The `StartIndex` is 1. In the *index view* in Figure 1.1.7.1, this is the index of the character 'm' in the string `s`.

The `EndIndex` is 3. In the *index view* in Figure 1.1.7.1, this is the index of the character 't' in the string `s`.

The substring returned is between index 1 and 3, inclusive, i.e. substring 'mit'.

```
s ← 'smith'
StartIndex ←1
EndIndex ← 3
SubOfs ← Substring(s, StartIndex, EndIndex)
Output SubOfs
```

Table 1.1.7.11 Pseudo-code showing a call to Substring

In the *offset view*,

- the first character of the substring, 'm' is reached by an offset of one character from the beginning of the string `s` as shown in Figure 1.1.7.24 - `StartOffset` is 1.
- the last character of the substring, 't' is included by an offset of four characters from the beginning of the string `s` as shown in Figure 1.1.7.24 (an offset of 0 is the first character 's' - `EndOffset` is 4. A slice can then occur between 1 and 4 as shown in Figure 1.1.7.24 to obtain the substring.

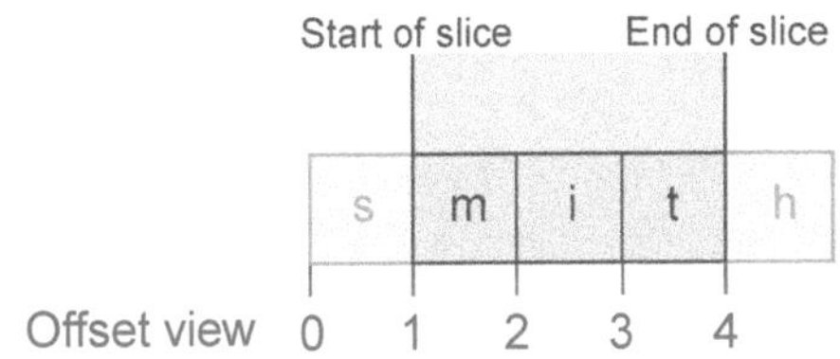

Figure 1.1.7.24 Taking a slice of the string 'smith' between StartOffset = 1 and EndOffset = 4

We can use `StartOfSlice` and `EndOfSlice` instead of `StartOffset` and `EndOffset`, to make it clearer that the selected substring is a slice through the string, i.e. `StartOfSlice = 1`, `EndOfSlice = 4`.

Table 1.1.7.12 shows examples of how a substring can be obtained in Pascal/Delphi, C#, Python, Java and VB.NET.

Python has no substring subroutine. Instead, we use slice syntax to get parts of existing strings.

<table>
<tr><th>Pascal/Delphi</th><th>C#</th></tr>
<tr><td><pre>Program SubstringExample;
{String indexing starts at 1}
Var
  s, SubOfs : String;
  StartIndex, Count : Integer;
Begin
  s := 'smith';
  StartIndex := 2;
  Count := 3;
  SubOfs := Copy(s,StartIndex,Count);
  Writeln(SubOfs);
  Readln;
End.
{Copy treats zero-based strings as if
they are 1-based In Delphi with zero-
based compiler option ON</pre></td><td><pre>using System;
namespace SubstringExample
{
  class Program
  {
    static void Main(string[] args)
    {
      String s = "smith";
      int startIndex = 1;
      int endIndex = 3;
      String subOfs = s.Substring(startIndex,endIndex);
      Console.WriteLine("Substring is {0}",subOfs);
      Console.ReadLine();
    }
  }
}</pre></td></tr>
<tr><th>Python</th><th>Java</th></tr>
<tr><td><pre>s = "smith"
start_offset = 1
end_offset = 4
sub_of_s = s[start_offset:end_offset]
print("Substring is ", sub_of_s)</pre></td><td><pre>public class SubstringExample {
  public static void main(String[] args) {
    String s = new String("smith");
    int startOffset = 1;
    int endOffset = 4;
    String subOfs = s.substring(startOffset,endOffset);
    System.out.println("Substring is " + subOfs);
  }
}</pre></td></tr>
<tr><th colspan="2">VB.Net</th></tr>
<tr><td colspan="2"><pre>Module Module1
  Sub Main()
    Dim s As String = "smith"
    Dim startIndex As Integer = 1
    Dim endIndex As Integer = 3
    Dim subOfs = s.Substring(startIndex, endIndex)
    Console.WriteLine("Substring is {0}", subOfs)
    Console.ReadLine()
  End Sub
End Module</pre></td></tr>
</table>

Table 1.1.7.12 Examples of how a substring can be obtained in Pascal/Delphi, C#, Python, Java and VB.NET

Concatenation

The concatenation of strings is the operation of joining character strings end-to-end.

For example, the concatenation of "john" and "smith" is "johnsmith".

The concatenation of "john" and " " and "smith" is "john smith".

The most common way of concatenating strings is to use the '+' operator.

For example in Java:

```
String a = "Hello";
String b = " World!";
String c = a + b;
System.out.print(c);
```

The concatenation operator '+' is common to all the programming languages covered in this chapter.

Programming tasks

1. Write a program which takes as input a string and prints out the number of characters in it.
2. Write a program which takes as input a word and checks if the first and last letters of the word are the same. The program should print either "The first and last letters are the same" or "The first and last letters are different".
3. Write a program which takes as input 2 words and prints the word made from the last 3 letters of the first word and the first 3 letters of the second word.
4. Write a program which takes as input a sentence and calculates how many words are in the sentence. The program should print this number (with appropriate message). Assume a word ends with a space, a sentence ends with a full stop.
5. Write a program which inputs two words, a master word and a test word. The program should check whether or not the test word appears anywhere in the master word and then print an appropriate message. For example "THE" appears inside the word "STRENGTHEN" but not inside "STEALTH". The program should first check that the test word is shorter than the master word; if not it should print the message "Test word too long" and request a new test word.
6. Write a program which takes as input a pair of words and prints a third word made from the letters at the end of the first word if they are the same as the letters at the beginning of the second word, e.g. IGNORANT and ANTLER are input, the output is ANT, otherwise the program should request another pair of words.
7. Write a program which takes as input a word and prints out a new word made from reversing the order of the letters in the input word, e.g. input word = "BEAR", output word = "RAEB".
8. Write a program which takes as input a pair of words and checks if one is an anagram of the other. The program should output the message "ANAGRAM" if it is and the message "NOT AN ANAGRAM" if it isn't.
9. Write a program which takes as input a word and determines whether or not the word is a palindrome. (A palindrome is a word that reads the same forwards and backwards. E.g. ROTOR.)
   Test your program on the following palindromes DAD, NOON, MADAM, REDDER, ROTOVATOR.
10. Write a program which takes a single word containing only upper case letters of the alphabet as input, and outputs an encrypted version of the word using the following simple encryption algorithm
    Character code for "A" + (((Character code of letter to encrypt - character code for "A") + 13) MOD 26)
11. Write a program to output the current date.
12. Write a program to output the current time.
13. Write a program which takes as input two dates in string form and calculates the number of days between the dates.

Position

Sometimes we may wish to discover if a given substring is present within a given string. For this we use a **position** function which returns the index within the given string of the first occurrence of the substring. If the substring is not present in the given string then a value is returned outside the index range, e.g. -1. *Table 1.1.7.13* shows how this can be done in Pascal/Delphi, C#, Python, Java and VB.NET.

Pascal/ Delphi	`Position := AnsiPos('ello', 'Hello World!');`
	`If Not (Position = 0)`
	`  Then Writeln('String contains ello')`
	`  Else Writeln('Not found');`
		The AnsiPos function finds the position of one string 'ello' within another 'Hello World'.
		If the string is not found, 0 is returned. The search is case sensitive.

C#	`string s = "Hello World!";`
	`if (s.IndexOf("ello") != -1)`
	`  {`
	`    Console.WriteLine("String contains ello");`
	`  }`
		Function `IndexOf` returns the index of a substring. First it scans the String. And if the substring is not found, it returns -1.

VB.NET	`Dim s As String = "Hello World!"`
	`If Not s.IndexOf("ello") = -1 Then`
	`  Console.WriteLine("String contains ello")`
		Function `IndexOf` returns the index of a substring. First it scans the String. And if the substring is not found, it returns -1.

Java	`String s = "Hello World!";`
	`if (s.indexOf("ello") >= 0){`
	`  System.out.println(" String contains ello")`
	`}`
		Function indexOf returns the index within this string of the first occurrence of the specified substring. If it does not occur as a substring, -1 is returned.

Python	`str1 = "Hello World!"`
	`str2 = "ello"`
	`if (str1.find(str2) != -1):`
	`  print ("String contains ello")`
		Function find returns the index within this string of the first occurrence of the specified substring. If it does not occur as a substring, -1 is returned.

Table 1.1.7.13 Examples of searching for a substring within a given string in Pascal/Delphi, C#, Python, Java and VB.NET

In this chapter you have covered:

- Using and becoming familiar with:
  - length
  - position
  - substring
  - concatenation
  - character → character code
  - character code → character
  - string conversion routines
    - string to integer
    - string to float
    - integer to string
    - float to string
    - date/time to string
    - string to date/time

1 Fundamentals of programming

1.1 Programming

Learning objectives:

- *Be familiar with, and be able to use, random number generation*

Figure 1.1.8.1 Rolling dice

Did you know?

The history of pseudorandom number generator algorithms began during the Manhattan project in the Second World War when John von Neumann devised the middle-square method of generating pseudorandom number sequences - the method was marked Top Secret initially.
A quick way of generating random numbers was needed for simulations for the nuclear bomb programme.
The middle-square method is flawed because it can go horribly wrong and generate sequences which are not very random but John Neumann was happy to work with this limitation because when things went wrong it was easy to spot.
In 1949, D.H Lehman came up with the linear congruential method, a far superior method still used today in some software systems although many now use the Mersenne Twister PRNG, e.g. Free Pascal and Python.

1.1.8 Random number generation in a programming language

Random number generation

Random numbers

An algorithm which generates a random, or apparently random, sequence of numbers is called a **random number generator**.

For example, suppose we require a method for selecting an integer at random from the set of integers 1, 2, 3, .., N.

For small values of N simple mechanisms exist.
For example:

- for N = 2 we can toss a coin
- for N = 6 we can roll a die - *Figure 1.1.8.1*
- for N = 12 we can roll a 12-sided die
- for N = 36 we can use a roulette wheel.

Every number in the chosen set of integers 1, 2, 3, .., N, is equally likely.

Statistically, each number from the set should appear on average the same number of times in a long sequence generated by coin tossing or dice rolling.

The sequence generated which satisfies these two conditions is called a **random sequence**.

Pseudorandom numbers

Most computer generated random numbers use pseudorandom number generators (PRNGs) which are algorithms that can automatically create long runs of numbers with good random properties but eventually the sequence repeats.

This kind of random number is adequate for many situations, e.g. computer simulations and cryptography.

However, pseudorandom generated number sequences are not as random as coin tosses and dice rolls or random sequences generated from physical phenomena such as electrical noise signals.

Pseudorandom number generator algorithms generate a random sequence which is completely determined by a shorter initial value known as a seed value or key.

As a result, the entire seemingly random sequence can be reproduced if the seed value is known.

For example, in the linear congruential method the next number in the pseudorandom sequence is calculated from its immediate predecessor as follows

next = (multiplier * predecessor + increment) MOD modulus

We can demonstrate this method by hand if we choose small values, e.g.

- multiplier = 13,
- increment = 0,
- modulus = 31

If we start the sequence with predecessor = 1, we get the pseudorandom sequence

1, 13, 14, 27, 10, 6, 16, 22, 7, 29, 5, 3, . . .

Information

If we choose the increment to be 0 then the generator is said to be a multiplicative linear congruential generator.
To obtain a maximal cycle with such a generator, we have to ensure the modulus is prime.

The first thirty terms in this sequence are a permutation of the integers from 1 to 30 and then the sequence repeats itself. It has a period equal to modulus − 1.

The starting value is called the seed.

If we divide each pseudorandom integer in the sequence by the modulus (31) we obtain numbers which are uniformly distributed between 0 and 1.

The pseudorandom sequence

1, 13, 14, 27, 10, 6, 16, 22, 7, 29, 5, 3, . . .

becomes

0.03226, 0.4194, 0.4516, 0.8710, 0.3226, 0.1935, ...

Questions

1. Calculate the first seven random numbers using the linear congruential method and multiplier = 7, increment = 0, modulus = 13 and starting value 1.
2. What is the maximum length of sequence in question 1 before the sequence hits 1 again?
3. Explain why, for a given starting value, the sequence of random numbers generated from the linear congruential method in question 1 eventually repeats itself.

Task

1. Set up a spreadsheet to calculate the first 37 random numbers generated by the linear congruential method and multiplier = 7, increment = 0, modulus = 13 and starting value 1.
   What do you observe?

   Change the starting value in the spreadsheet to 6. What do you observe?

Multiplicative linear congruential generator

Stephen Park and Keith Miller proposed a minimal standard random number generator in 1988 in which the increment was 0, the multiplier was 16807 and the modulus was 2147483647 (2^{31} -1).
The modulus was chosen to be as large as possible and at least the word size of operating system e.g. for a 32-bit operating system 32 bits in size.

The multiplier was chosen to be relatively prime to the modulus (two numbers are relatively prime if their greatest common divisor is 1).

Mersenne Twister generator

The Mersenne Twister generator algorithm (1998) based on a Mersenne prime is an alternative to the linear congruential generator algorithm.
The most commonly used version is based on the Mersenne prime $2^{19937}-1$.
It has a period of $2^{19937}-1$, i.e. the maximum sequence length before the sequence repeats is $2^{19937}-1$.
The standard implementation uses a 32-bit word length.

Key term

Mersenne Twister:
The Mersenne Twister generator has a better statistical distribution than a Linear Congruential generator algorithm, but is considerably slower than the latter.

Randomizing the seed

Although it is possible to set the seed manually, using the same seed will generate the same pseudorandom sequence of numbers.
Both linear congruential generators and Mersenne twister generators use algorithms which are deterministic, i.e. given the seed value, the algorithm and its parameter values, the sequence is predictable.
Truly random number generators are based on some physical phenomenon which is governed ultimately by quantum mechanics, a nondeterministic mechanics.

However, the choice of seed can be randomized. One method relies upon sampling the computer's system clock another chooses from a small set of truly random numbers.

For example, in Python one would call the procedure `random.seed(None)` to use the system clock to generate the seed for the Mersenne Twister generator. Next, function `random.random()` is called. It returns the next random floating point number in the interval [0.0, 1.0). "[" means 0.0 is included in the range. The symbol ")" means 1.0 is excluded.
For example, in one call to `random.seed(None)` followed by `random.random()`, 0.40488239522745517 was returned.

However, the pseudorandom number generated by the call `random.seed(1)` followed by `random.random()`, produced 0.13436424411240122 as the first number in the sequence every time and the same sequence of numbers on calling `random.random()` again and again.

Random number generators in programming languages

Table 1.1.8.1 shows pseudorandom number generator subroutines for Python, Java, Free Pascal, Delphi, C# and VB.NET. Table 1.1.8.2 shows how the seed value may be set in Python, Java, Free Pascal, Delphi, C# and VB.NET.

Table 1.1.8.3 shows the pseudorandom generator algorithm which is used for Python, Java, Free Pascal, Delphi, C# and VB.NET.

Language	Pseudorandom number generator subroutine	Explanation

Python	`random.random()`
	
	`random.randint(a, b)`
	
	`random.randint(N)`
		Returns the next random floating point number in the interval [0.0, 1.0)
		Returns a random integer N such that a <= N <= b
		Returns `Random integer` in interval [0,N]

Java	`import java.util.Random`
	`public class PRSG {`
	`  public static void main(String[] args){`
	`    System.out.println(Math.random())`
	`  }`
	`}`
		`Math.random()`
		Returns the next pseudorandom, double value in the interval [0.0, 1.0)

Java	`public class PRSG {`
	`  public static void main(String[] args){`
	`    Random pRSG = new Random();`
	`    System.out.println(pRSG.nextInt(10));`
	`  }`
	`}`
		Returns the next pseudorandom, `int` value in the interval [0, 10)

Free Pascal	`Uses`
	`  SysUtils;`
	`Var`
	`  Hours, Mins, Secs, Millisecs : Word;`
	`Begin`
	`  Randomize;`
	`  WriteLn(Random :20:18);`
	`  DecodeTime(Now, hours, mins, secs, milliSecs);`
	`  RandSeed := milliSecs;`
	`  WriteLn(Random :20:18);`
	`  WriteLn(Random(10));`
		`Randomize` changes the seed used to generate its range of pseudo random numbers.
		The `RandSeed LongInt` variable can be set directly.
		`Random` returns a random `real` number in the interval [0.0, 1.0)
		`Random(N)` returns a random number in `LongInt` integer interval [0, N)

Delphi	`Randomize;`
	`Writeln(Random :20:18);`
	`DecodeTime(Now, hours, mins, secs, milliSecs);`
	`RandSeed := milliSecs;`
	`Writeln(Random :20:18);`
	`Writeln(Random(10));`
		`Random` returns a random real number in range [0.0, 1.0)
		`Random(N)` returns a random number in `LongInt` integer interval [0, N)

C#	`Random n = new Random();`
	`Console.WriteLine("Randomly generated number in range [0.0, 1.0) : {0}", n.NextDouble());`
	`Console.WriteLine("Randomly generated number in range [0, 10) : {0}", n.Next(10));`
		`new Random()` initializes a new instance of the `Random` class, using a time-dependent default seed value.
		`NextDouble()` gets next `double` random no in interval [0.0, 1.0).
		`Next(N)` gets next integer random no in interval [0,N).

VB.NET	`Dim n As New Random()`
	`Console.WriteLine("Randomly generated number in range [0.0, 1.0) : {0}", n.NextDouble())`
	`Console.WriteLine("Randomly generated number in range [0, 10) : {0}", n.Next(10))`
		`new Random()` initializes a new instance of the `Random` class, using a time-dependent default seed value.
		`NextDouble()` gets next `double` random no.
		`Next(N)` gets next integer random no in interval [0,N).

Table 1.1.8.1 shows pseudorandom number generator subroutines for the languages

Language	Seed setting subroutines	Explanantion

Python	`import random`
	`random.seed(None)`
	`random.seed(seedvalue)`
		`random.seed(None)`, None means system clock sets seed
		Seed is `seedvalue`, e.g. 1.

Free Pascal	`Randomize`	Initializes the random number generator by giving a value to Randseed LongInt variable, calculated with the system clock.

Delphi	`Randomize`
	
	`DecodeTime(now, hours, mins, secs, milliSecs);`
	`RandSeed := milliSecs;`
		Randomize changes the seed used to generate its range of 2^{32} pseudo random numbers.
		
		The RandSeed LongInt variable can be set directly.

C#	`Random(N)`	Initializes a new instance of the `Random` class, using the specified seed value N of type `Int32`.
VB.NET	`Random(N)`	Initializes a new instance of the `Random` class, using the specified seed value N of type `Int32`.

Table 1.1.8.2 shows seed setting for Python, Free Pascal, Delphi, C# and VB.NET

Questions

4. What is the role of a seed in the generation of pseudorandom number sequences?

5. A certain online Poker site found that a group of players was winning every time against the computer-generated poker hands. On investigation, it was discovered that the group was familiar with the programming language used to program the poker game and had also worked out how to obtain the uptime of the server.
Explain one way this group could have accurately predicted the computer-generated poker hands?

Language	Pseudorandom number generator algorithm
Python	Mersenne Twister
Free Pascal	Mersenne Twister
Delphi	Multiplicative linear congruential generator
C#	Donald E. Knuth's subtractive random number generator algorithm
VB.NET	Donald E. Knuth's subtractive random number generator algorithm

Table 1.1.8.3 Pseudorandom number generator algorithms used in the languages

Programming tasks

1. Write a program to generate and display 10 random floating point numbers in the interval [0.0, 1.0), i.e. $0.0 \leq x < 1.0$.

2. Write a program to generate and display 10 random integers in interval [0, 10), i.e. $0 \leq x < 10$.

In this chapter you have covered:

- Using and becoming familiar with random number generation

1 Fundamentals of programming

1.1 Programming

Learning objectives:

- *Be familiar with the concept of exception handling*
- *Know how to use exception handling in a programming language with which students are familiar*

Key term

Exception:
An exception is an unexpected (or at least unusual) condition that arises during program execution, and which cannot be easily handled by the program.

Key concept

Exception handling:
The idea of exception handling is to move error-checking code "out-of-line", so that the source code can express the solution to the normal case without its intent being obscured by error-checking code.
When an exception does occur control branches "out-of-line" to a handler.
A handler performs some operation which, if recovery is possible, allows a program to recover from the exception and continue execution.
If recovery is not possible, a handler can print an informative error message before the program terminates.

1.1.9 Exception handling

The concept of exception handling

What is an exception?

An exception is an unexpected (or at least unusual) condition that arises during program execution, and which cannot be easily handled by the program.

The most common types of exceptions are various kinds of run-time errors such as *arithmetic overflow*, *division by zero*, *end-of-file on input*, *input conversion*, *subscript* and *subrange* errors.

For example, an input routine may find letters in the input when it is expecting digits.

To anticipate every unexpected condition is unrealistic. Attempts to include code to check for multiple error conditions is itself likely to introduce other errors.
It is also likely to obscure the normal control flow of the program, making the program difficult to read, understand and debug.
The resulting source code would resemble a veritable spaghetti junction of nested *If statements*.

Exception handling

Exception handling mechanisms address these issues by moving error-checking code "out-of-line", de-cluttering the source code which expresses the solution to the normal case.
To this source code must be added an arrangement for control to branch to a handler when an exception occurs.

A handler will perform some operation which, if recovery is possible, allows a program to recover from the exception and continue execution.

If recovery is not possible, a handler can print an informative error message before the program terminates.

Using exception handling in a programming language

In most programming languages an exception handler is attached to a statement or to a list of statements.

Delphi/Pascal

Table 1.1.9.1 shows an example in Delphi which catches a division by zero error. The block of statements between *Try* and *Except* are protected.

```
Readln(x);
y := 4 Div x;
Writeln(y);
```

If `yx` <> `0` then no exception occurs and the Except block is ignored.

However, if `x = 0` then an exception occurs when execution of `y := 4 Div x` is attempted.

Control is now transferred to the *Except* block to handle the exception. The `Writeln(y)` statement following `y := 4 Div x` is not executed.

Exceptions are usually objects in the object-oriented sense of the word - a value of some class type.

Most languages allow an exception to have parameters so that the code that raises the exception can pass information to the code that handles it.

In *Table 1.1.9.1* when an exception has occurred, an exception object is constructed and passed to the *Except* block.

In the *Except* block, *On E : EDivByZero* checks for a specific class type called *EDivByZero*.

If the class of the exception object matches the class *EDivByZero,* the exception object is assigned to the inline local variable *E*. The exception object has a field called *Message* which contains a pre-defined string, in the case of a divide by zero error it is the string 'Division by zero'.

This field is accessed with *E.Message* in the *Writeln* statement. *Figure 1.1.9.1* shows the output when this program is executed with input 0 for x.

```
Program DivByZeroException;
{$APPTYPE CONSOLE}
Uses
  SysUtils;
Var
  x : Integer;
  y : Integer;
Begin
  Try
    Readln(x);
    y := 4 Div x;
    Writeln(y);
  Except
    On E : EDivByZero
      Do
        Begin
          Writeln('Error: ', E.Message, '; Will recover by setting y to 1');
          y := 1;
        End;
  End;
  Writeln(y);
  Readln;
End.
```

```
Try
  // Do something that may raise an exception
Except
  // Handle any exception
End;
```

Table 1.1.9.1 Example of Exception handling in Delphi

```
Z:\ProductionChapters\Units1and2ASBook\NewVersion7\DelphiCode\DelphiException...
0
Error: Division by zero; Will recover by setting y to 1
1
```

Figure 1.1.9.1 Output from the exception handler when the Delphi program in Table 1.1.9.1 is executed with input 0 for x.

Table 1.1.9.2 shows a Delphi program with an *Except* block which checks for different specific exception types.

```
Program ExceptionHandling;
{$APPTYPE CONSOLE}
Uses SysUtils;
Var
  x, y : Integer;
  Date : TDate;
  DateStr : String;
Begin
  Try
    Readln(x);
    y := 4 Div x;
    Writeln(y);
    Readln(DateStr);
    Date := StrToDate(DateStr);
  Except
    On E:EDivByZero
      Do Writeln('Error 1 ', E.Message);
    On E: EInOutError
      Do Writeln('Error 2 ', E.Message);
    On EConvertError
      Do
        Begin
          DateStr := '01/01/2001';
          Date := StrToDate(DateStr);
        End;
  End;
  Writeln(y);
  Writeln(DateToStr(Date));
  Readln;
End.
```

```
Try
  // Do something that may raise an exception
Except
  On Identifier1 : ExceptionClass1
    Do Begin {Handle ExceptionClass1 exception}; End;
  On Identifier1 : ExceptionClass2
    Do Begin {Handle ExceptionClass2 exception}; End;
  On Identifier1 : ExceptionClass3
    Do Begin {Handle ExceptionClass3 exception}; End;
End;
```

```
Z:\Prod...
2
2
13/13/2016
01/01/2001
```

Figure 1.1.9.2 Output from the exception handler when the Delphi program in Table 1.1.9.2 is executed and an EConvertError exception occurs on converting a date string to date format

Table 1.1.9.2 Example of a Delphi program which checks for different specific exception types

VB.NET

Table 1.1.9.3 shows an example of exception handling in VB.NET.

VB.NET uses *Try ... Catch ... End Try* in a similar way that Delphi uses *Try ... Except ... End.*

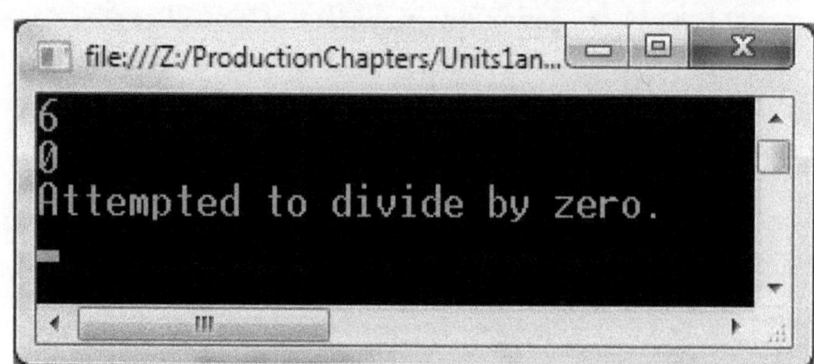

Figure 1.1.9.3 Output from the exception handler when the VB.NET program in Table 1.1.9.3 is executed with input 0 for y.

```
Module Module1
    Sub Main()
        DivideByZero()
        Console.ReadLine()
    End Sub
    Public Sub DivideByZero()
        Dim x As Integer
        Dim y As Integer
        Dim r As Integer = 0
        Try
            x = Console.ReadLine()
            y = Console.ReadLine()
            r = x \ y
            Console.WriteLine(r)
        Catch e As DivideByZeroException
            Console.WriteLine(e.Message)
        End Try
    End Sub
End Module
```

Table 1.1.9.3 Example of exception handling in VB.NET

C#

Table 1.1.9.4 shows an example of exception handling in C#.

C# uses *Try* {...} *Catch* {...} in a similar way that Delphi uses *Try* ... *Except* ... *End*.

```
using System;
namespace DivideByZeroExceptionHandling
{
    class Program
    {
        static void Main(string[] args)
        {
            int x, y, r;
            try
            {
                string input = Console.ReadLine();
                Int32.TryParse(input, out x);
                input = Console.ReadLine();
                Int32.TryParse(input, out y);
                r = x / y;
                Console.WriteLine(r);
            }
            catch (DivideByZeroException e)
            {
                Console.WriteLine(e.Message);
            }
            Console.ReadLine();
        }
    }
}
```

Table 1.1.9.4 Example of exception handling in C#

Java

Table 1.1.9.5 shows an example of exception handling in Java.

Java uses *try* {...} *catch* {...} in a similar way that Delphi uses *Try* ... *Except* ... *End*.

```
import java.util.Scanner;
public class DivideByZeroExceptionHandling {
    public static void main(String[] args) {
            int x, y, r;
            try
            {
                Scanner in = new Scanner(System.in);
                x = in.nextInt();
                y = in.nextInt();
                r = x / y;
                System.out.println(r);
            }
            catch (ArithmeticException e)
            {
                System.out.println(e);
            }

    }
}
```

```
6
0
java.lang.ArithmeticException: / by zero
```

Table 1.1.9.5 Example of exception handling in Java

Python

Table 1.1.9.6 shows an example of exception handling in Python.

Python uses *try: ... except ...* in a similar way that Delphi uses *Try ... Except ... End.*

```
try:
    x = int(input("Enter a number: "))
    y = int(input("Enter a number: "))
    result = x/y
    print(result)
except ZeroDivisionError:
    print("Division by zero detected")
else:

    print("Evaluation of x/y was successful")
```

Table 1.1.9.6 Example of exception handling in Python

Questions

1. What is the meaning of the terms *program exception* and *exception handling* in the context of programming?

Programming Task

1. Investigate exception handling in a programming language with which you are familiar.
   Explore the following:
   (a) Math exceptions
   (b) Input conversion exception caused by input of non-digit characters when character digits expected .

In this chapter you have covered:

- The concept of exception handling
- Using exception handling in a programming language with which students are familiar

1 Fundamentals of programming

1.1 Programming

Learning objectives:

- *Be familiar with subroutines and their uses*
- *Know that a subroutine is a named 'out of line' block of code that may be executed (called) by simply writing its name in a program statement*
- *Be able to explain the advantages of using subroutines in programs*

Information

Ord:
Ord applied to a character returns its character code.
Chr:
Chr applied to a character code returns the character.
Length:
Length applied to a string returns the no of characters in the string.

1.1.10 Subroutines (procedures/functions)

Subroutines and their uses

A subroutine is a named self-contained block of instructions, e.g. drawsquare. By encapsulating and naming a block of instructions in a program it becomes possible to call the block from other parts of the program.

This is very useful in situations where the same block of instructions or action or calculation needs to be repeated in multiple places in a program.

A program that references the subroutine `drawsquare` by name at a particular place in the program flow is said to call the subroutine `drawsquare`. It is sufficient to just use its name, `drawsquare`, to cause its block of instructions to execute.

Subroutines have been covered in depth in *Chapter 1.1.2*.

A subroutine may contain its own variable, type, label and const declarations.

A subroutine may also define subroutines which it may use and it may use subroutines defined elsewhere (usually library or language-defined subroutines).

Table 1.1.10.1 shows a pseudo-code procedure definition, `ConvertStringToUpper`, which itself contains a function definition, `Upper`, and a local variable declaration, `i : Integer`.

These procedure and function subroutines use library or language-defined subroutines, `Ord`, `Chr` and `Length`.

```
Procedure ConvertStringToUpper (INOUT Message : String)
  LocalVar
    i : Integer
  EndLocalVar
  Function Upper(Ch : Char) : Char
    If Ch In ['a'..'z']
      Then Ch ← Chr(Ord(Ch) - Ord('a') + Ord('A'))
    EndIf
    Return Ch
  EndFunction
  For i ← 1 To Length(Message)
    Message[i] ← Upper(Message[i])
  EndFor
EndProcedure
```

Table 1.1.10.1 Pseudo-code procedure definition, showing encapsulation of a block of instructions, a function and a local variable

A reference to a string is passed to procedure `ConvertStringToUpper` in the procedure parameter variable `Message`. The reference is to a string which exists in the calling program's variable memory space. Any changes made by `ConvertStringToUpper` are applied to this string. This is what is meant by `Message` being an INOUT parameter.

The function `Upper` is said to be nested inside procedure `ConvertStringToUpper`.

On encountering the name `ConvertStringToUpper`, the executing program transfers control to this subroutine. On finishing its execution `ConvertStringToUpper` transfers control back to the point in the program immediately following where it was called.

A subroutine is a named out of line block of code

Figure 1.1.10.1 shows the control structure of a program block consisting of program statements S1, S2, S3, a selection statement (shown as ?) controlling execution of two statements S4 and S5. This selection statement is followed by a loop which controls a block of statements S.
A procedure T consists of program statements S1, S2, S3 (different ones from the program block statements) and a loop controlling a block of statements S (also different from the program block S).

The flow of control in the program block is in line, forwards from the beginning to the end, except when statement S1 is encountered. This statement transfers control 'out of line' to procedure T.
Flow of control in procedure T is from its beginning to its end.
On reaching the end of T, control is transferred back to the program block.
Execution is resumed in the program block at statement S2, the statement immediately following S1, where the call to T occurred. If T was a function then control would be returned to statement S1 along with the function's result.

Procedure T is a subroutine.
In Pascal, statement S1 which is a call to a procedure T which doesn't use parameters is simply `T;`
In VB.NET, the call to a procedure T which doesn't use parameters would be `T()`
This example, shows that a subroutine is:

> **a named 'out of line' block of code which may be executed (called) by simply writing its name in a program statement.**

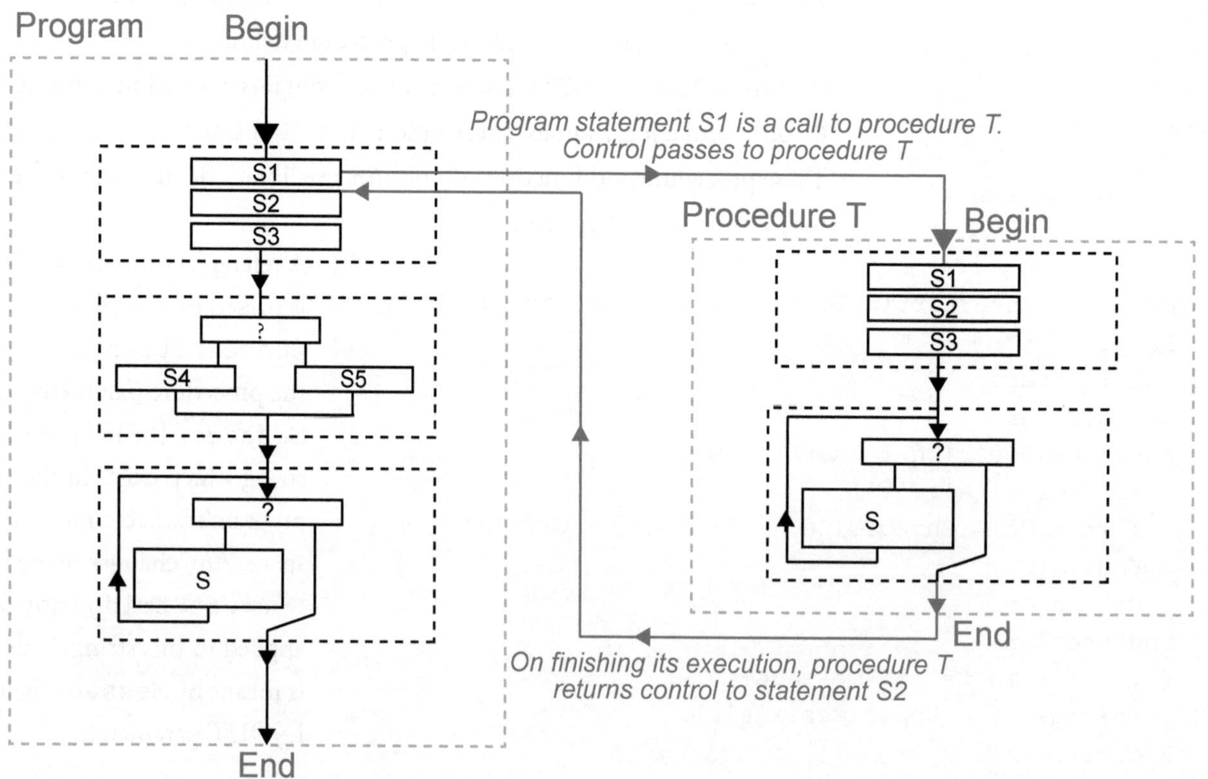

Figure 1.1.10.1 In line flow of control to out of line flow of control to a named out of line block of code

Questions

1. What is meant by "a subroutine is a named 'out of line' block of code that may be executed by simply writing its name in a program statement"?

Advantages of using subroutines in programs

Without programming language support for subroutines (procedures and functions), all programming would consist of inline blocks of program instructions.

This would make even programs of modest size

- difficult to understand
- difficult to debug.

Removing blocks of instructions from the program block and placing these in 'out of line', named subroutine blocks (Figure 1.1.10.1) separate from the control flow of the program block, reduces the intellectual demand needed to understand what the program does

The program block is reduced in length because where it relies on the instructions in subroutines these are referenced by a short and descriptive name (ideally).

If subroutines are self-contained they can be worked on separately.
This is useful when writing and debugging software.
In software projects involving a team of developers, different subroutines can be given to different members of the team to write and debug.
The more self-contained (independent) the subroutine the easier it is to write and debug without having to understand the program block in which it is called.

Subroutines written for one program may be reused in a different program. The more self-contained they are the easier it is to do this.

If a subroutine is particularly useful, it may be added to a library of subroutines which can be imported into any program which needs them.

Questions

2 State and explain **three** advantages of using subroutines in programs.

Did you know?

Inline code:

In defence applications such as missile homing heads, program code is often converted to inline code during the software construction stage.
Each subroutine call in the program block is replaced by the subroutine's block of instructions.
One reason this is done is to avoid a potential software crash caused by stack overflow.
A stack is used in subroutine calls.
A stack (or call stack) stores return addresses which are used by each executing subroutine to return to the place from where they were called. Specifically, to the statement following the call statement.
A stack is finite in size and is limited by the memory allocated to it.
A missile homing head is the part of a missile which guides the missile onto the target.
Missiles often cost upwards on £30000.
Once launched there is no opportunity to reboot if the computer crashes from stack overflow.

In this chapter you have covered:

- Subroutines and their uses
- A subroutine as a named 'out of line' block of code that may be executed (called) by simply writing its name in a program statement
- The advantages of using subroutines in programs

1 Fundamentals of programming

1.1 Programming

Learning objectives:

- *Be able to describe the use of parameters to pass data within programs*
- *Be able to use subroutines with interfaces*

1.1.11 Parameters of subroutines

Using parameters to pass data within programs

A subroutine parameter is one way of passing data into and out of a subroutine. When a subroutine is called, any data passed to it via the subroutine parameter mechanism is copied into the memory area reserved for subroutine formal parameters as shown in the memory schematic in *Figure 1.1.11.1*.

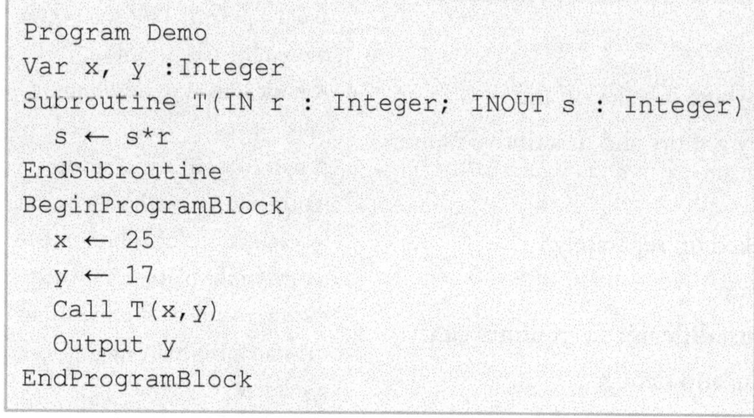

```
Program Demo
Var x, y :Integer
Subroutine T(IN r : Integer; INOUT s : Integer)
  s ← s*r
EndSubroutine
BeginProgramBlock
  x ← 25
  y ← 17
  Call T(x,y)
  Output y
EndProgramBlock
```

Table 1.1.11.1 An example of a pseudocode program with a subroutine call involving data associated with two program variables being passed to the subroutine

There are two ways that data may be passed via the subroutine parameter mechanism into a subroutine:

- Call by value
- Call by reference/Call by address

We illustrate both with data stored in two program variables, x and y.

The variable name x maps to value 25 and the variable name y maps to 17.

We can express this as follows where the symbol ↦ means 'maps to'

x ↦ 25 and y ↦ 17

This mapping is set up at the point in time when statements

```
x ← 25
y ← 17
```

are executed in the program shown in *Table 1.1.11.1*.

The subroutine memory area shows two variables, r and s, called **formal parameters** of the subroutine.

Figure 1.1.11.1 shows these mapping to 5674 and 25.

r ↦ 25 and y ↦ 5674

This mapping is set up at the point in time when

```
Call T(x, y)
```

is executed in the program shown in *Table 1.1.11.1*.

Close inspection of the memory map in *Figure 1.1.11.1* indicates that the datum associated with x has been copied into the location in the subroutine memory area associated with r.

Similarly, close inspection shows that the program memory address 5674 of the location in program memory associated with y has been copied into the location in the subroutine memory area associated with s.

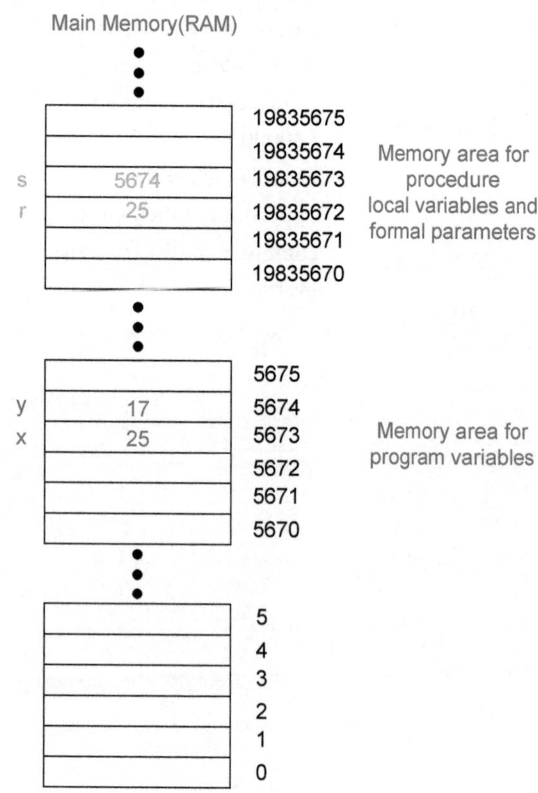

Figure 1.1.11.1 Memory map showing an area reserved for program variables and an area reserved for subroutine variables

Now when we look at the subroutine header we see that the r parameter is labelled an IN parameter and the s parameter is labelled an INOUT parameter:

```
Subroutine T(IN r : Integer; INOUT s : Integer)
```

The interpretation of IN r : Integer is as follows: a value is to be copied into the formal parameter r when the subroutine is called.
This is what is meant by Call by Value.
The interpretation of INOUT s : Integer is as follows: an address of where a value can be found in the program memory area is to be copied into the formal parameter s when the subroutine is called.
This is what is meant by Call by Reference/Call by Address.

This copying takes place when the subroutine is called with actual parameters x and y by the program statement

```
Call(x, y)
```

If a subroutine has the address of a datum in the program memory area then the subroutine may change the value in this area. The subroutine in Table 1.1.11.1 does this with an assignment statement

```
s ← s*r
```

Call by reference/address thus can have the side-effect of changing the value of a variable in another area of memory. This side-effect can be desirable and intended or undesirable.
Call by value cannot change the original value which has been copied.
Call by reference/address should be used as follows

- when a datum is too big to pass by value, i.e. it would take up a lot of space in subroutine memory or it would take too long (relatively speaking) to copy into subroutine memory
- when more than one result of executing the subroutine needs to be returned from the subroutine call
- when the data type of the result to be returned is not supported by the mechanism used by a function to return a result. Function return uses a different mechanism from subroutine parameters to return a result.

If only a single result needs to be returned and the data type of the result is supported by the function mechanism for returning results then a function should normally be used.

When a subroutine calls a subroutine, the subroutine memory area is used for both the calling subroutine and the called subroutine parameters/variables.

Table 1.1.11.2 shows Call by Value and Call by Reference/Address support in the programming languages Python, Java, Pascal/Delphi, C# and VB.NET.

Table 1.1.11.3 shows an example in Java of Call by Value.

Table 1.1.11.4 shows an example in Java of Call by Reference/Address.

Table 1.1.11.5 shows an example in Pascal of Call by Value and Call by Address.

Table 1.1.11.6 shows an example in C# of Call by Value and Call by Reference/Address.

Table 1.1.11.7 shows an example in VB.NET of Call by Value and Call by Reference/Address.

Key term

Subroutine parameter:
A subroutine parameter is a mechanism for passing data into and out of a subroutine.

Key term

Call by value:
Formal parameter of subroutine gets a copy of the datum associated with the actual parameter used in call to subroutine.

Call by address:
Formal parameter of subroutine is assigned the address in memory of the datum associated with the actual parameter used in call to subroutine.

Language	Call by Value	Call by Reference/Address
Python	Python is neither "call by value" nor "call by reference". In Python a variable is not an alias for a location in memory. It is a binding to a Python object.	

Java	void a(int r){
	    r = r +10;
	}
		There is no call by reference/address only call by value but a reference may be passed by value:
		class Test{
		  int x =5;
		  void c(Test r){
		    r.x = r.x+10; //object variable x is changed
		  }
		}

Pascal/ Delphi	Procedure A(r : Integer);
	  Begin
	    r := r + 10;
	  End;
	Function B(s : Integer) : Integer;
	  Begin
	    B := s + 10;
	  End;
		Procedure C(Var r : Integer);
		  Begin
		    r := r + 10;
		  End;

C#	static void a(int r)
	  {
	    r = r + 10;
	  }
		static void b(ref int s)
		  {
		    s = s + 10;
		  }

VB.NET	Sub A(ByVal r As Int)
	    r = r + 10
	End Sub
		Sub B(ByRef s As Int)
		    s = s + 10
		End Sub

Table 1.1.11.2 Call by Value and Call by Reference/Address support in the programming languages Python, Java, Pascal/Delphi, C# and VB.NET

```
public class CallByValue {
  public static void main(String[] args) {
    int x = 5;
    System.out.println("Before call to c " + x);
    c(x);
    System.out.println("After call to c " + x);
  }
  static void c(int r){
    r = r + 10;
  }
}
```

Table 1.1.11.3 Java example of Call by Value

```
public class CallByReference {
    int x = 5;
    void c(CallByReference s){
      s.x = s.x+10;//object variable x is changed
    }

    public static void main(String[] args) {
     CallByReference exampleCByR = new CallByReference();
     System.out.println("Before Before call to c " + exampleCByR.x);
     exampleCByR.c(exampleCByR);
     System.out.println("After call to c " + exampleCByR.x);
    }
}
```

Table 1.1.11.4 Java example of Call by Reference

```
Program CallByValueAndCallByAddress;
Procedure A(r : Integer);
  Begin
    r := r + 10;
  End;
Function B(s : Integer) : Integer;
  Begin
    B := s + 10;
  End;
Procedure C(Var s : Integer);
  Begin
    s := s + 10;
  End;
Var
  x, y : Integer;
Begin
  x := 5;
  y := 5;
  A(x);
  Writeln(x);
  Writeln(B(y));
  C(y);
  Writeln(y);
  Readln;
End.
```

Table 1.1.11.5 Pascal example of Call by Value and Call by Reference

```
using System;
namespace CallByValueAndCallByReference
{
    class Program
    {
        static void Main(string[] args)
        {
            int x;
            x = 10;
            a(x);
            Console.WriteLine(x);
            b(ref x);
            Console.WriteLine(x);
            Console.ReadLine();
        }

        static void a(int r)
        {
            r = r + 10;
        }

        static void b(ref int s)
        {
            s = s + 10;
        }
    }
}
```

Table 1.1.11.6 C# example of Call by Value and Call by Reference

```
Module Module1
    Sub Main()
        Dim x As Integer = 5
        A(x)
        Console.WriteLine(x)
        B(x)
        Console.WriteLine(x)
        Console.ReadLine()
    End Sub
    Sub A(ByVal r As Integer)
        r = r + 10
    End Sub
    Sub B(ByRef s As Integer)
        s = s + 10
    End Sub
End Module
```

Table 1.1.11.7 VB.NET example of Call by Value and Call by Reference

Questions

1. Explain the role of a subroutine parameter.
2. Explain
   (a) Call by value
   (b) Call by address

Using subroutines with interfaces

```
Subroutine T(IN r : Integer; INOUT s : Integer)
  s ← s*r
EndSubroutine
```

In the subroutine T, the part

```
IN r : Integer; INOUT s : Integer
```

is called the subroutine's interface. A subroutine interface is a mechanism by which data may be passed in and out of a subroutine via subroutine parameters. The use of subroutine interfaces is covered in Chapter 1.1.2 and Chapter 1.2.1.

In this chapter you have covered:

- The use of parameters to pass data within programs
- Using subroutines with interfaces

1 Fundamentals of programming

1.1 Programming

Learning objectives:

- *Be able to use subroutines that return values to the calling routine*

1.1.12 Returning a value(s) from a subroutine

Using subroutines that return values to the calling routine

Subroutines

A subroutine allows a block of instructions to be encapsulated, named and called by this name from other parts of a program.

This is particularly useful if the same block of instructions needs to be used in multiple places in a program or in several different programs.

After a subroutine is executed, control returns to the statement calling the subroutine. If the subroutine is a procedure then the calling statement's execution is complete. If the subroutine is a function, then the function returns a result to the calling statement which this statement may or may not deal with before it completes its execution.
For example, if the calling statement is as follows

```
x ← SquareOf(2)
```

the result 4 is returned by the call to function `SquareOf` and this result is then assigned to variable `x`.

Returning a result

If a result needs to be returned from an executing subroutine then a programmer may choose from two subroutine options:

- Procedure with the result returned via an INOUT or OUT parameter (call by address/reference)
- Function with the result returned via the function return mechanism

Procedure option

The procedure option has been covered in *Chapter 1.1.11*. An OUT parameter is similar to an INOUT parameter but some programming languages differentiate between the two by requiring an INOUT parameter to be initialised with a value whereas an OUT parameter can be passed uninitialized or undefined (see C#).

Information

In C# a value must be assigned to an OUT parameter within the subroutine, whereas an INOUT parameter can be left unchanged.

Function option

In some programming languages, e.g. Pascal, a function specifies a return value within the body of the function by executing an assignment statement whose left-hand side is the name of the function - *Table 1.1.12.1*.

```
Function SquareOf (Number : Integer) : Integer;
  Begin
    SquareOf := Number * Number;
  End;
```

Table 1.1.12.1 Pascal function SquareOf which returns an integer result to the calling statement

In Delphi, when a function is called, a variable is automatically created with the name Result of the same type as the return type of the function. It is available for the programmer to use to hold the result value to be returned by the function. Its value is passed back to the calling statement when the function returns.

The implicitly declared variable Result can be seen as equivalent to an OUT type parameter - where the value upon entry to the function is undefined. It is still possible in Delphi to use the Pascal convention of using the name of the function to assign the result. In Pascal, assigning a value to be returned to the name of the function does not automatically cause the function to return. Similarly, in Delphi assigning a value to be returned to the name of the function or to the variable Result does not automatically cause the function to return. In both Pascal and Delphi, usual practice is to use a temporary local variable to hold the result to be returned and assign this to Result or the function name at the end of the function, which is the place where control passes back to the calling statement.

In other programming languages, e.g. C#, functions use an explicit return statement

```
return expression
```

In addition to specifying a value, return causes the immediate termination of the function.

Table 1.1.12.2 shows a rather contrived C# function `Calculate` with three return expression statements.
The program executes when Main is called.
The logic of the program selects

```
return number * number
```

because parameter number is 2.
At this point control passes back to the calling statement

```
Console.WriteLine(Calculate(2));
```

This statement then outputs the value 4.
If control did not pass back at this point then `return 6`, the last statement in Calculate, would also be executed with the outcome that the return value would change to 6.
The fact that the output is 4 and not 6 confirms that return causes the immediate termination of the function.

```
using System;
namespace FunctionReturn
{
    class Program
    {
        static void Main(string[] args)
        {
            Console.WriteLine(Calculate(2));
            Console.ReadLine();
        }
        static int Calculate(int number)
        {
            if (number == 2)
            {
                return number * number;
            }
            if (number == 4)
            {
                return number * number * number;
            }
            return 6;
        }
    }
}
```

Table 1.1.12.2 C# function Calculate which returns an integer result to the calling statement

Type of result returned

Many programming languages place restrictions on the type of the result returned by a function.

Table 1.1.12.3 shows a Pascal program which defines and uses a function whose result type is a composite data type.
A composite data type or compound data type is any data type which can be constructed in a program using the programming language's primitive data types and other composite types.
It is sometimes called a structured data type, but this term is more commonly reserved for arrays and lists.
The act of constructing a composite type is known as composition.

When not to use a function to return a result

Although it is possible to return multiple separate results from a function, it is not normally considered good practice. For example, the following Pascal function returns one result in INOUT parameter s and another result via the function return mechanism:

```
Function D(Var s:Integer) : Integer;
  Begin
    ...
  End;
```

Both results in this example return a value which is a scalar data type, in this case, an integer. A scalar data type is a single value data type. It would be better to use a procedure with two INOUT parameters instead of a function.

```
Program FunctionReturnType;
Type
  TArrayType = Array[1..10] Of Integer;
Function Test (x : TArrayType) : TArrayType;
  Var
    i : Integer;
  Begin
    For i := 1 To 10
      Do x[i] := 2 * x[i];
    Test := x;
  End;
Var
  y : TArrayType = (1,2,3,4,5,6,7,8,9,10);
  z : TArrayType;
Begin
  z := Test(y);
  Writeln(z[2]);
  Readln;
End.
```

Table 1.1.12.3 Pascal function test which returns a result of composite type to the calling statement

Mathematical functions vs functions in a programming language

Loosely speaking, a function in mathematics is a rule that, for each element in some set A of inputs, assigns an output chosen from set B. For example, a function SquareOf takes input integer 2 and outputs its square 4 another integer.

Mathematics is very strict in its definition of a function:

- A function must return a single result
- A function must always return the same value for a given input, e.g. the square of 2 is always 4.
- A function must return a value for every value of input.

In programming languages, functions can break these rules:

- The Random (N) function covered in *Chapter 1.1.8* returns a different value in the interval [0, N) each time it is called. It would be useless as a random number generator if it returned the same value every time
- Multiple separate results may be returned from a function by using INOUT parameters as well as the function return mechanism
- The integer data type, e.g. int in C#, is a subset of the set of integers because computer memory is finite. If we attempt to square an integer which is larger than the square root of the maximum integer for the integer data type then overflow will result.

Programming tasks

1. Write and test a function which accepts a string as input and returns the string reversed.
2. Write and test a function which accepts a string as input and returns the number of words it contains, e.g. "Hello World" contains 2 words.

Programming tasks

3 Write and test a function which on each call returns a random number of data type integer in the interval (0, 12], i.e. 0 < number <= 12.
Use the generating relation and an appropriate value for k

NextRandomNo = Multiplier * PreviousRandomNo MOD k

and multiplier = 21. Seed the random number generator with the value 7, i.e. the first value of PreviousRandomNumber = 7.

4 Write and test a function which on each call returns a random number of data type real/float in the interval (0.0, 1.0].

In this chapter you have covered:

- Using subroutines that return values to the calling routine

1.1 Programming

Learning objectives:

- *Know that subroutines may declare their own variables called local variables, and that local variables:*
  - *exist only while the subroutine is executing*
  - *are accessible only within the subroutine*
- *Be able to use local variables and explain why it is good practice to do so*

1.1.13 Local variables in subroutines

Declaring local variables

A subroutine may declare its own variables and use these within the body of the subroutine as shown in the subroutine *DoExample* in Table 1.1.13.1.

```
Subroutine DoExample(IN x : Integer)
  Var
    s, t : Integer    ←— Declaration of two local variables, s and t
  Body
    Output x
    s ← 6
    t ← 7             ←— Using local variables, s and t in body of subroutine
    Output s + t
  EndBody
EndSubroutine
```

Table 1.1.13.1 Subroutine with local variables

The variables s and *t* are known as **local variables**. They are only visible inside subroutine *DoExample*, i.e. they cannot be accessed from outside the subroutine. In fact, they do not exist until the subroutine starts executing. They disappear when the subroutine stops executing. Thus any values that they hold are stored temporarily.

Lifetime

The lifetime of a local variable is the lifetime of an execution of the subroutine in which the local variable is declared.

Visibility

The scope of a local variable is the scope of the subroutine in which it is declared – scope means where the local variable is visible and can be used.

Using local variables

Table 1.1.13.2 shows the declaration and use of local variables (called `i` and `j`) in the programming languages Pascal/Delphi, C#, Python, Java and VB.NET.

Key term

Local variable:
These are variables declared inside a subroutine and used within the body of the subroutine.
The lifetime of a local variable is the lifetime of an execution of the subroutine in which the local variable is declared.
The scope of a local variable is the scope of the subroutine in which it is declared – scope means where the local variable is visible and can be accessed.

Programming tasks

1. Write and test a function which calculates x^n where $n \geq 1$.
   Use the following algorithm to calculate x^n

```
Power ← x
Count ← 1
While Count < n Do
  Power ← Power * x
  Count ← Count + 1
```

Your function should make use of local variables.

Pascal/Delphi	C#

`Procedure DoExample(n : Integer);`
`  Var`
`    i, j : Integer;`
`  Begin`
`    j := 6;`
`    For i : = 1 To n`
`      Do Writeln('Hello World!', i*j)`
`  End;`
	`static void DoExample(int n) {`
	`  int j = 6;`
	`  for (int i = 1; i <= n; i++)`
	`    {`
	`      Console.WriteLine("Hello World! {0}", i*j);`
	`    }`
	`}`

Python	**Java**

`def doExample(n):`
`    j = 6`
`    for i in range(n):`
`        print('Hello World!', j*(i + 1))`
	`public static void doExample(int n) {`
	`  int j = 6;`
	`  for (int i = 1; i <= n; i++) {`
	`    System.out.println("Hello World! " + j*i);`
	`  };`
	`}`

VB.Net	

```
Sub doExample(ByVal n As Integer)
   Dim j As Integer = 6
   For i As Integer = 1 To n
       Console.WriteLine("Hello World! {0}", i*j)
   Next
End Sub
```

Table 1.1.13.2 Declaring and using local variables

Why use local variables?

Support for modularisation

Subroutines enable modularisation of a program.

A solution to a problem can be divided into separate and independent modules. These modules can be implemented as subroutines.

The aim of modularisation is to have subroutines which can be worked on independently of the rest of the program.

This requires that each subroutine is self-contained and that its interaction with the rest of the program takes place only through the subroutine's interface, i.e. through its formal parameter(s).

Using local variables aids modularisation.

It also enables a subroutine to be reused because if a subroutine is self-contained and independent it may be lifted and used in another program.

Undesirable side-effects

In Table 1.1.13.3, the formal parameter of subroutine *DoExample* is x. However, instead of declaring local variables, the subroutine manipulates two global variables s and *t*.

These global variables come into existence when the program starts executing and only disappear when it finishes executing.

They are visible and therefore accessible inside procedure *DoExample*.

Unfortunately, this means that when *DoExample* is called and it executes the values of s and *t* are altered as shown.

This is called a side-effect of executing subroutine *DoExample*.

```
Program
  Var
    s, t, y : Integer        <---- Declaration of three global variables, s, t and y
  Subroutine DoExample(INOUT x : Integer)
    Body
      x ← 2 * x
      s ← 6                  <---- Using global variables, s and t
      t ← 7                        in body of subroutine
      Output s + t           <---- s + t = 13
    EndBody
  EndSubroutine
Begin
  s ← 3
  t ← 2
  y ← 9
  DoExample(y)               Expect output to be 3 + 2 = 5 but it
  Output s + t         <---- is 13. This is a side-effect of calling
  Output y                   subroutine DoExample
End
```

Table 1.1.13.3 Demonstrating the side-effect of using global variables inside a subroutine

Side-effects are undesirable because

- debugging a program is made harder - isolating the source of an error is made more difficult, the whole program may need to be examined
- the independence of the subroutine is reduced
  - it cannot be designed without considering the context in which it will be used
  - it cannot be debugged without considering the context in which it will be used
  - its reusability is reduced because it will be more difficult to use it in another program.

The only variable outside of *DoExample* which should be manipulated by *DoExample* is *y* because this variable is passed into *DoExample* through its INOUT interface, the formal parameter x.

Questions

1. What is a local variable?
2. What is the lifetime and scope of a local variable?
3. Explain why the use of local variables is considered good practice.

In this chapter you have covered:

- That subroutines may declare their own variables called local variables, and that local variables:
  - exist only while the subroutine is executing
  - are accessible only within the subroutine
- Using local variables and why it is good practice to do so

1.1 Programming

Learning objectives:

- *Be able to contrast local variables with global variables*

Key term

Static scoping:
In a programming language with static (lexical) scoping, the scope of a binding is determined at the compile time.

Key term

Binding:
A binding is an association between two things, such as a name and the thing its names.

Key term

Scope:
Scope is the the textual region in which a binding is active.

Key term

Binding time:
Binding time is the time at which a binding is created.

Key term

Compiler:
A compiler translates the source code form of a program into an independently executable object code form.

1.1.14 Global variables in a programming language

Contrasting local variables with global variables

Contrasting the scope of global and local variables

In Chapter 1.1.13 we learned that the scope of a local variable is limited to the subroutine in which it appears; it is not visible elsewhere.

Local variables are created when their subroutine is called and destroyed when it returns.

In a programming language with static scoping, the bindings between names and variables, etc, can be determined at compile time by examining the text of the program without consideration of the flow of control at run time.

Table 1.1.14.1 shows a program which declares two global variables s and *t*.

The compiler is able by inspection of the program text to determine at compile time that memory needs to be reserved for two integer variables, s and *t*.

The compiler builds this requirement into the executable form of the program which it produces. When the executable form of the program is loaded into memory, space is allocated to the two global variables, s and *t*.

A binding exists between global variables, s and *t* and the space allocated in memory to each.

The space allocated to s and *t* is retained throughout the program's execution.

We call this kind of allocation of memory static memory allocation and as a consequence the global variables are called static variables.

The space allocated to s and *t* is de-allocated on exit from the program.

```
Program GlobalVariables
  Var
    s, t : Integer          ←——— Declaration of two global
                                 variables, s and t
  Subroutine DoExample()
    Var
      s, t : Integer        ←——— Declaration of two local
                                 variables s and t
    Body
      s ← 6
      t ← 7
      Output s + t        ←—— Output 6 + 7 = 13
    EndBody
  EndSubroutine
Begin
  s ← 3
  t ← 2
  DoExample()
  Output s + t            ←—— Output 3 + 2 = 5
End
```

Table 1.1.14.1 Contrasting the scope of global variables and local variables

In contrast, the compiler will note that the variables s and *t* declared inside subroutine *DoExample* are local to this subroutine.

Memory is allocated for these local variables only when *DoExample* is called and this memory is de-allocated when the subroutine returns (control is passed back to the calling statement).
The compiler will set up the executable form of the program to allocate memory space for local variables s and *t* when *DoExample* is called.
Memory is allocated to local variables from an area of memory called stack memory. This is a different area of memory from the area used for global variables.
If the program in Table 1.1.14.1 is executing and control is currently in the block of the program between *Begin* and *End*, i.e.

```
s ← 3
t ← 2
DoExample()
Output s + t
```

Variables s and *t* in this block refer to the global variables s and *t*.
We say that the binding between s and *t* and the statically allocated memory is active.

If control passes to subroutine *DoExample* i.e. the block of program between *Body* and *EndBody*, i.e.

```
s ← 6
t ← 7
Output s + t
```

Variables s and *t* in this block refer to local variables s and *t*.

We say that the binding between s, and *t* and the allocated stack memory is active.

To avoid two variables s and two variables *t* being active at the same time, global s and global *t* go out of scope, and local variables s and *t* come into scope. We say their bindings are active and the binding of the global variables, temporarily inactive.

On exit from the subroutine, control returns to the *Begin End* block and the global variable bindings become active again.

Global scope

Table 1.1.14.2 shows the creation of two global variables s and *t* in various programming languages.

In Pascal/Delphi, variables declared at the outermost level with the language keyword *Var* are both global and static.
In C#, the keyword *static* creates a variable and statically binds it; the keyword *public* turns this variable into a global variable.
In Java, the keyword *static* creates a variable and statically binds it; the keyword *public* turns this variable into a global variable.
In VB.NET, the keyword *Public* in front of *variable name As datatype* creates a global variable.
In Python, two global variables s and *t* are created by the statements

```
s = 2
t = 3
```

To access these global variables inside subroutine *doExample*, the modifier *global* must be placed in front of each to indicate that it is global variables s and *t* which are to be used. Otherwise, Python will create two local variables of the same names.

Pascal/Delphi

```
Program GlobalVariables;
  Var
    s, t : Integer;
  Procedure DoExample();
    Begin
      s := 6;
      t := 7;
    End;
Begin
  s = 3;
  t = 2;
  Writeln("s = ", s, " t = ", t);
  DoExample();
  Writeln("s = ", s, " t = ", t);
End.
```

Accessing global variables *s* and *t*

C#

```
using System;
namespace GlobalVariables
{
  class Program
  {
    public static int s, t;
    static void DoExample()
    {
      s = 6;
      t = 7;
    }
    static void Main(string[] args)
    {
      s = 3;
      t = 2;
      Console.WriteLine("s = {0} t = {1}", s, t);
      DoExample();
      Console.WriteLine("s = {0} t = {1}", s, t);
      Console.ReadLine();
    }
  }
}
```

Python

```
def doExample():
    global s
    global t
    s = 6
    t = 7
s = 2
t = 3
print("s = ", s, " t = ",t)
doExample()
print("s = ", s, " t = ",t)
```

Java

```
public class GlobalVariables {
  public static int s, t;
  static void doExample() {
    s = 6;
    t = 7;
  }
  public static void main(String[] args) {
    s = 3;
    t = 2;
    System.out.println("s = " + s + " t = " + t);
    doExample();
    System.out.println("s = " + s + " t = " + t);
  }
}
```

VB.Net

```
Module Module1
    Public s As Integer
    Public t As Integer
    Sub DoExample()
        s = 6
        t = 7
    End Sub
    Sub Main()
        s = 3
        t = 2
        Console.WriteLine("s = {0} t = {1}", s, t)
        DoExample()
        Console.WriteLine("s = {0} t = {1}", s, t)
        Console.ReadLine()
    End Sub
End Module
```

Table 1.1.14.2 Demonstration of the use of global variables in various languages

Figure 1.1.14.1 shows the output when the C# program in *Table 1.1.14.2* is executed. Variables s and *t* are global and so are visible within the subroutine *DoExample*, i.e. they have *global scope*.

Variables with global scope are visible throughout the entire program and therefore can be accessed from anywhere in the program unless their binding is made inactive temporarily for the reason explained in the first section in this chapter. When variables binding is temporarily inactive the variable is said to be out of scope.

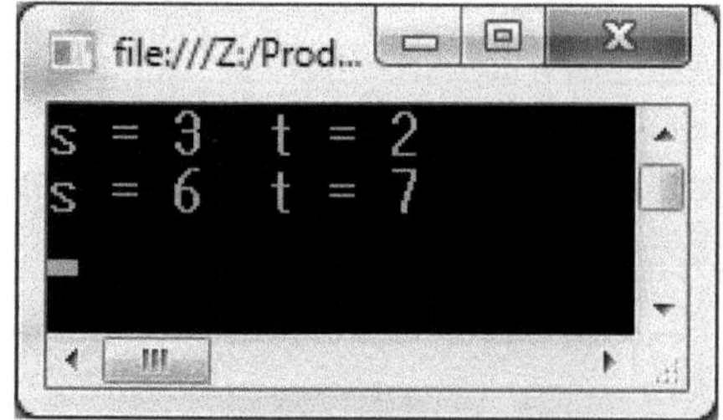

Figure 1.1.14.1 Screenshot of output from the C# program in Table 1.1.14.2 when executed

Questions

1. State **two** differences between global and local variables.

2. What does it mean to say that a global variable is out of scope?

3. What is the output when the program shown in *Table 1.1.14.3* is executed?
   Describe the action of this program in producing this output.

```
Program GlobalVariables
  Var
    s : Integer
  Subroutine DoExample()
    Var
      s: Integer
    Body
      s ← 6
    EndBody
  EndSubroutine
Begin
  s ← 3
  Output s
  DoExample()
  Output s
End
```

Table 1.1.14.3

In this chapter you have covered:

- Contrasting local variables with global variables

1 Fundamentals of programming

1.2 Procedural-oriented programming

Learning objectives:

- *Understand the structured approach to program design and construction*
- *Be able to construct hierarchy charts when designing programs*
- *Be able to explain the advantages of the structured approach*

1.2.1 Structured programming

The structured approach to program design and construction

Software artefact

The end result of program design and construction is an artefact, a piece of software that when executed solves some given problem, hopefully the one required to be solved.

Design

"Design" means to plan or mark out the form and method of solution.

All forms of engineering including software engineering are characterised by the engineer's dissatisfaction with the achievement of just any old solution. Engineering seeks the best solution (judged by factors such as efficiency, maintainability, reliability), within recognised constraints, while making compromises required by working in the real world.

Software design takes a real-world problem and produces a plan for a computer-based solution.

Structured design

Structured design is a disciplined process of deciding which components interconnected in which way will solve some well-specified problem.

Structured design relies on a principle known since the days of Julius Caesar:

DIVIDE and CONQUER

A problem is divided into smaller and smaller sub problems, so that each sub problem will eventually correspond to a component of the system which solves the problem.

The partitioning process into smaller and smaller sub problems is done until the sub problems are

- manageably small, and
- solvable separately, i.e. relatively independent of one another.

Good design

Good design is an exercise in partitioning and organising the pieces of the system so that each is

- cohesive, and
- loosely coupled

We call the pieces of the system, modules or components or units.

The modules/components/units are plugged together to create the system.Modules/components/units can be implemented as subroutines (procedures and functions).

Key term

Design:
To plan or mark out the form and method of solution.

Key term

Structured design:
Structured design is a disciplined process of deciding which components interconnected in which way will solve some well-specified problem.
A problem is divided into smaller and smaller sub problems, so that each sub problem will eventually correspond to a component of the system which solves the problem.
The partitioning process into smaller and smaller sub problems is done until the sub problems are

- manageably small, and
- solvable separately, i.e. relatively independent of one another.

Key principle

Good design:
Good design is an exercise in partitioning and organising the pieces of the system so that each is

- cohesive, and
- loosely coupled

Cohesive/Cohesion

Cohesion measures the strength of the interconnection between elements within a module.

To achieve cohesion, highly interrelated parts of the real-world **problem** should be in the same piece of the **software system**, i.e. things that belong together should go together.

Figure 1.2.1.1 shows a schematic mapping from a problem in a real-world system to a highly-cohesive software architecture of a structured design for a computer-based system to solve the problem.

Figure 1.2.1.2 shows a specific example of a simple calculator system. Note the one-to-one mapping between real-world system and the computer-based system.

To achieve a solution in which modules/components are highly-cohesive the software system needs to be broken down into modules

- which are highly independent and
- which accomplish a single objective.

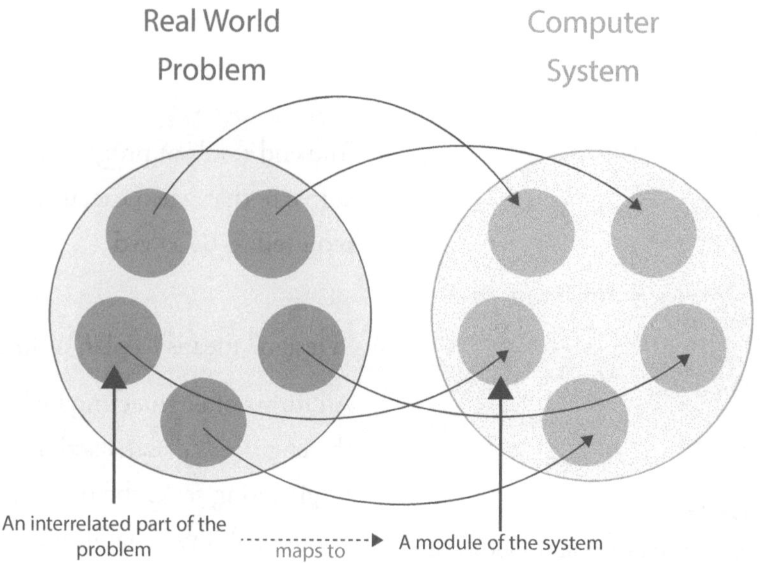

Figure 1.2.1.1 Mapping of problem parts to system modules

The aim is to achieve **functional cohesion**, i.e. modules which contain only one function or perform only one logically-related task.

For example,

- CalculateSquare
- GetDate

One good way to determine if modules are (functionally) cohesive is to write a phrase fully describing what the module does.

Analysis of this phrase can indicate whether or not the module is (functionally) cohesive. The module is not (functionally) cohesive if the result is one of the following:

- A compound sentence such as
  - Edit Student Name AND Test Scores
  - Get two operands AND Add these
- A lack of a specific object
  - Edit all Data
- Words relating to time such as
  - Initialisation
- Words such as "house-keeping" or "clean-up" because these imply more than one task.

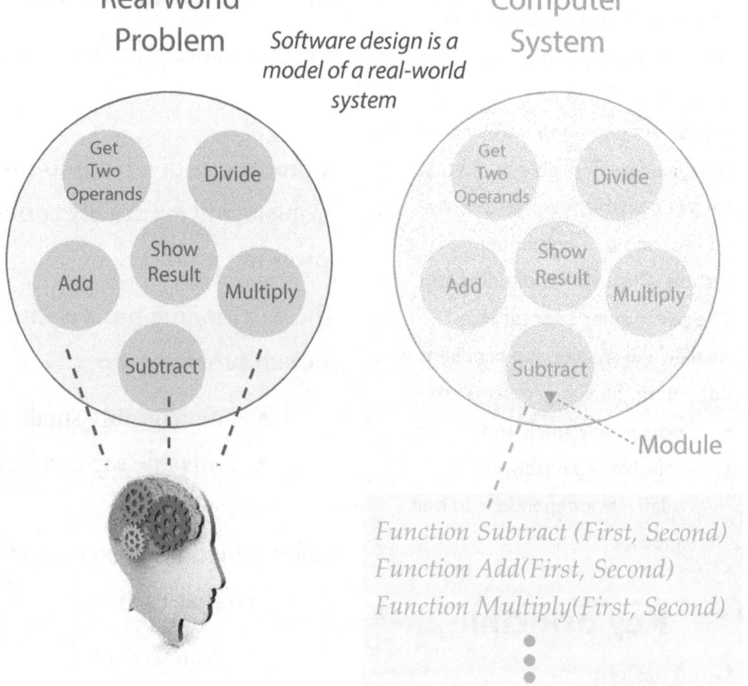

Figure 1.2.1.2 Highly interrelated parts of the problem should be in the same piece of the system

The functional description should not define the code within the module but how the module appears to the coder, e.g. `Subtract`.

The highest level of cohesion, referred to as functional cohesion, is a module in which

- every element is an integral part of a single function (task), and
- every element is essential to the performance of a single function (task)

Some advantages of using modules with high cohesion:

- The module can easily be replaced by any other serving the same purpose since what it does is localised within the module, i.e. it has no side-effects when it executes
- In the event of program failure,
  - it should be easier to locate the error as being in the module
  - it should be easier to discount the module as a source of error
- Different developers can work on individual modules because each is an independent unit.

Key terms

Cohesion:

Cohesion measures the strength of the interconnection between elements within a module.

Functional cohesion:

Functional cohesion is the highest level of cohesion. A functionally cohesive module is one in which

- every element is an integral part of a single function (task), and
- every element is essential to the performance of a single function (task)

Questions

1. What is the process known as design?
2. What is structured design?
3. What is meant by the term *cohesive* when applied to a module or component of a system?
4. A procedure in a calculator program is described as "Adding two operands and displaying the result".
   (a) Explain why this procedure is not considered functionally cohesive.
   (b) What can be done to achieve functional cohesion in this case?
5. State **two** advantages of using modules with high cohesion.

Loosely coupled

Coupling measures the strength of relationships between modules.

The objective of structured design is to minimise the coupling between modules, so that they will be as independent as possible.

The lower the coupling, the less likely that other modules will have to be considered in order to

- create a module
- understand a given module
- debug a given module
- change a given module.

Coupling results from connections.

A connection exists when an element of code references a location in memory defined outside the module.

Some connection must exist among modules in a program, or else they would not be part of the same program.

The objective is to minimise the coupling among modules.

Key term

Coupling:

Coupling measures the strength of relationships between modules. The objective of structured design is to minimise the coupling between modules, so that they will be as independent as possible. Coupling results from connections. A connection exists when an element of code references a location in memory defined outside the module.

To minimise coupling among modules:

- Subroutines or modules should only be allowed to access that data which they needs to perform their assigned task
- All data transfer between modules is visible in the module parameters
- There must be no hidden flows of data via global variables or shared data areas
- There should be no control information passing between modules, e.g. Boolean flags
- The number of module parameters should be minimal.

Loose coupling is achieved when a module's data interface with other modules is its module parameter list. Here we interpret module to mean a subroutine (procedure/ function).

In VB.NET, a procedure `DisplayMessage` is defined with the language keywords `Sub` and `End Sub` as shown in the example in *Figure 1.2.1.3*. In VB.NET, the term module can be interpreted as equivalent to program.

```
Module ProcedureInterface
    Sub Main()
        DisplayMessage("Hello World")
        Console.ReadLine()
    End Sub
    Sub DisplayMessage(ByVal Message As String)
        Console.WriteLine(Message)
    End Sub
End Module
```

Figure 1.2.1.3 VB.NET program with procedure DisplayMessage

Figure 1.2.1.4 shows a procedure `DisplayMessage` defined with the language keywords `Procedure` and `Begin` and `End`.

```
Program DisplayMessageExample;
Procedure DisplayMessage (Message : String);
  Begin
    Writeln(Message);
  End;
Begin
  DisplayMessage('Hello World');
  Readln;
End.
```

Figure 1.2.1.4 Pascal program with procedure DisplayMessage

The data interface for VB.NET `DisplayMessage` is the parameter list `ByVal Message As String`.

The data interface for Pascal `DisplayMessage` is the parameter list `Message : String`.
The procedure `DisplayMessage` is called with actual parameter value "Hello World" and 'Hello World', respectively, in *Figure 1.2.1.3* and *Figure 1.2.1.4*.
The Pascal program in *Figure 1.2.1.5* has declared a global variable `Message` which in Pascal is visible within procedure `DisplayMessage`. The procedure `DisplayMessage` has dispensed with a procedure parameter list and instead relies on accessing the global variable `Message`.
The procedure `DisplayMessage` in *Figure 1.2.1.5* has a higher coupling with its program than `DisplayMessage` does in *Figure 1.2.1.4*.

```
Program DisplayMessageExampleGlobal;
Var
  Message : String;
Procedure DisplayMessage;
  Begin
    Writeln(Message);
  End;
Begin
Message := 'Hello World';
  DisplayMessage;
  Readln;
End.
```

Figure 1.2.1.5 Pascal program with procedure DisplayMessage without a parameter list

Questions

6 What is *coupling* when applied to modules or components of a system?

7 Why should coupling between modules be minimised?

8 How does coupling between modules arise?

9 How can coupling between modules be minimised?

10 Give **two** reasons why the pseudo-code in Figure 1.2.1.6 could be considered a poor design by structured design standards.

11 Suggest **one** reason why the procedure `DisplayMessage` in Figure 1.2.1.7 could be considered poorly designed by structured design standards.

12 How could the design of procedure `DisplayMessage` and the program be changed to reflect good structured design?

```
Program Exercise1
Var
  No1, No2 : Integer
Procedure AddTwoNumbers
  Output No1 + No2
End Procedure
Begin
  No1 ← 4
  No2 ← 5
  AddTwoNumbers
End
```

Figure 1.2.1.6 Pseudo-code to add two numbers

```
Module Module1
   Sub Main()
       DisplayMessage("hello world", False)
       DisplayMessage("hello world", True)
       Console.ReadLine()
   End Sub
   Sub DisplayMessage(ByVal Message As String, ByVal UpperCase As Boolean)
         If UpperCase Then
             Console.WriteLine(StrConv(Message, vbUpperCase))
         Else Console.WriteLine(Message)
         End If
     End Sub
 End Module
```

Figure 1.2.1.7 VB.NET program that uses a procedure DisplayMessage with a flag parameter

13 A procedure `Initialise` is defined with a long parameter list of reference formal parameters, i.e. each formal parameter is a pointer type which when replaced by an actual parameter will point to a variable outside the procedure:

```
Procedure Initialise(Var a, b, c, d, e, f, g, h, i, j, k, l, m, n, p : Integer)
```

Why is this considered a poor design by the standards of structured design?

14 A program contains a module A, module B and other modules. Module A writes to a disk file and module B reads from a disk file. When module A is engaged in writing to a disk file no other module may access the same disk file. When module A has finished writing to a disk file it closes it. The program calls module A on file Z followed by module B on file Z. Would you describe the coupling between module A and module B as low or high? Explain.

Simple calculator example which illustrates cohesion and loose coupling

Suppose that we are required to demonstrate structured design in a simple way.

We choose to do this by designing and creating a very simple calculator that is limited to performing integer arithmetic on two given operands.

The arithmetic operations that must be supported are

1. Add
2. Subtract
3. Multiply
4. Divide (Integer division)

The major "pieces" of the system are

1. The system must display to the user the choices which are available for arithmetic operation
2. The system must obtain the user's choice of arithmetic operation
3. The system must obtain two operands from the user
4. The system must carry out the chosen on the two operands
5. The system must have a "piece" to do each of the following
   5.1 Add
   5.2 Subtract
   5.3 Multiply
   5.4 Divide (Integer division)
6. The system must display the result to the user.

> **Key term**
>
> **Hierarchy chart:**
> In structured design of software, the partition of a software system into its component parts can expressed as a hierarchy chart which shows the components (subroutines) and how they are interconnected.

Structured design is then used to decide which modules/components to use to solve this problem.

Structured design tells us that each piece identified above in 1, 2, 3, 4, 5.1, 5.2, 5.3, 5.4, 6 above should be a module of the system - *Figure 1.2.1.2*.

In this simple example, these modules/components can then be implemented in a programming language as subroutines.

Hierarchy charts

We show the **software architecture** of the simple calculator system resulting from the structured design approach in *Figure 1.2.1.8*. We call this a **hierarchy chart**.

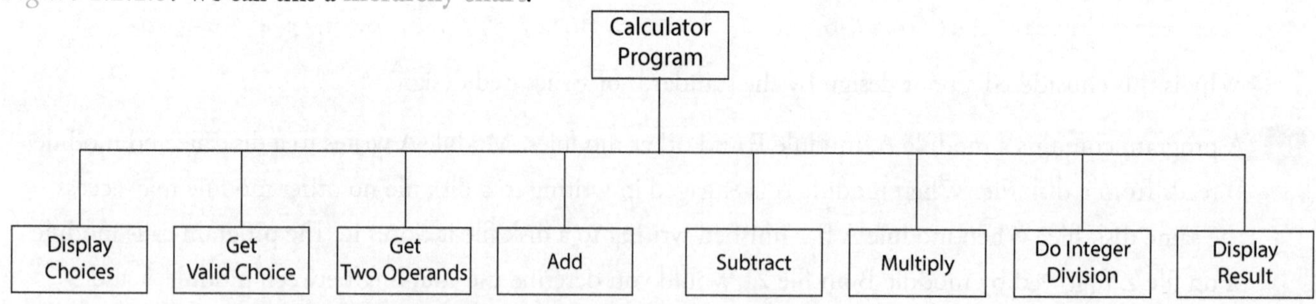

Figure 1.2.1.8 Hierarchy chart showing the software architecture of the simple calculator system

This doesn't tell the whole story because the chart doesn't show the coupling between the modules/components. Loose coupling is achieved when a module's data interface with other modules is its module parameter list. By adding the parameter list for each module to the chart we can show that its data interface is indeed that required for low coupling - *Figure 1.2.1.9*.

The meaning of the symbols used in *Figure 1.2.1.9* are shown in *Figure 1.2.1.10*.

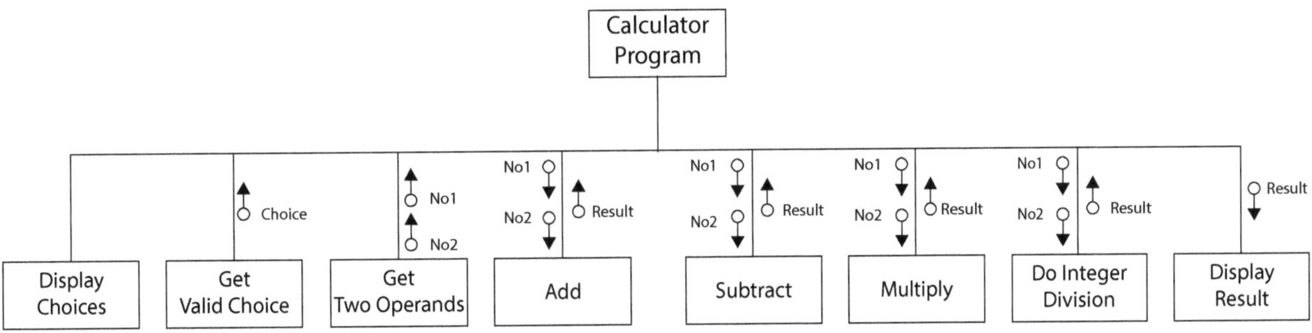

Figure 1.2.1.9 Hierarchy chart showing the software architecture of the simple calculator system and the parameter list/data interface of each module

The parameter `Choice` is the only parameter of module `GetChoice`. It is an OUT parameter. The value returned by `GetChoice` is used by the Calculator Program to choose from among modules `Add`, `Subtract`, `Multiply` and `DoIntegerDivision`.

Module `Add` has three parameters in its data interface: `No1`, `No2` and `Result`. `No1` and `No2` are IN parameters. `Result` is an OUT parameter.

OUT parameter symbol | IN parameter symbol | IN-OUT parameter symbol

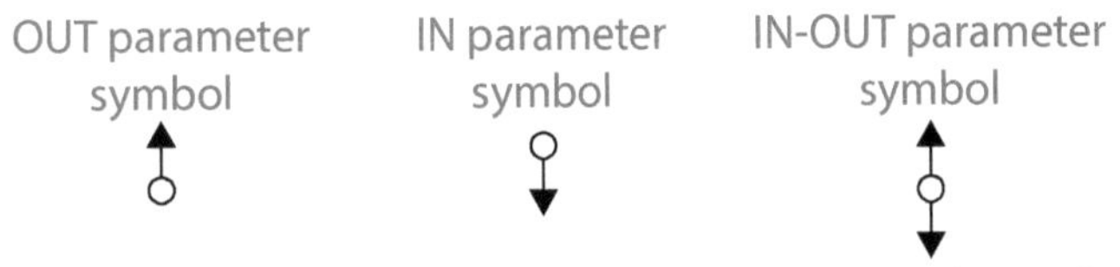

Figure 1.2.1.10 The meaning of the symbols shown in Figure 1.2.1.9

Sometimes a module needs to use an IN-OUT parameter because it processes the value passed in by an IN-OUT parameter and then exports a new value from the module in the same IN-OUT parameter.

The chart in Figure 1.2.1.9 just shows the architectural breakdown of the system into its software components and the data interfaces between these components. If we add control to the hierarchy chart as shown in Figure 1.2.1.11 we will get the program's structure, e.g. if the value of Choice is, say 'S' or 's', the program should choose to execute the `Subtract` module and not `Add`, `Multiply` or `DoIntegerDivision`. This is indicated with the option symbol o placed in the top-right corner of the module rectangle.

The **control hierarchy chart** shown in Figure 1.2.1.11 is read from left to right, i.e. module `DisplayChoice` is executed first followed by module `GetChoice`, and so on. A `Repeat Until Choice In ['Q', 'q']` has been added to indicate that the left to right sequence is repeated until the user chooses to quit.

Figure 1.2.1.12 shows the program structure in Pascal using procedures. The program structure could also have been written using functions if required. You can see that the control hierarchy chart maps one-to-one to the structure of its program equivalent.

The option symbol o placed in the top-right corner of the module rectangle for `Add`, `Subtract`, `Multiply` and `DoIntegerDivision` has been mapped to a Case statement (Select Case, if / elif in other languages) in Figure 1.2.1.12.

Key term

Control hierarchy chart:
A control hierarchy chart shows the structure of the program in chart form.
It can also show the parameter list for each module/subroutine in the chart.

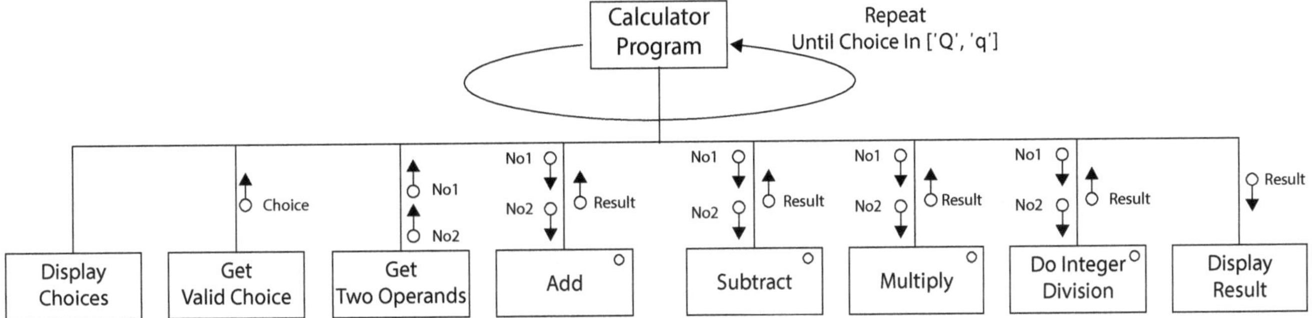

Figure 1.2.1.11 Control hierarchy chart showing the software architecture of the simple calculator system, the parameter list/data interface of each module and the program's structure

```
Program SimpleCalculator;
  Procedure DisplayChoices;
    Begin
    End;
  Procedure GetValidChoice(Var Choice : Char);
    Begin
    End;
  Procedure GetTwoOperands(Var No1, No2 : Integer);
    Begin
    End;
  Procedure Add(No1, No2 : Integer; Var Result : Integer);
    Begin
    End;
  Procedure Subtract(No1, No2 : Integer; Var Result : Integer);
    Begin
    End;
  Procedure Multiply(No1, No2 : Integer; Var Result : Integer);
    Begin
    End;
  Procedure DoIntegerDivision(No1, No2 : Integer; Var Result : Integer);
    Begin
    End;
  Procedure DisplayResult(Result : Integer);
    Begin
    End;
Var
  UsersChoice : Char = 'A';
  FirstNo : Integer = 0;
  SecondNo : Integer = 0;
  Answer : Integer = 0;
Begin
  Repeat
    DisplayChoices;
    GetValidChoice(UsersChoice);
    GetTwoOperands(FirstNo, SecondNo);
    Case UsersChoice of
      'A', 'a' : Add(FirstNo, SecondNo, Answer);
      'S', 's' : Subtract(FirstNo, SecondNo, Answer);
      'M', 'm' : Multiply(FirstNo, SecondNo, Answer);
      'D', 'd' : DoIntegerDivision(FirstNo, SecondNo, Answer);
      'Q', 'q' : ;
    End;
    DisplayResult(Answer);
  Until UsersChoice In ['Q', 'q'];
End.
```

Var denotes that parameter is IN-OUT but in this example it is used as an OUT parameter

Formal parameter

IN only parameters

Actual parameters

Figure 1.2.1.12 Program structure in Pascal of simple calculator written as procedures

Programming task

1. Create a simple calculator program based on the program structure shown in *Figure 1.2.1.12* in a programming language of your choice.

Structured design does not address the issue of how to write the program for the body of each procedure only the division of a system into its components and how those components fit together to produce a solution.

To write the program for the body of the procedures we use the principles of structured programming.

Structured programming

The principles

Structured programming advocates a *disciplined approach* to the construction of programs in order to avoid problems which can arise if the approach is not disciplined.

At the lowest level, the main principles of structured programming are concerned with the flow of control through a program unit such as shown in *Figure 1.2.1.13*. The most fundamental idea is that the main flow of control through a program unit should be from top to bottom of the program.

This translates to every block (sequence, selection and iteration) should have one entry point and one exit point.

In *Figure 1.2.1.13* this means that the flow of control enters at the top of a dotted block and exits at the bottom. Within a block, the flow doesn't have to be forward, e.g. iteration.

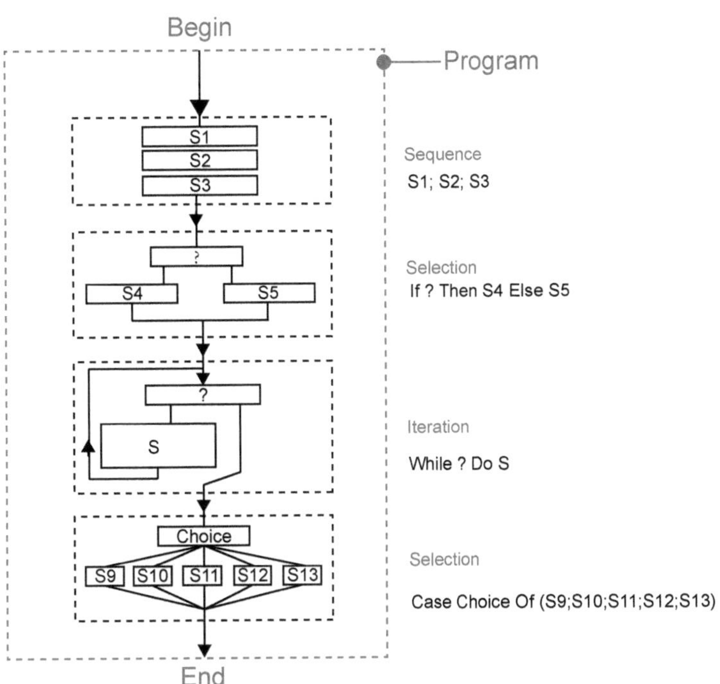

Figure 1.2.1.13 Program unit showing flow of control from top to bottom through the three basic control constructs, sequence, selection and iteration

There are three basic control constructs necessary to build any program:

- Sequence - a list of program statements which are executed one after another (i.e. in sequence),
  e.g. `x := x + 1; y := y + 2; z := 6;`
- Selection - a means of choosing between two or more sequences of statements depending on the value of some condition(s),
  e.g. `If Then Else`
- Iteration - a construct to allow controlled repetition of a sequence of statements, e.g. `While x < 5 Do Something.`

It can be shown that these three constructs are sufficient to implement the control structure of any algorithm.

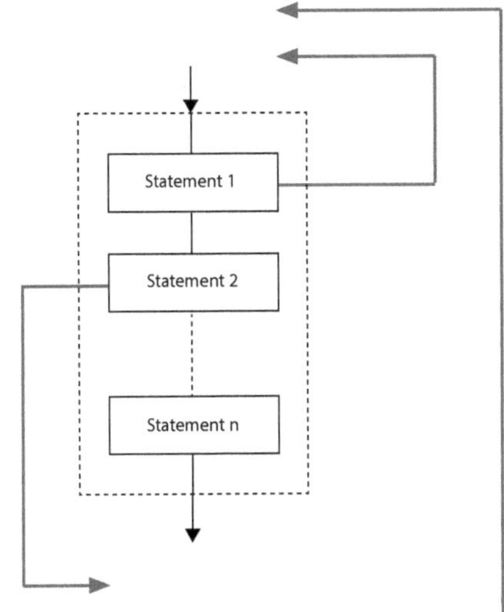

Figure 1.2.1.14 Part of a program unit showing flow of control jumping backwards and forwards between blocks

Structured programming is also known as *gotoless* programming because it avoids the use of the Go To control construct. If a label (e.g. `step1`) is attached to a statement in a program then the flow of control can jump to the labelled statement from anywhere in the program which references the label in a `Go To step1`. *Figure 1.2.1.14* shows how the flow of control can jump backwards and forwards when Go To statements are used; each red line is a transfer of control caused by a Go To statement.

In Pascal, a numeric label is declared using the language keyword `Label`. In *Figure 1.2.1.15* a numeric label 100 is declared with `Label 100` and then used by `GoTo 100` in the `Begin End` program block.
Structured programming doesn't mean that Go To should be avoided at all cost. There is one situation where it is the preferred solution. This is when something has gone wrong within the program, e.g. an attempt is made to open a nonexistent file. In this circumstance, it is often better to jump to the end of the program because to avoid use of Go To in this circumstance can often result in a difficult to understand and convoluted program.
The flow is still from top to bottom in this particular use of Go To and the structured programming principle, "*The main flow of control through a program unit should be from top to bottom of the program*" is not violated.

```
Program GoToExample;
Label 100;
Begin
  100:
  Writeln('Hello World');
  Writeln('Hello World');
  Writeln('Hello World');
  GoTo 100;
End.
```

Figure 1.2.1.15 Example of the use of Go To

We use structured programming because it leads to programs which are **easier to understand, maintain and reason about**.

In "Notes on Structured Programming" Edgar Dijkstra wrote:

> "*A program is never a goal in itself; the purpose of a program is to evoke computations and the purpose of the computations is to establish a desired effect. Although the program is the final product made by the programmer, the possible computations evoked by it-the "making" of which is left to the machine! - are the true subject matter of his trade. For instance, whenever a programmer states that his program is correct, he really makes an assertion about the computations it may evoke.*
>
> *The fact that the last stage of the total activity, viz. the transition from the (static) program text to the (dynamic) computation, is essentially left to the machine is an added complication. In a sense the making of a program is therefore more difficult than the making of a mathematical theory: both program and theory are structured, timeless objects. But while the mathematical theory makes sense as it stands, the program only makes sense via its execution.*"
>
> "*In vague terms we may state the desirability that the structure of the program text reflects the structure of the computation. Or, in other terms, "What can we do to shorten the conceptual gap between the static program text (spread out in "text space") and the corresponding computations (evolving in time) ?"*"
>
> Page 16, http://www.informatik.uni-bremen.de/agbkb/lehre/programmiersprachen/artikel/EWD-notes-structured.pdf

A goal of structured programming is **to reduce the conceptual gap between the program text and the corresponding computations**. In other words, how can you be sure that your program does what it is required to do, i.e. meets its specification?
Writing programs that are easy to understand contributes to achieving this goal even if it is done at the expense of efficiency, e.g. execution time and memory requirements.
Structured programming requires that

1. The main flow of control through a program unit should be from top to bottom of the program.
2. Program blocks should have one entry point and one exit point
3. Meaningful identifiers should be used for variables, subroutines (procedures and functions), etc, to aid readability and understanding
4. Indentation should be used that reflects the structure of the program and which aids readability and understanding
5. The following control constructs should be used: sequence, selection and iteration
6. Go Tos should be avoided in all but the one case of a major error in the computation which would require, if handled in a structured programming way, convoluted and difficult-to-understand program source code to be written
7. The use of global variables which are used in a global way should be avoided
8. Data should be passed to subroutines in subroutine parameters and results returned through subroutine parameters or preferable as a function return data type
9. Local variables should be used for handling data within subroutines.

Questions

15 What is meant by structured programming?

16 What does structured programming have to say about the flow of control in programs?

17 Give **two** benefits of using structured programming.

Stepwise refinement

The focus of structured design is the identification of the components of the system and how they interact, i.e. the software architecture of the computerised system, and not on the internal design of the components.

For the internal design of the components, i.e. the program source code for subroutines and the program which calls these subroutines, we use structured programming.

We take as our starting point the control hierarchy chart for the two-player game *noughts and crosses* - Figure 1.2.1.16.

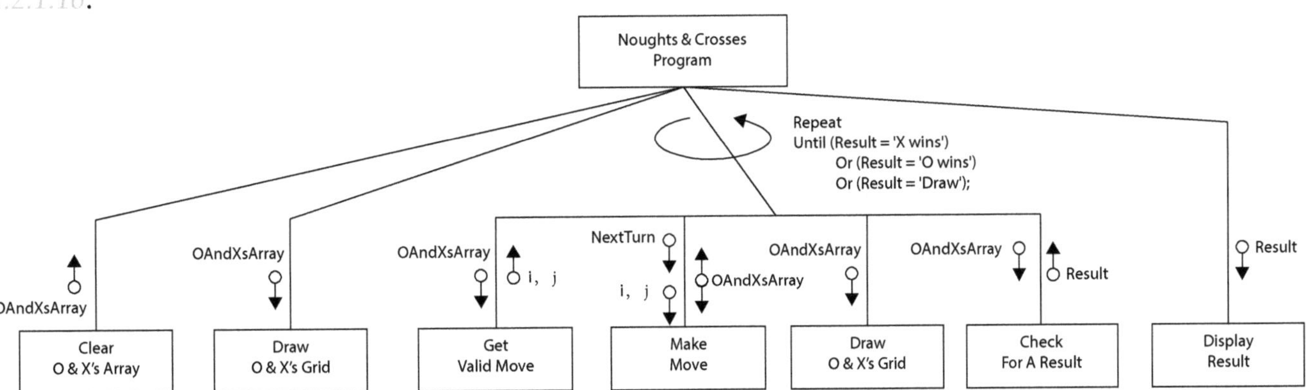

Figure 1.2.1.16 Control hierarchy chart for the game noughts and crosses

We model the two-dimensional grid of the noughts and crosses game in a two-dimensional array type `GridType` - Figure 1.2.1.17.

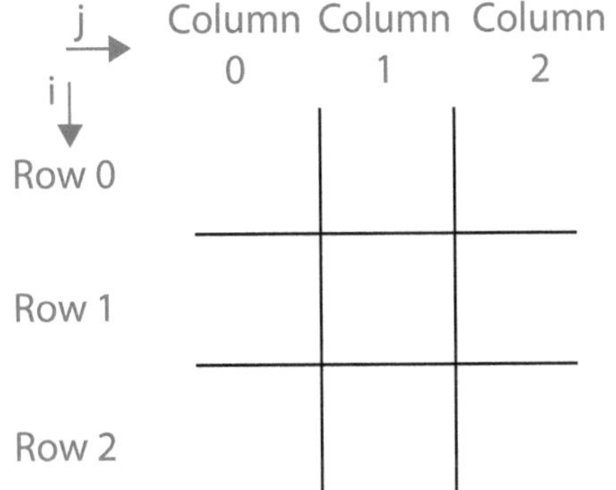


```
Type
   GridType = Array[0..2,0..2] Of Char;
Var
  OAndXsArray : GridType;
  Result : String;
  NextTurn : Char;
  i, j : Integer;
```

Figure 1.2.1.17 Modelling the game noughts and crosses

To reference a cell of this grid we will use integer variables `i` and `j`, e.g. the top-left cell will have `i`, `j` coordinates

`i = 0` and `j = 0`.

Each player of the two-player game takes it in turn to choose an unoccupied cell in which to place their symbol.
One player uses the symbol X and the other the symbol O.
In this game, the player with symbol X starts.
The symbol that is played next is stored in the character variable `NextTurn`.

For symbol X we use character value 'X', and for symbol O we use character value 'O'.

The result of a player's move is stored in string variable `Result`. The value of result could be one of

'X wins', 'O wins', 'Draw' or 'No result so far'.

Once we have designed data structures, we can design the program to process the data stored in these data structures.

The control hierarchy chart *Figure 1.2.1.16* already reflects the program structure so it is a relatively straightforward mapping task to produce the textual form of the program structure as shown in *Figure 1.2.1.18*.

The next task is to design the internal structure of each subroutine and then construct this structure in a programming language. We do this using the control structures of structured programming, sequence, selection and iteration and a technique called **stepwise refinement**.

```
ClearArray(OAndXsArray)
DrawGrid(OAndXsArray)
NextTurn ← 'X'
Repeat
  GetValidMove(i, j, OAndXsArray)
  MakeMove(i, j, OAndXsArray, NextTurn)
  DrawGrid(OAndXsArray)
  Result ← CheckForAResult(OAndXsArray)
  If Result = 'Win'
    Then
      If NextTurn = 'X'
        Then Result ← 'X wins'
        Else Result ← 'O wins'
  If Result = 'No result so far'
    Then
      If NextTurn = 'X'
       Then NextTurn ← 'O'
       Else NextTurn ← 'X'
Until (Result = 'X wins')
        Or (Result = 'O wins')
        Or (Result = 'Draw')
DisplayResult(Result)
```

Figure 1.2.1.18 Program structure for the game noughts and crosses

Stepwise refinement starts with the **major steps**.

Each major step is then refined into a **more detailed sequence of steps**.

Each one of these more detailed steps is then refined and so on until a stage is reached where the steps can be replaced by programming language statements.

For example, the possible stages of stepwise refinement for the subroutine `CheckForAResult` are shown in *Figure 1.2.1.19*, *Figure 1.2.1.20* and *Figure 1.2.1.21*.

Major steps:

```
1. Check rows
2. Check columns
3. Check diagonals
4. If No result
     Then check for a draw
```

Figure 1.2.1.19 Major steps

First level of refinement:

```
1. Check rows
  1.1 For row 0 To 2 Do check row
2. Check columns
  2.1 For column 0 To 2 Do check column
3. Check diagonals
  3.1 Check top left to bottom right diagonal
  3.2 Check top right to bottom left diagonal
4. If No result
     Then check for a draw
  4.1 If no result
        Then
          If grid full
            Then result a draw
          EndIf
        EndIf
```

Figure 1.2.1.20 First level of refinement

There are no hard and fast rules to apply to the process of refinement other than each level should be a step closer to the solution, i.e. the actual programming language statements. Rather than document each stage as has been done here, it is often better to do the refinement inside the actual subroutine in the program development environment. Applying the discipline of using successive refinements in constructing a program is more important than formally generating refinements on paper.

However, paper is a good place to start until you become more skilled and able to iterate the refinement process mentally as you apply the skill directly inside a program development environment.

Second level of refinement:

```
1. Check rows
   1.1 For row 0 To 2 Do check row
     1.1.1 For i ← 0 To 2 Do
             If (OAndXsArray[i,0] = OAndXsArray[i,1])
                  And (OAndXsArray[i,1] = OAndXsArray[i,2])
               Then
                 If (OAndXsArray[i,0] <> ' ') Then Outcome ← 'Win'
             EndIf
           EndFor
2.  Check columns
   2.1 For column 0 To 2 Do check column
     2.1.2 For j ← 0 To 2 Do
             If (OAndXsArray[0,j] = OAndXsArray[1,j])
                  And (OAndXsArray[1,j] = OAndXsArray[2,j])
               Then
                 If (OAndXsArray[0,j] <> ' ') Then Outcome ← 'Win'

           EndFor
3. Check diagonals
   3.1 Check top left to bottom right diagonal
     3.1.1 If (OAndXsArray[0,0] = OAndXsArray[1,1])
                And (OAndXsArray[1,1] = OAndXsArray[2,2])
             Then
               If (OAndXsArray[0,0] <> ' ') Then Outcome ← 'Win'
           EndIf
   3.2 Check top right to bottom left diagonal
     3.2.1 If (OAndXsArray[0,2] = OAndXsArray[1,1])
                And (OAndXsArray[1,1] = OAndXsArray[2,0])
             Then
               If (OAndXsArray[0,2] <> ' ') Then Outcome ← 'Win'
           EndIf
4. If No result Then check for a draw
   4.1 If no result
         Then
           If grid full Then result a draw
         EndIf
     4.1.1 If Outcome = 'No result so far'
             Then
               NoOfMovesSofar ← 0
               For i ← 0 To 2 Do
                 For j ← 0 To 2 Do
                   If OAndXsArray[i,j] <> ' ' Then NoOfMovesSoFar ← NoOfMovesSoFar + 1
                 EndFor
               EndFor
               If NoOfMovesSoFar = 9 Then Outcome ← 'Draw'
           EndIf
```

Figure 1.2.1.21 Second level of refinement

Programming task

2 Using stepwise refinement create a noughts and crosses program based on the program structure shown in *Figure 1.2.1.18* in a programming language of your choice.

Questions

18 Assuming that the sub tasks in the following are to be implemented as subroutines, create a hierarchy chart with control information and subroutine parameter lists for a program which

(a) collects three integers from the keyboard and calculates and displays their average.

(b) collects a letter from the keyboard, then tests and displays whether the letter is uppercase or not.

(c) collects an integer from the keyboard then calculates and displays its square, cube and fourth power.

Advantages of the structured approach

You have been introduced to the structured approach via very simple systems involving a small number of tasks where the "size" of the computation, i.e. the amount of information and the number of operations involved in it are relatively small.

When the problem to solve is really small, it would be easier not to use the computer at all and instead to do it by hand. The automatic computer is better employed on large computations which humans cannot do.

However, in order to manage such scale of computation successfully a disciplined approach to developing software is required.

The structured approach breaks the problem/system into manageable modules which have

- functional cohesion, i.e. modules which contain only one function or perform only one logically-related task. This enables a module to be easily replaced by another serving the same purpose.
- low coupling so that the modules are as independent as possible. The lower the coupling, the less likely that other modules will have to be considered in order to
    - create a module
    - understand a given module
    - debug a given module
    - change a given module.

Modules which are functionally cohesive, loosely coupled and for which all data transfer in and out of the modules is visible in the module parameters, enable programmers to work on individual modules without needing knowledge of the rest of the system.

The degree of intellectual effort (measured in some loose sense) to understand well-structured programs tends to be proportional to their program length (measured in some equally loose sense). This is important when reasoning about a program to check that it meets its specification. It is a more challenging task to do this with programs which are not well-structured.

Psychology research tells us that humans manage information in "chunks" and that the human brain is able to handle up to five pieces of information, maybe seven at a pinch. Stepwise refinement fits this limitation of the human brain well.

Questions

19 State **three** advantages of the structured approach and explain why these are advantages.

Information

There are two other software design paradigms:

- Object-oriented
- Function programming

In object-oriented design the nature of objects leads to the creation of loosely coupled systems.

In object-oriented design the representation of an object is concealed within that object and is not visible to external components.

The system does not have a shared state and therefore any object can be replaced by another object with the same interface.

Some of the skills you develop following a structured approach to constructing software and the principles of structured design and programming you acquire in AS Computer Science overlap with Object-Oriented Design (OOD) and Object-Oriented Programming (OOP) which is part of the A Level Computer Science course. This course will also introduce you to the functional programming paradigm and will lay the foundations for reasoning about program correctness.

In this chapter you have covered:

- The structured approach to program design and construction
- Constructing hierarchy charts when designing programs
- The advantages of the structured approach

2 Fundamentals of data structures

2.1 Data structures and abstract data types

Learning objectives:

- *Be familiar with the concept of data structures*

Figure 2.1.1.1 Queue Abstract Data Type

Key term

Composite data type:
In computer science, a composite data type or compound data type is any data type which can be constructed in a program using the programming language's primitive data types and other composite types.

Primitive data type:
In imperative languages, a primitive data type is one in which the set of values of the type are scalar values meaning "single" values e.g. integer, Boolean, character.

Key concept

Data structure:
A data structure is a named collections of variables, possibly of different data types, which are connected in various ways.
The collection consists of an aggregation of cells representing some abstract data type, e.g. a queue which models a real world entity, e.g. a supermarket queue.
The cell is the basic building block of data structures.

2.1.1 Data structures

The concept of data structures

Learning how to program is a process of developing the ability to model problems in such a way that a computer can solve them.

Array data structure

Suppose we needed to solve a problem which involved queueing. *Figure 2.1.1.1* shows an abstraction of a queue of people.

To represent this model in a computer programming language we use a data structure.

A data structure is a named collections of variables, possibly of different data types, which are connected in various ways. In the case of the queue, the person at the front of the queue is connected by relative position to the person next in the queue, this person is connected by relative position to the next and so on.

The cell is the basic building block of data structures. We can picture a cell as a box that is capable of holding a value drawn from some basic or composite data type. *Figure 2.1.1.2* shows a collection of or aggregation of cells representing a queue. This data structure is given a name, *Queue*, that refers to the aggregate of cells.

Each cell of *Queue* is designed to store a value of an integer data type.

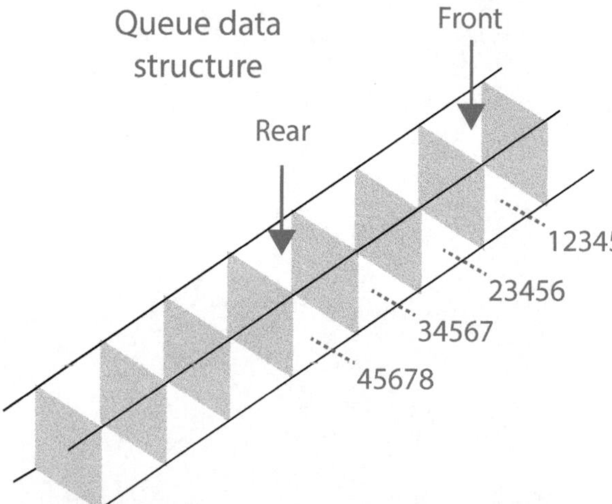

Figure 2.1.1.2 Queue data structure consisting of an aggregation of cells storing integers

The simplest aggregating mechanism available in many programming languages is the array which is a sequence of cells of a given type.

Record data structure

Another common mechanism for grouping cells in programming languages is the record data structure. A record is a cell that is made up of a collection of other cells, called fields, that may be of different data types. The record data structure can model a customer record from the real world and store such values in its fields such as customer name, address, age, salary, job position.

File data structure

A third grouping method is the file. A file is a collection of data of some particular data type stored on mass storage, e.g. magnetic disk.
In a sequential file, elements of the file can be accessed only in the order of their appearance in the file. The number of elements in the file data structure and the size of the file can vary in time and this size is not constrained by the available RAM in the way that array data structures are constrained by main memory (RAM) capacity.

The structure of the file refers to the way that data stored in the file is subdivided or structured, e.g. as records.

The array and file data structures are covered in depth in *Chapter 2.1.2* and *Chapter 2.1.3*.

Questions

1. What is meant by a data structure?

2. Customer orders in a fish and chip shop are queued in the order that they arrive by an assistant at the counter using a till receipt as a record of an order. Other assistants are responsible for retrieving till receipts from the queue and fulfilling each order.
Suggest a suitable a data structure to use to model this scenario by computer.

In this chapter you have covered:

- The concept of data structures

2 Fundamentals of data structures

2.1 Data structures and abstract data types

Learning objectives:

- *Use arrays (or equivalent) in the design of solutions to simple problems*

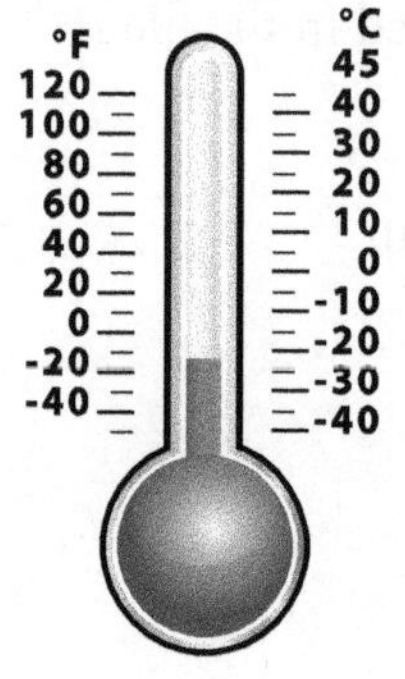

2.1.2 Single- and multi-dimensional arrays (or equivalent)

One-dimensional array

The problem

Suppose you are tasked with writing a computer program to keep a set of one hundred temperature readings in memory so that calculations may be performed on these readings in a uniform manner. A sample of the first 8 readings is shown in *Table 2.1.2.1*.

20.5	22.7	24.3	26.8	25.1	23.9	21.4	20.0

Table 2.1.2.1 Sample of temperature readings

We could store the first of the readings in a variable, `Temperature1`, the second in a variable, `Temperature2`, and so on as shown in *Table 2.1.2.2*. The data type chosen for `Temperature1` would be one that allows storage of a value possessing a fractional part, e.g. `float`. The same data type would be chosen for `Temperature2`, and each of the other 98 variables.

Variable	Value
`Temperature1`	20.5
`Temperature2`	22.7
`Temperature3`	24.3
`Temperature4`	26.8
`Temperature5`	25.1
`Temperature6`	23.9
`Temperature7`	21.4
`Temperature8`	20.0

Table 2.1.2.2 Variables for first 8 readings

Using 100 separate variables, each of which is only able to store a single value, is not ideal.

The solution

What is needed is a *single variable* which can store many values.

For this we use an array variable, `Temperature`, as shown in *Figure 2.1.2.1*.

Variable	Value
`Temperature`	20.5
	22.7
	24.3
	26.8
	25.1
	23.9
	21.4
	20.0
	•
	•
	•
	17.6

Figure 2.1.2.1 Array variable with storage for 100 temperature readings

1. An array is a data structure which is capable of storing many values, e.g. 100 temperature readings: 20.5, 22.7, ..., 17.6
2. An array is also a single entity, referred to by a single name, e.g. `Temperature`.
3. The values stored in an array are all of the same data type, e.g. `Float`.
4. The stored values are arranged in an order so that there is a first, a second, and so on.

Information

When we want to indicate that we have omitted numbers, etc, in a sequence of numbers or other entities we use a series of dots called an ellipsis • • • or ⋮

The omission is used where it would be unnecessary to include more numbers because these can be inferred from the context.

Questions

 A program is required to keep 10000 temperature readings in memory and to reference all the items in a uniform manner.
Explain why it would be preferable to use a one-dimensional array to store the value of each reading instead of 10000 separate variables.

Separate variables

In the separate variable approach, to extract, say, the value of the seventh temperature reading from among 100 separate variables, we need the name of the corresponding variable. We can construct this name by combining the name `Temperature` with the numeric name `7` to produce the name, `Temperature7`.

We then use this name to refer to the variable which contains the value of the seventh reading, i.e. 21.4 as shown in *Table 2.1.2.2*. Perhaps we might want to output the value of this variable to the console.
Pseudo-code that does this is as follows

```
Output Temperature7
```

Array index

Using an array to store 100 temperature readings, we retain the use of numeric naming 1, 2, 3, 4, ..., 100 and view the array as consisting of 100 elements with each element storing the value of a temperature reading.

To extract, say, the value of the seventh temperature reading, we construct a name by combining the name of the array, `Temperature`, with the numeric name `7` as follows `Temperature[7]` as shown in *Figure 2.1.2.2*.

We then use this name to refer to the **element** of the array which contains the seventh reading, i.e. 21.4 (see *Table 2.1.2.2*).

Variable	Index	Value
Temperature	[1]	20.5
	[2]	22.7
	[3]	24.3
	[4]	26.8
	[5]	25.1
	[6]	23.9
	[7]	21.4
	[8]	20.0
	⋮	⋮
	[100]	17.6

Figure 2.1.2.2 Use of an index in array variable Temperature

Perhaps we might want to output the value of this variable to the console. Pseudo-code that does this is as follows

```
Output Temperature[7]
```

Pseudo-code to output the first, second and third values of array `Temperature` is

```
Output Temperature[1]
Output Temperature[2]
Output Temperature[3]
```

Information

Square bracket notation:
Square bracket notation [ ] is used to access values in an array.

The name that we use inside the square brackets is called the **array index**, e.g. 3 in `[3]`.

Pseudo-code to output all 100 values is as follows

```
For i ← 1 To 100 Output Temperature[i]
```

Here the array index is a loop control variable `i` which ranges from 1 to 100.

We are not restricted to starting array indexing at 1. We can index from 0. In fact, many programming languages only offer array indexing from 0. Pascal and Delphi are exceptions. In fact, Pascal and Delphi allow indexing from any starting value of ordinal data type.

Questions

2 A one-dimensional array `Height` consists of 10 elements. Array indexing starts at 0 and ends at 9. The array stores the heights of 10 people. Write pseudocode using a *for loop* to output all 10 heights in the same order that they are stored in the array.

Numeric names and non-numeric names for array index

We used numeric names for the index of an array, e.g. 1, 2, 3, etc, in the previous section. We don't have to. Instead, we can use non-numeric names, e.g. A, B, C, D, etc. For example, to extract the first value stored in array `LetterCount` we would use `LetterCount[A]`, the second value, `LetterCount[B]`, and so on.

Note, however, that whatever names we use, they must be capable of being ordered and the next name must be the natural successor to the previous, e.g. B is the successor to A, 2 is the successor to 1. This is very important.

If this wasn't the case then the *for loop* on the previous page, which assumes an increment of 1, wouldn't be able to access every one of the 100 values.

Choosing to use as an array index a range of numbers drawn from the set of integers is thus a natural choice to make. For other scenarios, the array index may be chosen from values in a different data type, e.g. character.

Questions

A one-dimensional array `LetterCount` consists of 26 elements. Array indexing starts at letter A and ends at letter Z. The array stores the count for each uppercase letter of the alphabet occurring in a piece of text, e.g. `LetterCount[D]` stores the value 36. Write pseudocode using a *for loop* to output the count stored for each letter in the same order that they are stored in the array. Use a loop control variable, `Letter`, which uses values chosen from A, B, C, ..., X, Y, Z.

What kind of identifier is an array index?

There are three kinds of non-negative integral number[1] usage:

Quantities: 0, 1, 2, ...

Quantities are used to give the quantity (a count) of items. They include zero, because zero is a possible quantity. Quantities are **cardinal numbers**.

Position words: 1st, 2nd, 3rd, ...

Position words give the position of an item within a sequence with a beginning. The item at the beginning of the sequence is called the "first" item, the next the "second", and so on. "First" is written as 1st, "second" as 2nd, and so on. Position words are **ordinal numbers**.

Identification numbers: 0, 1, 2, ..., or 1, 2, 3, ..., or any other ordered sequence.

Identification numbers are just a methodical way to give numerical names to items such as the sequence of 100 temperature values. Identification numbers are therefore a way of numbering the temperature values.

Information

Identification numbers are used extensively in the world. For example, all vehicles registered in the UK must have a unique, stamped-in vehicle identification number (VIN). It is usually stamped into the chassis of the vehicle.

1 Integral numbers are whole numbers such as the integers

Figure 2.1.2.3 shows array `Temperature` together with the identification numbers which identify each value stored in the array.

1	2	3	4	5	6	7	8	• • •	100
20.5	22.7	24.3	26.8	25.1	23.9	21.4	20.0	• • •	17.6

Figure 2.1.2.3 Use of identification numbers in range 1 to 100 to index array `Temperature`

Questions

4 What kind of identifier is the array index in the Temperature array?

Basic operations that access arrays

The two basic operations that access the one-dimensional array `Temperature` are

- Extraction: this is achieved by evaluating `Temperature[i]` to identify a particular stored value in the array `Temperature`, e.g. if `i` = 5, then `Temperature[i]` evaluates to 25.1 - see Figure 2.1.2.3.
- Storing: this is achieved by executing the assignment `Temperature[i]` ← `x` which results in a copy of the value stored in `x` being assigned to the array `Temperature` at the location within this array identified by identification number `i`. Variable `x` holds the temperature reading to be stored in the array `Temperature`, e.g. if `i` = 5 and `x` = 25.1, then `Temperature[5]` ← 25.1 results in 25.1 being stored in the array location with identification number 5.

Questions

5 Describe with examples the **two** basic operations used to access elements of a one-dimensional array.

Addresses

Numbers as names are also called addresses. We are familiar with numbers being assigned to houses: "Such and such lives at no 42".

We can therefore think of an array index as an address. Using an address also implies a location. For example, `Temperature[5]` is a location with address 5 within array `Temperature`.

Figure 2.1.2.4 shows storage bays for Russian doll objects. We can think of this structure as an array used for storing objects. Each bay within this array is a location. The structure is divided into cells, one above another. So we can also use the synonym cell for location.

Each location/cell is assigned an address. In this numbering scheme we have chosen to start the numbering from 0 and to label the lowermost cell 0. We could have started the numbering from 1 and we could have chosen the uppermost cell as the first cell. The choice is arbitrary. All that we need to ensure is that the numbering is ordered, i.e. 0, 1, 2 , 3 or 1, 2, 3, 4, and each cell is assigned, in order, a unique number drawn from the range of numbers whether 0, 1, 2, 3 is chosen or 1, 2, 3, 4.

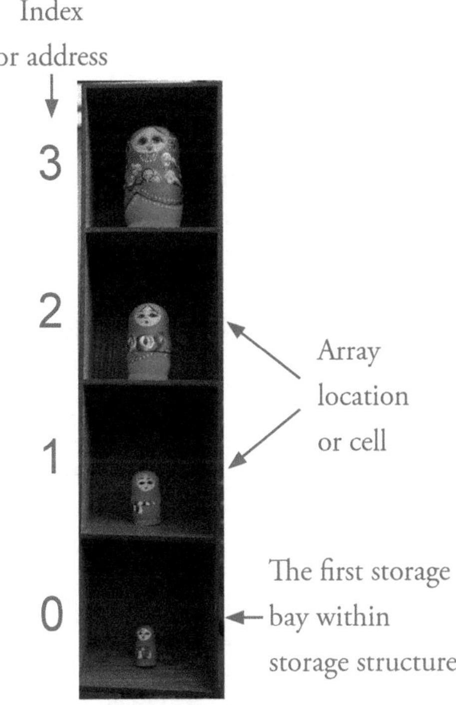

Figure 2.1.2.4 Location/cell view of an array with array index as a location address

We have now encountered three different terms for an array part that stores a value:

- element
- location
- cell

Questions

6 Explain why we can think of an array index as an address.

Why choose to start numbering array locations with the number zero?

Figure 2.1.2.5 shows array `Temperature` together with the identification numbers which identify each value stored in the array. This time the identification numbering/index starts at 0.

First ↓ 0	1	2	3	4	5	6	7	• • •	Last ↓ 99
20.5	22.7	24.3	26.8	25.1	23.9	21.4	20.0	• • •	17.6

Figure 2.1.2.5 Use of identification numbers from 0 to 99 to index array `Temperature`

The meaning in English of the ordinal-number word "first" is the first entry within a sequence, even if this first entry is labelled with identification number 0, as unnatural as it may seem. We are conditioned by everyday experience to use identification number 1 when referring to the first entity in a sequence, e.g. the first house in a street has address 1 not 0. However, if the house number was 0, it would still be the first - see *Figure 2.1.2.6*.

Figure 2.1.2.6 House with house number 0

0 Acacia Avenue
Dingley Dell
NeverNeverLand

ZX99 9ZZ

Questions

7 Array indexing starts at 0 for an array `Row` with 10 elements.
(a) What is the index of the last element?
(b) Write pseudo-code to output the value stored in the first cell of this array.

8 (a) Explain why the following pseudo-code will output the 10 values stored in the array `Row`.

```
i ← 0
While i < 10
  Output Row[i]
  i ← i + 1
EndWhile
```

(b) What is the value stored in `i` when the loop terminates?

9 Rewrite the *While loop* pseudo-code in Question 8 so that it uses a *Repeat loop* with the terminating condition at the end of the loop.

Offset

By starting array indexing at 0, the index takes on the role of an offset. If the physical address in memory of the base of the array is, say, 1500 then the first cell of the array has address 1500 + 0, the second 1500 + 1, and so on.

Questions

10 An array `Vector` has 10 elements with an index that starts at 0. The physical address in memory of the base of this array is 2300.
What is the physical address of the fifth element?

11 A collection of ropes of various lengths are wrapped in turn around a cylinder of circumference 10 units. All the ropes wrap around the cylinder at least once but never exactly. The total length of each rope is measured and the measurement truncated so that it is integral. The integral measurement `L` is stored in a one-dimensional 10 element array `ExcessRopeLength` according to whether the integral excess length is 0, 1, 2, ..., 8, 9 units.
The integral excess length can be calculated using the formula

L mod 10

For example, if the length L is 36 units then the excess length is 6 units.
You are required to choose between using array indexing that starts at 0 and array indexing that starts at 1. Justify your choice.

A one-dimensional array is a useful way of representing a vector

Most data processing and numerical simulations are nothing more than a succession of elementary operations, such as *add* and *multiply*, applied to large amounts of numerical data. Computers are extremely good at this provided that the data is structured in a way that facilitates computation. The typical structure of numerical data is that of vectors and matrices (plural of matrix), and more generally multi-dimensional arrays.

A vector represents a grouping of data values, e.g. 0, 0, 100, 100.

The group of values may be stored in a one-dimensional array, `exampleVector`, expressed in some languages as

[0, 0, 100, 100]

The array, `exampleVector` could represent a Euclidean vector (sometimes called a geometric or spatial vector, or simply a vector).
A Euclidean vector is a geometric object that has magnitude (or length) and direction and can be added to other vectors according to vector algebra.
Figure 2.1.2.7 shows a Python program created in Processing 3.1 (processing.org). The program sets the window used for output to 200 x 200 pixels. It then creates a list [0, 199, 100, 100] which groups 4 values. The first pair, 0, 199, represents the start coordinate (bottom left in Figure 2.1.2.8) and the second pair, 100, 100, the end coordinate of a vector. A list is not an array but in this example it is being used in a way that is equivalent to an array.
Figure 2.1.2.8 shows the geometric vector, a line, displayed in the output window of the executing program.
Figure 2.1.2.9 shows a Java program created in Processing 3.1. The program sets the window used for output to 200 x 200 pixels. It then creates an array of four integer elements using `new int[4]`, before initialising this array with the group of values 0, 199, 100, 100 representing a vector. The first pair, 0, 199, represents the start coordinate and the second pair, 100, 100, the end coordinate of a vector. Figure 2.1.2.10 shows the geometric vector, a line, displayed in the output window of the executing program.

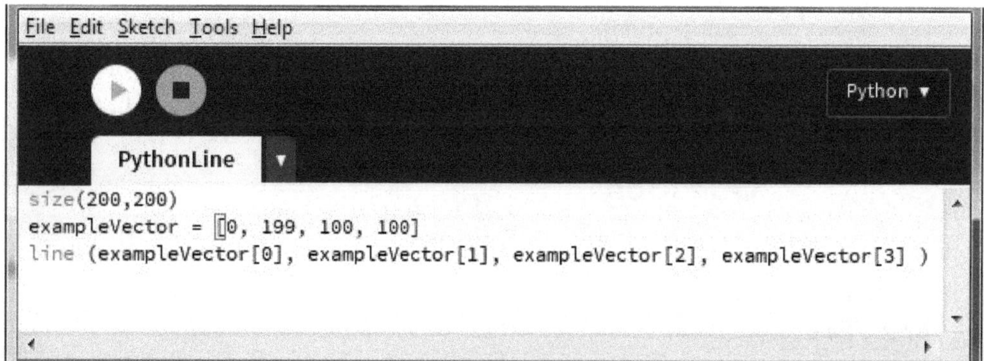

Figure 2.1.2.7 Python program in Processing 3.1 to draw a line for a given vector

Figure 2.1.2.8 Processing 3.1 graphical output for Python program

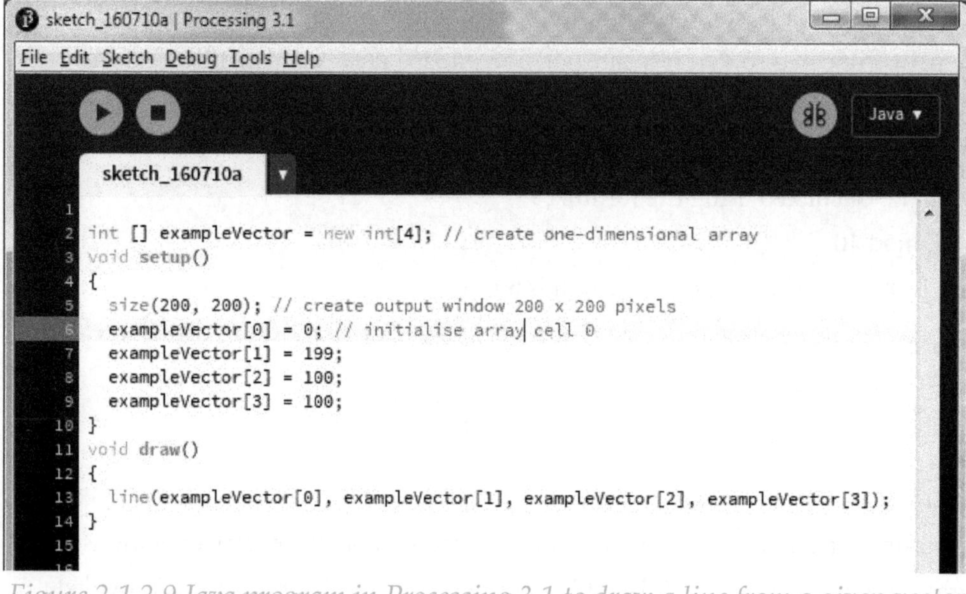

Figure 2.1.2.9 Java program in Processing 3.1 to draw a line from a given vector

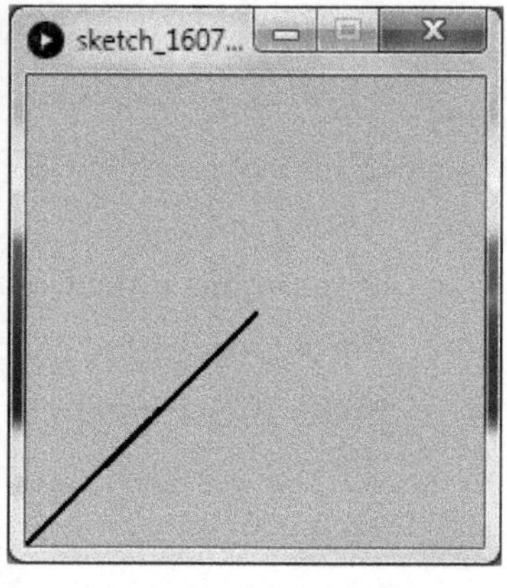

Figure 2.1.2.10 Processing 3.1 graphical output for Java program

Operations on vectors

It is useful to think of a vector in geometric terms. *Figure 2.1.2.11* shows two vectors realised as two lines in green. The vectors are expressed as two one-dimensional arrays as follows

[0, 0, 25, 75] and [0, 0, 100, 100]

If we add these two vectors element-wise we get a third vector expressed as a one-dimensional array as follows

[0, 0, 125, 75]

This vector is realised as the line in blue in *Figure 2.1.2.11*. Element-wise means that the first element of vector [0, 0, 25, 75] is added to the first element of vector [0, 0, 100, 100], and so on.

The red line drawn parallel to the shorter green line and started from the endpoint of the longer green line closes the triangle (of vectors). If we label this point A, then we have two ways to get to A: the first is along the long green line then along the red line; the second is along the blue line.

Figure 2.1.2.12 shows the Java program in Processing 3.1 which performs the vector addition and line drawing described above.

The term vector refers to a one-dimensional array of values to which operations such as add, subtract, multiple, divide can be applied to the array as a whole. The operations are applied in element-wise fashion so that the result is an array of the same size as the original array(s).

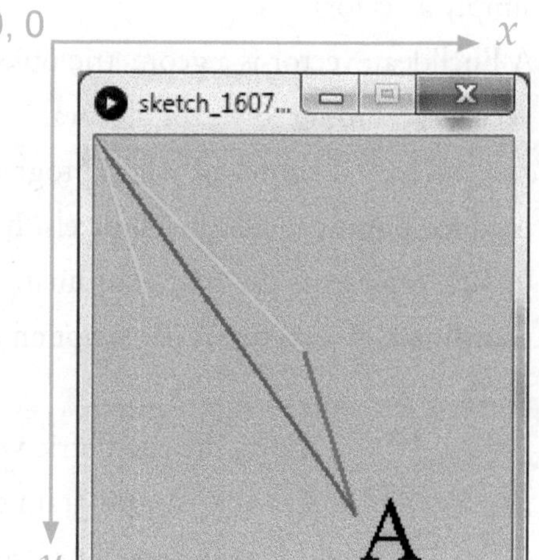

Figure 2.1.2.11 Processing 3.1 graphical output for Java program

The vector addition can be performed in parallel if a single ADD instruction can be applied to the four elements of each array simultaneously. Modern CPUs are capable of executing such operations by using **SIMD**[2] instructions, i.e. **S**ingle **I**nstruction **M**ultiple **D**ata stream instructions.

By creating and manipulating arrays, efficient vector computations can be performed with them.

The four elementary operations ADD, SUBTRACT, MULTIPLY, and DIVIDE can be applied to data in arrays provided they have compatible shapes, i.e. the same dimensions.

sketch_160712b | Processing 3.1.1

File Edit Sketch Debug Tools Help

Java ▾

sketch_160712b

```
int[] vector1 = {0,0, 100,100};
int[] vector2 = {0,0,25,75};
int[] vector3 = new int[4];
int[] vector4 = {100,100, 125,175};
void setup()
{
  size(200,200);
  vector3[0] = vector1[0] + vector2[0];
  vector3[1] = vector1[1] + vector2[1];
  vector3[2] = vector1[2] + vector2[2];
  vector3[3] = vector1[3] + vector2[3];
}
void draw()
{
  stroke(0,255,0);
  line(vector1[0], vector1[1],vector1[2],vector1[3]);
  line(vector2[0], vector2[1],vector2[2],vector2[3]);
  stroke(0,0,255);
  line(vector3[0], vector3[1],vector3[2],vector3[3]);
  stroke(255,0,0);
  line(vector4[0], vector4[1],vector4[2],vector4[3]);
}
```

Figure 2.1.2.12 Java program in Processing 3.1 which performs vector addition

Questions

 12 A one-dimensional array is a useful way of representing a vector. Use the multiplication of a one-dimensional array of integers, `ArrayOneD`, by 5 to explain what this means. Assume the array is initialised as follows `ArrayOneD = [3,6,7,2]`.

Creating a one-dimensional array

Table 2.1.2.3 shows examples of how integer and real/floating point one-dimensional arrays may be created in C#, Java, Pascal, Delphi, Python[3] and VB.NET. For Python two approaches are used. The first uses Python lists and the second arrays from the Numpy library.

Python lacks native support for creating an array data structure within the language. The closest that Python gets to a native data structure that can be used like a one-dimensional array is a list (a list is actually a dynamic array). A list is just a sequence of values (think of a shopping list).

However, it is possible to create an array in Python with the `NumPy` package if this package is loaded with the command `import numpy`.

`NumPy` is short for Numeric Python.

With `numpy` installed we can use the `array` function to create an array.

Information

Numpy:

NumPy is the fundamental package for scientific computing with Python.

Anaconda:

Installing some of the larger Python libraries, particularly those such as NumPy which depend on complex low-level C and Fortran packages, is made easy with Anaconda. Anaconda will do all the dependency checking and binary installs required. Anaconda is free to download and install from https://www.continuum.io/downloads

2 Not in the AQA specification

3 Spyder 2.3.1 the **S**cientific **PY**thon **D**evelopment **E**nvi**R**onment and Python 3.4

Language	Integer	Real/float
C#	`int[] vector = new int[4];` `int[] vector = {0,1,2,3};`	`float[] vector = new float[4];` `float[] vector = {0.0,1.5,2.3,3.4};`
Java	`int[] vector = new int[4];` `int[] vector = {0,1,2,3};`	`float[] vector= new float[4];` `float[] vector = {0.0,1.5,2.3,3.4};`
Pascal	`Vector : Array[0..3] Of Integer;` `Vector : Array[0..3] Of Integer = (0,1,2,3);`	`Vector : Array[0..3] Of Real;` `Vector : Array[0..3] Of Real = (0.0,1.5,2.3,3.4);`
Delphi	`Vector : Array[0..3] Of Integer;` `Vector : Array[0..3] Of Integer = (0,1,2,3);`	`Vector : Array[0..3] Of Real;` `Vector : Array[0..3] Of Real = (0.0,1.5,2.3,3.4);`

Python	`vector = [0,1,2,3,4] #list equivalent`
	`import numpy as np`
	`vector = np.array([0, 1, 2, 3])`
	`vector = np.empty([4],dtype=int)#empty array`
	`vector = np.zeros(4, dtype=int)`
		`vector = [0.0,1.5,2.3,3.4]`
		`import numpy as np`
		`vector = np.array([0, 1, 2, 3], dtype = float)`
		`vector = np.empty([4])#empty float array`
		`vector = np.zeros(4)`

VB.Net	`Dim vector(3) As Integer` `Dim vector = New Integer() {0,1,2,3}`	`Dim vector(3) As Double` `Dim vector = New Double() {0.0,1.5,2.3,3.4}`

Table 2.1.2.3 Creating one-dimensional arrays of different array element data type

In Table 2.1.2.3, the Python list [0, 1, 2, 3] is supplied as argument to the function `array` to create array x as follows

```
x = np.array([0,1, 2, 3])
```

In Table 2.1.2.3, the program code `x = np.zeros(4, dtype=int)` uses the `numpy` function `zeros` to create a four-element array with each element initialised to 0. The default array element data type is `float`.

In IPython (ipython.org), `%pylab` will install `numpy` as well as `matplotlib.pyplot`, a plotting library for displaying data visually - see Table 2.1.2.5.

IPython is an interactive python useful for trying out ideas.

Python lists are unsatisfactory as proxies for arrays for the following reasons:

1. Elements of a list can be of different data types, e.g. `[3, 4.5, 'hello', True, [34,56]]`
2. Lists may grow or shrink, e.g. `x = [0,1,2] x.append('a') x.pop()`
3. Processing of Python lists is considerably slower than processing arrays from Numpy

Tables 2.1.2.4, 2.1.2.5, and 2.1.2.6 show examples of one-dimensional array creation in C#, Java, Pascal, Delphi, Python and VB.NET. The Python example uses IPython. IPython already has `numpy` in its namespace so use of the prefix `np` is unnecessary.

Language	Integer

Python 3.4
(IPython)
	`In [1]: %pylab`
	`In [2]: vector2 = array([0,1,2,3]), dtype=int)`
	`In [3]: vector4 = array([0.0,1.5,2.3,3.4], dtype=float)`
	`In [4]: print(vector2[0])`
	`In [5]: print(vector4[3])`

Python 3.4
(Scipy)
	`vector = [1,2,3,4] # list equivalent of an array`
	`print (vector[2])`
	`import numpy as np`
	`vector2 = np.array([1,2,3,4])`
	`print (vector2[2])`

Table 2.1.2.4 Creating one-dimensional arrays of different array element data type

Language	Integer

C#	using System;
	namespace Arrays
	{
	class Program
	{
	static void Main(string[] args)
	{
	int[] vector1 = new int[4];
	int[] vector2 = { 0, 1, 2, 3 };
	float[] vector3 = new float[4];
	float[] vector4 = { 0.0f, 1.5f, 2.3f, 3.4f };
	double[] vector5 = { 0.0, 1.5, 2.3, 3.4 };
	vector1[0] = 45;
	vector3[0] = 45.8f;
	Console.WriteLine(vector1[0]);
	Console.ReadLine();
	}
	}
	}

Java	public class Arrays {
	public static void main(String[] args) {
	int[] vector1 = new int[4];
	int[] vector2 = {0,1,2,3};
	float[] vector3 = new float[4];
	float[] vector4 = { 0.0f, 1.5f, 2.3f, 3.4f };
	double[] vector5 = { 0.0, 1.5, 2.3, 3.4 };
	vector1[0] = 45;
	vector3[0] = 45.8f;
	System.out.println(vector1[0]);
	}
	}

Delphi	Program ArrayVector; {$APPTYPE CONSOLE} {$R *.res} Uses System.SysUtils; Var Vector1 : Array[0..3] Of Integer; Vector2 : Array[0..3] Of Integer = (0,1,2,3); Vector3 : Array[0..3] Of Real; Vector4 : Array[0..3] Of Real = (0.0,1.5,2.3,3.4); Begin Vector1[0] := 45; Vector3[0] := 45.8; Writeln(Vector1[0]); Writeln(Vector4[3] :6:1); Readln; End.
Pascal	Program ArrayVector; Var Vector1 : Array[0..3] Of Integer; Vector2 : Array[0..3] Of Integer = (0,1,2,3); Vector3 : Array[0..3] Of Real; Vector4 : Array[0..3] Of Real = (0.0,1.5,2.3,3.4); Begin Vector1[0] := 45; Vector3[0] := 45.8; Writeln(Vector1[0]); Writeln(Vector4[3] :6:1); Readln; End.

Table 2.1.2.5 Creating one-dimensional arrays of different array element data type

Language	Integer

VB.NET	`Module Arrays`
	`    Sub Main()`
	`        Dim vector1(3) As Integer`
	`        Dim vector2 = {0, 1, 2, 3}`
	`        Dim vector3(3) As Single`
	`        Dim vector4(3) As Double`
	`        Dim vector5 = {0.0, 1.5, 2.3, 3.4}`
	`        vector1(0) = 45`
	`        vector3(0) = 45.8F`
	`        vector4(3) = 45.8`
	`        Console.WriteLine(vector1(0))`
	`        Console.WriteLine(vector5(3))`
	`        Console.ReadLine()`
	`    End Sub`
	`End Module`

Table 2.1.2.6 Creating one-dimensional arrays of different array element data type

Iterating through the elements of a one-dimensional array

Iterating through the elements of an array is a common operation on arrays. Figure 2.1.2.13 shows the use of a *For loop* to access each element of array `Vector` starting with the first element `Vector[0]`. The index used is `i`, the loop control variable. Table 2.1.2.7 shows the value of `i` and the value of array `Vector[i]` in each iteration of the *For loop*.

The one-dimensional array `Vector` contains 4 elements with the following values 0.0, 1.5, 2.3, 3.4, respectively.

```
For i ← 0 To 3
  Output Vector[i]
EndFor
```

Figure 2.1.2.13 Pseudo-code For loop

Table 2.1.2.8 shows the loop pseudo-code expressed in the programming languages C#, Java, Delphi/Pascal, Python and VB.NET.

Value of i	Element accessed	Value of element
0	Vector[0]	0.0
1	Vector[1]	1.5
2	Vector[2]	2.3
3	Vector[3]	3.4

Table 2.1.2.7 Value of loop control variable and element of array Vector on each iteration

Programming task

1. Write a program which iterates through ArrayOneD outputting each value in turn starting at the first value contained in this array. Assume the array is initialised as follows `ArrayOneD = [3,6,7,2]`.

Language	Integer

C#	`int i;`
	`for (i = 0; i < 4; i++)`
	`  {`
	`    Console.WriteLine(vector[i]);`
	`  }`

Java	`int i;`
	`for (i = 0; i < 4; i++)`
	`  {`
	`    System.out.println(vector[i]);`
	`  }`

Delphi/ Pascal	`Var i : Integer;`
	`.....`
	`For i := 0 To 3`
	`  Do Writeln(Vector[i]);`

Python	`for i in range(4):` `    print(vector[i])`

VB.NET	`Dim i As Integer`
	`For i = 0 To 3`
	`    Console.WriteLine(vector(i))`
	`Next`

Table 2.1.2.8 Accessing the elements of a one-dimensional array by iteration with a For loop

Computing a single value from the contents of a one-dimensional array

To sum all the elements of a one-dimensional array, `Vector`, we must access each element of this array in turn adding its value to a running total `Sum`. The variable `Sum` is initialised to contain zero. Figure 2.1.2.14 shows pseudo-code that computes the sum of the elements of array `Vector`. Array `Vector` contains 4 elements with the following values 1, 3, 8, 9.

Table 2.1.2.9 shows the state of `Sum` before iteration begins and at the end of each iteration, e.g. after the first iteration variable `Sum` contains 1, after the second, 5.

```
Sum ← 0
For i ← 0 To 3
  Sum ← Sum + Vector[i]
EndFor
Output Sum
```

Figure 2.1.2.14 For loop

Value of i	Element accessed	Value of element	Sum
			0
0	Vector[0]	1	1
1	Vector[1]	3	4
2	Vector[2]	8	12
3	Vector[3]	9	21

Table 2.1.2.9 Summing the elements of a one-dimensional array

Programming tasks

2 Write a program which iterates through ArrayOneD and sums the values contained in this array. Assume the array is initialised as follows `ArrayOneD = [3,6,7,2]`.

3 Write a program which collects 6 integer values from the keyboard and stores them in an array called `IntegerArray`. The program is to display the contents of each cell of the array in turn, starting at the first cell, after all the values have been entered.

4 Using the same program structure, add code which calculates the average of the first three numbers stored in the array and the second three numbers.

5 Using the same program structure, add another array to the program of the same size and type as the first. Now add code to copy the contents of the first array to the second array so that the second array holds the contents of the first array in reverse order.

When to use a one-dimensional array?

When it is necessary to keep a large number of items in memory and reference all the items in a uniform manner.

Multi-dimensional arrays

Two-dimensional arrays

We have so far considered how data may be stored in a one-dimensional array. A one-dimensional array has, of course, one dimension. We can visualise the items of data in a one-dimensional array arranged along a single axis as shown by the example in Figure 2.1.2.15.

Figure 2.1.2.15 Visualising items of numerical data in a one-dimensional array arranged along a single axis

If we have two dimensions for storing data then we can visualise the data stored in a grid-like fashion defined by two axes as shown in *Figure 2.1.2.16*. The **structure** of 5 rows and 5 columns of data shown in *Figure 2.1.2.16* is called a **two-dimensional array** or **matrix**. The matrix contains 5 x 5 = 25 numbers.

In order to refer to a specific number, we need to specify both the **row** and **column** because the matrix has two dimensions. For example, the third value along in the second row in *Figure 2.1.2.16* is the number 27. This number has been marked by a red square in the figure.

row \ column	0	1	2	3	4
0	23	64	15	25	9
1	59	12	27	38	86
2	5	81	40	0	333
3	3	74	42	7	91
4	44	540	16	81	12

2-D Grid

Figure 2.1.2.16 Visualising items of numerical data stored in a two-dimensional array laid out in two dimensions

The axes in *Figure 2.1.2.16* have been labelled, `row` and `column` so that the first row has value 0 and the first column has value 0. Therefore, the `row` and `column` values of the number 27 marked by a red square are 1 and 2, respectively.

Loading a greyscale image into a two-dimensional array

A greyscale image can be loaded into a two-dimensional array of the same dimensions, e.g. if the image is 450 x 600 then its height is 450 and its width is 600 - see *Figure 2.1.2.17*.

A value representing the intensity of a pixel at a particular position in the image is stored in the array cell of the same row and column as the image pixel..

The Python 3.4 program shown in *Figure 2.1.2.17* loads a single channel greyscale image file, `PlaneBWSingleChannel.png`, into a two dimensional array `im` using the command

```
im = imread('C:\\Users\\drbond\\
PlaneBWSingleChannel.png')
```

(\\ is used and not \ because \ is used in Python strings as an escape character).

The values stored in array `im` are rendered by `imshow` to display in shades of grey the 450 x 600 greyscale image shown in *Figure 2.1.2.17*.

The size and shape of the array `im` is shown with the command

```
im.shape
```

Figure 2.1.2.17 shows that the array `im` has the dimensions `450` x `600`. This is a two-dimensional array.

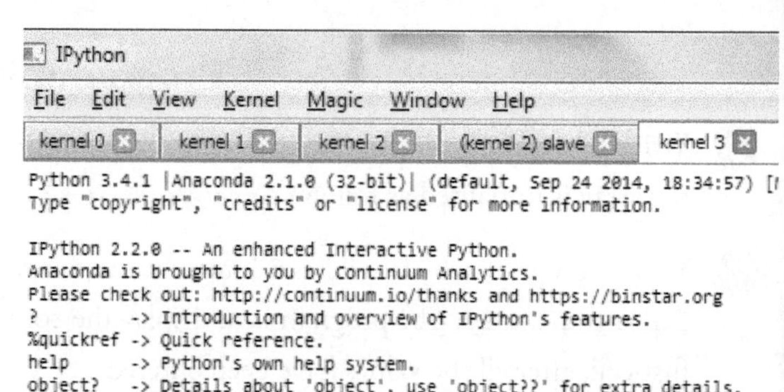


```
In [1]: %matplotlib qt

In [2]: %matplotlib inline

In [3]: import numpy as np

In [4]: import matplotlib.pyplot as plt

In [5]: from pylab import imread, imshow

In [6]: im = imread('C:\\Users\\drbond\\PlaneBWSingleChannel.png')

In [7]: im.shape
Out[7]: (450, 600)

In [8]: im[0,0]
Out[8]: 0.44705883

In [9]: imshow(im, cmap='Greys_r')
Out[9]: <matplotlib.image.AxesImage at 0x7d8a890>
```

Figure 2.1.2.17 Using Python 3.4. and library routines to load a greyscale image into a two-dimensional array, im

Information

Download: www.educational-computing.co.uk/Unit2/Images/Images2.rar to obtain PlaneBWSingleChannel.png

```
In [38]: matrix1 = np.ones([1104, 927])

In [39]: matrix2 = imread('C:/Users/drbond/KRB.png')

In [40]: matrix3 = matrix1 - matrix2

In [41]: matrix1.shape
Out[41]: (1104, 927)

In [42]: matrix2.shape
Out[42]: (1104, 927)

In [43]: imshow(matrix2, cmap='Greys_r')
Out[43]: <matplotlib.image.AxesImage at 0x78f5950>
```

```
In [44]: imshow(matrix3, cmap='Greys_r')
Out[44]: <matplotlib.image.AxesImage at 0x792a730>
```

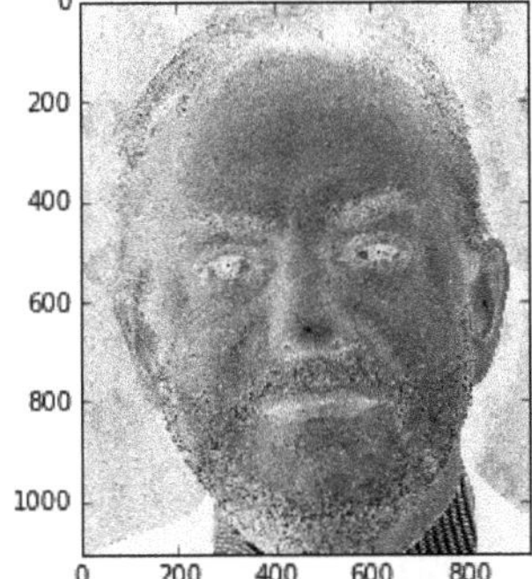

Figure 2.1.2.19 Subtracting an image matrix from a ones matrix to invert the image

The value stored in this array at `0, 0` is revealed with the command `im[0, 0]`. The `imread` function normalises each pixel intensity read from the image file to a value between 0 and 1.

The procedure `imshow` converts the array values to numbers in the range 0 to 255 when it displays an image. The library `matplotlib` handles the plotting of the image and the `inline` directive causes the image to be displayed in the IPython window in line with the Python code. `imshow(im, cmap='Greys_r')` renders the values in array `im` using a mapping which produces a greyscale image display.

Matrix algebra

We reserve the term two-dimensional array for a data structure which stores data in rows and columns in two dimensions.

The term matrix refers to a two-dimensional array of values to which operations such as add, subtract, multiple, divide can be applied to the array as a whole. For example, suppose that we have a 5 x 4 array `matrix1` consisting of all ones and another 5 x 4 array `matrix2` consisting of values between 0 and 1 as shown in *Figure 2.1.2.18* and we subtract `matrix2` from `matrix1`. We get `matrix3` as shown in *Figure 2.1.2.18*.

In effect we have done `matrix3 = matrix1 - matrix2.`

Figure 2.1.2.19 shows the result of subtracting an image matrix from a ones matrix: the image is inverted.

Two image matrices (plural of matrix), `image1` and `image2`, are shown in *Figure 2.1.2.20* and *Figure 2.1.2.21*. We can add these in different proportions so that we can fade one into the other as shown in *Figures 2.1.2.22, 2.1.2.23, 2.1.2.24, 2.1.2.25*.

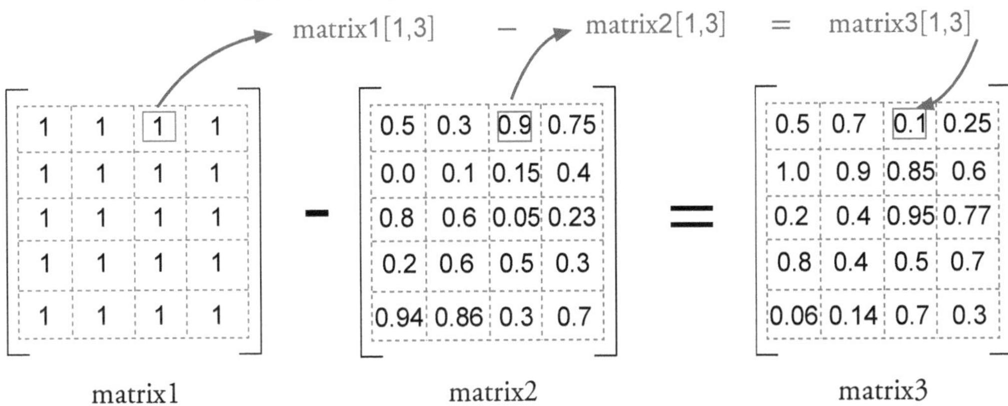

Figure 2.1.2.18 Subtracting one matrix from another

Information

Download: www.educational-computing.co.uk/Unit2/Images/Images2.rar to obtain images used above.

Questions

13 A two-dimensional array is a useful way of representing a matrix. Use the multiplication of a two-dimensional array of integers, `ArrayTwoD`, by 5 to explain what this means. Assume the array is initialised as follows `ArrayTwoD` = $\begin{bmatrix} 3,6,7 \\ 4,8,1 \\ 9,3,8 \end{bmatrix}$

```
In [6]: image1 = imread('C:/Users/drbond/Poh2017P1Cropped.png')

In [7]: image1.shape
Out[7]: (1104, 927)

In [8]: imshow(image1, cmap='Greys_r')
Out[8]: <matplotlib.image.AxesImage at 0x73bc930>
```

1104 x 927 pixels

1104 x 927 array

=1104 rows &

927 columns

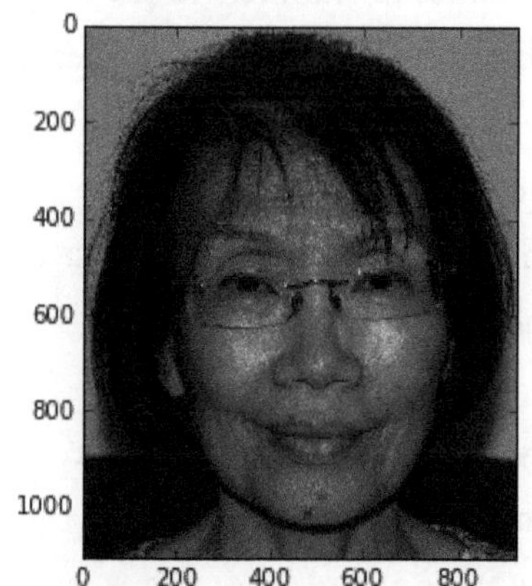

Figure 2.1.2.20 Loading array image1 with a greyscale image

```
In [8]: image2 = imread('C:/Users/drbond/KRB.png')

In [9]: imshow(image2, cmap='Greys_r')
Out[9]: <matplotlib.image.AxesImage at 0x545abf0>
```

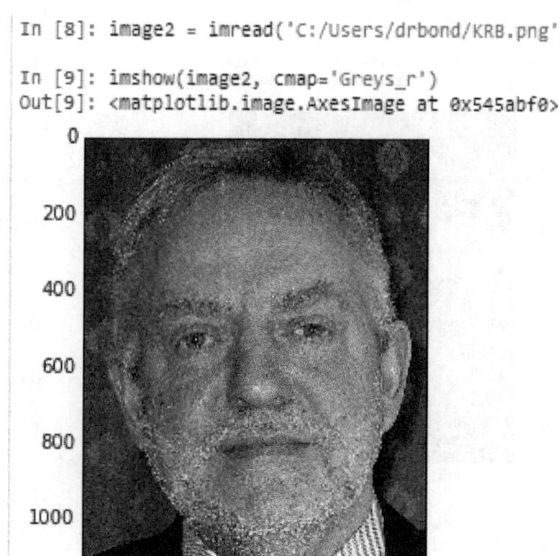

Figure 2.1.2.21 Loading array image2 with another greyscale image

```
In [16]: image = 0.7*image1 + 0.3*image2

In [17]: imshow(image, cmap='Greys_r')
Out[17]: <matplotlib.image.AxesImage at 0x557b350>
```

*Figure 2.1.2.22 0.7*image1 + 0.3*image2*

```
In [10]: image = 0.5*image1 + 0.5*image2

In [11]: imshow(image, cmap='Greys_r')
Out[11]: <matplotlib.image.AxesImage at 0x549a430>
```

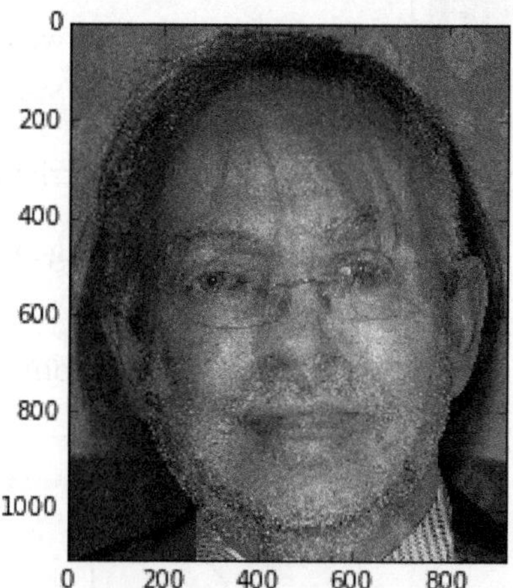

*Figure 2.1.2.23 0.5*image1 + 0.5*image2*

```
In [18]: image = 0.3*image1 + 0.7*image2

In [19]: imshow(image, cmap='Greys_r')
Out[19]: <matplotlib.image.AxesImage at 0x55b30f0>
```

*Figure 2.1.2.24 0.3*image1 + 0.7*image2*

```
In [45]: image = 0.0*image1 + 1.0*image2

In [46]: imshow(image, cmap='Greys_r')
Out[46]: <matplotlib.image.AxesImage at 0x79634d0>
```

*Figure 2.1.2.25 0.0*image1 + 1.0*image2*

Creating two-dimensional arrays in some programming languages

Table 2.1.2.10 shows the creation of two-dimensional arrays in C#, Java, Pascal, Delphi, Python 3.4 and VB.NET.

Language	Integer	Real/float
C#	`int[,] array2D = new int[4,2];` `int[,] array2D = {{1,2},{3,4},{5,6},{7,8}};`	`float[,] array2D = new float[4,2];`
Java	`int[][] array2D = new int[4][2];` `int[][] array2D = {{1,2},{3,4},{5,6},{7,8}};`	`float[][] array2D=new float[4][2];`
Pascal	`Array2D : Array[0..3,0..1] Of Integer;` `Array2D : Array[0..3,0..1] Of Integer = ((1,2),(3,4),(5,6),(7,8));`	`Array2D: Array[0..3,0..1] Of Real;`
Delphi	`Array2D : Array[0..3,0..1] Of Integer;` `Array2D : Array[0..3,0..1] Of Integer = ((1,2),(3,4),(5,6),(7,8));`	`Array2D : Array[0..3,0..1] Of Real;`

Python	`array2D = []`
	`for row in range(4):`
	`    array2D.append([])`
	`    for column in range(2):`
	`      array2D[row].append(0)#creating a 4 x 2 list equivalent`
	`import numpy as np`
	`array2D = np.array([[1,2], [3,4], [5,6], [7,8]])`
	`array2D = np.empty([4,2],dtype=int)# creates a 4 x 2 empty array`
		`array2D = []`
		`for row in range(4):`
		`    array2D.append([])`
		`    for column in range(2):`
		`      array2D[row].append(0.0)`
		
		`import numpy as np`
		`array2D =`
		`np.empty([4,2],dtype=float)`

VB. NET	`Dim array2D(3, 1) As Integer` `Dim array2D = New Integer(3, 1) {{1, 2}, {3, 4}, {5, 6}, {7, 8}}`	`Dim array2D(3,1) As Double`

Table 2.1.2.10 Creating two-dimensional arrays of different array element data type

C#

The following creates a two-dimensional integer array of 4 rows and 2 columns

```
int[,] array2D = new int[4,2];
```

The following creates and initialises a two-dimensional integer array of 4 rows and 2 columns

```
int[,] array2D = new int[4,2] {{1,2},{3,4},{5,6},{7,8}};
```

If the array is being initialised, `new int[4,2]` can be omitted. Array indexing is zero-based.

Java

The following creates a two-dimensional integer array of 4 rows and 2 columns

```
int[][] array2D = new int[4][2];
```

The following creates and initialises a two-dimensional integer array of 4 rows and 2 columns

```
int[][] array2D = {{1,2},{3,4},{5,6},{7,8}};
```

Array indexing is zero-based.

Pascal/Delphi

The following creates a two-dimensional integer array of 4 rows and 2 columns

```
Array2D : Array[0..3,0..1] Of Integer;
```

The following creates and initialises a two-dimensional integer array of 4 rows and 2 columns

```
Array2D : Array[0..3, 0..1] Of Integer = ((1,2),(3,4),(5,6),(7,8));
```

Array indexing is more flexible in Pascal and Delphi. It may begin at any value, e.g. -1, 1. Array is a keyword in the Pascal and Delphi.

Python

The following creates an equivalent of a two-dimensional integer array of 4 rows and 2 columns by using lists within a list and initialises it with zeros

```
array2D = []
for row in range(4):
    array2D.append([])
    for column in range(2):
      array2D[row].append(0)
```

List indexing is zero-based.

The following creates an empty two-dimensional integer array of 4 rows and 2 columns by using the numpy library

```
import numpy as np
array2D = np.empty([4,2],dtype=int)
```

The following creates and initialises a two-dimensional integer array of 4 rows and 2 columns

```
array2D = np.array([[1,2], [3,4], [5,6], [7,8]])
```

VB.NET

The following creates a two-dimensional integer array of 4 rows and 2 columns

```
Dim array2D(3, 1) As Integer
```

Array indexing is zero-based. 3 and 1 are the upper bound index values.

The following creates and initialises a two-dimensional integer array of 4 rows and 2 columns

```
Dim array2D = New Integer(3, 1) {{1, 2}, {3, 4}, {5, 6}, {7, 8}}
```

Using two-dimensional arrays

Tables 2.1.2.11, 2.1.2.12 and 2.1.2.13 show the creation and use of two-dimensional arrays in C#, Java, Pascal, Delphi, Python 3.4 and VB.NET.

Language	Integer

C#	`using System;`
	`namespace TwoDimensionalArrays`
	`{`
	`    class Program`
	`    {`
	`        static void Main(string[] args)`
	`        {`
	`            int[,] array2D = new int[4, 2];`
	`            int[,] array2D1 = {{1, 2}, {3, 4}, {5, 6}, {7, 8}};`
	`            Console.WriteLine(array2D1[1,1]);`
	`            array2D[0,0] = 1;`
	`            Console.ReadLine();`
	`        }`
	`    }`
	`}`

Java	`public class TwoDArray {`
	`    public static void main(String[] args) {`
	`       float[][] array2D = new float[4][2];`
	`       int[][] array2D1 = {{1,2},{3,4},{5,6},{7,8}};`
	`       System.out.println(array2D1[1][1]);`
	`       array2D[0][0] = 1;`
	`       System.out.println(array2D[0][0]);`
	`    }`
	`}`

Table 2.1.2.11 Creating and using two-dimensional arrays

<table>
<tr><th>Language</th><th>Integer</th></tr>
<tr><td>Delphi</td><td><pre>Program TwoDimensionalArrays;
{$APPTYPE CONSOLE}
{$R *.res}
Uses
  System.SysUtils;
Var
  Array2D : Array[0..3,0..1] Of Integer;
  Array2D1 : Array[0..3,0..1] Of Integer = ((1,2),(3,4),(5,6),(7,8));
Begin
  Array2D[0,0] := 1;
  Writeln(Array2D[0,0]);
  Writeln(Array2D1[1,1]);
  Readln;
End.</pre></td></tr>
<tr><td>Pascal
(Lazarus)</td><td><pre>Program TwoDimensionalArrays;
Var
  Array2D : Array[0..3,0..1] Of Integer;
  Array2D1 : Array[0..3,0..1] Of Integer = ((1,2),(3,4),(5,6),(7,8));
Begin
  Array2D[0,0] := 1;
  Writeln(Array2D[0,0]);
  Writeln(Array2D1[1,1]);
  Readln;
End.</pre></td></tr>
<tr><td>Python
3.4
(Scipy)</td><td><pre>import numpy as np
array2D = np.array([[1,2], [3,4], [5,6], [7,8]])
for row in range(4):
    for column in range(2):
        print(array2D[row,column], end= '')
    print(end='\n')
array2D1 = np.empty([4,2],dtype=int)
array2D1[0,0] = 1
array2D1[0,1] = 2
array2D1[1,0] = 3
array2D1[1,1] = 4
array2D1[2,0] = 5
array2D1[2,1] = 6
array2D1[3,0] = 7
array2D1[3,1] = 8
for row in range(4):
    for column in range(2):
        print(array2D1[row,column], end= '')
    print(end='\n')</pre></td></tr>
</table>

Table 2.1.2.12 Creating and using two-dimensional arrays

Language	Integer

VB.NET	`Dim array2D(3, 1) As Integer`
	`Dim array2D1 = New Integer(3, 1) {{1, 2}, {3, 4}, {5, 6}, {7, 8}}`
	`Dim array2D2(3, 1) As Double`
	`array2D(0, 0) = 1`
	`array2D(0, 1) = 2`
	`array2D(1, 0) = 3`
	`array2D(1, 1) = 4`
	`array2D2(0, 0) = 1.5`
	`array2D2(0, 1) = 2.3`
	`array2D2(1, 0) = 3.6`
	`array2D2(1, 1) = 4.8`
	`Console.WriteLine(array2D(1, 0))`
	`Console.WriteLine(array2D1(1, 0))`
	`Console.WriteLine(array2D2(1, 0))`

Table 2.1.2.13 Creating and using two-dimensional arrays

Programming task

6 Write a program which creates a two-dimensional array `ArrayTwoD` and displays the values contained in the second row of this array. The array `ArrayTwoD` should be created with values arranged into rows and columns as follows

$$\texttt{ArrayTwoD} = \begin{bmatrix} 3,6,7 \\ 4,8,1 \\ 9,3,8 \end{bmatrix}$$

Iterating through the elements of a two-dimensional array

Iterating through the elements of an array is a common operation on arrays. Figure 2.1.2.26 shows the use of nested *For loops* to access each element of array `Array2D` starting with the first element `Array2D[0,0]`. The outer *For loop* uses the loop control variable, `i`. The inner *For loop* uses the loop control variable, `j`.

The two-dimensional array `Array2D` contains 3 x 3 = 9 elements with values as shown in Table 2.1.2.14.

```
For i ← 0 To 2
  For j ← 0 To 2
    Output Array2D[i,j]
  EndFor
EndFor
```

Figure 2.1.2.26 Pseudo-code that iterates through the elements of array Array2D

	0	1	2
0	12	45	6
1	9	23	65
2	2	18	33

Table 2.1.2.14 Array2D

The **trace table**, Table 2.1.2.15, shows the value of array `Array2D[i,j]` and the output for each value of `i` and `j`. A trace table is a table which shows the current values of variables used by the pseudo-code and its output whilst the pseudo-code is executed (traced) by hand. This execution by hand is called a **hand-trace**.

i	j	Array2D[i,j]	Output
0	0	12	12
0	1	45	45
0	2	6	6
1	0	9	9
1	1	23	23
1	2	65	65
2	0	2	2
2	1	18	18
2	2	33	33

Table 2.1.2.15 Trace table for pseudo-code

Table 2.1.2.16 shows the nested loop pseudo-code expressed in the programming languages C#, Java, Delphi/Pascal, Python and VB.NET.

Language	Integer

C#	`int[,] array2D = new int[3, 3] {{12,45,6},{9,23,65},{2,18,33}};`
	`int i, j;`
	`for (i = 0; i < 3; i++)`
	`{`
	`    for (j = 0; j < 3; j++)`
	`    {`
	`        Console.Write(array2D[i,j]);`
	`        Console.Write(" ");`
	`    }`
	`    Console.WriteLine();`
	`}`
	`Console.ReadLine();`

Java	`int [][] array2D = {{12,45,6},{9,23,65},{2,18,33}};`
	`int i, j;`
	`for (i = 0; i < 3; i++)`
	`{`
	`    for (j = 0; j < 3; j++)`
	`    {`
	`        System.out.print(array2D[i][j]);`
	`        System.out.print(' ');`
	`    }`
	`    System.out.println();`
	`}`

Delphi/ Pascal	`Var`
	`  i, j : Integer;`
	`  Array2D : Array [0..2, 0..2] Of Integer = ((12,45,6),(9,23,65),(2,18,33));`
	`.....`
	`For i := 0 To 2`
	`  Do`
	`    Begin`
	`      For j := 0 To 2`
	`        Do Write(Array2D[i, j], ' ');`
	`      Writeln;`
	`    End;`
	`Readln;`

Python	`import numpy as np`
	`array2D = np.array([[12,45,6], [9,23,65], [2,18,33]])`
	`for i in range(3):`
	`    for j in range(3):`
	`        print( array2D[row,column], end= ' ')`
	`    print(end='\n')`

VB.NET	`Dim array2D = New Integer(2, 2) {{12, 45, 6}, {9, 23, 65}, {2, 18, 33}}`
	`For i = 0 To 2`
	`    For j As Integer = 0 To 2`
	`        Console.Write(array2D(i, j))`
	`        Console.Write(" ")`
	`    Next`
	`    Console.WriteLine()`
	`Next`
	`Console.ReadLine()`

Table 2.1.2.16 Accessing the elements of a two-dimensional array by iteration with a nested For loop

Programming task

7 Write a program which iterates through `ArrayTwoD` and sums the values contained in this array. The array `ArrayTwoD` should be created with values arranged into rows and columns as follows

$$\texttt{ArrayTwoD} = \begin{bmatrix} 3,6,7 \\ 4,8,1 \\ 9,3,8 \end{bmatrix}$$

Programming tasks

8 Write a program which iterates through `ArrayTwoD` multiplying each value by 5. The result of each multiplication should replace the original value.
The array `ArrayTwoD` should be created with values arranged into rows and columns as follows

$$\texttt{ArrayTwoD} = \begin{bmatrix} 3,6,7 \\ 4,8,1 \\ 9,3,8 \end{bmatrix}$$

A particular black and white image contains a single simple convex shape, such as a circle, represented as a dark area on a light background. Such images are commonly represented in computers as two-dimensional arrays, where each element has the value 1 or 0. A dark area on a light background becomes a group of 1's surrounded by 0's. Figure 2.1.2.27 shows a two-dimensional array representation of a lower resolution image of a black circle on a white background.

```
0,0,0,0,0,0,0
0,0,0,1,0,0,0
0,0,1,1,1,0,0
0,1,1,1,1,1,0
0,0,1,1,1,0,0
0,0,0,1,0,0,0
0,0,0,0,0,0,0
```

Figure 2.1.2.27

9 Write a program with a two-dimensional array initialised with the values shown in Figure 2.1.2.27.
The program should display the shape of the dark region by displaying the points of the image which represent dark regions as 1's and the background as spaces.
Hint: Scan the image row-wise or column-wise.

10 Write a program with a two-dimensional array initialised with the values shown in Figure 2.1.2.27.
The program should display the shape of the dark region by displaying the points in the image on the boundary between the dark region and the surrounding white region as 1's and the background and interior points as spaces.
Hint: Scan the image row-wise or column-wise. For a given 1, if **any** of the surrounding points are 0's then that 1 represents a boundary point.

11 Write a program with a two-dimensional array initialised with the values shown in Figure 2.1.2.27.
The program should calculate the ratio of the area of the dark region to its perimeter. As a measure of the area, count the number of ones. A (rather inaccurate) measure of the perimeter can be obtained by counting the number of boundary points.

When to use a two-dimensional array?

When it is necessary to keep a large number of items in memory and reference all the items in a uniform manner.

When the structure of the data is two-dimensional.

N-dimensional arrays

If we add a third axis at right-angles to the two axes in Figure 2.1.2.16 we obtain a three dimensional storage grid, i.e. a three-dimensional array.

In Pascal, a three-dimensional array variable, `Array3D`, is created as follows

```
Array3D : Array[0..3,0..4,0..3] Of Integer;
```

We can store the pixel intensity of each pixel of an RGB image in a three-dimensional array as illustrated by the schematic in Figure 2.1.2.28.

Figure 2.1.2.29 shows an RGB image 'plane.png' loaded into a three-dimensional array `im1`. This array has 450 rows, 600 columns and in the third dimension, 3 colour planes, one for the red intensity, one for the blue intensity and one for the green intensity of a pixel.

We can continue to add dimensions but we will not be able to visualise the array geometrically because we live in a three-dimensional world. It is quite rare, however, to work on arrays with more than four dimensions.

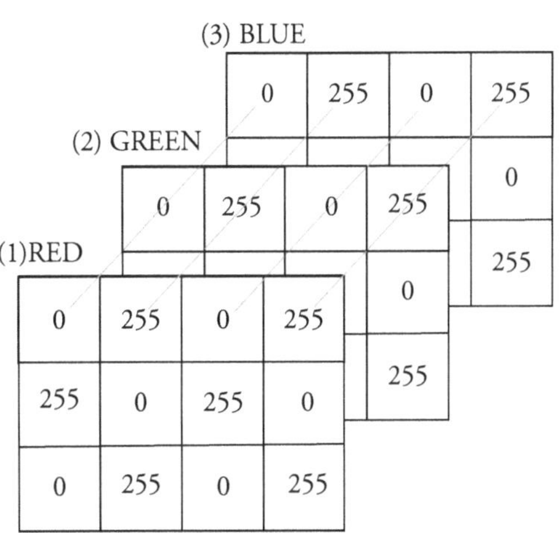

Figure 2.1.2.28 Colour planes of an RGB image, each plane is a two-dimensional array

A n-dimensional array is a multi-dimensional array of n dimensions where n could be, say 4.

All the elements of the n-dimensional array are of the same data type which is why it is an array. The index consists of a tuple of *n* integers in a zero-based indexed array, e.g. in C#, a four-dimensional array, `array4D`, could be declared as follows

```
int[,,,] array4D = new int[4,4,4,4];
```

The index part of the four-dimensional array declaration is the tuple of 4 integers 4, 4, 4, 4.

```
In [5]: im1 = imread('C:/Users/drbond/Plane.png')

In [6]: im1.shape
Out[6]: (450, 600, 3)

In [7]: imshow(im1)
Out[7]: <matplotlib.image.AxesImage at 0x4c64b70>
```

Figure 2.1.2.29 The RGB image 'plane.png' is loaded into a three dimensional array `im1` of dimensions 450 x 600 x 3

Questions

14 What is an n-dimensional array?

Key concept

Array:
An array is a container for a fixed number of values of a single data type. An array may be organized into several dimensions.

Length of an array:
The length of an array is established when the array is created. After creation, its length is fixed.

One-dimensional array:
A one-dimensional array is a data structure containing an ordered sequence of elements (e.g. numbers) that are indexed with a single integer.

Two-dimensional array:
A two-dimensional array is a data structure containing elements indexed by a pair of integers, that is, the row index and the column index.

n-dimensional array:
More generally, an n-dimensional array is a set of elements with the same data type that are indexed by a tuple of n integers.

Key concept

Element data type:
All elements in an array must have the same data type

Storage:
Elements in an array are stored internally in a contiguous block of memory.
For example, the elements in a vector of size 5 occupy 5 consecutive memory addresses. When the dimension of the array is two or more, there is more than one way of ordering of the elements in memory but this is hidden from user.

In this chapter you have covered:

- What is an array?
  - An array is a container for a fixed number of values of a single data type
  - An array may be organized into several dimensions.
- Square bracket notation
  - Square bracket notation [ ] is used to access values in an array.
- Array index
  - The name that we use inside the square brackets is called the **array index**, e.g. 3 in [3].
- Length of an array
  - The length of an array (static array) is established when the array is created. After creation, its length is fixed
  - All elements in an array must have the same data type
  - Elements in an array are stored internally in a contiguous block of memory. For example, the elements in an array of size 5 occupy 5 consecutive memory addresses.
- One-dimensional arrays
  - A one-dimensional array is a data structure containing an ordered sequence of elements (e.g. numbers) that are indexed with a single integer
  - It is a container for a fixed number of values of a single data type
  - A one-dimensional array is a useful way of representing a vector
  - The term vector refers to a one-dimensional array of values to which operations such as add, subtract, multiple, divide can be applied to the array as a whole in an element-wise way. The result is a vector with the same dimension.
- Two-dimensional arrays
  - A two-dimensional array is a data structure containing elements indexed by a pair of integers, that is, the row index and the column index.
  - The term matrix refers to a two-dimensional array of values to which operations such as add, subtract, multiple, divide can be applied to the array as a whole in an element-wise way. The result is a matrix with the same dimensions.
- Higher dimensional arrays: n-dimensional arrays
  - An n-dimensional array is a set of elements with the same data type that is indexed by a tuple of n integers (a tuple is a sequence of data that does not change. A sequence is simply an ordered collection of things, e.g. 0 1 2 . . .).

Key concept

Vector:

The term vector refers to a one-dimensional array of values to which operations such as add, subtract, multiple, divide can be applied to the array as a whole. The operations are applied in element-wise fashion so that the result is an array of the same size as the original array(s).

Matrix:

The term matrix refers to a two-dimensional array of values to which operations such as add, subtract, multiple, divide can be applied to the array as a whole. The operations are applied in element-wise fashion so that the result is an array of the same size as the original array(s).

2 Fundamentals of data structures

2.1 Data structures and abstract data types

Learning objectives:

- *Be able to read/write from/to a text file*
- *Be able to read/write data from/to a binary (non-text) file*

2.1.3 Fields, records and files

Files

A file is a data structure for storing data. The number of items of data stored in the file can vary in time and the amount of data is not limited in the way that other data structures are because files rely on secondary storage such as magnetic disk for their storage unlike arrays which rely on RAM storage.

By using secondary storage, files persist in time because secondary storage is non-volatile whereas RAM is volatile.

A file is assigned a name called its *filename* so that it can be referenced by name.

Files have structure which is either defined by the programmer at creation time, a file of some record type or is a commonly used structure such as text.

Key term

File:
A file is a data structure for storing data. The number of items of data stored in the file can vary in time and the amount of data is not limited in the way that other data structures are because files rely on secondary storage such as magnetic disk for their storage unlike arrays which rely on RAM storage.

Text files

Text files are files whose contents are sequences of characters organised on a line by line basis. For example, Shakespeare's Sonnet 116 shown in Table 2.1.3.1 consists of 14 lines as do almost all of Shakespeare's sonnets.

Key term

Text file:
Text files are files whose contents are sequences of characters organised on a line by line basis.

Let me not to the marriage of true minds
Admit impediments. Love is not love
Which alters when it alteration finds,
Or bends with the remover to remove:
O, no! it is an ever-fixed mark,
That looks on tempests and is never shaken;
It is the star to every wandering bark,
Whose worth's unknown, although his height be taken.
Love's not Time's fool, though rosy lips and cheeks
Within his bending sickle's compass come;
Love alters not with his brief hours and weeks,
But bears it out even to the edge of doom.
If this be error and upon me prov'd,
I never writ, nor no man ever lov'd.

Table 2.1.3.1 Shakespeare's Sonnet 116

Questions

1. What is a file?
2. What is a text file?

Text files may be opened and read in a text editor such as Microsoft's WordPad. Text editors expect files to be organised on a line-by-line basis and to consist of characters that can read when displayed with the exception of some specific control characters.

Each line ends with a special control character called the end of line or *newline* character (character code 10 or character codes 10 and 13).

The only control characters that text editors are able to handle are characters called *whitespace* characters, i.e. characters with ASCII or UTF-8 character codes 32 (space), 10 (line feed), 13 (carriage return) and 9 (tab). Other control characters have an effect on a text editor which is unpredictable and usually render the display unreadable.

Non-text files do not display well in text editors because they often contain control character codes which text editors are unable to handle because they are not control character codes 32, 10, 13 or 9.

Not only can text files be read by text editors but they may also be created and edited in a text editor.

We turn to computer programs when we wish to manipulate text files in ways that text editors do not support.

Reading from a text file

Table 2.1.3.2 shows a Python program which opens a text file with the filename 'sowpods.txt' for reading. The contents of this file is read one line at a time from the beginning of this file. Each line which is read is stored temporarily in the string variable `line`. The line of characters stored in this variable is displayed on the console by `print(line)`. Finally the file is closed.

The first thing that this Python program does is open the specified file in a particular mode, in this case, for reading.

```
f = open("sowpods.txt", "r")
for line in f:
    print(line)
f.close()
```

Table 2.1.3.2 Python program which opens a text file 'sowpods.txt' for reading and displaying

The call to `open("sowpods.txt", "r")` returns a file handle which is assigned to file handle variable `f`. `"r"` specifies that the mode is reading.

The contents of file `"sowpods.txt"` are now accessed through file handle `f`.

aa
aah
aahed
aahing
aahs
aal
aalii
aaliis
aals
aardvark
aardvarks

Table 2.1.3.3 The first few lines of the text file 'sowpods.txt'

Next, `for line in f` iterates through the file line-by-line. The file handle `f` is aware of the file structure, and is able to keep track of which line in the file is currently selected so that string variable `line` is able to receive the next line of the file.

The print statement `print(line)` outputs the line it currently stores followed by a newline character. A *newline* character is the line feed character (character code 10)

Unfortunately, this results in a blank line between lines appearing on the output because each line ends with a *newline* character as well.

```
>>>line = line.readline()
>>>line
'aa\n'
```

The solution is to delete the *newline* character ('\n') from the end of the string in variable `line` before `print(line)` is reached. Table 2.1.3.4 shows the revised Python program.

The action of strip() removes the *whitespace* at the end of the line, i.e. the *newline* character.

Summarising, reading from a text file takes the following form:

```
open the text file for reading
read the text file line-by-line
do something with each line
close the file
```

```
f = open("sowpods.txt", "r")
for line in f:
    line = line.strip()
    print(line)
f.close()
```

Table 2.1.3.4 Python program which opens a text file 'sowpods.txt' for reading and displaying

We can also read from the file in the following ways:

`line = f.readline()` will read one line of the file into variable `line`.

`all_lines = f.read()` will read the entire contents of a file into variable `all_lines`.

Table 2.1.3.5 and Table 2.1.3.6 show how to read from a text file in Pascal/Delphi, Java, VB.NET and C#.

Java requires try catch around the code because the methods which are called under the hood are designed to throw exceptions which have to be trapped (or caught).

Two ways of reading a file are shown for Java, VB.NET and C#.

Pascal/Delphi

```
Program ReadingATextFile;
Var
  f : TextFile;
  Line : String;
Begin
  AssignFile(f, 'Sonnet116.txt');
  Reset(f);
  While Not Eof(f)
    Do
      Begin
        Readln(f, Line); {Read line of text from file into string variable Line}
        Writeln(Line); {Write line of text in string variable Line to output}
      End;
  CloseFile(f);
  Readln;
End.
```

Java

```
import java.io.FileReader;
import java.io.BufferedReader;
public class ReadATextFile {
    public static void main(String[] args) {
       try{
                FileReader f = new FileReader("Sonnet116.txt");
                BufferedReader textReader = new BufferedReader(f);
                String line;
                while (( line = textReader.readLine()) != null ) {
                     System.out.println(line);
                }
            }
        catch (IOException e)
        {
             System.out.println(e);
        }

        FileReader inputStream = null;

        try {
            inputStream = new FileReader("Sonnet116.txt");
            int ch;
            System.in.read();
            while ((ch = inputStream.read()) != -1) {
                System.out.print((char)ch);
            }
        }
               catch (IOException e)
        {
             System.out.println(e);
        }
    }
}
```

Table 2.1.3.5 Reading from a text file "Sonnet116.txt" in Pascal/Delphi and Java

VB.NET

```
Imports System
Imports System.IO
Module Module1
    Sub Main()
      ' Reads the entire file at once
        ' Open the file using a stream reader.
        Using f As New StreamReader("Sonnet116.txt")
            Dim line As String
            ' Read the stream string variable line and write the string to the console.
            line = f.ReadToEnd() ' Reads to end of file
            Console.WriteLine(line)
        End Using ' Dispose of all the resources
        Console.ReadLine()
      ' Reads the file line-by-line.
        ' Open the file using a stream reader.
        Using f As New StreamReader("Sonnet116.txt")
            Dim line As String
            line = f.ReadLine()
            While Not (line Is Nothing)
                Console.WriteLine(line)
                line = f.ReadLine()
            End While
        End Using
        Console.ReadLine()
    End Sub
End Module
```

C#

```
using System;
namespace ReadingATextFile
{
    class Program
    {
        static void Main(string[] args)
        {
         // Read the whole file into a string array lines.
            string[] lines = System.IO.File.ReadAllLines("Sonnet116.txt");
            foreach (string line in lines)
            {
                Console.WriteLine(line);
            }
            Console.ReadLine();
            string nextLine;
            // Read the file and display it line by line.
            System.IO.StreamReader f = new System.IO.StreamReader("Sonnet116.txt");
            while ((nextLine = f.ReadLine()) != null)
            {
                System.Console.WriteLine(nextLine);
            }

            f.Close();
            Console.ReadLine();
        }
    }
}
```

Table 2.1.3.6 Reading from a text file "Sonnet116.txt" in VB.NET and C#

Writing to a text file

In Python, if we want to write to a file with filename `"studentresults.txt"`, we open this file in write mode (`"w"`) with

```
open("studentresults.txt", "w")
```

This will create a new file `"studentresults.txt"` or overwrite this file if it exists already.

The program in *Table 2.1.3.7* collects a student name and the student's exam score typed at the keyboard and then using the file handle `f` to the opened file, writes student name then a comma then exam score on the same line to the opened text file

```
f.write(student_name + "," + exam_mark + "\n")
```

`"\n" is the` special control character called the end of line or *newline* character.

This ensures that the file handle `f` is ready to write the next student name, comma, exam score combination on the next line.

Entering the student name "quit" causes the program to exit the *while loop* but not before printing "Quitting...". Finally the file is closed.

```
f = open("studentresults.txt", "w")
while True:
    student_name = input("Name: ")
    if student_name == "quit":
        print("Quitting...")
        break
    exam_mark = input("Exam score for " + student_name + " : ")
    f.write(student_name + "," + exam_mark + "\n")
f.close()
```

Table 2.1.3.7 Python program which creates and writes lines of text to a text file 'studentresults.txt'

Table 2.1.3.8 shows the contents of `"studentresults.txt"` produced by executing the program in *Table 2.1.3.7*.

Bond K, 95
Cheadle P, 85
Gunawardena P, 90
Khan M, 88
De Silva S, 75
Smith E,55
Teng P, 85
Tipp S,30

Table 2.1.3.8 Contents of "studentresults.txt" created by program in Table 2.1.3.7

Appending to a text file

Changing the file mode to `"a"` allows new lines to be appended to the end of `"studentresults.txt"` if it exists or to an empty newly created `"studentresults.txt"` - *Table 2.1.3.9*.

```
f = open("studentresults.txt", "a")
while True:
    student_name = input("Name: ")
    if student_name == "quit":
        print("Quitting...")
        break
    exam_mark = input("Exam score for " + student_name + " : ")
    f.write(student_name + "," + exam_mark + "\n")
f.close()
```

Table 2.1.3.9 Python program which appends lines of text to an existing text file 'studentresults.txt'

Table 2.1.3.10 shows two ways of writing to text files in Pascal/Delphi, Java and one way in VB.NET.

Pascal:

1. Line-by-line:

```
For Line in Lines
  Do Writeln(f, Line);
```

2. Writing all the lines in one go

```
Lines.LoadFromFile('Sonnet116.txt');
Lines.SaveToFile('AnotherNewFile.txt');
```

Java:

1. Using java.io.PrintWriter
2. Using java.io.PrintWriter and java.io.File

VB.NET: Using StreamWriter and WriteLine.

Table 2.1.3.11 shows one way of writing to text files in C#.

Pascal/Delphi

```
Program WriteToATextFile;
Uses Classes;
Var
  f : TextFile;
  Lines : TStringList;
  Line : String;
Begin
  AssignFile(f, 'NewFile.txt');
  Rewrite(f);
  Lines := TStringList.Create;
  Lines.Add('Let me not to the marriage of true minds');
  Lines.Add('Admit impediments. Love is not love');
  Writeln(Lines.text);
  For Line in Lines
    Do Writeln(f, Line); {Write a line of text to text file}
  CloseFile(f);
  Lines.Clear;
  Lines.LoadFromFile('Sonnet116.txt');
  Lines.SaveToFile('AnotherNewFile.txt');
  Readln;
End.
```

Java

```
import java.io.IOException;
import java.io.PrintWriter;
import java.io.File;
public class WriteToATextFile {
  public static void main(String[] args) {
    try{
        PrintWriter printLine = new PrintWriter("Z:/NewFile.txt");
        String line = "Let me not to the marriage of true minds";
        printLine.println(line); // Write a line of text to the file
        printLine.close(); // Close the file
        File f = new File("Z:/AnotherNewFile.txt");
        if (!f.exists()) {
          if (f.createNewFile()) {
            PrintWriter newPrintLine = new PrintWriter(f);
            newPrintLine.println("Let me not to the marriage of true minds");
            newPrintLine.println("Admit impediments. Love is not love");
            newPrintLine.close();
          }
        }
    }
    catch (IOException e){
        System.out.println(e);
    }
  }
}
```

VB.NET

```
Imports System
Imports System.IO
Imports System.Text
Module Module1
    Sub Main()
        Try
            Dim w As StreamWriter = New StreamWriter("NewFile.txt")
            w.WriteLine("Let me not to the marriage of true minds")
            w.WriteLine("Admit impediments. Love is not love")
            w.Close()
        Catch e As Exception
            Console.WriteLine("The process failed: {0}", e.ToString())
        End Try
    End Sub
End Module
```

Table 2.1.3.10 Writing to a text file in Pascal/Delphi, Java and VB.NET

C#

```
using System;
using System.Text;
using System.IO;
namespace WriteToATextFile
{
    class Program
    {
        public static void Main()
        {
            try
            {
                using (StreamWriter w = new StreamWriter("NewFile.txt"))
                {
                    w.WriteLine("Let me not to the marriage of true minds");
                    w.WriteLine("Admit impediments. Love is not love");
                }
            }
            catch (Exception e)
            {
                Console.WriteLine("The process failed: {0}", e.ToString());
            }
        }
    }
}
```

Table 2.1.3.11 Writing to a text file in C#

Programming tasks

1. Write a program which makes a copy of a text file. Your program should prompt the user to enter the names of the input and output text files.

2. Write a program that reads a text file and displays it with the corresponding line number at the beginning of each line. Start line numbering from 1.

3. The text file "Dict5LetterWords.txt" (download from www.educational-computing.co.uk/CS/Textfiles.html) contains 5 letter words. Write a program which finds all 5 letter words in this file which contain the substring 'oe'.

4. The text file "sowpods.txt" is an official Scrabble dictionary (download from www.educational-computing.co.uk/CS/Textfiles.html). Write a program to find all words containing a particular substring in the text file "sowpods.txt". The program should prompt the user to enter a substring to search for.

5. Write a program to create a Geography quiz which tests a user's knowledge of country capitals.
   Use the text file "countriescapitals.txt" (download from www.educational-computing.co.uk/CS/Textfiles.html) which is a comma separated file of countries and their capitals.
   The program should display the name of a country chosen at random from this text file and prompt the user to supply the name of the capital of this country. The program should then check the user's answer. If the user's answer is correct the program should respond "Well done, you got it right!". If the user's answer is incorrect the program should respond "Incorrect answer, the correct answer is ???????" where the correct answer is substituted for the string "???????" when the program executes.

Binary files

A binary file is considered to be any file that is not a text file.

Binary files can only be processed by applications that know about the file's structure.

For example, the Pascal program shown in Table 2.1.3.12 creates a file with the structure *file of integer*.

If we want to write to a file with filename 'FileOfIntegers.int', we open this file in write mode with `Rewrite(f);`

This will create a new file 'FileOfIntegers.int' or overwrite this file if it exists already.

The file handle, f, to the file 'FileOfIntegers.int' is created with

```
AssignFile(f, 'FileOfIntegers.int');
```

Each integer is written to this file by the statement

```
Write(f, NextInteger);
```

```
Program FileOfIntegers;
Var
  f : File Of Integer;
  n, i : Integer;
  NextInteger : Integer;
Begin
  AssignFile(f, 'FileOfIntegers.int');
  Rewrite(f);
  Write('How many integers? ');
  Readln(n);
  For i := 1 To n
    Do
      Begin
        Write('Input next integer: ');
        Readln(NextInteger);
        Write(f, NextInteger);
      End;
  CloseFile(f);
  Writeln('File of ', n, ' integers created');
End.
```

Table 2.1.3.12 Pascal program which creates a file with the structure file of integer

The file 'FileOfIntegers.int' is closed with `CloseFile(f);`

The program in Table 2.1.3.12 creates a *file of integer* containing n integers.

If we want to read the contents of the file with filename 'FileOfIntegers.int' we open this file in reading mode as shown in Table 2.1.3.13 with

```
Reset(f);
```

The file handle, f, to the file 'FileOfIntegers.int' is created as before with

```
AssignFile(f, 'FileOfIntegers.int');
```

Each integer is read from this file by the statement

```
Read(f, NextInteger);
```

The end of file is checked for by `Eof(f)` which returns **True** when the end of file is reached otherwise it returns False.

We can create a file with a different structure by changing `File Of Integer` to a `File Of` *a different type*, e.g. `File Of Real` or `File Of Byte` or `File Of SomeArrayType` or `File of SomeRecordType`.

```
Program ReadingFileOfIntegers;
Var
  f : File Of Integer;
  NextInteger : Integer;
Begin
  AssignFile(f, 'FileOfIntegers.int');
  Reset(f);
  While Not Eof(f)
    Do
      Begin
        Read(f, NextInteger);
        Writeln(NextInteger);
      End;
  CloseFile(f);
  Writeln('End of file reached, press return to close
DOS window');
  Readln;
End.
```

Table 2.1.3.13 Pascal program which reads a file with the structure file of integer

`File of Byte` is interesting because every file consists of bytes.

Viewing the structure of a file as other than `File Of Byte` applies an **abstraction** to the file contents. This abstraction occurs when the file is created.

The file type declaration sets the unit of data that will be written to a file of this type, e.g. for a file type `File Of`

Integer, the unit of data is *integer* which typically is four bytes.

However, we can open any file with a handle which has been declared as File Of Byte and read the contents of the file byte by byte.
This is very useful when the file's data structure is unknown or when we might want to manipulate its contents, e.g. in an application of steganography. Steganography is the science of hiding messages in pictures and other media.

The program in Table 2.1.3.14 is written to treat any file as a File Of Byte, in particular bitmap files.

```
Program ReadABitMap;
Type
  BitMapFilePipeType = File Of Byte;
Var
  BitMapFilePipe: BitMapFilePipeType;
  Filename: String;
  NextByte : Byte;
Begin
  Write('Input name of file to be opened for reading: ');
  Readln(Filename);
  Assign(BitMapFilePipe, Filename);
  Reset(BitMapFilePipe);
  While Not Eof(BitMapFilePipe)
    Do
      Begin
        Read(BitMapFilePipe, NextByte);
        If NextByte In [32..126]
          Then Write(NextByte : 1, ' ');
          {Note the single space character}
      End;
End.
```

Table 2.1.3.14 Pascal program which intended for reading a bitmap files, byte by byte (it can read any file type)

Table 2.1.3.15 shows a program for hiding a message in the pixel area of a bitmap file by replacing a pixel byte with a message byte.

```
Program HideMessageInABitMap;
Type
  BitMapFilePipeType = File Of Byte;
Var
  BitMapFilePipe, BitMapFileCodedPipe : BitMapFilePipeType;
  Filename, Message : String;
  NextByte : Byte;
  n, i : Integer;
Begin
  Write('Input name of file to be opened for reading: ');
  Readln(Filename);
  Assign(BitMapFilePipe, Filename);
  Reset(BitMapFilePipe);
  Assign(BitMapFileCodedPipe, 'c' + Filename);
  Rewrite(BitMapFileCodedPipe);
  Write('Input message up to 30 characters in length: ');
  Readln(Message);
  If Length(Message) < 30
    Then
      For i := 1 To 30 - Length(Message)
        Do Message := Message + ' ';
  {Pads message with spaces so that it is always 30 characters in length}
  n := 0;
  i := 0;
  While Not Eof(BitMapFilePipe)
    Do
      Begin
        Read(BitMapFilePipe, NextByte);
        If (n >= 1078) And (n <= 1078 + Length(Message)-1)
          Then
            Begin
              i := i + 1;
              NextByte := Ord(Message[i]);
            End;
        n := n + 1;
        Write(BitMapFileCodedPipe, NextByte);
      End;
End.
```

Table 2.1.3.15 Pascal steganography program which reads a bitmap file and a 30 character message which hides in the bitmap

Table 2.1.3.16 shows samples of code in C#, VB.NET, Java and Python for writing data to and reading data from non-text files, i.e. binary files.

C#

```
using (BinaryWriter writer = new BinaryWriter(File.Open(fileName, FileMode.Create)))
{
    writer.Write(3.142F);
    writer.Write("Hello World!");
    writer.Write(10);
    writer.Write(true);
}
If (File.Exists(fileName)) Then
{
    using (BinaryReader reader = new BinaryReader(File.Open(fileName, FileMode.Open)))
    {
        pi = reader.ReadSingle();
        greeting = reader.ReadString();
        score = reader.ReadInt32();
        flag = reader.ReadBoolean();
    }
}
```

VB.NET

```
Using writer As BinaryWriter = New BinaryWriter(File.Open(fileName, FileMode.Create))
    writer.Write(3.142F)
    writer.Write("Hello World!")
    writer.Write(10)
    writer.Write(true);
End Using
If (File.Exists(fileName)) Then
    Using reader As BinaryReader = New BinaryReader(File.Open(fileName, FileMode.Open))
        pi = reader.ReadSingle()
        greeting = reader.ReadString()
        score = reader.ReadInt32()
        flag = reader.ReadBoolean()
    End Using
End If
```

Java

```
import java.io.IOException;
import java.nio.file.Files;
import java.nio.file.Path;
import java.nio.file.Paths;
public class WritingToABinaryFile {
    public static void main(String[] args) throws IOException {
        WritingToABinaryFile binary = new WritingToABinaryFile();
        byte[] bytes = binary.readFromBinaryFile("C:/Javacode/SmallJPG.jpg");
        binary.writeToBinaryFile(bytes,"C:/Javacode/SmallJPG2.jpg");
    }
    byte[] readFromBinaryFile(String aFileName) throws IOException {
        Path path = Paths.get(aFileName);
       return Files.readAllBytes(path);
    }

  void writeToBinaryFile(byte[] aBytes, String aFileName) throws IOException {
    Path path = Paths.get(aFileName);
    Files.write(path, aBytes); //creates, overwrites
  }
}
```

Python

```
from struct import pack
with open("c:/Javacode/test.bin", "wb") as file:
  file.write(pack("IIIII", *bytearray([120, 3, 255, 0, 100])))
with open("c:/Javacode/foo.bin", "rb") as f:
    byte = f.read(1)
    while byte:
        byte = f.read(1)
        print(byte)
```

Table 2.1.3.16 Writing data to and reading data from a binary file in C#, VB.NET, Java and Python

Questions

3 What is a binary file?

Programming tasks

6 Write a program which creates a file of decimal numbers (e.g decimal number 12.67) with filename "FileOfDecimals.int". Your program should prompt the user to enter n, the number of decimal numbers to store in the file. The program should then collect n decimal numbers from the user.

7 Investigate steganography with the programs in *Table 2.1.3.14* and *Table 2.1.3.15* recreated in a programming language with which you are familiar.

In this chapter you have covered:

- Reading/writing from/to a text file
- Reading/writing data from/to a binary (non-text) file

3 Software development

3.1 Aspects of software development

Learning objectives:

- *Be aware that before a problem can be solved, it must be defined, the requirements of the system that solves the problem must be established and a data model created*
- *Be aware that before constructing a solution, the solution must be designed, for example planning data structures for the data model, designing algorithms, designing an appropriate modular structure for the solution and designing the human user interface*
- *Be aware that the models and algorithms need to be implemented in the form of data structures and code (instructions) that a computer can understand*
- *Be aware that the implementation must be tested for the presence of errors, using selected test data covering normal (typical), boundary and erroneous data*
- *Know the criteria for evaluating a computer system.*

3.1.1 Analysis

Introduction to analysis

You have been tasked to create a computer-based system to solve a problem. The process will involve designing and coding a solution which solves the problem. You have to start somewhere so you set about trying to find out more about the problem. This stage of problem solving is known as **problem analysis**. Its objective is to answer the question:

Exactly what must the system do to solve the problem?

This is a different question from the question that asks "how should what the system does be done?". How it must be done is answered when the system is designed and coded in a programming language. However, prototyping a design and program solution will help to build up an understanding of the problem being solved as well as aiding the process of establishing the requirements of the system that solves the problem.

For example, analysing what a system is expected to do that implements a simple computer-based calculator is carried out before a full solution is designed, written in program code, tested and evaluated. Although aspects of the calculator system may be prototyped to aid the analysis process.
Perhaps when analysis is carried out it is established that the simple calculator is required to do the following:

1. work with numbers with a fractional part, e.g. 5.6.
2. perform the following arithmetic operations on these numbers:
    - i. add
    - ii. subtract
    - iii. multiply
    - iv. divide (real division)
    - v. square
    - vi. cube
    - vii. square root

and more.....
Note that this list of things does not in any way describe how these things are to be done:

there are no references to

- any particular programming language
- data structures to use
- algorithms expressed in program code.

This is because the focus of analysis is on reporting what the system that solves the problem is expected to do, e.g. have large buttons, not on how it should be done, e.g. using Java and the Swing GUI widget toolkit to solve the problem.

Problem definition

The requirement for a simple computer-based calculator is in response to some need which we call the problem to be solved. Problems and their solutions vary in nature, scope and difficulty.

For example, consider the following problem to be solved.

Problem definition:

Computer systems that play the Chinese game of Go struggle to beat even novice human players of the game.

Analysis of the game will tell you why:

The average 150-move game contains more possible game configurations - 10^{170} - than there are atoms in the Universe.

Game configurations are states of the board when the game is played.

However, a computer system using an Artificial Intelligence (AI) technique called Deep Learning has now beaten the 2016 European champion.

Defining the problem to be solved helps

- analysts, designers and coders to understand the problem that has to be solved
- set the scope for what follows.

Did you know?

Google masters Go:
A computer has beaten a human professional for the first time at Go - an ancient board game that has long been viewed as one of the greatest challenges for Artificial Intelligence (reported January 2016).
See www.nature.com/polopoly_fs/1.19234!/menu/main/topColumns/topLeftColumn/pdf/529445a.pdf.

The challenge is in designing a computer-based system which will solve the problem defined in the problem definition. In the case of the Chinese game of Go, the problem definition points to a need for a solution which is an improvement on the current systems that play Go.

Once the problem has been defined the process of establishing the requirements of the system that solves the problem can begin.

Requirements of the system

Requirements need to be prescriptive and unambiguous. A requirement that simply specifies "better than the current systems" is not very helpful. We need something measurable so that designers and coders have something concrete to aim for. A better requirement is "a computer-based system that is capable of beating the current World champion at the Chinese game of Go".

Simple example

A problem definition for a computer-based simple calculator could be:

I teach maths to partially-sighted students and I have been unable to find a calculator which fits the needs of my students. In particular with regard to layout, size, colour of buttons, and font sizes of what is displayed on buttons and in the accumulator.

If this definition does not convey the problem with sufficient clarity then it needs to be revised until it is does.

Most of the requirements for a system that solves this problem are shown in *Table 3.3.1.1*.

1. The calculator should work with real numbers (in Computing this means numbers with a fractional part).
2. The calculator should perform the following arithmetic operations on real number operands:
   (i) add (ii) subtract (iii) multiply (iv) divide (real division) (v) square (vi) cube (vii) square root
3. The calculator should have
   i. an accumulator
   ii. a memory
4. The calculator should perform the following operations
   i. clear the accumulator (zero the contents of the accumulator)
   ii. clear the memory (zero the contents of memory)
   iii. store the result of every arithmetic operation in the accumulator
   iv. recall the contents of memory to the accumulator (accumulator contents overwritten with contents of memory
   v. add the contents of the accumulator to the current contents of memory, storing the result in the memory
5. The calculator should display the contents of the accumulator continuously
6. The calculator should display the contents of the memory continuously
7. The calculator should prompt the program user to enter an operator or command
8. An operator/command is one of the following characters:
   i. '+' Add
   ii. '-' Subtract
   iii. '*' Multiply
   iv. '/' Divide (real division)
   v. 'S' Square
   vi. '*' Multiply
   vii. '/' Divide (real division)
   viii. 'C' Cube
   ix. 'R' Square root
   x. 'A' Clear accumulator
   xi. 'Z' Clear memory
   xii. 'M' Add to memory
   xiii. 'F' Recall memory
9. The list of operators/commands should be displayed continuously
10. The calculator should collect the user's choice of operator/command
11. The calculator should determine whether the operation is a zero operand, single operand, double operand operation
12. The calculator should execute a zero operand operation
13. The calculator should prompt the user to enter
    i. one operand if the operation is a single operand operation
    ii. two operands if the operation is a double operand operation
14. The calculator should collect the appropriate number of operands for a single operand/double operand operation
15. Users may enter operands as real or integer but an integer will be converted to real before being stored
16. The calculator should execute the single operand/double operand operation storing the result in the accumulator
17. The calculator should initialise the accumulator to zero when it starts up
18. The calculator should initialise the memory to zero when it starts up
19. The calculator should initialise the operator to the space character when it starts up

Table 3.1.1 Requirements for a computer-based simple calculator

Key term

Data model:
Data models are abstractions of the real world which are produced by omitting unnecessary details of the real world scenario. The focus of data modelling is on identifying the fundamental or base elements, their structure and the relationships with each other. The base elements are the names of real-world things. The real-world base elements may be structured out of sub-elements, e.g. a car has a make, model, body colour and registration number. A car registration number is a string of characters.

Key term

Structure of base elements in a data model:
This structure can be

- sequences: things before and after each other, either unordered or ordered on some property
- tables: things arranged in rows of columns
- arrays: things accessed by indices.

Question

1. Do you think that the list of specific requirements for the computer-based simple calculator will solve the problem specified in the problem definition? If not, in what way do they not address the problem. How could they be extended to satisfy the problem definition?

Data model

Figure 3.1.1 shows some car parks and their parking bays. Individual parking bays are similar in size but differ in how they are positioned in relation to their immediate neighbours. For example, in *Figure 3.1.1(a)* the bays are arranged in a rectangular grid whilst in *Figure 3.1.1(b)* opposite bays are placed at an angle to each other in a herringbone pattern.

Figure 3.1.1(a) Car park with bays arranged in a rectangular grid

Suppose car parking has become a problem for staff at your school or college and one proposal to solve this problem is to allocate specific parking bays to individual staff and to employ a computer-based system to record this allocation.

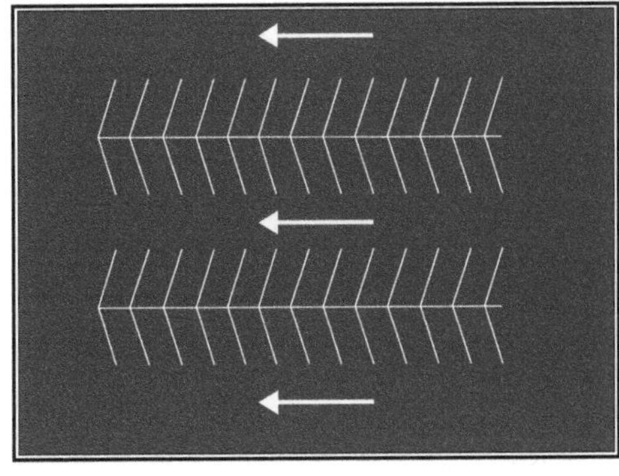

Figure 3.1.1(b) Car park with bays arranged in a herringbone pattern

For the purposes of exploring how this might be done, it is useful to model the data that will need to be recorded so that a request for information such as "who has been allocated Bay 6?" can be answered.

This aspect of analysis is known as **data modelling**, its output is a **data model**. Data models are abstractions of the real world which are produced by omitting unnecessary details of the real world scenario.

The focus of data modelling is on identifying the fundamental or base elements, their structure and the relationships with each other.

Base elements

The base elements are the names of things in the real world that are relevant to solving the problem, e.g.

- a car park
- a parking bay
- the number that labels a parking bay

- a car allocated to a particular parking bay
- a car's registration mark (registration plate number)
- the name of the owner of the car
- a row of parking bays
- the number of parking bays in a row
- the number of rows

The angle of a parking bay in relation to its immediate neighbours is irrelevant to the problem being solved so this information is omitted from the model. Are the dimensions of a parking bay relevant? It is pertinent to ask and the role of the analyst is to obtain an answer to this question, e.g. staff may have big cars or require disabled access. For the moment, let's assume that it isn't. Analysis will seek answers to many questions when deciding what should be included and what should be excluded from the data model.

Structure

A car that parks in a bay has a make, model, body colour, engine size, registration mark, etc. Of these, only the registration mark (car/vehicle plate number) would appear to be relevant to solving the problem. A registration

Figure 3.1.3 Modelling car park as a table

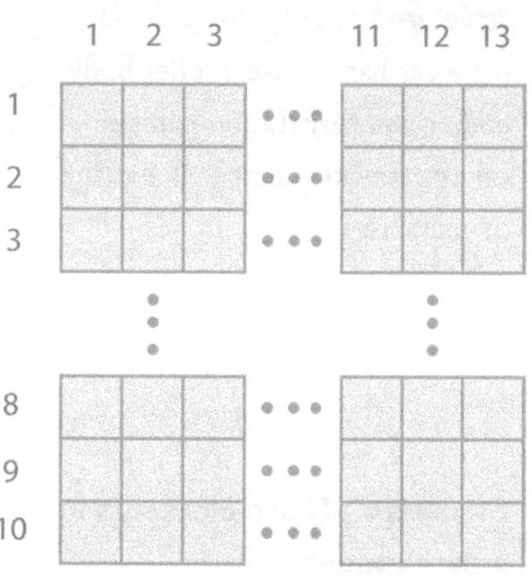

Figure 3.1.4 Modelling car park as a two-dimensional array

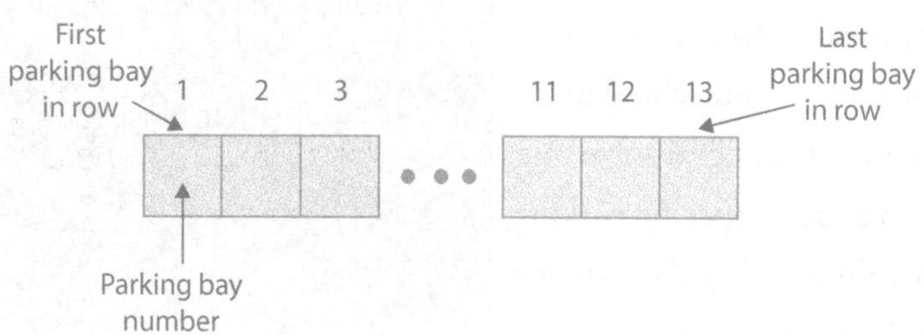

Figure 3.1.2 Modelling a row of the car park by a one-dimensional array

mark has structure: it is a sequence of characters, e.g. OY08 BYO, collectively known as a string (length 8 characters including the space character).

The owner of the car has a name which is also a string up to 25 characters in length.

The number that labels a parking bay is a positive integer greater than zero. The first bay is labelled one, the second two, and so on consecutively.

A row of the car park could be modelled as a one-dimensional array with each cell of this array storing the parking bay number. An array is a structure in which access to the things it stores is by an index. For example, in *Figure 3.1.2* which shows the modelling of a row of parking bays, the first bay in the row has index 1, the second index 2 and so on.

The car park itself could be modelled as a table of rows with columns (*Figure 3.1.3*) which itself could be modelled as a two-dimensional array (*Figure 3.1.4*).

The table is a model of the car park arrived at by ignoring certain physical details such as the angle of parking bays and the proximity of bays to each other. The model uses the fact that the bays are arranged physically in rows and numbered in sequence.

Be careful not to interpret the structures used above in a programming language data type sense. A program data type is a concept to do with representing and implementing problem information in a particular programming language.

When we talk about, for example, the fifth row in our data model of the car park, and the first bay in this row we are using indices as they would be used in the real world. In the car park itself, bays in this row are numbered 53, 54, 55, and so on whilst bays in the first row are numbered 1, 2, 3, etc.

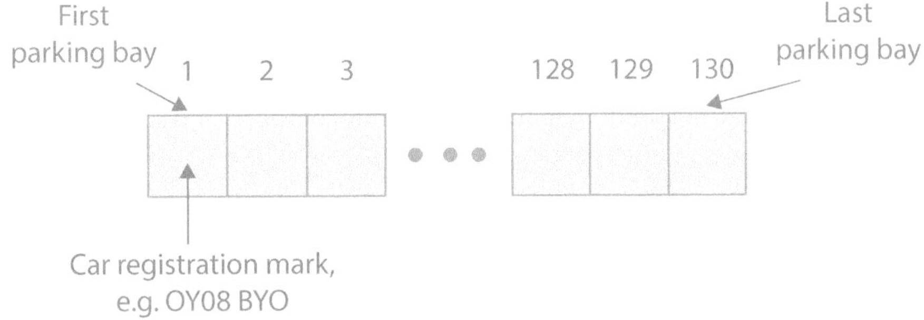

Figure 3.1.5 Data model for associating a parking bay with a particular car

The data model needs to capture information on the range of numbers, the length of strings for car registration mark and car owner name, the number of bays per row and the number of rows because this information will be needed when designing, programming and testing a solution.

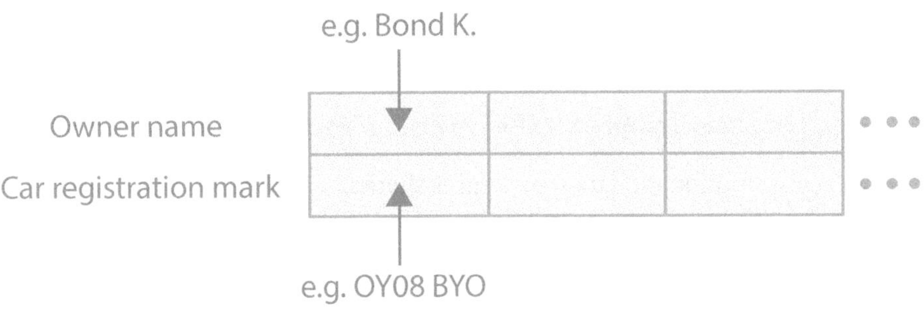

Figure 3.1.6 Data model for associating a car owner with a particular car

Relationship

Clearly a relationship exists between a parking bay and the car allocated to the parking bay. This association could be modelled as a one-dimensional array as shown in *Figure 3.1.5*.

A relationship also exists between car owner (name) and the car (registration mark) that they own. This could be modelled as a table as shown in *Figure 3.1.6*.

Question

A school production of a play is put on once a year in the school hall. The production is scheduled to run for three nights with one performance per night. The seats for the audience are arranged in 40 rows facing the stage in two blocks each 25 seats wide with a central aisle between the blocks. The seats are numbered by row number (1 to 40) and position in row (1 to 50). The seats are available for sale for each performance all at a single price. The name of the person purchasing a seat or seats for a particular performance is recorded. Create a data model for this scenario.

3.1.2 Design

Design answers the question

How should the solution to the problem be constructed?

It involves planning data structures for the data model, designing algorithms, designing an appropriate modular structure for the solution and designing the human computer interface.

Planning data structures

For example, a data type `TCarPark` to represent the car park data model could be designed as follows

```
TCarPark[1] = Array[1..10,1..13] Of TCarBayNumber
```

where data type `TCarBayNumber` is designed to be a subrange

```
TCarBayNumber = 1..130
```

The data model for the relationship between an allocated parking bay and the car allocated to the parking bay could be represented by the following programming language data type

```
TCarParkingBayNoToRegistrationMark = Array[1..130] Of TRegistrationMark
```

The car registration mark data type is an 8 character string, `TRegistrationMark`, designed as follows

```
TRegistrationMark = String[8]
```

The owner name data type is a 25 character string, `TOwnerName`, designed as follows

```
TOwnerName = String[25]
```

The data model for the relationship between between car owner and the car that they own could be represented by the following programming language data types

```
TRegistrationMarkArray = Array[1..130] Of TRegistrationMark
TOwnerNameArray = Array[1..130] Of TOwnerName
```

The arrays based on these data types will be populated with data which will need to be stored permanently. This can be done by saving each array in a file. The programming language file data types for these files are as follows

```
TCarParkingBayNoToRegistrationMarkFile = File of TCarParkingBayNoToRegistrationMark
TRegistrationMarkArrayFile = File Of TRegistrationMarkArray
TOwnerNameArrayFile = File Of TOwnerNameArray
```

If the `TCarPark` array is used then its data can be reconstructed from the `TCarParkingBayNoToRegistrationMark` array.

Designing algorithms

The arrays of data type `TCarParkingBayNoToRegistrationMark`, `TRegistrationMarkArray` and `TOwnerNameArray` will need to be searched in response to the following queries:

- What is the name of the owner of the car with registration mark, e.g. OY08 BYO?
- What is the registration mark of the car allocated to car park bay *n* where *n* is in the range 1..130?
- What is the registration mark of the car belonging to owner with name, e.g. Ahmed M.?

In each case a linear search algorithm could be used (*Figure 3.1.7*).

---

1 Array indexing starts from 0 normally but using 1 preserves correspondence with the problem scenario

Linear Search Algorithm

```
j ← 0
Found ← False
Repeat
  j ← j + 1
  If Vector[j] = ElementSought
    Then Found ← True
Until Found Or j = NoOfElementsInVector
If Found
  Then Result ← j
  Else Result ← 0
```

Figure 3.1.7 Linear search algorithm

Algorithm to display car park in tabular form

```
For i ← 0 To 9
  For j ← 1 To 13
    Write(i * 13 + j, '    ')
  EndFor
  WriteLn
  For j ← 1 To 13
    RegMark ←CarParkingbayNoToRegistrationMark [ i * 13 + j]
    Write(RegMark, ' ')
  EndFor
  WriteLn
EndFor
```

Figure 3.1.8 Algorithm to display car park in tabular form

To display a table of parking bays labelled with the registration mark of the car allocated to the bay together with the bay number the algorithm shown in *Figure 3.1.8* could be used.

Algorithms will also be required to

- find a free slot in the `TCarParkingBayNoToRegistrationMark` array when allocating a parking bay to a car
- find a free slot in the `TOwnerNameArray` array when adding a new name
- delete a name from `TOwnerNameArray` array and the corresponding registration mark in `TCarParkingBayNoToRegistrationMark` array and `TRegistrationMarkArray` array when a member of staff leaves

Task

1. Write algorithms for the three bulleted points above.

Designing an appropriate modular structure for the solution

Figure 3.1.9 is a hierarchy chart with some control information added to it. It shows a possible modular structure for the solution. *Figure 3.1.10* shows pseudo-code corresponding to this hierarchy chart.

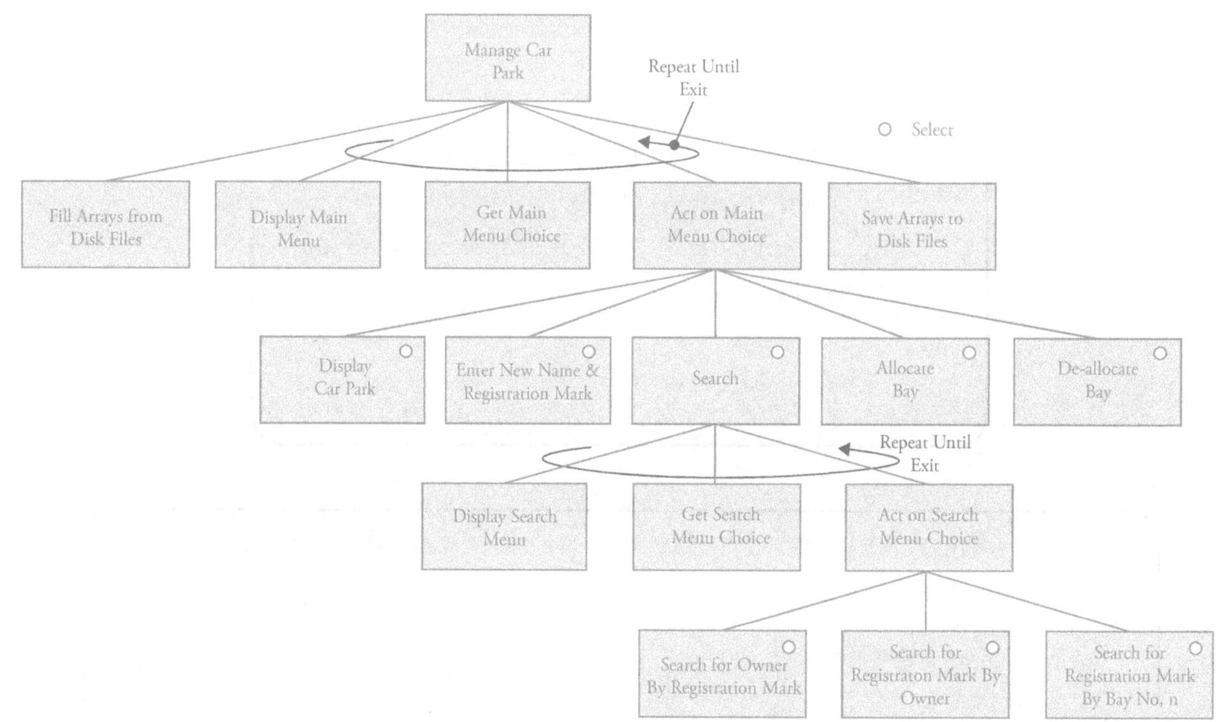

Figure 3.1.9 Hierarchy chart with some control information added to it

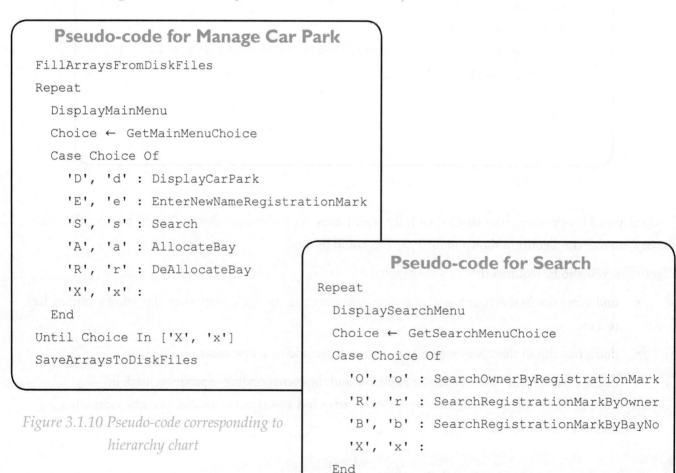

Pseudo-code for Manage Car Park

```
FillArraysFromDiskFiles
Repeat
  DisplayMainMenu
  Choice ← GetMainMenuChoice
  Case Choice Of
    'D', 'd' : DisplayCarPark
    'E', 'e' : EnterNewNameRegistrationMark
    'S', 's' : Search
    'A', 'a' : AllocateBay
    'R', 'r' : DeAllocateBay
    'X', 'x' :
  End
Until Choice In ['X', 'x']
SaveArraysToDiskFiles
```

Pseudo-code for Search

```
Repeat
  DisplaySearchMenu
  Choice ← GetSearchMenuChoice
  Case Choice Of
    'O', 'o' : SearchOwnerByRegistrationMark
    'R', 'r' : SearchRegistrationMarkByOwner
    'B', 'b' : SearchRegistrationMarkByBayNo
    'X', 'x' :
  End
Until Choice In ['X', 'x']
```

Figure 3.1.10 Pseudo-code corresponding to hierarchy chart

Designing the human interface

Figure 3.1.11 and *Figure 3.1.12* show some aspects of the user interface design.

User Interface Design

Car Park Management System
Main Menu

(D)isplay car park - 'D', 'd '

(E)nter new name & registration mark - 'E', 'e'

(S)earch by owner name, registration mark, bay no - 'S', 's'

(A)llocate a parking bay - 'A', 'a'

(R)emove a parking bay allocation - 'R', 'r'

e(X)it - 'X', 'x'

Enter choice:

User Interface Design

Car Park Management System
Search Menu

Search (O)wner by registration mark - 'O', 'o '

Search (R)egistration mark by owner name - 'R', 'r'

Search registration mark by (B)ay no - 'B', 'b'

e(X)it - 'X', 'x'

Enter choice:

Figure 3.1.11 User interface design: Menus

User Interface Design

Car Park Management System

1	2	3	4	5	6	7	8	9	10	11	12	13
OY08 BYO	ZZZZ ZZZ	ZZZZ ZZZ	ZZZZ ZZZ	ZZZZ ZZZ	ZZZZ ZZZ	ZZZZ ZZZ	ZZZZ ZZZ	ZZZZ ZZZ	ZZZZ ZZZ	ZZZZ ZZZ	ZZZZ ZZZ	ZZZZ ZZZ
14	15	16	17	18	19	20	21	22	23	24	25	26
OY08 BYO	ZZZZ ZZZ	ZZZZ ZZZ	ZZZZ ZZZ	ZZZZ ZZZ	ZZZZ ZZZ	ZZZZ ZZZ	ZZZZ ZZZ	ZZZZ ZZZ	ZZZZ ZZZ	ZZZZ ZZZ	ZZZZ ZZZ	ZZZZ ZZZ
27	28	29	30	31	32	33	34	35	36	37	38	39
OY08 BYO	ZZZZ ZZZ	ZZZZ ZZZ	ZZZZ ZZZ	ZZZZ ZZZ	ZZZZ ZZZ	ZZZZ ZZZ	ZZZZ ZZZ	ZZZZ ZZZ	ZZZZ ZZZ	ZZZZ ZZZ	ZZZZ ZZZ	ZZZZ ZZZ
40	41	42	43	44	45	46	47	48	49	50	51	52
OY08 BYO	ZZZZ ZZZ	ZZZZ ZZZ	ZZZZ ZZZ	ZZZZ ZZZ	ZZZZ ZZZ	ZZZZ ZZZ	ZZZZ ZZZ	ZZZZ ZZZ	ZZZZ ZZZ	ZZZZ ZZZ	ZZZZ ZZZ	ZZZZ ZZZ
53	54	55	56	57	58	59	60	61	62	63	64	65
OY08 BYO	ZZZZ ZZZ	ZZZZ ZZZ	ZZZZ ZZZ	ZZZZ ZZZ	ZZZZ ZZZ	ZZZZ ZZZ	ZZZZ ZZZ	ZZZZ ZZZ	ZZZZ ZZZ	ZZZZ ZZZ	ZZZZ ZZZ	ZZZZ ZZZ
66	67	68	69	70	71	72	73	74	75	76	77	78
OY08 BYO	ZZZZ ZZZ	ZZZZ ZZZ	ZZZZ ZZZ	ZZZZ ZZZ	ZZZZ ZZZ	ZZZZ ZZZ	ZZZZ ZZZ	ZZZZ ZZZ	ZZZZ ZZZ	ZZZZ ZZZ	ZZZZ ZZZ	ZZZZ ZZZ
79	80	81	82	83	84	85	86	87	88	89	90	91
OY08 BYO	ZZZZ ZZZ	ZZZZ ZZZ	ZZZZ ZZZ	ZZZZ ZZZ	ZZZZ ZZZ	ZZZZ ZZZ	ZZZZ ZZZ	ZZZZ ZZZ	ZZZZ ZZZ	ZZZZ ZZZ	ZZZZ ZZZ	ZZZZ ZZZ
92	93	94	95	96	97	98	99	100	101	102	103	104
OY08 BYO	ZZZZ ZZZ	ZZZZ ZZZ	ZZZZ ZZZ	ZZZZ ZZZ	ZZZZ ZZZ	ZZZZ ZZZ	ZZZZ ZZZ	ZZZZ ZZZ	ZZZZ ZZZ	ZZZZ ZZZ	ZZZZ ZZZ	ZZZZ ZZZ
105	106	107	108	109	110	111	112	113	114	115	116	117
OY08 BYO	ZZZZ ZZZ	ZZZZ ZZZ	ZZZZ ZZZ	ZZZZ ZZZ	ZZZZ ZZZ	ZZZZ ZZZ	ZZZZ ZZZ	ZZZZ ZZZ	ZZZZ ZZZ	ZZZZ ZZZ	ZZZZ ZZZ	ZZZZ ZZZ
118	119	120	121	122	123	124	125	126	127	128	129	130
OY08 BYO	ZZZZ ZZZ	ZZZZ ZZZ	ZZZZ ZZZ	ZZZZ ZZZ	ZZZZ ZZZ	ZZZZ ZZZ	ZZZZ ZZZ	ZZZZ ZZZ	ZZZZ ZZZ	ZZZZ ZZZ	ZZZZ ZZZ	ZZZZ ZZZ

Figure 3.1.12 User interface design: Parking bay allocation

Task

2 Create a design for the computer-based simple calculator whose requirements are specified in Table 3.1.1.

3.1.3 Implementation

Turning a design into a working program

Tackling Programming Task 1 will give you an opportunity to practice writing, debugging and testing a program.

Programming Task

1 Given the design for the car park management system in the previous section, program this in the programming language of your choice.

Debugging programs

Program compilers catch syntax and type mismatch errors. They can warn if a variable is uninitialised. However, a compiled program may fail to work because of errors in the logic of the program. An error in the logic of the code can lead to incorrect results being calculated or to the program failing in some way. This type of error is difficult to detect. Under these circumstances, we have to resort to testing the program or to conducting a visual inspection of the code called hand-tracing. In hand-tracing, the source code is executed by hand one statement at a time as it would be executed by machine. Hand-trace the code in questions **4** and **5** to find the bug in each

Questions

3 Find the bug in the following section of code which counts letters A through E and F through K:

```
CountAtoE ← 0
CountFtoK ← 0
For Ch ← 'A' To 'K'
  Case Ch Of
    'A', 'B', 'C', 'D', 'E' : CountAtoE ← CountAtoE + 1
    'F', 'G', 'I', 'J', 'K' : CountFtoK ← CountFtoK + 1
  End
EndFor
```

4 Find the bug in the following section of code which finds the average of `HowMany` numbers:

```
ReadLn(HowMany)
For i ← 1 To HowMany
  Sum ← 0 {Initialise Sum}
  Read (Number) {Get a number)
  Sum ← Sum + Number {Add it to the running total}
EndFor
WriteLn('The average is ', Sum/HowMany)
```

The programming environment that you use to develop programs in your preferred programming language may have a built-in debugger which will enable you to set breakpoints in your program code. You will need to compile your program with the debug option enabled because debugging features such as breakpoints require extra code to be inserted into the executable version of the program. In debugging mode, you should be able to run the code to a breakpoint at which point execution should pause to enable the state of variables to be examined and if necessary altered.

Debuggers support single-step execution so it should be possible to single step through parts or all of your program and examine the state of variables at any point.

If you do not want to use the resident debugger then you can embed debugging in your code:

- Comment out statements or blocks of statements that you suspect contain a bug(s)
- Insert Output statements at positions in your code where you want to know the current values of a variable(s)
- Insert Input statements to pause the execution of the program just before the part(s) of the program where you suspect the bug(s) resides. This is especially useful if the program is actually falling over or is getting stuck in a loop.

Correctness of a program

We can only say that a program is correct if we can show that it will work for all possible input data.

Proving that an entire program is correct requires a mathematical approach which is beyond AS/A Level. However, there are some useful guidelines that will help you to minimise errors.

- Always initialise variables before they are used.
- Pay particular attention when writing loops.

  Three potential situations should be considered when writing loops:

  1. The loop will not be entered when it should
  2. The loop will never exit
  3. The loop will terminate after the wrong number of iterations

  The first and last situations can be avoided by a careful examination of the loop's boundary conditions:

  Entry into the loop:

  - Can the entry condition be met?
  - Is a Repeat loop or a While loop required? Does the loop have to be conditional? Would a For loop work?

  Exit from the loop:

  - Can the exit conditions be met?
  - Is there at least one statement in the loop body that will guarantee that the exit condition will be met?

  Off-by-one:

  - Will all variables have their expected values when the loop terminates?
  - Is it possible that that loop executes one more time or one less time than it should?
- Check that values read into the program fall within the expected range and are of the correct type.
- All keyboard input enters the computer as text and can be a source of error if a text representation of, say, a decimal digit is expected and instead a letter of the alphabet is read.
- Case statements (multiple-way selection) should be guarded to ensure only values which can be matched enter the Case block.
- Avoid division by zero.

Questions

5 Check for an error in the boundary condition of the loop in the following snippet of code which is supposed to add the numbers 1 through 50:

```
Sum ← 0
NextNumber ← 1
Repeat
  Sum ← Sum + NextNumber
  NextNumber ← NextNumber + 1
Until NextNumber >= 50
```

6 Rewrite the snippet of code in question 6 to use (a) a While loop (b) a For loop

7 Why does the loop in the following snippet of code fail to terminate?

```
Counter ← 1
Repeat
  Counter ← 2*Counter + 1
Until Counter = 100
```

8 Rewrite the loop terminating condition so that it will terminate.

Efficiency

If in carrying out an identical task on the same machine, e.g. finding prime numbers between 2 and some number *n*, one program takes ten times longer than another program, the conclusion to be drawn is that the faster program is more efficient in time than the slower program. Assignments, comparisons such as <=, logical operations such as AND, etc..., take a finite amount of time to execute in a computing machine. A program that consists of more operations/instructions than another program will take longer to execute on a given machine under identical circumstances.

Which of the two snippets of code in Figure 3.1.13 would you expect to take less time to execute and why?

Pseudo-code for finding the smallest of three values, x, y, z

```
If (x <= y) And (x <= z)
  Then Smallest ← x
  Else
    If (y <= z) And (y <= x)
      Then Smallest ← y
      Else Smallest ← z
```

Figure 3.1.13(a) One way of finding the smallest of three values, x, y, z

In Figure 3.1.13(a) there are

- 4 comparisons, e.g. (x <= y)
- 2 logical And operations

Pseudo-code for finding the smallest of three values, x, y, z

```
Smallest ← x
If y < Smallest
  Then Smallest ← y
If z < Smallest
  Then Smallest ← z
```

Figure 3.1.13(b) Another way of finding the smallest of three values, x, y, z

In Figure 3.1.13(b) there are

- 2 comparisons, e.g. (x < Smallest)
- 0 logical And operations

The code with fewer operations will execute faster. The above examples are trivial. However, where loops are involved we have to be a little more careful. For example, the snippet of code in Figure 3.1.14 is very sensitive to the size of *n*. Execution of this snippet of code will slow noticeably if *n* grows significantly in size.

```
List
  2
  3
  4
  5
  6
  7
  8
  9
  etc...
```

Pseudo-code of a nested loop

```
Write down all numbers between 2 and n into a list
For j ← 2 To n
  For k ← 2 To n
    remove the number j * k from the list
  EndFor
EndFor
```

Figure 3.1.14 Nested loop that removes non-prime integers from a list

Table 3.1.2 shows some execution times on a Windows PC (3.2 GHz) for different values of *n* in the program equivalent of the pseudo-code in Figure 3.1.14.

n	10^3	10^4	10^5	10^6
Time	negligible	0.19 s	18.6 s	1862.3 s

Table 3.1.2 Execution times for different values of n

The programmed pseudo-code in Figure 3.1.15 executes fewer operations and takes considerably less time than the programmed pseudo-code in Figure 3.1.14.
For comparison Table 3.1.3 shows some new times for given values of *n*.
It is possible to improve the algorithm (pseudo-code) even further but this is left as an exercise for the reader.

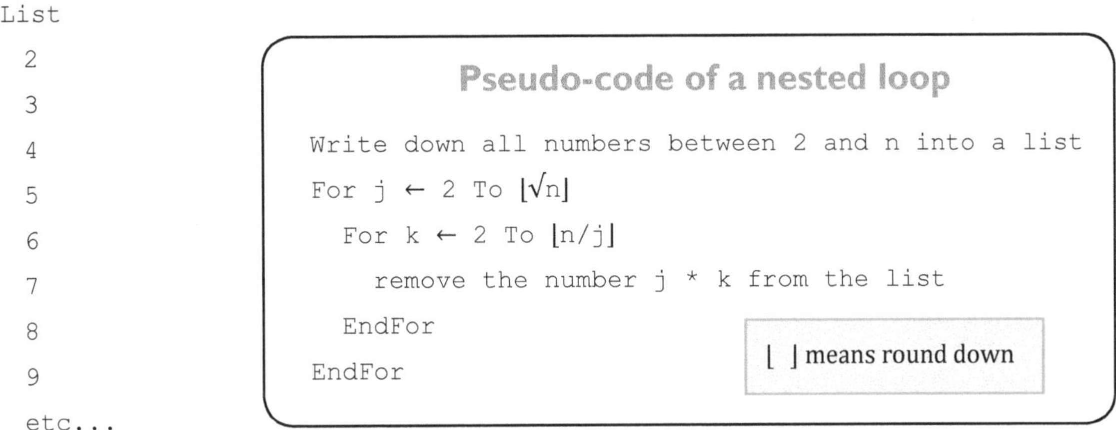
List
2
3
4
5
6
7
8
9
etc...
Pseudo-code of a nested loop
Write down all numbers between 2 and n into a list
For j ← 2 To ⌊√n⌋
For k ← 2 To ⌊n/j⌋
remove the number j * k from the list
EndFor
EndFor
⌊ ⌋ means round down

Figure 3.1.15 More efficient nested loop that removes non-prime integers from a list

n	10^4	10^5	10^6	10^7
Time	negligible	0.01 s	0.01 s	2.1 s

Table 3.1.3 Execution times for different values of n

Articulating how programs work

Often there is a need to explain what a particular program or piece of program code does. If you have written the program then hopefully you know what it is supposed to do. However, if it is another person's program then it may not be immediately obvious what it does, especially if it is written in a particularly obscure way. Running the program might give some clue but sometimes this is not enough on its own. You suspect that the program has not been written with efficiency in mind and you have been charged with improving this efficiency. It might also be the case that you have been charged with the task of adapting the program for another purpose. Either way there is no alternative but to hand-trace the execution of the program to see what it does and how well it does it. Once you understand what the purpose of the program and how it achieves that purpose, you should be able to articulate how the program works. To articulate is to explain.

It is helpful when hand-tracing the execution of a program or snippet of code to use a table called a trace table to keep track of the state of the variables. The pseudo-code in Figure 3.1.16 (Figure 3.1.15 with *n* = 5) has been hand-traced using the trace table in Table 3.1.4. If you suspect that the purpose of this snippet of code is to find prime numbers then changing *n* to 11 or 17 and retracing the code might help to confirm your suspicions. It is clear from the trace table that the code is not very efficient. Table 3.1.4 shows that only one value of `j*k` results in an integer being removed from (red lined one) the list.

Pseudo-code of a nested loop

```
Write down all numbers between 2 and 5 into a list
For j ← 2 To 5
  For k ← 2 To 5
    remove the number j * k from the list
  EndFor
EndFor
```

Figure 3.1.16 Algorithm to finds the first n prime numbers where n = 5

List			
2	3	~~4~~	5 (n)

j	k	j*k
2	2	4
	3	6
	4	8
	5	10
3	2	6
	3	9
	4	12
	5	15
4	2	8
	3	12
	4	16
	5	20
5	2	10
	3	15
	4	20
	5	25

Table 3.1.4 Trace table for n = 5

Questions

9. Hand-trace the following pseudo-code by completing a trace table similar to that shown in Table 3.1.4. Comment on the efficiency of this algorithm compared with the algorithm shown in Figure 3.1.16.

Pseudo-code of a nested loop

```
Write down all numbers between 2 and 7 into a list
For j ← 2 To ⌊√7⌋
  For k ← 2 To ⌊7/j⌋
    remove the number j * k from the list
  EndFor
EndFor
```

⌊ ⌋ means round down

3.1.4 Testing

Testing a program can never adequately prove or demonstrate the correctness of the program. Generally speaking, testing can only reveal the existence of errors. The purpose of testing is to find errors. However, it is not the purpose of testing to find solutions to errors discovered, that is the job of debugging.

Specific sets of data are chosen to test a program to reveal errors. These sets of data are known as test data and each test is known as a test case.

Test cases should be chosen to find errors. When designing test cases you should consider trying to find if the program:

- fails to do what it is supposed to do.
- fails to trap and report invalid input, e.g. a letter of the alphabet is entered when the program expects an integer or input not in the expected range.
- fails to trap input which the logic of the program is not designed for or fails in its logic to cater for all logical pathways through the program.

The design of test cases can be categorised as follows:

- normal data – typical values.
- erroneous data – data that is invalid e.g. a letter of the alphabet is entered when an integer is expected.
- boundary values – test cases are designed to probe the boundary regions: just valid (on the boundary and just inside the boundary) and just invalid values (just outside the boundary) are tried. For example, programs are often written with sub-ranges of some native data type, e.g. 0..9 is a sub-range type of the integer data type. It is with such sub-ranges that programmers often make mistakes, e.g. a programmer has used 1..9 when they meant 0..9.

A necessary part of a test case is a definition of the expected output or result.

Information

Test case example template:
When drawing up test cases it is useful to use a template similar to the one found at http://cdn2.softwaretesting-help.com/wp-content/qa/up-loads/2012/12/Test-case-example.jpg

Question

10 A program reads three integers typed at a keyboard. The three integers are interpreted as representing the lengths of the sides of a triangle. The program prints a message which states whether the triangle is scalene (all sides unequal in length), isosceles (two sides equal) or equilateral (three sides equal).
Write a set of test cases that you feel would adequately test the program and reveal the existence of errors. For example, one test case could be an integer value of zero. The program should trap this and report that the integer entered is invalid.

11 A program to determine the number of days in a month, given the number of the month in the range 1..12 and the year needs to be tested. A leap year is a year which is exactly divisible by 4 and not a century year unless the century year is exactly divisible by 400. Write test cases to adequately test this program.

12 A program to calculate car insurance premiums uses information from a guidance table, Table 3.1.5, to decide the loading to apply to an insurance policy. Age and engine size are integers.

Age	Engine size	Message
>=21	>= 2000	Policy loaded by 10%
< 21	>=2000	Policy loaded by 50%
< 21	< 2000	Policy loaded by 25%

Table 3.1.5 Policy guidance table

Write test cases to adequately test that the program applies the guidance correctly.

Usability (User) testing

An important category of system test cases is one that attempts to find human-factor, or usability, problems.

An example of some categories of test case in usability testing is

> *Has each user interface been tailored to the intelligence, educational background, and environmental pressures of the end user?*
>
> *Are the outputs of the program meaningful, non-insulting to the user, and devoid of computer gibberish?*
>
> *Are the error diagnostics, such as error messages, straightforward, or does the user need to be an expert in computer science to comprehend them?*
>
> *From the user perspective—real people using the software in a real-world environment - does the software perform according to its specifications?*

3.1.5 Evaluation

The computer system that was developed to solve the problem specified in the problem definition is now finished. You hope that your solution has solved the problem but you are not quite sure whether it has or, if it has, how well it has solved the problem. Testing so far has demonstrated that your system is robust, i.e. it doesn't fall over easily if at all.

The problem for which the computer system is the solution belonged to someone. For argument's sake, let's call this someone the client. The first step in evaluation is to get the client to use the system to answer the questions that need answering:

1. Does the developed system
   - i. solve the problem and how well?
   - ii. meet all the requirements established at the analysis stage (see *Table 3.1.1*) and how effectively?
2. How well does the developed system perform?

   (Criteria: speed of execution; amount of memory consumed; errors are trapped and error messages are informative)
3. How easy is the system to use? One that is easy to use will have:
   - i. an uncluttered layout.
   - ii. menus that communicate well.
   - iii. clear instructions/guidance on how to carry out an action.
   - iv. good use of prompts to guide user.
   - v. error messages are straightforward and at the appropiate level for the user.

Task

3 Evaluate the computer-based calculator program or the car park program you have implemented from earlier in the chapter.

In this chapter you have covered:

- Before a problem can be solved, it must be defined, the requirements of the system that solves the problem must be established and a data model created.
- Before constructing a solution, the solution should be designed and specified, for example planning data structures for the data model, designing algorithms, designing an appropriate modular structure for the solution and designing the human user interface.
- The models and algorithms need to be implemented in the form of data structures and code (instructions) that a computer can understand.
- The implementation must be tested for the presence of errors, using selected test data covering normal (typical), boundary and erroneous data.
- The criteria for evaluating a computer system.

4 Theory of computation

4.1 Abstraction and automation

Learning objectives:

- *Be able to develop solutions to simple logic problems.*
- *Be able to check solutions to simple logic problems.*

Key term

Proposition:
A proposition can be defined as a statement which can be either true or false, e.g. "Today is Friday"

Information

An argument:
An argument in propositional logic is a sequence of propositions. All but the final proposition in the argument are called premises and the final proposition is called the conclusion.
An argument is valid if the truth of all its premises implies that the conclusion is true.

Argument form:
An argument form in propositional logic is a sequence of propositions involving propositional variables, e.g. P, Q. An argument form is valid if no matter which particular propositions are substituted for the propositional variables in its premises, the conclusion is true if the premises are all true.
For example, a given set of propositions $P_1, P_2, P_3, \ldots P_n$, called premises, yields another proposition Q called the conclusion. Such an argument is denoted by the argument form

$$P_1, P_2, P_3, \ldots P_n \vdash Q$$

$P_1, P_2, P_3, \ldots P_n$ and Q are propositional variables. The symbol $\vdash$ denotes an assertion.

4.1.1 Problem solving

Developing and checking solutions to simple logic problems

It is well-known that it snows only if it is cold. "It snows only if it is cold" is called a **proposition**.

> **A proposition can be defined as a statement which can be either *true* or *false*.**

For example, "Today is Friday" is a proposition which is *true* or *false*. If today is Friday then it is *true*, if it isn't Friday today it is *false*.

The following are alternative phrasings of the proposition "It snows only if it is cold":

- "If *it snows, it is cold*"
- "If *it is snowing, it is cold*"
- "If *it snows* then *it is cold*"
- "If *it is snowing* then *it is cold*"
- "A necessary condition for *it to snow* is *it must be cold*"
- "*Being cold* is necessary for *it to be snowing*".
- "*It is cold* when *it snows*"
- "*It is cold* whenever *it snows*"
- "*It is cold* if *it snows*"
- "*It is snowing* implies *it is cold*"
- "*It is cold* follows from *it is snowing*"
- "a sufficient condition for it *to be cold* is *it is snowing*".

Question

1 Write each of these statements in the form "*If P, then Q*".
(a) It snows whenever the wind blows from the north.
(b) Getting unfit follows from not exercising enough.
(c) Leaves on the trees turning brown implies it is autumn.
(d) Being at a temperature of 100 °C is necessary for water to boil.
(e) A sufficient condition for a refund is that you bought the goods in the last two weeks.

Compound proposition

Actually, "It snows only if it is cold" is a compound proposition because it is made up of

- two simpler propositions "It snows" and "It is cold" and
- the conditional connective, "only if".

If we know that "It snows only if it is cold" is *true* then "It snows" or "It is snowing" is *true* only if "it is cold" is *true*.

We use the major proposition and the minor proposition as shown below to infer or argue by deduction that if "*If it is snowing then it is cold*" is *true* and if "*It is snowing*" is *true* we may conclude that "*It is cold*" is *true*.

Major proposition: *If it is snowing then it is cold*

Minor proposition: *It is snowing*

Conclusion: *Therefore, it is cold*

Now consider

Major proposition: *If it is snowing then it is cold*

Minor proposition: *It is cold*

Conclusion: *Therefore, it is snowing*

Is this a valid conclusion?

The answer is no. It can be cold and not snowing at the same time. We are not entitled to deduce that it is snowing just because it is cold.

Question

2 Given that the two propositions are true

- If it is cold, he wears a hat
- It is cold

What conclusion can you draw?
Layout your argument in the form of a major and a minor proposition followed by a conclusion as shown above.

3 Given that the two propositions are true

- If it is cold, he wears a hat
- He wears a hat

Are you entitled to deduce that "it is cold"?
Explain your answer.

4 A politician says in his manifesto:
"*If I am elected, then I will lower taxes.*"
The politician is elected.
Assuming that the two statements are true, what conclusion are you entitled to draw?

5 A politician says in his manifesto:
"*If I am elected, then I will lower taxes.*"
The politician manages to get taxes lowered.
Assuming that the two statements are true, are you entitled to deduce that the politician got elected? Explain your answer.

6 A politician says in his manifesto:
"*If I am elected, then I will lower taxes.*"
The following are true statements:
The politician is elected.
The politician doesn't lower taxes.
Is the politician's manifesto statement a true statement?

7 A student, Alice, says to another student, Ben:
"*If you have a valid network password, then you can log onto the network.*"
Ben replies
"*I have a valid network password.*"
What are the logical conditions that must apply to these two statements for the conclusion "*Ben can log onto the network*" to be true?

Suppose without looking, you take a card from a pack of 52 playing cards and place it face down on the table and say "If the card is the King of Diamonds, then it is red." Anyone familiar with the colour of playing card suits (Diamonds and Hearts are red, Spades and Clubs are black) will know that this statement is true.

If you now turn over this card to reveal that it is the Queen of Spades, a black card, is it still true that "If the card is the King of Diamonds, then it is red"? The answer is, of course, yes.

Table 4.1.1 shows the truth table for the proposition "If the card is the King of Diamonds, then it is red." The only case when this proposition is *false* is when "The card is the King of Diamonds" is true and "It is red" is false.

If the card is not the King of Diamonds then it could be red or black in colour but the column headed "If the card is the King of Diamonds, then it is red." will still be *true* for these rows.

The card is the King of Diamonds	It is red	If the card is the King of Diamonds, then it is red
True	True	True
True	False	False
False	True	True
False	False	True

Table 4.1.1 Truth table for the truth of the proposition "If the card is the King of Diamonds, then it is red"

Major proposition: The card is the King of Diamonds only if it is red

Minor proposition: The card is the King of Diamonds

Conclusion: *Therefore, it is a red card*

Figure 4.1.1 Valid argument and a conclusion which is true

Major proposition: The card is the King of Diamonds only if it is red

Minor proposition: The card is not the King of Diamonds

Conclusion: Therefore, *?*

Figure 4.1.2 Valid argument but the conclusion is inconclusive

In *Figure 4.1.1*, the conclusion "*It is a red card*" is true because both major and minor propositions are true.

In *Figure 4.1.2*, both major and minor propositions are true. However, we cannot draw any conclusion other than the card could be red or black because we know that cards are either red or black. But restricting ourselves to the evidence supplied, we are not entitled to use this additional knowledge.

Question

Draw the truth table for the proposition "*If I am elected, then I will lower taxes.*"
State the truth values for the row of your table which corresponds to the politician breaking his promise?

Conditional connective ⇒

If we know that "*It is snowing*" is true only if "*It is cold*" is true then using propositional variables, P and Q, where P = "It is snowing", Q = "It is cold", we write P $\Rightarrow$ Q which reads P is true only if Q is true or P implies Q.
In the conditional statement P $\Rightarrow$ Q, P is called the hypothesis (or antecedent or premise) and Q is called the conclusion (or consequence). So if the conditional statement is true and hypothesis is true then the conclusion is true.

The argument

Major proposition: *If it is snowing then it is cold*

Minor proposition: *It is snowing*

Conclusion: *Therefore, it is cold*

is a valid argument with a conclusion which is true.

Information

Conditional connective ⇒:

If we know that "*It is snowing*" is true only if "*It is cold*" is true then using propositional variables, P and Q, where P = "*It is snowing*", Q = "*It is cold*" we write

$$P \Rightarrow Q$$

which reads P is true only if Q is true.
In the conditional statement P $\Rightarrow$ Q, P is called the hypothesis (or antecedent or premise) and Q is called the conclusion (or consequence). So if the conditional statement is true and the hypothesis is true then the conclusion is true.

Using propositional variables, the equivalent argument form of the above argument is $P \Rightarrow Q$

where ∴ is the symbol that denotes "therefore". P

Whenever, both P and $P \Rightarrow Q$ are true then Q is also true. $\therefore Q$

The form of the argument that uses propositional logic variables, e.g. P and Q, is called the argument form to differentiate it from the argument which uses actual statements such as "It is snowing".

Is the conclusion always true if the argument is valid?

Consider the following valid argument

Major proposition: *If computer program A compiles then it will terminate when run*

Minor proposition: *Computer program A compiles*

Conclusion: *Therefore, it will terminate when run*

Even though this is a valid argument because the argument form is $P \Rightarrow Q$

the conclusion is not true if the major proposition is not true. P

It is a fact that some programs can get stuck in a loop and therefore $\therefore Q$ will not terminate.

Question

9 Consider the following argument involving propositions:
"*If the card is the King of Diamonds, then it is red.*"
"*The card is the King of Diamonds.*"
Therefore, "The card is red."
Write the argument form using the propositional variables, P and Q, where P = "*The card is the King of Diamonds*" and Q = "*It is red.*" Is this a valid argument? Is the conclusion true?

10 The following argument consisting of two propositions and another proposition, the conclusion, is a valid argument but the conclusion is not true even though it is snowing. Why is the conclusion not true?

If it is snowing, it is warm.
It is snowing.

Therefore, it is warm.

11 The following valid argument consists of three propositions, one of which is the conclusion. The first two propositions are true. Is the conclusion true?

If it is snowing then it is cold.
It is not cold.

Therefore, it is not snowing.

12 The following valid argument consists of three propositions, one of which is the conclusion. The first two propositions are true. Is the conclusion true?

It is snowing or it is cold or it is both.
It is not snowing.

Therefore, it is cold.

Logical reasoning

A fundamental principle of logical reasoning states:

If P then Q, If Q then R, therefore, If P then R

that is, the following argument is valid

$$P \Rightarrow Q,\ Q \Rightarrow R \vdash P \Rightarrow R$$

Consider the following statements

- If it is freezing, the streets are icy.
- If the streets are icy, accidents will happen

Applying the fundamental principle of logical reasoning we get

It is freezing implies the streets are icy	*It is freezing ⇒ the streets are icy*	$P \Rightarrow Q$
the streets are icy implies accidents will happen	*the streets are icy ⇒ accidents will happen*	$Q \Rightarrow R$
It is freezing implies accidents will happen	*It is freezing ⇒ accidents will happen*	$\therefore P \Rightarrow R$

Question

13 *If it snows today, then I will not go to school today. If I do not go to school today, I can catch up on my homework.*
Use logical reasoning to draw a conclusion.

14 *If the train arrives early then Jamin will be early for his meeting. If Jamin is early for his meeting, he can call in on his friend John.* What conclusion can you draw?

15 *If I don't watch the late night film, I will go to bed early. If I go to bed early, I will wake up feeling refreshed.* What conclusion can you draw?

16 Consider the following scenario:

If Alex is allowed a TV in his bedroom, he will neglect his homework. If he neglects his homework, he will fall behind at school. If he falls behind at school, he will not progress at school. If he does not progress at school, he will need extra tution.

Use logical reasoning to draw a conclusion.

17 *If the plane arrives late and there are no taxis at the airport then Jack is late for his meeting. Jack is not late for his meeting. The plane did arrive late.* What conclusion can you draw?

18 *If it is raining and Isla does not have her raincoat with her, then she will get wet. Isla is not wet. It is raining.* What conclusion can you draw.

19 Consider this rule about a set of cards:

"If a card has a vowel on one side, then it has an even number on the other side."

Look at the cards below and answer the question which cards do I need to turn over to tell if the rule is actually true? Explain your reasoning.

Did you know?

Mathematical induction:
Unfortunately, the term "mathematical induction" clashes with the terminology used in reasoning by logic. Deductive reasoning uses rules of inference to draw conclusions from premises, whereas inductive reasoning makes conclusions only supported, but not guaranteed, by evidence. Proofs that use mathematical induction are deductive, not inductive.

Did you know?

Rationalism and empiricism:
Rationalism is the philosophy that believes that the senses deceive and that logical reasoning is the only sure path to knowledge.
Empiricism is the philosophy that believes that all reasoning is fallible and that knowledge must come from observation and experimentation.
Empiricism gave birth to the scientific method during the Enlightenment.
Rationalism was responsible for the invention of some fundamental mathematical techniques such as calculus but on theories of the universe did not do so well. The empiricists' approach of generalising from what has been observed and measured has been more successful. This approach has also proved useful in machine learning.

From deduction to induction

Newton is well known for his three laws of motion. He is less well known for his four rules of induction. His third rule of induction is said to be at the heart of the Newtonian revolution and modern science. This rule, known as Newton's Principle, can be expressed in modern parlance as follows

> *Newton's Principle: Whatever is true of everything before our eyes is true of everything in the universe.*

Newton's principle allows scientists to draw conclusions of a general nature from the results of experiments involving a limited set of observations and measurements.

We have learned so far about deductive reasoning, e.g.

John Smith is a footballer

All footballers kick a football when playing soccer

Therefore, ...?.............

The first statement is a fact about John Smith and the second is a general rule about footballers. We can infer from these two statements that *John Smith kicks a football when playing soccer* by applying the general rule to John.

Inductive reasoning is the inverse of deductive reasoning. In inductive reasoning we start instead with the initial and the derived facts, and look for a rule that allows the derived fact(s) to be inferred from the initial fact(s). For example,

John Smith is a footballer

..........?.............

Therefore, John Smith kicks a football when playing soccer

One such rule is: *If John Smith is a footballer, then he wears football boots when playing soccer*

This is a rule but not a very useful one because it is specific to John Smith. We use Newton's principle to generalise this rule to make a more useful general rule:

If x is a footballer, then x wears football boots when playing soccer

where x can be anyone including people who are not footballers.

Another way of expressing this is

All footballers wear football boots when playing soccer

We would need more evidence to have faith in this general rule. This could be obtained by observing more than just one footballer playing soccer and noting over and over again that they wear football boots when playing soccer.

Note that the statement

If x is a footballer, then x wears football boots when playing soccer

is neither true nor false whilst the value of x is unknown, but if x = *John Smith* then it becomes

If John Smith is a footballer, then John Smith wears football boots when playing soccer

This is either true or false depending on whether John is a footballer. It is therefore a proposition.

In this logic we have statements that are not propositions until a value has been assigned to the variable(s) in the propositional function.

If we denote

If x is a footballer, then x wears football boots when playing soccer by P(x)

then P("John Smith") is a proposition. P(x) is said to be the value of the propositional function P at x.

Question

20 Let P(x) denote the statement "x > 5". What are the truth values of P(3) and P(7)?

21 The following statements are true:

Gerry is a computer science student.

All computer science students drink coffee.

What conclusion can you draw?

22 The following statements are true:

Deemei is in class CS1.

Every student in class CS1 *has learned at least one programming language.*

What conclusion can you draw?

Extension Question

23 A boy and a girl, whose names we do not know, are sitting next to each other. One of them has fair hair, and the other dark hair. The dark-haired one says "*I am a girl.*" The fair-haired one says, "*I am a boy*". We are told at least one of them is lying. What is your conclusion?

In this chapter you have covered:

- Developing solutions to simple logic problems.
- Checking solutions to simple logic problems.

4 Theory of computation

4.1 Abstraction and automation

Learning objectives:

- *Understand the term algorithm*
- *Be able to express the solution to a simple problem as an algorithm using pseudo-code, with the standard constructs:*
  - *sequence*
  - *assignment*
  - *selection*
  - *iteration*
- *Be able to hand-trace algorithms*
- *Be able to convert an algorithm from pseudo-code into high level language program code*
- *Be able to articulate how a program works, arguing for its correctness and its efficiency using logical reasoning, test data and user feedback.*

4.1.2 Following and writing algorithms

What is an algorithm?

An algorithm is a precise description of steps necessary to accomplish a certain task or solve a particular problem.

The notion of an algorithm is not peculiar to computer science.

Algorithms have been around for thousands of years.

Mathematics is full of algorithms, some of which we rely on today, e.g. the algorithm we use for adding two numbers column-by-column.

Table 4.1.2.1 shows some fields of human activity in which algorithms are used. In each case the process is carried out by a human being.

Process	Algorithm	Example steps
Knitting a cardigan	Knitting pattern	1st row: Pearl9, Knit2, ...
Putting together flat pack furniture	Assembly instructions	Screw side panel to front panel
Bisecting an angle with compass and ruler	Drawing instructions	Place the point of the compass on A, and swing an arc ED
Playing music	Musical score	

Table 4.1.2.1 Some fields of human activity in which algorithms are used

Figure 4.1.2.1 shows that the process of knitting a cardigan consists of

- an input - balls of wool of a particular colour and yarn
- an output - the finished cardigan
- a processor - a human
- a precise finite sequence of steps expressed in a code which a human can interpret

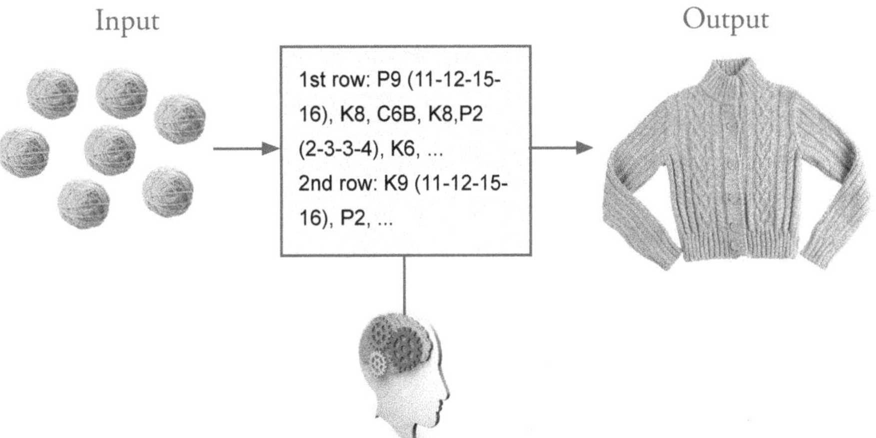
Input
Output
1st row: P9 (11-12-15-16), K8, C6B, K8,P2 (2-3-3-4), K6, ...
2nd row: K9 (11-12-15-16), P2, ...

Figure 4.1.2.1 The process of knitting a cardigan

Information

Derivation of term algorithm:
The term algorithm is a corruption of the name al-Khowarizmi, a mathematician of the ninth century (see below), whose book on Hindu numerals is the basis of modern decimal notation. He coined the term *algorism* to describe the rules for performing arithmetic using decimal notation. By the eighteenth century, *algorism* had evolved into the word algorithm. With the advent of machines that could compute, the concept of an algorithm was given a more general meaning to include all definite procedures for solving problems, not just procedures for performing arithmetic.

Abu Ja'Far Mohammed Ibn Musa Al-Khowarizmi (C. 780 -C. 850) an astronomer and mathematician, was a member of the House of Wisdom, an academy of scientists in Baghdad.
He wrote many books. Western Europeans first learned about algebra from his works.
The word algebra comes from al-jabr, part of the title of the book Kitab al-jabr w'al muquabala which he wrote.

An algorithm is a method for solving a problem (a task).
It describes an effective path that leads to the problem solution.
Interesting algorithms are ones which involve repeating instructions many times, something which a digital computer is capable of doing.

All but the simplest of algorithms are challenging to design because:

- The description of the algorithm has to be absolutely unambiguous in the sense that different interpretations are excluded
- Each application of the algorithm has to reach the same result
- An algorithm must be designed in a such a way that it works correctly for each of the possible inputs/problem instances and finishes in a finite time
- An algorithm may have many problem instances as possible inputs, too many to test everyone.

Cooking recipes are not algorithms. They are expressed too imprecisely and rely too much on the knowledge, experience and skill of the cook to be correctly interpreted. A less experienced cook may easily misinterpret the recipe's instructions or worse still not understand some. The range of input is also limited.

Task

This task illustrates the difficulty of writing an algorithm which is not open to misinterpretation.
Using pen/pencil and paper execute the following instructions by hand:

1. Draw a diagonal line
2. Draw another diagonal line connected to the top of the first one
3. Draw a straight line from the point where the diagonal lines meet
4. Draw a horizontal line over the straight line
5. At the bottom of the straight line, draw a curvy line
6. Draw a diagonal line from the bottom of the first diagonal to the straight line
7. Draw a diagonal line from the bottom of the second diagonal to the straight line

What object have you drawn?
Compare your result with a friend's.
(CSInside, Algorithm Development, reproduced with kind permission of Professor Quintin Cutts, Glasgow university)

The following constructs are sufficient for constructing algorithms:

- sequence
- assignment
- selection
- iteration

Key concept

Algorithm:
A description, independent of any programming language, of a procedure that solves a problem or task.
It consists of a precisely described sequence of steps for solving a problem or completing a task.
The algorithm must terminate and its action must be capable of completing in a finite amount of time.

Writing algorithms

Problem

Describe an algorithm for finding the maximum (largest) value in a finite sequence of integers.

Solution

Even though the solution to this problem is very straightforward it provides a good illustration of the concept of an algorithm.

It is possible to express a method for solving this problem in several ways. One method is simply to use the English language to describe the sequence of steps used.

English description of algorithm

The following steps must be performed:

1. *Set the temporary maximum equal to the first integer in the sequence. (The temporary maximum will be the largest integer examined at any stage of the procedure)*
2. *Compare the next integer in the sequence to the temporary maximum, if it is larger than the temporary maximum, set the temporary maximum equal to this integer*
3. *Repeat the previous step if there are more integers in the sequence*
4. *Stop when there are no integers left in the sequence. The temporary maximum at this point is the largest integer in the sequence*

English is notoriously ambiguous, relying on context to resolve ambiguity.
For example, the grammatically correct sentence

Fruit flies like a banana

could refer to fruit such as bananas or alternatively "fruit flies" which are members of the genus Drosophila of small flies.

It is also verbose and too complex to be easily understood by computers.

If you are French then the steps above would be written in French.

One solution is to use a programming language.

Programming language description

An algorithm can be written in a computer programming language.
However, when this is done, only those instructions allowed in the language may be used. The result can be more complicated and difficult to understand than necessary.
Also, there are many computer languages so it would be inappropriate to favour one particular language over another.

Pseudo-code description

Therefore, instead of using a particular programming language to write algorithms, pseudo-code is used.

Pseudo-code provides an intermediate step between an English language description of an algorithm and an expression of this algorithm in a particular programming language.
In pseudo-code, the steps of the algorithm are expressed using instructions resembling those used in a programming language. However, the writer has the freedom to choose how closely or how loosely the pseudo-code resembles a programming language.

A computer program can then be produced in any computer language using the pseudo-code description as a starting point.

The principle aim of writing in pseudo-code is to communicate with the reader, a human being, so the syntax should be sufficiently informal to satisfy this aim but it must not lose the ability to be mapped accurately and relatively effortlessly into a program in one of the currently used programming languages.

Table 4.1.2.2 shows a pseudo-code description of the algorithm for finding the maximum element in a finite sequence of *n* integers.

The first step in this algorithm assigns the first integer in the sequence, a_1, to the variable Maximum.

```
Input: a1, a2, a3, a4, a5, ..., an : Integer
Algorithm:
  Maximum ← a1
  For i ← 2 To n Do
    If Maximum < ai
      Then Maximum ← ai
    EndIf
  EndFor
Output: Maximum is the largest element
```

Table 4.1.2.2 Algorithm expressed in pseudo-code to find the maximum element in a finite sequence of n integers

The *For loop* is used to examine the integers of the sequence, in turn. If the next integer examined is larger than the current value of Maximum, it is assigned to Maximum replacing the current value.

Programming task

1. Write and test a program that implements the algorithm in Table 4.1.2.2.

Question

1. Complete the algorithm shown in Table 4.1.2.3 which relies on addition to calculate the product of two integers, *x* and *y*. Replace each instance of *?* by an appropriate addition step expressed in pseudo-code.

2. Complete the algorithm shown in Table 4.1.2.4 which calculates integer *x* raised to the power of integer *m* by replacing each instance of *?* by an appropriate step expressed in pseudo-code.

3. Write an algorithm to find the positive integer m such that $2^m \leq N$ but also such that $2^{m+1} > N$.
   Input is N. Output is m.

4. Write an algorithm to find the sum of the first *n* natural numbers, i.e. 1 + 2 + 3 + ... + n.

5. Write an algorithm to find the product of the first *n* natural numbers, i.e. 1 x 2 x 3 x ... x n.

```
Input: x                          [Integer > 0]
       y                          [Any integer]
Algorithm:
  Product ← 0
  NoOfTimes  ← 0
  Repeat
    ?
    ?
  Until NoOfTimes = x
Output: product of x and y
```

Table 4.1.2.3 Incomplete algorithm expressed in pseudo-code to calculate the product of x and y

```
Input: m                          [Integer > 0]
       x                          [Any integer]
Algorithm:
  Power ← x
  Count  ← 1
  While Count < m Do
    ?
    ?
  EndWhile
Output: x^m
```

Table 4.1.2.4 Incomplete algorithm expressed in pseudo-code to calculate x^m

Hand-tracing algorithms

Integer division was studied in Chapter 1.1.3.

In integer division the quotient q and the remainder r are obtained when dividing an integer x by an integer y.

In integer division, the relationship between x, y, q and r is as follows

$$x = y * q + r$$

For example, when the dividend x = 5, the divisor y = 2, the quotient q = 2, and the remainder r = 1.

To verify this computation, we substitute the given values of x, y, q and r in

$$x = y * q + r$$

and check that the left hand side is equal to the right hand side

$$5 = 2 * 2 + 1$$

Task

2 Complete Table 4.1.2.5 for x = y * q + r.

Dividend x	Divisor y	Quotient q	Remainder r
5	2	2	1
6	3	2	0
25	4	6	1
36	6		
121	7		
23	3		
1	3		
5	10		

*Table 4.1.2.5 Values of x, y, q, r which satisfy x = y * q + r*

```
r ← x
q ← 0
While r > y Do
  r ← r - y
  q ← q + 1
EndWhile
```

Table 4.1.2.6 Algorithm for calculating quotient q and remainder r

A first attempt at writing an algorithm in pseudo-code for calculating q and r is shown in Table 4.1.2.6. Table 4.1.2.7 is a completed trace table which shows the result of executing the algorithm in Table 4.1.2.6 by hand.

Iteration No	x	y	r	q	r > y
0	5	2	5	0	True
1	5	2	3	1	True
2	5	2	1	2	False

Table 4.1.2.7 Shows a completed trace table for the algorithm in Table 4.1.2.6

Extracting the value for q and r from the last row of Table 4.1.2.7 and plugging these into x = y * q + r along with dividend x and divisor y, we get confirmation that q and r have been calculated correctly

$$5 = 2 * 2 + 1$$

Task

3 Complete Table 4.1.2.8 by hand-tracing the algorithm shown in Table 4.1.2.6. (Hand-trace = execution by hand).

4 (a) Does your completed table in question 3 demonstrate that

$$x = y * q + r ?$$

(b) Is your answer correct, i.e. are q and r correct?

Iteration No	x	y	r	q	r > y
0	6	3	6	0	True

Table 4.1.2.8 Incomplete trace table of a hand trace of the algorithm shown in Table 4.1.2.6

Task

5 Complete Table 4.1.2.9 by hand-tracing the algorithm shown in Table 4.1.2.6.

6 Does the algorithm in Table 4.1.2.6 terminate when x = 6 and y = 0?

Iteration No	x	y	r	q	r > y
0	6	0	6	0	True

Table 4.1.2.9 Incomplete trace table of a hand trace of the algorithm shown in Table 4.1.2.6

Articulating how a program works

Correctness

It can be concluded from the outcome for Task 5 and Task 6, that before the algorithm is executed, input y to the algorithm must be constrained such that y > 0 is true for the algorithm to terminate and for x = y ∗ q + r to be true after execution of the algorithm - Table 4.1.2.10.

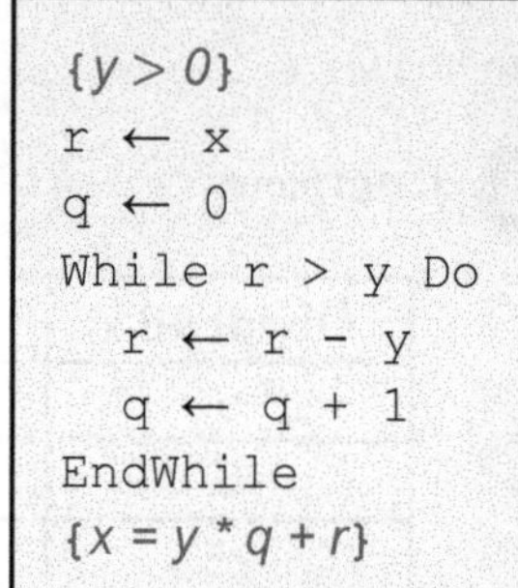

```
{y > 0}
r ← x
q ← 0
While r > y Do
  r ← r - y
  q ← q + 1
EndWhile
{x = y * q + r}
```

Table 4.1.2.10 Require y > 0 to be true at beginning, and x = y ∗ q + r true at end

In Task 4, x = 6, y = 3, q = 1 and r = 3 makes x = y ∗ q + r true but something is wrong in the algorithm because q should be 2.

Table 4.1.2.11 shows a trace of the values of x, y, q, r.

```
{y > 0}                 {x = 6, y = 3}
r ← x                   {r = 6}
q ← 0                   {q = 0}
While r > y Do
  r ← r - y             {r = 3}
  q ← q + 1             {q = 1}
EndWhile
{x = y * q + r}         {x = 6, y = 3, q = 1, r = 3}
```

Table 4.1.2.11 Trace of the values of x, y, q, r

Close inspection of the algorithm reveals that the *While condition* is incorrect - Table 4.1.2.12.
It should be r >= y, not r > y.

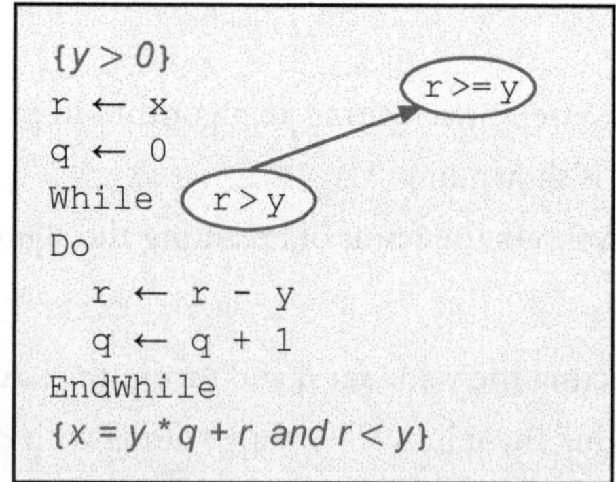

```
{y > 0}
r ← x
q ← 0
While (r > y)          (r >= y)
Do
  r ← r - y
  q ← q + 1
EndWhile
{x = y * q + r and r < y}
```

Table 4.1.2.12 Error in the algorithm revealed

Table 4.1.2.13 shows the corrected algorithm.

The *While loop* is now exited when r < y.

We can now assert that if *y > 0* is true before the algorithm is entered then it will terminate with *x = y * q + r and r < y* true.
The quotient q is now calculated correctly, i.e. q = 2 when x = 6, y = 3, q = 1 and r = 3.

Also x = y ∗ q + r is true and r < y is true.

```
{y > 0}
r ← x
q ← 0
While r >= y Do
  r ← r - y
  q ← q + 1
EndWhile
{x = y * q + r and r < y}
```

Table 4.1.2.13 Corrected algorithm

Task

7 Complete Table 4.1.2.14 by hand tracing the algorithm shown in Table 4.1.2.13.

8 Is x = y * q + r for the values recorded in Table 4.1.2.14?

9 Is negative remainder r allowed?

Iteration No	x	y	r	q	r >= y
0	-2	1			

Table 4.1.2.14 Incomplete trace table of a hand trace of the algorithm shown in Table 4.1.2.13

Task 7 calculates a negative remainder. A negative remainder is impossible! - see Figure 4.1.2.2.

We must therefore constrain input x to be greater than or equal to zero to avoid a negative remainder.

Table 4.1.2.15 shows the correct input constraints to make condition $\{x = y * q + r \text{ and } 0 \le r < y\}$ true after execution of algorithm. The algorithm will now terminate with the value of q and r calculated correctly.

```
{x ≥ 0 and y > 0}
r ← x
q ← 0
While r >= y Do
  r ← r - y
  q ← q + 1
EndWhile
{x = y * q + r and 0 ≤ r < y}
```

Table 4.1.2.15 Correct input constraints to make condition $\{x = y * q + r \text{ and } 0 \le r < y\}$ at end of algorithm true

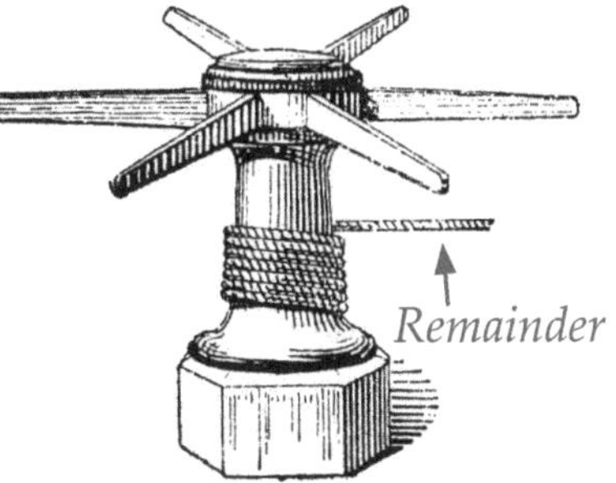

Figure 4.1.2.2 Rope remainder after winding rope on capstan

Key concept

Specifying the range of inputs of an algorithm:
The range of inputs are specified as a pre-condition of executing the algorithm.
Pre-condition:
A pre-condition specifies the state of the computation that must be true before the algorithm is executed.
For example,
{x ≥ 0 and y > 0}

Programming task

2 Write and test a program that implements the algorithm expressed in Table 4.1.2.15.

Key concept

Specifying the desired effect of an algorithm:
The desired effect of executing an algorithm can be specified as a post-condition that must be true after executing the algorithm.
Post-condition:
A post-condition specifies the state of the computation after the algorithm is executed.
For example,
$\{x = y * q + r \text{ and } 0 \le r < y\}$ must be true.

Efficiency

Given an integer *n*, compute its prime factorisation[1].
For example, if *n* is 60, its prime factorisation is 2 x 2 x 3 x 5.

Table 4.2.1.16 shows an algorithm expressed in pseudo-code for finding the prime factors of *n*.
The algorithm checks if *i* is a factor. If it is, it outputs this factor before dividing it out of *n*.

Table 4.1.2.17 shows another algorithm expressed in pseudo-code for finding the prime factors of *n* in fewer steps than the algorithm shown in Table 4.1.2.16.

1 Prime factorization of a number is the determination of the set of prime numbers which multiply together to give the original integer.

Input: n [Integer ≥ 1]

Algorithm:

```
For i ← 2 To n Do
   While n MOD i = 0  Do
      Output i
      n ← n DIV i
   EndWhile
EndFor
```

Output: prime factors of n

Table 4.1.2.16 Algorithm expressed in pseudo-code to find prime factors of n

Programming task

3 Write and test a program that implements the algorithm expressed in *Table 4.1.2.16*.

If *n* has a factor then this must be one less than or equal to the square root of *n*.

Input: n [Integer > 1]

Algorithm:

```
SqrtOfn ← Floor(Sqrt(n))
For i ← 2 To SqrtOfn Do
  While (n MOD i) = 0 Do
    Output i
    n ← n DIV i
  EndWhile
EndFor
If n > 1
  Then Output n
EndIf
```

Output: prime factors of n

Table 4.1.2.17 Algorithm expressed in pseudo-code to find prime factors of n using fewer iterations of for loop than algorithm in Table 4.1.2.16

For example, suppose n = 9. Its square root is 3. The first factor that is found is 3, the second is 3. The *for loop* in the algorithm in *Table 4.1.2.17* finds and outputs the prime factor 3 when i = 3. Next *n* is divided by *i* and the result 3 is assigned to *n*. The *for loop* now exits with n = 3. The next step *If n > 1* is true so 3 is output. The two prime factors of 9 have now been output.

Now suppose n = 10. Its square root is 3.1623 to 4 decimal places. This becomes 3 after applying the operation *Floor*.
The first factor that is found is 2, the second is 5.
The *for loop* in the algorithm in *Table 4.1.2.17* finds and outputs the prime factor 2.
It then divides *n* by *i* and assigns the result 5 to *n*.
The next step *If n > 1* is true so 5 is output.

When using this method on a number *n*, only divisors up to ⌊sqrt(n)⌋ (where ⌊x⌋ is the *floor* function) need be tested.

This algorithm when programmed in a programming language should therefore consume less execution time than the program equivalent of the algorithm in *Table 4.1.2.16*.

We say that this algorithm is more **time-efficient** than the algorithm in *Table 4.1.2.16*.

Information

Floor function:
The floor function returns the largest (closest to positive infinity) value that is less than or equal to the argument and is equal to a mathematical integer.

Programming task

4 Write and test a program that implements the algorithm expressed in *Table 4.1.2.17*.

In this chapter you have covered:

- The term algorithm
- Expressing the solution to a simple problem as an algorithm using pseudo-code, with the standard constructs:
  - sequence
  - assignment
  - selection
  - iteration
- Hand-tracing algorithms
- Converting an algorithm from pseudo-code into high level language program code
- Articulating how a program works, arguing for its correctness and its efficiency using logical reasoning, test data and user feedback

4.1 Abstraction and automation

4.1.3 Abstraction

Learning objectives:

- *Be familiar with the concept of abstraction as used in computations and know that:*
  - *representational abstraction is an abstraction arrived at by removing unnecessary details*
  - *abstraction by generalisation or categorisation is a grouping by common characteristics to arrive at a hierarchical relationship of the 'is a kind of' type.*

What is abstraction?

The human brain is an exceptional piece of biological machinery capable of recognising objects even when most of their detail has been removed.

This is illustrated in *Figure 4.1.3.1* which is an abstraction of an image of a child.

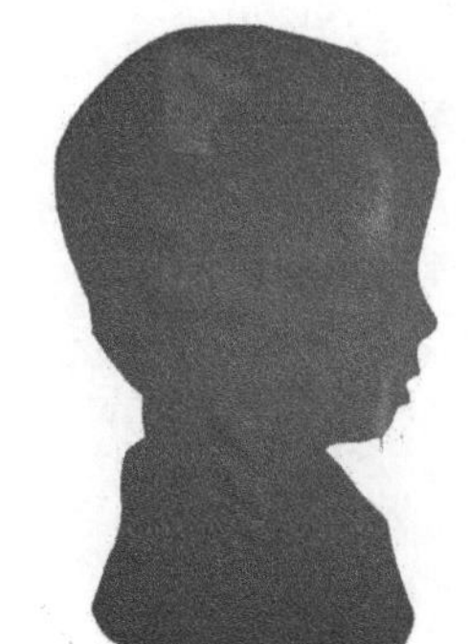

Figure 4.1.3.1 Silhouette image of a child

Representational abstraction

Humans deal with abstractions all the time, because they are useful in everyday problem solving.

For example, travelling from Marylebone to Russell Square by London Underground involves taking the Bakerloo line from Marylebone as far as Piccadilly Circus then changing to the Piccadilly line and travelling as far as Russell Square (*Figure 4.1.3.2*). It is not necessary to include more details than these to succeed in reaching the desired destination. In fact, this example of Harry Beck's London Underground map is itself an abstraction. Unnecessary details have been removed and the layout of the stations adjusted to make the map easy to use. Ease of use is a very good reason to work with an abstraction rather than the real thing. Abstraction means **omitting unnecessary details**. What we end up with when unnecessary details are removed is an example of **representational abstraction**.

Key term

Representational abstraction: Means omitting unnecessary details.

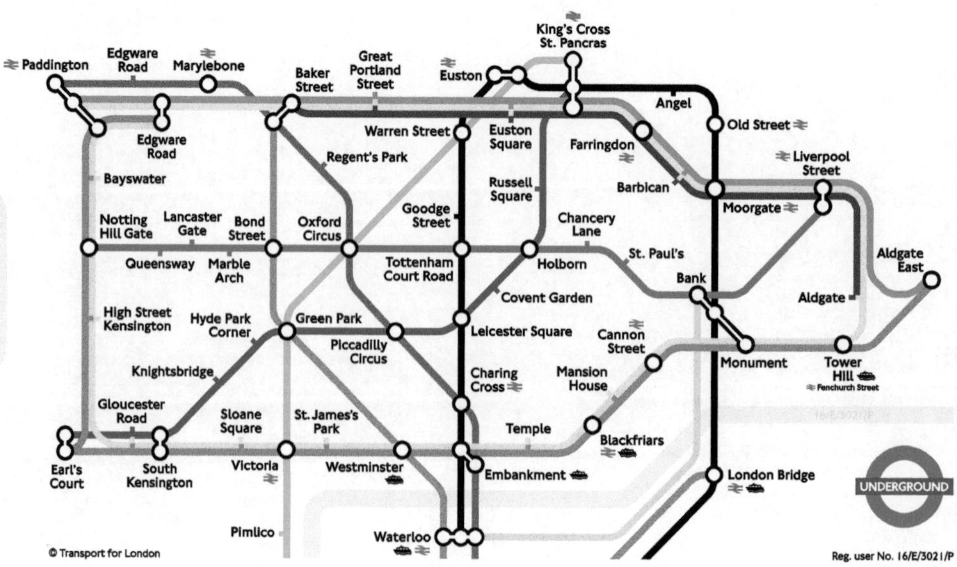

Figure 4.1.3.2 London underground map based on a design by Harry Beck

Abstraction as used in computations

Modelling

Ease of use is a very good reason to work with an abstraction rather than the real thing. The London tube map is a model of the real underground system. Models are used to understand the world by removing complexity and focussing on details relevant to the task in hand. The process of abstraction allows problems to be solved by separating the logical and physical views. To navigate the London underground, we just need information consisting of stations, their links and the classification of links, e.g. Marylebone, Oxford Circus are connected directly by the Bakerloo line. This is the logical view. To take in the physical view requires going to these stations and travelling on the underground.

Figure 4.1.3.3 Car park with bays arranged in a rectangular grid

Data modelling

Figure 4.1.3.3 shows parking bays in a car park. These could be modelled by an abstraction known as an array as shown in Figure 4.1.3.4. An array is a logical element. It has a meaning which crops up in everyday life, e.g. an array of solar panels as shown in Figure 4.1.3.5.

Figure 4.1.3.5 Solar panel arrays

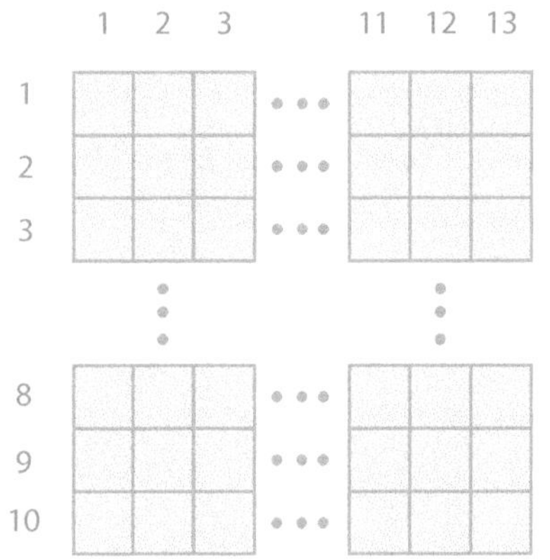

Figure 4.1.3.4 Modelling car park as a two-dimensional array

A programmer would find it more convenient to work with the two-dimensional array model of the car park than to work directly with the electronic units from which the memory of a computer is built. This separation of the physical view of the computer's memory from the programmer's logical view of an array is an example of (representational) abstraction.

Layers of abstraction

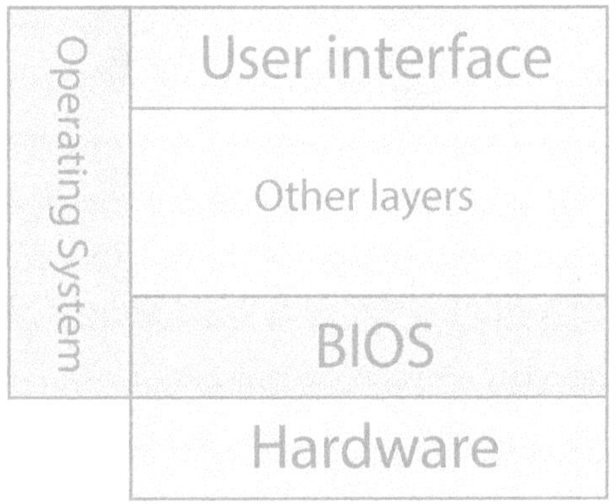

Figure 4.1.3.6 Layers of abstraction

The complexities of the hardware of a computer make it difficult for users to interact directly with the hardware. The solution is to progressively hide these complexities by layers of abstraction as shown in Figure 4.1.3.6. The BIOS (Basic Input Output System) which resides in firmware interfaces directly with the layer below, the hardware, and the operating system software layer above the BIOS. The operating system is multilayered. The user interacts with the user interface layer of the operating system which in turn interacts with the operating system layer immediately below. A computation submitted to the computer through the user interface is carried out by the user interface layer calling on services from the layer immediately below which in turn does something similar with the layer below it and so on. Eventually, the computation reaches the hardware where it is executed. The result of the computation is returned up through the layers until it reaches the user interface where it is presented to the user. This distinguishes abstraction in Computer Science from abstraction in mathematics. Mathematics only ever deals with one layer of abstraction, e.g. 5 x 6 + 4 is abstracted to a x b + c. Computer Science deals with two layers at a time: the layer above which calls on services from the layer below.

Abstraction and subprograms

Figure 4.1.3.7(a) shows pseudo-code for a method that swaps the contents of variables `x` and `y` using a temporary variable `temp` in the process. We are able to abstract away the detail of this method by creating a subprogram `swap(a, b)` shown in *Figure 4.1.3.7(b)* whose body contains this pseudo-code. To swap the contents of two variables `x` and `y` we would substitute `x` and `y` for the formal parameters `a` and `b` and call subprogram `swap(x, y)`.

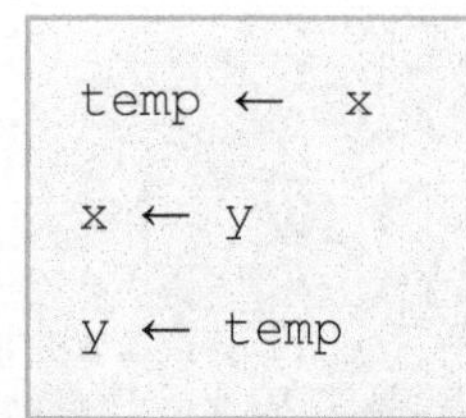

Figure 4.1.3.7(a) Pseudo-code to swap the contents of two variables x, y

```
swap(a, b)
```

Figure 4.1.3.7(b) Subprogram to swap the contents of two variables, a, b

Generalisation

Figure 4.1.3.8 illustrates what is meant by abstraction by **generalisation** or **classification** (by category).

> **Key term**
>
> **Abstraction by generalisation:** Means grouping by common characteristics to arrive at a hierarchical relationship of the 'is a kind of' type

Mammal

Cat   Dog

....   Siamese   Alsatian   Labrador

Bert   Sooty   ....   Fido   Rover

Figure 4.1.3.8 An example of abstraction by generalisation

Rising up the hierarchy, we go from specific examples of mammals to categories they belong to.

The relationship is classified as '*is a kind of*'. For example, Rover is a kind of Labrador, which is a kind of dog, etc.

All Labrador dogs have characteristics in common. Similarly, all types of dog have dog characteristics in common.

This grouping together by identifying common characteristics is a feature of generalisation.

Figure 4.1.3.9 shows how the dog part of this hierarchy could be modelled with arrays.

Table 4.1.3.1 shows the data structures that could be used to model the dog part of the hierarchy.

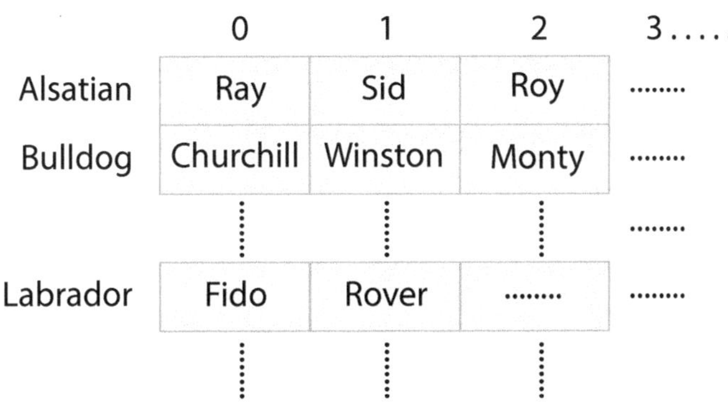

Figure 4.1.3.9 An array of one-dimensional arrays

Data structure	Variable
`TDogArray = Array[0..100] Of TString`	
`TDogBreedArray = Array[TDogBreed] Of TDogArray`	`DogBreedArray : TDogBreedArray`

Table 4.1.3.1 Data structures for modelling the Dog part of the hierarchy in Figure 4.1.3.7

The Array `DogBreedArray` could itself be an array element of a `MammalArray`.

These data structures use a user-defined data type

```
TDogBreed = (Alsation, Bulldog, ...., Labrador, ....)
```

This is an enumerated data type which enables meaningful names Alsation, Bulldog, ... to be used in place of 0, 1, 2, 3, ...

Figure 4.1.3.10 shows assignment of the names of some dogs to array `DogBreedArray`.

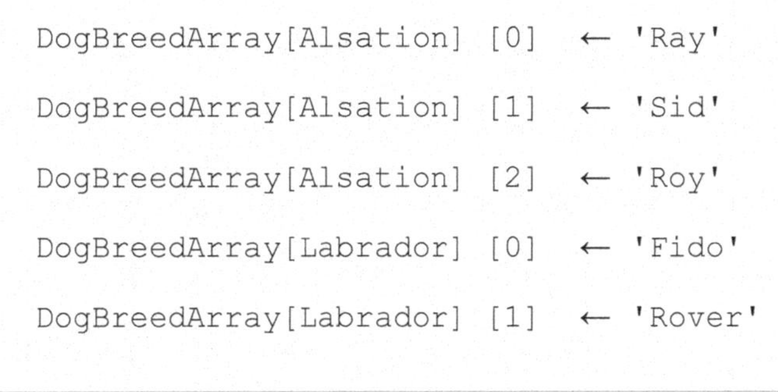

```
DogBreedArray[Alsation] [0]  ← 'Ray'
DogBreedArray[Alsation] [1]  ← 'Sid'
DogBreedArray[Alsation] [2]  ← 'Roy'
DogBreedArray[Labrador] [0]  ← 'Fido'
DogBreedArray[Labrador] [1]  ← 'Rover'
```

Figure 4.1.3.10 Assigning names of dogs to array DogBreedArray

Question

1. What is meant by
   (a) representational abstraction
   (b) abstraction by generalisation?

2. Why is it useful to work with an abstraction of reality when problem solving?

In this chapter you have covered:

- The concept of abstraction as used in computations:
  - representational abstraction - an abstraction arrived at by removing unnecessary details
  - abstraction by generalisation or categorisation - a grouping by common characteristics that produces a hierarchical relationship of the 'is a kind of' type.

4.1 Abstraction and automation

Learning objectives:

- *Information hiding:*

  Be familiar with the process of hiding all details of an object that do not contribute to its essential characteristics.

Key concept

Information hiding:
Information hiding means hiding design details behind a standard interface.

4.1.4 Information hiding

Modules

Large programs, or systems, benefit from being decomposed into modules. Modules can be separately-compilable units consisting of several subroutines (procedures and functions) or they be a single subroutine (which itself can be composed of other subroutines nested inside it).

Decomposing a software system into separate modules is considered the key to good design. However, there are many ways that a software system can be decomposed into modules. It is the job of design to decide how exactly the system should be decomposed.

Several guiding design principles inform the process of achieving good design:

- Each task that a software system or program is required to carry out should form a separate, distinct program module
- Each module and its inputs and outputs should be well-defined so it is clear to other modules how to use the module
- Each module should know as little as possible about how the other modules are designed internally.

When the design for the software system follows these principles, it should be possible to

- work independently on each module
- change the internal design of a module without affecting other modules which rely on the changed module, i.e. the other modules will not require changing as well
- understand how a particular module works without needing to know how other modules work internally
- test modules independently of other modules
- trace errors of the whole system or limitations of the whole system to individual modules thus limiting the scope of searching for errors.

Information hiding

Following the guiding design principles mentioned above means applying the principle of information hiding.

This means that each module should know as little as possible about how other modules with which it interacts are designed internally. The temptation to design a module using knowledge of some aspect of the internal design of another module is minimised if this is the case. Modules then can interact only through well-defined interfaces. Also, modules can be worked on independently of other modules.

Module interface(s)

Interfaces hide the complexities of a module and force interaction to take place only through an interface as illustrated in Figure 4.1.4.1. **Information hiding** means hiding design details behind a standard interface.

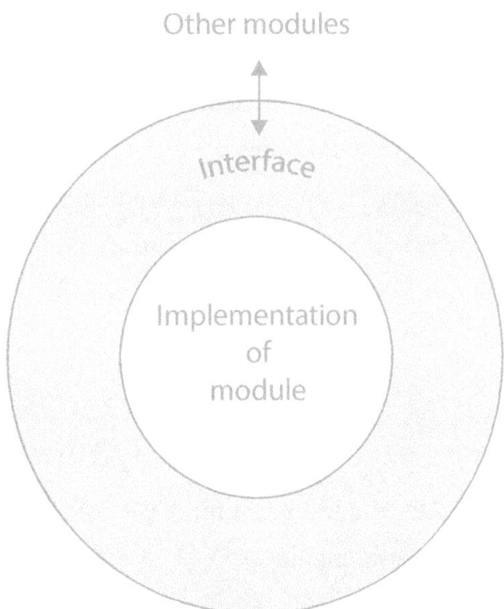

Figure 4.1.4.1 Hiding the complexity of a module behind an interface

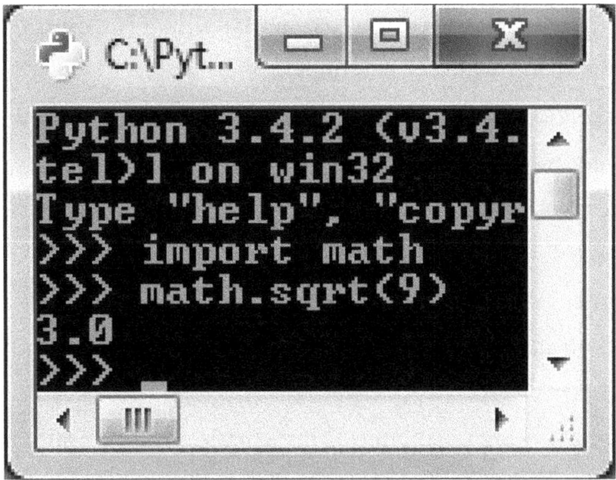

Figure 4.1.4.2 Importing the Python Math module and applying the sqrt function to argument 9

Figure 4.1.4.2 shows a Python example which imports a Python module *math*. Module *math* implements several mathematical routines each of which has its own interface.

The example uses one of these mathematical routines called *sqrt* and applies it to the argument 9. This routine calculates the positive square root of 9 without revealing how it does it. This is because Python hides the implementation of the mathematical routines in module *math* behind interfaces. If we only need

Information

Information hiding:

David Parnas first introduced the concept of information hiding around 1972 in a seminal paper 'On the Criteria to Be Used in Decomposing Systems into Modules'.

There are many ways to decompose a system into modules. A guiding principle is to minimise the number of "connections" between modules. This means that each module should know as little as possible about how other modules it interacts with are designed internally. The temptation then to design this module using knowledge of some aspect of the internal design of another module is minimised.

Adopting this design principle means that modules can only interact through well-defined interfaces. Hiding information (design information) in this manner:

- isolates other modules from the effects of changing the internal design decisions of a module.
- allows modules to be worked on independently of other modules
- means an intimate knowledge of the design of a module is not needed in order to use it.

to calculate the positive square root of a number, we don't need to know how the square root is being calculated. This is a form of abstraction known as functional abstraction.

The routines then are known as functions. To use mathematical routines in module *math* we need to know

- the name of each routine, e.g. *sqrt*
- the argument(s) that needs to be supplied
- what will be returned.

In the case of a module such as math, we call these three things in each case, the **interface** to the module. *Figure 4.1.4.3* shows the interface to Python's math module which is made up of maths functions, a sample of which are shown in the figure.

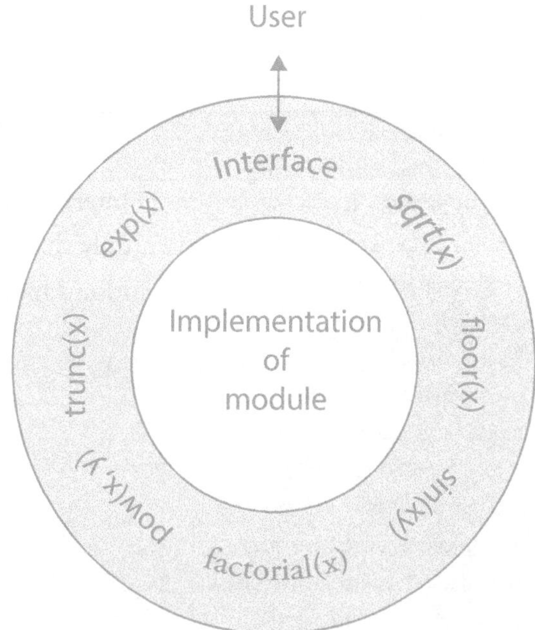

Figure 4.1.4.3 Some functions available in the Python Math module

Question

1 The modular design of a modern motor car consists among other things of the following major units:
An internal combustion engine

- a gear box
- a drive shaft
- wheels that are connected to the drive shaft

The engine is connected to the gear box which is connected to the drive shaft which in turn is connected to the wheels and which drives the wheels.

A driver controls the driving of the car through the following:

- a steering wheel
- a gear stick to select a gear, low gears for climbing uphill or pulling away and higher gears for cruising
- an accelerator pedal with which to accelerate the car
- a brake pedal with which to slow and stop the car
- various instruments including a speedometer which indicates the speed of the car.

Explain the design principle of information hiding using the design of a motor car. In your answer, you should consider whether the following benefits of information hiding are achieved in the design of a motor car and if they are, exactly how:

- isolates other modules from the effects of changing the internal design decisions of a module.
- an intimate knowledge of the design of a module is not needed in order to use it
- allows modules to be worked on independently of other modules.

Subroutine interface

The design principles embedded in the principle of information hiding were arrived at by studying how large scale software systems were developed. Nevertheless, these design principles can be usefully applied to even small scale projects. Figure 4.1.4.4 shows a very simple problem broken down into three modules which are actually the subroutines *Getn*, *CalculateSum* and *DisplayResult*. The problem posed is how to "*sum the natural numbers from* 1 *to n*", for example, if n = 6, Sum = 1 + 2 + 3 + 4 + 5 + 6 = 21.

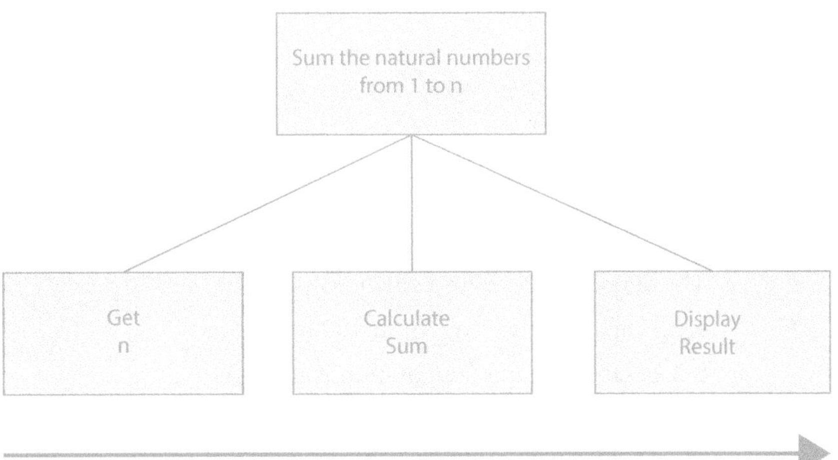

Figure 4.1.4.4 Hierarchy chart for Sum natural numbers from 1 to n with an arrow indicating the order of execution

We view the subroutine *CalculateSum* as a black box with one input and one output as shown in Figure 4.1.4.5. In the case, we call the input and the output the interface because the module is a single subroutine.

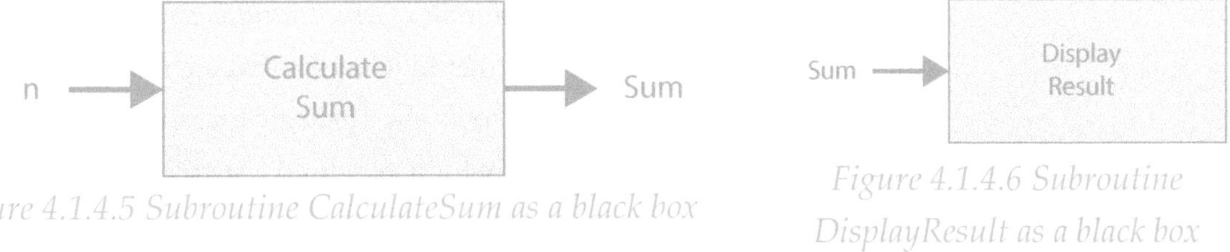

Figure 4.1.4.5 Subroutine CalculateSum as a black box

Figure 4.1.4.6 Subroutine DisplayResult as a black box

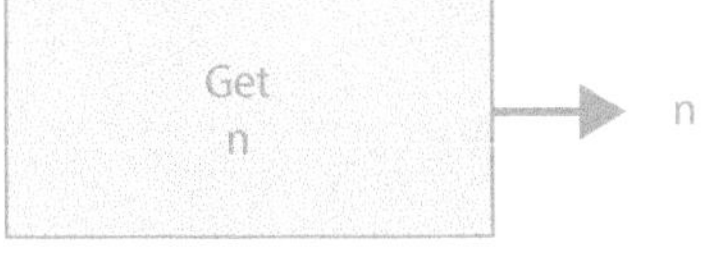

Figure 4.1.4.7 Subroutine Getn as a black box

Figure 4.1.4.6 shows subroutine *DisplayResult* as a black box. It accepts as input the value of *Sum* which it then displays on the console. In this case, we call the input the interface because the module is a single subroutine

Figure 4.1.4.7 shows subroutine *Getn* as a black box. It outputs the value of *n* which it has read from the keyboard. In this case, we call the output the interface because the module is a single subroutine.

The implementation details of each subroutine is hidden when we view each as a black box. This means that we should be able to substitute subroutine *CalculateSum* by one which calculates the sum in a different way, but without affecting how subroutine *CalculateSum* is used in the program as long as its interface is the same.

Task

1. Using a programming language of your choice, implement a program that uses the three subroutines *Getn*, *CalculateSum*, *DisplayResult* to sum the natural numbers from 1 to *n*. For example, n = 6, Sum = 1 + 2 + 3 + 4 + 5 + 6 = 21. You should use Gauss' method of summing natural numbers in *CalculateSum* (see Chapter 5.1.1).
2. Now without altering *CalculateSum*'s interface replace Gauss's method by the brute force method of summing natural numbers in *CalculateSum*, i.e. Sum = 1 + 2 + 3 + 4 + 5 + 6 + ...

Data encapsulation

We may hide the implementation of a queue behind an interface (*Figure 4.1.4.8*) and restrict access to the queue to the following subroutines:

- AddItem(x)
- RemoveItem
- IsEmpty
- IsFull
- Flush

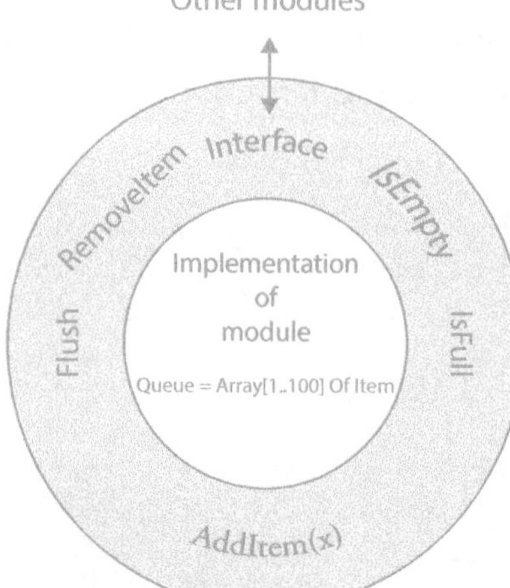

Figure 4.1.4.8 Interface for the queue

This is called **data encapsulation**, another form of information hiding.

The queue could be implemented as an array capable of storing up to 100 items but because the implementation is hidden, modules which use the queue module would not be given this information.

They would interact with the queue through the module's interface routines. The implementation of these would also be hidden.

Information

Queue:

A queue is a first in first out data structure for storing data items. Data items are removed in turn from the front of the queue. Data items join the queue at the rear in the order of their arrival.

Hiding all details of an object that do not contribute to its essential characteristics

The Python *math* module, the modules *Getn*, *CalculateSum*, *DisplayResult*, and the *queue* module are all objects that hide details that are not essential for other modules which use this module to know. These are examples of information hiding by which design details are hidden behind a standard interface.

Question

2 Explain with examples drawn from software systems what is meant by information hiding.

In this chapter you have covered:

- Information hiding:
  - the process of hiding all details of an object that do not contribute to its essential characteristics.

4.1 Abstraction and automation

Learning objectives:

- *Know that procedural abstraction represents a computational method.*

4.1.5 Procedural abstraction

Computations

The arithmetic expression 3 × 4 + 2 represents a computation which can be described with reductions as follows

$$3 \times 4 + 2 \rightarrow 12 + 2 \rightarrow 14$$

The given expression describes a single computation.

Key term

Computation:
An arithmetic expression such as

3 × 4 + 2

describes a single computation.

Formula

A formula is an expression containing variables. It represents a whole class of computations, since the variable(s) can assume different values.

For example, the formula corresponding to the computation above

`a x b + c`

uses the variables `a, b, c`.

Substituting integers for the variables, `a, b, c`, produces an expression whose value can be computed. For example, a = 3, b = 4, c = 2

$$3 \times 4 + 2 \rightarrow 12 + 2 \rightarrow 14$$

The formula `a x b + c` describes one computation for each possible combination of values for `a, b, c`.

Since there are an infinite number of integers, the formula represents an infinite number of computations.

Key term

Formula:
A formula is an expression containing variables. It represents a whole class of computations, since the variable(s) can assume different values, e.g.

`a x b + c`

Procedural abstraction

The formula `a x b + c` is an abstraction because it omits the actual numbers to be used in the computation. The formula `a x b + c` represents a computational method, a procedure. Such an abstraction is called a procedural abstraction, since the result of the abstraction is a procedure, a method.

In general, there are many methods for obtaining a desired result.

The result of a procedural abstraction is a procedure.

For example, suppose we wished to calculate the `sum` of the first `n` natural numbers. We have two choices of method or formula for calculating this sum:

$$\frac{n \times (n + 1)}{2}$$

and

$$1 + 2 + 3 + 4 + \ldots + (n - 1) + n$$

The above two methods are examples of procedural abstraction.

Key term

Procedural abstraction:
The formula a x b + c represents a computational method, a procedure. Such an abstraction is called a procedural abstraction, since the result of the abstraction is a procedure, or method.

Question

1. Using words and phrases such as computation, formula, and computational method explain procedural abstraction.

In this chapter you have covered:

- Procedural abstraction which represents a computational method.

Learning objectives:

- Know that functional abstraction the particular computation method is hidden.

4.1.6 Functional abstraction

Functional abstraction

The result of a procedural abstraction is a procedure, not a function. To get a function another abstraction, which disregards the particular computation method, must be performed.

The result of this abstraction is a function and the abstraction is called functional abstraction. The focus is then on the input(s) and the output.

For example, suppose we wished to calculate the sum of the first n natural numbers. We have two choices of method or formula for calculating this sum:

$$\frac{n \times (n + 1)}{2}$$

and

$$1 + 2 + 3 + 4 + \ldots + (n - 1) + n$$

The above two methods are examples of procedural abstraction.

The black box in Figure 4.1.6.1 hides the particular method used to calculate the sum for a particular n and so is an example of functional abstraction.

Figure 4.1.6.1 Calculation of sum of first n natural numbers

All that a user needs to know are the number and order of the inputs and the name of the function in order to be able to apply the function to these inputs.

Key term

Functional abstraction: By disregarding the particular computation method we get an abstraction known as a function, By knowing the number and order of the inputs and the name of the function we are able to apply the function to these inputs.

Parameters

The formula used to define a function is sometimes called the body of the function. The name used for the quantity that can vary is called the parameter of the function. Therefore in the example above n is the parameter.

The function associated with the formula $\frac{n \times (n + 1)}{2}$ is given a name, e.g. sum.

To use the sum function, we apply it to an argument.

For instance, to find the sum of the first 6 natural numbers, the function sum is applied to the argument 6.

Thus the parameter, n, is the name used in the function body to refer to the argument, 6.

To compute the value of the function for some argument, replace the parameter in the body of the function by the argument and compute the expression.

For example,

$$n = 6 \longrightarrow \frac{n \times (n + 1)}{2}$$

$$= \frac{6 \times (6 + 1)}{2}$$

$$= 21$$

Question

1 What is functional abstraction?

In this chapter you have covered:

- Functional abstraction which hides the particular computation method.

4 Theory of computation

4.1 Abstraction and automation

Learning objectives:

- *Know that details of how data are actually represented are hidden, allowing new kinds of data objects to be constructed from previously defined data types*

4.1.7 Data abstraction

Isolating the use of a compound data object from its construction details

Creating a compound object

Learning how to program is a process of developing the ability to model problems in such a way that a computer can solve them.

Suppose that we want to model a queue at an ATM such as shown in *Figure 4.1.7.1*. People join the queue at the rear and leave from the front to use the ATM to withdraw cash.

Figure 4.1.7.1 Queue of people at an ATM

To model the queue, we first ignore all but the essential details of each person which are necessary to solve the problem. The problem might be to know how much money to load the ATM with at the beginning of each day.

We reduce each person to a single uniform object illustrated in *Figure 4.1.7.2*. We have abstracted away unnecessary details of a person.

Figure 4.1.7.2 Queue of people with unnecessary details removed

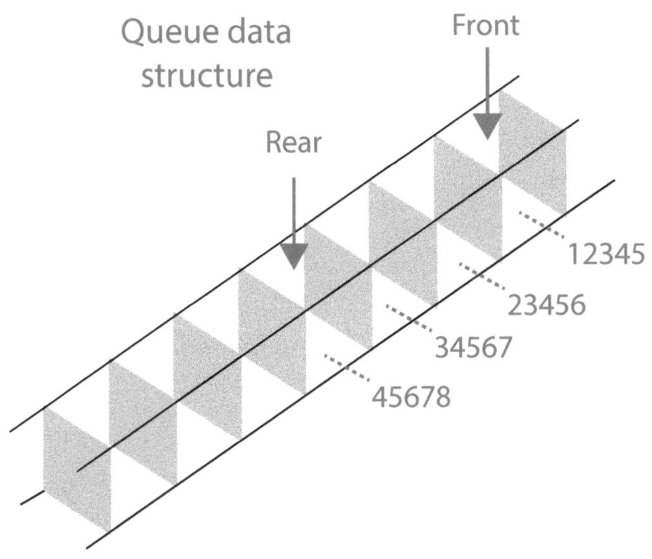

Figure 4.1.7.3 Queue data structure

The next stage models a person joining the queue by adding their values for these essential details (e.g. card number, card expiry date, name on card) to the queue. We use a data structure to store these details as illustrated in *Figure 4.1.7.3*.

The data structure must have storage space for the essential details of each person currently in the queue and for persons who join the queue subsequently.

It is a **compound object** because it is constructed to store the details of more than one person, e.g. `Person1` with card number '12345', `Person2` with card number '23456', etc.

Using the queue compound object

We could use a subroutine, `AddItem(Person)` to add a person's details to the rear of the queue, passing the person's essential details in the variable `Person`.

To model a person leaving the queue to use the ATM, we could use a subroutine `RemoveItem` which returns the person's essential details.

This would remove the person's essential details from the front of the queue.

Of course, we need to apply constraints to this model:

1. A person may only join the queue at the rear
2. A person may only leave the queue from its front
3. A person cannot join a full queue[1]
4. A person cannot be removed from an empty queue

Therefore, we need subroutines to test whether the queue is full or not and to test whether the queue is empty or not:

- `IsFull`
- `IsEmpty`

Finally we need to be able to clear the queue so that we can start with an empty queue. For this we use a subroutine `Flush`.

Figure 4.1.7.4 shows a Pascal program which uses a queue. However, the details of the queue's construction are hidden in a module `HiddenQueueDetails`.

```
Program QueueExample;
{$APPTYPE CONSOLE}
Uses HiddenQueueDetails;
Var
  Person1 : String = '12345';
  Person2 : String = '23456';
  Person3 : String = '34567';
  Person4 : String = '45678';
Begin
  Flush;
  AddItem(Person1);
  AddItem(Person2);
  AddItem(Person3);
  If Not IsEmpty
    Then Writeln(RemoveItem)
    Else Writeln('Queue Empty');
  Readln;
End.
```

Figure 4.1.7.4 Pascal program which uses a queue

The program can only access the queue by calling subroutines defined in the module `HiddenQueueDetails` and made available through the module's interface - see *Figure 4.1.7.5* and *Figure 4.1.7.6*.

The module is also written in Pascal but it is only available to the program in object code form so that how it has been constructed is hidden.

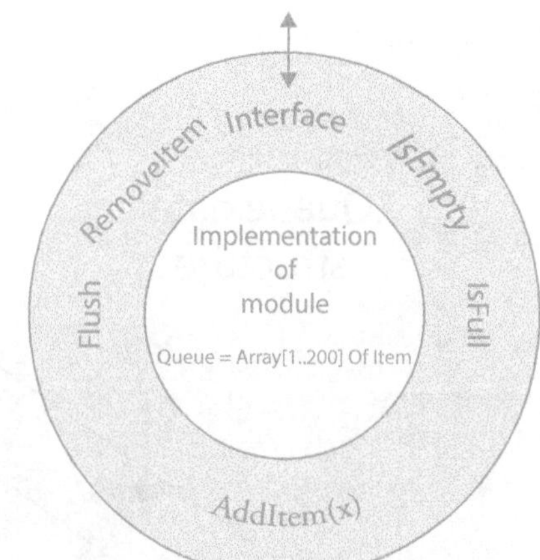

Figure 4.1.7.5 Interface to the implementation of a queue of 200 items

Constructing and hiding the queue compound object

In module `HiddenQueueDetails`, the queue is constructed from an array of 200 cells. The cell data type is string in this example. A more realistically application of queues might use a record type.

The module/unit implements a circular queue (*Figure 4.1.7.7*).

In *Figure 4.1.7.6* the only part of the module/unit which is exposed to other modules is placed in the *Interface* section.

The hidden part of the module/unit is placed in the *Implementation* section.

This includes the `type` definition `TQueue = Array[1..200] Of String` and the variable declaration

```
Var Queue : TQueue; Front, Rear : Integer;
```

`Front` and `Rear` are queue pointers.

1 There is a waiting area and people are not allowed to wait for the ATM unless they are standing in the waiting area and the waiting area can only hold X people.

```
Unit HiddenQueueDetails;
Interface
  Procedure Flush;
  Procedure AddItem (Item : String);
  Function RemoveItem : String;
  Function IsEmpty : Boolean;
  Function IsFull : Boolean;
Implementation
  Uses System.Contnrs;
  Type
    TQueue = Array[1..200] Of String;
  Var
    Queue : TQueue;
    Front, Rear : Integer;
  Procedure Flush;
    Begin
      Front := 0;
      Rear := 0;
    End;
  Procedure AddItem (Item : String);
    Begin
      If (Front=0) And (Rear=0)
        Then
          Begin
            Front := 1;
            Rear := 1;
            Queue[Rear] := Item;
           End
        Else
          Begin
            If (Rear Mod 200) + 1 = Front
              Then Writeln('Queue Full!')
              Else
                Begin
                  Rear := (Rear Mod 200) + 1;
                  Queue[Rear] := Item;
                End;
          End;
    End;
  Function RemoveItem : String;
    Begin
      If (Front=0) And (Rear=0)
        Then Writeln('Queue Empty!')
        Else
          Begin
            RemoveItem := Queue[Front];
            If Front=Rear
              Then
                Begin
                  Front := 0;
                  Rear := 0;
                End
              Else Front := (Front Mod 200) + 1;
          End;
    End;
  Function IsEmpty : Boolean;
    Begin
      If Front = 0
        Then IsEmpty := True
        Else IsEmpty := False;
    End;
  Function IsFull : Boolean;
    Begin
      If (Rear Mod 200) + 1 = Front
        Then IsFull := True
        Else IsFull := False;
    End;
End.
```

The only part of this unit which is exposed to other modules/programs is placed in the Interface section.

The hidden part of this unit is placed in the Implementation section.

Figure 4.1.7.6 Pascal module which creates a queue of 200 items by declaring an array of 200 cells, with each designed to store a string.

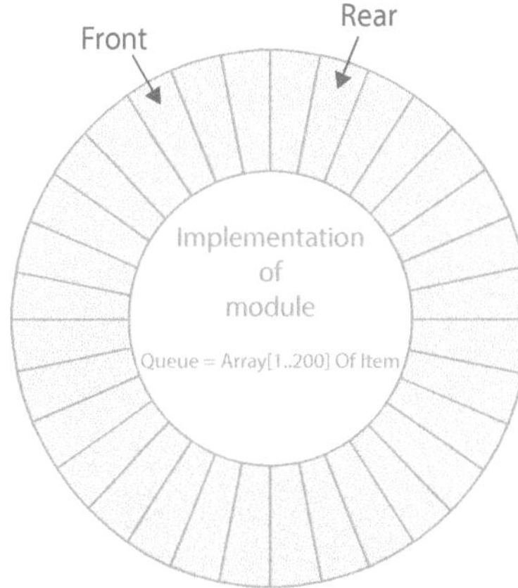

Figure 4.1.7.7 The unit implements a circular queue

Key point

Data abstraction:

Data abstraction is a methodology that enables us to isolate how a data object is used from the details of how it is constructed.

Information

Keyboard buffers are usually implemented as circular buffers. The buffering allows typing ahead. and lazy I/O. Lazy I/O means that a line typed at the keyboard is not processed until the return key is pressed. Until this happens the line may be changed.

Figure 4.1.7.8 A stack of books

Questions

1. What is meant by *data abstraction*?

2. *Figure 4.1.7.8* shows a stack of books. Books are added and removed from a stack at one end only which is called the top of stack.
   (a) Suggest one way that the stack of books could be modelled in a computer.
   (b) What operations might be needed for this stack?
   (c) Explain how you would isolate the compound data object which models the stack from its construction.

Programming tasks

1. Model the stack exercise described in Question 2 in a programming language with which you are familiar. The stack should just store a string representing the ISBN of the book recorded on the stack (use a made-up truncated ISBN that is easy to type).
   The details of how the stack is constructed and the details of the operations which access this stack should be hidden from the program which uses the stack in a separate module/unit - see queue code example in *Figure 4.1.7.6*.
   The program should use the operations exported from the stack module/unit to add and remove books from the stack.

In this chapter you have covered:

- That details of how data are actually represented are hidden, allowing new kinds of data objects to be constructed from previously defined data types

4 Theory of computation

4.1 Abstraction and automation

4.1.8 Problem abstraction/reduction

Learning objectives:

- *Know that the details are removed until the problem is represented in a way that is possible to solve because the problem reduces to one that has already been solved.*

Pigeonhole principle

Generalisation can be applied to problem solving by identifying a principle that is shared among solutions to different problems.

This is an example of **problem abstraction or reduction**.

One example of this is the **pigeonhole principle**, which states that, given two natural numbers n and m with n > m, if n items are put into m pigeonholes, then at least one pigeonhole must contain more than one item (*Figure 4.1.8.1*).

A simple application of this principle is a situation where there are six people who want to play football (n = 6 objects) but there are only five teams available that they can play for (m = 5 holes).

This would not be a problem except that each of the six refuses to play on a team with any of the other five.

To prove that there is no way for all six people to play football together, the pigeonhole principle says that it is impossible to allocate six people among five teams without putting two of the people on the same team. Since they refuse to play on the same team, at most five of the people will be able to play.

Why is this principle applicable to more than just the football team problem? The reason is that when **unnecessary details of specific problems are ignored**, **the problems reduce to the common problem** of fitting n items into m holes. For example, there must be at least two people in London with the same number of hairs on their head. Is this true or false?

We will use the pigeonhole principle to answer this as follows.

A typical head of hair has around 150 000 hairs; it is reasonable to assume that no one has more than 1 000 000 hairs on his or her head (m = 1 000 000 holes) but there are more than 1 000 000 people in London (n is bigger than 1 million objects). If we assign a pigeonhole for each number of hairs on a head and assign people to the pigeonhole with their number of hairs on it, there must be at least two people with the same number of hairs on their head.

Figure 4.1.8.1

Question

1. If there are n persons (where n > 1) who can shake hands with one another, explain using the pigeonhole principle why there is always a pair of persons who shake hands with the same number of people. Here the holes correspond to the number of hands shaken.

2. Assume that in a box there are 10 black socks and 12 blue socks and you need to get one pair of socks of the same colour. Supposing you can take socks out of the box only once and only without looking. How many socks do you have to pull out together? Use the pigeonhole principle.

Data representation

Representation abstraction is applied to problem solving. It is also known as **problem abstraction or reduction**. Details are removed until it becomes possible to represent the problem in a way that is possible to solve.

For example, mobile phone networks consist of a series of base stations, each of which provides coverage over a limited range for mobile phones as shown in *Figure 4.1.8.2*.

A mobile phone signal is not strong enough to reach across the country. Instead, a mobile phone communicates with its nearest base station, usually mounted on a mast. The nearest base station then relays the signal over a cabled network to a base station in a neighbouring cell, which in turn passes the signal onto another base station.

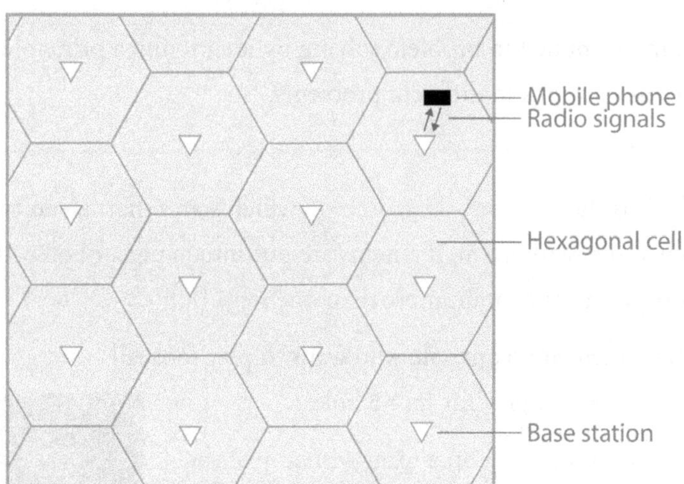

Figure 4.1.8.2 Mobile phone cellular network

The mobile phone company needs to buy the radio frequencies used by its customers and base stations. These frequencies are very expensive, so the company needs to buy as few as possible and reuse them.

The problem is that if mobile phones and base stations in neighbouring cells use the same broadcast frequency, calls will interfere with each other, resulting in poor communications.

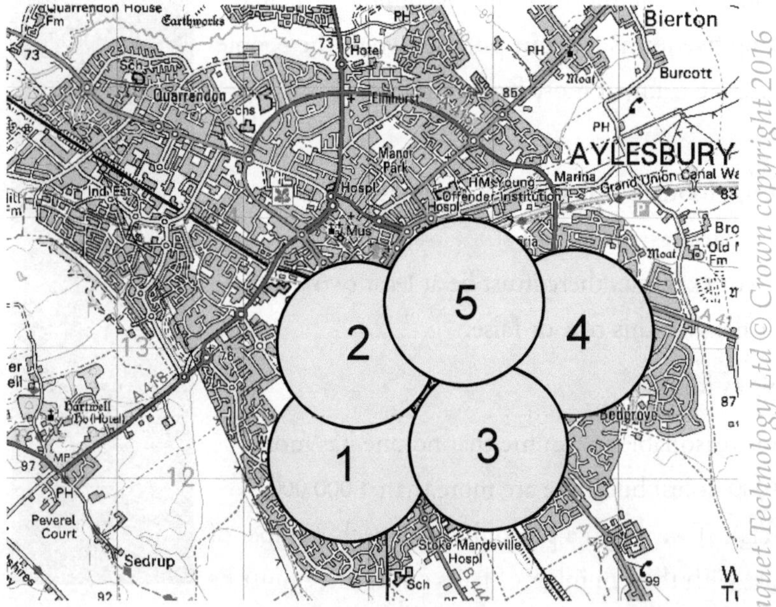

Figure 4.1.8.3 Locations and mobile coverage of the mobile phone masts

Suppose that you are required to work out the minimum number of frequencies that a mobile phone company must buy in order to provide interference-free coverage of the area covered by phone masts located as indicated in *Table 4.1.8.1* and *Figure 4.1.8.3*.

How could you represent the information from *Figure 4.1.8.3* and *Table 4.1.8.1* to make it easier to understand?

The solution is to remove unnecessary detail and represent it as a collection of circles (vertices) and connecting lines (edges)

Mobile phone masks	Location	Potential for interference with
1	Stoke Mandeville Road	2, 3
2	Town centre	1, 5
3	Wendover Road	1, 4, 5
4	Broughton	3, 5
5	Canal Walk	2, 3, 4

Table 4.1.8.1 Mobile phone mast potential signal interference

(Figure 4.1.8.4). Figure 4.1.8.4 is known as a graph. This is a model of the mobile phone network shown in Figure 4.1.8.3.

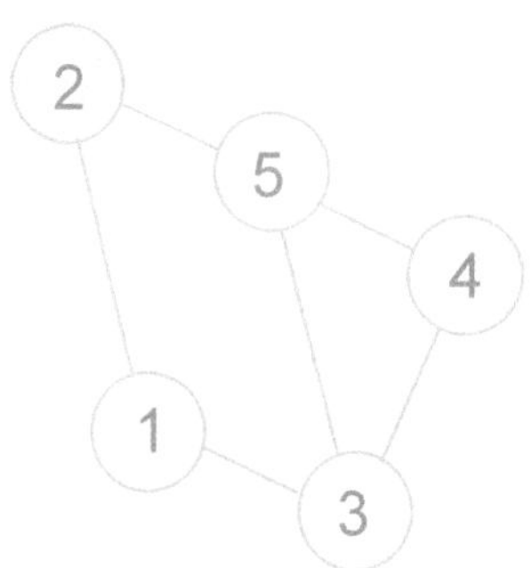

Figure 4.1.8.4 Abstract representation of mobile phone network

Next represent Figure 4.1.8.4 in table form (Table 4.1.8.2). Table 4.1.8.2 shows that mobile phone masts labelled 2 and 3 are adjacent to mobile phone mast labelled 1. By adjacent is meant that the transmissions from mobile phone masts 2 and 3 overlap with those from mobile phone mast 1.

Vertex	Adjacent
1	2, 3
2	1, 5
3	1, 4, 5
4	3, 5
5	2, 3, 4

Table 4.1.8.2 Shows the adjacency of mobile phone masts to each other

Figure 4.1.8.5 shows a solution to this problem. Different frequencies are represented by different colours in this figure. The solution shows that only three frequencies are required. Every vertex (base station) uses a frequency that will not interfere with a neighbouring vertex (base station) with which it is connected by an edge, i.e. mobile transmissions overlap.

Map colouring problem

Figure 4.1.8.6 shows a map divided into numbered sections.

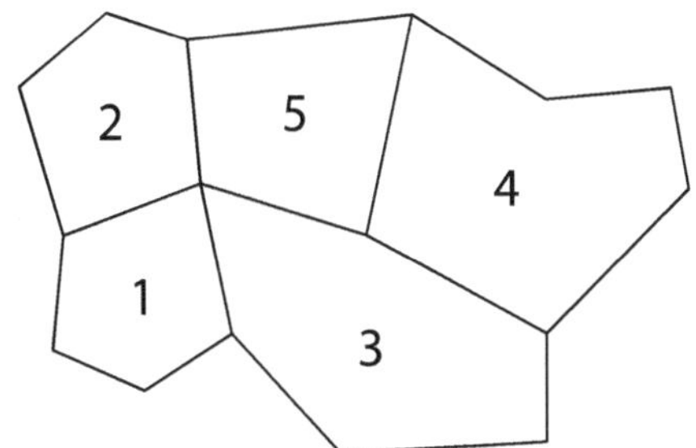

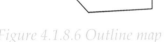

Figure 4.1.8.6 Outline map

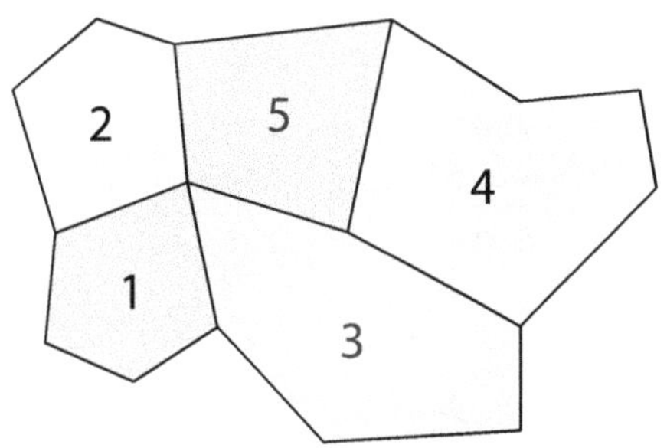

Figure 4.1.8.7 Outline map with countries coloured

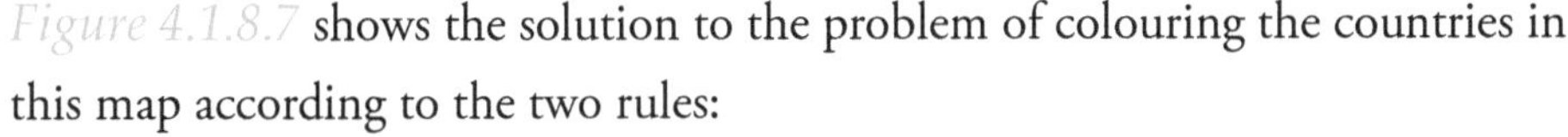

Figure 4.1.8.7 shows the solution to the problem of colouring the countries in this map according to the two rules:

- No countries that share a border should be the same colour.
- As few colours as possible should be used.

If we abstract away the shape of each section of the outline map of Figure 4.1.8.6 and represent each section by a circle (vertex) and each boundary between two countries by a connecting line (edge) we obtain a similar graph to Figure 4.1.8.4. If we do the same for the solution to the map colouring problem shown in Figure 4.1.8.7, we obtain a similar graph to that shown in Figure 4.1.8.5.

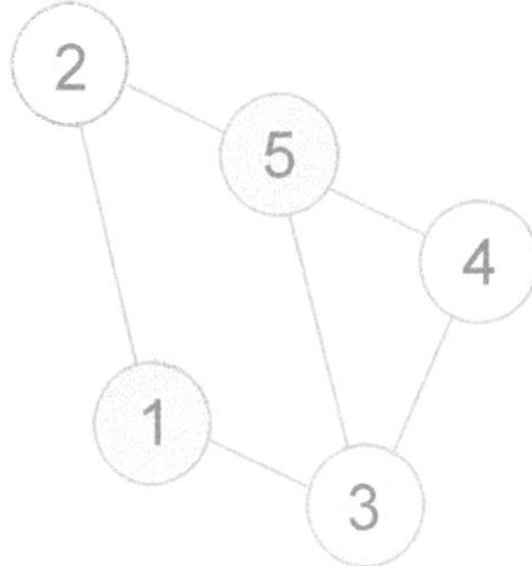

Figure 4.1.8.5 Solution to the mobile phone frequency allocation problem

Both problems - allocation of mobile phone frequencies and map colouring - share a common representation when unnecessary details are removed. Both reduce to a similar abstraction, a graph - Figure 4.1.8.4. If a problem can be transformed into a representation of another for which a solution exists then this solution can be used to solve the problem. Simply apply the algorithm of the existing solution to the new problem.

Algorithm to solve mobile phone mast frequency selection and map colouring problem

Table 4.1.8.3 shows the algorithm to allocate mobile phone mast frequencies and to colour map sections.

```
Repeat
  Remove vertex with lowest connectivity and its links from graph
  Add this vertex and its list of connected vertices to a record of those removed,
    held in order of removal
Until graph empty
Repeat
  Replace vertices in graph in reverse order of removal, noting a legal colour each time
Until Stack of records empty
```

Table 4.1.8.3 Frequency selection and map colouring algorithm

Figure 4.1.8.8 shows the first stage of this algorithm being traced. *Figure 4.1.8.9* shows the second stage of this algorithm being traced.

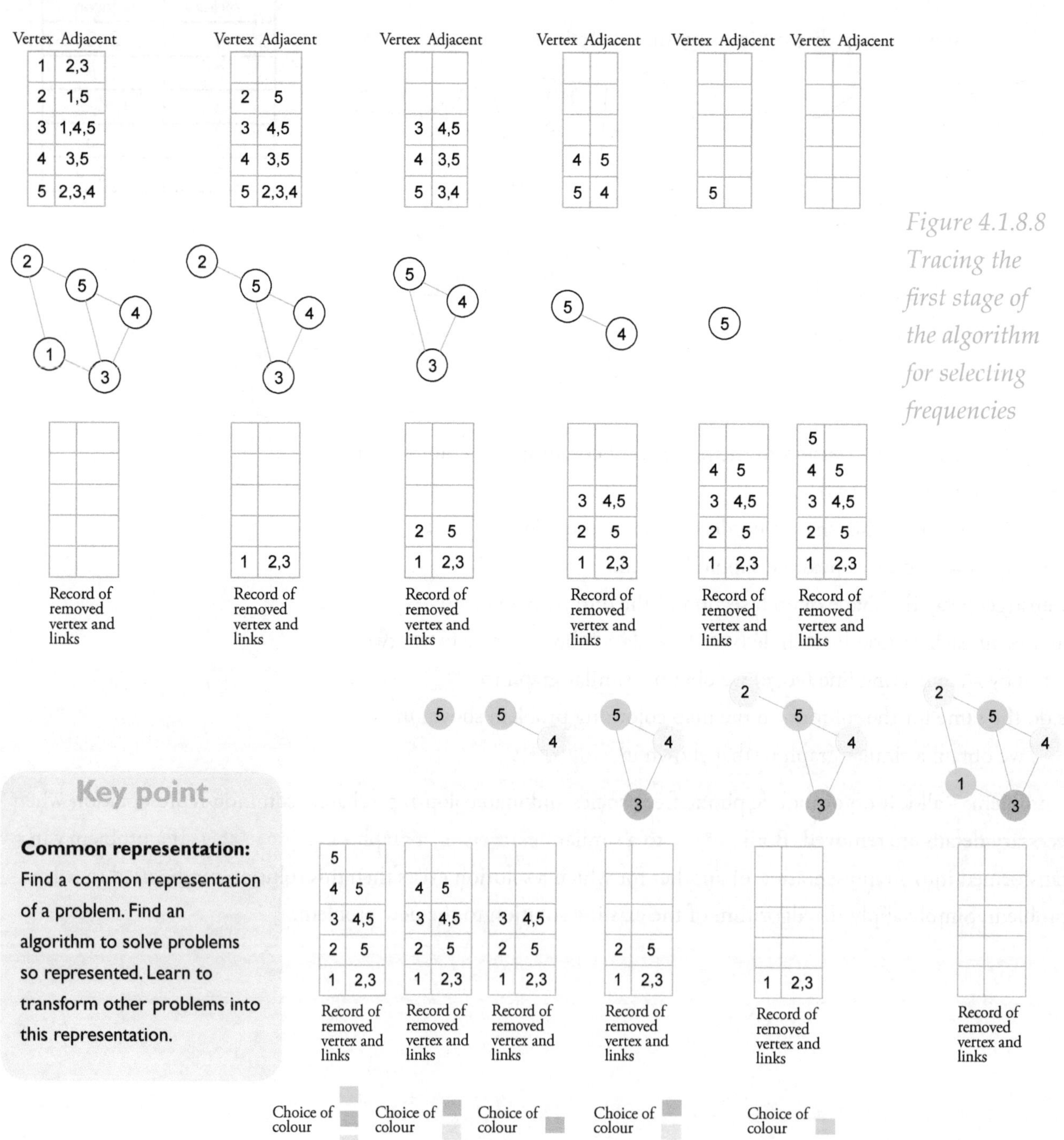

Figure 4.1.8.8 Tracing the first stage of the algorithm for selecting frequencies

Figure 4.1.8.9 Tracing the second stage of the algorithm for selecting frequencies

Key point

Common representation:
Find a common representation of a problem. Find an algorithm to solve problems so represented. Learn to transform other problems into this representation.

Question

3 Using a map of South America, draw a representation that would help in the task of colouring this map with the minimum number of colours so that no two countries sharing a border would have the same colour.

Task

1 Watch Professor Paul Curzon's video on Graphs https://www.youtube.com/watch?v=xRKCDcRVpQg. This video illustrates problem abstraction/reduction by considering a puzzle game based the Knight's tour problem which can be reduced to the same problem of visiting tourist attractions in which each is visited only once.

In this chapter you have covered:

- Problem abstraction/reduction whereby *details of the problem are removed until the problem is represented in a way that is possible to solve because the problem reduces to one that has already been solved.*

4 Theory of computation

4.1 Abstraction and automation

Learning objectives:

- *Know that procedural decomposition means breaking a problem into a number of sub-problems, so that each sub-problem accomplishes an identifiable task, which might itself be further subdivided*

4.1.9 Decomposition

Procedural decomposition

Breaking big problems into smaller problems, or sub-problems, is called a top-down strategy. It may be far easier to deal with a number of smaller problems each of which accomplishes a single identifiable task than one large problem.

When the top-down strategy is used to plan a solution it is called **top-down design**.

The process of breaking a problem down through successive steps into smaller problems is also known as **stepwise refinement**.

Stepwise refinement has been covered in detail in *Chapter 1.2.1* on structured programming.

In essence, a problem is sub-divided into a number of sub-problems.
If these can be solved directly then the decomposition is complete. If not then sub-problems are further divided and so on until small enough problems result which identify a single task and which can be directly coded in a functionally cohesive subroutine (see *Chapter 1.2.1*).

The solution to the problem now consists of a sequence of subroutine calls each of which contributes to a part of the solution.

Key concept

Procedural decomposition:
Procedural decomposition is a top-down strategy in which big problems are broken into smaller problems by a process of stepwise refinement which continues until small enough problems result identifying a single task which can be directly coded as a functionally cohesive subroutine.

Questions

1. What is meant by decomposition in the context of problem solving?

In this chapter you have covered:

- *Procedural decomposition which means breaking a problem into a number of sub-problems, so that each sub-problem accomplishes an identifiable task, which might itself be further subdivided*

4 Theory of computation

4.1 Abstraction and automation

Learning objectives:

- *Know how to build a composition abstraction by combining procedures to form compound procedures*
- *Know how to build data abstractions by combining data objects to form compound data.*

4.1.10 Composition

Composition abstraction

Composition

In the process known as bottom-up development, a solution is developed by "plugging" together existing components whose reliability and usefulness have been demonstrated already, e.g. assorted Lego® bricks as shown in Figure 4.1.10.1 can be used to build structures such as model toy houses. A model toy house built of Lego bricks is an example of composition.

There is little abstraction in Lego bricks, "what you see is what you get". However, in something as complex as a motor car, the building blocks that most people can identify are the engine, the gearbox, the brakes, etc which a car is composed of. Each of these components is an abstraction hiding considerable complexity. Workers on car production lines can put cars together without needing to focus on the internal workings of the components because the engine comes as a unit as does the gearbox and so on. These components just need to be "plugged" together correctly to make a motor car.

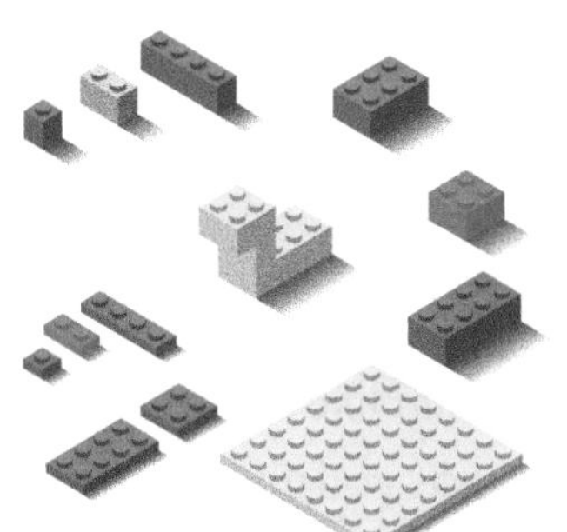

Figure 4.1.10.1 Various types of Lego bricks which have proved useful and which are used by millions to construct Lego® buildings, etc

Combining procedures to form compound procedures

In a similar manner, software can be assembled from tried and tested components. Writing correct software is a demanding, time-consuming activity. It makes sense therefore to reuse software wherever possible. If the software is modular, then modules can be combined in different ways to solve new problems. The procedure is one form of module.

> *"By June 1949, people had begun to realize that it was not so easy to get a program right as had at one time appeared. It was on one of my journeys between the EDSAC[1] room and the punching equipment that the realization came over me with full force that a good part of the remainder of my life was going to be spent in finding errors in my own programs."*
>
> Maurice Wilkes, computing pioneer

Did you know?

David Wheeler, University of Cambridge, Computer Laboratory, was the inventor of closed subroutines and the subroutine call in 1949.

Maurice Wilkes was director of this laboratory at the time and led a team of people tasked with building of a library of subroutines for the EDSAC 1 and subsequent digital stored program computers.

Suppose a programmer relies upon a routine task again and again in different programs that he or she writes. This task might be to sort a list of integers or to extract all English words of length *n* from a given text file.

After using and debugging these procedures in many programs, the programmer might be confident in the reliability of these procedures and decide that a better approach would be to combine together the procedures needed, say, for the sorting operation, into a compound procedure called *Sort*.

1 EDSAC 1 was the world's first complete and fully operational regular electronic digital stored program computer.

```
Procedure Sort (List)
  Procedure A
    Begin
      ...
      ...
    End;
  Procedure B
    Begin
      ...
      ...
    End
Begin
  ...
  A
  ...
  ...
  B
  ...
  ...
End
```

Table 4.1.10.1 Compound procedure called sort which defines other procedures within itself

This procedure could itself contain subordinate procedures called nested procedures which it could rely upon for the task of sorting a list.
Table 4.1.10.1 shows an example outline structure for such a compound procedure.

The detail of the sorting operation has been abstracted away by creating this named compound procedure, *Sort*. This is a form of **encapsulation**.
The example shown in Figure 4.1.10.1 is one way that encapsulation can be achieved.
If this compound procedure is provided in object form, i.e. compiled form, then whenever the programmer needs to sort a list of integers at a particular place in a program, it is sufficient to write the compound procedure name *Sort* at this point in the source code form of the program.
When this program is compiled, its object form will need to be linked to the object form of the compound procedure *Sort* for the executable program produced from the linking process to call *Sort* at runtime.

Libraries of (compound) generally useful procedures

It may transpire that the compound procedure *Sort* is so useful that other programmers would like to use it. To do this, the programmer could add it to a library of useful compound procedures which is made available for others to incorporate into their programs.
The standard Java graphics library, Java Swing, is quite challenging to use.
By wrapping Java Swing operations in higher-level procedures, access to graphics in Java can be made much easier.

Table 4.1.10.2 shows an example in which simpler "compound procedures" e.g. *StdDraw.line*, available in a Java class file (object file) *StdDraw* are used by the class *Plot*.
These "compound procedures" have abstracted away the messier detail of the Java Swing drawing procedures. Figure 4.1.10.2 shows the output from the Java program in Table 4.1.10.2 when it is executed.

```
public class Plot {
    public static void main(String[] args) {
          StdDraw.setPenRadius(0.05);
          StdDraw.setPenColor(StdDraw.BLUE);
          StdDraw.point(0.5, 0.5);
          StdDraw.setPenColor(StdDraw.MAGENTA);
          StdDraw.line(0.2, 0.2, 0.8, 0.2);
    }
}
```

Table 4.1.10.2 Java program which uses compound procedures in an object class file StdDraw

Table 4.1.10.3 shows a Delphi program that uses a compound procedure *Map* which can take a function, e.g. *Sqr* and apply (map) this to each element of an array, *A*, whose length is not specified until runtime.
In Table 4.1.10.3 *Map* is called as follows

```
Map(Sqr, MyArray);
```

The output of this program is shown in Figure 4.1.10.3.

Figure 4.1.10.2 Drawing created by Java program in Table 4.1.10.2

Procedure *Map* is passed array *MyArray* by reference and function *Sqr*.
Map applies function *Sqr* to each element of *MyArray*. On return from procedure *Map*, the *For loop* iterates through *MyArray* element by element, displaying each element's value on its own line.

Table 4.1.10.4 shows the Delphi Unit in which compound procedure *Map* is defined.

Although in this example, *Map* has been designed to work with any function that takes a single integer input and returns an integer result, *Map* could have been written to use a procedure instead of a function.

The details of how procedure *Map* is implemented are hidden by being placed in the implementation section of the unit. Only items placed in the interface section are visible outside the unit.

The program *ArrayTypeMap* in Table 4.1.10.3 only needs access to the object form of *Unit1* when it is compiled and linked into an executable.

```
Program ArrayTypeMap;
{$APPTYPE CONSOLE}
{$R *.res}
Uses
  System.SysUtils,
  Unit1 in 'Unit1.pas';
Var
  MyArray : Array[1..5] Of Integer = (1,2,3,4,5);
  i : Integer;
Function Sqr(x : Integer) : Integer;
  Begin
    Sqr := x * x;
  End;
Procedure Map(F : FunctionPtr; Var A : Array Of Integer);
  Var
    i : Integer;
  Begin
    For i := 1 To Length(A)
      Do A[i] := F(A[i]);
  End;
Begin
  Map(Sqr, MyArray);
  For i :=1 To Length(MyArray)
    Do Writeln(MyArray[i]);
  Readln;
End.
```

```
1
4
9
16
25
```

Figure 4.1.10.3

Table 4.1.10.3 Delphi program that uses a compound procedure Map which can take a function, e.g. Sqr and applies this to each element of an array, A

The compiler uses the interface information of *Unit1* to compile program *ArrayTypeMap* and the linker, which "stitches" object files together, requires the object forms of *ArrayTypeMap* and *Unit1* to produce an executable file, *ArrayTypeMap.Exe*.

```
Unit Unit1;
Interface
  Type
    FunctionPtr = Function(x : Integer) : Integer;
    Procedure Map(F : FunctionPtr; Var A : Array Of Integer);
Implementation
  Procedure Map(F : FunctionPtr; Var A : Array Of Integer);
    Var
      i : Integer;
    Begin
      For i := 1 To Length(A)
        Do A[i] := F(A[i]);
    End;
End.
```

Table 4.1.10.4 Delphi Unit in which compound procedure Map is defined.

Programming tasks

1. Combine procedures together to form a compound procedure which opens a given text file, A, for reading, opens a new text file for writing, B, reads the contents of A separating words from the surrounding white space (e.g. space character(s)), writes each word on a separate line to B.
   Write and test a program which uses your compound procedure on text files. The program should prompt the user for the name of the text file to be read and the name of the text file to be created and written to. Your compound procedure should be written to accept as parameters the filenames of the reading and writing text files and nothing else.

Data abstraction

Combining data objects to form compound data

Chapter 2.1.2 introduced arrays. An array is a compound or composite data type which allows a collection of data objects of the same type to be grouped into a single object. The objects placed in the cells of an array must be of the same data type but this can be any data type including another composite data type.

By aggregating data objects in this way we can compose named data structures which can be referenced collectively by their name. For example, it is possible to create queue data structures and stack data structures in this way.

This is data abstraction which has been covered in depth in Chapter 4.1.7.

In this chapter you have covered:

- *How to build a composition abstraction by combining procedures to form compound procedures*
- *How to build data abstractions by combining data objects to form compound data*

4 Theory of computation

4.1 Abstraction and automation

Learning objectives:

- *Understand that automation requires putting models (abstraction of real world objects/phenomena) into action to solve problems. This is achieved by*
    - *creating algorithms*
    - *implementing the algorithms in program code (instructions)*
    - *implementing the models in data structures*
    - *executing the code*

4.1.11 Automation

Models into action

The key process in Computer Science is **abstraction** which means building models which represent aspects of behaviour in the real-world which are of interest. For example, if we wanted to build an automated recommendation system for an online book store, we might choose to record the types of book and number of each type purchased as well as details that identify the respective customer.

Computer Science is not alone in building abstractions, mathematics and the natural sciences also build abstractions but their models only serve to describe and explain whereas Computer Science must, in addition, perform actions on and with the data that has been modelled if it is to solve problems. These actions are described by **algorithms** or step-by-step instructions which form what is called the **automation** stage of problem solving.

Whilst it is true that automation of tasks existed before Computer Science, their nature involved concrete, real-world objects, e.g. the Jacquard loom, not informational abstractions such as an online book recommendation system.

Computer scientists must turn their models into data structures which are supported in the programming language that will be used to implement the algorithms.

When the program-coded algorithms execute, the information stored in the data structures is transformed into new forms of information. This is the automation stage.

The scale and speed of processing of informational abstractions made possible by modern digital computers surpasses by many orders of magnitude anything that could be achieved by manual means.

Questions

1. Describe **two** informational abstractions in which automation plays a large rôle.

In this chapter you have covered:

- Automation requires putting models (abstraction of real world objects/phenomena) into action to solve problems. This is achieved by
    - creating algorithms
    - implementing the algorithms in program code (instructions)
    - implementing the models in data structures
    - executing the code

4 Theory of computation

4.2 Finite state machine (FSM)

Learning objectives:

- *Be able to draw and interpret simple state transition diagrams and state transition tables for FSMs with no output.*

Figure 4.2.2 Combination lock

Key term

Finite state machine (FSM): A finite state machine is a machine that consists of a fixed set of possible states, a set of allowable inputs (input symbol alphabet) some of which can change the machine's state, and, if it is a finite state machine with output, a set of possible outputs.

Key term

State transition diagram: A way of describing an FSM graphically. Each state is represented by a circle and each transition by an arrow labelled with the input that causes the transition.

4.2.1 Finite state machines (FSM)

What is a finite state machine?

A **finite state machine** is a machine that consists of a fixed set of possible states, a set of allowable inputs some of which can change the machine's state, and, if it is a finite state machine with outputs, a set of possible outputs[1]. *Figure 4.2.1* is the **state transition diagram** for a combination lock with combination code 537. A state transition diagram is a way of describing a FSM graphically.

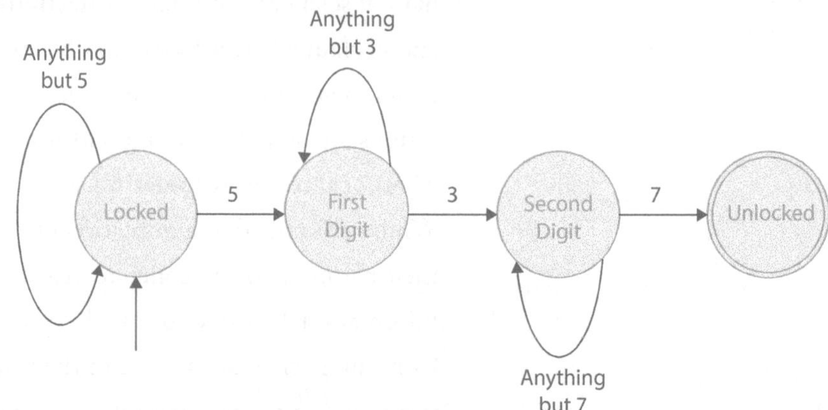

Figure 4.2.1 State transition diagram for a combination lock with combination code 537

The combination lock is an example of a finite state machine (FSM) with the following states

- Locked
- First Digit
- Second Digit
- Unlocked

and the set of allowable inputs {0-9} of which 5, 3 and 7 can change the state of the machine when entered in the right sequence. This FSM is without outputs.

The initial state of the combination lock is indicated by an arrow pointing to the state 'locked'. When the lock is in state 'locked' and it receives the input 5, the lock moves to the state 'First Digit'. When it receives the input 3, the lock moves to the state 'Second Digit'. When it receives the input 7, the lock moves to the state 'Unlocked'. At any stage, if a digit other than the required digit is entered, the lock remains in its current state. The final or halting state is reached when the combination lock is unlocked. The state 'Unlocked' is indicated by a double circle because it is the goal state. The goal state is more commonly known as the **accepting state**.

1 Not covered at AS Level

Key term

Finite state machine with no output:
A finite state machine with no output is an FSM that produces no output while processing the input but which responds YES/ACCEPT or NO/REJECT when it has finished processing the input.

FSMs with no output have an initial state and one or more accepting or goal states.
State transition diagrams use a special arrow to indicate the initial or starting state and a double circle to indicate the accepting states or goal states.

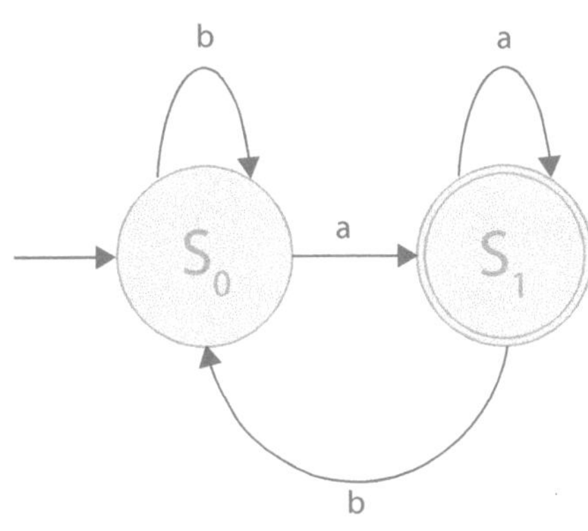

Figure 4.2.3 A finite state machine with no output that accepts a sequence of a's and b's which end in the symbol a

Key point

FSMs with no output solve decision problems, i.e. problems where the outcome is either YES or NO.

Key point

The states which cause the FSM to produce a YES or ACCEPT response are called accepting states. All other states cause the FSM to produce a NO or reject response.

Finite state machine with no output

A finite state machine with no output is an FSM that produces no output while processing the input.
Finite state machines with no output solve decision problems such as "does the input string end in the symbol a?".
Decision problems are ones where the outcome is either YES or NO.
A finite state machine with no output simply runs through the input sequence of symbols, one by one, changing state or not as a result of the current state and the current symbol from the input it sees.
On reaching the end of the input, it stops and, depending on which state it stopped in, accepting state or a non-accepting state, it is able to decide whether the input sequence has met the criteria or not, e.g. "does the input sequence of a's and b's end in the symbol a?".

The states which cause the FSM to indicate YES, the criteria have been met, are called accepting states. All other states are, by default, states that cause the FSM to indicate NO, the criteria have not been met. Accepting states are indicated by putting two rings round them, like S_1 in *Figure 4.2.3*. An FSM with no output always has one or more accepting states.

Figure 4.2.3 is a finite state machine with no output which accepts a sequence of a's and b's which end in the symbol a. The finite state machine uses an alphabet {a, b}.

Its start state is state S_0 indicated by →. It has one accepting state, S_1. The arrow-headed arcs represent transitions between states or a transition which starts and ends on the same state or the start state.

Figure 4.2.4 shows this finite state machine in a simulator accepting bbbbabbaaa because this sequence ends in the symbol a.

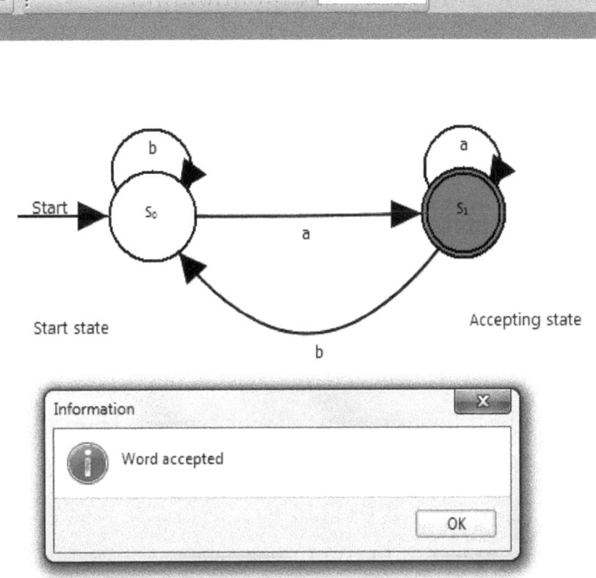

Figure 4.2.4 A finite state machine simulator FSMSim showing that the sequence bbbbabbabaaaa is accepted

Figure 4.2.5 shows this finite state machine in a simulator rejecting bbbbabbaab because the sequence of symbols does not end in the symbol a.

One reason that FSMs are so useful is that they can recognise sequences, e.g. the set of valid strings for some application.

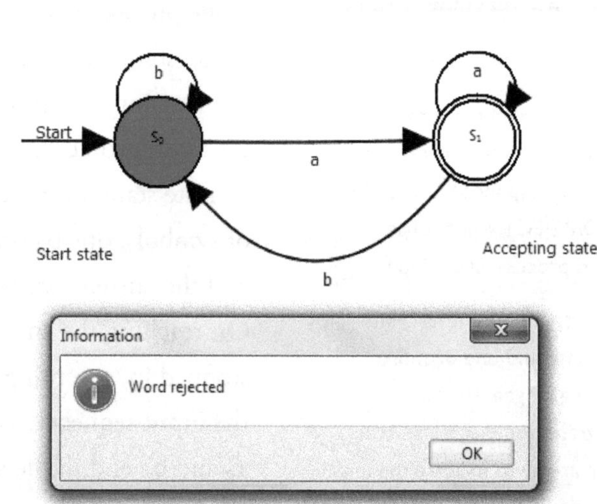

Figure 4.2.5 A finite state machine simulator FSMSim showing that the sequence bbbbabbaab is rejected

Key point

To avoid an FSM having to report an error, ensure that for each state there is an outgoing transition for every symbol in the machine's input alphabet.

Question

1. *Figure 4.2.6* is a finite state machine with alphabet {a, b}. State whether the following sequences of symbols from this alphabet are accepted or rejected:
(a) aa (b) ab (c) ba (d) bbaa (e) aaabbbbaa
(f) aabbbabbba

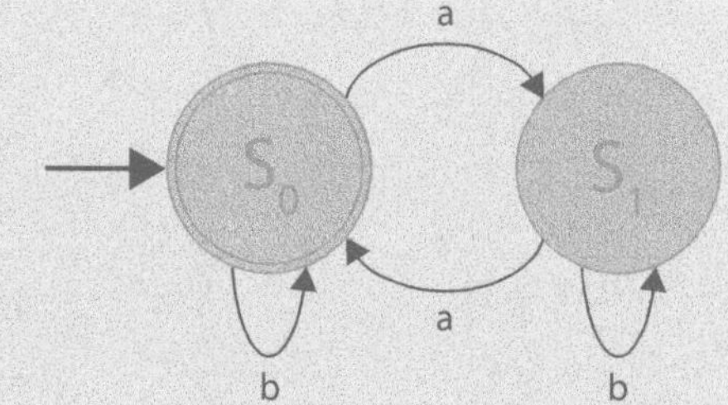

Figure 4.2.6 A finite state machine with no output for alphabet {a, b}

2. *Figure 4.2.7* is a finite state machine with alphabet {a, b}. State whether the following sequences of symbols from this alphabet are accepted or rejected:
(a) abaa (b) ababa
(c) abababababaa
(d) abababababa
(e) abababaa (f) abababaab
(g) ababaabaa

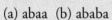

Figure 4.2.7 A finite state machine with no output for alphabet {a, b}

3. Draw the state transition diagram for a finite state machine which accepts a sequence of symbols containing an odd number of 1's. The alphabet for this machine is {0, 1}.

4. Draw the state transition diagram for a finite state machine which accepts a sequence of symbols beginning with an a followed by zero or more a's or b's. The alphabet for this machine is {a, b}. For example, abbbaababb is a valid sequence of symbols from the alphabet.

5. *Figure 4.2.8* is a finite state machine with alphabet {0, 1}. State whether the following sequences of symbols from this alphabet are accepted or rejected:
(a) 0 (b) 1 (c) 0111 (d) 0111110
(e) 11111 (f) 1011 (g) 111000

Figure 4.2.8 Finite state machine with no output and alphabet {0, 1}

Key term

State transition table:
A state transition table shows the effect of particular inputs on the current state of an FSM with no output.

State transition table

We use a table as shown in *Table 4.2.1* to select the next state given the current state and the current input symbol. For example, if the current state is S_0 and the input symbol is a then the FSM moves to state S_1 because the table shows that this is as the next state. If the current state is S_0 and the input symbol is b then the FSM moves to state S_3. This table is called a **state transition table** or just a **state table**. The state transition table in *Table 4.2.1* corresponds to the state transition diagram shown in *Figure 4.2.7*.

Current state	S_0	S_0	S_1	S_1	S_2	S_2	S_3	S_3
Input symbol	a	b	a	b	a	b	a	b
Next state	S_1	S_3	S_2	S_0	S_3	S_3	S_3	S_3

Table 4.2.1 A state transition table for finite state machine with no output

Question

6 Draw the state transition table for the finite state machine in *Figure 4.2.9*.

Figure 4.2.9 Finite state machine with no output and alphabet {a, b}

7 Draw the state transition table for the finite state machine in *Figure 4.2.10*.

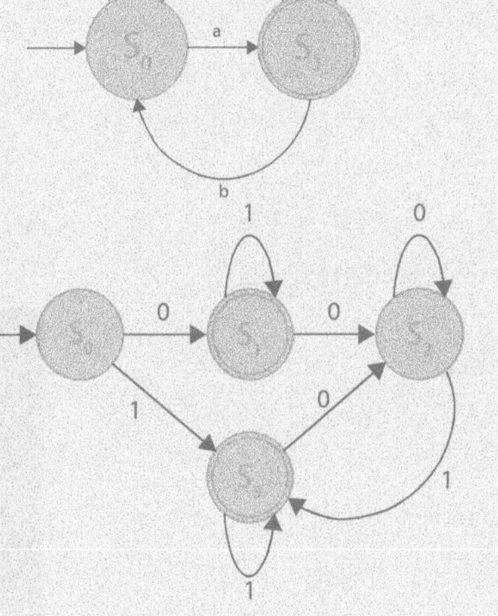

Figure 4.2.10 Finite state machine with no output and alphabet {0, 1}

Did you know?

Why are finite state machines useful?
Finite state machines (FSMs) are used extensively in applications in computer science. For example, finite state machines are the basis for

- Any kind of controller, e.g. traffic lights
- Specifying a language, e.g. given any string, an FSM determines if that string is in the language or not
- Programs for
  - spell checking
  - grammar checking
  - indexing or searching large bodies of text
  - recognising speech
  - processing text containing mark-up languages such as XML and HTML
- networking protocols that specify how computers communicate.

In this chapter you have covered:

- Drawing and interpreting simple state transition diagrams and state transition tables for FSMs with no output.

5 Fundamentals of data representation

5.1 Number systems

Learning objectives:

- *Concept of number*
- *The natural numbers*
- *Numerals*

5.1.1 Natural numbers

What does it mean to count?

We learn to count from an early age. We notice that in the real world objects can be grouped together in collections, for example three apples. In doing so, we use abstraction in ignoring the differences between the individual apples in the collection – for example, one of them is green, the other two are red.

Task

1. Try your hand at counting: https://www.youtube.com/watch?v=vJG698U2Mvo video.

The concept of number

By considering collections of items we can get an understanding of the concept

of number. For example, a collection of three oranges, a collection of three bananas. If we choose to ignore the differences between these collections and concentrate on their similarity, then we can form a relatively abstract concept of the number three. The same process could lead to the concept of the number 4, 5 and so on.

Key principle

Abstraction:
An abstraction is a representation that is arrived at by ignoring or removing unnecessary detail.

Numerals – representation of number

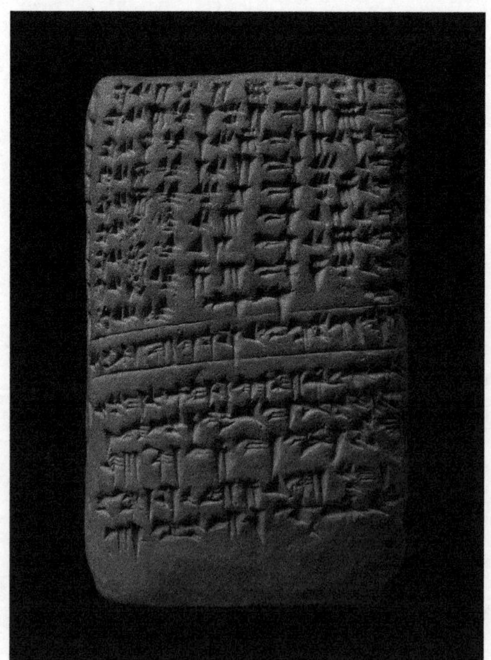

Representations of the concept of number have been carved in stone, and scratched on clay tablets since early times. The representation of a number is called a numeral. The early Roman numerals were originally pictorial. For example, three strokes carved in stone, III, represented the number three.

Figure 5.1.1.1 Late Babylonian clay tablet: table of numerals representing lunar longitudes

Key concept

Number:
Quantity of things.
Numeral:
The representation of a number is called a numeral.
Numerals are written symbols for numbers.

Task

2. Investigate the Babylonian numeral system.
What symbols did the Babylonian numeral system use?
Evaluate the following:

(Use http://en.wikipedia.org/wiki/Babylonian_numerals)

The Arabic (decimal) representations are less pictorial, but again there is some choice in the numerals to represent a number. For example, both 3 and 03 (and indeed 003 and so on) are all recognised as valid numerals, representing the same number.

0 0 3

Numeral systems

V A numeral system (or system of numeration) is
VI a writing system for expressing numbers, using
VII symbols in a consistent manner.

Questions

1. For the following numbers represented by Roman numerals, change the symbols from Roman numeral representation to the equivalent Arabic numeral representation:

   (a) VII (b) LXXVII (c) MCMXCVI

Digits of numerals

In a basic digital system, a numeral is a sequence of digits, which may be of arbitrary length. The most commonly used system of numerals is the Hindu–Arabic numeral system, based on Hindu numerals. It uses ten symbols called digits (0, 1, 2, 3, 4, 5, 6, 7, 8, and 9) to represent any number, no matter how large or how small. This system is referred to as the decimal or denary system.

Key concept

Natural number:
Natural numbers are the counting numbers, either {1, 2, 3, ... }, or {0, 1, 2, 3, ... }.

The symbol $\mathbb{N}_1$ is used to denote the set {1, 2, 3, ... }, and the symbol $\mathbb{N}_0$ is used to denote the set {0, 1, 2, 3, ... }.

Where it is clear which set applies, the symbol $\mathbb{N}$ is used.

What is a counting number?

We use the counting numbers {1, 2, 3, 4, ... } to keep track of things such as how much money we have in our pocket. The braces {} indicate a set (a collection of objects). The objects in the set are written inside the braces. "..." indicates that there are infinitely more objects. Informally, the counting numbers are all the numbers you can get to by counting, starting at 1.

What is a natural number?

Counting numbers are known as natural numbers.

$\mathbb{N}$

Thus natural numbers can mean either "Counting Numbers" {1, 2, 3, ... }, or the "Counting Numbers" and zero, {0, 1, 2, 3, ... }. Sometimes the special symbol $\mathbb{N}$ or $\mathbb{N}_1$ is used to denote {1, 2, 3, ... } and the special symbol $\mathbb{N}_0$ is used to denote {0, 1, 2, 3, ... }.

Did you know?

What is the sum of the first 100 natural numbers?

The mathematician Karl Friedrich Gauss when in elementary school in the eighteenth century amazed his teacher by finding, in a few minutes, the sum of the natural numbers from 1 to 100. Gauss wrote the sum down twice as shown below, once in ascending order, the second time in descending order, directly beneath the first.

1 + 2 + 3 + 4 + 5 + ... + 96 + 97 + 98 + 99 + 100
100 + 99 + 98 + 97 + 96 + ... + 5 + 4 + 3 + 2 + 1

Each vertical pair adds up to 101.
In total, there are 100 vertical pairs.
This makes the sum of all the natural numbers across the two rows = 100 × 101 = 10100.
The sum for one of the rows is one-half of this, i.e. 5050.

The alternative to Gauss' method involves laboriously performing 99 addition steps, adding 1 to 2 then 3 to the resulting sum and so on. This long-winded and laborious calculation is an example of a **brute-force** approach.

Questions

2. Find the sum of the following range of natural numbers using Gauss's method

   (i) 1 to 50 (ii) 1 to 200

3. Write a formula, in terms of n, to calculate the sum of all the natural numbers from 1 to n.

Programming tasks

1. Write a program to find the sum of the natural numbers from 1 to n. Your program should use the brute-force approach. Test your program with the following values of n

   (i) 100 (ii) 1000 000

2. Write a program to find the sum of the natural numbers from 1 to n. Your program should use the formula approach. Test your program with the following values of n.

   (i) 100 (ii) 1000 000

Investigation

1. Compare the execution times of programming tasks 1 and 2 for the two test values. What do you observe?

In this chapter you have covered:

- What it means to count
- The concept of number
- Numerals – representation of number
- Numeral systems
- Digits of numerals
- What is a counting number?
- What is a natural number?

5 Fundamentals of data representation

5.1 Number systems

Learning objectives:

- *Integer numbers*

Key concept

Integer numbers:
Integer numbers are the natural numbers, ℕ, plus the negative numbers formed by subtracting one natural number from another.

The special symbol ℤ is used to denote the set of integers

ℤ = { ..., -5, -4, -3, -2, -1, 0, 1, 2, 3, 4, 5, ... }

5.1.2 Integer numbers

Is the set of natural numbers, ℕ, enough?

Are the natural numbers sufficient for all simple arithmetic? What about 3 – 5? The answer is clearly not a counting number so negative numbers have to be added to the set of natural numbers to create the integers.

Integers are like the set of natural numbers, ℕ, but they also include negative numbers. For example, when the temperature is 10 degrees below zero, it is -10 degrees.

So, integers can be negative {-1, -2, -3, -4, -5, ... }, positive {1, 2, 3, 4, 5, ... }, or zero {0}.

The special symbol ℤ is used to denote the set of integers

ℤ = { ..., -5, -4, -3, -2, -1, 0, 1, 2, 3, 4, 5, ... }

ℤ

There are infinitely many elements in this set.

Questions

1. Are the following numbers (Hindu-Arabic numerals representing numbers) integers?

   (a) -10 (b) 5⅓ (c) 3.5?

2. Is the result of evaluating the following expression an integer?

   (367 × 42) / 7

Programming Task

1. What are the maximum and minimum integers for the programming language that you use?

   If your programming language has several integer data types, find these values for all the supported integer data types.

Whole numbers

Key concept

Whole number:
Whole number is another name for an integer number.

What are whole numbers?

We will consider whole numbers to be numbers without a fractional part although other definitions of whole numbers exist which take a different interpretation. A fractional part is a fraction. A fraction is any number greater than 0 and less than 1. For example, a slice of cake is a part of the whole, say $^1/_{10}$ and clearly not the whole. On the other hand, we may have 3 whole cakes or 3 whole degrees of temperature below zero, i.e. -3.

Whole numbers can be positive, negative or zero according to this interpretation. Whole number is another name for integer.

In this chapter you have covered:

- Integer numbers which are numbers which belong to the set
  { ..., -5, -4, -3, -2, -1, 0, 1, 2, 3, 4, 5, ... }
- Whole number is another name for integer

5 Fundamentals of data representation

5.1 Number systems

Learning objectives:

- *Rational numbers*
- *The set $\mathbb{Q}$ of rational numbers*

Key concept

Rational number:
A rational number, x, is one that can be expressed in the form $x = {}^{m}/_{n}$ where m and n are integers, excluding zero for n.

Key point

Simplest form:
A rational number in its simplest or lowest form is one that cannot be reduced any further because the only common factor of m and n, the numerator and denominator respectively, is 1.

Information

The word "rational" comes from the word "ratio" because a rational number can always be written as the ratio, or quotient, of two integers.

5.1.3 Rational numbers

Is the set of integers, $\mathbb{Z}$, enough for all arithmetic operations?

$\frac{10}{7}$ If we carry out an arithmetic operation of division such as 3 ÷ 5 the result is not a natural number or an integer. Therefore, we need to extend our number system to include the rational numbers, e.g. ½, ⅓, ¼, ⅜, ⅛, ${}^{10}/_{7}$ and so on. $\frac{1}{4}$

The definition of a rational number is as follows

"For x to be a rational number it must be expressible in the form

$$x = {}^{m}/_{n}$$

where m and n are integers, excluding zero for n."

By this definition, ${}^{2}/_{1}$, ${}^{11}/_{1}$, ${}^{3}/_{2}$, ${}^{4}/_{1}$, ${}^{5}/_{3}$, $-{}^{3}/_{2}$, ${}^{24}/_{11}$, ${}^{9}/_{7}$, $-{}^{1}/_{2}$, are rational numbers as are ${}^{8}/_{4}$, ${}^{6}/_{3}$, ${}^{24}/_{3}$. $\frac{11}{1}$

For x to be a unique rational number then we need to insist that m and n have no common factor except 1. ${}^{8}/_{4}$, is not a unique rational number because 8 and 4 have the common factors 2 and 1. ${}^{8}/_{4}$, can be reduced to ${}^{2}/_{1}$ which is a unique rational number because the only common factor is 1. A rational number in its simplest form is one that cannot be reduced any further because the only common factor of m and n, the numerator and denominator respectively, is 1. Such rational numbers are called simple fractions.

Formally, $\mathbb{Q}$ is the set of rational numbers.

There are infinitely many elements in this set.

Questions

1. Determine whether each of the following statements is true or false:

   (a) $-13 \in \mathbb{N}$ (b) ${}^{36}/_{77} \in \mathbb{Q}$ (c) $-11 \in \mathbb{Q}$?

Key term

Set of rational numbers, $\mathbb{Q}$:
Formally, the symbol $\mathbb{Q}$ is used to mean the set of rational numbers.

Information

Read Unit 1 section 4.2.2 for more background on sets and set comprehension:

$\mathbb{Q} = \{^m/_n : m \in Z \text{ and } n \in \mathbb{N}_1\}$

Programming Task

1 A program that computes the quotient q and the remainder r when dividing an integer x by an integer y must satisfy the following two conditions as follows:

1) $x \geq 0$ and $y > 0$

2) $x = y * q + r$ and $0 \leq r < y$

Pseudo-code for the algorithm to compute q and r when dividing an integer x by an integer y:

```
r ← x
q ← 0
While r >= y
  r ← r - y
  q ← q + 1
```

Write a program for this algorithm. Does your program meet the two conditions? If your programming language supports assertions, then use assertions to check that the two conditions are met. If not use appropriate tests.

Is the set of rational numbers $\mathbb{Q}$ countable?

Just for the moment, consider the set of positive rational numbers

$\{^1/_1, ^2/_1, ^1/_2, ^1/_3, ^3/_1, ^4/_1, ^3/_2, ^2/_3, ^1/_4, ^1/_5, ^5/_1, \ldots\}$

arrived at by following the arrows in *Table 5.1.3.1*.

This set is represented by the symbol $\mathbb{Q}^+$.

Key point

Simplest form:
The entries in Table 1.3.1 that have common factors greater than 1 are greyed out because they can be reduced to their simplest form which is already in the table e.g. $^2/_8$ becomes $^1/_4$.

	1	2	3	4	5	6	7	8	...
1	1/1	1/2	1/3	1/4	1/5	1/6	1/7	1/8	
2	2/1	2/2	2/3	2/4	2/5	2/6	2/7	2/8	
3	3/1	3/2	3/3	3/4	3/5	3/6	3/7	3/8	
4	4/1	4/2	4/3	4/4	4/5	4/6	4/7	4/8	
5	5/1	5/2	5/3	5/4	5/5	5/6	5/7	5/8	
6	6/1	6/2	6/3	6/4	6/5	6/6	6/7	6/8	
7	7/1	7/2	7/3	7/4	7/5	7/6	7/7	7/8	
8	8/1	8/2	8/3	8/4	8/5	8/6	8/7	8/8	
...									

Table 5.1.3.1

If you think about it all possible positive rational numbers will be generated, e.g. $^{147}/_{91457}$ will be in the table at the intersection of row 147 and column 91457 and will get added in turn. Therefore, it is possible to order the rational numbers of the set $\mathbb{Q}^+$ and to show a one-to-one correspondence with the natural numbers as indicated in Table 5.1.3.2.

1	2	3	4	5	6	7	8	9	10	11	...
1/1	2/1	1/2	1/3	3/1	4/1	3/2	2/3	1/4	1/5	5/1	...

Table 5.1.3.2

To generate $\mathbb{Q}$, we can place zero /1 before 1/1 and insert the negative of each positive rational number other than zero immediately after the positive rational number as shown in Table 5.1.3.3.

1	2	3	4	5	6	7	8	9	...
0/1	1/1	-1/1	2/1	-2/1	1/2	-1/2	1/3	-1/3	...

Table 5.1.3.3

Table 5.1.3.3 shows that it is possible to order the rational numbers $\mathbb{Q}$ and to place them in a one-to-one correspondence with the natural numbers. Therefore, the set of rational numbers $\mathbb{Q}$ is countable. It is also infinite because the set of natural numbers is infinite.

In addition, all integers are in $\mathbb{Q}$ because every integer n can be expressed as n/1.

Representing rational numbers as terminating decimals

Long division is used to convert a rational number into decimal form.

Examples: (a) 189/9 = 189 ÷ 9 = 21 (b) 13/20 = 13 ÷ 20 = 0.65

9 goes into 189
21 times remainder 0

20 goes into	13
0 times remainder	13
• 20 goes into	130
6 times remainder	10
20 goes into	100
5 times remainder	0

If the final remainder is 0, e.g. 189/9, the quotient is a whole number, e.g. 21, or a finite or terminating decimal, i.e. a decimal with a finite number of digits after the decimal point, e.g. 0.65.

The rational numbers in lowest form whose only prime factors in their denominator are 2 or 5 or both, convert to terminating decimals.

Key point

$\mathbb{Q}$ is countable:
It is possible to order the rational numbers, $\mathbb{Q}$, and to show a one-to-one correspondence with the natural numbers. Therefore, $\mathbb{Q}$ is countable.

Key point

The rational numbers in lowest form whose only prime factors in their denominator are 2 or 5 or both, convert to **terminating decimals**.

Examples: (a) $^1/_2 = {}^1/_2 \times {}^5/_5 = {}^5/_{10} = 0.5$

(b) $^1/_4 = {}^1/_2 \times {}^1/_2 \times {}^5/_5 \times {}^5/_5 = {}^{25}/_{100} = 0.25$

Key point

All **recurring decimals** are **infinite decimals.** This occurs when the denominator involves the prime factors from the set {3, 7, 11, 13, 17, 19, ...}.

Questions

2 Without performing a decimal conversion, determine whether the following rational numbers will convert to a terminating decimal

(a) $^5/_{125}$ (b) $^{16}/_{1024}$ (c) $^2/_3$

Representing rational numbers as recurring decimals

Sometimes when converting a rational number by long division, the division never stops as there is always a remainder. Such rational numbers convert to a recurring decimal.

All recurring decimals are infinite decimals.

This occurs when the denominator involves the prime factors from the set

{3, 7, 11, 13, 17, 19, ...}

Examples: (a) $^{19}/_{12} = 19 \div 12 = 1.58333...$ (b) $^1/_3 = 1 \div 3 = 0.333...$

	(a)	(b)
Remainder	70	10
	100	10
	40	10
	40	1
	40	...
	4	
	...	

The repeating pattern may consist of just one digit or of any finite number of digits. The number of digits in the repeating pattern is called the period. The repeating pattern is indicated by placing a period mark or a bar over each digit in the repeating pattern, e.g.

(a) $^1/_3 = 0.333... = 0.\dot{3}$

(b) $^8/_{11} = 0.727272... = 0.\overline{72}$

Questions

3 Convert the following rational numbers to decimal:
(a) $^{16}/_3$ (b) $^{10}/_7$ (c) $^{13}/_{11}$

4 What is the repeating pattern for each decimal in Q3?

Rational numbers are terminating or recurring decimals

A rational number is either a terminating or recurring decimal. Every terminating or recurring decimal can be converted to $^a/_b$ where $a \in \mathbb{Z}$ and $b \in \mathbb{N}_1$.

Key point

A **rational number** is either a terminating decimal or a recurring decimal.

Questions

5. Convert the following decimals to their rational number equivalent:
(a) 5.25 (b) $0.\overline{90}$

In this chapter you have covered:

- The set of integers $\mathbb{Z}$ is not enough for all arithmetic operations
- A rational number, x, is one that can be expressed in the form x = m/n where m and n are integers, excluding zero for n.
- The set of rational numbers $\mathbb{Q}$ is countable
- The rational numbers in lowest form whose only prime factors in their denominator are 2 or 5 or both, convert to **terminating decimals**.
- Rational numbers are terminating or recurring decimals
- Recurring decimals are infinite decimals

5 Fundamentals of data representation

5.1 Number systems

Learning objectives:

- *Irrational numbers*
- *Decimal expansion of an irrational number*

5.1.4 Irrational numbers

Are rational numbers sufficient to model all numbers?

The answer is no. The following boxed yellow section explains why but this is for information only.

Figure 5.1.4.1 shows a rectangle with sides of length a, and b. We use multiplication to work out the area of the rectangle as follows

$$\text{Area} = ab$$

where ab means a times b. To measure the length of the sides we use a ruler marked with the rational numbers as shown in *Figure 5.1.4.2*. The integers were marked first. Next the multiples of $^1/_2$ were added followed by the multiples of $^1/_3$ and so on. It would seem that this process would leave little room for any further points on the line.

b

a

Figure 5.1.4.1 Rectangle of sides a and b

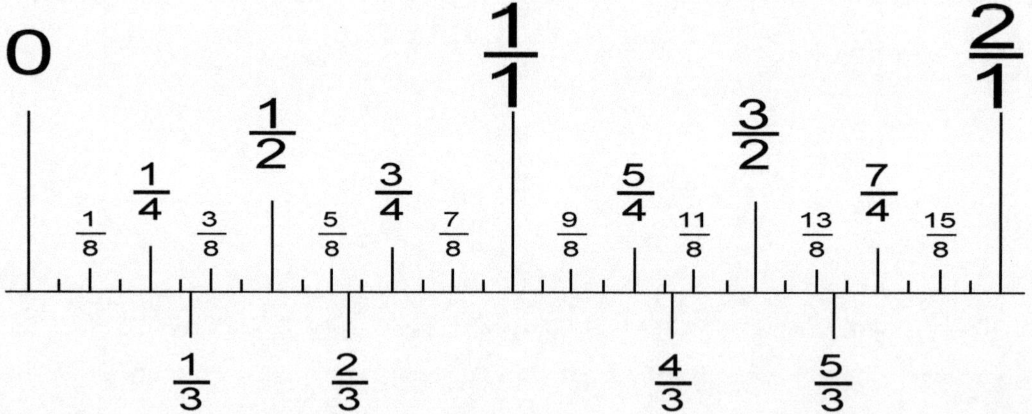

Figure 5.1.4.2 Ruler of the rational numbers

Information

Pythagoras' theorem states that the square on the hypotenuse of a right-angled triangle is the sum of the squares on the other two sides.

However, this intuition is not consistent with Pythagoras' theorem which requires that the length *h* of the hypotenuse in the right-angled triangle in *Figure 5.1.4.3* should satisfy

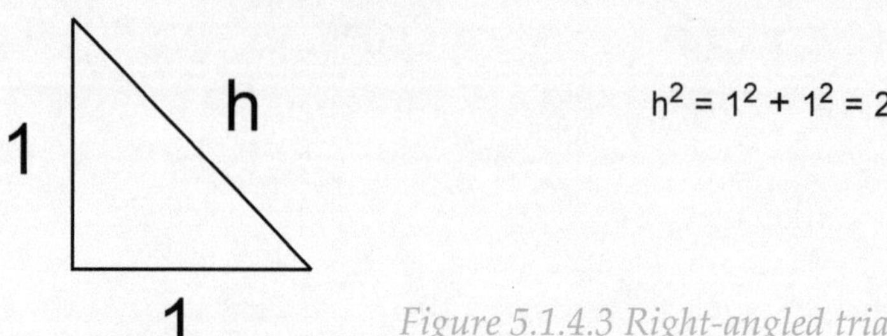

$$h^2 = 1^2 + 1^2 = 2$$

Figure 5.1.4.3 Right-angled triangle sides 1, 1, h

Information

Euclidean geometry is the geometry described by Euclid in his textbook the Elements and which we have used for over 2000 years.

If it is true that every length in Euclidean geometry can be measured by a rational number, then it must be true that there is a positive rational number such that $x = h$, $x^2 = 2$, and $x = \sqrt{2}$. That makes $\sqrt{2}$ a rational number but we will discover that it can't be.

If x is rational then it can be expressed as the ratio of two integers, m and n with common factor 1 only and n <> 0.

$$x = {}^{m}/_{n}$$

Information

Proof by contradiction: We assume that what we want to prove is not true, and then show the consequences contradict either what we have just assumed, or something we already know to be true (or both).

It follows that $\quad x^2 = {}^{m^2}/_{n^2} \quad$ because $x = \sqrt{2}$

Therefore, $\quad m^2 = 2n^2$

And so m^2 is even. This implies that m is even.

We may therefore write $m = 2k$ (Multiplying k, any natural number, by 2 ensures evenness).

Substituting 2k for m in $m^2 = 2n^2$

we get $\quad (2k)^2 = 2n^2$

Or $\quad 4k^2 = 2n^2$

$$2k^2 = n^2$$

Rearranging $\quad n^2 = 2k^2$

Thus n is even.

For both m and n to be even they must be divisible by 2 but by definition ${}^{m}/_{n}$ is a rational number divisible by 1 only.

Therefore, $\sqrt{2}$ cannot be defined as a rational number and therefore it is not a member of the set of rational numbers.

What is the set of irrational numbers?

Conclusion, we need more than the set of rational numbers. We require in addition, a new set which contains those numbers that like $\sqrt{2}$ are not rational numbers. We call this new set the set of irrational numbers. $\sqrt{2}$ is therefore an irrational number.

Irrational numbers are numbers that can be written as decimals but not as simple fractions. Irrational numbers have decimal expansions that neither terminate nor are periodic with some repeating sequence. For example, the decimal expansion of $\sqrt{2}$ to 50 decimal places is

1.41421356237309504880168872420969807856967187537694

To see more decimal places go to

http://apod.nasa.gov/htmltest/gifcity/sqrt2.1mil

> **Key point**
>
> **Irrational number:**
> Irrational numbers are numbers that can be written as decimals but not as simple fractions.
>
> Irrational numbers have decimal expansions that neither terminate nor are periodic with some repeating sequence.

Square roots and irrational numbers?

If a number could be the area of a square with a side that is a whole number, then the number is called a "perfect square", e.g. 4. However, if the area of a square is not a perfect square, then the side of the square is an irrational number, i.e. the square root of the area. For example, if the area is 3 cm^2 then 1.73205..... is an irrational number.

Questions

1 Which of the following numbers are irrational?

(a) $\sqrt{8}/2$ (b) $\sqrt{8}$ (c) $\sqrt{300}$
(d) $\sqrt{361}$ (e) $3.777... = 3.\overline{7}$
(f) 0.12112111211112... (g) 325/7

In this chapter you have covered:

- The set of rational numbers $\mathbb{Q}$ is not enough to model all numbers
- An irrational number is a number that can be written as a decimal but not as a simple fraction.
- Irrational numbers have decimal expansions that neither terminate nor are periodic with some repeating sequence

5 Fundamentals of data representation

5.1 Number systems

Learning objectives:

- *Real numbers*
- *Real numbers form a continuum*
- *Real number line*
- *Set of real numbers*
- *Decimal expansion of a real number*

Key concept

Real number:
A real number is either a rational number or an irrational number.
Real numbers are represented by decimals using an infinite decimal expansion.

Key point

The real number system of rational numbers and irrational numbers forms a continuum.

Key point

Real number line:
The real number line is a useful way of modelling the set of real numbers.

Key concept

Set of real numbers:

The set of real numbers, $\mathbb{R}$, is formed from the union of the set of rational numbers and the set of irrational numbers.

5.1.5 Real numbers

Real number system forms a continuum

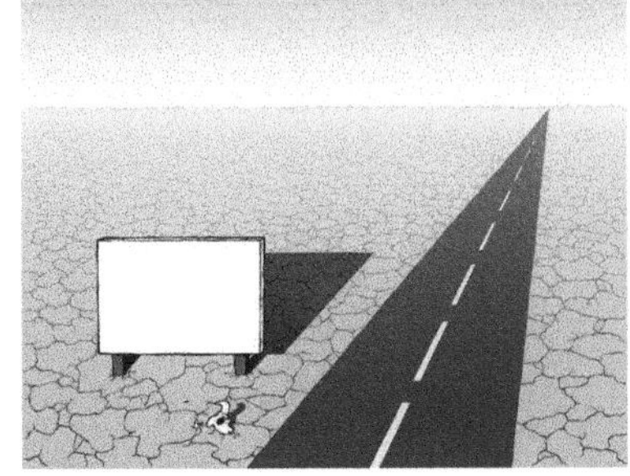

We need more than the set of rational numbers to model numbers because marking a straight line with the rational numbers will still leave points of the line unmarked. These 'holes' are filled by irrational numbers. When both rational and irrational numbers are marked on the line, they fill it completely and stretch unbroken in both directions to form the real number system. The real number system of rational numbers and irrational numbers forms a continuum.

What is the real number line?

The real number line is a useful way of modelling the set of real numbers. It is an infinite line on which points are taken to represent the real numbers by their distance from a fixed point labelled O and called the origin. Every point of this line represents a real number. Some real numbers are shown on this line in *Figure 5.1.5.1*.

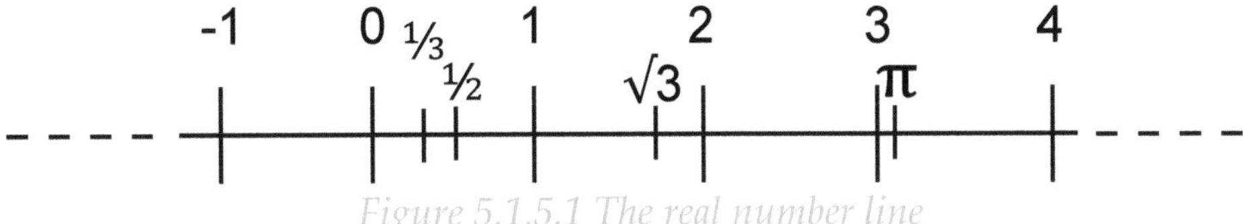

Figure 5.1.5.1 The real number line

Ideally, one would like to show and label every point on the number line, but no matter how dense one makes the points there are always points in between.

What is the set of real numbers?

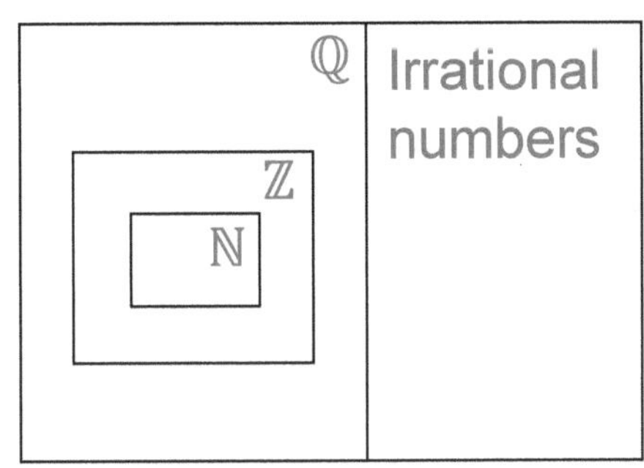

The set interpretation of real numbers is an alternative to thinking of real numbers as points on an infinitely long line. The special symbol $\mathbb{R}$ is used to denote the set of real numbers. It is a set formed from the union of the set of rational numbers and the set of irrational numbers – *Figure 5.1.5.2*.

Figure 5.1.5.2 The composition of the set of real numbers, $\mathbb{R}$

Key point

The set $\mathbb{R}$ is an uncountable set. Real numbers have the property that between any two of them, no matter how close, there lies another real number.

Questions

1. Determine whether each of the following statements is true or false:
   (a) $^{16}/_{3} \in \mathbb{R}$ (b) $3.142 \in \mathbb{R}$
   (c) $^{1}/_{4} \in \mathbb{Q}$ and $^{1}/_{4} \in \mathbb{R}$ (d) $\pi \in \mathbb{R}$ (e) $\sqrt{2} \in \mathbb{Q}$
   (f) $\sqrt{361} \in \mathbb{N}$ and $\sqrt{361} \in \mathbb{R}$ (g) $-3 \in \mathbb{R}$

What is a real number?

Key point

Real numbers describe real-world quantities such as distances, amounts of things, temperature, and so on.

Real numbers describe real-world quantities such as distances, amounts of things, temperature, and so on. They are represented by decimals using an infinite decimal expansion and which define a real number.

Using this definition a real number is an expression of the form

$$\pm\, a_1a_2a_3 \ldots a_k \bullet b_1b_2b_3 \ldots$$

For example, −4328.5000000... where ... indicates infinitely many zeroes.

± represents a choice between plus and minus.

Each of the digits a_1, a_2, a_3, ..., a_k is an integer between 0 and 9 inclusive except a_1 when there is more than one digit in which case a_1 is restricted to being between 1 and 9, since it is the leading digit, e.g. 13•56....

The infinitely many b digits are integers between 0 and 9 inclusive.

Key point

Every real number has a unique decimal expansion unless it is a rational number of the form

$$^{m}/_{10^n}$$

For the latter number, there are two forms of the decimal expansion, e.g. 0.9999... and 1.0000..., 4.9999... and 5.0000... with no real number existing between each form.

Questions

2. A line of exact length 1 is repeatedly shortened an infinite number of times by cutting exactly $^{9}/_{10}$ths from the line each time. Each bit removed is added to the end of its immediate predecessor to make a new and separate line. How much in total is removed after
   (a) one cut (b) two cuts (c) four cuts
   (d) a very large but finite number of cuts
   (e) infinitely many cuts

Investigation

Find out why 0.9999... and 1.0000... represent the same real number.

Programming Task

1 The ratio of the circumference of a circle to its diameter, π can be calculated using the formula below. The more terms in the sequence the more accurate the calculated value for π will be.

$$\pi = 3 + \frac{4}{2\cdot3\cdot4} - \frac{4}{4\cdot5\cdot6} + \frac{4}{6\cdot7\cdot8} - \frac{4}{8\cdot9\cdot10} + \cdots$$

··· means that there are more terms modelled on what is given already, e.g. the next two terms in the sequence are

$$\frac{4}{10\cdot11\cdot12} - \frac{4}{12\cdot13\cdot14}$$

Write a program that uses this formula to calculate π for a given number of terms, n. Test your program with the following values of n

(a) 2 (b) 3 (c) 5 (d) 7

If we evaluate

$$1 + \frac{1}{1!} + \frac{1}{2!} + \frac{1}{3!} + \frac{1}{4!} + \cdots + \frac{1}{r!} + \cdots$$

the result tends towards the value 2.718... which is given the symbol *e*.

We can arrive at a value for *e* by evaluating the formula

$$e = \sum_{0}^{n} \frac{(2n+2)}{(2n+1)!}$$

Using a value for n of 6 we can evaluate *e* to 9 decimal places of accuracy.

Write a program that uses this formula to calculate *e* for the following values of n.

(a) 1 (b) 3 (c) 6 (d) 8

In this chapter you have covered:

- Real number system forms a continuum
- A real number is either a rational number or an irrational number
- Real numbers are represented by decimals using an infinite decimal expansion
- Every real number has a unique decimal expansion unless it is a rational number of the form $^{m}/_{10^n}$

Information

$\sum_{1}^{n=6} n$ is shorthand for

$1 + 2 + 3 + 4 + 5 + 6$.

$\sum$ means summate or sum.

! means factorial, e.g. $3! = 3\times2\times1$.

This special number e was known in the early 17th century, and probably was discovered around this date in connection with the growth of money with time when invested.

Did you know?

There are some irrational numbers that can be contemplated in their entirety. For example,

0.2200022200000222222000000022...

defines an irrational number in which each string of 0's and 2's increases in length each time by two of each. Thus we have a rule for constructing the decimal expansion of this irrational number. The rule can be expressed as an algorithm to generate successive digits.
Real numbers whose expansions can be generated by algorithms are called **computable numbers.** They are the real numbers that can be computed to within any desired precision by a finite, terminating algorithm.
However, there are also many real numbers that are not computable in this sense.

- The set of real numbers, $\mathbb{R}$, is formed from the union of the set of rational numbers and the set of irrational numbers
- The set $\mathbb{R}$ is an uncountable set
- Real numbers describe real-world quantities such as distances, amounts of things, temperature, and so on.

5 Fundamentals of data representation

5.1 Number systems

Learning objectives:

- *Ordinal or ordinal number*

Key concept

Ordinal or ordinal number: Ordinals or ordinal numbers are used to label the positions of objects in a list, ordered set or sequence of objects.

5.1.6 Ordinal numbers

What is an ordinal number?

The natural numbers are used for counting or quantifying something, i.e. how much of something we have, but we have another type of number which we use when we need to talk about where something comes in relation to something else, e.g. first or second and so on. This number type is called ordinal number or just ordinal.

Ordinal numbers are therefore used when we need to position something. Ordinal numbers are used to label the positions of objects in a list, ordered set or sequence of objects. The objects must be ordered so that there is a first element, a second element and so on. We use the natural numbers to describe the position of an element in a sequence as follows

$$1^{st},\ 2^{nd},\ 3^{rd},\ 4^{th},\ 5^{th}, \text{etc.}$$

In English, this is

first, second, third, fourth, fifth, etc.

We could also have started at 0 and labelled the first element as the zeroth element in which case we use the natural numbers including zero as follows

$$0^{th},\ 1^{st},\ 2^{nd},\ 3^{rd},\ 4^{th},\ 5^{th}, \text{etc.}$$

Information

An array index is a way of labelling a cell of an array. The term subscript is also used to mean the same thing.

Questions

1. An index is used in programming to specify the position of an element in an ordered collection, e.g. an array. An index may start from 0 or 1 depending on programming language used or programmer preference.
   (a) If you were told that i was the 100th element of an array:
      (i) How many elements would you consider come before this element?
      (ii) What would be the index for this 100th element if the indexing starts at 0?
      (iii) What would be the index for this 100th element if the indexing starts at 1?
   (b) If you were told that there are 100 elements in an array:
      (i) What would be the index of the last element if the indexing starts at 0?

(ii) What would be the index of the last element if the indexing starts at 1?

2 An element's ordinal (index) equals the number of elements preceding it in the sequence, e.g. an array or a string.
Should the index start with 0 or 1 to make this statement true?

3 The length of a range is the difference of its endpoints, e.g. 0 <= i < 5 has 5 elements, as does 5 <= i < 10.
Give the length of these two ranges if in each case '<' is replaced by '<='. Comment on your answer.

Discussion

4 Some programming languages only allow array indexing to begin from zero whilst other languages are more flexible and allow the programmer to choose whether to start indexing from 0, 1 or any integer, e.g. -2.
Discuss the advantages and disadvantages of each.

Programming Task

1 Write a program that accepts a letter of the alphabet typed at the keyboard, uppercase or lowercase, and outputs its numeric position in the alphabet followed by either "st", "nd", "rd" or "th" as appropriate.

In this chapter you have covered:

- Ordinals or ordinal numbers which are used to label the positions of objects in a list, ordered set or sequence of objects.

5 Fundamentals of data representation

5.1 Number systems

Learning objectives:

- *Be familiar with the use of*
  - *natural numbers for counting*
  - *real numbers for measurement*

Key point

The process of counting is known as enumeration. To enumerate is to count. Enumeration is counting with natural numbers.

Information

url for Cantor's diagonal argument:
Su, Francis E., et al. "Cantor Diagonalization."
Math Fun Facts.
https://www.math.hmc.edu/funfacts/ffiles/30001.4.shtml

5.1.7 Counting and measurement

Enumeration

When we count things we start at 1 for the first item, 2 for the second and so on. Anything that can be counted out is said to be enumerable. The process of counting is known as enumeration and we use the natural numbers for counting.

Can we count the integers? If we can they can be said to be enumerable. We can in actual fact. Similarly, we can enumerate, i.e. count, the positive rational numbers greater than 0 using a for loop as follows

```
for i ← 1 to infinity
  for j ← 1 to i
    display i/j
```

By a similar for-loop argument we could enumerate all rational numbers and thereby count them. We conclude that the set of rational numbers is also countable.

We are not so lucky when it comes to the irrational numbers. The irrational numbers cannot be enumerated (for a formal proof see Cantor's diagonal argument).

Using real numbers for measurement

When we make a physical measurement, we use a measuring instrument. For example, for measuring the lengths of pieces of wood we could use a ruler such as the one shown in Figure 5.1.7.1. This ruler is marked off in whole centimetres and tenths of centimetres. A tenth of a centimetre in the decimal numeral system is the fraction $^1/_{10}$.

Figure 5.1.7.1 Ruler marked in centimetres and tenths of a centimetre

Key point

When making measurements we are limited to using a rational number approximation to a real number.

Clearly, using this ruler, we would not be able to measure the length of a piece of wood to hundredths of a centimetre, but instead are limited to measuring to tenths of a centimetre. We conclude that when dealing with fractions, we shall have to approximate some by using a suitably close fraction that does have a representation on the ruler, e.g. $^1/_9$ would be approximated by $^1/_{10}$ with an error of $^1/_9 - {}^1/_{10} = {}^1/_{90}$. The more divisions that we have on the ruler, the better our approximation can be, but the need for approximation cannot be removed. Between one tenth and two tenths, for example, there are infinitely many fractions. We are limited therefore to using a rational number approximation to a real number.

Key point

All fractional representations run the risk of being imprecise.

Questions

1. Calculate the decimal expansion of $^1/_9$.

2. If the decimal expansion of $^1/_9$ is restricted to each of the following number of decimal places, what fraction results in each case

   (a) 2 (b) 3 (c) 6?

3. What is the difference between $^1/_9$ and each of the fractions that result from answering (a), (b), (c) in Q2?

Programming task

1. Write a program that outputs the result of performing the following calculations:
   (a) $^1/_3$
   (b) $^1/_7$
   (c) $^1/_5$
   (d) $^1/_{10}$
   Comment on the results.

Rational number approximation to a real number

Any real number can be approximated to any desired degree of accuracy by rational numbers with finite decimal representations, i.e. terminating decimals. If the real number is x and assuming

$$x \geq 0$$

Then for every integer $n \geq 1$ there is a finite decimal

$$r_n = + a_1a_2a_3\ldots a_k \bullet b_1b_2b_3\ldots b_n$$

such that $$r_n \leq x < r_n + {}^1/_{10^n}$$

For example, assuming $x = 368.78456789123\ldots\ldots\ldots$

then for $n = 2$, $r_2 = 368.78$ and $r_2 + {}^1/_{100} = 368.79$

That is, x, lies somewhere between 368.78 and 368.79.

Questions

4 For each real number x where $x \geq 0$ write down

r_n and $r_n + {}^1/_{10^n}$

where $r_n = + a_1a_2a_3\ldots a_k \bullet b_1b_2b_3\ldots b_n$ and $n \geq 1$

(a) $x = 0.3245995632\ldots\ldots\ldots$ and $n = 4$

(b) $x = 85.994467285\ldots\ldots\ldots$ and $n = 3$

Key point

Any real number can be approximated to any desired degree of accuracy by rational numbers having finite decimal representations.

Rounding off

We usually apply the process of rounding off to real numbers when using a rational number approximation. The rules for rounding off to n decimal places are:

- If the value of the $(n + 1)^{th}$ digit is less than five (0, 1, 2, 3, or 4), we leave the nth digit alone.
- If the value of the $(n + 1)^{th}$ digit is greater than or equal to five (5, 6, 7, 8, or 9), we increase the value of the nth digit by one.

For example, if the real number is 368.78456789123.........

then rounding off to 2 decimal places, it becomes 368.78.

Whilst if the real number is 368.78546789123.........

then rounding off to 2 decimal places, it becomes 368.79.

Questions

5 Round off the following real numbers to the specified number of decimal places

(a) x = 0.3245995632......... to 4 decimal places

(b) x = 85.994467285......... to 3 decimal places

(c) x = 5.884467285......... to 3 decimal places

In this chapter you have covered:

- To count is to enumerate.
- Enumeration is counting with natural numbers.
- When making measurements we are limited to using a rational number approximation to a real number.
- All fractional representations run the risk of being imprecise.
- Any real number can be approximated to any desired degree of accuracy by rational numbers having finite decimal representations.
- We usually apply the process of rounding off to real numbers when using a rational number approximation.

5 Fundamentals of data representation

5.2 Number bases

Learning objectives:

- *Number base*
- *Decimal (base 10)*
- *Binary (base 2)*
- *Hexadecimal (base 16)*
- *Converting between decimal, binary and hexadecimal*
- *Hexadecimal as a shorthand for binary and why*

Background

The abacus is a calculating tool based on moving beads in a counting frame to positions that represent the size of a number. It was invented long before the adoption of the written modern numeral system and is still in use today.

Information

Base 10 system is an example of a positional number system. This type of system was first used by the Babylonians over 4000 years ago in Mesopotamia, modern day Iraq. Positional number systems are good for doing arithmetic with.

5.2.1 Number base

Meaning of number base

The number base system specifies how many digits are used in constructing a numeral (representation of a number) and by how much to multiply each digit.

For example, in the decimal system the numeral 734 is interpreted as meaning

$$7 \times 100 + 3 \times 10 + 4 \times 1$$

Decimal (base 10)

The number base of the decimal system is ten because it has ten digits 0, 1, 2, 3, 4, 5, 6, 7, 8, 9 and the digit multiplier is a power of ten, 10^n where n is

$\cdots -3, -2, -1, 0, 1, 2, 3, \cdots$

The number represented by the numeral 734 in base 10 is

constructed using the place values indicated in *Table 5.2.1.1* as follows

$$7 \times 100 + 3 \times 10 + 4 \times 1$$

...	10^2	10^1	10^0	...
...	100	10	1	...
	7	3	4	

Table 5.2.1.1 Place values for the decimal system

Table 5.2.1.2 shows how the place values can be extended to include fractions, thousands and ten thousands.

...	10^4	10^3	10^2	10^1	10^0	10^{-1}	10^{-2}	...
...	10000	1000	100	10	1	$^1/_{10}$	$^1/_{100}$	...
	2	7	7	3	4	3	5	

Table 5.2.1.2 Some more place values for the decimal system

The number represented by the numeral 27734•35 in base 10 is

constructed using the place values shown in *Table 5.2.1.2* as follows

$$2 \times 10000 + 7 \times 1000 + 7 \times 100 + 3 \times 10 + 4 \times 1 + 3 \times {}^1/_{10} + 5 \times {}^1/_{100}$$

To indicate the base we use a suffix attached to the numeral, e.g. 34_{10}.

Binary (base 2)

The number base of the binary system is two because it has two digits 0, 1 and the digit multiplier is a power of two, 2^n where n is $\cdots -3, -2, -1, 0, 1, 2, 3, \cdots$

Key concept

Decimal:
The number base of the decimal system is ten because it has ten digits 0, 1, 2, 3, 4, 5, 6, 7, 8, 9 and the digit multiplier is a power of ten, 10^n where n is ···, −3, −2, −1, 0, 1, 2 , 3, ···

...	2^4	2^3	2^2	2^1	2^0	2^{-1}	2^{-2}	...
...	16	8	4	2	1	$^1/_2$	$^1/_4$	...
	1	0	1	1	1	1	1	

Table 5.2.1.3 Place values for the binary system

The number in decimal represented by the binary numeral 10111•11 is constructed using the place values in *Table 5.2.1.3* as follows

$$1 \times 16 + 0 \times 8 + 1 \times 4 + 1 \times 2 + 1 \times 1 + 1 \times {}^1/_2 + 1 \times {}^1/_4$$

To indicate the base we use a subscript attached to the numeral, e.g. $10111{\bullet}11_2$.

Now the "There are 10 types of people in the world those that understand binary and those that don't" quote might make more sense because

$$10_{Binary} = 2_{Decimal}$$

Key point

To indicate the base we use a suffix attached to the numeral, e.g. 34_{10}.

Questions

1. Write out each of the following in the form

   digit × multiplier + digit × multiplier + ...

   (a) 1010_2 (b) $1111{\bullet}11_2$ (c) $10{\bullet}0101_2$

2. Convert the following numbers expressed in binary to their decimal equivalent:

   (a) 1010_2 (b) 1111_2 (c) 10010111_2 (d) 11111111_2

3. Convert the following numbers expressed in binary to their decimal equivalent:

   (a) $10{\bullet}10_2$ (b) $0{\bullet}1111_2$ (c) $100{\bullet}10111_2$ (d) $1{\bullet}1111111_2$

Key concept

Binary:
The number base of the binary system is two because it has two digits 0, 1 and the digit multiplier is a power of two, 2^n where n is ···, −3, −2, −1, 0, 1, 2 , 3, ···

Hexadecimal (base 16)

The number base of the hexadecimal system is sixteen because it has sixteen digits 0, 1, 2, 3, 4, 5, 6, 7, 8, 9, A, B, C, D, E, F and the digit multiplier is a power of sixteen, 16^n where n is ···, −3, −2, −1, 0, 1, 2 , 3, ···

The number in decimal represented by the hexadecimal numeral D4 is constructed using the place values in *Table 5.2.1.4* as follows

$$13 \times 16 + 4 \times 1$$

where D has been replaced by 13.

...	16^1	16^0	...
...	16	1	...
	D	4	

Table 5.2.1.4 Place values for the hexadecimal system

The hexadecimal digits A, B, C, D, E and F are in decimal 10, 11, 12, 13, 14 and 15 respectively.

The number in decimal represented by the hexadecimal numeral 38AD4•95 is constructed using the place values in Table 5.2.1.5 as follows

$$3 \times 65536 + 8 \times 4096 + 10 \times 256 + 13 \times 16 + 4 \times 1 + 9 \times 1/16 + 5 \times 1/256$$

To indicate the base we use a subscript attached to the numeral, e.g. $38AD4{\bullet}95_{16}$.

...	16^4	16^3	16^2	16^1	16^0	16^{-1}	16^{-2}	...
...	65536	4096	256	16	1	$^1/_{16}$	$^1/_{256}$	...
	3	8	A	D	4	9	5	

Table 5.2.1.5 Some more place values for the hexadecimal system

Questions

4 Write out each of the following in the form

digit × multiplier + digit × multiplier + ···

(a) 1023_{16} (b) $1F_{16}$ (c) $F{\bullet}13_{16}$

5 Convert the following numbers expressed in hexadecimal to their decimal equivalent:

(a) 1023_{16} (b) $1F_{16}$ (c) $FFFF_{16}$ (d) $DEAD_{16}$

Key concept

Hexadecimal:
The number base of the hexadecimal system is sixteen because it has sixteen digits 0, 1, 2, 3, 4, 5, 6, 7, 8, 9, A, B, C, D, E, F and the digit multiplier is a power of sixteen, 16^n where n is
···, −3, −2, −1, 0, 1, 2 , 3, ···

Information

In some programming languages, e.g. Java, a number represented in hexadecimal is indicated by placing 0x before the numeral, e.g. 0x3c4 or 0x3C4.

Converting from decimal to binary

Method 1

Take the decimal number to be converted and find between which two column place values it lies, e.g. 35_{10} lies between columns with place values 32 and 64, respectively. Place 1 in the column with the lower of the two place values and 0 in the higher of the two as shown in Table 5.2.1.6. With the given example, take the place value 32 away from the decimal number, leaving 3_{10}. Place 0 in all the columns with place values greater than 3_{10}. It is then trivial to see that we need one 2 and one 1 to match 3_{10}.

...	2^6	2^5	2^4	2^3	2^2	2^1	2^0	...
...	64	32	16	8	4	2	1	...
	0	1	0	0	0	1	1	

Table 5.2.1.6 Some place values for the binary system

Questions

6 Convert the following numbers expressed in decimal to their binary equivalent using Method 1.

(a) 33_{10} (b) 24_{10} (c) 58_{10} (d) 127_{10}

Key method

Example:
Decimal to decimal by successive division, picks out the individual digits
e.g. $n = 462_{10}$

n	$^{n}/_{10}$	r
462	46	2
46	4	6
4	0	4

Where r is the remainder.
The remainder supplies the individual digits, one at a time, e.g. 2.

Method 2 - the method of successive division

Take the decimal number and repeatedly divide by 2 writing down the remainder each time as shown in *Table 5.2.1.7*, stopping when zero is reached.

The binary equivalent of 35_{10} is read from the remainder column beginning at the last row and working up the table.

Quotient	New number	Remainder
35/2	17	1
17/2	8	1
8/2	4	0
4/2	2	0
2/2	1	0
1/2	0	1

Table 5.2.1.7 Successive division by 2 method

Questions

7 Convert the following numbers expressed in decimal to their binary equivalent using Method 2. Show the intermediate results in a table with structure similar to Table 2.1.7.

(a) 33_{10} (b) 24_{10} (c) 58_{10} (d) 127_{10}

Why does the method of successive division work?

We note that if a decimal number, n, is even then there is some integer, k for which

$$n = 2k \quad \text{i.e.} \quad n = 2k + 0$$

e.g. $n = 62$, $k = 31$,

$$\therefore 62 = 2 \times 31 + 0$$

We call 0 the remainder. In this example, 2 goes into 62, 31 times exactly.

On the other hand, if a decimal number, n, is odd then there is some integer, k for which

$$n = 2k + 1$$

e.g. $n = 63$, $k = 31$

$$\therefore 63 = 2 \times 31 + 1$$

We call 1 the remainder. In this example, 2 does not divide 63 exactly.

The first 1 or 0 remainder is the least significant bit of the decimal number's binary equivalent and the final remainder 1 or 0 remainder, the most significant bit of the binary equivalent.

Successive division algorithm decimal to binary

For decimal number, n.

```
Make k the value of n
If k is equal to 0 write down the answer 0
While k is not equal to 0
  Make the new value of k the old value
          divided by 2 using integer division
  If this is the first pass write down remainder
  Else write down remainder to the left
          of the previous remainder
```

Programming task

1 Code this successive division algorithm in a programming language with which you are familiar. Test your program by converting the following decimal numbers

(a) 0_{10} (b) 24_{10} (c) 59_{10} (d) 127_{10} (e) 33_{10}

Converting from decimal to hexadecimal

We can use the method of successive division similar to the one used for decimal to binary conversions, this time dividing by 16. Table 5.2.1.8 shows a worked example for $n = 319_{10}$. The last column is read from the last row upwards giving $13F_{16}$.

Quotient	New number	Remainder
319/16	19	15 (F)
19/16	1	3
1/16	0	1

Table 5.2.1.8 Successive division by 16 method

Questions

8 Convert the following numbers expressed in decimal to their hexadecimal equivalent using the algorithm above. Show the intermediate results in a table with structure similar to Table 2.1.8.

(a) 47_{10} (b) 302_{10} (c) 65517_{10} (d) 285562_{10}

Successive division algorithm decimal to hexadecimal

For decimal number, n.

```
Make k the value of n
If k is equal to 0 write down the answer 0
While k is not equal to 0
  Make the new value of k the old value
          divided by 16 using integer division
  If this is the first pass write down remainder
                         using hexadecimal digit
  Else write down remainder to the left
         of the previous remainder
                         using hexadecimal digit
```

Programming task

2 Code this successive division algorithm in a programming language with which you are familiar. Test your program by converting the following decimal numbers

(a) 0_{10} (b) 47_{10} (c) 302_{10} (d) 65517_{10} (e) 285562_{10}

Use of Microsoft® Windows® programmer calculator

It is possible to use Microsoft Windows' calculator to perform number conversions by selecting the programmer view mode, entering a value in the chosen base and then by changing to one of the other available bases.

You could use this calculator to check your answers to questions about number bases.

Figure 5.2.1.1 Screenshot of Microsoft® Windows® calculator in decimal mode

Converting from hexadecimal to binary

This can be done in a straightforward way as follows:

```
Write down the number in hexadecimal
Replace each hexadecimal digit
by its binary equivalent
using 4 binary digits
```

$B47A_{16} = 1011010001111010_2$

The method relies on the fact that the hexadecimal digits 0 to F map to 0 to 15 in decimal and this decimal range can be coded by just four binary digits. When a number represented in four binary digits is multiplied by 16_{10}, it becomes a number represented by eight binary digits with zeroes in the least significant four bit positions, twelve binary digits when multiplied by 16_{10} again and so on.

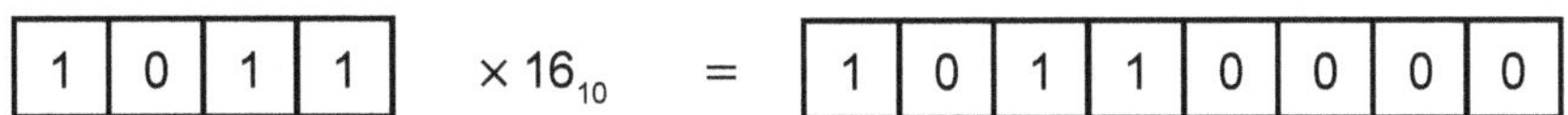

Questions

9 Convert the following numbers expressed in hexadecimal to their binary equivalent using the method described above.

(a) 47_{16} (b) $3A2_{16}$ (c) $6FE7_{16}$ (d) $BEEF_{16}$

Converting from binary to hexadecimal

This can be done in a straightforward way as follows:

```
Write down the number in binary
Add leading 0s to the left-hand side of
     the bit pattern so that the number of bits
              is a multiple of 4 (if necessary)
Replace each block of four binary digits
                by their hexadecimal equivalent
```

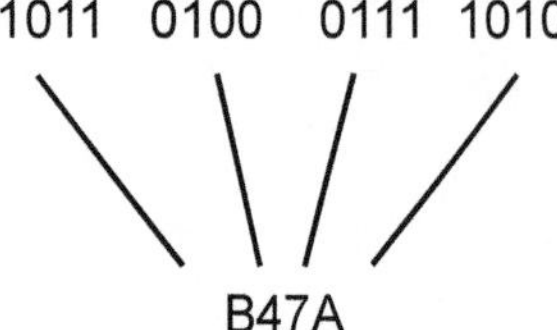

$1011010001111010_2 = B47A_{16}$

Questions

Convert the following numbers expressed in binary to their hexadecimal equivalent using the method described above.

(a) 1111_2 (b) 10101101_2 (c) 101100_2

(d) 110011100011_2

Hexadecimal as shorthand for binary

Long strings of 1s and 0s are difficult for a human to read so programmers often switch to the hexadecimal equivalent because it is much easier to read. If the strings of 1s and 0s represent executable code then debugging this code is much easier if the code is displayed in hexadecimal form. Its meaning is easier to determine than its binary form.

0000011000010000	0000000000000101	0000000001000001
0000011000010000	0000000000000110	0000000001110011
0000011000010000	0000000000000111	0000000001101101
0000011000010000	0000000000001000	0000000001010100
0000011000010000	0000000000001001	0000000001110101
0000011000010000	0000000000001010	0000000001110100
0000011000010000	0000000000001011	0000000001101111
0000011000100000	0000000000000000	0000000001110010
0000011011000000	0000000000000000	0000000000001100
0000001100000000	0000000000000000	0000000000000000
0000000000000000	0000000000000000	0000000000000000
0000000000000000	0000000000000000	0000000000000000
0000000000000000	0000000000000000	0000000000000000
0000000000000000	0000000000000000	0000000000000000
0000000000000000	0000000000000000	0000000000000000
0000000000000000	0000000000000000	0000000000000000

Figure 5.2.1.2 Machine code displayed in binary

Similarly, writing numbers in hexadecimal form is less error prone than writing the same numbers in binary especially if the binary form consists of long strings of 1s and 0s. For example, it would be cumbersome and error prone to specify the colour for text on a page of HTML in 24 binary digits, better to use the shorthand form of hexadecimal, e.g. #1F040A. Here the # symbol is used to indicate that the numeral is in hexadecimal.

The contents of memory or registers of a computer system can be displayed for debugging purposes. It is usual for the software that does this to display these contents in hexadecimal because it is much easier for a human to read the numbers in this form as well as taking up less space on the display screen. Software is needed because the numbers are actually stored in the memory locations and the registers in base 2 form.

0610	0005	0041
0610	0006	0073
0610	0007	006D
0610	0008	0054
0610	0009	0075
0610	000A	0074
0610	000B	006F
0620	0000	0072
06C0	0000	000C
0300	0000	0000
0000	0000	0000
0000	0000	0000
0000	0000	0000

Figure 5.2.1.3 The same machine code expressed in hexadecimal

Memory addresses are more conveniently expressed in hexadecimal than binary. For example, the memory limit of Windows 7 is 4 GiB. This requires the use of 32 binary digits to express the address of a particular memory word or location but in hexadecimal it requires only 8 hexadecimal digits. Incidently, it would require 10 decimal digits. However, hexadecimal is more suitable when working with digital hardware than decimal because hexadecimal uses 4x fewer digits than binary ($^{32}/_{4}$) but decimal uses 3.2x fewer ($^{32}/_{10}$), an awkward factor to work with.

Key point

Long strings of 1s and 0s are difficult for a human to read so programmers often switch to the hexadecimal equivalent because it is

- much easier to read
- more compact, 4x fewer digits
- less error prone
- easier to debug code expressed in hexadecimal
- suitable for working with digital hardware because an integral factor relationship with binary unlike decimal.

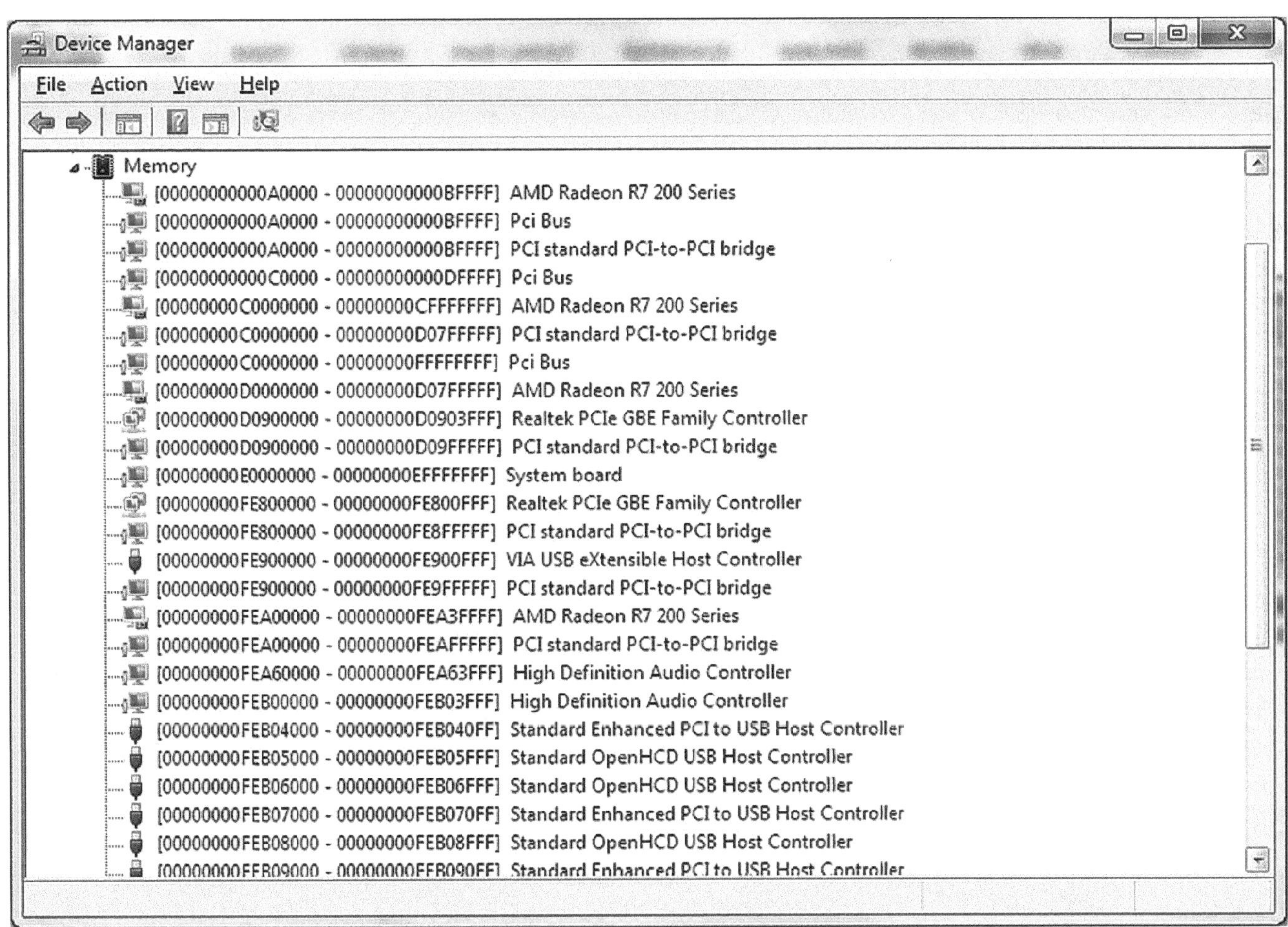

Figure 5.2.1.4 Microsoft® Windows® Device manager showing the allocation of memory

Task

1. Explore memory with the memory viewer of a debugger in the programming language environment that you use, e.g. memory window in Visual Studio 2013, Xcode on Apple Mac, or use a command line tool such as
cat /proc/<processid>/maps in Linux, e.g. using Raspberry Pi.

In this chapter you have covered:

- The meaning of number base
- The decimal number base
- The binary number base
- Converting from decimal to binary
- The method of successive division
- Converting from decimal to hexadecimal
- Converting from hexadecimal to binary
- Converting from binary to hexadecimal
- Hexadecimal as a shorthand for binary.

5.3 Units of information

Learning objectives:

- *The bit is the fundamental unit of information*
- *A byte is a group of 8 bits*
- *Know that 2^n different values can be represented with n bits*

Background

Sounds can have symbolic meaning i.e. are symbols for something.

Gestures or movement can have symbolic meaning i.e. are symbols for something.

Key point

Symbols communicate information.

A symbol is an information carrier.

Key principle

A representation is a pattern of symbols that conveys information, e.g. a pattern of 1s and 0s.

Background

The words *sign* and *symbol* are equivalent.

5.3.1 Bits and bytes

Information

The number of penguins can be represented by many symbols,

e.g. 6 VI six 0110 |||||| 3 + 3 六

We use symbols all the time when we communicate. Animals also use symbols to communicate. Special sounds or movements are used by animals to attract a partner and other sounds and movements are used to warn of danger. *Figure 5.3.1.1* shows a peacock with its tail fully extended. This display of tail feathers is a form of communication.

Figure 5.3.1.1 Peacock display

Special sounds are made by humans too when we speak but our use of such symbols is considerably more advanced than that of animals.

Humans also use symbols when writing words and sentences on paper and on electronic devices; when drawing pictures on paper and painting paintings. We also use gestures and write music using musical notation and so on.

The use of the symbols is not decorative instead their use is to communicate something. That something is **information**. In other words, the symbol is an **information carrier**.

Questions

1. State the information conveyed by the following symbols:

   ♩ ♪ ☺ He Ar [battery symbol]

2. The word sign is sometimes used in place of the word symbol. *Figure 5.3.1.2* shows road signs. State the information conveyed by these signs.

   (a) (b) (c)

Figure 5.3.1.2 Road signs

Information and data

Information is made of data put together according to the rules (*syntax*) that govern the way the chosen symbols are used. Syntax determines the form, construction, composition, or structuring of something. The data must also have meaning or be meaningful. This means that data must comply with the meanings (*semantics*) of the chosen symbol system, code, or language in question. It is not restricted to language but could, for example, be pictorial. The data-based definition of information is thus summarised as

Information = data + meaning

Types of information

The road signs shown in Q2(a), (b) and (c) are informational of a factual kind, e.g. Q2(a) has the meaning, the road ahead narrows, that is a fact. On the other hand, information of the instructional kind is supplied by, for example, the GIVE WAY sign. The sign has a meaning but that meaning is an instruction.

Both factual and instructional data belong to a category of information called **semantic content**. Semantic content is associated with an intelligent producer/consumer pair. *Figure 5.3.1.3* shows the datum *True* being sent from a producer to a consumer. This datum has the status of information at the producer end and at the consumer end where the information = *it is raining*. If the datum *False* was sent instead, then this would be interpreted at the producer and the consumer ends as the information = *it is not raining*.

The datum *True* in transit is an uninterpreted symbol, i.e. its meaning is not yet processed. It is the responsibility of the consumer to interpret this datum and extract its meaning.

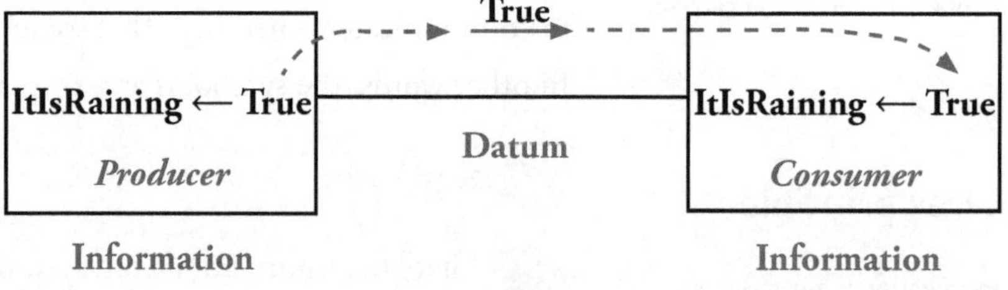

Figure 5.3.1.3 Semantic content information = data + meaning

Environmental information on the other hand is information that is defined relative to an observer who relies on it instead of having direct access to the original data, e.g. the concentric rings visible in the wood of a cut tree trunk provide information on the age of the tree and the growing conditions at the time a ring was laid down. Note, environmental doesn't mean it has to be natural, e.g. the low battery indicator in Q1 is environmental information because it reflects the state of the battery but it is not the battery.

Key concept

Datum:
A datum (plural data) is any physical phenomenon or object that carries information, e.g. road sign object, speech.
There can be no information without data. Data is how information is represented.

Key concept

Physical phenomenon:
A natural phenomenon involving the physical properties of matter and energy, e.g. production or transmission of sound.

Background

Genetic information in the form of genes are instructions which together with other essential ingredients serve the purpose of controlling and guiding the development of organisms very much in the way that procedures in an imperative programming language control the physical state in which an imperative program executes.

Key point

Information as semantic content can also be described as *queries + data*, e.g. *IsItRaining?* + *Yes*, where the query is *IsItRaining?* and the datum is *Yes*.
Yes can be coded as 1. *No* as 0.

Bits

Figure 5.3.1.4 A collection of apples

We have seen how to represent the natural numbers in the decimal and the binary numeral systems.
In the binary system, we use just two symbols, the binary digits 0 and 1 to represent a natural number, for example, the number of apples shown in Figure 5.3.1.4 in binary is 101_2. Rather than use the term **binary digit** we can abbreviate it to **bit**. So we need three bits to count five apples.

This digital data 101_2 encodes the information that we have five apples. If we remove one apple, our digital data must change to 100_2 to convey the new information that we have four apples. Note that digital data always changes in discrete steps. The minimum step in our apples' example is one. Removing more apples, say three, leaves just one apple and to convey this information we must change our digital data to 1_2. Removing the last apple leaves none and our digital data becomes 0_2 to convey this information.

In a similar manner, the datum True and the datum False in Figure 3.1.3 could be encoded as 1 and 0, respectively.

Did you know?

Bit is derived from the *b* of binary and the *it* of digit.

Coin tossing

Now rather than counting objects and recording their number, let's suppose that we wish to convey the outcome of a coin tossing experiment. For the experiment, assume our coin will land either head up (h) or tail up (t) with equal probability when tossed and we will call a single toss of the coin, a trial.

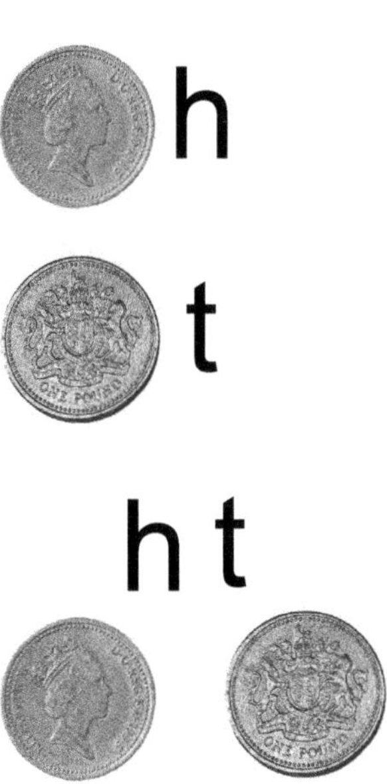

Now before we toss the coin, we cannot say that the outcome is (h) or the outcome is (t). We are in a state of *data deficit* and therefore, in possession of no information about the outcome. However, as soon as the coin is tossed we have an outcome, (h) or a (t) which we can represent as 1 or 0. We now have data, a single bit of data which conveys information, the result of the trial. We say that to represent the outcome we require **one bit of information** or **one bit of information per symbol** where a symbol is either (h) or (t).

Outcome	2-bit encoding
(tt)	00
(th)	01
(ht)	10
(hh)	11

Table 5.3.1.1

Now let's conduct a coin tossing experiment using two unbiased coins. We have four possible outcomes, encoded as the symbols (hh), (tt), (ht) and (th). Before conducting the experiment, the data deficit is four units, the four symbols, because we have no information about which outcome will actually occur. However, when we have an outcome, say the symbol (ht), we remove a greater data deficit than we do for the single coin experiment because each symbol in the two coin experiment provides more information by excluding more alternatives.

We need two bits to encode the possible two-coin experiment outcomes as shown in *Table 5.3.1.1*, or **two bits of information per symbol**.

Questions

3. Complete a copy of *Table 5.3.1.2* by replacing the blanks in the Alphabet column and entering the missing information in the Bits of information per symbol column.

No of coins	Alphabet	Bits of information per symbol
1	2 equiprobable symbols (h), (t)	1
2	4 equiprobable symbols (hh), (ht), (th), (tt)	2
3	8 equiprobable symbols (hhh), (___), (___), (___) (thh), (___), (___), (ttt)	
4	16 equiprobable symbols (hhhh), (____), (____), (____) (hthh), (____), (____), (____) (thhh), (____), (____), (____) (tthh), (____), (____), (tttt)	

Table 5.3.1.2

Key principle

Unit of information:
The bit is the fundamental unit of information.

The bit is the fundamental unit of information

Imagine a machine that can answer only "42" to any question. There is no data deficit because the answer to any question can be predicted with absolute certainty, it is always the symbol "42". Therefore, the machine produces an amount of information which is zero.

The smallest amount of information occurs when we have two equally likely choices which we know requires one bit. We therefore use the **bit as the fundamental unit of information**.

Key concept

Byte:
The name used for a group of 8 bits is *byte*.

A byte is a group of 8 bits

It is convenient to group together bits and refer to the group by name. The name used for a group of 8 bits is byte.

Task

1. Investigate whether or not the programming language that you use has a byte data type. If it doesn't how could one be created for use in programs that you might write?

How different arrangements of n bits are there?

Figure 5.3.1.5 shows all possible arrangements for 1, 2, 3, 4 bits. Notice that the number of arrangements doubles each time we add another bit. Starting at one bit, the number of arrangements is 2 or 2^1. To double the number of arrangements to 4 or 2^2 we just add another bit making 2 bits. To double again from 4 to 8 or 2^3 we add another bit making 3 bits. Doubling again we obtain 16 or 2^4 different arrangements and we now have used 4 bits.

This suggests the relationship between number of bits and number of different arrangements is as follows

2 ways
0
1

4 ways	
0	0
0	1
1	0
1	1

8 ways		
0	0	0
0	0	1
0	1	0
0	1	1
1	0	0
1	0	1
1	1	0
1	1	1

16 ways			
0	0	0	0
0	0	0	1
0	0	1	0
0	0	1	1
0	1	0	0
0	1	0	1
0	1	1	0
0	1	1	1
1	0	0	0
1	0	0	1
1	0	1	0
1	0	1	1
1	1	0	0
1	1	0	1
1	1	1	0
1	1	1	1

Figure 5.3.1.5 No of different arrangements of n bits where n = 1, 2, 3, 4

Key point

Bit arrangements or bit patterns can represent natural numbers.

3 bits	Decimal value
000	0
001	1
010	2
011	3
100	4
101	5
110	6
111	7

Number of different arrangements of n bits = 2^n

If each arrangement represents a value, e.g. a natural number, then we can also say that

Number of different values that can be represented in n bits = 2^n

No of bits	Decimal integers	No of integers	Binary integers
1	0, 1	2	0, 1
2	0, 1, 2, 3	4	00, 01, 10, 11
3	0, 1, 2, 3, 4, 5, 6, 7	8	000, 001, 010, 011, 100, 101, 110, 111

Table 5.3.1.3 Number of different values for a given number of bits

Key concept

Bit pattern:
An arrangement of bits is called a bit pattern, e.g. 100101.

Key point

Number of different values that can be represented in n bits = 2^n

Questions

4 How many different arrangements are possible if the number of bits is
(a) 5 (b) 8 (c) 16 (d) 24 (e) 32?
Express your answers as both powers of 2 and fully evaluated.

5 How many different values are possible for the following number of bytes
(a) 1 (b) 2 (c) 8?
Express your answers as powers of 2.

Questions

6. Write all possible bit patterns for 4 bits and their corresponding decimal natural number values in table format.

In this chapter you have covered:

- Symbols are used to communicate information
- The data-based definition of information:

  Information = data + meaning
- Data is how information is represented
- Information can be factual or instructional
- A bit is a single binary digit, 0 or 1
- The bit is the fundamental unit of information
- Byte: The name used for a group of 8 bits is byte.
- Number of different values that can be represented in n bits = 2^n

5.3 Units of information

Learning objectives:

- *Naming quantities of bytes*
- *kibi, mebi, gibi, tebi*
- *kilo, mega, giga, tera*

5.3.2 Units

Quantities of bytes

Storage device manufacturers measure capacity using the decimal system (base 10), so 1 gigabyte (GB) is calculated as exactly 1,000,000,000 bytes or 1 billion bytes.

Figure 5.3.2.1 shows the reporting of the capacity of a Western Digital hard disk.

Figure 5.3.2.1 Image of a part of the exterior of a hard disk showing storage capacity of 160.0 GB quoted to 4 significant figures

On the other hand, the memory capacity of RAM installed in machines and quoted in GB is usually reported by the OS using the binary system (base 2) of measurement. In binary, 1 GB means 1,073,741,824 bytes, 2 GB is therefore 2147483648 bytes as shown in *Figure 5.3.2.2*. The RAM capacity GB is therefore a different unit from the disk storage GB.

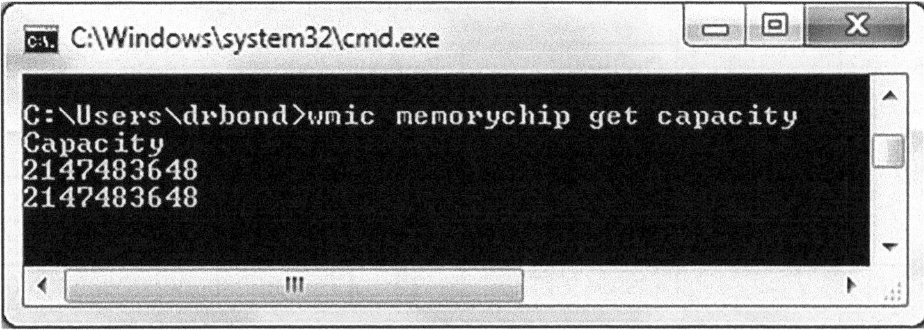

Figure 5.3.2.2 Command line Microsoft® Windows® 7 showing capacity in bytes of RAM chips – 2 in total each 2GB

Background

The *bi* in prefix *gibi* refers to binary.

This rather confusing situation has been resolved by the gradual adoption of the International Electrotechnical Commission (IEC) standard for binary prefixes, which specify the use of **gigabyte (GB)** to strictly denote **1000000000 bytes** and **gibibyte (GiB)** to denote **1073741824 bytes**. This standard is now part of the International System of Quantities.

Figure 5.3.2.3 shows the use of Gi and Ki for reporting disk storage capacity using the command *df –h* in terminal mode on an Apple® MacBook Pro® running operating system OS X® 10.8.5. The About This Mac window is also shown.

```
Kevin-Bonds-MacBook-Pro:~ drbond$ df -h
Filesystem                                   Size
/dev/disk0s2                                232Gi
devfs                                       184Ki
map -hosts                                    0Bi
map auto_home                                 0Bi
```

Figure 5.3.2.3 shows the use of the units Gi and Ki

Task

1. Using the command line of your computer, investigate the capacity of the
   (a) hard disk drive attached to your computer
   (*wmic diskdrive get size* on Microsoft Windows,
   wmic diskdrive get /? for more options)
   (b) RAM installed in your computer
   (*hostinfo | grep memory* on Apple Mac computers,
   wmic memorychip get capacity on Microsoft Windows)

Information

The following command to obtain disk capacity is available at the command line in Windows:

wmic logicaldisk get size, freespace, caption

Powers of 2

Table 5.3.2.1 shows some numbers in decimal numerals expressed as powers of 2 and their equivalent binary numeral. In 2 raised to the power of 10, 10 is known as the exponent. The exponents 10, 20, 30, 40 specify the number of zeroes in the binary numeral.

Decimal numeral	Power of 2	Binary numeral
1024	2^{10}	10000000000
1048576	2^{20}	100000000000000000000
1073741824	2^{30}	1000000000000000000000000000000
109951162776	2^{40}	100000000000000000000 00000000000000000000

Questions

1. Express the following binary numerals in the form 2^n.
   (a) 1000_2 (b) 1000000_2 (c) 1000000000000000_2

2. Express the following decimal numerals in the form 2^n.
   (a) 1024 (b) 512 (c) 2048 (d) 4096 (e) 2097152

To avoid writing out long strings of zeroes, the names, symbols and corresponding powers of 2 are used as shown in Table 5.3.2.2.

If the binary numeral refers to a quantity of bytes then we can express the quantity using the units of Ki, Mi, Gi and Ti as shown in Table 5.3.2.3.

B refers to byte.

Name	Symbol	Power of 2
kibi	Ki	2^{10}
mebi	Mi	2^{20}
gibi	Gi	2^{30}
tebi	Ti	2^{40}

Table 5.3.2.2 Unit name, symbol and corresponding power of 2

Decimal numeral	Power of 2	Using units	Using symbol form of unit for quantities of bytes	Using named unit for quantities of bytes
1024	2^{10}	1Ki	1KiB	1 kibibyte
1048576	2^{20}	1Mi	1MiB	1 mebibyte
1073741824	2^{30}	1Gi	1GiB	1 gibibyte
109951162776	2^{40}	1Ti	1TiB	1 tebibyte

Table 5.3.2.3 Quantities of bytes expressed in units

Key fact

kibi, Ki - 2^{10}
mebi, Mi – 2^{20}
gibi, Gi – 2^{30}
tebi, Ti – 2^{40}

kilo, k - 10^3
mega, M – 10^6
giga, G – 10^9
tera, T – 10^{12}

Questions

3 Convert the following to bytes
(a) 1MiB (b) 1.5KiB (c) 1.75GiB

4 Convert the following quantities in bytes to KiB
(a) 1024 (b) 512 (c) 2048 (d) 4096

5 Convert the following quantities in bytes to MiB
(a) 1048576 (b) 6291456 (c) 4718592 (d) 9437184

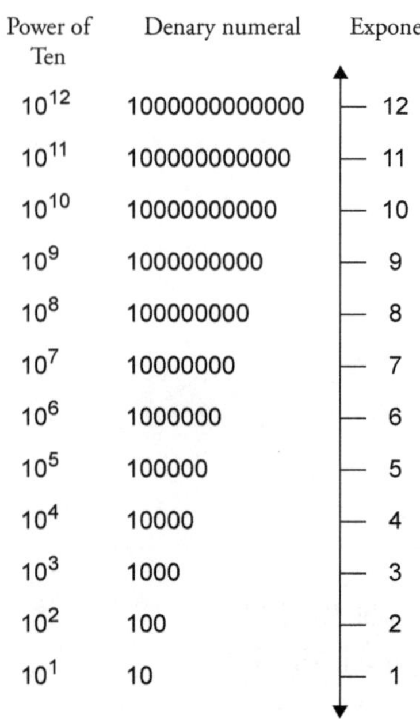

Power of Ten
Denary numeral
Exponent
10^12 1000000000000 12
10^11 100000000000 11
10^10 10000000000 10
10^9 1000000000 9
10^8 100000000 8
10^7 10000000 7
10^6 1000000 6
10^5 100000 5
10^4 10000 4
10^3 1000 3
10^2 100 2
10^1 10 1

Figure 5.3.2.4 Powers of 10

Powers of 10

Figure 5.3.2.4 shows the decimal numeral corresponding to a given power of 10. The power is known as the exponent. The exponent specifies the number of zeroes in the decimal numeral.

To avoid writing out long strings of zeroes, the names, symbols and corresponding powers of 10 are used as shown in Table 5.3.2.4.

Name	Symbol	Power of 10
kilo	k	10^3
mega	M	10^6
giga	G	10^9
tera	T	10^{12}

Table 5.3.2.4 Unit name, symbol and corresponding power of 10

Table 5.3.2.5 shows how to express a decimal numeral which is a power of 10 in units of k, M, G and T.

If the decimal numeral refers to a quantity of bytes then we can express the quantity using the units of k, M, G and T.

Decimal numeral	Power of 10	Using units	Using symbol form of unit for quantities of bytes	Using named unit for quantities of bytes
1000	10^3	1k	1kB	1 kilobyte
10000	10^4	10k	10kB	10 kilobytes
100000	10^5	100k	100kB	100 kilobytes
1000000	10^6	1M	1MB	1 megabyte
10000000	10^7	10M	10MB	10 megabytes
100000000	10^8	100M	100MB	100 megabytes
1000000000	10^9	1G	1GB	1 gigabyte
10000000000	10^{10}	10G	10GB	10 gigabytes
100000000000	10^{11}	100G	100GB	100 gigabytes
1000000000000	10^{12}	1T	1TB	1 terabyte

Table 5.3.2.5 Quantities of bytes expressed in units k, M, G and T

Questions

6 Express the following decimal numerals in the form 10^n
(a) 1000 (b) 1000000 (c) 10000000

7 Convert the following quantities in bytes to kB
(a) 1000 (b) 10000

8 Convert the following quantities in bytes to MB
(a) 500000 (b) 2000000 (c) 30000000

Data transfer units

Data transfer rates are normally expressed in bits per second using the units k, M, G, T, e.g. 1Mb/s, where the meaning of 1Mb/s is 1 megabit per second or 1000000 bits per second. A lowercase b is used to indicate bits.

Questions

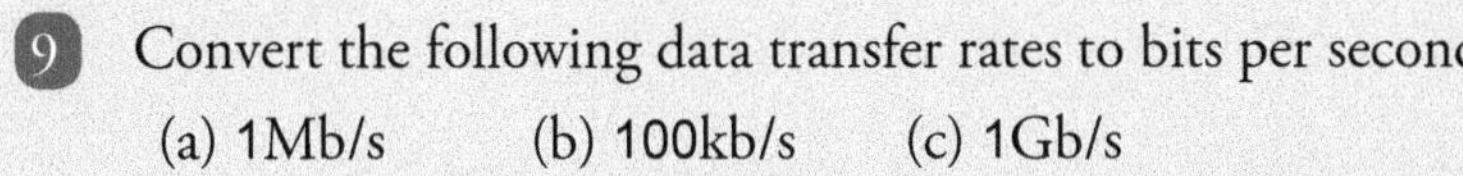

9 Convert the following data transfer rates to bits per second
(a) 1Mb/s (b) 100kb/s (c) 1Gb/s

In this chapter you have covered:

- *How quantities of bytes are named*
- *The use of the prefixes kibi, mebi, gibi, tebi*
- *The use of the prefixes kilo, mega, giga, tera*

5.4 Binary number system

Learning objectives

- *Unsigned binary*
- *Range of unsigned binary*
  Min value = 0
  Max value = $2^n - 1$ for n bits

Key fact

Unsigned binary:
In unsigned binary numbers are limited to non-negative values.

5.4.1 Unsigned binary

Non-negative values

In this coding scheme, the numbers that can be coded are limited to nonnegative values. For example, the numbers expressible in four bits for unsigned binary are as shown in *Figure 5.4.1.1*. This figure also shows the decimal equivalent values.

Decimal value	Unsigned binary value	Decimal value	Unsigned binary value
0	0000	8	1000
1	0001	9	1001
2	0010	10	1010
3	0011	11	1011
4	0100	12	1100
5	0101	13	1101
6	0110	14	1110
7	0111	15	1111

Figure 5.4.1.1 Table of unsigned binary codes in four bits and their decimal equivalent values.

When coding numbers in unsigned binary, the weights of each binary position in decimal are as shown in *Figure 5.4.1.2*. Notice that the next significant digit weighting in decimal is obtained from the previous one by multiplying by 2.

Figure 5.4.1.2 shows that the number with decimal representation 12 has an unsigned binary representation of 00001100 in 8 bits.

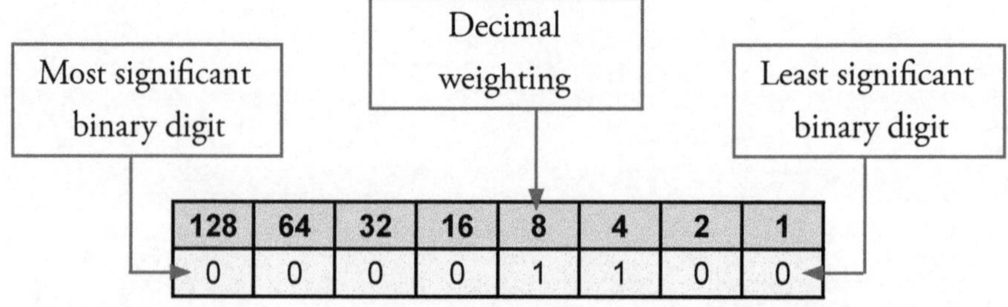

Figure 5.4.1.2 Decimal weighting of binary digits in unsigned binary coding.

Questions

1. Convert the following decimal values to unsigned binary using 8 bits:
   (a) 5   (b) 129   (c) 253

2. Convert the following unsigned binary numbers to decimal:
   (a) 10100001   (b) 01111010   (c) 11111111

Key fact

Range of numbers in unsigned binary in n bits:
Min value = 0
Max value = $2^n - 1$

Minimum and maximum values

The range of numbers that can be coded in unsigned binary depends upon the number of bits that are allocated to represent the number. Obviously, with just one bit only two numbers can be coded, zero and one, giving a range of

$$\text{minimum} = 0_2$$

$$\text{maximum} = 1_2$$

With two bits, four numbers can be coded in unsigned binary as follows:

00, 01, 10, 11, giving a range with

$$\text{minimum} = 00_2$$

$$\text{maximum} = 11_2$$

The minimum number is always zero but the maximum varies with the number of bits used to represent the number. Figure 5.4.1.3 shows the maximum binary numeral for 1, 2, 3, 4, 5, 6, 7 and 8 bits and the weighting in decimal for each bit position.

128	64	32	16	8	4	2	1
1	1	1	1	1	1	1	1
	1	1	1	1	1	1	1
		1	1	1	1	1	1
			1	1	1	1	1
				1	1	1	1
					1	1	1
						1	1
							1

Figure 5.4.1.3 Maximum binary numeral for a given number of bits

Figure 5.4.1.4 shows the maximum number expressed as a decimal numeral for 1, 2, 3, 4, 5, 6, 7, 8 and n bits.

No of bits	Maximum number in decimal	In unsigned binary	In compact decimal form
1	1	1	$2^1 - 1$
2	3	11	$2^2 - 1$
3	7	111	$2^3 - 1$
4	15	1111	$2^4 - 1$
5	31	11111	$2^5 - 1$
6	63	111111	$2^6 - 1$
7	127	1111111	$2^7 - 1$
8	255	11111111	$2^8 - 1$
n		1111...1111	$2^n - 1$

Figure 5.4.1.4 Maximum number for a given number of bits

Generalising, the minimum and maximum values expressible in unsigned binary for a given number of bits n is in decimal as follows

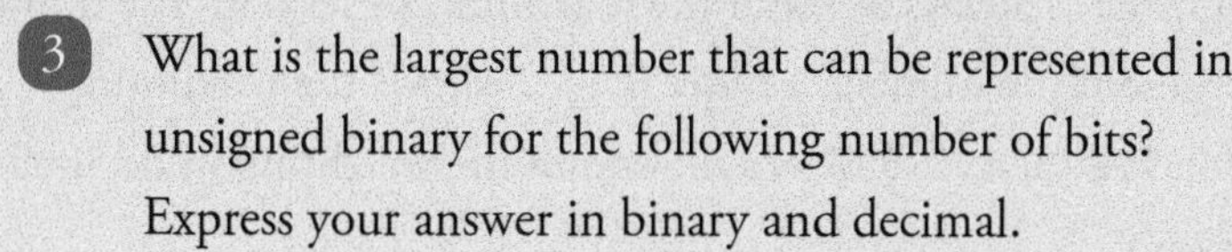

Questions

3 What is the largest number that can be represented in unsigned binary for the following number of bits? Express your answer in binary and decimal.

(a) 6 bits (b) 10 bits (c) 16 bits

In this chapter you have covered:

- Unsigned binary
- Range of unsigned binary
  Min value = 0
  Max value = $2^n - 1$ for n bits

5.4 Binary number system

Learning objectives

- *Adding two unsigned binary integers*
- *Multiplying two unsigned binary integers*

5.4.2 Unsigned binary arithmetic

Adding two unsigned binary integers

The rules for adding numbers expressed in the binary numeral system are basically the same as for any other system. We add the contents of each column in turn, starting from the right with the least significant digit column and moving progressively leftward. Any carry from a column must be added to the sum of the digits in the next column as shown in *Figure 5.4.2.1* which shows the sum $01101100_2 + 00101010_2$ of two 8-bit unsigned binary integers.

Key principle

Addition of two unsigned binary integers:
Apply the following rules to each digit column

$0_2 + 0_2 = 0_2$
$0_2 + 1_2 = 1_2$
$1_2 + 0_2 = 1_2$
$1_2 + 1_2 = 0_2$ carry 1_2
$0_2 + 0_2$ + carry $1_2 = 1_2$
$0_2 + 1_2$ + carry $1_2 = 0_2$ carry 1_2
$1_2 + 0_2$ + carry $1_2 = 0_2$ carry 1_2
$1_2 + 1_2$ + carry $1_2 = 1_2$ carry 1_2

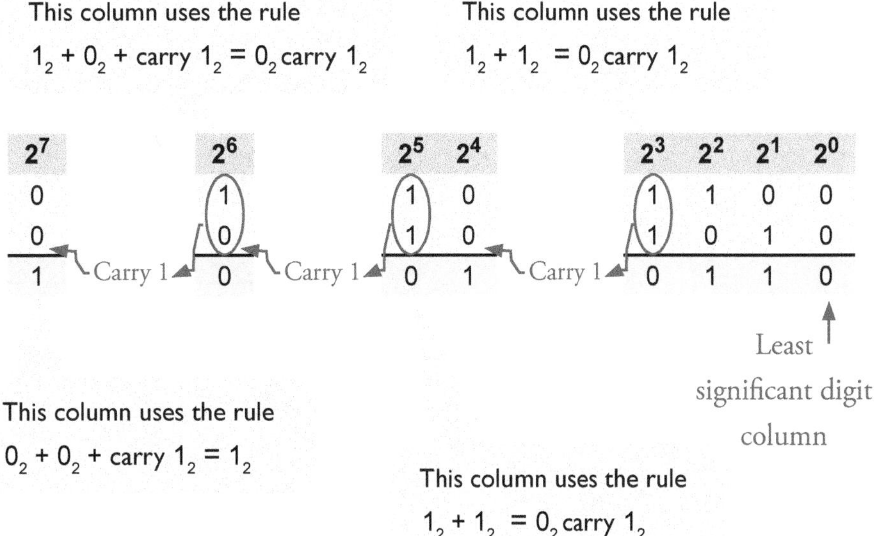
This column uses the rule
$1_2 + 0_2$ + carry $1_2 = 0_2$ carry 1_2
This column uses the rule
$1_2 + 1_2 = 0_2$ carry 1_2
2^7 2^6 2^5 2^4 2^3 2^2 2^1 2^0
0 1 1 0 1 1 0 0
0 0 1 0 1 0 1 0
1 0 0 1 0 1 1 0
Carry 1
Carry 1
Carry 1
Least significant digit column
This column uses the rule
$0_2 + 0_2$ + carry $1_2 = 1_2$
This column uses the rule
$1_2 + 1_2 = 0_2$ carry 1_2

Figure 5.4.2.1 Addition of two 8-bit unsigned binary integers

The basic rules are as follows

$0_2 + 0_2 = 0_2$

$0_2 + 1_2 = 1_2$

$1_2 + 0_2 = 1_2$

$1_2 + 1_2 = 0_2$, carry 1_2 to the next column since there is no symbol for 2.

The last rule states that $1_2 + 1_2 = 10_2$.

If we have a carry from the previous column then the carry must be added to the sum of the two digits of the current column. So we have the additional rules

$0_2 + 0_2 + \text{carry } 1_2 = 1_2$

$0_2 + 1_2 + \text{carry } 1_2 = 0_2 \text{ carry } 1_2$

$1_2 + 0_2 + \text{carry } 1_2 = 0_2 \text{ carry } 1_2$

$1_2 + 1_2 + \text{carry } 1_2 = 1_2 \text{ carry } 1_2$

Normally addition of two binary numerals representing unsigned binary integers is set out in the manner of the example below

```
  01101011
+ 00011011
  --------
  10000110
```

Questions

1 Complete the following additions of two 4-bit unsigned binary integers:

(a)
```
  0110
+ 0001
  ----
```

(b)
```
  0101
+ 0101
  ----
```

2 Complete the following additions of two 8-bit unsigned binary integers:

(a)
```
  01101011
+ 00011011
  --------
```

(b)
```
  11010101
+ 01011101
  --------
```

Multiplication of two unsigned binary integers

Multiplication in binary is performed in a similar manner to a decimal long multiplication problem. For example, the decimal long multiplication problem $456_{10} \times 43_{10}$ would be done as follows

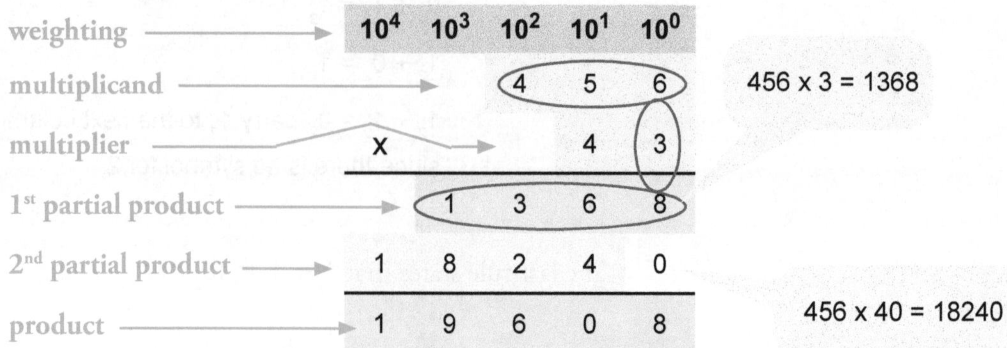

The multiplicand 456_{10} is multiplied by each digit of the multiplier 43_{10} separately and then the partial products are added giving appropriate weighting to the implied power of 10 of each digit of the multiplier.

If we wanted the result of $101_2 \times 11_2$ where each numeral represents an unsigned binary integer then the binary long multiplication would be done as follows

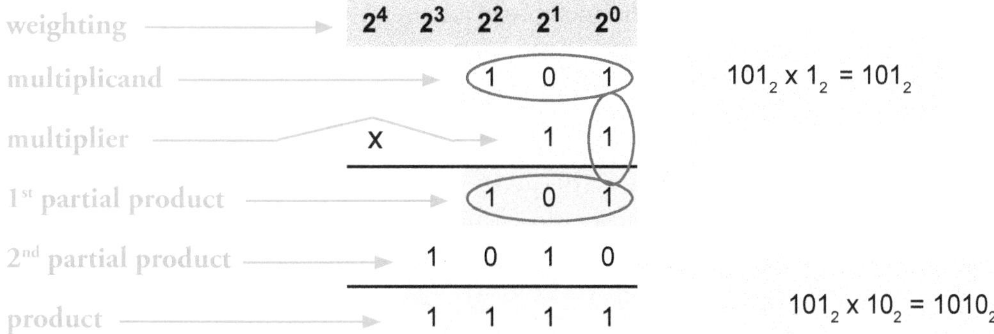

Notice that because each digit of the multiplier 11_2 in the above example is a 1, the multiplicand 101_2 is just copied and then shifted either zero or one places to the left to produce the corresponding partial product, 101_2 or 1010_2. The number of shifts to perform is the same as the exponent of the weighting, i.e. 0 or 1.

Extending this to a multiplication of larger numbers we see that binary multiplication consists of copying and shifting the multiplicand, e.g. $11011101_2 \times 1011_2 = 100101111111_2$ as shown in Figure 5.4.2.2.

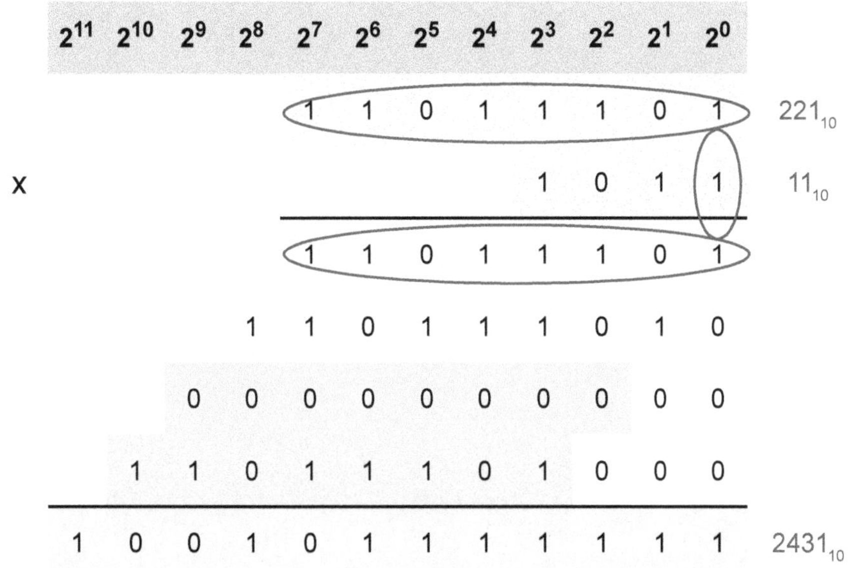

Figure 5.4.2.2 Long multiplication of 11011101_2 by 1011_2

Key principle

Multiplication of two unsigned binary integers:

For each 1 in the multiplier, copy the multiplicand and place below the last partial product but shifted left by a number of columns equal to the exponent of the weight for this 1.

For each 0 in the multiplier, change every digit in a copy of the multiplicand to 0 and place the copy as before.

Sum the partial products to obtain the product.

$1_2 + 1_2 + \text{carry } 1_2 = 1_2 \text{ carry } 1_2$

Questions

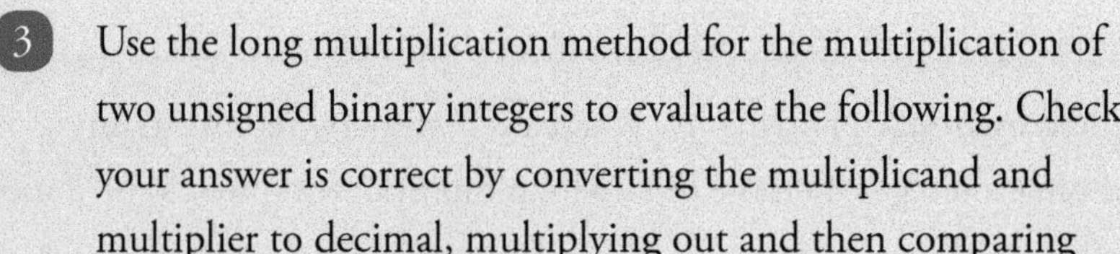

3 Use the long multiplication method for the multiplication of two unsigned binary integers to evaluate the following. Check your answer is correct by converting the multiplicand and multiplier to decimal, multiplying out and then comparing with your unsigned binary answer.

(a) $101_2 \times 10_2$ (b) $101_2 \times 11_2$ (c) $1001_2 \times 10_2$

(d) $1001_2 \times 11_2$ (e) $1001_2 \times 101_2$

(f) $1001011_2 \times 1101_2$ (g) $1011100_2 \times 1010_2$

(h) $10111101_2 \times 11101_2$

In this chapter you have covered:

- Adding two unsigned binary integers
- Multiplying two unsigned binary integers

5.4 Binary number system

Learning objectives

- *Two's complement representation of negative and positive integers*
- *Converting between signed binary and decimal and vice versa*
- *Subtraction using two's complement*
- *Range of two's complement representation for a given number of bits*

5.4.3 Signed binary using two's complement

Representing negative integers

Numbers smaller than zero are called negative numbers. Most humans but not all, accountants are the exception, place the symbol, '-', before a natural number greater than zero, e.g. 2, to indicate a negative integer, e.g. -2.

-2 -1 0 1 2 3 4

The term, negative or minus sign, is used for '-'. The '+' symbol used to indicate a positive integer, is called the positive or plus sign. If there is no sign before the number, it is assumed to be positive. Integers can be positive or negative or zero.

Computations are carried out in digital computers using binary to represent numbers because the binary system is ideally suited to the electronic circuits in digital computers. These circuits operate using two different levels of voltage which map easily to the two symbols, 0 and 1, of the binary system. However, there is no third level of voltage to map to the symbol '-'. Therefore, we have to rely on the two symbols, 0 and 1 to indicate both the magnitude (size) and the sign of a number.

Did you know?

Accountants are different, they place brackets around a natural number to indicate a negative integer, e.g. (567) means -567.

There are several choices of representation for positive and negative integers in binary one of which is two's complement.

Bin	Dec
0 0 0	0
0 0 1	1
0 1 0	2
0 1 1	3
1 0 0	-4
1 0 1	-3
1 1 0	-2
1 1 1	-1

Table 5.4.3.1 Two's complement representation of negative and positive integers

In *Table 5.4.3.1*, the column headed `Bin` contains 3-bit binary integer numerals and the column headed `Dec` contains the corresponding decimal numerals for these integers. If you study *Table 5.4.3.1* carefully, you will observe that `Dec` is a negative integer only when the most significant digit of `Bin` is 1 and `Dec` is a positive integer or zero only when the most significant digit of `Bin` is 0. This representation in binary of integers is known as **two's complement**.

Key fact

For integers represented in two's complement binary:

- 1 in the most significant bit position indicates a negative integer and a 0, a positive integer
- The most negative integer occurs with 1 in the most significant bit position and all 0s in the other positions
- For -1, every bit is 1
- For the most positive integer every bit is 1 except the most significant bit which is 0.

Bin	Dec
0000	0
0001	1
0010	2
0011	3
0100	4
0101	5
0110	6
0111	7
1000	-8
1001	-7
1010	-6
1011	-5
1100	-4
1101	-3
1110	-2
1111	-1

Table 5.4.3.2 Two's complement representation of negative and positive integers

Key fact

Two's complement sign bit:

The most significant bit is the sign bit.

Its weighting is always negative.

Table 5.4.3.2 shows `Bin` using 4 bits to represent integers in binary. Again, negative numbers are represented in binary with the most significant digit 1 and positive numbers with the most significant digit 0.

Whatever the number of bits:

- 1 in the most significant bit position indicates a negative integer and a 0, a positive integer
- The most negative integer occurs with 1 in the most significant bit position and all 0s in the other positions
- For -1, every bit is 1
- For the most positive value every bit is 1 except the most significant bit which is 0.

The sign bit in two's complement is always the most significant digit.

To achieve the range -8_{10} to $+7_{10}$ the weighting for each bit must be as shown in *Table 5.4.3.3*. Notice that the most significant digit, the sign bit, also has magnitude or size, i.e. a weighting of -8_{10}.

-8	4	2	1
0	0	0	0
0	0	0	1
0	0	1	0
0	0	1	1
0	1	0	0
0	1	0	1
0	1	1	0
0	1	1	1
1	0	0	0
1	0	0	1
1	0	1	0
1	0	1	1
1	1	0	0
1	1	0	1
1	1	1	0
1	1	1	1

Table 5.4.3.3 4-bit two's complement representation of integers

Table 5.4.3.4 shows how the weighting of each bit position varies for integers in two's complement binary for a given number of bits, e.g. for 5 bits the most significant bit has a weighting of -16 in decimal. The most significant digit is always the sign bit and its weighting is always negative.

The bit positions are labelled starting with the least significant digit which is given bit position 0.

The most significant bit has weighting, -2^{n-1} where n is the number of bits,

e.g. n = 8, $-2^{8-1} = -2^7 = -128_{10}$.

No of bits	Weighting							
8	-128	64	32	16	8	4	2	1
7		-64	32	16	8	4	2	1
6			-32	16	8	4	2	1
5				-16	8	4	2	1
4					-8	4	2	1
3						-4	2	1
2							-2	1
Bit position	7	6	5	4	3	2	1	0

Table 5.4.3.4 Two's complement representation of integers showing weighting of bit positions for different numbers of bits

Questions

1. What is the weighting in decimal of the most significant bit if the following number of bits are used to represent integers in two's complement binary
(a) 3 (b) 5 (c) 8 (d) 10 (e) 16?

2. Express your answers to Q1 in 2^x format.

3. What is the binary numeral for the most negative integer in two's complement binary when the number of bits for the numeral is as follows
(a) 3 b) 5 (c) 8 (d) 10 (e) 16?

4. What is the binary numeral for the most positive integer in two's complement binary when the number of bits for the numeral is as follows
(a) 3 (b) 5 (c) 8 (d) 10 (e) 16?

Converting an integer from decimal to two's complement binary

We have two cases to consider, negative integers and non-negative integers.

Non-negative integers

Treat the integer as unsigned and convert using one of the available methods for converting unsigned decimal numerals such as Repeated Division By Two.

Write down the result in binary and place one or more zeroes in front of the binary numeral up to the specified number of bits. For example, convert $+13_{10}$ to two's complement binary using 5 bits as follows

$$+13_{10} \rightarrow 1101_2 \rightarrow 01101_2$$

The most significant bit will always be 0 for non-negative integers.

Negative integers

Treat the integer as unsigned and convert using one of the available methods for converting unsigned decimal numerals such as Repeated Division By Two.

Write down the result in binary and place one or more zeroes in front of the binary numeral up to the specified number of bits.

Now there are two possible methods for the next stage.

Method 1

- Flip the bits
- Then add 1.

Key principle

To convert from decimal to 2's complement binary:
Non-negative
- Treat the integer as unsigned
- Convert to unsigned binary
- Pad out with leading zeroes up to the specified number of bits

Negative
Method 1
- As for non-negative
- Flip the bits
- Add 1

Method 2
- As for non-negative
- Starting from the right, leave all the digits alone up to and including the first 1
- Flip all the other digits

For example, if the specified number of bits is 5 proceed as follows

	Change to unsigned decimal		Convert		Insert 0		Flip bits		Add 1	
-13_{10}	→	13_{10}	→	1101_2	→	01101_2	→	10010_2	→	10011_2

Check: $10011_2 = -16_{10} + 2_{10} + 1_{10} = -13_{10}$

Method 2

- Starting from the right, leave all the digits alone up to and including the first 1
- Then flip all the other digits.

For example,

	Change to unsigned decimal		Convert		Insert 0		Leave 1st bit alone		Flip all other bits	
-13_{10}	→	13_{10}	→	1101_2	→	01101_2	→	$0110 \mid 1_2$	→	10011_2

Questions

5. Convert the following integers expressed in decimal to 5-bit two's complement binary.

   (a) +12 (b) -12 (c) +7 (d) -7 (e) -1

6. Convert the following integers expressed in decimal to 8-bit two's complement binary.

   (a) +12 (b) -12 (c) -7 (d) +32 (e) -32 (f) -128
   (g) -1 (h) -63 (i) -76

Key principle

Two's complement to decimal: Sum the products of each bit value and the corresponding decimal weighting.

Converting an integer from two's complement binary to decimal

- Set out the decimal weighting for each binary digit remembering that the most significant digit's weighting is negative.
- Sum the products of each bit value and the corresponding decimal weighting.

For example, for 11110001_2 proceed as follows

-128_{10}	64_{10}	32_{10}	16_{10}	8_{10}	4_{10}	2_{10}	1_{10}
1	1	1	1	0	0	0	1

$1 \times -128 + 1 \times 64 + 1 \times 32 + 1 \times 16 + 0 \times 8 + 0 \times 4 + 0 \times 2 + 1 \times 1 = -15_{10}$

Questions

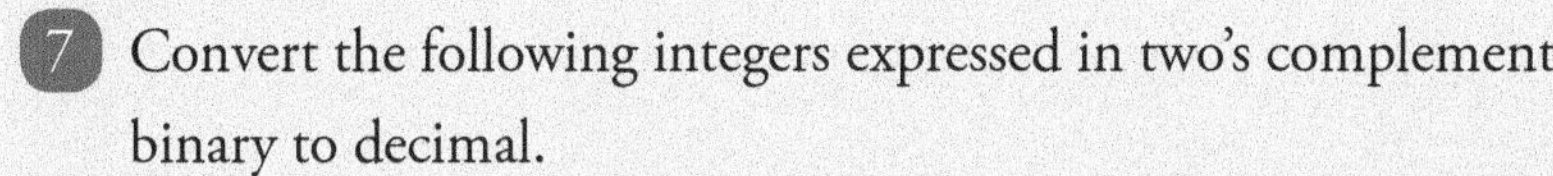

7 Convert the following integers expressed in two's complement binary to decimal.

(a) 01011100 (b) 10100100 (c) 1000000 (d) 11111111
(e) 10000000 (f) 01111111

Subtraction in two's complement

Given two integers in two's complement binary, it is possible to subtract one, B, from the other, A, by two's complementing B and then adding the result to A.

$$A - B \rightarrow A + (-B)$$

For example, $0101_2 - 0011_2$ would be evaluated as follows

$$0101_2 - 0011_2 \rightarrow 0101_2 + (-0011_2) \rightarrow 0101_2 + 1101_2 \rightarrow (1)0010_2$$

The addition carried out is just binary addition but this can generate a carry (1) which is ignored because we restrict the answer to the same number of bits as we started with, i.e. 4.

Check: $0101_2 - 0011_2 = 5_{10} - 3_{10} = +2_{10} = 0010_2$

Another example, $0101_2 - 1111_2$ would be evaluated as follows

$$0101_2 - 1111_2 \rightarrow 0101_2 + (-1111_2) \rightarrow 0101_2 + 0001_2 \rightarrow 0110_2$$

Check: $0101_2 - 1111_2 = 5_{10} - (-1_{10}) = +6_{10} = 0110_2$

Key principle

Subtraction:
Perform addition with 2's complement of B

$$A - B \rightarrow A + (-B)$$

Questions

8 Evaluate the following 4-bit two's complement binary integer expressions using steps that involve only binary.

(a) 0111 - 0100 (b) 0100 - 1110 (c) 1101 - 1110
(d) 1111 - 1100 (e) 1100 - 0011

Computer hardware engineers like to use two's complement binary for arithmetic because they only need to design addition circuits and circuits that flip bits (complement), no subtraction circuitry is required. The addition and complementing circuits are easy to design.

Computer engineers also like to use two's complement binary because there is only one binary numeral for zero. Other representations have two binary numerals for zero. Comparisons of two numerals is often done by subtracting one from the other and checking to see if the answer is zero or not. Zero means that the two numerals represent the same number.

Key fact

Range:

For 2's complement the range of a given number of bits, n is

-2^{n-1} to $2^{n-1} - 1$

Range for a given number of bits

The range of integers that can be coded in two's complement binary depends upon the number of bits that are allocated to represent the integer.

For example, in 8 bits, the most negative integer that can be represented in two's complement binary is 10000000_2 whose bits are associated with the following decimal weightings:

-2^7	2^6	2^5	2^4	2^3	2^2	2^1	2^0
-128_{10}	64_{10}	32_{10}	16_{10}	8_{10}	4_{10}	2_{10}	1_{10}
1	0	0	0	0	0	0	0

and the most positive integer is 01111111_2 whose bits are associated with the following decimal weightings:

-2^7	2^6	2^5	2^4	2^3	2^2	2^1	2^0
-128_{10}	64_{10}	32_{10}	16_{10}	8_{10}	4_{10}	2_{10}	1_{10}
0	1	1	1	1	1	1	1

Thus, the range in decimal is

$$-2^7 \text{ to } (2^6 + 2^5 + 2^4 + 2^3 + 2^2 + 2^1 + 2^0)$$

but $(2^6 + 2^5 + 2^4 + 2^3 + 2^2 + 2^1 + 2^0) = 127_{10} = 128_{10} - 1 = 2^7 - 1$

Therefore,

the range for 8 bits is -2^7 to $2^7 - 1$

In general,

for n bits the range is -2^{n-1} to $2^{n-1} - 1$

Questions

9 What is the range in decimal of integers represented in two's complement binary using

(a) 4 bits (b) 6 bits (c) 10 bits
(d) 16 bits?

Express your answers first in 2^x format before evaluating.

In this chapter you have covered:

- Two's complement representation of negative and positive integers
- Converting between signed binary and decimal and vice versa
- Subtraction using two's complement
- Range of two's complement representation for a given number of bits

5.4 Binary number system

Learning objectives

- *Representing numbers with a fractional part in*
  - *Fixed point form*
  - *Floating point form*
- *Decimal to binary fixed point*
- *Binary to decimal fixed point*

5.4.4 Numbers with a fractional part

Fixed point form

Calculations often produce results that are not whole numbers, e.g. 5¼, so there is a need to represent values that have a fractional part in the language of the digital computer, i.e. binary. The decimal system gives a clue to how to do this in binary

```
100    10     1      1/10  1/100
------------------------------
  1     3     6   •   7     5
```

The number 136 • 75 represents 1 hundred, 3 tens, 6 units, 7 tenths and 5 hundredths.

Figure 5.4.4.1 shows how unsigned numbers with a fractional part can be represented in binary using 8 bits. The weighting of each bit has been selected to allow three bits for the fractional part but we could have chosen a different number of bits for the fractional part, if we had wanted to. Notice that the weighting decreases by a factor of 2 between adjacent columns as shown.

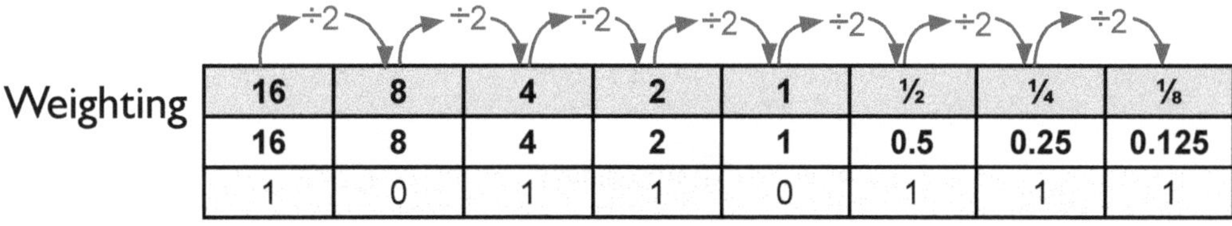

Weighting	16	8	4	2	1	½	¼	⅛
	16	8	4	2	1	0.5	0.25	0.125
	1	0	1	1	0	1	1	1

Figure 5.4.4.1 Interpreting a bit pattern when it represents an unsigned number with a fractional part

$$10110 \cdot 111_2 = 16 + 4 + 2 + \tfrac{1}{2} + \tfrac{1}{4} + \tfrac{1}{8} = 22\tfrac{7}{8} = 22.875_{10}$$

This coding is known as **fixed point coding** because the binary point is fixed in position, in this example between the third and fourth bits from the right.

Questions

1. Given 8 bits with the binary point fixed in position between the third and fourth bits from the right as in Figure 5.4.4.1, what is the decimal representation for each of the following unsigned binary numbers?

   (a) 00011•100 (b) 00101•110 (c) 10000•101
   (d) 11111•111

Questions

2 Given 8 bits with the binary point fixed in position between the fourth and fifth bits from the right what is the decimal representation for each of the following unsigned binary numbers?

(a) 0001•0001 (b) 0010•0011 (c) 1111•0100 (d) 1010•0111

3 Given 12 bits with the binary point fixed in position between the sixth and seventh bits from the right what is the decimal representation for each of the following unsigned binary numbers?

(a) 100000•000001 (b) 111000•000010
(c) 001111•000011 (d) 110001•000111

Fixed point form of signed numbers

We use two's complement representation to represent signed numbers with a fractional part in binary as shown in the example in *Figure 5.4.4.2*.

-16	8	4	2	1	½	¼	⅛
1	0	1	1	0	1	1	1

Figure 5.4.4.2 Interpreting a bit pattern when it represents a signed number with a fractional part

$$10110 \bullet 111_2 = -16 + 4 + 2 + \tfrac{1}{2} + \tfrac{1}{4} + \tfrac{1}{8} = -9\tfrac{1}{8} = -9.125_{10}$$

Questions

4 Given 8 bits with the binary point fixed in position between the third and fourth bits from the right as in Figure 5.4.4.2, what is the decimal representation for each of the following signed binary numbers?

(a) 11100•100 (b) 11010•010 (c) 10111•011
(d) 11100•001

Converting from decimal to fixed point binary

Unsigned decimal to unsigned fixed point binary

To convert an unsigned decimal number, W . F, e.g. 5.75_{10} where W = 5 and F = 0.75, to fixed point binary proceed as follows

1. Consider the whole number part, W, and the fractional part, F separately.
2. Convert the whole number part, W, from decimal to binary using, for example, the repeated division by two algorithm.
3. Convert the fractional part, F, from decimal to binary in a given number of bits using the following algorithm.

Repeated multiplication by two algorithm:

```
n ← 0
OrigF ← Fractional part F
Repeat
  R ← F x 2
  Write down the digit to the left of the
  decimal point of R, call it D
  n ← n + 1
  F ← R - D
Until F = 0 Or F = OrigF
      Or n = AllocatedFractionalNoOfBits
```

Table 5.4.4.1 shows how the fractional part 0.75_{10} is converted to 0.11_2 by this algorithm. The algorithm terminates for 0.75_{10} on the condition `F = 0`. It will always terminate on `F = 0` when the denominator of the fractional part involves the prime factor 2 only, if a sufficient number of bits are allocated to the fractional part.

Fractional part, F	R	Digit D
0.75	0.75 x 2 = 1.5	1
0.5	0.5 x 2 = 1.0	1
0		

Most significant bit

Table 5.4.4.1 Conversion of fractional part, 0.75_{10} to 0.11_2

Table 5.4.4.2 shows an example where the algorithm terminates on the condition `F = OrigF`. Under these circumstances, the fractional decimal part converts to a repeating binary part, e.g. 0.8_{10} is converted to $0 \bullet \overline{1100}_2$.

Key principle

Decimal to binary fixed point:

1. Consider the whole number part, W, and the fractional part, F separately.
2. Convert the whole number part, W, from decimal to binary using the repeated division by two algorithm.
3. Convert the fractional part, F, from decimal to binary in a given number of bits using the repeated multiplication by two algorithm.

Fractional part, F	R	Digit D
0.8	0.8 x 2 = 1.6	1
0.6	0.6 x 2 = 1.2	1
0.2	0.2 x 2 = 0.4	0
0.4	0.4 x 2 = 0.8	0
0.8	(Previous 4 steps now repeat)	

Most significant bit

Table 5.4.4.2 shows an example of a conversion which results in a repeating binary pattern.

Table 5.4.4.2 shows an example of a conversion which results in a repeating binary pattern.

Table 5.4.4.3 shows an example of a conversion which results in a repeating binary pattern for which `F ≠ 0` and `F ≠ OrigF` so condition

`n = AllocatedFractionalNoOfBits` is necessary to terminate loop.

Fractional part, F	R	Digit D
0.1	0.1 x 2 = 0.2	0
0.6	0.2 x 2 = 0.4	0
0.2	0.4 x 2 = 0.8	0
0.4	0.8 x 2 = 1.6	1
0.6	0.6 x 2 = 1.2	1
0.2	0.2 x 2 = 0.4	0
0.4	0.8 x 2 = 1.6	1
0.6	0.6 x 2 = 1.2	1
0.2	(Previous 3 steps now repeat)	

Most significant bit

Table 5.4.4.3 Repeating binary pattern for which F ≠ 0 and F ≠ OrigF.

Repeating bit patterns occur whenever the denominator of the fractional part involves prime factors other than 2, e.g. 0.8 = $^8/_{10}$ = $^4/_5$ so the denominator has a prime factor (5) other than 2.

Questions

5 Convert the following decimal numbers to fixed point binary using the *repeated multiplication by two algorithm*.

(a) 0.375 (b) 0.4 (c) 0.7 (d) 0.703125 (e) 0.1

6 Convert the following decimal numbers to fixed point binary using the repeated division by two algorithm for the whole number part and the *repeated multiplication by two algorithm* for the fractional part.

(a) 101.875 (b) 333.55

Programming tasks

1. Write a program that implements the repeated multiplication by two algorithm. Test your program for cases (a) to (e) in Question 6.

Signed decimal to signed two's complement fixed point binary

To convert a signed non-zero decimal number to two's complement fixed point binary:

- Ignoring the sign, convert decimal number to two's complement fixed point binary in given number of bits
- If the sign was negative

  Use one of the following two methods

  Either

  Method 1: Flip all bits then add 1 to the least significant bit

  Or

  Method 2: Starting from the right, leave all the digits alone up to and including the first 1 then flip all the other digits.

For example, -3.75_{10} becomes in 8-bit fixed point binary 11100.010_2 if three bits are allocated to the fractional part.

Using method 1:

$$3.75_{10} \rightarrow 00011.110_2 \rightarrow 11100.001_2$$

$$\rightarrow 11100.001_2 + 1_2 \rightarrow 11100.010_2$$

Key principle

Signed decimal to signed 2's complement binary:

Method 1: Flip all bits then add 1 to the least significant bit

Method 2: Starting from the right, leave all the digits alone up to and including the first 1 then flip all the other digits.

Questions

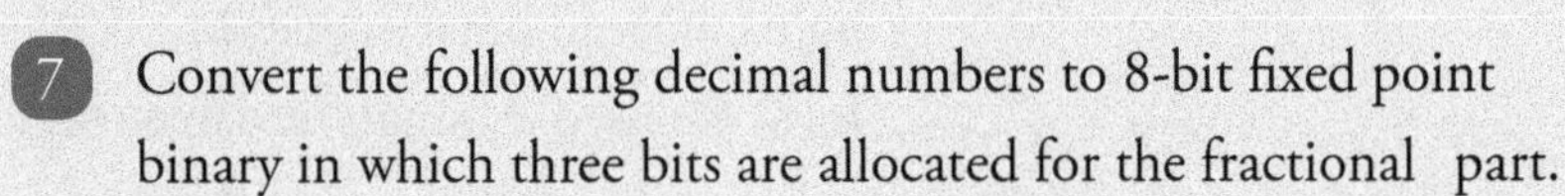

7. Convert the following decimal numbers to 8-bit fixed point binary in which three bits are allocated for the fractional part.

   (a) -1.25 (b) -7.5 (c) -1 (d) -15.875

In this chapter you have covered:

- Representing numbers with a fractional part in
  - Fixed point form
  - Floating point form
- Decimal to binary fixed point
- Binary to decimal fixed point

5 Fundamentals of data representation

5.5 Information coding systems

Learning objectives:

- *Describe the following coding systems for coding character data*
  - *ASCII*
  - *Unicode*
- *Explain why Unicode was introduced*
- *Differentiate between the character code representation of a decimal digit and its pure binary representation*
- *Describe and explain the use of:*
  - *parity bits*
  - *majority voting*
  - *check digits*

5.5 Information coding systems

ASCII

Figure 5.5.1 shows the states of traffic lights, *amber*, *green*, *red* & *amber*, *red*. Each state encodes a message using light codes, e.g. green means GO, red means STOP.

Figure 5.5.1 Traffic lights and their states

Traffic lights are able to use light codes successfully to convey information of an instructional form to road users because the communication is between machine, the traffic lights, and humans in control of another kind of machine, e.g. a motor car. Humans can interpret the light codes from the traffic lights and decide whether to proceed through the junction controlled by the lights or not.

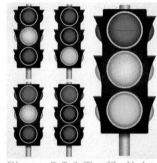

Figure 5.5.2 Two computing machines communicating in binary

In computing, we often want to send data between one computer or part of one computer and another, e.g. between the central processing unit (CPU) and a flat screen display, that map to symbols which humans use for communication, i.e. letters of an alphabet. Light codes are not used because the language of digital computers is binary not coloured lights, instead binary codes in electrical form are used. Human readable text and their binary-coded equivalent are mapped to each other in terminal devices such as keyboards and their controllers, and visual display units and their controllers. Two coding schemes that map between human readable symbols and binary codes that represent them are ASCII and Unicode.

In ASCII, the symbols corresponding to the letters of the alphabet (upper case and lower case), punctuation marks, special symbols and the decimal digits 0 to 9 are assigned different 7-bit binary codes according to a look up table, *Table 5.5.1* which shows 96 of the possible 128 codes (2^7). For example, the ASCII code for the letter A is 1000001 in binary and 65 in decimal.

All 128 codes are called character codes because they encode what is collectively known as characters. However, only 95 codes are actually used for symbols, the other 33 are control codes, codes 0 to 31 and the code 127 which is reserved for an instruction *delete a character code.*

Key concept

Machine to machine communication of human readable text:

Digital computers and their components send and receive binary codes that are mapped in terminal devices such as keyboards and visual display units to symbols which humans use to communicate, i.e. letters of an alphabet. Two such coding schemes that do this are ASCII and Unicode.

ASCII was invented in the 1960s so that information could be exchanged over telephone wires between data processing equipment. ASCII stands for American Standard Code for Information Interchange. Messages were prepared on paper tape, similar to that shown in Figure 5.5.3, by punching holes in the tape (a hole = 1, an absence of a hole = 0) and then the tape was read by a sending machine connected to a telephone line. At the other end of the line was another machine that would interpret the received ASCII codes and then print the corresponding message in symbol form on paper for a human to read.

Figure 5.5.3 5-bit Punched paper tape large black dot = a hole = 1, absence of a hole = 0

Code in decimal	Character	Code in decimal	Character	Code in decimal	Character	Code in decimal	Character
32	Space	56	8	80	P	104	h
33	!	57	9	81	Q	105	i
34	“	58	:	82	R	106	j
35	#	59	;	83	S	107	k
36	$	60	<	84	T	108	l
37	%	61	=	85	U	109	m
38	&	62	>	86	V	110	n
39	‘	63	?	87	W	111	o
40	(	64	@	88	X	112	p
41	)	65	A	89	Y	113	q
42	*	66	B	90	Z	114	r
43	+	67	C	91	[	115	s
44	,	68	D	92	\	116	t
45	-	69	E	93	]	117	u
46	.	70	F	94	^	118	v
47	/	71	G	95	_	119	w
48	0	72	H	96	`	120	x
49	1	73	I	97	a	121	y
50	2	74	J	98	b	122	z
51	3	75	K	99	c	123	{
52	4	76	L	100	d	124	|
53	5	77	M	101	e	125	}
54	6	78	N	102	f	126	~
55	7	79	O	103	g	127	DEL

Table 5.5.1 ASCII code lookup table

Table 5.5.2 shows a lookup table for ASCII control codes, 0 to 31. The codes with a blank character field are codes used for controlling communication over a telephone line. Line feed and carriage return are used to break a long string of characters into separate lines. When characters are organised on a line-by-line basis we call this text, e.g. the text that you are reading on this page.

Text files therefore consist of one long string of ASCII character codes with the line breaks marked by a combination of ASCII code 10 (line feed) and ASCII code 13 (carriage return). These control codes reposition a VDU's cursor at the beginning of the next line when displaying a text file on a VDU.

Code in decimal	Character	Code in decimal	Character
0	Null	16	
1		17	
2		18	
3		19	
4		20	
5		21	
6		22	
7	Bell	23	
8	Backspace	24	
9	Horizontal tabulation	25	
10	Line feed	26	
11	Veetical tabulation	27	Escape
12	Form feed	28	
13	Carriage return	29	
14		30	
15		31	

Table 5.5.2 ASCII code lookup table for some control codes

Questions

1. What is the ASCII character code for
   (a) the letter H (b) the decimal digit 3 (c) the symbol ?
2. What is the symbol or character corresponding to the following ASCII character codes
   (a) 97 (b) 37 (c) 48?
3. Encode the message "Hello" in ASCII.
4. Why is ASCII code 127 the control code for the instruction delete a character code (HINT: a clue is in the holes punched in 5-bit paper tape - see *Figure 5.5.3*)?
5. Encode the text

   "Hello
   World!"

   in ASCII.
6. Convert the following string of ASCII character codes to its equivalent text form

   72 101 108 108 111 10 13 87 111 114 108 100 33

Unicode

ASCII provides only 128 numeric values, and 33 of those are reserved for special functions - the control codes and delete. Many of the control codes are no longer needed because they have their origin in the days of the teletype, punched cards and paper tape. ASCII does not cater for many Western European languages which have accented letters, and special symbols such as £, as it was designed for the North American market and it certainly doesn't cater for Asian languages which are logogram-based (symbols represent concepts), not alphabetic. The 95 ASCII codes for characters found in text are wholely inadequate for a universal standard for information interchange.
Unicode was designed to provide a single character set that covers the languages of the world. Unicode UTF-16 uses either one or two 16-bit code units for its character codes. A single 16-bit unit supports 2^{16} or 65536 different codes. Unicode UTF-32 uses 32-bit code units each representing a single character code. Unicode includes all the ASCII codes in addition to codes for characters in foreign languages (e.g. complete sets of Chinese characters), and many mathematical and other symbols.

UTF-8 encodes each of the 1,112,064 valid code points in the Unicode code space using one to four bytes. The first 128 characters of Unicode, which correspond one-to-one with ASCII, are encoded using a single byte with the same binary value as ASCII.

Key concept

ASCII or American Standard Code for Information Interchange:
In ASCII, the symbols corresponding to the letters of the alphabet (upper case and lower case), punctuation marks, special symbols and the decimal digits 0 to 9 are assigned different 7-bit binary codes according to a look up table.

Information

Extended ASCII:
This is the 8-bit version of ASCII consisting of 2^8 or 256 character codes or code points. The code points beyond 127 use the eighth bit. These map to symbols that are not covered in 7-bit ASCII, e.g. £ sign.
A code point or code position is any of the numerical values that make up the code space.

Information

Scan codes:
When a key on a keyboard is pressed a scan code is generated. Scan codes are binary codes as well. The scan code that is generated is converted into an ASCII code that corresponds to the current setting for the keyboard's keys. The mapping between scan codes and ASCII codes can be changed. For example, the mapping for a key marked in one currency symbol can be changed so that when pressed it maps to the ASCII code for another currency symbol, e.g. $ to £ (extended ASCII code 163_{10}). This was the only way to overcome ASCII's limited character set until the adoption of Unicode.

Character form of a decimal digit

Table 5.5.3 has been constructed by copying the code points for the decimal digits 0 to 9 from Table 5.5.1.

Humans work with numerals consisting of decimal digits, e.g. 261, when they do a calculation or record a number. If a decimal numeral sent from one computer or computer component to another is used by a human at the receiving end for a calculation, the decimal digits of the numeral must first be mapped to their ASCII code equivalents before sending, and mapped back on receipt from ASCII code to decimal digit form.

Code in decimal	Symbol
48	0
49	1
50	2
51	3
52	4
53	5
54	6
55	7
56	8
57	9

Table 5.5.3 ASCII codes for the decimal digit symbols 0 to 9

For example, if 261 is typed at the keyboard, the sequence of ASCII codes 50, 54, 49 is generated and sent. A visual display unit (VDU) receiving these ASCII codes knows that it should display 261 on its screen - see Figure 5.5.4.

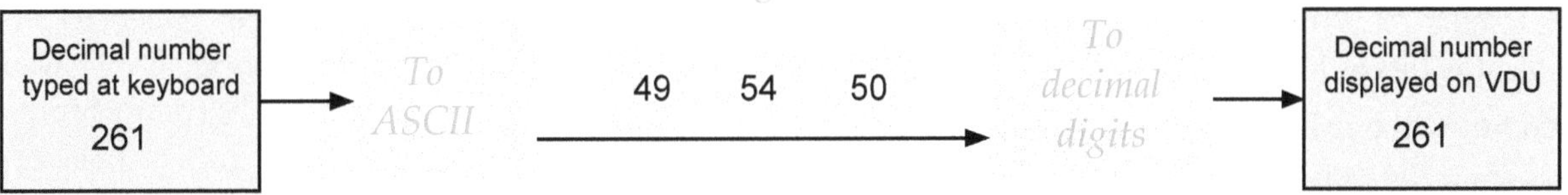

Figure 5.5.4 From decimal numeral to ASCII codes and back to decimal numeral

The ASCII codes 50, 54, 49 are called the character code form of the decimal digits 261 e.g. 50 is the character code form of the decimal digit 2. To convert this character code form 50 into the number 2 we need to subtract 48. The character code form of the decimal number 2 in 7-bits is 0110010 whereas its pure binary representation is 000 0010 in 7-bits.

Symbolically, the character code form 50, 54, 49 can be written as '2' '6' '1'. The single apostrophes around each digit are used to differentiate the character form from the decimal digit form.

Questions

7 What needs to be done to convert the following ASCII codes to their equivalent decimal digit
(a) 53 (b) 48 (c) 57?

8 What is the ASCII character code form of the following decimal digits and combination of decimal digits
(a) 6 (b) 34 (c) 908 (d) 444?

9 Why is it difficult to do arithmetic with the character form of a decimal numeral?

10 What would need to be done with the character form of a decimal numeral in order to do arithmetic in the conventional way?

11 What is the ASCII character code form of the following characters and character strings
(a) '6' (b) '54'?

Error checking and correction

Every time information is transmitted it may get corrupted by electrical interference or faulty hardware, and result in errors in the information received. Faulty hardware may also cause errors to suddenly appear in information stored in a storage device.

Figure 5.5.5 Error detected in data bits

The solution to this problem is to use redundancy to add reliability to information in transit or in storage. The data (data is how information is represented) is extended by including additional data used for error checking and correction.

Majority voting

Majority voting is an error correction method that duplicates or copies each bit in the message an odd number of times before sending these copies. For example, if the message consists of three bits, 101, then the thrice duplicated message would consist of nine bits as follows 111 000 111. The size of the message is thus increased but without increasing the amount of information. The message therefore contains additional redundancy (it may already be redundant, e.g. message = " It is hot. It is hot."). However, this additional redundancy can be used for error correction.

Let's first see how error detection can be achieved by just duplicating the message bits twice. If the data 1011 have to be transmitted then the bits 11 00 11 11 are sent instead. If the receiver receives a pair of bits with non-identical bits then it knows an error has occurred but it won't know if, for example, 01 was originally 00 or 11. Duplication twice has allowed error detection but not correction.

To allow for error correction, we need to copy the message bits an odd number of times. For example, 1011 becomes 111 000 111 111.

On receipt of this redundant bit pattern, the receiver compares the three bits of each triplet. If for each triplet all three bits are identical then the receiver assumes that they are correct (it is possible but very unlikely that 111 gets corrupted to 000). If only two bits in a triplet are the same and the third is different, the receiver assumes that the two bits the same are correct and the third bit is in error. This is what is meant by majority voting. The message bits need to be duplicated an odd number of times, *n*, for majority voting to make a decision.

For the above example, if transmission errors change 111 000 111 111 to 110 010 101 111, majority voting applies error correction producing 111 000 111 111 and the recovered message 1011.

Key fact

Errors:
Every time information is transmitted it may get corrupted by electrical interference or faulty hardware, and result in errors in the information received.
Faulty hardware may also cause errors to suddenly appear in information stored in a storage device.

Key concept

Majority voting:
Majority voting is an error correction method that duplicates or copies each bit in the message an odd number of times before sending these copies, e.g. 101 becomes 111 000 111.
If for each triplet all three bits are identical then the receiver assumes that they are correct (it is possible but very unlikely that 111 gets corrupted to 000). If only two bits in a triplet are the same and the third is different, the receiver assumes that the two bits the same are correct and the third bit is in error.
Majority voting does not guarantee absolute reliability.

Majority voting does not guarantee absolute reliability. Careful consideration of this example will tell you that majority voting can get it wrong, but the probability of this happening can be minimised if it isn't already low enough by choosing a bigger value for *n*.

Parity bits

Key concept

Parity bit:
The parity bit is computed from a group of *n* data bits and then added to the group, making it *n* + 1 bits long.
The parity bit is computed by counting the number of ones in the *n* bit data group, and then setting the parity bit to make the count for the *n* + 1 group (parity + data) either even or odd. The former is called even parity and the latter odd parity.
A transmission or disk read is judged reliable if the parity bit regenerated from the *n* data bits agrees with the received parity bit.
Parity bit checking only works if an odd number of bits have been flipped.

If error detection rather than error correction is sufficient then the parity bit method can be used. The parity bit is computed from a group of *n* data bits and then added to the group, making it *n* + 1 bits long. For example, a 7-bit ASCII code becomes 8 bits long after a parity bit is added. The parity bit is computed by counting the number of ones in the *n* bit data group, and then setting the parity bit to make the count for the *n* + 1 group (parity + data) either even or odd. The former is called even parity and the latter odd parity.

Figure 5.5.6 7-bit ASCII character code

For example, the count of 1s for the 7-bit ASCII code 0101101 is 4.

With even parity this becomes the 8-bit code 00101101 with the parity bit set to 0 to make the count of 1s across the 8 bits an even number. With odd parity this becomes the 8-bit code 10101101 with the parity bit set to 1 to make the count of 1s across the 8 bits an odd number. Now suppose that even parity is used and 00101101 is sent. If the pattern 01101101 is received then an error has occurred because the count of 1s is now odd.

The parity bit can be computed by applying the exclusive-OR (XOR) to the *n* data bits because an XOR operation performs modulo-2 addition. Thus a series of XOR operations can perform the counting.

Suppose the data is the 7-bit ASCII code, 0101101, and the XOR operation is denoted by ⊕ then

$$0 \oplus 1 \oplus 0 \oplus 1 \oplus 1 \oplus 0 \oplus 1 = 1 \oplus 1 \oplus 1 \oplus 1 = 0 \oplus 0 = 0$$

Information

Exclusive-OR (XOR):
This performs modulo-2 addition, i.e. integer addition modulo 2.

+	0	1
0	0	1
1	1	0

The XOR-computed parity bit for the 1011010 is 0 for even parity. Inverting the computed XOR-computed result gives 1 for odd parity. The result for parity + data is thus as follows

EVEN parity: 00101101 ODD parity: 10101101

Now suppose that the byte 00101101 (most significant bit(MSB) a parity bit) is read from disk and even parity is used. To check that this byte has been read reliably, the parity bit for its 7 data bits is computed (by hardware or software) using XOR (0) and compared with the MSB using XOR again (0 ⊕ 0 = 0). The transmission or disk read is judged reliable if the regenerated parity bit agrees with the received parity bit. This judgement is not always correct as two bits or an even number of bits may be corrupted during transmission. However, use of a single parity bit is usually sufficient except when circumstances dictate that full error-detection capability is required.

Questions

12 Calculate the parity bit using even parity for the following 7-bit codes (a) 0111000 (b) 1110010

13 Calculate the parity bit using odd parity for the following 7-bit codes (a) 0111000 (b) 1110010

14 Explain how a receiver of a data transmission consisting of one parity bit and 7 data bits can detect that an error has occurred affecting an odd number of the 8 received bits.

Check digits

Check digits and parity bits are special cases of checksums. The maths used for parity bits works for binary numbers but not decimal numbers. Thus different methods must be used for making decimal number data such as credit card numbers and book ISBNs reliable.

A check digit is a decimal digit added to a number (either at the end or the beginning) to validate the number, e.g. a valid book ISBN.

Figure 5.5.8 ISBN-13 book code 978-0-9927536-2-7 showing check digit 7

For example, the check digit in ISBN 978-0-9927536-2-7 shown in *Figure 5.5.8*, is the rightmost 7 digit. This 7 is computed by an algorithm applied to the information digits of the number, i.e. 978-0-9927536-2. On entering this ISBN into a computer, the check-digit generating algorithm is applied to the information digits of the ISBN as before, and the re-computed check digit compared with the check digit that was entered (see later for a more efficient way of doing this). In this way it is possible to check that the book ISBN has been read correctly.

The three most common errors made by humans when keying numbers into a computer, or reading and saying them, are omitting or adding a digit, transposing adjacent digits and changing a single digit.

For example, transposing the digits 2 and 7 in 978-0-9927536-2-7 or changing the triplet 992 to 922. The omission or addition of a digit is easily detected without a check digit. Therefore, the main task of a check digit is to detect a single corrupted digit and a transposition of two adjacent digits. Other types of error are rare.

> **Key concept**
>
> **Check digit:**
> A check digit is a decimal digit added to a number (either at the end or the beginning) to validate the number, e.g. a valid book ISBN.
> The main task of a check digit is to detect a single corrupted digit and a transposition of two adjacent digits.

Check digits normally use modular arithmetic. The mathematical function a mod b returns the remainder of the integer division a / b, an integer in the range 0 to b - 1. Given a number N that consists of decimal digits $d_1 d_2 d_3 ...$, the simplest way to compute a check digit C for N is to solve the equation

$$(C + d_1 + d_2 + d_3 + ...) \bmod p = 0$$

choosing an appropriate value for p. Note that for the lefthand side of this equation to be 0

$$(C + d_1 + d_2 + d_3 + ...) \text{ must be a multiple of } p$$

Therefore, this equation can be solved by first computing the sum S as follows

$$S = (d_1 + d_2 + d_3 + \cdots) \bmod p$$

and then using the fact that if C is restricted to the range 0 to p - 1,

$$C + S = p$$

Rearranging,

$$C = p - S$$

Example

Suppose N is a three-digit number and each digit is in the range 0 to 4, inclusive, then a good choice for p is 5.

If N = 342, $S = (3 + 4 + 2) \bmod 5 = 4$

then $C = 5 - 4 = 1$

The check digit 1 is appended to the number N and the 4-digit number 3421 is given over the telephone, stored in a computer or transmitted over a communication line. At the receiving end, the 4-digit number is checked. If no digits have been corrupted, the calculation (3 + 4 + 2 + 1) mod 5 will yield 0 (remember $(C + d_1 + d_2 + d_3 + \dots) \bmod p = 0$). However, if the received 4-digit number has been corrupted in a single digit, e.g. it became 3221, then the calculation (3 + 2 + 2 + 1) mod 5 yields 3 when it should be 0. Detection of single-digit errors are possible with this simple check digit mechanism.

However, it is not possible to detect any transposition of digits.

Therefore, the check digit is calculated by applying weights to each digit as follows

$$(C + w_1 \cdot d_1 + w_2 \cdot d_2 + w_3 \cdot d_3 + \dots) \bmod p = 0$$

or

$$S = (w_1 \cdot d_1 + w_2 \cdot d_2 + w_3 \cdot d_3 + \dots) \bmod p$$

and

$$C = p - S$$

Example

Suppose N is a three-digit number and each digit is in the range 0 to 4, inclusive, then a good choice for p is 5. The weights chosen are 2, 3, and 4 because they are relatively prime to 5, i.e. 5 does not divide any of them evenly.

If N = 342, $S = (2{\cdot}3 + 3{\cdot}4 + 4{\cdot}2) \bmod 5 = 1$

then $C = 5 - 1 = 4$

The check digit 4 is appended to the number N and the 4-digit number 3424 is read over the telephone, stored in a computer or transmitted over a communication line. At the receiving end, the 4-digit number is checked. If no digits have been corrupted, the calculation (2·3 + 3·4 + 4·2 + 4) mod 5 will yield 0. However, if two adjacent digits of the 4-digit number have been swapped because of an error, e.g. it became 3244, then the calculation (2·3 + 3·2 + 4·4 + 4) mod 5 yields 2 when it should be 0, thereby detecting an error.

ISBN

ISBN-13 has a total of 13 digits and includes a check digit. It conforms to EAN-13, the European Article Numbering barcode system. The commonly used ISBN-10 book codes have been turned into ISBN-13 by prepending 978. ISBN-13 book codes can use an EAN-13 barcode and therefore be barcode scanned. For example, ISBN-13 book code 978-0-9927536-2-7 has 978 followed by language/country code 0, publisher code 9927536, book number 2, and check digit 7.

To calculate the check digit:

Add up all the even numbered positions and multiply the sum by 3.

Sum the odd numbered positions.

Total the two sums.

Add a number that rounds up this total to the nearest multiple of ten.

This number is the check digit.

Algebraically

$S = (1 \cdot 9 + 3 \cdot 7 + 1 \cdot 8 + 3 \cdot 0 + 1 \cdot 9 + 3 \cdot 9 + 1 \cdot 2 + 3 \cdot 7 + 1 \cdot 5 + 3 \cdot 3 + 1 \cdot 6 + 3 \cdot 2) \bmod 10 = 3$

$C = p - S$

$C = 10 - 3 = 7$

The check digit C is therefore 7.

Questions

15 What is a check digit?

16 What are the **three** most common errors made by humans when keying numbers into a computer, or reading and saying them?

17 Using an example, describe how a check digit is calculated so that it can be used to detect two of these commonest errors?

In this chapter you have covered:

- The following coding systems for coding character data
  - ASCII
  - Unicode
- Why Unicode was introduced
- The difference between the character code representation of a decimal digit and its pure binary representation
- The meaning of and uses of
  - parity bits
  - majority voting
  - check digits

5 Fundamentals of data representation

5.6 Representing images, sound and other data

Learning objectives:

- *Describe how bit patterns may represent other forms of data, including graphics and sound*

5.6.1(1) Bit patterns, images, sound and other data

Binary, the language of the machine

The language of digital computers is binary. Whether the communication is instructions, e.g. calculate the square of 9, or data, e.g. speech, the communication must be transformed into discrete signals of a binary nature for the hardware of the computer to be able to process them.

Instructions or data at this level are seen logically as sequences of bit patterns or bits, e.g. 01101010 10001111 11000010 …., although physically they are patterns of electrical voltage (or electric charge) in the memory of a computer, for example zero volts and five volts.

A bit pattern is just a unit of bits (binary digits) such as a byte. 01101010 is an 8-bit bit pattern. For convenience, bit patterns are usually shown in hexadecimal or decimal form to make viewing easier for humans - *Figure 5.6.1.1*.

0000011000010000	0000000000000101	0000000001000001	0610	0005	0041
0000011000010000	0000000000000110	0000000001110011	0610	0006	0073
0000011000010000	0000000000000111	0000000001101101	0610	0007	006D
0000011000010000	0000000000001000	0000000001010100	0610	0008	0054
0000011000010000	0000000000001001	0000000001110101	0610	0009	0075
0000011000010000	0000000000001010	0000000001110100	0610	000A	0074

Figure 5.6.1.1 Binary bit patterns and their equivalent hexadecimal

We can view a sequence of bit patterns representing instructions or data as just a sequence of numbers. Each bit pattern can be treated as a binary value with an equivalent hexadecimal or decimal value, e.g. 01101010_2 is $6A_{16}$ or 106_{10} if treated as an unsigned integer.

When data or instructions are organised as files and stored on a computer's backing store, e.g. magnetic disk, a stream of bits is sent to the backing store device. Similarly, when a file is opened for reading and its contents transferred to the CPU or main memory of a computer, the contents are transferred as a stream of bits. To interpret a bit stream of bit patterns as a digitised image/digitised sound/text/instructions, for example, requires that the sequence of bit patterns is organised into an appropriate structure for viewing/playing/displaying/executing. Applying the wrong structuring can have unintended consequences, e.g. interpreting data as code and vice versa.

Questions

1. Explain why instructions, e.g. calculate square of 9, and data, e.g. speech, must be transformed before the hardware of a digital computer is able to process these instructions or data.

2. What is a bit pattern?

Graphics

One way of structuring bit patterns is the Joint Photographic Experts Group (JPEG) method for images produced by digital photography.

A JPEG file stores a digitised image as a sequence of bit patterns obtained, for example, from a digital camera that captures a scene photographically by sampling the brightness (or intensity) of the colour components of the scene before digitising the result in numbers to produce a JPEG formatted digital image representation of the scene – see Figure 5.6.1.2.

0	255	255	255	255	255	255
255	255	255	255	255	255	255
255	255	255	255	255	255	255
255	255	255	255	255	20	0
255	255	255	255	255	255	255
255	255	255	255	255	255	255
255	255	255	255	255	255	255
255	255	255	21	0	255	255

Figure 5.6.1.2 Image data taken from a section of the JPEG formatted file, Redang.jpg and displayed in decimal for ease of viewing.

When this JPEG file's contents are accessed and processed correctly the digitised recording of the original scene can be displayed as shown in Figure 5.6.1.3. The sequence of bit patterns serves to convey both the digitised image itself plus information (metadata) about the image such as its dimensions, in this case 600 x 800.

Figure 5.6.1.3 600 × 800 digital image stored in file Redang.jpg

Information

MatLab:
http://uk.mathworks.com/products/matlab

GNU Octave:
http://mxeoctave.osuv.de/

Redang.jpg:
www.educational-computing.co.uk/CS/Images/Redang.jpg

Questions

3. Outline a method by which an image of a scene can be captured in digital form so that it can be displayed on an image display device.

Information

Octave:
You will need to add the command disp(info); to output the value of the info.

A relatively easy way to explore digital images is to use either Matlab from MathWorks or GNU Octave, an open source system. The same scripts and commands execute in either. For example, the following script

```
Z = imread('Redang.jpg');
info=imfinfo('Redang.jpg');
image(Z);
```

executes in either Matlab or GNU Octave and extracts and displays image and format information data from `Redang.jpg`.

Figure 5.6.1.4 shows the extracted format information and Figure 5.6.1.5 the image displayed by the command

```
image (Z).
```

```
Filename: 'C:\Images\Redang.jpg'
FileModDate: '11-Jul-2003 12:12:16'
FileSize: 58014
Format: 'jpg'
FormatVersion: ''
Width: 800
Height: 600
BitDepth: 24
ColorType: 'truecolor'
FormatSignature: ''
NumberOfSamples: 3
CodingMethod: 'Huffman'
CodingProcess: 'Progressive'
Comment: {}
```

Figure 5.6.1.4 Produced in MatLab's command window by >>info

The digital image is actually made of three separate monochrome digital images, one red, one green and one blue that are combined by the command `image(Z)` to produce the 600 × 800 image shown in Figure 5.6.1.5 with labelled x and y axes.

When the digital camera snapped the scene it sampled the scene through three filters: a red filter, recording each red sample's intensity value in 8 bits, a green filter recording each green sample's intensity value in 8 bits and a blue filter recording each blue sample's intensity value in 8 bits.

The red, green and blue samples are combined to produce an RGB image of 600 × 800 samples in all. For each sample, a total of 8 + 8 + 8 = 24 bits is used as indicated by the `BitDepth` field.

Figure 5.6.1.5 The output of the script command image(Z). Z contains the image data.

A quick calculation indicates by comparison with the format information `FileSize` that the whole collection of digital samples has undergone compression. The JPEG format uses compression throwing away image information that the viewer would not notice.

To process the bit patterns from the file `Redang.jpg` appropriately, i.e. according to the JPEG standard, the bit patterns must be structured as follows using two-dimensional arrays of the following dimensions:

- The 600 × 800 red samples into a 600 × 800 array
- The 600 × 800 green samples into a 600 × 800 array
- The 600 × 800 blue samples into a 600 × 800 array

It is the metadata on image dimensions 600 × 800 extracted from this file that is used to determine the dimensions 600 × 800 of the arrays.

Therefore when all three two-dimensional arrays are stacked together we obtain a 600 × 800 × 3 three-dimensional array as shown in Figure 5.6.1.6.

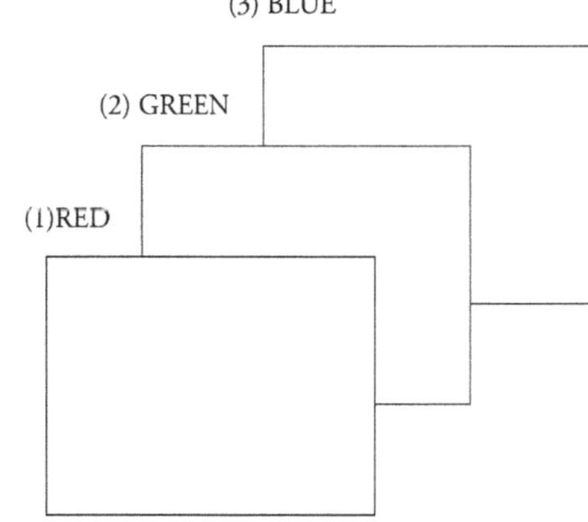

Figure 5.6.1.6 Three-dimensional array Z with dimensions 600 × 800 × 3.

The script command:

```
Z = imread('Redang.jpg');
```

reads the contents of `Redang.jpg`, decompresses it and performs the processing just described, storing the image samples' intensity values in a three-dimensional array `Z` with dimensions 600 × 800 × 3.

Using MatLab's Pixel region Image Tool as shown in *Figure 5.6.1.7*, the Red (R), Green (G) and Blue (B) sample values of any region of the displayed image can be retrieved.

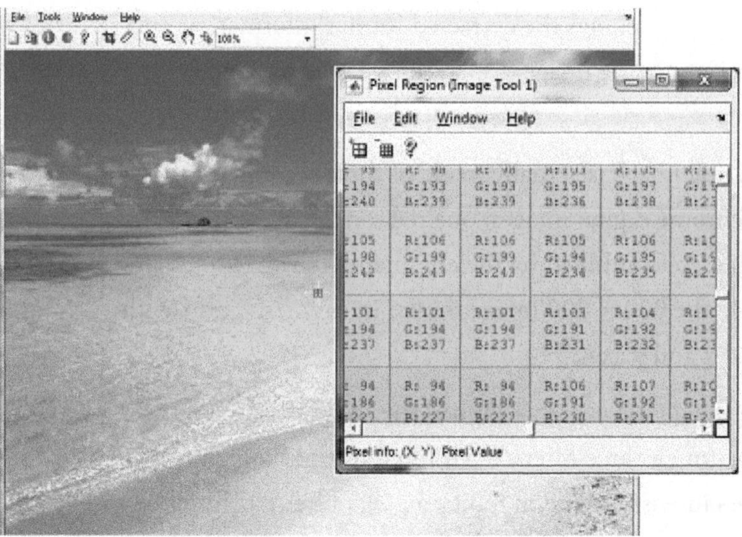

Figure 5.6.1.7 Pixel Region Image Tool showing Red (R), Green (G) and Blue (B) values in a region of the image.

Questions

4 A digital image file stores bit patterns representing intensity values of samples of the scene captured by the imaging device. What other information about the image is also stored in the image file and why?

In this chapter you have covered:

- *How bit patterns may represent graphics*

Learning objectives:

- *Describe how bit patterns may represent other forms of data, including graphics and sound*

Information

MatLab:
http://uk.mathworks.com/products/matlab

GNU Octave:
http://mxeoctave.osuv.de/

Redang.jpg:
www.educational-computing.co.uk/CS/Images/Redang.jpg

5.6.1(2) Bit patterns, images, sound and other data

Manipulating digital images

Having digitised an image, it is now just a sequence of numbers (bit patterns) to which arithmetic operations may be applied to produce new numbers and new forms of the digital image. For example, the following MatLab/ GNU Octave script will double every value in the Red array, `C(:, :, 1)` obtained after reading the JPEG image file Redang.jpg with the command

```
W = imread('Redang.jpg');
```

and storing a copy of `W` in `C` with the command

```
C = W;
```

```
% Introduces a comment in the script
close all; % Closes all figures
clear all; % Deletes all stored variables in workspace
clc; % Removes all lines in the command window
W = imread('Redang.jpg'); % Populate 3-D array W
figure(1); % Draw contents of W as figure 1 appropriately rendered as an image
image(W); % Renders the digital image for values in W
C = W; % makes a copy of W and assigns it to C
% Every value in the 600 x 800 Red array (1) of C is now doubled and written
back into the corresponding cell of this array. This will enhance the redness
of the image
% :, :, means the entire 600 x 800 array
C(:,:,1) = 2*C(:,:,1);
figure(2); % Draw the result as Figure 2
image(C); % Render C as a digital image
% Write C to a new JPEG file RedangChanged.jpg.
imwrite(C, 'RedangChanged.jpg');
```

The outcome is shown in *Figure 5.6.1.8(b)* alongside the original image, *Figure 5.6.1.8(a)*.

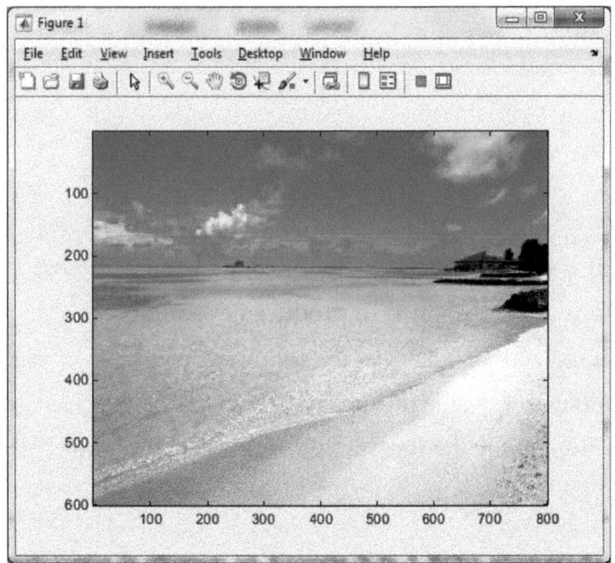

Figure 5.6.1.8(a) Array W rendered.

Figure 5.6.1.8(b) Array C rendered showing the effect of doubling every red value in W

Questions

Explain how each of the red and the green components of an RGB image can be reduced by 50% in MatLab or GNU Octave.

Information

PlaneGrey.jpg:
www.educational-computing.co.uk/CS/Images/PlaneGrey.jpg

Information

Octave:
You will need to add the command disp(info); to output the value of the info.

The greyscale digitised image shown in *Figure 5.6.1.9(a)* occupies a single 480 × 640 two-dimensional array, C, when loaded by the MatLab/GNU Octave script

```
clear all;
C = imread('PlaneGrey.jpg');
figure(1);
image(C);
C(:,:) = 255 - C(:,:);
figure(2);
imshow(C);
imwrite(C, 'PlaneGreyNegative.jpg');
```

If the intensity values in array C are subtracted from 255 then an intensity value of 255 becomes an intensity value of 0, and an intensity value of 0 becomes an intensity value of 255, and so on.

Thus we get the negative of this image when we update C as follows

```
C(:,:) = 255 - C(:,:);
```

Figure 5.6.1.9(b) shows the result.

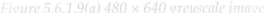

Figure 5.6.1.9(a) 480 × 640 greyscale image

Figure 5.6.1.9(b) 480 x 640 negative greyscale image

Programming tasks

1. Whenever the red, green and blue components of an image sample have the same value, the colour displayed is a shade of grey. This means that a digitised image of sampled red, green and blue colours has the potential for 256 shades of grey if each colour is encoded with 8 bits (0..255). We can use the intensity of the overall colour, i.e. red + green + blue, to assign a shade or level of grey. The intensity of a colour called the luminance is calculated as follows

$$\frac{\text{red} + \text{green} + \text{blue}}{3}$$

   Write a program or script in MatLab or GNU Octave that uses this formula to set the colour of each pixel of an RGB image to a shade of grey to produce an equivalent greyscale image.

2. If you succeeded in turning an RGB image into a greyscale image you may have noticed that the result is not as expected. This is because the formula method used in Programming task 1 did not take into account the way that the human eye perceives luminance, e.g. the eye is less sensitive to blue light than red. We need to adjust for this by weighting as follows

$$\frac{0.299 \times \text{red} + 0.587 \times \text{green} + 0.114 \times \text{blue}}{3}$$

   Change your program or script to take account of this new formula.

3. Write a program or MatLab/GNU Octave script to rotate an image through 180 degrees, i.e. turn the image upside down.

A digital image can be created without using a camera. We can instead create a digital coloured image by creating a three-dimensional array of numbers, D, as shown in Figure 5.6.1.10. D is populated with values, 0 and 255 or in binary 00000000 and 11111111, representing the intensity of red, green and blue with 255 being the strongest and 0 the weakest.

The MatLab/GNU Octave script to generate this array, to render it as an image and write the data to a file Squares.jpg is as follows

```
close all; % Closes all figures
clear all; % Deletes all stored variables in workspace
D(:,:,1) = [0 255 0 255; 255 0 255 0; 0 255 0 255];
D(:,:,2) = [0 255 0 255; 255 0 255 0; 0 255 0 255];
D(:,:,3) = [0 255 0 255; 255 0 255 0; 0 255 0 255];
figure(4);
image(D);
imwrite(D, 'Squares.jpg');
```

`[0 255 0 255; 255 0 255 0; 0 255 0 255]` is the way that MatLab/GNU Octave creates a two-dimensional array, each sequence of numbers is a row vector with rows separated by ' ; ' so putting the row vectors together we get, in this instance,

0	255	0	255
255	0	255	0
0	255	0	255

As we have three primary colours, three of these 2-D arrays are required, one for each colour, Red, Green, Blue.

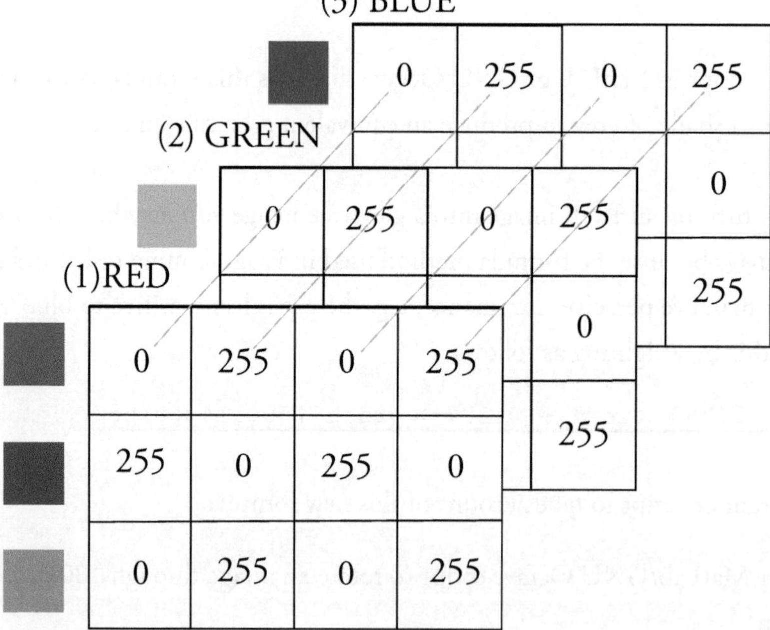

Figure 5.6.1.10 Three-dimensional array, D, containing cells values, 0 or 255.

The outcome when the command image(D) is executed is a 3 x 4 grid of black and white squares on the screen. The black square is produced by the triplet 0, 0, 0 taken from the arrays for (1) RED, (2) GREEN, (3) BLUE. The white square is produced by the triplet 255, 255, 255 taken from the arrays for (1) RED, (2) GREEN, (3) BLUE.

The command:

```
imwrite(D, 'Squares.jpg')
```

scans array D,as it does so writing its values to a bit stream for file Squares.jpg using the format required by JPEG.

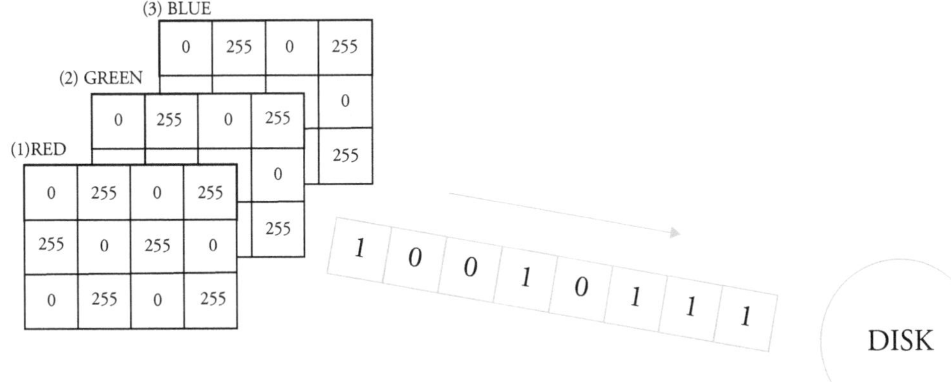

Figure 5.6.1.12 Writing array D to disk

Figure 5.6.1.11 Outcome of executing image(D), an image of 3 by 4 squares.

Reading file contents byte by byte

Files of any type, e.g. JPEG, BMP, XLS, TXT, can be opened as a file of byte and their contents read as bit patterns of unit size one byte. For example, given access to a bitmapped file `Fruit1.bmp` the following Python 3.4 script will open, read and display both a running count and each byte of this file in decimal.

Information

Spyder python:
https://store.continuum.io/cshop/anaconda/
Spyder is part of the Anaconda system that gives access to scientific routines including support for arrays and digital signal processing in Python.

Programming tasks

4. Write a script for execution in MatLab or GNU Octave that creates a file Squares.bmp for a black and white chequer board image with dimensions 4 × 4 with white as the colour of the top left square.

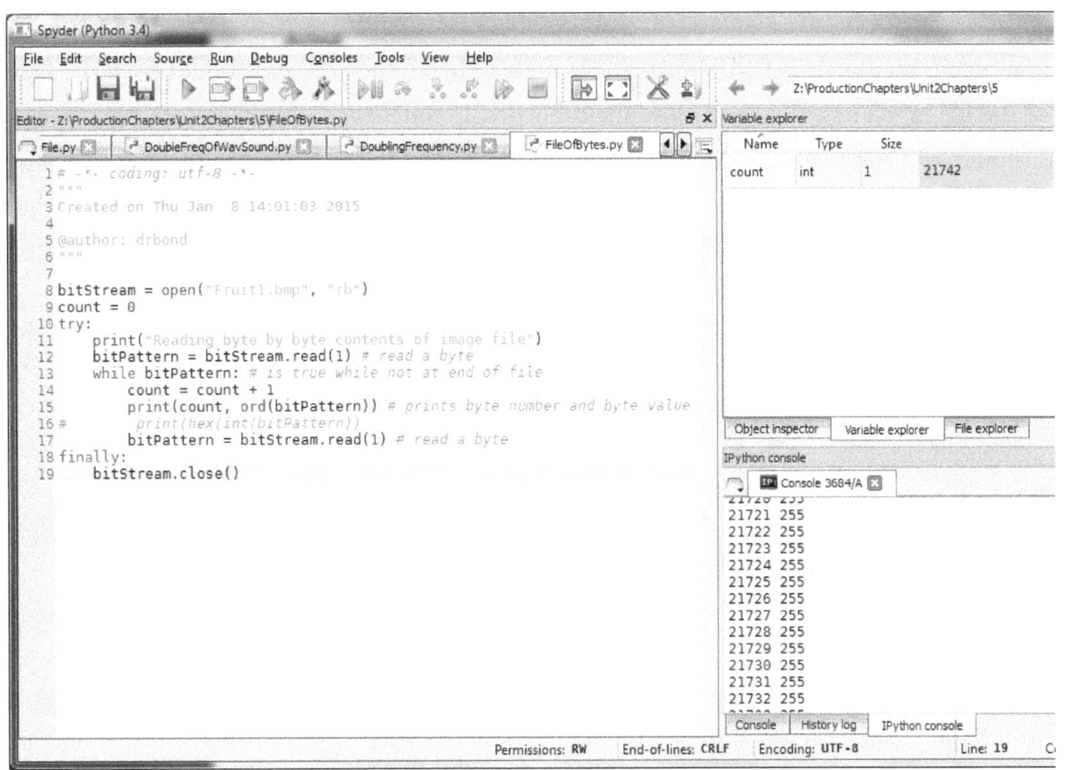

Figure 5.6.1.13 Python 3.4 script to read byte by byte contents of a bitmap file Fruit1.bmp

The size of this file is calculated as follows.

The total number of bytes necessary to store one row of pixels is

$$\texttt{RowSize} = \frac{\texttt{BitsPerPixel} \times \texttt{ImageWidth}}{8}$$

where `ImageWidth` is expressed in pixels. A pixel is a picture element and is the smallest area of the picture that is sampled and digitised.

The total number of bytes to store an array of pixels, `ArraySize`, is

$$\texttt{RowSize} \times \texttt{ImageHeight}$$

where `ImageHeight` is measured in pixels.

Image Fruit1.bmp when displayed has dimensions 126 × 161, i.e. 126 rows each of 161 pixels. This bitmap stores 8 bits per pixel.

Therefore, $\texttt{RowSize} = (8 \times 161) / 8 = 161$

and

$$\texttt{ArraySize} = 161 \times 126 = 20286 \text{ bytes}$$

The metadata occupies 1078 bytes

Therefore, total size in bytes of `Fruit1.bmp` = 20286 + 1078 = 21364

This calculation is close to the result obtained from running the Python 3.4 script in *Figure 5.6.1.13* above. The discrepancy is caused by the fact that RAM stores bytes in groups of four so our calculation for the `RowSize` is an underestimate. It should be 164 bytes. This gives 164 × 126 bytes for total file size, i.e. 20664 + 1078 = 21742 bytes. This agrees exactly with the output of the Python 3.4 script.

Programming tasks

5. Write a program that opens a BMP image file as a file of byte. The program should copy the first 1078 bytes of the file into a new file, then write the 8-bit ASCII codes for `"HELLO WORLD"` to the new file after this. It should skip copying the next 11 bytes of the original file (which are effectively replaced by `"HELLO WORLD"`) and then copy the rest of the data in the original file into the new BMP file. Note where the message starts. View the new BMP file in an image viewer. Can you detect where the original image has been altered?

   Now write a program to extract the message that has been stored in the image file. The program should use the same message starting position as was used in the program that stored the message.

Tasks

1. Investigate steganography and digital watermarking.

In this chapter you have covered:

- *How bit patterns may represent graphics*

Learning objectives:

- *Describe how bit patterns may represent other forms of data, including graphics and sound*

Information

Audacity:
http://audacity.sourceforge.net/

JES:
http://coweb.cc.gatech.edu/mediaComp-teach

Information

The beginning of a WAVE file comprises a "header" storing information about the sound data :

- number of channels
- number of sample frames
- word size (16bit, 24bit, etc)
- sample type (int, float)
- sample rate

5.6.1(3) Bit patterns, images, sound and other data

Sound

A WAV file, `Me2.wav`, is just a sequence of bit patterns or numbers recording the sampled and digitised waveform of a sound.

File `Me2.wav` was sampled, and recorded in digitised form, using a microphone connected to a computer running Audacity, the free, open source, cross-platform software for recording and editing sounds.

This WAV file was then read from disk as a bit stream of bit patterns using JES, free, cross-platform software for interacting with graphics and sound files. The sequence of bit patterns read from the disk was stored in `sound`, a one-dimensional array. JES' Sound Tool is able to render the bit patterns stored in array `sound` as an on screen waveform of amplitude against sample number as shown in Figure 5.6.1.14. Each sample value can be shown on screen using this tool. The samples are stored in `as` 16-bit twos' complement integers (–32768 to 32767). JES displays the sample values in decimal.

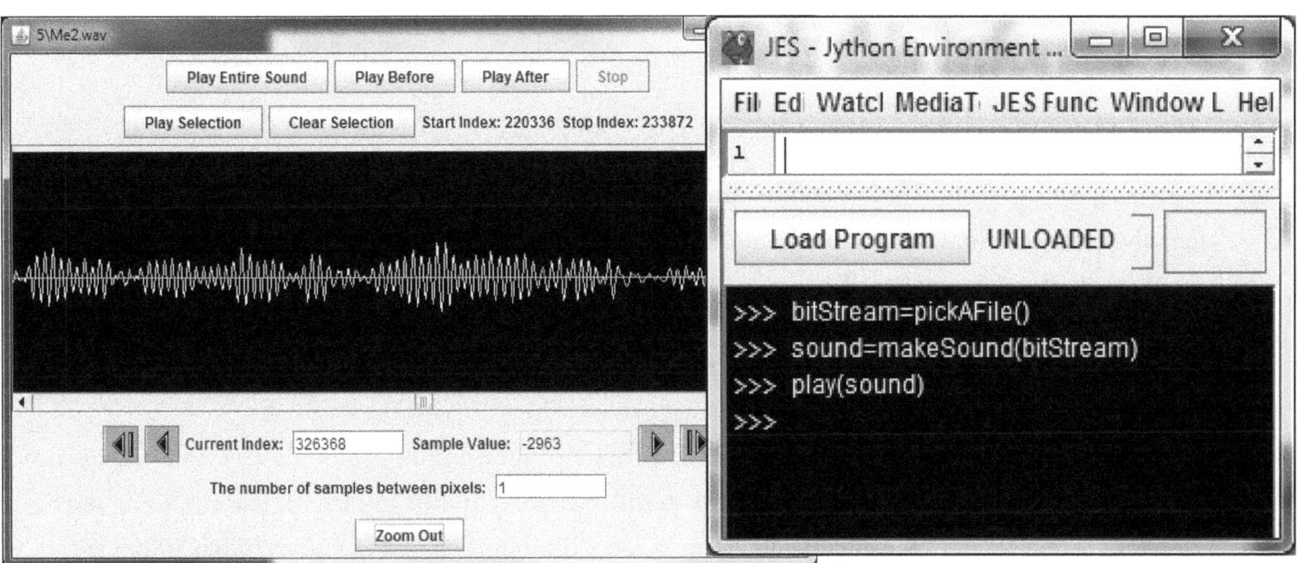

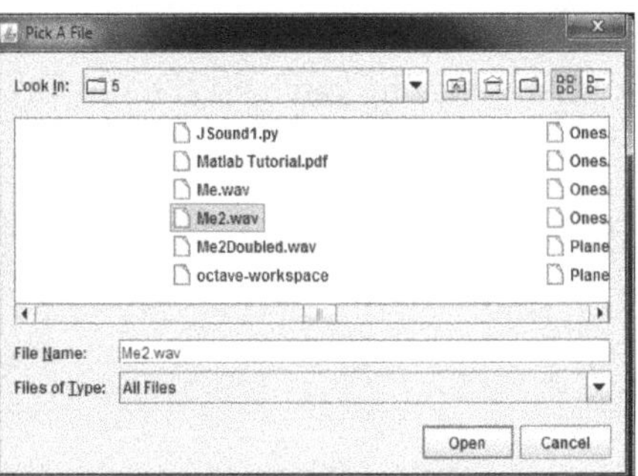

Figure 5.6.1.14 JES GUI showing the Command window and the Sound Tool window and sample 326368 whose value is -2963.

The command `makeSound(bitStream)` reads the bit patterns from bit stream `bitStream` which itself is connected to WAV file `Me2.wav`. It extracts the sampling rate, the number of bits per sample and the type of recording (mono or stereo) all of which are stored in this file. With this information, `makeSound(bitStream)` constructs either a one-dimensional

Information

For sound file I/O by far the best add-in module for Python is "pysoundfile". http://pysoundfile.readthedocs.org/en/0.8.1/

array (mono) or a two-dimensional array (stereo) and then stores the bit stream bit patterns in the constructed array.

Figure 5.6.1.15 shows `Me2.wav` opened by a Python 3.4 script running in Spyder. It extracts the sampling rate and assigns this to variable `samplingRate` and the sound data which it assigns to variable `soundData`. Before printing both, samples per second (44100) and array `soundData` [9 -2 12 ..., -50, -48 -47].

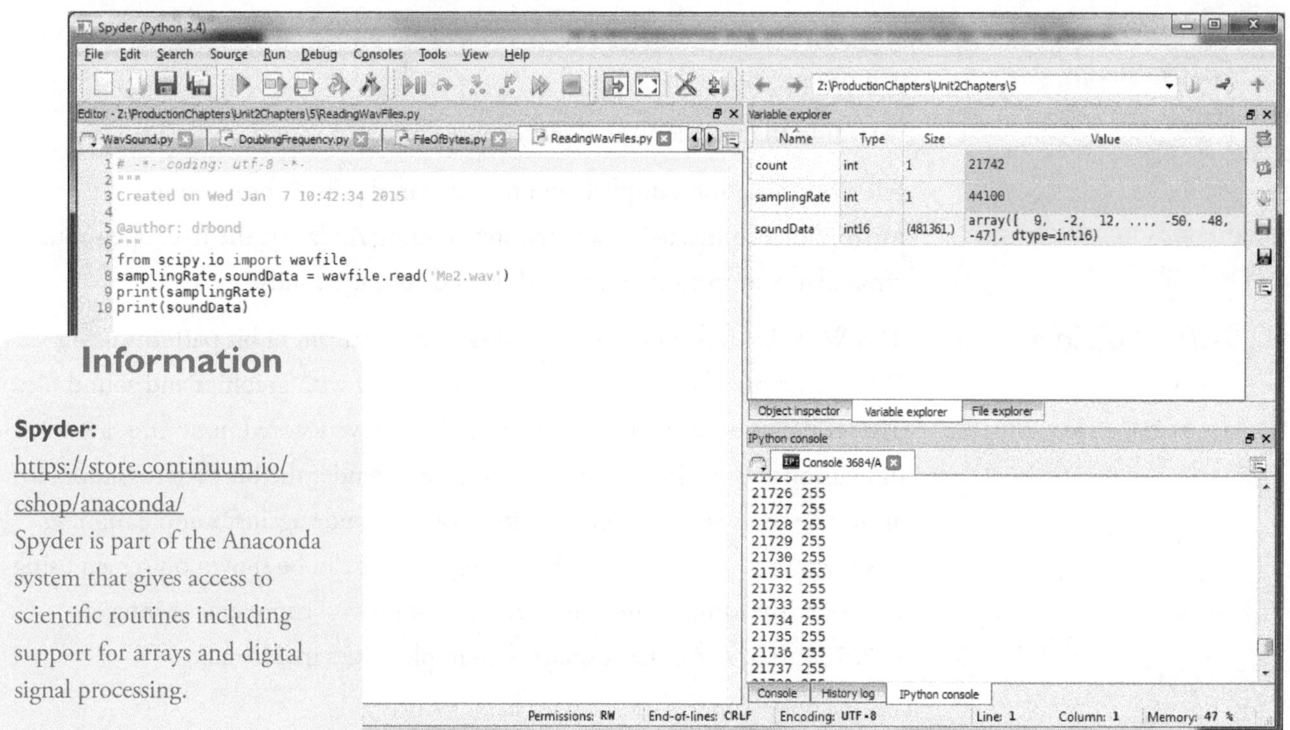

Figure 5.6.1.15 WAV file Me2.wav opened in Spyder by a Python 3.4 script.

Information

Spyder:
https://store.continuum.io/cshop/anaconda/
Spyder is part of the Anaconda system that gives access to scientific routines including support for arrays and digital signal processing.

Programming tasks

6. Using JES, Spyder Python 3.4 or another programming/scripting system that supports exploration of digitally recorded sound, write a program/script/commands to open WAV files, read the stored sampled sound values and display these. Try also to extract the sampling rate and bits per sample.

Information

MatLab
http://uk.mathworks.com/products/matlab

GNU Octave
http://mxeoctave.osuv.de/

Creating digital sound files

The MatLab/GNU Octave script shown in *Figure 5.6.1.16* creates a sequence of numbers or bit patterns, allocating 16 bits to each bit pattern, to represent the digital equivalent of a continuous tone of a frequency/pitch 1000 Hz sampled every $\frac{1^{th}}{20000}$ of a second. The bit patterns or numbers are stored in WAV format in file `Tone.Wav` together with the sampling rate and the bits per sample.

`Tone.wav` can be played using Windows Media Player or any other suitable media player.

```
SampleRate = 2e4; % 20000 samples per second
t = 0:1/2e4:1-(1/2e4); % time step 1/2e4 from 0 to 1 - 1/2e4
x = 1/2*cos(2*pi*1000*t); % cosine value at time t
% write the signal x to Tone.wav file using 16 bits per sample
wavwrite(x, SampleRate,16, 'Tone.wav');
```

Figure 5.6.1.16 Generating mathematically a sequence of numbers that represent a time sequence of samples of a continuous tone of frequency 1000 Hz sampled at a rate of 20000 samples per second or one every 1/20000th of a second. The sequence is written together with the sampling frequency and the bits per sample, to file Tone.wav.

Programming tasks

7 Using MatLab or GNU Octave, mathematically generate separate WAV files of the following tones (use trigonometric function cosine and then repeat using trigonometric function sine)

(a) 500 Hz (b) 2000 Hz (c) 4000 Hz (d) 8000 Hz

Use sampling rate 20000 samples per second, bits per sample 16 and collect 20000 samples (0 to 1 – 1/20000 in time steps of 1/20000 second).

Play your generated tones in a media player.

Manipulating digital recordings of sounds

Just as it is possible to manipulate digital images because they are represented by bit patterns/numbers so it is possible to manipulate digital recordings of sounds because they too can be accessed as a sequence of bit patterns/numbers. A simple way of demonstrating this is to create a WAV file using a script similar to that shown in Figure 5.6.1.16.

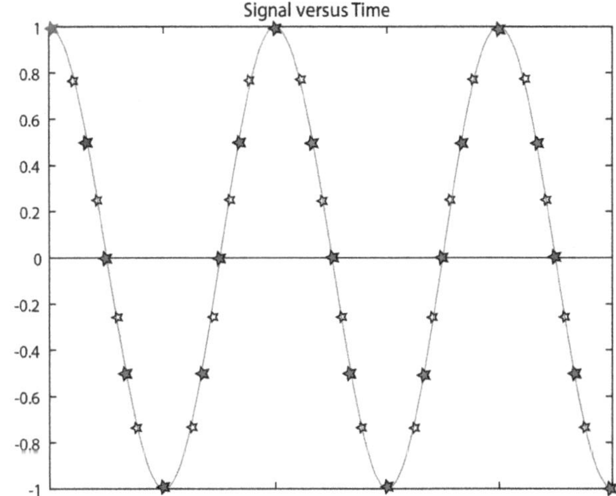

Figure 5.6.1.17 Cosine wave marked with sample points ☆ and ★

The sampled points of the wave are indicated in Figure 5.6.1.17 with ☆ and ★. The height (amplitude) of the wave is normalised (adjusted to a desired value) in the figure for convenience, 1 corresponds to +32767 and -1 to -32768.

The chosen frequency for this explanation is deliberately low in order that the numbers are manageable.

Using normalised values we have a sequence of samples

1.0, 0.9239, 0.707, 0.3826, 0.0, -0.3826, -0.707, -0.9239, -1.0, -0.9239, -0.707, -0.3826, 0.0, 0.3826, 0.707, 0.9239, etc

The values in this sequence are separated in time by $\frac{1^{th}}{20000}$ of a second because the sampling rate used was 20000 samples per second. The "sampling interval" or "sampling period" for this sample rate is $\frac{1^{th}}{20000}$.

If we read this sequence from the beginning and write the sequence to a new WAV file, `ToneFreqDoubled.wav`, omitting every other value, then the sequence in the new file is

1.0, 0.707, 0.0, -0.707, -1.0, -0.707, 0.0, 0.707, 1, etc

These are the samples indicated by ★ in Figure 5.6.1.17.

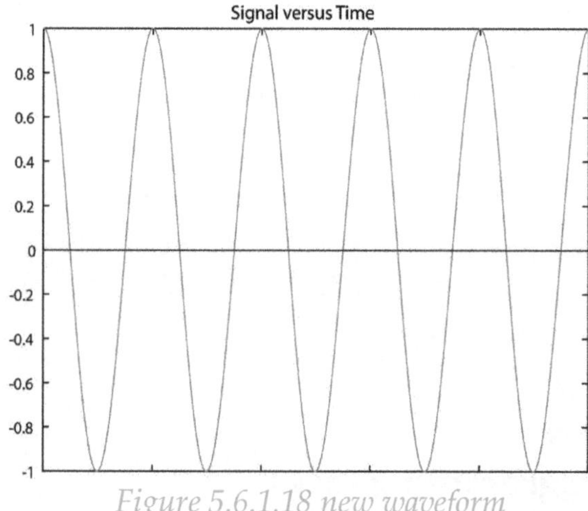

Figure 5.6.1.18 new waveform

If we record the sampling frequency as 20000 samples per second in this new file, then when it is read back, a sample will be separated in time from the next sample by $\frac{1^{th}}{20000}$ of a second. If the sequence of numbers is plotted on the same time scale as Figure 5.6.1.17 then we get the waveform shown in Figure 5.6.1.18. This has 5 complete waves to the 2.5 waves in Figure 5.6.1.17, i.e. the frequency of the wave has been doubled. A script to double frequencies of digitally recorded sounds in WAV files is shown in Figure 5.6.1.19. We appear to have brought about a doubling of frequency of the sound by halving the sampling rate. We have to be careful when sampling a waveform to sample at a sufficiently high rate to avoid creating frequencies which don't exist in the waveform, i.e. spurious frequencies. If we get spurious frequencies we have produced a situation called aliasing.

```
#Spyder (Python 3.4) script
import numpy as np
import scipy.io.wavfile
samplingRate, soundSamples = scipy.io.wavfile.read('Tone.wav')
soundSamplesNew = []
for i in range(len(soundSamples)):
  if (i % 2) == 0:
    soundSamplesNew.append(soundSamples [i])
#Convert from soundSamplesNew list to array
soundSamplesNew = np.asarray(soundSamplesNew)
scipy.io.wavfile.write('ToneFreqDoubled.wav', samplingRate, soundSamplesNew)
```

Figure 5.6.1.19 Spyder Python 3.4 script to double frequencies of digitally recorded sounds in a WAV file.

Play `Tone.wav` and `ToneFreqDoubled.wav` in a media player such as Windows Media Player and note the difference in frequency.

Questions

6. Writing every other sample is one way of doubling frequencies of digitally recorded sound. Can you think of another way that this could be done without having to omit sampled values and which could alter frequencies by factors other than 2?

Programming tasks

8 Using JES, Spyder Python 3.4 or another programming/scripting system that supports exploration of digitally recorded sound, write a program/script/commands to double frequencies of digitally recorded sounds in WAV files.

Test your results in a media player.

Sound and text files

The numbers representing samples of digitised sound may be read from a WAV file, converted to their string equivalent and then written to a text file, one sample per line (text files are strings of characters organised on a line-by-line basis). The text file may now be opened in a spreadsheet and the numbers displayed on a chart as shown in *Figure 5.6.1.20*.

A Python script that creates the text file equivalent of a sound file, `Tone.wav`, is shown in *Figure 5.6.1.21*.

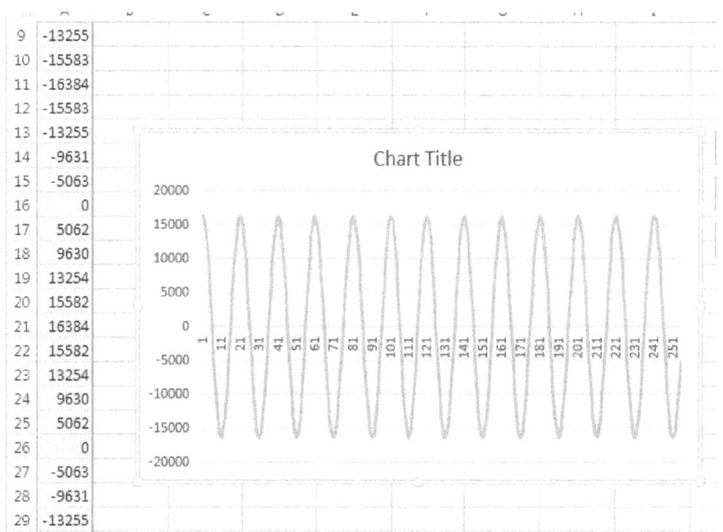

9	-13255
10	-15583
11	-16384
12	-15583
13	-13255
14	-9631
15	-5063
16	0
17	5062
18	9630
19	13254
20	15582
21	16384
22	15582
23	13254
24	9630
25	5062
26	0
27	-5063
28	-9631
29	-13255

Figure 5.6.1.20 Excel spreadsheet that displays and charts Tone.txt

```
#Spyder (Python 3.4) script
import scipy.io.wavfile
samplingRate, soundSamples = scipy.io.wavfile.read('Tone.wav')
bitStream = open('Tone.txt', "wt") # open file in write text mode
for i in range(len(soundSamples)):
  # str converts number to string representation, \n add end of line
  bitStream.write(str(soundSamples[i]) + "\n")
bitStream.close()
```

Figure 5.6.1.21 Spyder Python 3.4 script to transfer sound samples to a text file

Likewise, it is possible to convert a text file into a sound file. Using `Tone.txt` for convenience, the Spyder Python 3.4 script shown in *Figure 5.6.1.22* creates a WAV file, `TextToSound.wav`, of digitised sound samples. It sets the sampling rate to 20000 samples per second but this can be changed easily to change the frequency of the tone represented by this file and it sets the number of bits per sample to be 16.

```
#Spyder (Python 3.4) script
import numpy as np
import scipy.io.wavfile
bitStream = open('Tone.txt', "rt")
contents = bitStream.readlines()
bitStream.close()
fileIndex = 0
soundData = []
samplingRate = 20000
while (fileIndex < len(contents)):
  sample = int(contents[fileIndex].replace("\n", ""))
  soundData.append(sample)
  fileIndex = fileIndex + 1
soundData = np.asarray(soundData, dtype='int16')
scipy.io.wavfile.write('TextToSound.wav', samplingRate, soundData)
```

Figure 5.6.1.22 Spyder Python 3.4 script to create a sound file from a text file

The Matlab command `audioinfo` can be used as shown in *Figure 5.6.1.23* to obtain the metadata stored in file `TextToSound.wav`.

Information

audioinfo:
The audioinfo command is not yet implemented in Octave

```
>> info = audioinfo('TextToSound.wav')
info = Filename: 'TextToSound.wav'
       CompressionMethod: 'Uncompressed'
       NumChannels: 1
       SampleRate: 20000
       TotalSamples: 20000
       Duration: 1
       Title: []
       Comment: []
       Artist: []
       BitsPerSample: 16
```

Figure 5.6.1.23 MatLab command line >>info = audioinfo('TextToSound.wav')

Principle

Text, digitised sound and images:
Text, digitised sound and images are all just bits or bit patterns under the hood. As such they can be mapped between each other by transforming the way that the bit patterns are arranged and interpreted.

Programming tasks

9 Using JES, Spyder Python 3.4 or another programming/scripting system that supports exploration of digitally recorded sound and text files, write a program/script/commands to convert WAV files to text files and vice versa.

Test your results in a media player.

Questions

7 It has been demonstrated that it is possible to transform sound and image files to text files and back again. Give **three** reasons why this is useful.

In this chapter you have covered:

- *How bit patterns may represent sound*

Learning objectives:

- *Understand the difference between analogue and digital*
  - *data*
  - *signals*

5.6.2 Analogue and digital

What is data?

Recording your body weight over time, say six months, would generate a set of values of a quantitative and discrete nature. Discrete because the values are not recorded continuously but sampled at intervals of time. The recorded values are known individually by the term **datum** and collectively as **data**. The data is quantitative in nature because it is obtained by measurements performed by some measuring instrument calibrated by reference to some continuous scale of values.

Data may also be qualitative and discrete. For example, recording name and eye colour of every individual in a class of students, e.g. "John Smith, blue", "Carol Jennings, green", produces a set of values or value-pairs of a qualitative nature. The recorded values or value-pairs are also known collectively as data and a single value or value-pair as a datum. The data is qualitative because it is descriptive in nature and constitutes a characteristic, e.g. eye colour or a property, e.g. a person has a name rather than a measurement.

Key concept

Analogue data:
Data that varies in a continuous manner or is recorded in a continuous form and that is similar to its original structure.

What is analogue data?

Air temperature and air pressure vary in a continuous manner. For example, if you were to climb a mountain you would find that as you rose in height the air pressure would lessen in a continuous manner as the total amount of air pressing down on you from above became less – see *Figure 5.6.2.1*.

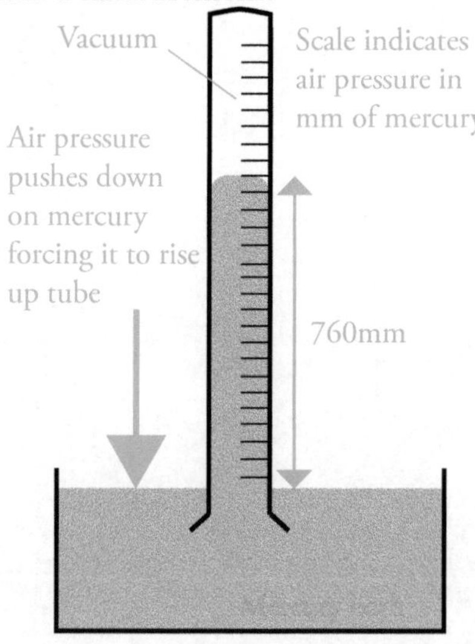
Vacuum
Scale indicates air pressure in mm of mercury
Air pressure pushes down on mercury forcing it to rise up tube
760mm
Figure 5.6.2.1 Toriccelli barometer

The relationship between air pressure and height above sea level is shown in *Figure 5.6.2.2*. This variation in pressure could have been observed with a Torricellian barometer carried up the mountain. The height of the column of mercury, the data, would have been observed to vary in a continuous manner. Data that varies in a continuous manner is known as **analogue data**. The barometer is a source of analogue data.

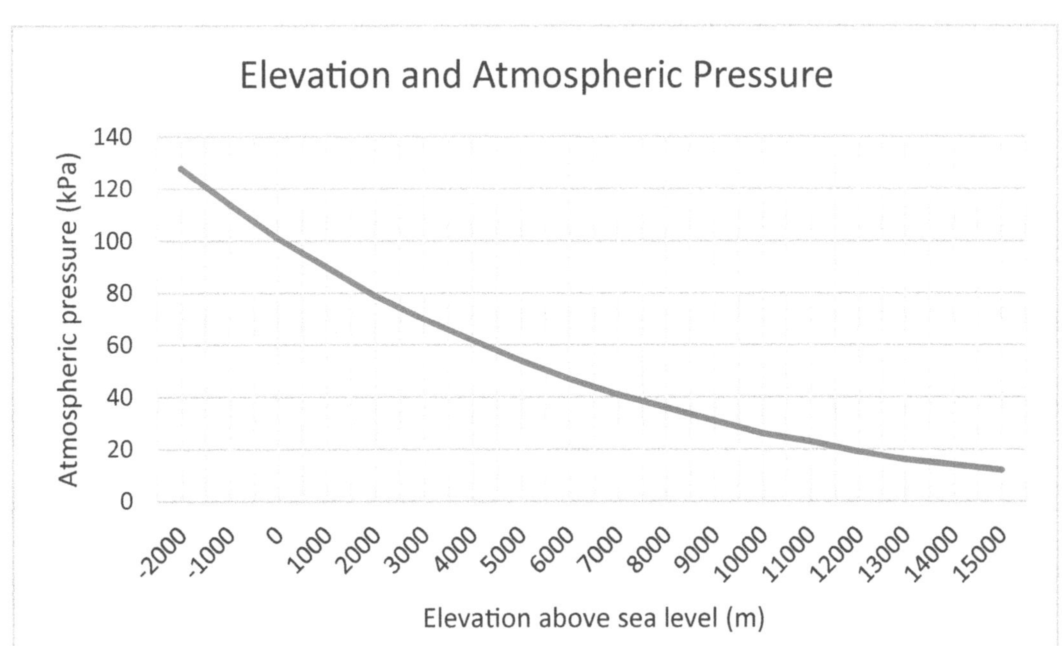

Figure 5.6.2.2 Relationship between air pressure and height above sea level (Adapted from www.engineeringtoolbox.com/air-altitude-pressure-d462.html with kind permission of the editor)

Key concept

Discrete data:
Information represented by separate values is discrete. We say that these values are discrete data.

Information that is recorded in a continuous form and that is similar to its source's original structure is also analogue data. The phonograph invented in 1877 by Thomas Edison, known today as a record player, recorded speech directly onto wax cylinders by making physical deviations of a groove, impressed into the wax, a replica of the variation in air pressure caused by the speech.

The pattern of variation recorded on the wax cylinder is an example of analogue data because it varies in a continuous fashion and is similar in form to that which caused it, the variation in air pressure caused by the spoken word. The modern equivalent of the wax cylinder is the vinyl LP.

What is discrete data?

Information represented by separate values (quantities), e.g. words in a list, is "discrete". Here are three sets of discrete quantities:

- 1, 2, 3, 4 (set 1)
- 0, 1, 0, 1, 1, 0 (set 2)
- A, B, C, D (set 3)

Hour	Temperature	Hour	Temperature
1	8	7	13
2	7	8	14
3	6	9	16
4	8	10	16
5	10	11	17
6	10	12	16

Table 5.6.2.1 Discrete temperature data (sampled from analogue data)

When analogue data are sampled and their values recorded, in the appropriate units, they become **discrete data**. The decimal number 45 is discrete because it belongs to a set of discrete numbers, the set of all positive integers. Table 5.6.2.1 shows discrete data in the form of temperature readings taken at hourly intervals.

What is digital data?

To store data digitally in a computer, it has first to be represented in discrete form, and then converted (encoded) to digital (binary) values.

Figure 5.6.2.3 shows discrete data being encoded in binary by a process which represents each discrete datum by a specific binary value, e.g. 4.70_{10} and 4.93_{10} are both represented by 100_2. This digitising process introduces errors called quantisation errors, e.g. 4.70_{10} is represented by 100_2 which is 4_{10}.

> **Key concept**
>
> **Digital data:**
> Digital data is discrete data which has been encoded in digital form, i.e. binary, using some algorithm.
> Since discrete information is conveyed by the sequence in which the encoding symbols are ordered, there must be some way of determining the beginning of a sequence. This is known as synchronisation. Synchronisation is a property of digital data that distinguishes it from analogue data. Machine communications typically use special synchronization sequences to enable machines to extract discrete information represented by digital data.

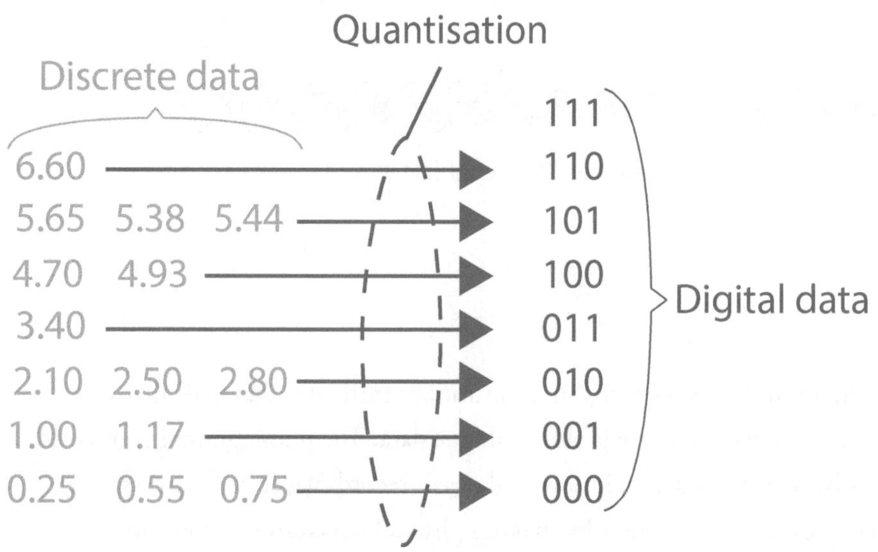

Figure 5.6.2.3 Digitising discrete data by encoding the data in 3 bits

> **Key concept**
>
> **Signal:**
> A signal is that which conveys a message or information from one place to another.

What is a signal?

Many countries around the world have used beacons, i.e. bonfires, strategically sited, to warn of or signal danger. Some animals use sound for a similar purpose. Internally, the human body uses both electrical and chemical means to convey signals some of which are in response to danger, e.g. to cause an adrenaline response to a threatening situation.

Signals are used for all sorts of purposes. Essentially a signal is that which conveys a message or information from one place to another. As such, signals are subject to the laws of Physics, in particular Einstein's special theory of relativity that states that signals or the information that they carry cannot travel faster as a group than the speed of light which is 3×10^8 metres per second in a vacuum.

The information carried by a signal is in the form of energy that can activate a detector or sensor in a receiver of the signal. For example, the light from a warning beacon is conveyed as photons or light particles, each of which carries a certain amount of electromagnetic energy, enough to stimulate cells in the retina of the eyes of the receiver. This stimulation of the retina results in an electrical signal to the receiver's brain which responds accordingly.

Key concept

Analogue signal:
In telecommunications and computer engineering, an analogue signal is an electrical or electromagnetic signal that varies in a continuous manner.

What are analogue signals?

In order to process analogue data it must be sensed and then converted into an equivalent electrical form. The electrical equivalent for this purpose is called an analogue electrical signal or just analogue signal. In telecommunications and computer engineering, an analogue signal is an electrical or electromagnetic signal that varies in a continuous manner. The conversion process takes place in a device known as a transducer. A transducer is designed to convert energy from one form to another. A microphone is an example of a transducer. It converts continuously varying sound pressure waves into an equivalent continuously varying electrical signal. Another example of a transducer is a loudspeaker. A loudspeaker converts electrical energy into sound energy.

Figure 5.6.2.4 shows an electrical circuit for converting sound energy into electrical energy. Figure 5.6.2.5 shows the variation in pressure produced by the speaker whistling a pure tone. Figure 5.6.2.6 shows the equivalent analogue signal.

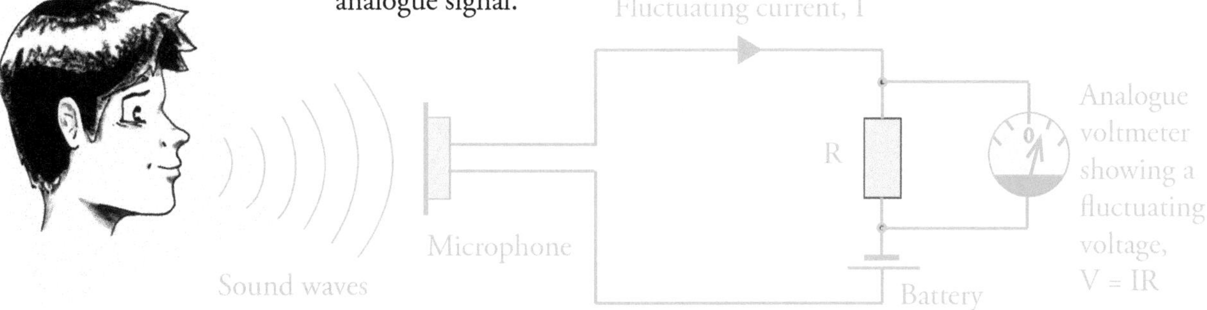

Figure 5.6.2.4 Electrical circuit for converting sound energy into electrical energy

Information

Speech:
When a person speaks, they emit a continuous stream of sound, essentially - the final syllable of one word prefixes the starting syllable of the next. However, the words spoken are nevertheless semantically discrete, and can be written down accordingly. The "raw" data is arguably the (continuous) sound. The information it carries is discrete – the words and their meaning.

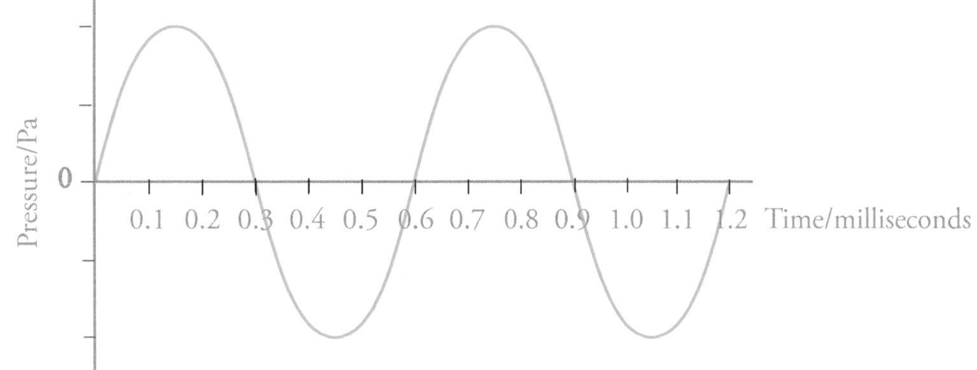

Figure 5.6.2.5 Variation in pressure produced by speaker whistling a pure tone

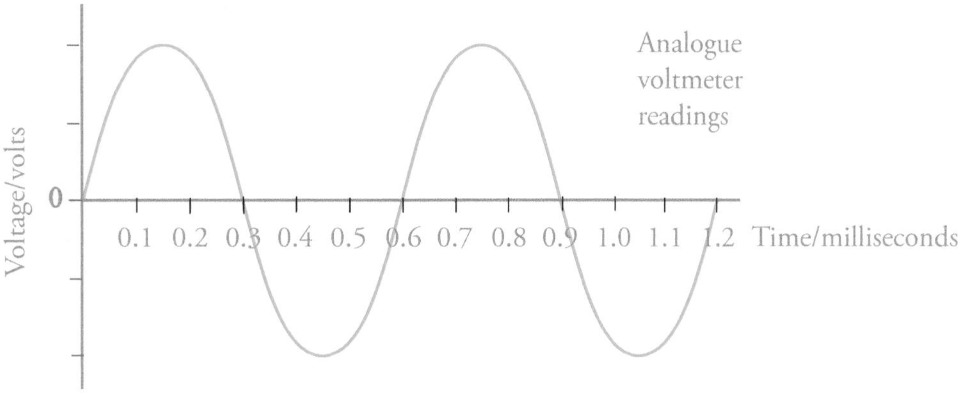

Figure 5.6.2.6 Equivalent analogue electrical signal

What are digital signals?

In contrast to analogue signals, a **digital signal** is a signal that represents a sequence of discrete values. It may be considered to be a sequence of codes represented by a physical quantity such as an alternating current or voltage, the signal strength of a radio signal, the light intensity of an optical signal, etc.

> **Key concept**
>
> **Digital signal:**
> A digital signal is a signal that represents a sequence of discrete values. It may be considered to be a sequence of codes represented by a physical quantity such as an alternating current or voltage or the signal strength of a radio signal or the light intensity of an optical signal.

Figure 5.6.2.7 shows a digital signal with 7 distinguishable voltage levels. In this example, the voltage levels available to the signal were -7.5, -5 , -2.5, 0, 2.5, 5, 7.5.

Each voltage level encodes a binary datum (single item of binary data) as shown in *Table 5.6.2.2*. The most significant binary digit is a sign bit with 0 representing + and 1 representing −. Unfortunately this leads to two binary patterns representing zero.

Figure 5.6.2.7 Digital signal

Voltage level	Binary
+7.5	011
+5	010
+2.5	001
0	000
0	100
−2.5	101
−5	110
−7.5	111

Table 5.6.2.2 Using digital signals to encode binary data

It is possible to use just two distinguishable levels of voltage, 0 volts and 5 volts as shown in *Figure 5.6.2.8*. The digital signal is then a binary digital signal. The shape in *Figure 5.6.2.8* is called a voltage pulse.

Each voltage represents a binary datum, binary datum 1 by +5 volts and binary datum 0 by 0 volts as shown in *Table 5.6.2.3*.

Voltage level	Binary
5	1
0	0

Table 5.6.2.3 Using binary digital signals to encode binary data

The stream of voltage pulses shown in *Figure 5.6.2.8* encodes the binary data 0110101010 (the least significant digit is the first pulse to be produced).

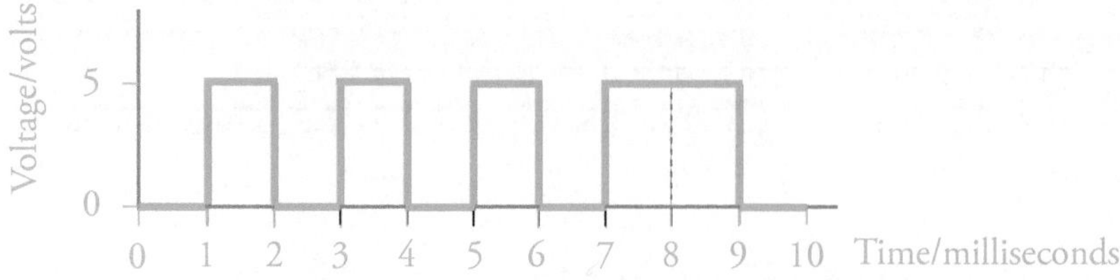

Figure 5.6.2.8 Using binary digital signals to encode binary data

Questions

1. What is analogue data?
2. What is digital data? Give an example.
3. What is a signal?
4. Differentiate between analogue and digital signals.

In this chapter you have covered:

- The difference between
  - analogue data: data that varies in a continuous manner or is recorded in a continuous form and that is similar to its original structure

  and

  - digital data: discrete data which has been encoded in digital form, i.e. binary, using some algorithm
- The difference between
  - analogue signals: in telecommunications and computer engineering, an analogue signal is an electrical or electromagnetic signal that varies in a continuous manner

  and

  - digital signals: a digital signal is an electrical signal which conveys information represented by digital data, i.e. it is a signal that represents a sequence of discrete values. It may be considered to be a sequence of codes represented by a physical quantity such as an alternating current or voltage or the signal strength of a radio signal or the light intensity of an optical signal. The digital signal can also change voltage level or amplitude in an abrupt manner or in abrupt steps.

5.6 Representing images, sound and other data

Learning objectives:

- *Describe the principles of operation of:*
  - *An analogue to digital converter (ADC)*
  - *A digital to analogue converter (DAC)*
- *Know that ADCs are used with analogue sensors*
- *Know that the most common use for a DAC is to convert a digital audio signal to an analogue signal*

Key principle

Analogue to digital converter (ADC):
Converts an analogue signal into an equivalent digital signal.

Key principle

Pulse Amplitude Modulation(PAM):
Pulse Amplitude Modulation is a process of measurement of the amplitude (height) of an analogue signal at fixed and regular intervals of time determined by the sampling frequency. The process outputs a series of pulses whose amplitudes correspond to these measurements and whose duration in time is the time elapsed between one sampling and the next (the sampling interval).

5.6.3 Analogue/digital conversion

Analogue to digital converter (ADC)

Using a transducer to generate an analogue signal

Sound waves travel through air causing vibrations in your ear that you perceive as sound. **Sound waves** are classified as **analogue data** because they vary continuously in shape and size. Sound waves may be converted into an **equivalent analogue electrical current or voltage** using a microphone which is an example of a transducer, a device for converting energy from one form to another. The variation in frequency (pitch) and amplitude (loudness) of the sound is converted to an equivalent electrical form in the microphone to produce an **analogue signal**.

Converting to digital form

An **analogue signal** representing a sound may be recorded by converting it with an **analogue to digital converter (ADC)** into a digital signal suitable for transmitting and storing in a digital computer system. Figure 5.6.3.1 shows an analogue signal plotted on a voltage-time graph.

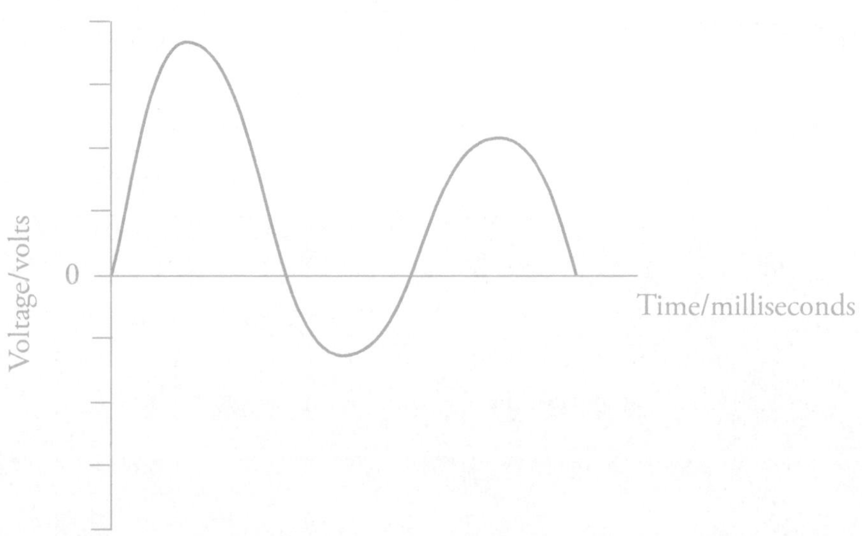

Figure 5.6.3.1 Analogue signal plotted on a voltage-time graph

The analogue to digital conversion process consists of several stages:

1. The analogue signal is sampled at fixed and regular intervals of time using sample and hold circuitry – see Figure 5.6.3.2 - to produce an equivalent digital signal as shown in Figure 5.6.3.3.
   This form of digital signal is known as a **Pulse Amplitude Modulation (PAM) signal**.

2. The size or amplitude of each sample is measured and coded in binary in a given number of bits, e.g. 4 bits, as shown in Figure 5.6.3.4.
3. The binary form of the measurements is represented by electric pulses suitable for transmission over a bus system, serial or parallel, connected to the ADC. This form of the digital signal is known as a **Pulse Code Modulation (PCM) signal**.

Key principle

Pulse Code Modulation (PCM):
Pulse Code Modulation is a process for coding sampled analogue signals by recording the amplitude of each sample in a binary electrical equivalent.

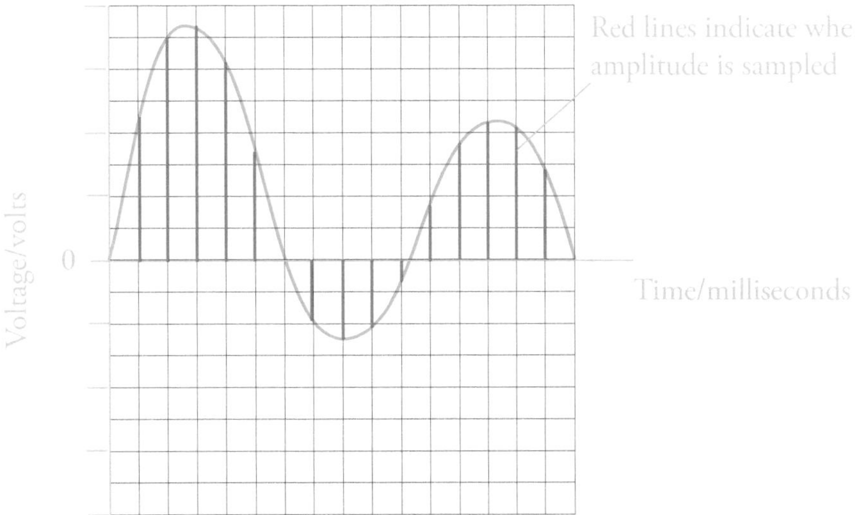

Figure 5.6.3.2 Analogue signal sampled at fixed and regular intervals of time

Figure 5.6.3.2 shows this analogue signal sampled at fixed and regular time intervals. A **sample is a single measurement of amplitude**. The number of measurements of amplitude per second is known as the **sampling rate**. Sampling rate is expressed as **number of samples per second**, e.g. 1000 samples per second. Sampling rate is also called **sampling frequency**. Sampling frequency is expressed in Hz, e.g. 1000 Hz is the equivalent of 1000 samples per second, and 1 KHz, which is the equivalent of 1000 samples per second.

Figure 5.6.3.3 shows the digital signal produced from the sampled analogue signal by a circuit that holds the current sampled value steady until the next sampled value is obtained.

Questions

1. What is a sample?
2. What is the sampling rate for the following sampling frequencies
(a) 20000 Hz (b) 40 kHz
(c) 44.1 kHz?

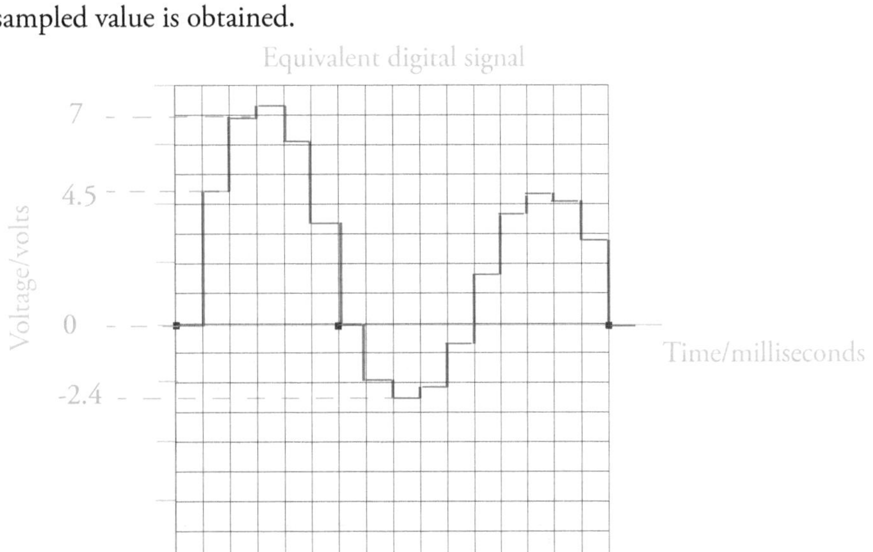

Figure 5.6.3.3 Digital signal produced from the sampled analogue signal.

A 4-bit ADC is helpful in explaining how the measurements of voltage are converted to binary but not very useful in practice; commercially available ADCs use a higher number of bits, e.g. 8, 10, 12, 16.

If we are dealing with a bipolar signal, i.e. one where the voltage may be positive or negative then the ADC must be set to work across a voltage range that includes both positive and negative values. For the conversion shown in Figure 5.6.3.4 the range is set from −8.5 to +7.5 volts i.e. 16 volts.

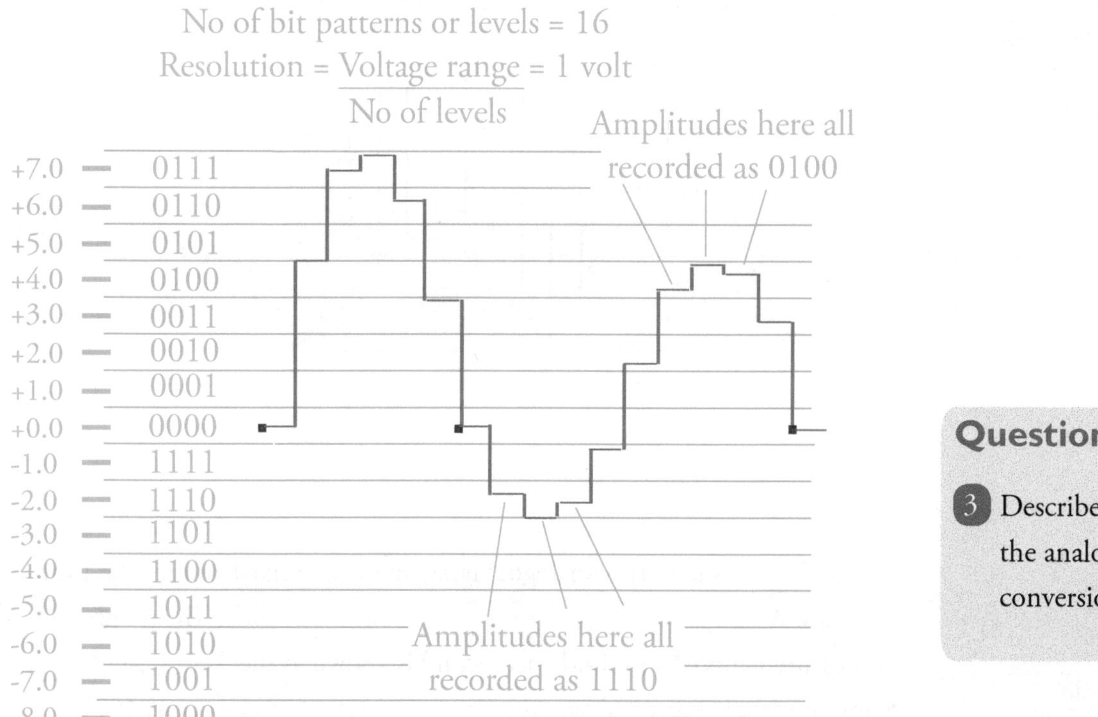

Figure 5.6.3.4 Levels for a 4-bit ADC and voltage range -8.5 to + 7.5 volts coded in 4-bit two's complement binary

Questions

3 Describe the stages of the analogue to digital conversion process.

Encoding samples using 4 bits gives 16 different bit patterns from 0000 to 1111. To cover both positive and negative values of voltage, these bit patterns are interpreted as representing two's complement binary, so voltages in the range −0.5 to +0.5 are coded as 0000, −0.5 to -1.5 volts are coded as 1111, +6.5 to +7.5 volts as 0111 and −7.5 volts to −8.5 volts as 1000. Table 5.6.3.1 shows the correspondence between voltage and binary code.

Sample value in volts	Binary Two's Complement	Voltage equivalent of code	Sample value in volts	Binary Two's complement	Voltage equivalent of code
-0.5 to +0.5	0000	0	-0.5 to -1.5	1111	-1.0
+0.5 to +1.5	0001	+1.0	-1.5 to -2.5	1110	-2.0
+1.5 to +2.5	0010	+2.0	-2.5 to -3.5	1101	-3.0
+2.5 to +3.5	0011	+3.0	-3.5 to -4.5	1100	-4.0
+3.5 to +4.5	0100	+4.0	-4.5 to -5.5	1011	-5.0
+4.5 to +5.5	0101	+5.0	-5.5 to -6.5	1010	-6.0
+5.5 to +6.5	0110	+6.0	-6.5 to -7.5	1001	-7.0
+6.5 to +7.5	0111	+7.0	-7.5 to -8.5	1000	-8.0

Table 5.6.3.1 4-bit ADC set to range -8.5 to +7.5 volts

We can imagine that the ruler shown in Figure 5.6.3.5 has been used to measure the amplitude of the digital signal shown in Figure 5.6.3.4, rounding up or down to a value from the set {–8.0, –7.0, …, +6.0, +7.0}. For example, 3.6 volts would be rounded up to 4.0 volts and coded as 0100, as would 3.5 volts. But 3.4 volts would be rounded down to 3.0 volts and coded as 0011.

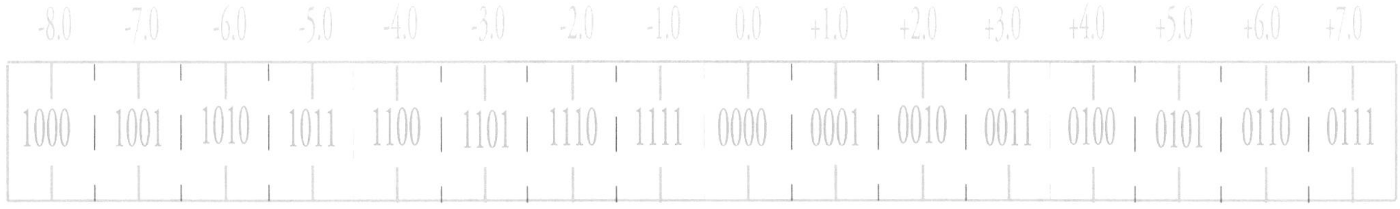

Figure 5.6.3.5 Ruler for a 4-bit ADC

The ADC stores the binary code, e.g. 0110, for the current measurement of amplitude in an internal register before transfer to the processor of the computer to which the ADC is connected. ADCs may be connected by serial (SIP or I2C) or parallel interface depending on its design. Figure 5.6.3.6 shows the pulse code form of one 4 bit sample. Binary code 1 is a 5 volts high pulse and binary code 0 is a 0 volts high pulse.

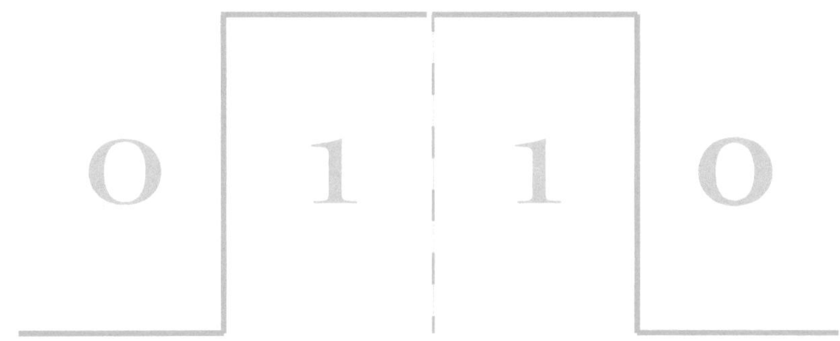

Figure 5.6.3.6 Pulse Code Modulation (PCM) form of one four bit sample.

Questions

4. Draw a ruler for a 3-bit ADC to measure an analogue signal that varies from –9.0 to +7.0 volts over a range of 16 volts. The ruler uses two's complement representation (HINT: see Figure 5.6.3.5).

5. What binary code would be used for a voltage of
(a) +2.0 volts (b) +2.9 volts (c) –2.9 volts (d) +5.0 volts?

6. Draw a ruler for a 3-bit ADC to measure an analogue signal that varies within the range 0.0 to 8.0 volts. The ruler uses unsigned binary representation (HINT: see Figure 5.6.3.5).

Resolution

The purpose of an ADC is to output a PCM digital signal that represents measurements of the amplitude of an analogue signal at fixed and regular intervals of time. The accuracy of the measurements are determined by the number of bits that the ADC uses for its measurements, the more bits the greater the accuracy. Stating the resolution of the ADC is one way of expressing this accuracy.

Resolution of an ADC is measured in terms of the number of bits per sample. The number of bits per sample is referred to as the bit depth of the ADC or word length.

Resolution for a given analogue signal is defined in terms of the range of voltage measured and the number of levels or bit patterns available as follows

$$\text{Resolution} = \frac{\text{Voltage range}}{\text{No of levels}}$$

where No of levels = $2^{\text{No of bits}}$

Table 5.6.3.2 shows resolution for a voltage range 0 to +8 volts and various number of bits

No of bits available to ADC	No of levels $2^{\text{No of bits}}$	Resolution in volts
4	16	0.5
8	256	0.03125
12	4096	0.001953125
16	65536	0.0001220703125

Table 5.6.3.2 Resolution for a voltage range of 0 to +8 volts

Quantisation

The measurement process can be visualised using a ruler to measure the amplitude of an analogue signal to the nearest binary code or corresponding voltage. Imagine that the range of voltage for the analogue signal is from 0 to 4 volts and the number of bits available to represent the measurement is 2 then the ruler would be marked as shown in *Figure 5.6.3.7* with 0.5 volts corresponding to 00, 1.5 volts to 01 and so on.

Figure 5.6.3.7 Ruler for measuring voltages in range 0 to 4 volts in 2 bits.

A voltage measurement that lies between 0 and 1 volts would be therefore be coded as 00, a voltage measurement between 1 and 2 volts as 01, and so on. The **resolution** is $\frac{4 \text{ volts}}{4} = 1$ volt . However, given, for example, 01 as the coded measurement, we can only say that the analogue signal's amplitude at the time of measurement was in the range 1 to 2 volts or 1.5 ± 0.5 volts.

If the actual amplitude was 1.7 volts then the measurement would be rounded down to 1.5 volts and coded as 01.

If the actual amplitude was 1.2 volts then the measurement would be rounded up to 1.5 volts and coded as 01.

> **Key concept**
>
> **Quantisation error:**
> The error in measurement introduced by an ADC because of rounding down or up when measuring the amplitude of an analogue signal.

Therefore, the ADC can introduce errors when it converts an analogue signal to a PCM signal.

The error in measurement introduced by an ADC because of rounding down or up is known as **quantisation error**. The process of rounding up or down is called **quantisation**. It results in a distorted recording of the true shape of the original analogue signal. This is known as **quantisation distortion**.

The maximum possible error because of rounding down or up is, in this example, ± 0.5 volts. This is known as the **maximum quantisation error**.

The effects of quantisation errors produced by an ADC are most apparent when the number of bits is small. The greater the number of bits the smaller the effects of quantisation error. Unfortunately, more bits means the quantity of digital data is greater and therefore file sizes that store this data are greater too. Quantity of data is calculated as follows

Quantity of data = No of bits per sample × Sample rate × Length in time of analogue signal

Music CDs are PCM recordings of analogue signals sampled at 44,100 samples per second using ADCs with a resolution of 16 bits. So three minutes of mono sound would occupy 15.876 MB of storage according to Table 5.6.3.3. If two channels are used then three minutes of stereo sound would occupy 31.752 MB of storage.

No of bits per sample	Sample rate (samples per second)	Length in time of analogue signal (seconds)	Quantity of data (megabytes)
8	40000	60	2.4
16	40000	60	4.8
16	44100	180	15.876

Table 5.6.3.3 Quantity of data for various no of bits per sample and sample rates

Questions

7 (a) Draw a ruler for a 4-bit ADC to measure an analogue signal that varies in the voltage range 0 to 4 volts.

(b) What is the resolution of this ADC?

(c) What is the resolution in volts for the measurements of this analogue signal?

(d) What is the maximum quantisation error?

8 An ADC with a resolution of 10 bits is used to digitize an analogue signal of duration 180 seconds using a sampling rate of 40000 samples per second. How many bytes will the ADC's PCM produce?

9 A CD-ROM has a capacity of 737 MB (1MB = 1000000 bytes). How many 3 minute two-channel stereo music recordings can be stored on this CD-ROM if the recordings were made in PCM from an ADC with a resolution of 16 bits using a sampling rate of 44,100 samples per second per channel?

Digital to analogue converter (DAC)

To turn a PCM signal back into an analogue signal requires the use of a digital to analogue converter (DAC). The DAC produces an analogue signal which is an approximation of the original analogue signal as illustrated in Figure 5.6.3.9. The PCM signal is first turned into a PAM signal - Figure 5.6.3.8. The staircase effect is a result of the approximation at the PCM quantisation stage of the analogue to digital conversion of the original analogue signal. The deviation from the original is known as quantisation noise. The DAC applies smoothing to the PAM signal before it is output as shown in Figure 5.6.3.9.

Key principle

Digital to analogue converter:
Converts a digital signal into an analogue signal approximately equivalent to the original analogue signal from which the digital signal is derived.

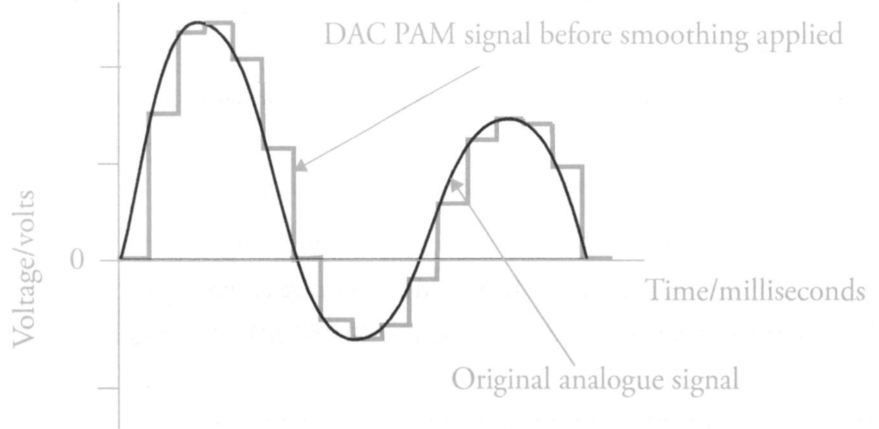

Figure 5.6.3.8 DAC reconstructed analogue signal and the original analogue signal

Key concept

Quantisation noise:
The deviation in the DAC – produced analogue signal from the original analogue signal.

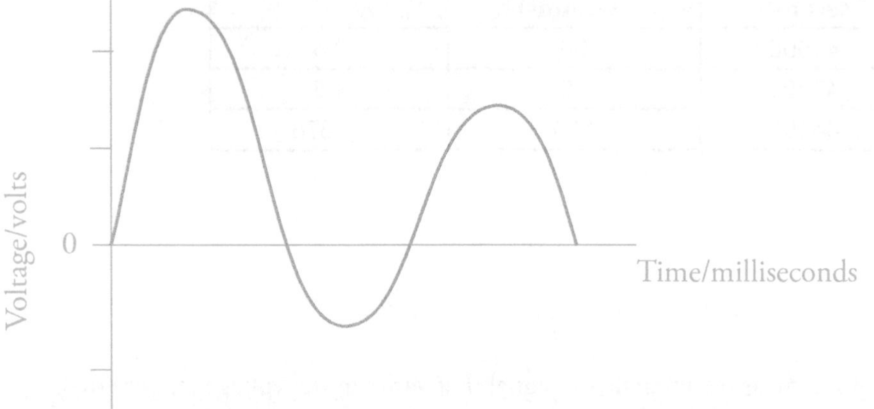

Figure 5.6.3.9 Output of DAC after smoothing applied

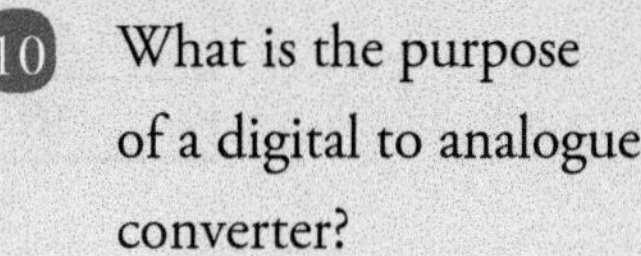

10 What is the purpose of a digital to analogue converter?

Key concept

Sensor:
A sensor is a device that measures something of interest in the physical world and using a transducer converts what is sensed into an equivalent electrical signal.

ADCs and analogue sensors

What is a sensor?

A sensor is a device that measures something of interest using a variety of mechanisms. A sensor is usually integrated with a transducer which converts the output of the sensing into a signal as shown in *Figure 5.6.3.10*. This conversion process is known as transduction. Sensors play a key role in connecting the physical world (temperature, light level, pressure, moisture, concentration levels of gases such as CO_2) with the digital world.

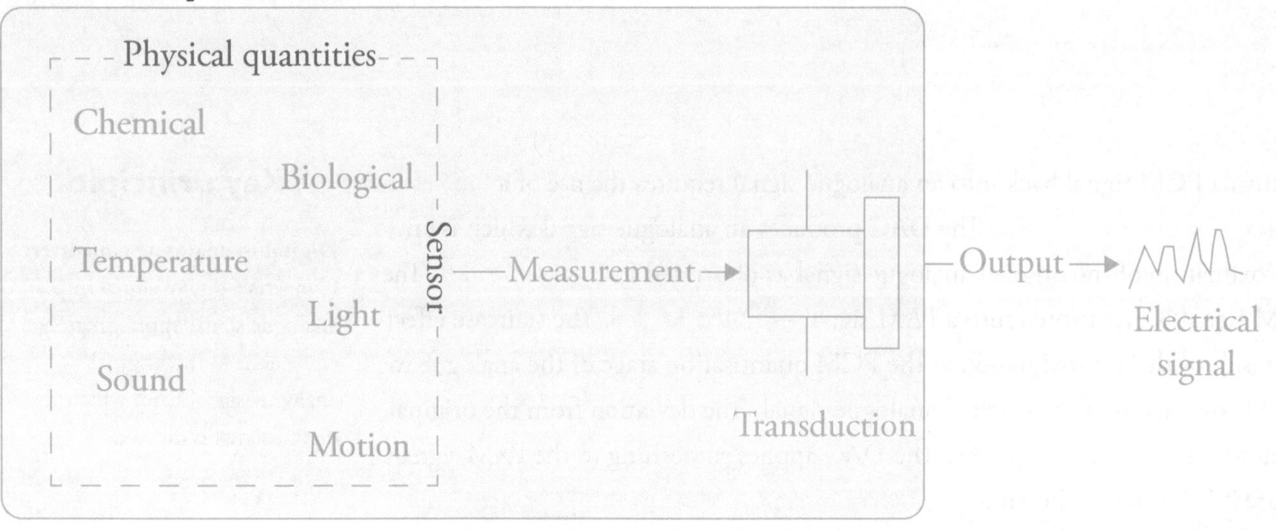

Figure 5.6.3.10 The sensing process

Analogue sensors

The output signal from the majority of sensors is analogue so the signal must first be converted into a digital signal before it can be passed to a digital computer system for recording and further processing.

Key concept

Analogue sensor:
A sensor whose output is an analogue signal.

To convert the analogue signal from an analogue sensor, the signal is fed to an analogue to digital converter (ADC). The output of the ADC is a PCM signal (digital) suitable for transmission to a digital computer system.

Transmitting the PCM signal to a digital computer system is usual done through a serial interface such as a UART or I2C or SPI (see Chapter 9.1.1).

The analogue signal may also need to undergo some conditioning before being applied to the ADC.

This signal conditioning takes the form of filtering

- to remove unwanted frequency components
- signal conversion to ensure its voltage range is correct for the ADC
- signal isolation for safety reasons in healthcare applications where there may be direct contact between a patient's body and the sensor.

The need to perform sense-transduce-signal condition-signal convert-output PCM onto a serial bus with analogue sensors has led to the development of integrated circuits called MEMS that do all this.

Information

MEMS

MEMS stands for microelectromechanical systems. They consist of mechanical microstructures, microsensors, microactuators, and microelectronics, all integrated onto the same silicon chip. Figure 5.6.3.11 shows a schematic for a MEMS integrated circuit digital gyroscope and an actual MEMS 3-axis gyroscope that can be connected to a Raspberry Pi.

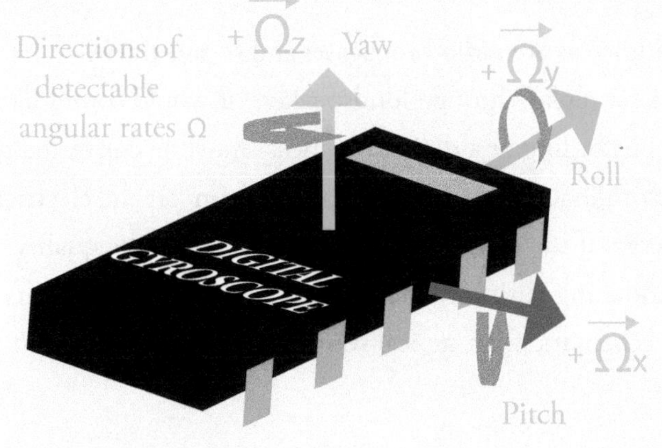

Figure 5.6.3.11 MEMS 3-axis gyroscope

MEMS are known as smart sensors because they incorporate into a single integrated package or chip,

- sensing + transduction with an analogue signal conditioning interface circuit
- an integrated analogue-to-digital converter (ADC)
- a microcontroller and an I/O bus to provide serial output to other computer systems.

Figure 5.6.3.12 shows a simplified block diagram of a smart sensor on a chip.

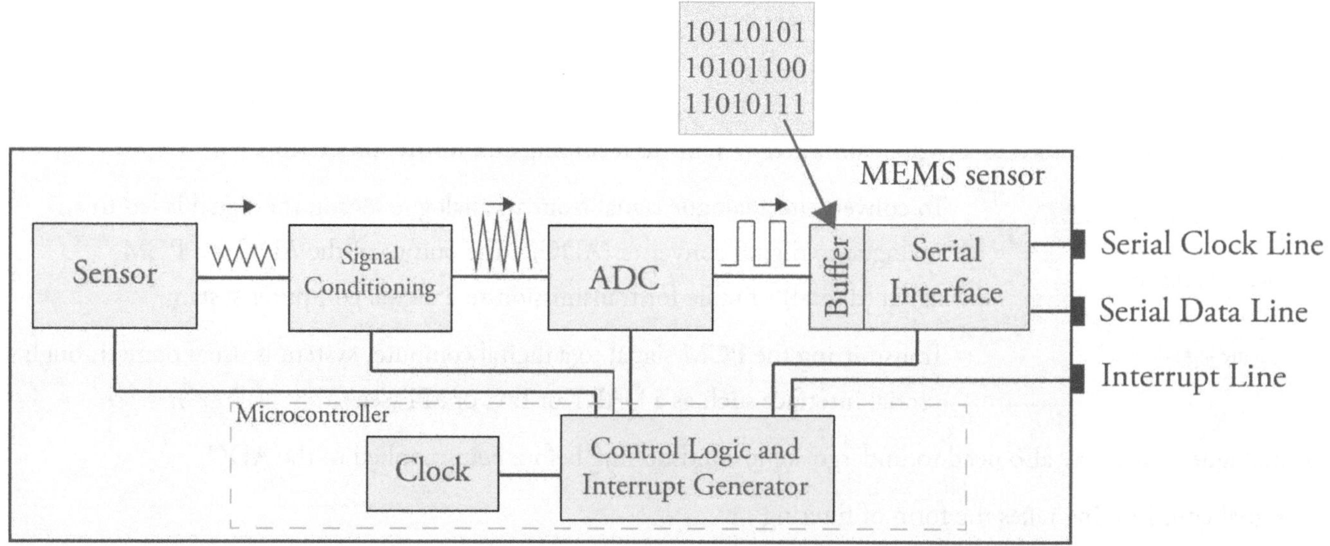

Figure 6.5.3.12 Single integrated circuit smart sensor

MEMS applications

MEMS can be found in smartphones, tablets, game console controllers, digital cameras and camcorders as well as healthcare devices such as pacemakers. Two of the most important and widely used forms are accelerometers and gyroscopes.

Smartphones often have embedded within them a range of analogue smart sensors such as accelerometers, gyroscopes, magnetometers, pressure sensors, optical sensors, silicon microphones, etc.

Sensor platforms

Sensor platforms are a subset of smart sensors. Like smart sensors they feature a microcontroller, a wired/wireless interface, and memory. However, sensor platforms are designed for non-specific platforms, i.e. not just dedicated to generating a PCM signal from an analogue sensor such as a gyroscope. Sensor platforms can provide their services to a range of sensors that may be optionally connected to them by direct wiring, Wi-Fi or Bluetooth. Examples are the Arduino, smartphones, and the electric imp.

Converting digital audio signals to analogue using a DAC

Much of today's music is available in digital format (digital audio) as are radio broadcasts and sound tracks accompanying video. The digital format is not suitable for direct replay through loudspeakers, it would sound like a morse code transmission, so the digital signal from a digital recording or a digital broadcast must be converted by a DAC into an analogue signal that approximates closely the original audio. The loudspeakers convert the electrical energy in the DAC-produced analogue signal into sound energy. If the quantisation noise is low then the quality of the sound produced in the loudspeakers will be high, reproducing faithfully the original analogue sound from which the digital form was created. *Figure 6.5.3.13* shows a schematic for a typical sound card.

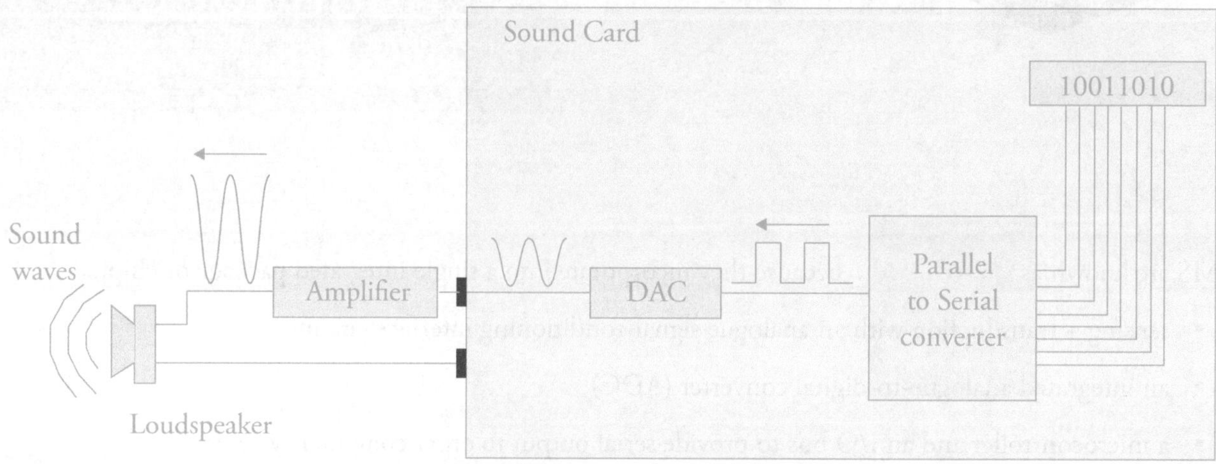

Figure 6.5.3.13 Use of a DAC in a sound card

Questions

11 What is the most common use for a Digital to Analogue Converter (DAC)?

12 What is a sensor? Why is an Analogue to Digital Converter (ADC) often required before the signal from a sensor can be processed by a digital computer?

13 Name **three** analogue sensors found in smartphones.

14 Name **four** components of a single integrated circuit smart sensor.

15 Why is a Digital to Analogue Converter (DAC) needed in order to play digitally recorded sound?

16 With the aid of diagrams, describe the process of converting a PCM signal into its equivalent analogue signal.

17 An audio signal from a microphone was converted into a PCM signal using an 8-bit ADC and replayed through a loudspeaker via a sound card employing an 8-bit DAC. A listener complained that the quality of the reproduced sound was inferior to a PCM signal generated from the same audio signal using a 16-bit ADC and replayed through the same loudspeaker via a sound card employing a 16-bit DAC. Explain why the quality of the reproduced sound could have been perceived as different for the two systems.

In this chapter you have covered:

- The principles of operation of:
  - An analogue to digital converter (ADC)
    - Sample analogue signal
    - Measure amplitude of sample
    - Encode amplitude in binary to produce PCM signal
  - A digital to analogue converter (DAC)
    - Convert PCM signal into a PAM signal
    - Smooth PAM signal to produce analogue signal
- ADCs are used with analogue sensors
  - Analogue sensors produce analogue signals which must be converted into digital form to be stored and processed by a digital computer. The conversion is performed by an ADC.
- The most common use for a DAC is to convert a digital audio signal into an analogue signal
  - Digital audio signals are not suitable for direct replay through loudspeakers. This form of signal would sound through a loudspeaker like morse code. Therefore, a DAC is required to convert the digital audio signal into an analogue signal that approximates closely the original audio. The output of the DAC when played through a loudspeaker should then resemble the sound of the original audio signal.

Learning objectives:

- *Explain how bitmaps are represented*
- *Explain the following for bitmaps*
    - *resolution*
    - *colour depth*
    - *size in pixels*
- *Calculate storage requirements for bitmapped images*
- *Be aware that bitmap image files may also contain metadata*
- *Be familiar with typical metadata*

Did you know?

Digital single-lens reflex cameras:
These use an aspect ratio of 3:2. Aspect ratio is the ratio of the width of the image to its height. The Canon EOS 600D (released February 2011) uses an APS-C CMOS sensor consisting of a sensor array of dimensions 5184 x 3456.

Tasks

1. Digital cameras currently use either a CCD or a CMOS light sensor array. How does each work and why are two types used?
2. Find out the dimensions of the array of photosensors for a digital camera that you have access to (it will be specified in pixels).

5.6.4 Bitmapped graphics

Image sensing and acquisition

If an object is illuminated by a source of light it will reflect that light to varying degrees, reflecting some colours more than others. If the reflected light is captured in, say, a digital camera then the energy in the light is converted by light-sensitive sensors (photosensors) into an analogue electrical voltage as shown in *Figure 5.6.4.1*.

This analogue electrical voltage must then be digitised to produce digital output.

In a digital camera, many such photosensors are arranged as shown in *Figure 5.6.4.1*. The whole array is just called a sensor.

Figure 5.6.4.1 Sensor and its array of photosensors

Sampling and quantisation

When, for example, a digital camera takes a picture of an object such as shown in *Figure 5.6.4.2*, light from the object is projected through the imaging system onto an array of light sensitive sensors (photosensors).

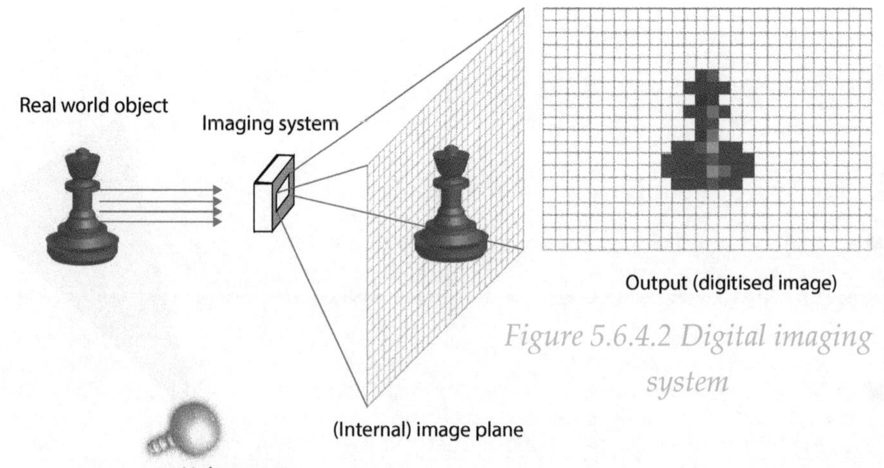

Figure 5.6.4.2 Digital imaging system

The intensity of the image is sampled in the photosensor array at specific X- and Y-coordinate positions. Each photosensor produces a voltage proportional to the intensity of the light falling on it. Making intensity measurements at specific X- and Y- coordinates positions is called **sampling**. Digitising the analogue voltages representing intensity of light is called **quantisation**.

Key concept

Pixel:
A pixel is the smallest addressable region or element of a digital image. Each pixel is a sample of the original image.

Key concept

Pixel:
A pixel is also the smallest controllable element of a digital image represented on the screen i.e. the smallest element or region of a digital image that can be changed or edited when editing bitmapped images using software such as iPhoto, Photoshop, Windows Paint, and other "paint" style packages.

Key fact

Pixel-based graphics:
Pixel-based graphics are made up of small individual pieces of the whole, and each can be changed via editing.
Its strength is in creating complex patterns and displaying photographs with many colour changes.

Its weakness is in changing size. Pixel images can be reduced in size, but lose quality when they are increased in size.

Pixel

Figure 5.6.4.3 shows the result of sampling the image in *Figure 5.6.4.2* at discrete coordinate positions ranging in the X-direction from 0 to 27 and the Y-direction from 0 to 19, and digitising the analogue voltage representing the intensity of the light of the primary colours Red(R), Green(G) and Blue(B) in this light, e.g. at X = 18, Y = 12.

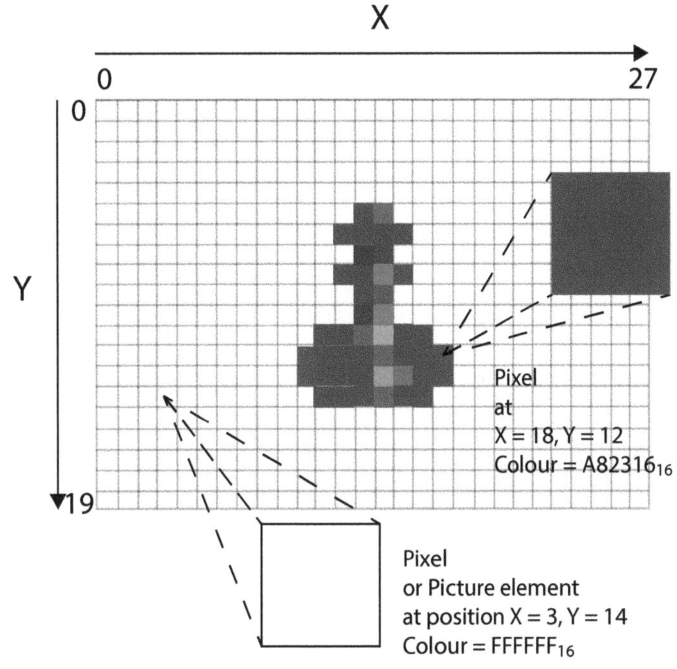

Figure 5.6.4.3 Result of sampling the image plane and digitising the intensity of light of the primary colours for each sample.

Each coordinate position in this discrete coordinate space is known as a pixel or picture element. It is the smallest addressable region of the image plane that can be sampled and the intensity of light falling on it quantised.

At the position (18, 12),

- the red component has an 8-bit value representing its intensity of $A8_{16}$ or 168_{10} (measured on a scale that ranges from 0 to 255)
- the green component has an intensity of 23_{16} or 35_{10}
- the blue component has an intensity of 16_{16} or 22_{10}

At position X = 3 and Y = 14, the corresponding red, green and blue intensities are each represented by FF_{16} or 255_{10}, the maximum value.

Figure 5.6.4.4 shows a smiley face drawn in pixel mode using Photoshop. The pixels for the eyes, nose and mouth were drawn individually by selecting the relevant pixel and changing its colour.

Figure 5.6.4.4 Smiley face drawn in Photoshop in pixel mode at 50 x 50 pixels

Questions

1. What is a pixel?

2. Explain sampling and quantisation in the context of a taking a picture with a digital camera.

3. How many pixels make up a digitised image if the image plane is sampled over the following X and Y coordinates:

   (a) X from 0 to 719, Y from 0 to 479?
   (b) X from 0 to 1919, Y from 0 to 1279?
   (c) X from 0 to 5183, Y from 0 to 3455?

4. Express the result for 3(c) in megapixels by dividing your answer by 1,000,000.

Bitmapped image or bitmap

If we wish to store a digitised image, such as the one shown in *Figure 5.6.4.2* then each quantised sample must be stored, i.e. pixel by pixel, by recording the bit pattern representing the digitised intensity of each pixel.

Figure 5.6.4.5 shows a section of memory from locations 308 to 335 and the corresponding row of pixels that it maps to. Note that the white pixels are stored as FFFFFF and the red pixels as A82316, CA1719, F29476.

We say that the digitised image is mapped to bits in memory.

The stored bits in memory are a digital representation of the image or just a **bitmap**. We say that the image has been **bitmapped**.
A **bitmapped image** is a pixel-based digital image.

Key concept

Bitmapped image or bitmap:
A bitmapped image is a pixel-based digital image.
The digitised image is mapped to bits in memory representing the intensity and colour of light of each pixel.

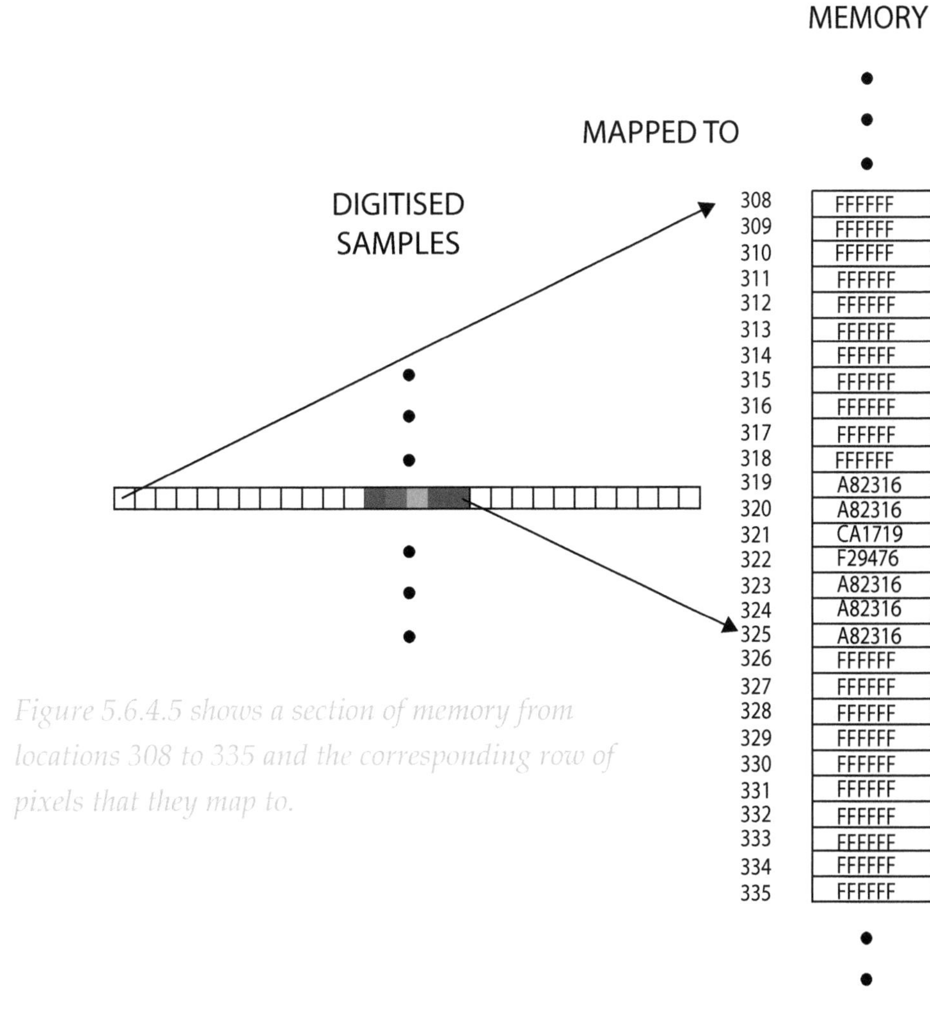

Figure 5.6.4.5 shows a section of memory from locations 308 to 335 and the corresponding row of pixels that they map to.

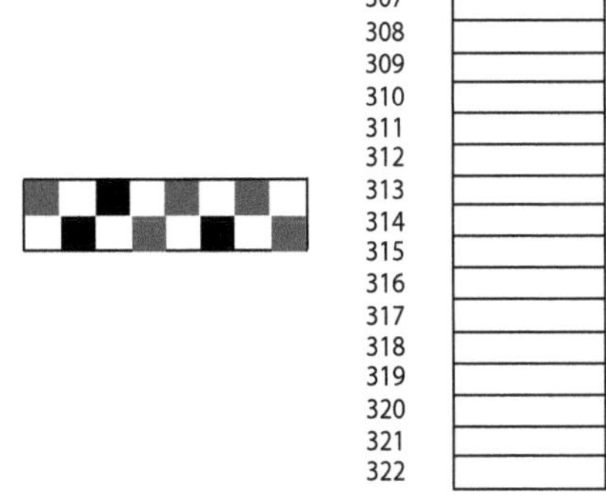

Figure 5.6.4.6

Questions

5 *Figure 5.6.4.6* shows an image of a section of a chequered board and a section of memory for storing the bitmap for this image. The pixel size is defined as the size of a single square. Each memory cell, e.g. cell 311, can store one byte. A bitmap is to be created in the memory that will record the colour of each pixel as any one of 256 different colours. White will be coded as 255, black as 0 and the red used in the image as 125.

(a) Show how this image could be stored as a bitmap. Use the given memory cells in your explanation.

(b) With each memory cell still representing one pixel the memory is changed so that each cell can store 3 bytes. How many different colours can be coded in one memory cell? Express your answer as a power of 2.

Bitmap size in pixels

The output of the sampling and quantisation processes is a sequence of digital values, one per sample, corresponding to each discrete coordinate position or pixel. Image size is usually expressed as number of pixels in the X-direction by number of pixels in the Y-direction, e.g. 28 × 20 in the example in *Figure 5.6.4.3*.

Tasks

3 What is the image size in pixels produced by the digital camera in a typical smartphone? Use number of columns (X) × number of rows (Y) notation.

Colour depth or bit depth

Colour depth, also known as **bit depth**, is expressed as the number of bits used to indicate the colour of a single pixel, e.g. 8 bits, in a digitised image.

When the voltage representing intensity of light is quantised, it is represented by an integer number chosen from some range beginning at zero, e.g. 0 to 255 in decimal.

255

192

128

64

0

Figure 5.6.4.7

A range of 0 to 255 can be represented in binary by 8 bits.

If the range was instead 0 to 65535 then 16 bits would be required to represent the colour of a single pixel.

The example shown in *Figure 5.6.4.5* allocates 8 bits to represent red intensity, 8 bits to green and 8 bits to blue, a total of 24 bits. *Figure 5.6.4.7* shows the intensity of red, coded in 8 bits, for some selected values.

Each possible combination of quantised red, green and blue intensities represents a different resultant colour.

The number of different bit patterns that 24 bits can represent is

$$2^{24} = 16777216$$

Therefore, the number of different intensities of colour that can be recorded using 24 bits for each is 16777216.

Questions

6 How many different intensities of colours can be represented for an individual pixel if the number of bits used for each quantised sample is

(a) 12 (b) 15 (c) 18?

Express your answer as a power of 2.

Did you know?

Digital cameras, and scanners (both film and paper type) capture information in pixel format.

Key concept

Bitmap size in pixels:
Bitmap size = w x h
where
w = width of image in pixels
h = width of image in pixels

Key concept

Colour depth or bit depth:
Colour depth, also known as bit depth, is expressed as the number of bits used to indicate the colour of a single pixel, e.g. 8 bits, in a digitised image.

Information

Did you know?
The Hubble telescope used a CCD detector array size of 4096 x 4096 and a field of view of 160 x 160 arcsecs. This gave a pixel size of 160/4096 or 0.04 arcsec, i.e. a pixel for every 1/90000 degrees of view.

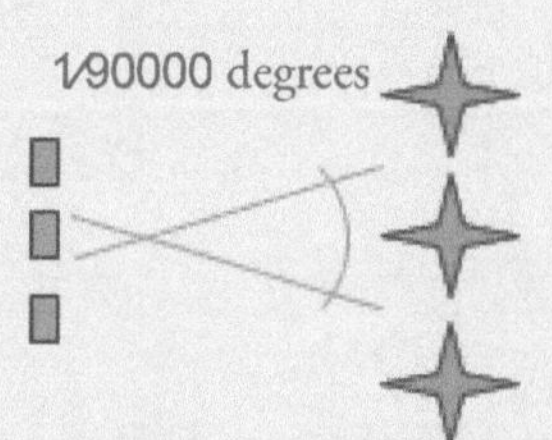

This is approximately the angle subtended by a penny viewed at 52 km, meaning it could be distinguished from another penny immediately next to it.

Key principle

Resolution of a bitmapped image:
Image resolution = w x h
where
w = width of image in pixels
h = width of image in pixels

Key principle

Displayed or printed resolution of a bitmapped image:
This is expressed as pixels per inch or ppi.

The choice of ppi for a clear, sharp image depends on the viewing distance.

Key fact

Scanned and digital camera images:
For images produced by scanning or by a digital camera, the clarity and resolution of a captured image is determined by the size of the photosensors (one photosensor = one pixel). This can be expressed as ppi.

Resolution

A popular convention is to describe the resolution of a bitmapped image as the number of pixel columns (width) by the number of pixel rows (height), for example, 3264 × 2448.

Image resolution = width of image in pixels × height of image in pixels

For a given dimension of image, say 1.5 inches by 1 inch, the more samples that are taken across the image the smaller the pixels and the greater the recorded detail.

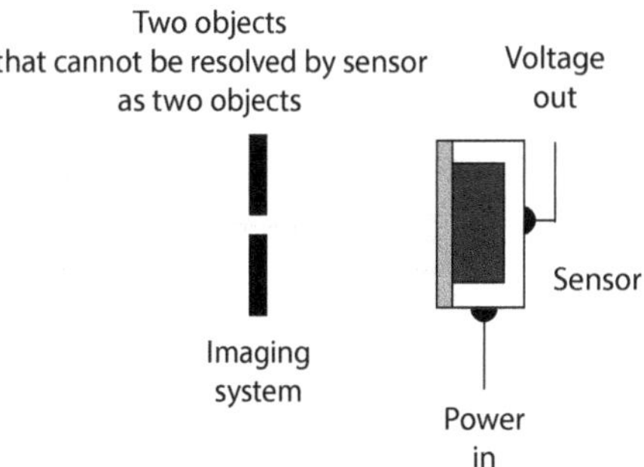

Figure 5.6.4.8 Sensor too large to resolve two objects

To resolve the detail in a barcode, for example, it must be possible to pick out both white and black bands in the image. If the photosensors are too big then this detail will be missed.

However, the pixel dimensions of a bitmapped image, such as 5184 × 3456 pixels, doesn't give the image a physical size. The bitmapped image's dimensions in pixels state only how many pixels there are, not how big each is.

Display and print resolution

The size of each pixel is set by specifying how many pixels should be fitted into an inch when the bitmapped image is displayed or printed.

This is expressed as pixels per inch or ppi.

The choice of ppi for a clear, sharp image depends on the viewing distance.

At the viewing distance, it should not be possible to see individual pixels.

For example, a 4"× 6" standard photographic print, printed at 300 ppi and viewed at about 11 inches appears fine, whereas a billboard-sized photograph also appears fine because its viewing distance is so much greater, even though it is only printed at about 15 ppi.

Figure 5.6.4.9 shows a bitmapped image originally prepared for printing at (a) 10 ppi, (b) 50 ppi and (c) 300 ppi.

The image in (a) of 40 × 30 pixels still reveals its pixels at normal viewing distance. We say that the image is pixelated because the individual pixels are visible. Image (b) is 200 × 150 pixels and shows much less pixelation but the sharpest image is (c) which has dimensions 1200 × 900 pixels.

(a)

(b)

(c)

Figure 5.6.4.9 bitmapped image printed at (a) 10 ppi, (b) 50 ppi and (c) 300 ppi

Physical dimensions of printed images

It should be clear that for practical purposes, the clarity of the image displayed or printed is decided by its spatial resolution, not the number of pixels in an image.

In effect, when a digital image is displayed or printed, resolution refers to the number of independent pixel values per unit length, e.g. pixels per inch or ppi. This is also known as pixel density.

This is an alternative meaning of digital image resolution or bitmap resolution.

Bitmap resolution is measured in number of pixels per inch (ppi).

This definition determines the size of the pixel of the display unit when displaying digital images or the number of image pixels that will fit inside each inch of paper when printed.

Specifying a resolution gives a size to the pixels of the printed image.

Scanned and digital camera images

For images produced by scanning or by a digital camera, the clarity and resolution of a captured image is determined by the size of the photosensors (one photosensor = one pixel).

Resolution of computer displays

A bitmapped digital image produced by a digital camera is composed of digitised or quantised samples that a computer screen displays as pixels because the screen of a computer display is divided into pixels.

The pixels are the addressable units of the screen that are individually illuminated to create an image or text on the screen. Pixels per inch (ppi) or pixels per centimetre (ppcm) is a measure of pixel density and therefore screen or display resolution. It is defined as the number of pixels in the horizontal direction per unit measurement, e.g. inch, or the number in the vertical direction per unit measurement which is the same thing for square pixels. The ppi of a computer display is therefore related to the size of the display in inches and the total number of pixels in the horizontal or vertical directions.

1920 pixels
1080 pixels
20″
11.25″

Figure 5.6.4.11 LCD monitor with screen dimensions 20 inches by 11.25 inches, filled with 1920 x 1080 pixels.

For the display in *Figure 5.6.4.11*,

Resolution = 1920 pixels/20 inches

= 1080 pixels/11.25 inches

= 96 ppi

PPI is a display resolution not an image resolution.

Information

Spatial resolution:
Spatial resolution is the capability of the sensor to observe or measure the smallest object clearly and distinctly, distinguishing it from other objects that surround it.
Figure 5.6.4.10 is composed of two objects which are straight lines separated from each other by a small amount of white space. At the distance at which you are viewing this page, most people will be able to see these as two separate objects, i.e. lines. The sensor in this case is your eye.
However, if you gradually increase the distance between your eye and the page, you will reach a distance at which the two lines are seen as just one thicker line. You are no longer able to resolve the two lines spatially (i.e. in space). Thus spatial resolution depends upon object separation and viewing distance, ignoring any deficiencies of the sensor itself.

Figure 5.6.4.10

Did you know?

Retina displays:
Retina displays use 326 ppi
When introducing the iPhone 4, Steve Jobs said that the number of pixels needed for a Retina Display is about 326 ppi for a device held 10 to 12 inches from the eye. At a distance of 12 inches, the average eye will not be able to resolve the individual pixels of the screen and therefore the display will be acceptable for viewing.

Image resolution is measured in samples per inch or loosely in horizontal pixels × vertical pixels. Display screens used by desktop computers typically have a resolution of 96 ppi or lower.

For the LCD monitor in Figure 5.6.4.11, 96 ppi is the maximum pixel density. Display devices usually allow the display settings to be changed, e.g. for the given display, choosing 1280 pixels by 720 pixels changes the pixel density or resolution to

1280 pixels/20 inches or 720/11.25 = 64 ppi

for the same screen real estate of 20 × 11.25 inches.

Did you know?

Screen resolution:

The iPhone 5s (released September 2012) has a screen resolution of 326 ppi and a screen size of 1136 by 640-pixel. Sony's Xperia Z's screen has a screen size of 1080 × 1920 pixels and a resolution or pixel density of approximately 441 ppi.

Figure 5.6.4.12 shows the same section of a digitised image at different screen resolutions or ppi. The dimensions of the image in pixels is unchanged but the image's size in the display goes from small to large as the resolution of the screen is reduced. The displayed pixels become larger as the screen resolution is lowered.

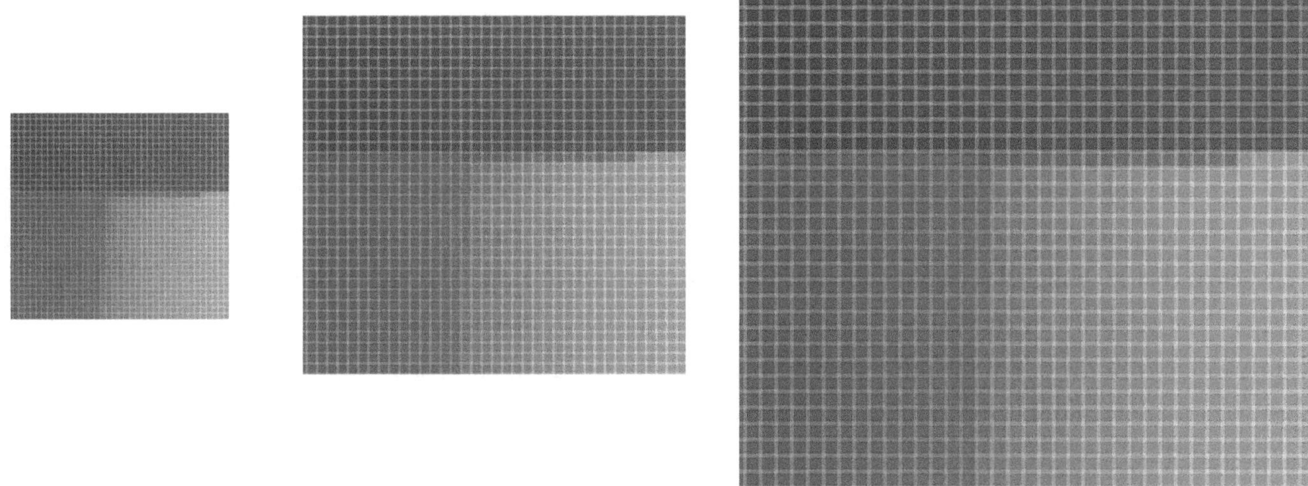

Figure 5.6.4.12 The same section of a digitised image at different screen resolutions, with the pixel density of the screen or ppi decreasing from left to right.

Questions

7 Calculate the screen resolution in number of pixels per inch for the following

(a) Apple MacBook Pro Retina 13.3"

screen size in pixels = 2560 × 1600 screen dimensions = 11.3 × 7.04 inches

(b) Microsoft Surface Pro 3 12"screen size in pixels = 2160 x 1440 screen dimensions = 10.0 × 6.67 inches

(c) Dell Ultrasharp U2414M 24 inch monitor

screen size in pixels = 1920 × 1200 screen dimensions = 20.43 × 12.77 inches

(d) Google Nexus 6

screen size in pixels = 2560 × 1440 screen dimensions = 5.19 × 2.92 inches

8 Large screens can get away with lower pixel densities because viewing distance is important with regards to resolution. Use your answers for question 7 to justify this statement.

Camera resolution

The iPhone 5s' iSight camera uses a chip with light sensors of width and height 1.5×10^{-6} metre in size, giving dimensions for each pixel of 1.5×10^{-6} metres (1.5µm where µm is a micrometre) . This camera uses an aspect ratio of 4:3 and therefore is 3264 pixels across by 2448 pixels down (3264 × 2448) or 7990272 pixels in total. Expressed to 2 decimal places this is 7.99 megapixels or to none, 8 megapixels.

Apple actually increased pixel size in the iPhone 5s to 1.5µm (from 1.4 µm in iPhone 5) and kept the pixel count the same by using a 15% larger sensor. The slightly larger sensor size and therefore pixel size improved low light sensitivity and reduced the ratio of image signal to noise emanating from within the sensor in low light conditions. This actually improved the quality of the image.

Sony Xperia 's primary camera uses a chip of width and height 4128 × 3096 pixels. The total quoted number of pixels is 13.1 megapixels. This is actually greater than the number which contribute to the final image because some pixels are unused or are shielded from the light because they are around the edges of the sensor.

Questions

Why is it useful for smartphone cameras to have 4 megapixels or greater?

Printing a bitmapped image on paper

Paper is an analogue material so it differs from a typical computer screen which is digital, i.e. divided up into pixels. The coordinate system for drawing by hand on paper is a continuous one whereas that for a digital screen is a discrete one. However, when a digital image is printed on paper, it is pixels which are printed, i.e. discrete units. There is a difference, however, for the printer controls the size of the printed image pixel, all that the digitised image supplies by way of control is the number of pixels horizontally and the number of pixels vertically.

For example, a 100 × 100 pixel image that is printed in a 1 inch square has a resolution of 100 pixels per inch (ppi). To produce good quality printed photographs, the printer must be capable of printing 300 pixels per inch, at 100% size, and the paper printed on must be coated paper stock.

A printer creates an image on paper by laying down a series of dots of ink or toner. Its resolution is therefore measured in number of dots per inch (DPI).

A pixel made up of 16 blue dots

An ink-jet printer prints by moving a printhead across and down the paper. It has a basic movement of 1200 steps across and 1200 steps down, typically. Each pixel of the image is created by a series of tiny dots and every pixel output is made up of different coloured inks (usually 4 colours, CMYK - Cyan, Magenta, Yellow, and Key which is black - though professional printing uses more) deposited by the print head on the paper.

If the printer can print 1200 dots of ink per inch (1200 dpi) and a bitmapped image is sent to the printer for printing at 300 pixels per inch, then each printed pixel will be consist of 16 smaller ink dots.

> **Key fact**
>
> **Printer resolution and Dots per inch (DPI):**
> Dots per inch is a measure of the resolution of a printer. It properly refers to the dots of ink or toner used by an imagesetter, laser printer, or other printing devices to print text and graphics. In general, the more dots, the better and sharper the image. DPI is printer resolution.

Questions

10 An image of size 640 × 480 pixels is to be printed at 300 pixels per inch. What will be the size of the printed image in inches to one decimal place?

11 The size of a photographic print printed at 300 ppi is 4.2 × 3.2 inches. What was the size in pixels of the digital image that was printed?

Stretch & challenge question

12 A bimapped image is produced by scanning a 35mm film slide (0.94 inches by 1.42 inches) with a scanner designed for this purpose. A print of size 9.4 × 14.2 inches is to be made of the bitmapped image on a printer that prints at 300 pixels per inch, i.e. photographic quality.

(a) How many pixels are printed in a 9.4 inch wide row?

(b) If the scanning resolution is n samples per inch, how many samples, in terms of n, would be taken in a scan of one row across the film slide (0.94 inches)?

(c) What must the minimum value of the scanning resolution be in samples per inch to produce a print of acceptable quality?

(d) Using your answer to part (c), what is the size of the bitmap in pixels produced by the scanner? Express your answer in the form of number of pixel columns (width) by the number of pixel rows (height). Both numbers are integers.

Key concept

Metadata:
The header part of the bitmap file contains information about the bitmap data part of the file, such as number of bits per pixel. This is metadata because it is data about data, i.e. the data in the bitmap part of the file.

HEADER
BITMAP DATA

Figure 5.6.4.13 Structure of a Windows bitmap file

Metadata

Microsoft's Paint program that comes with the Windows operating system enables bitmaps to be created and saved. Bitmap files saved in Windows Paint with file extension ".bmp" have a file structure which conforms to the Windows bitmap format shown in *Figure 5.6.4.13*. The header contains information about the bitmap data part of the file, such as

- number of bits per pixel
- horizontal width of bitmap in pixels
- whether it is compressed or not, etc.

This is called metadata because it is data about data.

The actual detailed structure and content of the header is shown in *Figure 5.6.4.14* for an uncompressed, RGB, 24 bits per pixel, 4 × 2 pixel bitmap produced with Microsoft Paint and shown in *Figure 5.6.4.15*.

Figure 5.6.4.16 shows the data part of the bitmap file for *Figure 5.6.4.13*. Bytes 54, 55 and 56 correspond to the first pixel in the bottom row of the image. The colour of each pixel is controlled by three bytes, the first in the triplet controls red, the second green, and the third blue. Thus this first pixel of the bottom row is green because its colour is controlled by the triplet 0, 255, 0. The second pixel in the bottom row is black because it is controlled by the triplet, 0, 0, 0.

Figure 5.6.4.16, byte 10 states that the bitmap data begins at byte 54. Byte 34 states that the length of the bitmap data is 24 bytes, which indeed it is as *Figure 5.6.4.15* shows. Microsoft chose to store the bytes in little-endian fashion. In little-endian, the least significant byte is stored in the smallest address. For example, "Where the data starts" is four bytes long and has value 0, 0, 0, 54 which in decimal is just 54.

77	0	Top row fourth pixel BLACK 0, 0, 0
76	0	
75	0	
74	0	Top row third pixel BLUE 0, 0, 255
73	0	
72	255	
71	255	Top row second pixel RED 255,0 ,0
70	0	
69	0	
68	0	Top row leftmost pixel BLACK 0, 0, 0
67	0	
66	0	
65	0	Bottom row fourth pixel BLUE 0, 0, 255
64	0	
63	255	
62	255	Bottom row third pixel RED 255, 0, 0
61	0	
60	0	
59	0	Bottom row second pixel BLACK 0, 0, 0
58	0	
57	0	
56	0	Bottom row leftmost pixel GREEN 0, 255, 0
55	255	
54	0	

Figure 5.6.4.14 Bytes 54 to 77 of bitmap file represent bitmap data for 4 x 2 pixels image, 24-bit Windows bitmap.

Questions

13 Using *Figure 5.6.4.16* as a reference, list **nine** items of metadata found in the header of a bitmap file.

Figure 5.6.4.15 Image produced when 24-bit bitmap rendered on screen

Information

Reading and writing bytes: The source code of programs to read and write a file of bytes can be downloaded from www.educational-computing.co.uk.

0	identifier	The file type	66	'B'	← Bitmap, BM
1	identifier	must be 'BM'.	77	'M'	
2	file size	The size, in bytes, of the bitmap file.	78		4 bytes, 0, 0, 0, 78
3	file size		0		
4	file size		0		
5	file size		0		
6	reserved	Reserved; must be zero.	0		
7	reserved		0		
8	reserved		0		
9	reserved		0		
10	bitmap data offset	The offset, in bytes, from the	54		← Where the data starts 0, 0, 0, 54
11	bitmap data offset	beginning of the	0		
12	bitmap data offset	BITMAPFILEHEADER	0		
13	bitmap data offset	structure to the bitmap bits.	0		
14	bitmap header size		40		4 bytes, 0, 0, 0, 40
15	bitmap header size		0		
16	bitmap header size		0		
17	bitmap header size		0		
18	Horizontal width of bitmap in pixels		4		4 bytes, 0, 0, 0, 4
19	Horizontal width of bitmap in pixels		0		
20	Horizontal width of bitmap in pixels		0		
21	Horizontal width of bitmap in pixels		0		
22	Vertical width of bitmap in pixels	If Height is positive, the	2		4 bytes, 0, 0, 0, 2
23	Vertical width of bitmap in pixels	bitmap is a bottom-up DIB.	0		
24	Vertical width of bitmap in pixels	DIB = Device Independent	0		
25	Vertical width of bitmap in pixels	Bitmap.	0		
26	Number of planes in the bitmap	The number of planes for the target	1		
27	Number of planes in the bitmap	device.This value must be set to 1.	0		
28	Bits per pixel		24		2 bytes, 0, 24
29	Bits per pixel		0		
30	Compression	The type of compression for a	0		
31	Compression	compressed bottom-up bitmap	0		
32	Compression	RGB uncompressed= 0x0000	0		
33	Compression	JPEG = 0x0004, PNG = 0x0005	0		
34	Bitmap data size	Size in bytes	24		4 bytes, 0, 0, 0, 24
35	Bitmap data size		0		
36	Bitmap data size		0		
37	Bitmap data size		0		
38	Horizontal resolution in pixel/metre of the target device	An application can use this value to select a bitmap from	0		
39	Horizontal resolution in pixel/metre	a resource group that best	0		
40	Horizontal resolution in pixel/metre	matches the characteristics	0		
41	Horizontal resolution in pixel/metre	of the current device.	0		
42	Vertical resolution in pixel/metre of the target device		0		
43	Vertical resolution in pixel/metre		0		
44	Vertical resolution in pixel/metre		0		
45	Vertical resolution in pixel/metre		0		
46	Number of colours used	If zero, the bitmap uses the maximum	0		
47	Number of colours used	number of colours corresponding to the	0		
48	Number of colours used	value of the bits per pixel.	0		
49	Number of colours used		0		
50	Number of important colours used	If zero, all colours are important.	0		
51	Number of important colours used		0		
52	Number of important colours used		0		
53	Number of important colours used		0		

Figure 5.6.4.16 Header part of bitmap file. It contains metadata.

Programming Tasks

1. Using Microsoft Paint (or equivalent), create and save a 4 × 2 pixels 24-bit uncompressed Windows bitmap similar to Figure 5.6.4.15. Use the pencil tool to change the colour of individual pixels. You will need to zoom in to make the pixels large enough to manipulate.

2. Write a program that opens and reads the contents of this file, byte by byte, displaying each byte as a decimal integer on the console. Number these bytes starting from 0 so that the console output displays number followed by byte value read from file. Check that your output shows similar values to those shown in *Figures 5.6.4.14* and 5.6.4.16.

3. Using Paint, change the colours of the pixels in the bitmap, noting the RGB values and re-run your program. Check that the output from your program now reflects the new RGB values of the colours.

4. Using Paint, create and save an 8 x 2 pixels 24-bit uncompressed Windows bitmap, with differently coloured pixels.

5. Re-run you program and note the relevant changes in the header (metadata) and the data part of the bitmap displayed on the console. Do the displayed changes agree with what you expect?

6. Edit your program so that it also writes each byte that it reads from the opened bitmap file to a new file. Save your edited program under a new name. The new bitmap file produced by running the new program should be given a suitable name and the extension ".bmp". At the moment it should be just a copy of the original.

7. Edit your new program so that it alters the three bytes of a chosen pixel before writing these to the new bitmap file. Now open the changed bitmap file in Paint and check that your program has changed the colour of a pixel.

8. How could a short sequence of 8-bit ASCII character codes be placed in a bitmap file? Choose a much larger image bitmap file than you have been working with, e.g. 640 x 480 pixels, and use your program suitably modified to replace pixel bytes in this bitmap with a sequence of 8-bit ASCII codes. Check the result by displaying the new image bitmap file in an image viewer, e.g. Paint. Can you detect the ASCII codes?

9. Write a program that reads an altered image bitmap file and recovers the sequence of 8-bit ASCII codes. Display these as characters on the console.

Key fact

Storage requirements for bitmapped images):

Storage requirements = width in pixels × height in pixels × colour depth

Calculating storage requirements for bitmapped images

Ignoring the storage space taken up by metadata, the storage requirements of the data part of a bitmapped image is calculated as follows

Storage requirements = width in pixels × height in pixels × colour depth

This is sometimes referred to as being the minimum file size for a bitmapped image.

For example, a bitmapped image has dimensions 5184 × 3456 pixels and uses 24-bit colour. What is the size of the data part of the bitmap in bits? In bytes? What is it in megabytes (1000000 bytes), to 1 decimal place?

Size in bits = 5184 × 3456 × 24 = 429981696

Size in bytes = (5184 × 3456 × 24)/8 = 53747712

Size in megabytes = (5184 × 3456 × 24)/(8 x 1000000) = 53.7

Questions

14. What is the minimum file size in bytes, for a bitmapped image that has a colour depth of 12 bits and dimensions 640 × 480 pixels?

In this chapter you have covered:

- *How bitmaps are represented*
- *For bitmaps the meaning of*
  - *resolution*
  - *colour depth*
  - *size in pixels*
- *How to calculate storage requirements for bitmapped images*
- *Bitmap image files may also contain metadata*
- *Typical metadata*

6 Representing images, sound and other data

Learning objectives:

- *Describe the digital representation of sound in terms of:*
  - *sample resolution*
  - *sampling rate and Nyquist theorem.*
- *Calculate sound sample sizes in bytes*

5.6.5 Digital representation of sound

Classification of waveforms

Periodic and aperiodic

It is useful when working with sounds to graph their waveforms (amplitude of air pressure, or voltage from a microphone, as a function of time). *Figure 5.6.5.1(a)* shows the waveform of the sound "Laa" spoken into a microphone. *Figure 5.6.5.1(b)* shows the waveform of white noise, the sort of sound heard from an analogue radio not tuned to any radio station.

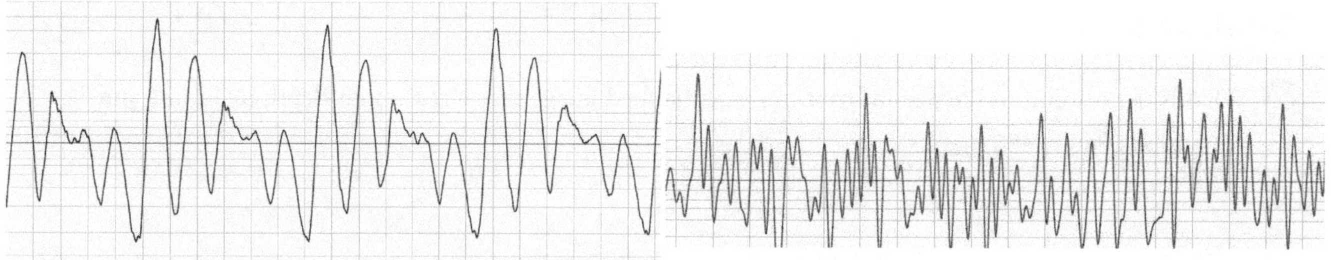

Figure 5.6.5.1(a) "Laa" sound recording

Figure 5.6.5.1(b) White noise sound recording

Key concept

Frequency of a sound:
The pitch of a sound is what humans perceive as frequency. Frerquency is measured as the number of cycles per second of a repeating pattern in a periodic waveform or vibration or oscillation. Its unit is the Hz which is one cycle per second.

Sounds are caused by vibrations or oscillations of a column of air in a woodwind instrument or in a stretched string such as a violin or guitar string when bowed or plucked.

The waveform in *Figure 5.6.5.1(a)* consists of a repeating pattern called a **periodic** oscillation, with maybe a few minor deviations. This is characteristic of sounds that have **pitch**. Pitch is what humans perceive as **frequency** and recognise by its position in a range of audible frequencies that range from low to high. The pitch of a sound is varied when you sing or whistle a song melody. Musicians use a notation for indicating the pitch of a sound to be played.

The waveform in *Figure 5.6.5.1(b)* does not repeat in time (**aperiodic**) because it is essentially random in nature.

Waveforms are broadly divided into two classes:

1. periodic (repeat in time)
2. aperiodic (don't repeat in time)

The first class is subdivided into simple (sinusoidal) and complex (non-sinusoidal) waveforms. It turns out that these complex (non-sinusoidal) waveforms are composed of sinusoidal waveforms of different frequencies and amplitudes added together. This means that complex waveforms can be synthesised by selecting the right sinusoids to add together.

The second class is subdivided into impulsive (occur once) and noise (continuous but random) waveforms.

Sinusoids

If we imagine the red dot inside the circle in Figure 5.6.5.2 is a cyclist cycling round the circle at constant speed of, say, one complete loop of the circle per minute then we are imagining a periodic system because it has a repeating pattern. If we were to lie down in the plane of the circle, i.e. view the circle sidewise-on, then looking along the time axis across the page we would see the vertical distance of the cyclist from this axis vary in time as shown in red. Mathematically, this waveform is called a sine waveform or sine wave.

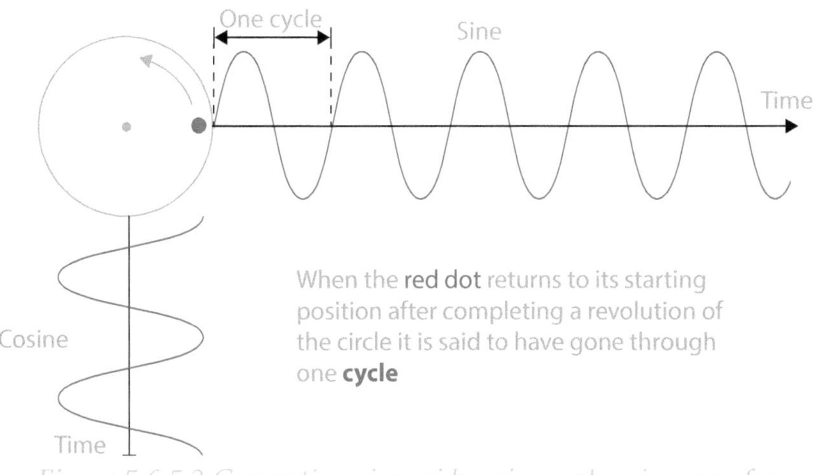
One cycle
Sine
Time
Cosine
Time
When the red dot returns to its starting position after completing a revolution of the circle it is said to have gone through one **cycle**

Figure 5.6.5.2 Generating sinusoids - sine and cosine waveforms

If we look along the time axis going down the page we see the vertical distance of the cyclist from this new axis also vary in time as shown in red. Mathematically, this waveform is called a cosine waveform or cosine wave. Both sine and cosine waveforms are called sinusoids. A sinusoid is characterised by three quantities:

1. Peak amplitude or just amplitude which is the maximum vertical distance of the waveform from the time axis. In circle terms this is the radius of the circular path that the cyclist follows.
2. Frequency which in circle terms is the number of cycles of the circle per second, e.g. 60 loops of the circle per second. In pitch or frequency terms it is expressed in Hz, e.g. 60 Hz.
3. Phase which in circle terms is where the red dot starts. Conventionally, this is measured in angle from the time axis, e.g. for the sine waveform time axis, angle = 0 degrees; for the cosine waveform time axis this is 90 degrees.

Task

To see a demonstration of generating a sinusoid from circular motion visit http://treeblurb.com/dev_math/sin_canv00.html

Task

Download and install SFS/ESynth from https://www.phon.ucl.ac.uk/resource/sfs/esynth.php Experiment with generating sinusoids using ESythn.

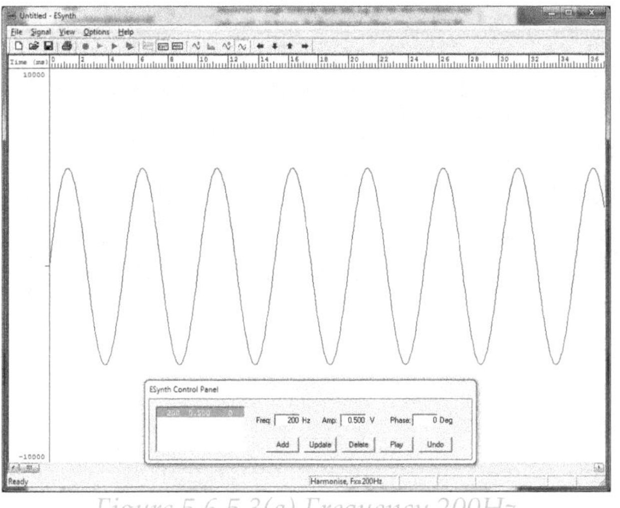

Figure 5.6.5.3(a) Frequency 200Hz, amplitude 0.5, phase 0 degrees

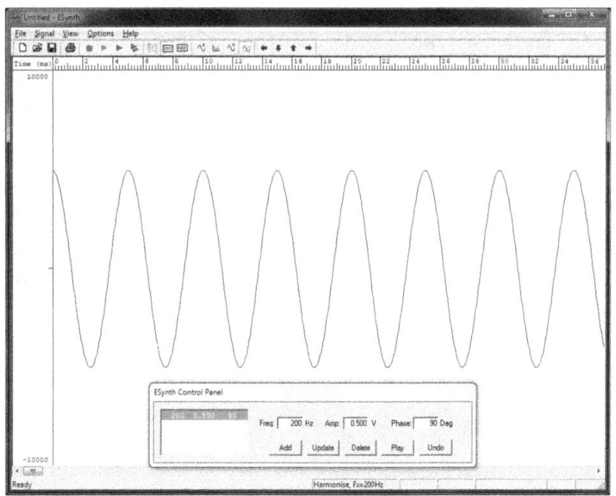

Figure 5.6.5.3(b) Frequency 200Hz, amplitude 0.5, phase 90 degrees

Figure 5.6.5.3 shows waveforms generated by ESynth with frequency 200 Hz, amplitude 0.5 and phases 0 and 90 degrees.

Key concept

Sampling rate:
Sampling rate or sampling frequency is the number of samples taken per second.

Bit depth:
Bit depth or sampling resolution is the number of bits allocated to each sample.

Sampling a waveform

Sampling rate and bit depth (sample resolution)

We have learned that the term periodic refers to any waveform that can be described in terms of going round in a circle.

Figure 5.6.5.4 shows one cycle of a sine wave generated along the time axis by recording the vertical distance of the clock hand from this axis in time. The clock hand rotates anticlockwise and the recording starts when this hand is pointing along the time axis (phase = 0 degrees).

To create a sine-wave generator (oscillator) in a digital computer all that is needed is to store, at successive intervals of time, the vertical distance of the clock hand from the time axis. This is called **sampling**.

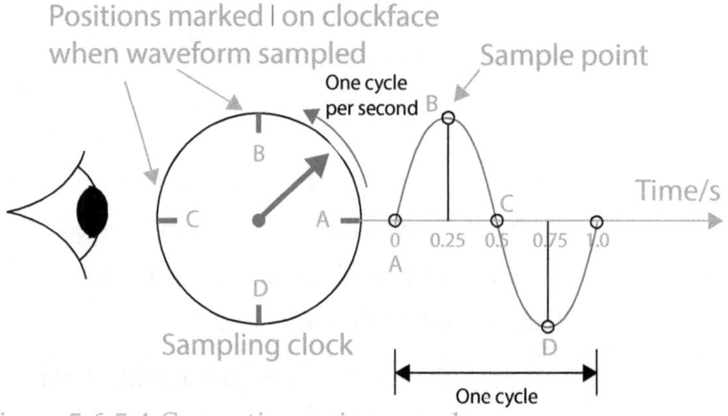

Figure 5.6.5.4 Generating a sine wave by the circle method and sampling it 4 times per cycle

The positions marked in red on the clock face indicate the moments in time when the vertical distance is sampled.

Let's suppose that the clock hand rotates at 1 revolution per second, i.e. 1Hz, then in one revolution 4 samples are taken at A, B, C and D, measured and recorded, i.e. a **sampling rate** of 4 samples per second (4 Hz).

Each measurement made by the digital computer is stored in binary. This is the process of quantisation. The number of binary digits used for each measurement is called the **bit depth**. Bit depth is one way of specifying **sample resolution**.

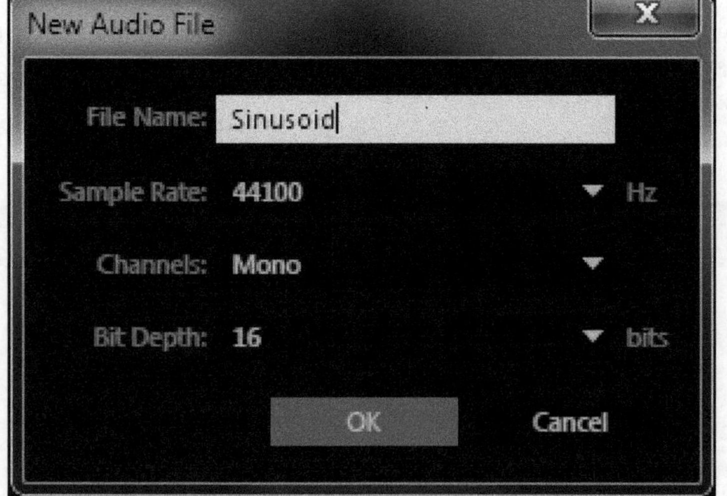

Figure 5.6.5.5 Setting sampling rate and bit depth

Figure 5.6.5.5 shows the first stage in the process of generating a sine wave digitally with Adobe® Audition CC 2015. At this stage, the sampling rate is set at 44100 Hz and the bit depth at 16 bits.

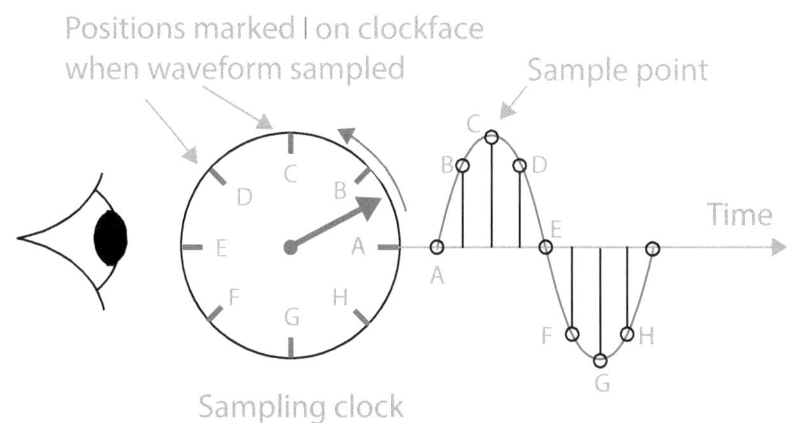

Figure 5.6.5.6 Generating a sine wave by the circle method and sampling it 8 times per cycle

Figure 5.6.5.6 shows sampling occurring at a rate of 8 samples per cycle. If the clockhand rotates at 1 revolution per second then the sampling rate is 8 samples per second, i.e. one sample every ⅛ second.

To convey an important point about sampling frequency Figure 5.6.5.7 and Figure 5.6.5.8 have been simplified by omitting any filtering which would normally be applied during the reconstruction process.

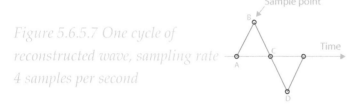

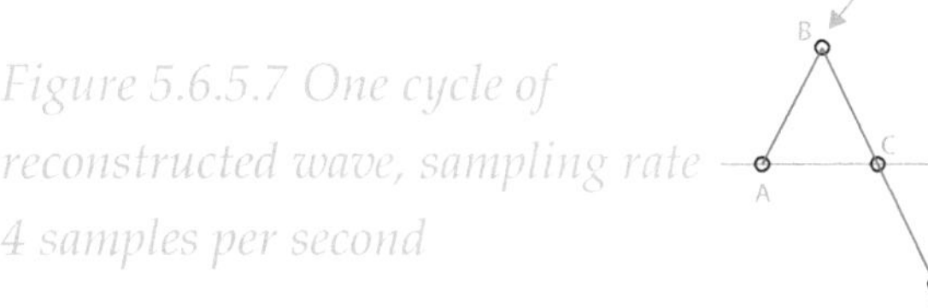

Figure 5.6.5.7 One cycle of reconstructed wave, sampling rate 4 samples per second

Figure 5.6.5.7 shows one cycle of the reconstructed wave for a sampling rate of 4 samples per second - see Figure 5.6.5.4.

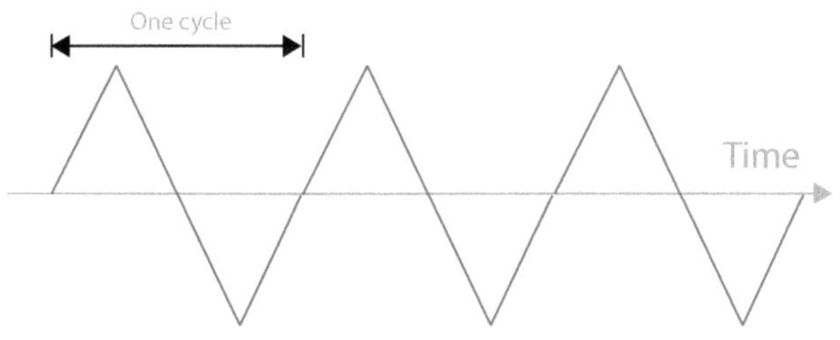

Figure 5.6.5.8 Three cycles of reconstructed wave

Figure 5.6.5.8 shows several cycles of the reconstructed wave for a sampling rate of 4 samples per second. It is still periodic with a frequency of 1 Hz, the same frequency as the original sine wave. However, its shape is no longer a sine wave. The waveform is now triangular in shape. We need to **sample at a higher rate** to get a better approximation to a sine wave - see Figure 5.6.5.6.

Key concept

Jean Baptiste Joseph Fourier (1768-1830), introduced the concept by which a signal can be synthesised by adding up its constituent frequencies.

He introduced the concept of frequency for elementary signals that belong to a set of sinusoidal signals (sines and cosines) with various periods of repetition.

However, if this triangular waveform was played through a sound card and loudspeakers it would still have a pitch of 1 Hz (we would need to work with higher frequencies to make a sound that the ear would perceive in a tone-like way, e.g. 200 Hz) but it would sound different from a sine wave of the same frequency. We say that its **timbre** is different. Higher frequencies have been added which are whole number multiples of the frequency with which the waveform repeats. These are called **harmonics**. The repetition frequency of the waveform is called the **fundamental frequency**.

The triangular waveform is thus made up of a fundamental frequency plus harmonics of the fundamental frequency. Figure 5.6.5.9 shows that adding two harmonics, $3f$ and $5f$ to the fundamental frequency f in just the right amounts and phase produces a triangle-like waveform.

Figure 5.6.5.10 shows a screenshot of a triangle-like waveform being synthesised in ESynth using a fundamental of 200 Hz and harmonics of 600 Hz and 1000 Hz. Joseph Fourier was the first person to realise that complex periodic waveforms could be synthesised in this way.

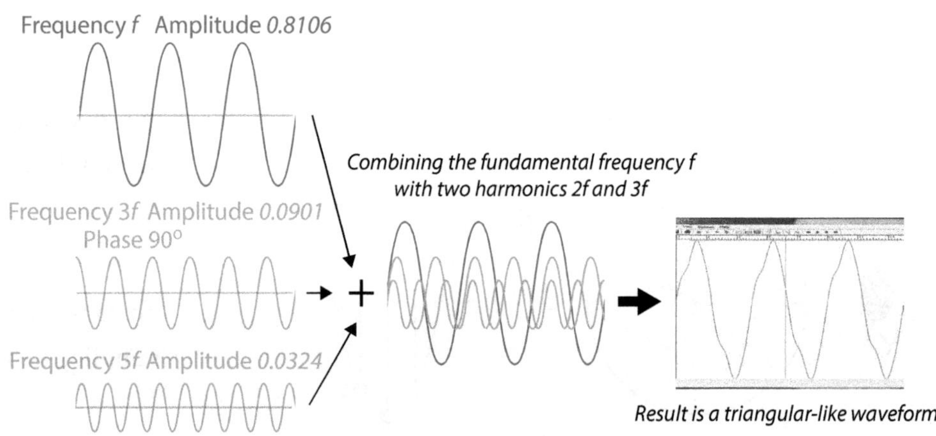

Figure 5.6.5.9 Fundamental + two harmonics = triangle-like waveform

It led to the concept of **bandwidth**. To preserve the shape of this signal any communication system through which it passes must pass not only the fundamental frequency but also its harmonics, 600 Hz and 1000 Hz, i.e. frequencies located in the band 0 to 1000 Hz.

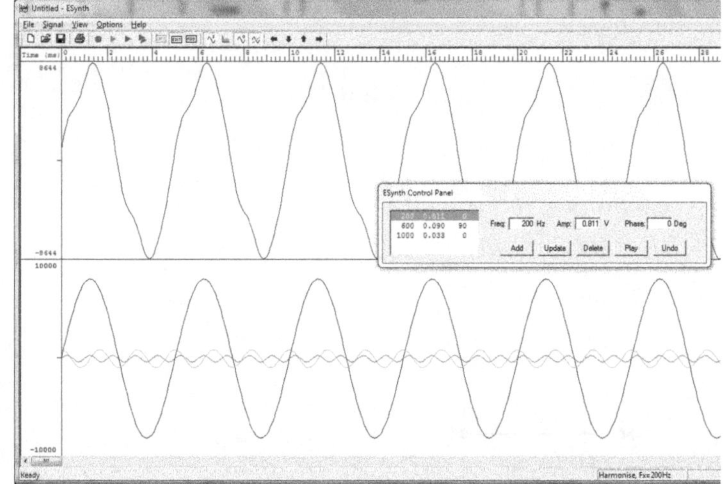

Figure 5.6.5.10 ESynth screenshot

Lower limit on sampling rate - Nyquist's theorem

We have seen that to achieve a better approximation to the original signal we need to sample at a higher rate but is there a lower limit? The answer is yes. *Figure 5.6.5.11* shows a 2.5 Hz sine waveform sampled at 4 samples per second (4 Hz). The sampling points in the sampling cycle are A, B, C, D.

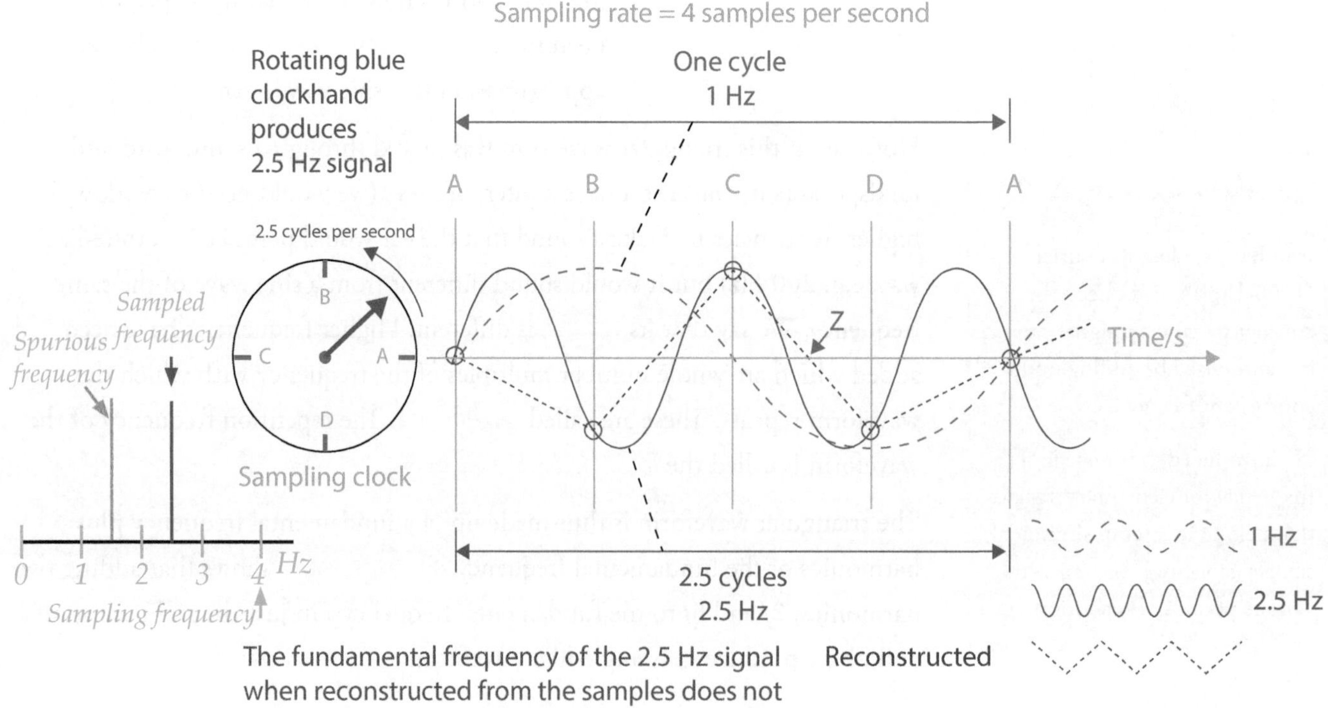

Figure 5.6.5.11 Sampling a waveform at a sampling frequency which is less than twice the waveform's frequency results in an alias (spurious) frequency replacing the sampled waveform's frequency

Key principle

Nyquist's theorem:
When sampling a (complex) periodic waveform, we must sample at twice the highest frequency present in the waveform, at least, if all the frequencies present in the (complex) periodic waveform are to be preserved.

Task

Sampling a rotating image at too low a frequency can result in the rotating image appearing to rotate at a lower frequency than it actually is.
Try observing rotating ceiling fan blades whilst blinking your eyes. The fan blades may appear to rotate at a lower frequency than they really are. We call the false frequency of rotation a spurious frequency. It is a consequence of Nyquist's theorem.

However, the waveform constructed from these samples has a repeating pattern frequency which is not 2.5 Hz. Its frequency is approximately 1.25 Hz. This is an artifact called a spurious or alias frequency, i.e. one that does not really exist. This known as aliasing. However, the waveform that could be constructed from samples of the 1 Hz sine waveform (red dotted curve) does have a repeating pattern frequency of 1 Hz.

It turns out that when sampling a (complex) periodic waveform, we must sample at twice the highest frequency present in the waveform, at least, if all the frequencies present in the (complex) periodic waveform are to be preserved. This is known as Nyquist's theorem. Figure 5.6.5.12 illustrates this with a sinusoid (cosine waveform) of frequency 1 Hz. The sampling rate is twice this at 2 samples per second but it is still possible to construct a waveform with fundamental frequency, 1 Hz, the same frequency as the original.

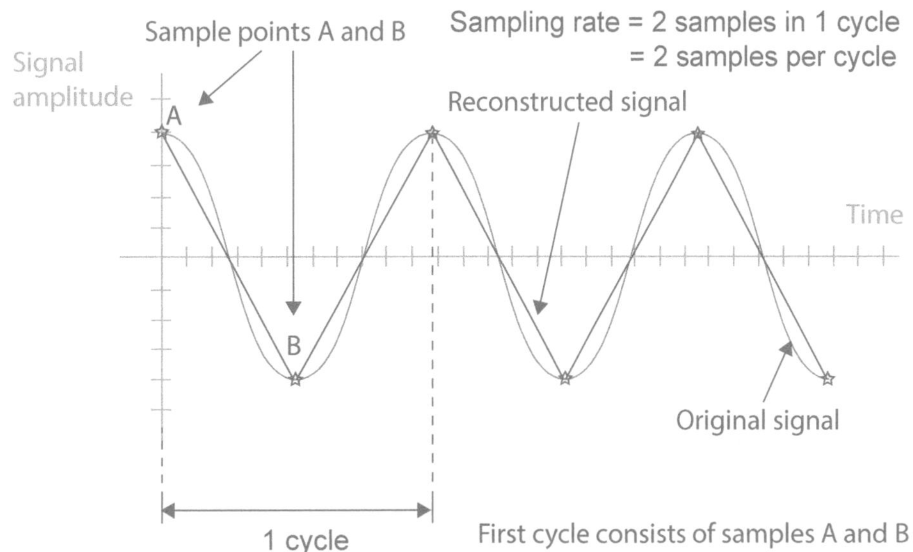

Figure 5.6.5.12 Applying Nyquist's theorem, sampling rate is at least twice highest frequency in waveform

Questions

1. Explain the terms (a) sampling rate (b) bit depth or sample resolution.
2. An analogue waveform made up of the following sinusoids with frequencies 1 kHz, 5 kHz, and 10 kHz is sampled and the samples digitised. When the digitised result is processed, it is discovered that it is made up of sinusoids with frequencies, 1 kHz, 5 kHz and 7.5 kHz but not 10 kHz. Suggest the most likely reason why this has happened and suggest one possible solution.
3. Why are music CDs recorded at a sampling rate of 44100 samples per second?
4. State Nyquist's theorem.

Nyquist's theorem and recording sound

Music CDs are recorded at a sampling rate of 44100 samples per second for a good reason. The human ear is capable of hearing sound over a frequency range of 20 Hz to 20 kHz with its greatest sensitivity to frequencies between 2000 and 5000 Hz. Thus the sampling rate at which music is recorded for music CD production is greater than the minimum sampling frequency according to Nyquist's theorem. A note from a violin pitched at 2000 Hz still must be sampled at 44100 samples per second because what makes the note sound like a violin note are the harmonic frequencies that are also present. This is called the quality of the note or timbre that distinguishes it from other sounds of the same pitch and volume, e.g. a violin note from a trumpet note. The fundamental plus harmonics of a sound are called the spectral content. *Figure 5.6.5.13* shows the spectral content of a recording of the sound "Laa". A Discrete Fourier Transform(DFT) has been applied to the recorded waveform to reveal a fundamental at 155 Hz and 22 harmonics, some of which are not displayed because their amplitude is too small. The highest harmonic frequency is 3895 Hz. Fourier analysis is the process of finding which sine waves need to be added together to make a particular waveform shape. The DFT works with digital samples. If the sound "Laa" had been sampled at, say 4000 samples per second, which is not at least twice the frequency of the highest frequency and ten other harmonics, the recording would have been distorted by including frequencies not in the original - see *Figure 5.6.5.11*.

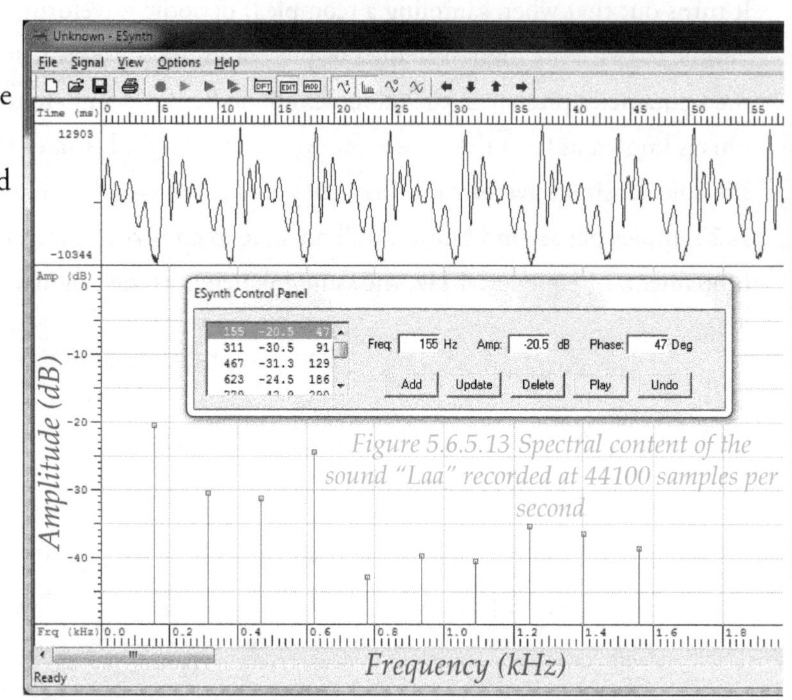

Figure 5.6.5.13 Spectral content of the sound "Laa" recorded at 44100 samples per second

Calculate sound sample sizes in bytes - See *Chapter 5.6.3*.

Did you know?

The seemingly arbitrary choice of 44100 Hz arose in order to accommodate early Video Tape recorders.
See e.g. https://en.wikipedia.org/wiki/44,100_Hz

Did you know?

The most general term for a frequency component of a complex tone is a "partial" or "overtone". All harmonics are partials, but partials can be either harmonic or inharmonic. Instruments such as bells, and other metallophones, generate a multitude of inharmonic partials. Waveforms containing inharmonic partials will not be periodic at the fundamental frequency, but may or may not be over a longer time.

Did you know?

Modified Shannon-Nyquist Theorem:
States that the highest frequency component in the source must be less than half the sampling frequency.

Information

Discrete Fourier Transform:
Converts from the time domain to the frequency domain and lists the frequency components of the signal.

In this chapter you have covered:

- The digital representation of sound in terms of:
    - sample resolution or bit depth which is the number of bits allocated to each sample.
    - sampling rate or sampling frequency is the number of samples taken per second.
    - Nyquist theorem -when sampling a (complex) periodic waveform, we must sample at twice the highest frequency present in the waveform, at least, if all the frequencies present in the (complex) periodic waveform are to be preserved. If we don't then spurious(false) frequencies appear called alias frequencies and their corresponding original frequencies do not.

Learning objectives:

- *Describe the purpose of MIDI and the use of event messages in MIDI*
- *Describe the advantages of using MIDI files for representing music*

5.6.6 Musical Instrument Digital Interface(MIDI)

What is MIDI?

MIDI stands for Musical Instrument Digital Interface. It is a hardware/software protocol adopted in the 1980s to enable electronic instruments to communicate with each other using the same set of agreed-upon codes and numbers. For example, a Korg keyboard (MIDI controller) can instruct suitable software running on a computer (MIDI instrument) to play a note by sending the software a "Note On" message. Figure 5.6.6.1 shows a Korg MIDI 61-key keyboard connected via USB (using a USB-MIDI driver) to a computer running an emulator for a Korg synthesiser called Wavestation.

Key principle

MIDI: MIDI stands for Musical Instrument Digital Interface. It is a hardware and software specification for the exchange of information (musical notes, expression control, etc) between different musical instruments or other devices such as sequencers, computers, lighting controllers, etc.

Korg Wavestation synthesiser emulator running on Windows 7

USB cable

Figure 5.6.6.1 Korg 61-key keyboard connected to Korg's Wavestation synthesiser emulator

Information

Introduction to computer music:
http://www.indiana.edu/~emusic/etext/toc.shtml

Pressing a key on the Korg keyboard sends a message to the computer program to play the note corresponding to this key. A note number is assigned to each key on a MIDI keyboard. For the keyboard in Figure 5.6.6.1, note numbering starts at 36 and runs consecutively up to 95 as shown in Figure 5.6.6.2.

MIDI note number 60 has been assigned to middle C on this keyboard. Note, number 60 corresponds to frequency 261.63 Hz but the MIDI specification allows this mapping to be changed.

Table 5.6.6.1 shows the usual correspondence between MIDI note number and frequency for this and some other MIDI note numbers. The name given to each note is also shown. Note that musical pitch (note frequency) is not embedded in any way in MIDI Note messages, thereby allowing mapping from note number to pitch to be changed. Nor is note name tied to a specific frequency (tuning a musical instrument adjusts frequency).

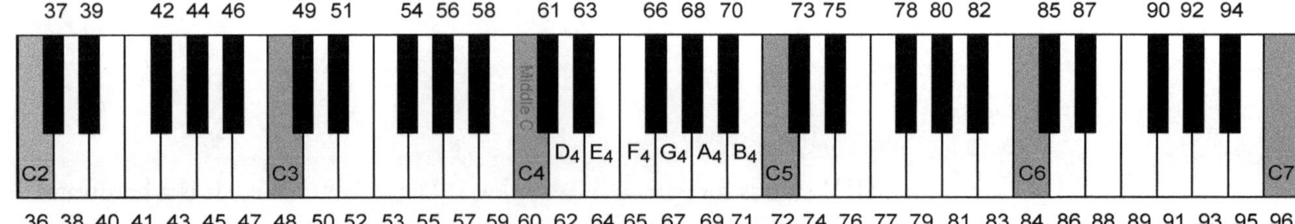

Figure 5.6.6.2 Some notes from an octave (white and grey keys only), their MIDI note number and one possible assignment of frequencies

MIDI note no	60	62	64	65	67	69	71	72
Frequency Hz	261.63	293.67	329.63	349.23	392.00	440	493.88	523.25
Note name	C4	D4	E4	F4	G4	A4	B4	C5

Table 5.6.6.1 MIDI note no, its usual corresponding frequency in Hz and its usual note name

MIDI itself does not make sound. It is just a **series of messages** to turn notes on and off, etc. These messages are interpreted by a MIDI instrument to produce sound. A MIDI instrument can be a piece of hardware (a synthesizer) or a software tool (Wavestation emulator, MuLab, Logic Pro).

The most common tool used to generate MIDI messages is an electronic keyboard. These messages may be routed to a digital synthesiser inside the keyboard or they may be patched (wired) to some other MIDI instrument such as a computer running synthesiser software. Almost all MIDI devices are equipped to receive MIDI messages on one or more of 16 selectable MIDI Channel numbers, labelled 1 to 16 (supports "multi-timbral" performance).

> **Information**
>
> **Octave:**
>
> The range from C4 to C5 is an octave. The grey keys indicate the musical interval of an octave (12 semitones) between notes. An octave has the property that the ratio of the frequencies at the ends of the range is 2:1. In equal temperament, an octave is defined to be 12 equal semitones in the modern scale. Each semitone therefore has a ratio of $2^{1/12}$ (approximately 1.059). Note A4 is assigned frequency 440 Hz. Therefore, the frequency of the nth semitone above or below A4 is
>
> $2^{n/12}$ x 440 Hz.

MIDI messages

The most common MIDI messages are **Voice Channel messages**. Voice Channel messages convey information about whether to turn a note on or off on a particular channel, what instrument sound to change to, and so on.

Voice Channel MIDI messages consist of two or three bytes as shown in Figure 5.6.6.3 (Status byte followed by one or two Data bytes). For the serial hardware interface, each byte is surrounded by a start bit and a stop bit, making each packet 10 bits long. Within a MIDI software system data is 8-bit bytes. The first byte, called the **Status byte**, takes on values ranging from 0x80 to 0xFF in hexadecimal or 128 to 255 in decimal - most significant bit (MSB) is '1'. The **Data bytes**, take on values in the range 0x00 to 0x7F or 0 to 127 - most significant bit of each byte is a '0'.

The transmission bit rate of the hardware interface in the MIDI standard is 31,250 bits per second. Therefore, one start bit, eight data bits, and one stop bit result in a maximum transmission rate of 3125 bytes per second.

MIDI uses the fact that the Status byte is in a different range from the Data bytes. If MSB = 1, the byte is a "Status" byte. If MSB = 0, the byte is a "Data" byte. The first four bits of a Status byte are the code for the command, and the last four bits the channel to which the command applies (e.g. 0000_2 is Channel 1, 1111_2 is Channel 16).

For example, when a key is pressed, the keyboard creates a "Note On" (Status byte = 0x91, 145_{10}, 10010001_2) message for Channel 2 consisting of three bytes, e.g. 145 45 100. The first four bits of the Status byte (1001_2) tell MIDI that the message is a Note On command, while the last four bits tell MIDI what MIDI channel the message is for (0001_2= MIDI Channel 2).

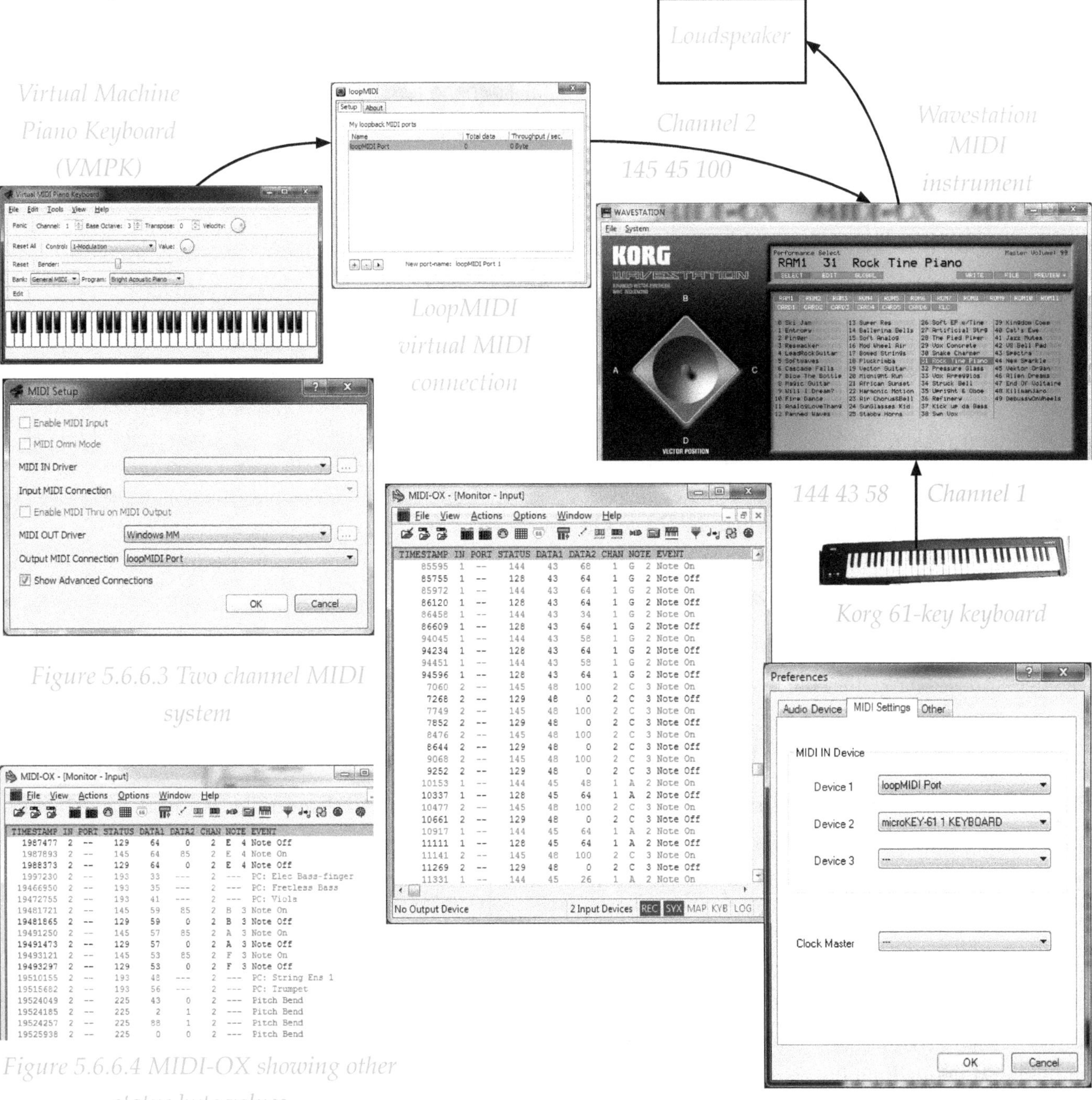

Figure 5.6.6.3 Two channel MIDI system

Figure 5.6.6.4 MIDI-OX showing other status byte values

The second byte, the nore number 60, selects the frequency used by the receiving instrument, in this example middle C (261.63 Hz). The third byte, 85, specifies how fast the key was pressed (velocity).

Velocity is a number that is used mainly to describe the volume (gain) of a MIDI note (higher velocity = greater volume or loudness) because it refers to how hard a key was pressed. The harder a key is pressed the greater will be the volume or loudness but the mapping is performed by the receiving instrument.

Information

VMPK:

Information on VMPK can be viewed at http://vmpk.sourceforge.net/.

It can be downloaded from http://vmpk.sourceforge.net/#Download

Information

MIDI-OX:

http://www.midiox.com/

To generate messages that use different velocities requires a MIDI keyboard. Computer keyboards are not velocity sensitive. Using a computer's keys to play notes into a software synthesiser will generate note messages that all have the same velocity.

When a key is released the keyboard creates another MIDI message, a "Note Off" message, e.g. 129 60 85. The first byte, 129, is the Status byte - the first four bits of the Status byte (1000_2) correspond to "Note Off", the second four bits (0001_2) to the channel, i.e. Channel 2 (0000 is Channel 1). The second byte is the key, 60 (middle C) in this example, and the third byte is the velocity which indicates how quickly the key was released. The MIDI instrument can use the velocity value of 85 to know how quickly it should dampen the note.

Information

LoopMIDI:

Information on LoopMIDI can be viewed at http://www.tobias-erichsen.de/software/loopmidi.html where it can also be downloaded.

Figure 5.6.6.3 shows an on screen piano keyboard (VMPK) connected via a virtual MIDI connection (LoopMIDI) to a running copy of the Wavestation emulator. A Korg 61-key keyboard is connected via USB to the computer and Wavestation emulator. The output from Wavestation goes to a loudspeaker. The input channels 1 & 2 are monitored by a piece of software called MIDI-OX.

Information

Korg Wavestation:

Information on the Korg Wavestation is available at http://www.korg.com/us/products/software/korg_legacy_collection/. It is not free software. MULAB is an alternative that is free - http://www.mutools.com/mulab-downloads.html

In *Figure 5.6.6.3* MIDI-OX shows that the "Note On" and "Note Off" Status bytes for Channel 1 have codes 144 and 128, respectively, whilst for Channel 2, these are 145 and 129, respectively. Wavestation uses the Channel values to route the messages on each Channel to different voices.

Messages can also have other purposes, e.g. to change the instrument sound. *Figure 5.6.6.4* shows messages that do this, e.g. 193 41 which is a two-byte code to change the MIDI instrument for Channel 2 (code 193 - $1100\ 0001_2$, 1100_2 is the change code and 0001_2 is the Channel) to a viola (code 41). Such messages are control messages.

Pitch Bend (control to vary pitch) is another type of control message that a MIDI controller can send, e.g. 225 43 0 (*Figure 5.6.6.4*), causes pitch bend in a Channel 2 note. For Channel 1 the same control message would use a leading byte with value 224 ($1110\ 0000_2$). There are many more ways to control the playing of a note and each has a corresponding control code.

The playing of multiple notes "together" events in MIDI are sent as a string of serial commands so, for example, a 2-note chord will be transmitted as two separate messages, *Status(Note On, Ch 1) key1-velocity Status(Note On, Ch 1) key2-velocity* unless the synthesiser supports Running Status. In this case, a single Status byte's action is allowed to persist for an unlimited number of Data byte pairs which follow.

```
While True
  Do
    Wait for message
    Process message
```

Figure 5.6.6.5 Event handler

MIDI messages

A MIDI message is the means by which an event in one system, e.g. key pressed on a keyboard, is communicated or transported to another to produce an event in the receiving system, e.g. a synthesiser plays a note.

Keyboard-event → MIDI message → synthesiser event.

Information

Chuck download:

http://chuck.cs.princeton.edu/release/

For example, the "Note On" message sent by a MIDI controller to a MIDI instrument causes an event to take place, i.e. the synthesiser plays the note specified in the message by note number. The Virtual MIDI Piano Keyboard shown in Figure 5.6.6.3 is a MIDI events generator and receiver. Event-driven systems rely upon a piece of software called an event handler which consists of a non-terminating loop that "sleeps" when there are no messages to process, i.e. is suspended - Figure 5.6.6.5 - and springs into action when there is (in Chuck the loop takes the form of a "polling loop").

Extension material

Chuck is an open-source and freely available programming language for real-time sound synthesis and music creation. Figure 5.6.6.6 shows an event handler written in Chuck.

```
MidiIn midiIn; //create an event object
0 => int port; // select MIDI port 0
if( !midiIn.open(port) ) // if MIDI port 0 not open exit
  {
    <<< "Error: MIDI port did not open on port: ", port >>>;
    me.exit();
  }
MidiMsg msg; // makes object to hold next MIDI message
Wurley piano => dac; // select Wurley piano to play with MIDI controller
while( true ) // loop forever
{
  midiIn => now; // wait on MIDI event, shred suspended but time advances
  while( midiIn.recv(msg) )
  {
    if (msg.data1 == 144) //check that status byte = 144 which is Note On Channel 1
    {
      Std.mtof(msg.data2) => piano.freq; //convert MIDI no to corresp. frequency
      msg.data3/127.0 => piano.gain; //set piano gain (data3 in range 0 to 127)
      1 => piano.noteOn; //trigger note on
    }
    else //status byte not equal to 144 so switch note off
    {
      1 => piano.noteOff; //trigger note off
    }
  }
}
```

Figure 5.6.6.6 Event handler written in Chuck programming language

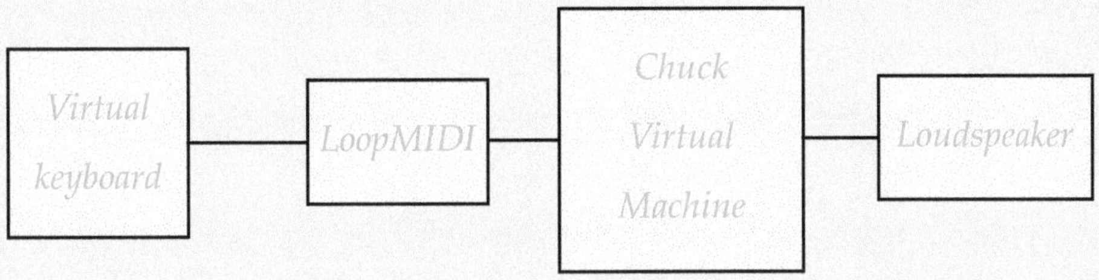

Figure 5.6.6.7 Playing music via an executing Chuck event handling program

Figure 5.6.6.7 shows the use of VMPK virtual piano connected via LoopMIDI to the running Chuck event handler shown in Figure 5.6.6.6. The output of the Chuck program is sent to a loudspeaker connected to the computer.

Advantages of using MIDI files for representing music

MIDI consists of a series of event messages that instruct a MIDI controlled instrument how to play music. These messages can be stored in a file before being read from the file and transmitted serially byte by byte to a MIDI-controlled instrument.

This has four main advantages over audio data produced from analogue sounds by sampling thousands of times per second and recording the digitised samples (sounds) in, for example, a .wav file.

- compact compared to sampled audio data. With MIDI, an entire song can be stored within a few hundred MIDI messages saving on memory whilst the equivalent sampled audio data would occupy many more bytes, possibly millions
- easy to modify/manipulate notes, e.g. change pitch, duration, and other parameters without having to record the sounds again which would be the case with sampled audio data recordings
- easy to change instruments - MIDI only describes which notes to play, these notes can be sent to any instrument to change the overall sound of the composition whilst with sampled audio data the sampling and recording process would have to be repeated
- it offers a simple means to compose and notate algorithmically which sampled audio does not. MIDI data is mostly a glorified note list, and such lists can easily be generated by code, and translated as needed into MIDI, whether for live output or via a MIDI file.

Questions

1. What is MIDI?
2. "MIDI itself does not make sound". Explain this statement.
3. The following MIDI message consisting of three bytes is generated when a key is pressed on a MIDI keyboard: 144 60 64
   Explain the purpose of each of three bytes.
4. Note On is one example of a MIDI message. Give **three** other examples, each must be a different type.
5. Explain the statements "A MIDI keyboard is an events generator" and "MIDI messages are associated with events". What is the fundamental structure of event-handling software such as that found running in a MIDI instrument?
6. State **three** main advantages of MIDI file representation of music over audio data file representation, e.g. .wav file

In this chapter you have covered:

- The purpose of MIDI - to instruct via messages a MIDI controlled instrument how to make sound, e.g. Note On, Note Off, pitch, duration of note, loudness
- The use of event messages in MIDI - MIDI controller sends messages to a MIDI controlled instrument to turn notes on and off, etc. These are events that a MIDI controlled instrument responds to. It waits in a loop for messages and then acts on these received messages accordingly
- The advantages of using MIDI files for representing music - compact, easy to modify/manipulate and change instruments compared with sampled audio data stored in, e.g., .wav files

6 Representing images, sound and other data

Learning objectives:

- *Know why images and sound files are often compressed and that other files, such as text files, can also be compressed*
- *Understand the differences between lossless and lossy compression and explain the advantages and disadvantages of each*
- *Explain the principles behind the following techniques for lossless compression:*
  - *run length encoding (RLE)*
  - *dictionary-based methods*

Key principle

Compression:
Data can be compressed because its original representation is not the shortest possible. The original data has redundancies and compressing the data reduces or eliminates these redundancies.
Non-random data is non-random because it has structure in the form of regular patterns. It is this structure that is the cause of redundancy in the data. Random data has no structure and therefore has no redundancy. Therefore, random data cannot be compressed.

5.6.7 Data compression

Why are images, sound files and other files compressed?

There are two main reasons why files are compressed:

- To reduce the amount of storage space required to store the data
- To reduce the time taken to transmit the data because fewer bytes need to be transmitted.

Essentially, the purpose of data compression is to squeeze the data into a smaller number of bytes than the data would occupy if uncompressed.

For example, text may be compressed by replacing each common character/letter combination with a single byte-coded integer number from Table 5.6.7.1.

Integer Code	Character Combination
1	'TH'
2	'BL'
3	'CK'
4	'AT'
5	'ON'

Table 5.6.7.1 Codes for common character combinations

Uncompressed text = 'THE BLACK CAT SAT ON A MAT'

Compressed text = '1E 2A3 C4 S4 5 A M4.'
If each character in the uncompressed text is coded in one byte (including spaces and full stop) then this text requires 27 bytes of storage. For the compressed text the storage requirement is just 20 bytes, a saving of seven bytes. This represents a 26% saving, approximately.
Not every file can be compressed significantly, in fact most files cannot.

The redundancies in data depend on the type of data (text, images, audio, etc) which is why different compression methods have been developed. Each works best with a particular data type.

Questions

1. What does it mean to compress data?
2. Why is it possible to compress data that has structure without losing information?
3. Give two reasons why files are compressed.
4. Can random data be compressed?
5. Why is it necessary to have different compression methods?

Key principle

Lossless and lossy compression:
Data is how information is represented.
It is possible using compression to alter the representation without losing information - this is called **lossless compression.**
It is also possible using compression to alter the representation and lose information - this is called **lossy compression.**

Key concept

Lossless compression and redundancy:
In general, information can be compressed if it is redundant. Lossless compression is possible when information is redundant.

Key concept

Lossy compression and irrelevancy:
Even when no redundancy exists it is still possible to compress by removing irrelevant information, e.g. removing image features to which the eye is not sensitive.

What are the differences between lossless and lossy compression?

Lossless compression

In lossless compression, the compression algorithm does not remove information from the original uncompressed data only redundancies. This allows the original uncompressed data to be restored by reversing the process. Lossless compression is used for text because it must be compressed without any loss of information. Imagine uncompressing an essay that you wrote for an assignment and finding that it looked nothing like the original that you spent hours constructing.

Lossy compression

In lossy compression, the compression algorithm may remove information which is irrelevant from the original uncompressed data. For example, in audio data, harmonics to which the human ear is not sensitive may be removed because they are not important to the listener. However, this means that the original uncompressed data cannot be fully restored when the reverse process is carried out. This does not matter for most images, video and audio data because these can tolerate much loss of data when compressed and later decompressed. Some exceptions are text files, executable files, and medical X-ray images where artefacts introduced into lossy compressed images could matter.

Advantages and disadvantages of lossless and lossy compression

Better compression ratios can be achieved with lossy compression than with lossless compression. Compression ratio is the size of the compressed file as a fraction of the uncompressed file, e.g. 50% expressed as a percentage.

This means that data compressed with a lossy compression method will occupy less storage space than with a lossless compression method. The time taken to transmit the data will also be less, e.g loading a file from disk.

However, a disadvantage with lossy compression is that the lost data are not retrievable. The compressed data will have very limited potential for adjustments or changes and every time the compressed data is uncompressed, edited, compressed again and saved, more data is lost.

With lossless compression the original uncompressed data is always recoverable.

Online high-quality image retailers often display their images in low quality form, i.e. they use a lossy, compressed version of high compression ratio, so potential customers can view what is on offer before purchasing. This protects against theft of data as it prevents customers from accessing and downloading a higher-quality version. It is the ability of lossy compression methods to allow the compression ratio to be varied from low to high that supports this way of marketing images. Alternative, an uncompressed or lossless version can be made available to customers on receipt of payment.

Questions

6 What is meant by lossless compression?

7 What is meant by lossy compression?

8 State **one** advantage that lossy compression has over lossless compression.

9 State **one** advantage that lossless compression has over lossy compression.

10 For each of lossless and lossy compression, give **one** example where it is used and why.

Principles of lossless compression

Run length encoding (RLE)

In run length encoding a run of contiguous bytes all with the same value can be condensed into two bytes, one byte that stores the count or run length and a second byte that stores the value in the run. These two bytes are called an RLE packet. *Figure 5.6.7.1* shows run length encoding applied to a run of six contiguous bytes each of value 128.

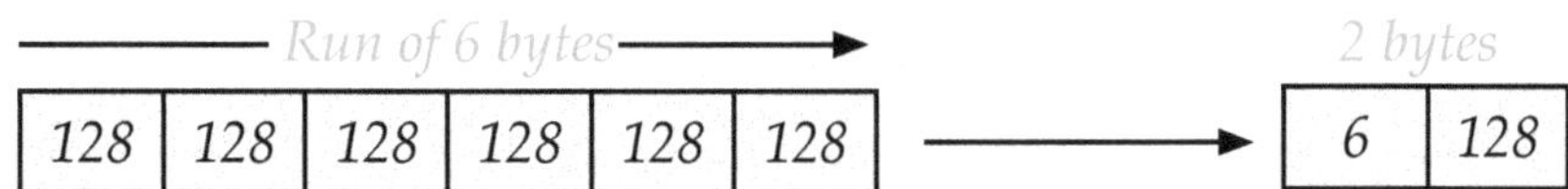

Figure 5.6.7.1 Run length encoding compression of 6 bytes into 2 bytes

RLE can be used to compress greyscale images. Each run of pixels of the same intensity (gray level) is encoded as a pair (run length pixel value). It doesn't make sense to encode a run of one and so the raw value is used. The following example shows how RLE could be applied to a greyscale bitmap that encodes the gray level of each pixel in 8 bits and that starts with the sequence

15, 15, 15, 15, 15, 15, 15, 15, 46, 81, 123, 58, 98, 98, 98, 98, 7, 7, 7, 8, ...

Information

Contiguous:
Means next to each other or together in sequence.

The compressed sequence of bytes is

8, 15, 46, 81, 123, 58, 4, 98, 3, 7, 8, ...

where the red values indicate counts. The problem is to distinguish a byte containing a greyscale value (such as 15) from one containing a count (such as 8). There are several possible solutions.

In one solution, the 256 different greyscale values are reduced to 255 so that the 256th can be used as a flag to precede every byte containing a count. Suppose this flag value is 255 then the sequence above becomes

255, 8, 15, 46, 81, 123, 58, 255, 4, 98, 255, 3, 7, 8

RLE works well with images that contain large areas of the same colour e.g. black and white images which are mostly white, such as the page of a book. This is due to the large amount of contiguous bytes that are all the same colour.

However, an image with many colours and relatively few runs of the same colour such as a photograph containing a high degree of colour variation will not lend itself to compression using RLE so well.

The direction of scan can also affect the compression ratio. For example, an image that has lots of vertical lines will not compress well if it is scanned horizontally for same-pixel runs but will if scanned vertically. A good RLE image compressor should be able to scan a bitmap by rows, columns, or in a zig-zag pattern and be able to choose the scan output that produces the best compression ratio.

Questions

11 Explain the principles of run length encoding lossless compression.

12 The following numbers, restricted to the range 0..254, represent the intensities of a contiguous block of pixels in a greyscale bitmap

15, 112, 112, 112, 98, 76, 76, 15, 46, 46, 46, 46, 46, 19, 101, 6, ...

Using run length encoding, compress this block of pixels using 255 as the flag that prefixes an RLE packet.

13 Run length encoding works well, i.e. achieves a good compression ratio, with some images but not others. Why?

14 Why is run length coding normally not a good choice for text compression?

Dictionary-based methods

We compress naturally in everyday life when, for example, referring to months of the year by number, e.g. September by the number 9. Dictionary-based methods compress by using this technique. The dictionary is a kind of look-up table, e.g. entry 9 is September. Dictionary-based compression methods vary in how the dictionary is constructed and represented but they all use the principle of replacing substrings in a text, e.g. 'th' in 'the' with a codeword, e.g. 1, that identifies that substring in a dictionary or codebook - see *Table 5.6.7.1*. The substring is called a phrase. Codewords for the dictionary are chosen so that they need less space than the phrase that they replace, thus achieving compression. The process of compression is called encoding. The reverse process is called decoding. The compressor is an encoder and the decompressor is a decoder.

Key concept

Token:
A unit of data written on the compressed file. A token consists of two or more fields. In LZ78, the token consists of two fields, the first is a pointer to an entry in the dictionary and the second is the code of a symbol, e.g. "A".
A token is sometimes written surrounded by chevrons < and > e.g. <2, A>

If we have to use a dictionary containing a large number of entries then the overhead of storing or transmitting the dictionary is significant, and choosing which substrings to place in the dictionary to maximise compression is also difficult.The solution is to use an adaptive dictionary scheme based on methods developed by Jacob Ziv and Abraham Lempel in the 1970s.

In the 1978, Ziv and Lempel described a dictionary-based algorithm (LZ78) that encodes a phrase (substring) of n characters from the input in a codeword that points back to an earlier phrase in the input which it matches in all but the last character, e.g. the B in BA matches B at position 2 in the example shown in *Figure 5.6.7.2* so is encoded as the two-field token 2, A. The first field of the token is the pointer 2 and the second the code of the symbol, e.g. ASCII A.

The dictionary starts empty with the empty string at position 0 (not shown in Figure 5.6.7.2). As substrings or phrases are read and encoded, phrases are added to the dictionary at positions 1, 2, and so on. For the given input string, ABAABABAA, the first phrase consisting of the single character A is added at position 1, the next, B, at position 2.

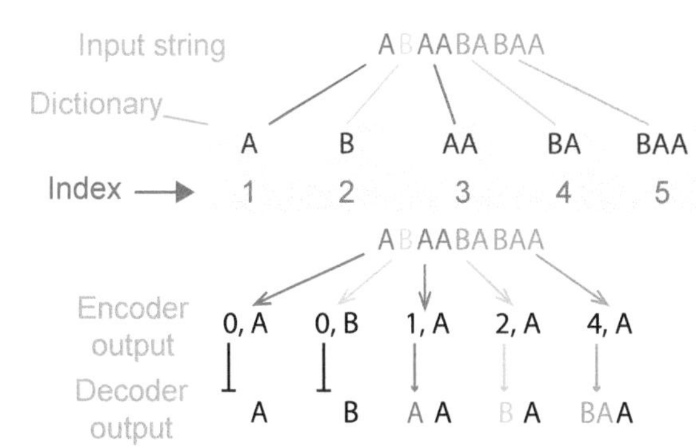

Figure 5.6.7.2 Lev-Zimpel 1978 (LZ78) compression simple example

This happens because when the first substring, A, is read from the input, no dictionary entry with the one-character string A is found, so A is added at the next available position in the dictionary which is 1, and the token 0, A is output. This token indicates the string *empty string* followed by A.

The next symbol read from the input is the character B but there is no entry yet in the dictionary for this phrase, and so B is added at position 2.

The third character read from the input, is A. This is matched with the A at position 1 in the dictionary. The goal of dictionary encoding is to find the longest dictionary substring that matches the input so the next symbol is read. This is another A. The dictionary is now searched for an entry containing the two-symbol string AA.

None is found, so the string AA is added to the next available position in the dictionary which is 3, and the token 1, A is output. This is the "compressed" version of the substring AA. We actually need to build up phrases in the dictionary with at least three characters before we can replace a phrase with something shorter. Figure 5.6.7.3 shows that this happens at entry 5 in the dictionary.

An efficient way of representing the dictionary is a tree-like structure called a trie as shown in Figure 5.6.7.3 which grows as more characters of the input are processed. All strings that start with the empty string (dictionary index 0) are added as children of the root which is labelled 0.

Information

Trie:

A tree data structure in which the string of characters represented by node n is the sequence of characters along the path from the root to n. Given a string, the trie consists of nodes for exactly those substrings that are prefixes of some other substring.
The word 'trie' comes from the middle of the word 'retrieval'.

In the example, all strings that begin with A are located in the subtree with node labelled 1 (index 1 in the dictionary).
All strings that begin with B are located in the subtree with root labelled 2.
All strings that begin with AA are located in subtree with root labelled 3 and so on.

Extension material

The example in Figure 5.6.7.2 is too trivial to achieve a reduction in the number of bytes (assuming each character is represented in one byte). We need a much longer input string to achieve compression.

The dictionary shown in Figure 5.6.7.2 and Figure 5.6.7.3 is constructed as the input string is parsed (processed). This dictionary is empty when the first character, A, of the input string is read. The characters about to be encoded are used to traverse the tree until the path is blocked, either because there is no onward path for the current character or because a leaf is reached.

The node at which the block occurs gives the index/phrase number to be used in the output, e.g. 1 in <1, A>.

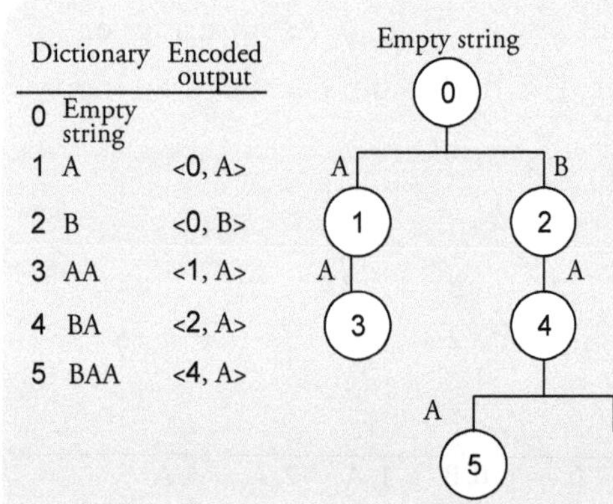

Dictionary	Encoded output
0 Empty string	
1 A	<0, A>
2 B	<0, B>
3 AA	<1, A>
4 BA	<2, A>
5 BAA	<4, A>

Figure 5.6.7.3 Data structure for LZ78 coding - numbers in nodes refer to dictionary index

A new node, e.g. 3, is added and joined by a new branch to the node at which the block occurred.

The new branch is labelled with the last character of current string, e.g. A.

For example, suppose we append BAB to the input string to form the new input ABAABABAA**BAB**. We need to add a new node 6 to *Figure 5.6.7.3* and connect it to node 4. The path from node 4 to node 6 is labelled BAB.

The encoder output is now the string of tokens

0, A 0, B 1, A 2, A 4, A 4, B

If we extend the input with BABB to form input ABAABABAABAB**BABB** the encoder output is now the string of tokens

0, A 0, B 1, A 2, A 4, A 4, B 6, B

The compressed form (ignoring commas which have been included to aid readability) occupies less space than the uncompressed form, 14 bytes compared with 16 bytes.

On decoding, the decoder reconstructs the tree data structure so it can decode the token string - *Figure 5.6.7.4*.

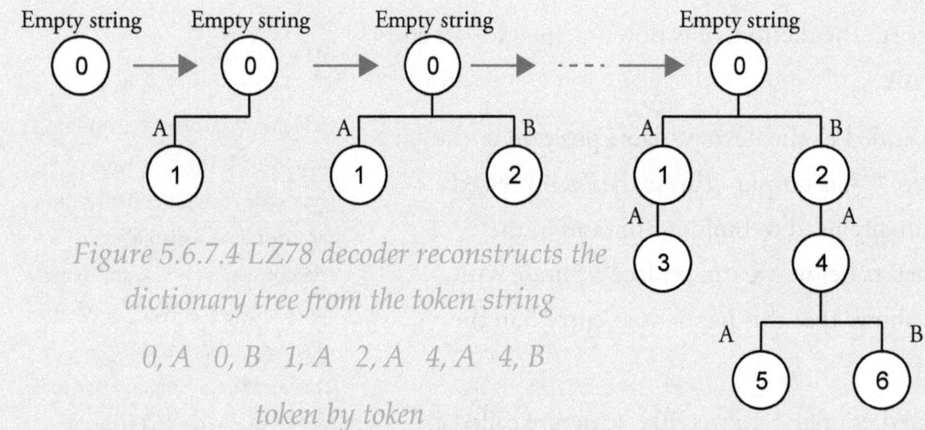

Figure 5.6.7.4 LZ78 decoder reconstructs the dictionary tree from the token string

0, A 0, B 1, A 2, A 4, A 4, B

token by token

Our examples have used an alphabet of two symbols A and B but what if the alphabet of symbols was A, B, C, D, E?

The tree data structure dictionary would then consist of a root for the empty string and then all strings that start with the empty string (strings for which the token pointer is zero) are added to the tree as children of the root.

Figure 5.6.7.5 shows the dictionary tree for the input string ABAAEACBDCBBDE.

Using the token structure <pointer, symbol> the output of the encoder for this input string is,

<0, A> <0, B> <1, A> <0, E> <0, A> <0, C> <2, D> <5, B> <6, E>

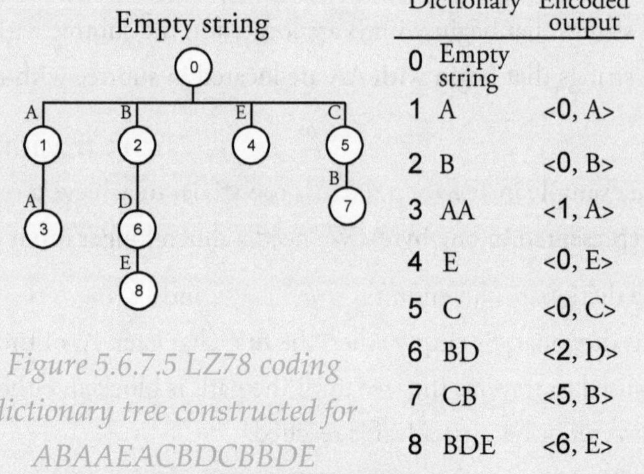

Dictionary	Encoded output
0 Empty string	
1 A	<0, A>
2 B	<0, B>
3 AA	<1, A>
4 E	<0, E>
5 C	<0, C>
6 BD	<2, D>
7 CB	<5, B>
8 BDE	<6, E>

Figure 5.6.7.5 LZ78 coding dictionary tree constructed for ABAAEACBDCBBDE

Questions

15 Explain the principles of dictionary-based lossless compression.

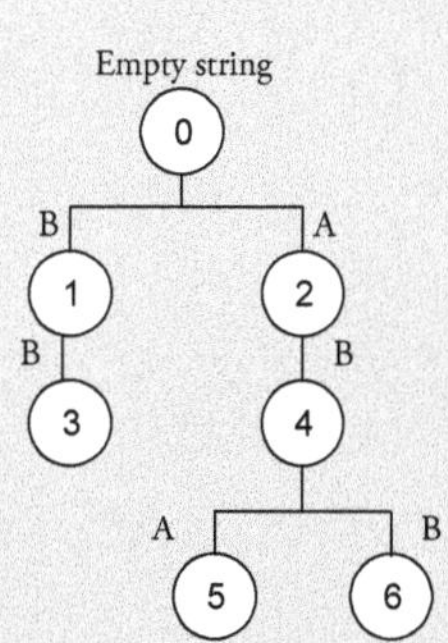

16 This tree data structure was created when encoding a string using a dictionary-based lossless compression technique.

(a) What is the dictionary?

(b) What was the input if the encoded output was

<0, B>, <0, A>, <1, B>, <2, B>, <0, B>, <1, B> <4, A> <4, B>

17 The output from a dictionary-based encoder is

<0, B> <1, B> <0, A> <1, B> <3, A> <1, D> <1, A> <2, B>

Draw the dictionary tree for this output and then decode the output.

In this chapter you have covered:

- Why images and sound files are often compressed and that other files, such as text files, can also be compressed
  - to reduce the amount of storage space required to store the data
  - to reduce the time taken to transmit the data
- The differences between lossless and lossy compression and the advantages and disadvantages of each
  - In lossless compression,
    - the compression algorithm does not remove information from the original uncompressed data only **redundancies**
    - the original uncompressed data is always recoverable.
  - In lossy compression,
    - the compression algorithm may remove information which is **irrelevant** from the original uncompressed data
    - the original uncompressed data cannot be fully restored when the reverse process is carried out but compression ratios are higher than for lossless compression.
    - limited potential for adjustments or changes and every time the compressed data is uncompressed, edited, compressed again and saved, more data is lost
- The principles behind the techniques for lossless compression:
  - run length encoding (RLE)
  - dictionary-based methods

Learning objectives:

- *Understand what is meant by encryption and be able to define it*
- *Be familiar with Caesar cipher and be able to apply it to encrypt a plaintext message and decrypt a ciphertext*
- *Be able to explain why it is easily cracked*
- *Be familiar with Vernam cipher or one-time pad and be able to apply it to encrypt a plaintext message and decrypt a ciphertext*
- *Explain why Vernam cipher is considered as a cipher with perfect security*
- *Compare Vernam cipher with ciphers that depend on computational security*

5.6.8 Encryption

What is cryptography?

Cryptography has typically concerned itself with methods of protecting information by transforming the contents of messages and documents into representations called "secret codes" that make the message and document contents incomprehensible except to those granted the means to reverse the process. A **cryptosystem**, or **cipher**, is a system or method for achieving this.

Figure 6.8.1 illustrates this with two pieces of similar-looking text, one an encrypted message and the other gobbledegook. The text on the left hand side is a message rendered incomprehensible by a process called **encryption**, i.e. turned into text that resembles random gibberish, whilst the text on the right hand side is random gibberish. The reverse of the encryption process is known as **decryption**. Decryption restores the message to a form that is comprehensible.

Encrypting a message is one way to keep the message's contents secret from others who are not authorised to view its contents. The encrypted messages look just like random gibberish as illustrated in *Figure 5.6.8.1*.

VWXGHQWV VKRXOG EH IDPLOLDU ZLWK WKH WHUPV FLSKHU SODLQWHAW DQG FLSKHUWHAW FDHVDU DQG YHUQDP FLSKHUV DUH DW RSSRVLWH HAWUHPHV RQH RIIHUV SHUIHFW VHFUHFB WKH RWKHU GRHVQW	LUBD YEAQJFF TEW PBDNJKFD FDSFD ND JQHD JBDCJBC EQBVAX VSS MCVN VAJGOTH HGVCCB HSXGWEFR GVCBC BCB BC W APQV VXVBBSCX YREGEVD NHEPHJVBBSP NDJ BGBWRSE SFDHJ GDHJBD MJOVQZXGT VBSH HBSV

Figure 5.6.8.1 A secret message and random gibberish

A **cryptographer** is someone who uses and studies secret codes (encrypted messages). On the other hand, someone who analyses other peoples' secret codes in order to discover the secret message is a **cryptanalyst**. Cryptanalysts are also known as **code breakers**. The most famous of code breakers is Alan Turing who during the Second World War was a key member of the team which broke the German's Enigma machine coded messages daily during World War 2, revealing important information that aided the war effort.

What is encryption?

Encryption is the process of obtaining ciphertext from plaintext. Before it is encrypted, the understandable (English) text is normally referred to as **plaintext** and after encryption it is referred to as **ciphertext**. The left hand side of *Figure 5.6.8.1* is an example of ciphertext.

The encryption process requires two inputs: the **plaintext** and the **key**.

The **decryption** process also requires two inputs, the **ciphertext** and the **key**, in order to produce as output the plaintext equivalent of the ciphertext.

The processes of encryption and decryption are called the **cryptosystem** or **cipher**. Thus a cryptosystem is a set of rules for converting between plaintext and ciphertext.

> **Key concept**
>
> **Encryption:**
> Encryption is the process of obtaining ciphertext from plaintext.

> **Key concept**
>
> **Decryption:**
> Decryption is the process of obtaining plaintext from ciphertext.

> **Key concept**
>
> **Cipher:**
> The processes of encryption and decryption are called the cryptosystem or cipher.

Codes versus ciphers

Common parlance and the media apply the term *code* to the practice and science of transforming messages in order to protect a secret when in fact the correct term is **cipher**.

Morse code and ASCII are examples of codes.

Morse code is a system which was designed to allow communication across a telegraph link by translating English into electrical pulse codes in a process called encoding and electrical pulse codes into English in a process called decoding. Unlike a cipher system, codes are intentionally understandable and publicly available so cannot be used to protect a secret.

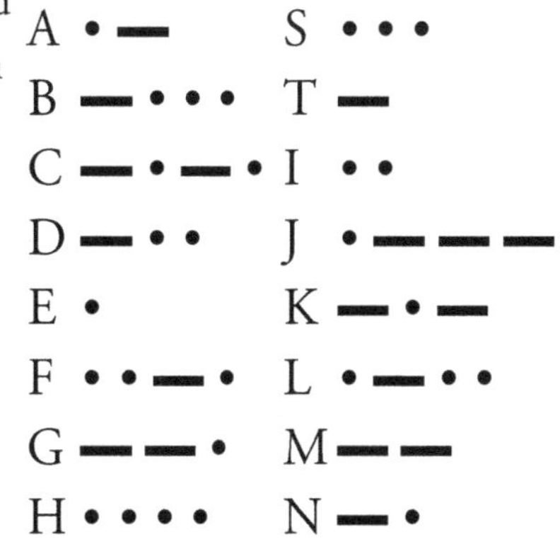

Figure 5.6.8.2 Sample of Morse code

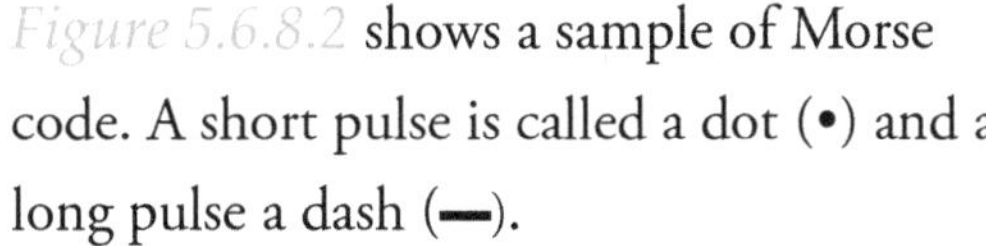

Figure 5.6.8.2 shows a sample of Morse code. A short pulse is called a dot (•) and a long pulse a dash (—).

> **Key point**
>
> Encoding and decoding are processes that are applied using coding systems that are publicly available and open, e.g. ASCII, whereas encrypting and decrypting are processes in a cipher system which is by definition closed to all but the participants using it to exchange secret or private messages or information.

Caeser cipher

The ciphertext (secret message) shown in *Figure 5.6.8.1* was produced using a cipher called the **Caesar cipher**, so named because it is believed that it was first used by Julius Caesar two thousand years ago. A writer at the time, Suetonius, wrote that Julius Caesar's cryptosystem replaced the plaintext letter **A** by the letter **D**, **B** by **E** and so on. The last three letters of the alphabet were replaced, respectively, by the first three letters of the alphabet. The Caesar cipher is a type of cipher called a **shift cipher** because the plaintext letters are shifted to produce the ciphertext.

> **Key concept**
>
> **Caesar cipher:**
> The Caesar cipher is a shift cipher which shifts plaintext letters by an amount called the key to produce ciphertext.

The easiest way of visualising this is to use something called a **cipher wheel** or disk to convert plaintext to ciphertext. The wheel consists of an inner wheel of letters + numbers and an outer wheel of letters as shown in *Figure 5.6.8.3*.

The outer wheel in *Figure 5.6.8.3* is set to map the plaintext letter to its equivalent ciphertext letter, e.g. letter **A** maps to letter **D** for the current setting. The encryption key is the number on the inner wheel corresponding to the letter **A** on the outer wheel. For the current wheel setting it is the number **3**. The dot under the letter **A** in the outer wheel is to remind the user that the encryption key is the corresponding number on the inner wheel.

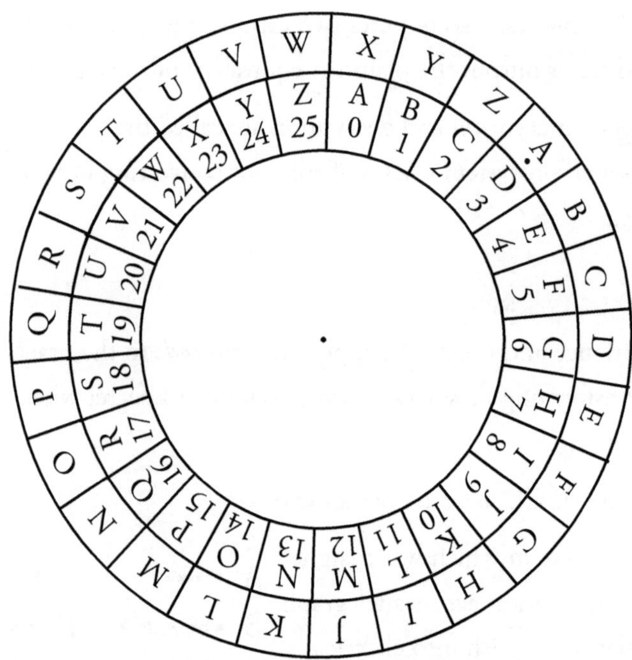

Figure 5.6.8.3 Cipher wheel showing inner and outer wheels

You can make your own cipher wheel by downloading copies of the inner and outer wheels from www.educational-computing.co.uk/cipherwheels and cutting out and pinning these shapes with a brad fastener or you can try an online version at https://www.khanacademy.org/computing/computer-science/cryptography/ciphers/a/ciphers-vs-codes.

How to encrypt with the cipher wheel

First write down the plaintext form of the message to be encrypted across the page, as shown below. Set the cipher wheel for the given key, let's say 3. For each letter of the message find the corresponding letter on the outer cipher wheel then read off the corresponding letter from the inner wheel. Write this below the plaintext letter as shown below.

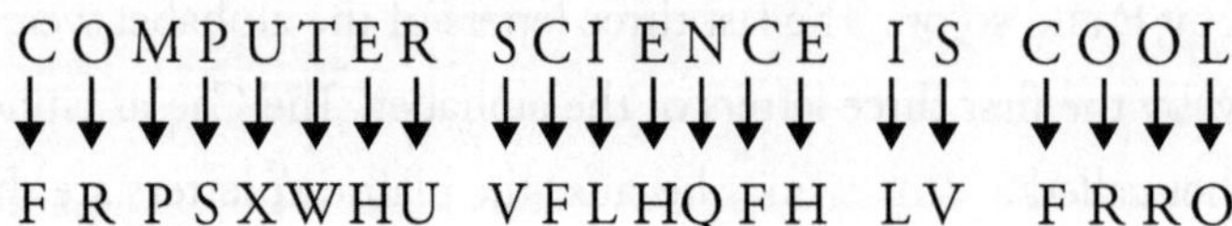

Decrypting with the cipher wheel

To decrypt ciphertext, first write it down as shown below. Set the cipher wheel to the key used to encrypt the plaintext. For each letter of the ciphertext, find the corresponding letter on the inner cipher wheel then read off the corresponding letter from the outer wheel. Write this below the ciphertext letter as shown below. When finished you have the decrypted message.

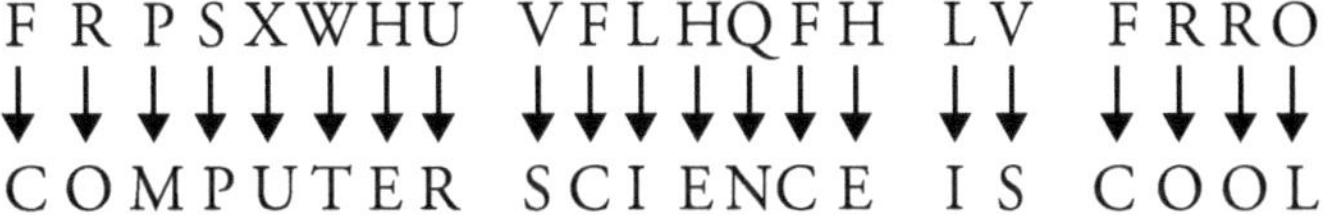

Questions

1. Convert the following plaintext message using the Caesar cipher and a key of 7:

   THE SUN HAS GOT ITS HAT ON

2. Decrypt the following ciphertext which was produced using Caeser's cipher and a key of 5:

   MNU MNU MTTWFD

3. Decrypt the ciphertext shown in the left hand side of Figure 5.6.8.1 which was produced by Caesar cipher using a key of 3.

   Online exercises for encryption and decryption using the Caesar cipher are available at
   https://www.khanacademy.org/computing/computer-science/cryptography/ciphers/e/

Mathematical description

To describe the Caesar cipher mathematically, we represent each letter of the alphabet by an integer between 0 and 25:

0 for A, 1 for B, …, 25 for Z as shown in Figure 6.8.4.

A	B	C	D	E	F	G	H	I	J	K	L	M	N	O	P	Q	R	S	T	U	V	W	X	Y	Z
0	1	2	3	4	5	6	7	8	9	10	11	12	13	14	15	16	17	18	19	20	21	22	23	24	25

Figure 5.6.8.4 alphabet and integer equivalent representation

To encrypt the plaintext COMPUTER SCIENCE IS COOL with key 8, first convert the plaintext letters to their integer equivalent using Figure 5.6.8.4. Next add the key 8 to each integer. If the resulting integer is 26 or greater then subtract 26 to convert 26 to 0, 27 to 1, 28 to 2, and so on, otherwise leave alone. Finally, convert each resulting integer to its equivalent letter using Figure 5.6.8.4 again. The steps of the process are shown in Figure 5.6.8.5.

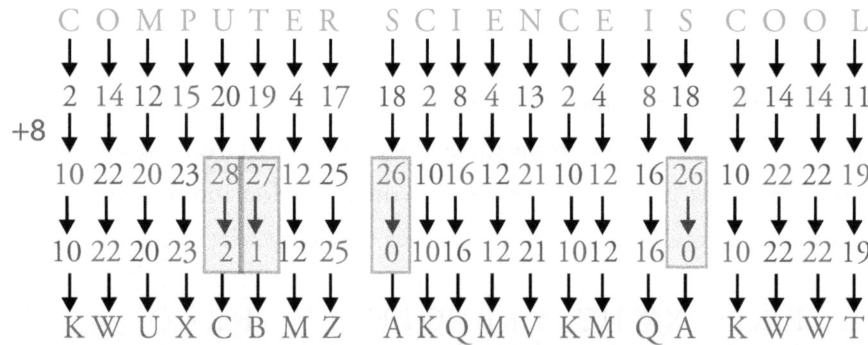

Figure 5.6.8.5 Encrypting with key 8

To decrypt the ciphertext KWUXCBMZ AHQMVKM QA KWWT with key 8, first convert the plaintext letters to their integer equivalent using *Figure 5.6.8.4*. Next subtract the key 8 from each integer. If the resulting integer is less than 0 then add 26 to convert −1 to 25, −2 to 24, −3 to 23, and so on. Finally convert each integer to its equivalent letter using *Figure 5.6.8.4* again. The steps of the process are shown in *Figure 5.6.8.6*.

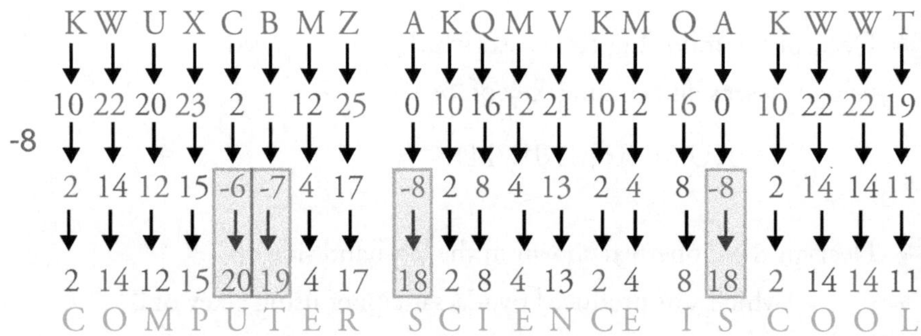

Figure 5.6.8.6 Decrypting with key 8

The number circle

The number circle shown in *Figure 5.6.8.7* is useful for visualising addition and subtraction performed in the Caesar cipher.

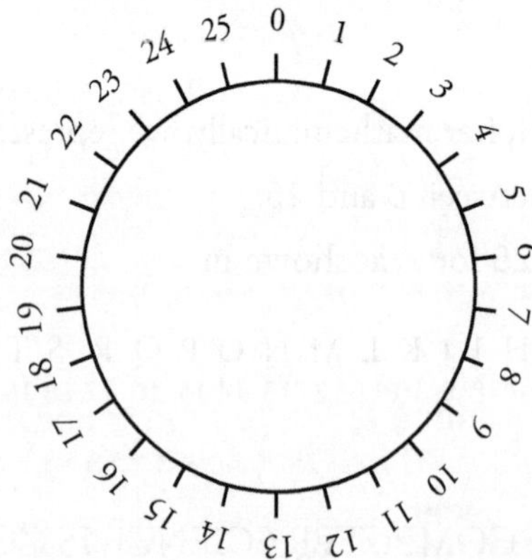

Figure 5.6.8.7 Number circle

If we add 6 to 22 then we move to position 2 on the number wheel. If we subtract 6 from 2 then we end up at position 22 on the number wheel as shown in *Figure 5.6.8.8*.

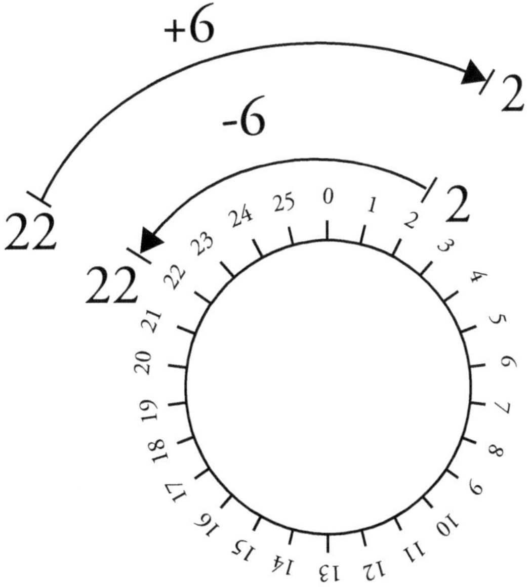

Figure 5.6.8.8 Number circle

Modular arithmetic

Addition using this number circle is called modulo 26 addition. Likewise subtraction using this number circle is called modulo 26 subtraction. In the world of modulo 26, there are exactly 26 numbers, {0, 1, 2, …, 23, 24, 25}. These are indicated on the number circle as 0 through 25. The number 26 is called the **modulus**. This particular arithmetic is called **modular arithmetic**.

Key concept

Modular arithmetic:
Addition using the number circle is called modulo *n* addition where *n* is the modulus. Likewise subtraction using the number circle is called modulo *n* subtraction.

Questions

4. Evaluate the following using modulo 26 addition:

   (a) 13 + 13 (b) 20 + 16 (c) 19 + 26 (d) 10 + 26

5. Evaluate the following using modulo 26 subtraction:

   (a) 6 – 12 (b) 11 – 20 (c) 13 – 26 (d) 18 – 26

6. (a) How many numbers are there in the world of modulo 12 arithmetic?

   (b) What are the numbers in modulo 12 arithmetic?

It is conventional to indicate modulo arithmetic as follows

$$13 + 13 = 0 \text{ (mod 26)}$$

Where (mod 26) indicates that modulo 26 arithmetic has been used.

Modular arithmetic in daily life

People use modular arithmetic in their daily lives often without realising that they are doing so. For example, consider the clock face shown in *Figure 6.8.9*, ignore the fact that 12 has been replaced by 0. Suppose it is eight o'clock, and you want to know what time it will be in 7 hours. You would use modulo 12 arithmetic: $8 + 7$ is 3 (mod 12).

Figure 5.6.8.9 Unconventional 12 hour clock

In the case of days of the week represented by numbers as shown in *Table 5.6.8.1* it is useful to use modulo 7 arithmetic.

Day	Number
Sunday	0
Monday	1
Tuesday	2
Wednesday	3
Thursday	4
Friday	5
Saturday	6

Table 5.6.8.1 Numbered days of the week

Suppose today is Wednesday.

What will the day of the week be in 6 days?

To answer this we add 6 to 3, the latter being the number for Wednesday, obtaining 9. But 9 modulo 7 is 2 (mod 7) which is Tuesday.

What day of the week will it be in 490 days?

To solve this, imagine travelling around the number circle for modulo 7. How many times does one travel around in 490 days, i.e. how many times does 7 go into 490? The answer is 70 times. This means we would arrive on a Wednesday, i.e. $3 + 490 = 3$ (mod 7).

Congruence

This last example illustrates that adding 7 has the same effect as adding 14, as adding 21 or adding 0 or subtracting 7 and so on. We call this congruence (remember congruent triangles from maths lessons, it is a similar idea).

Questions

7. Suppose today is Tuesday.
   (a) What day of the week will it be in 492 days?
   (b) What day of the week was it 210 days ago?

8. In dealing with compass bearings, the modulus to use is 360. Whole number bearings are chosen from the set
   {0, 1, 2, ..., 358, 359}.
   Suppose that you are headed due East, your bearing is 90 degrees. You turn right 130 degrees onto a bearing 220 degrees. You then turn right 150 degrees, what is your new bearing?

9. Suppose that you are headed due East, your bearing is 90 degrees. You turn left 130 degrees, what is your new bearing?

Key concept

Congruence:
Two integers are said to be congruent with respect to a given modulus if they differ by a multiple of that modulus. For example, if the modulus is 12 then 2, 14, 26, 38 are congruent.

Two integers are said to be **congruent** with respect to a given modulus if they differ by a multiple of that modulus. For example, if the modulus is 12 then 2, 14, 26, 36 are congruent. *Figure 5.6.8.10* shows some more congruence for modulus 12.

A statement that two expressions are congruent is called a **congruence**.

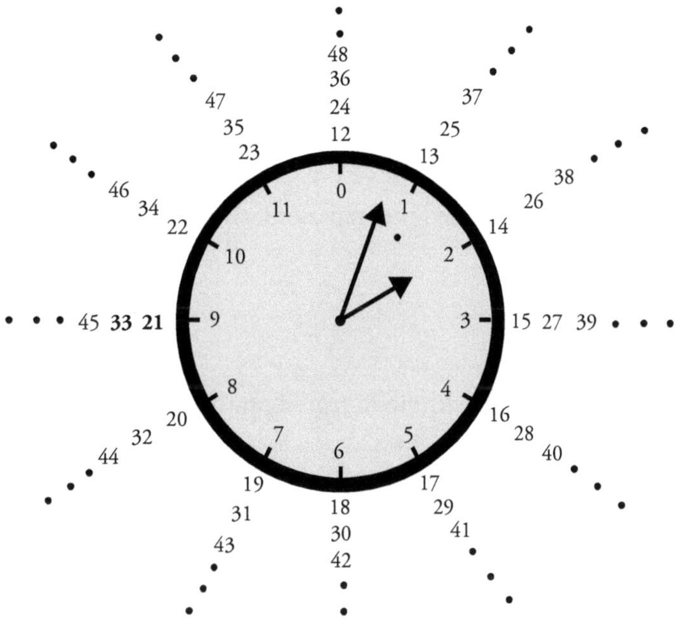

Figure 5.6.8.10 Unconventional 12 hour clock showing congruence

Congruence modulo 12

Two integers are congruent modulo 12 if they differ by a multiple of 12.

For example 5 is congruent to 17 (which is $5 + 12$) and to 29 (which is $5 + 2 \cdot 12$).

5 is also congruent to -7 (which is $5 + (-1) \cdot 12$).

The mathematical notation for writing a congruence is similar to the mathematical notation for writing an equation but where the equality symbol has two horizontal bars ("="), the congruence symbol has three ("≡").

For example, we write the congruence

$$5 \equiv 17 \pmod{12}$$

to state that 5 is congruent (modulo 12) to 17.

The notation requires that the modulus is specified in brackets together with the word "mod" short for "modulo".

Here are more modulo 12 examples. To verify that the numbers are indeed congruent check that the difference between them is a multiple of 12:

$$6 \equiv 42 \pmod{12}$$

$$-13 \equiv 11 \pmod{12}$$

$$-13 \equiv -1 \pmod{12}$$

$$-21 \equiv 3 \pmod{12}$$

$$12 \equiv 0 \pmod{12}$$

$$7 + 5 \equiv 12 \pmod{12}$$

Representative theorem

Every integer is congruent modulo m to exactly one of the integers

$$0, 1, 2, 3, \ldots, m - 1.$$

For example, modulo 7: every integer is congruent to exactly one of the integers 0, 1, 2, 3, 4, 5, 6.

The 0, 1, 2, 3, …, $m - 1$ are called the representatives.

Questions

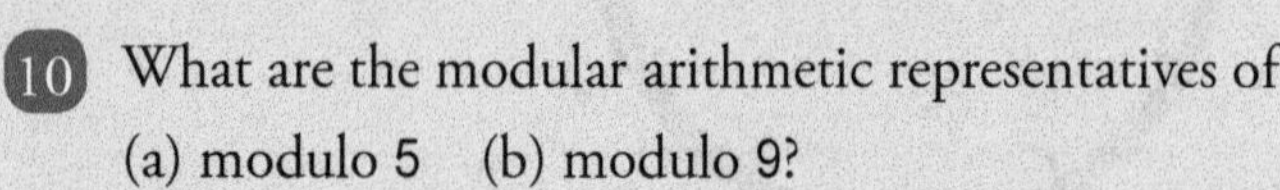

10 What are the modular arithmetic representatives of
(a) modulo 5 (b) modulo 9?

Key principle

Quotient and remainder theorem:
For every integer b and every positive integer m, there is exactly one integer q and exactly one integer r among 0, 1, 2, 3, …, m – 1 such that

$$b = q \bullet m + r$$

r is the remainder when b is divided by m.
q is the quotient.

The equation $b = q \bullet m + r$ shows that b and r differ by a multiple of m, which shows that b is **congruent** to r (mod m).

Quotient and remainder theorem

For every integer b and every positive integer m, there is exactly one integer q and exactly one integer r among 0, 1, 2, 3, …, m – 1 such that

$$b = q \bullet m + r$$

Example:

Let b = 23 and let m = 7.
Then the above equation is satisfied by q = 3 and r = 2
(That is, $23 = 3 \bullet 7 + 2$)

As this example suggests, r is the remainder when b is divided by m.

q is the quotient.

The remainder r is thus the value of (b mod m)'s representative.

The equation $b = q \bullet m + r$ shows that b and r differ by a multiple of m, which shows that b is **congruent** to r (mod m).

Questions

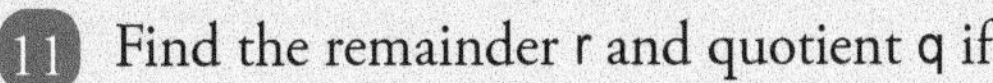

11 Find the remainder r and quotient q if
(a) b = 37 m = 12 (b) b = 38 m = 24 (c) b = 76 m = 60
(d) b = 576 m = 365

Representatives and negative integers

What is the remainder for –15 mod 7?

To answer this we must remember that the result must be a mod 7 representative, i.e. one of 0, 1, 2, 3, 4, 5, 6.

–15 divided by 7 is –2 with –1 left over.

The representative that is congruent to –1 is 6
(difference between 6 and –1 is 7).

Therefore –15 mod 7 = 6.

Questions

12 Find the remainder r and quotient q if
(a) b = –37 m = 12 (b) b = –38 m = 24 (c) b = –76 m = 60
(d) b = –576 m = 365

Programming Tasks

1 Write a program to encrypt a line of uppercase text using the Caesar cipher. Represent each character by a number between 0 and 26 (A ↦ 0, B ↦ 1, ..., Z ↦ 25, space ↦ 26).
Use only these characters. Allow a user to choose a key within the range 0...26.
Encrypt each character of the text using the equation

ciphertext_character = (plaintext_character + key) mod 27

2 Write a program to decrypt a line of text encrypted using the Caesar cipher. Assume that each character was represented by a number between 0 and 26 (A ↦ 0, B ↦ 1, ..., Z ↦ 25, space ↦ 26) and only these characters were used when producing the line of encrypted text. The user should enter a key in range 0...26.

Decrypt each character of the text using the equation

ciphertext_character = (plaintext_character − key) mod 27

Questions

13 What is it unnecessary to use a key range wider than 0..26 for the Caesar cipher in this case?

Breaking the Caesar cipher

Brute force approach

The Caesar cipher is easily broken by an attacker thus revealing the plaintext and the key used to produce the ciphertext. A brute-force search is sufficient. Assuming that the plaintext consisted of the 26 uppercase letters of the alphabet. A brute force search on the ciphertext consists of just trying all the possible keys except 0 on the ciphertext until the plaintext is discovered. It is assumed that key 0 would not have been used when encrypting the plaintext because it doesn't alter the plaintext.

For example, take a five letter name, choose a key between 1 and 25 and then, with this key, use the Caesar cipher to encrypt the name. If we choose ALICE for the name and 3 for the key then the ciphertext is DOLFH. *Table 5.6.8.2* shows the outcome of the brute force search from which it can be deduced that the key was 3 and the plaintext was ALICE.

Key	Plaintext	Key	Plaintext	Key	Plaintext
1	CNKEG	10	TEBVX	19	KVSMO
2	BMJDF	11	SDAUW	20	JURLN
3	ALICE	12	RCZTV	21	ITQKM
4	ZKHBD	13	QBYSU	22	HSPJL
5	YJGAC	14	PAXRT	23	GROIK
6	XIFZB	15	OZWQS	24	FQNHJ
7	WHEYA	16	NYVPR	25	EPMGI
8	VGDXZ	17	MXUOQ		
9	UFCWY	18	LWTNP		

Table 5.6.8.2 Brute force attack on ciphertext DOLFH

Task

1. Choose a four letter name and a key. Use the key and the Caesar cipher to encrypt the name. Now give the ciphertext to another student and ask them to use a brute force attack to discover the name and the key used.

Letter frequency attack

The Caesar cipher is also susceptible to letter frequency analysis. If an attacker knows that the plaintext was written in English then because the Caesar cipher applies the same shift to each plaintext letter, the frequencies of occurrence of the letters in the ciphertext match those in the plaintext shifted by the key. When the plaintext is sufficiently long or a series of ciphertexts are intercepted, a good guess is that the ciphertext(s) matches the relative frequency of letters common to a large number of English texts when shifted by the key.

Frequency analysis of a large number of English texts has revealed that each letter of the alphabet occurs with unequal likelihood as shown in *Figure 5.6.8.11*. The letter E occurs most frequently, 12.7% of the time on average, and so is roughly twice as likely on average to occur in a piece of text as the letter S which has relative frequency of approximately 6.3%.

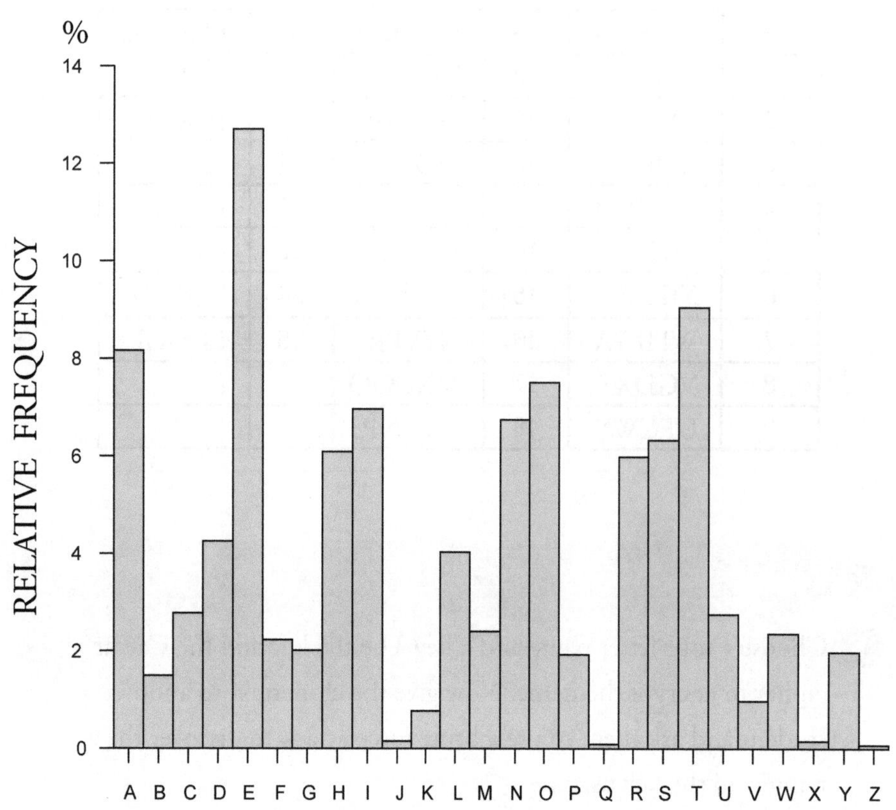

Figure 5.6.8.11 Relative frequency analysis for English

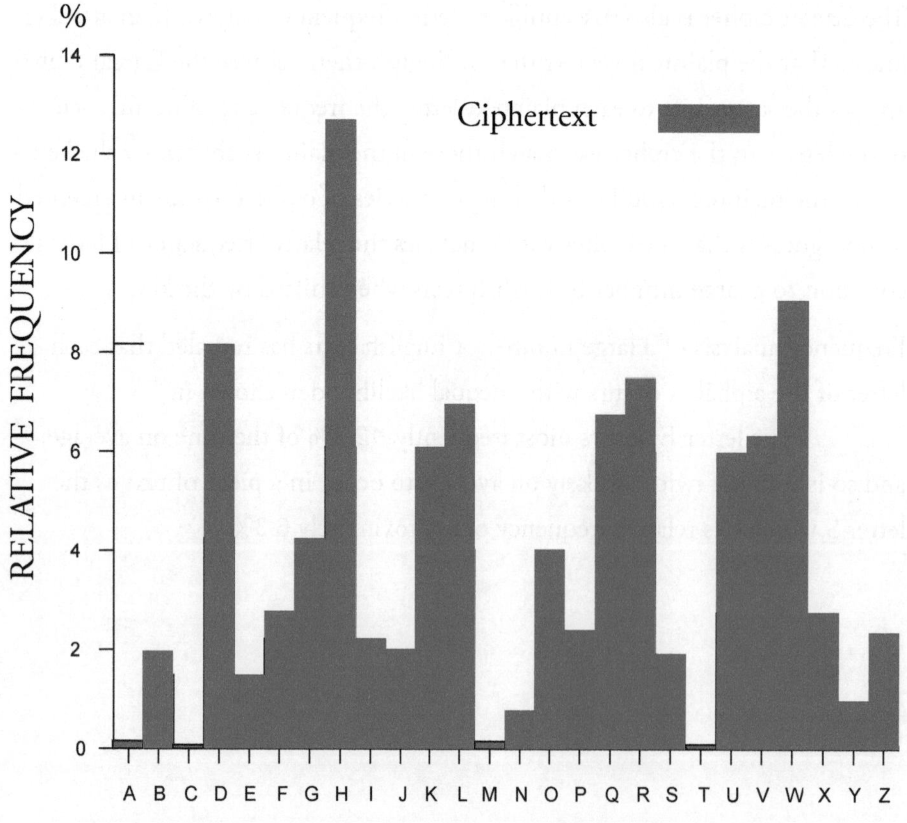

Figure 5.6.8.12 Ciphertext relative frequency analysis

Figure 5.6.8.12 shows what the relative frequency distribution would be if the Caesar cipher was applied with key 3 to plaintext with relative letter frequency distribution as shown in *Figure 5.6.8.11*. It is relatively easy to see that an E has been shifted to become an H, therefore the key must be 3. The ciphertext is said to leak information about the plaintext.

Task

2 Try the Caesar frequency analysis exercise at https://www.khanacademy.org/computing/computer-science/cryptography/ciphers/e/

Programming Task

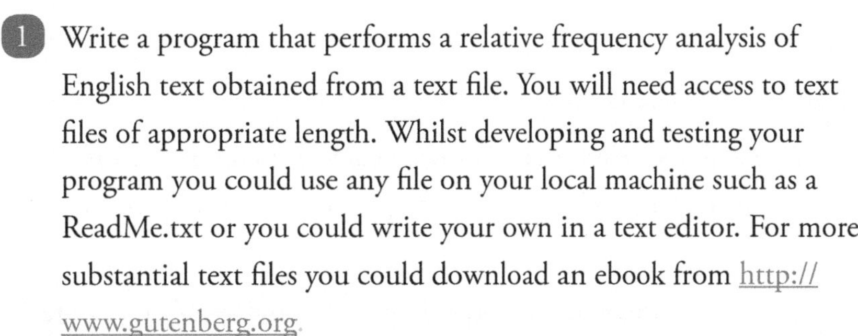

1 Write a program that performs a relative frequency analysis of English text obtained from a text file. You will need access to text files of appropriate length. Whilst developing and testing your program you could use any file on your local machine such as a ReadMe.txt or you could write your own in a text editor. For more substantial text files you could download an ebook from http://www.gutenberg.org.
The NLTK toolkit from www.nltk.org written for Python is a very powerful text processing resource that could be used for this and other work.

Key point

Caesar cipher weaknesses:

1. The number of possible keys is too small
2. The same shift is applied to each character making it easy to use relative letter frequency analysis.
3. The same shift is likely to be used for each message.

Caesar cipher weaknesses

Summarising, the Caesar cipher has three major weaknesses:

1. The number of possible keys is too small
2. The same shift is applied to each character making it easy to use relative letter frequency analysis.
3. The same shift is likely to be used for each message.

The solution:

4. Make the number of possible keys so large that it becomes infeasible to employ a brute force approach of trying all possible keys
5. Arrange for the occurrence of each letter/character in the ciphertext to be equally likely by applying a random shift to each.

One-time pad

One way of making the number of possible keys large is to choose a new key value for each letter/character of the plaintext message and a new set of key values for each new message. If key values are chosen randomly then the second bullet point above can also be satisfied.

For example, if the plaintext message is

CLOCK TOWER USUAL TIME TONIGHT J

then 32 key values are needed because there are 32 characters – 27 letters and 5 spaces in this message. We randomly choose a different combination of 32 key values for each new 32 character long message from the set of all possible permutations of 32 key values. Each key value can be one of 26 possible letters or a space. This is done 32 times therefore there are 27^{32} different key patterns to choose from at random.

Applying a random shift to each letter/character in the plaintext ensures that each ciphertext character is equally likely.

For our example, first convert each plaintext character to numeric form. The 26 letters of the alphabet are coded as 0...25, respectively and the space character as 26.

If we use p_i to refer to the numeric code for the ith character of the plaintext, and c_i for the numeric code of the corresponding letter in the ciphertext, then to obtain c_i from p_i and key k_i we use

$$c_i = (p_i + k_i) \bmod 27$$

To obtain the ciphertext character we convert c_i into its equivalent character.

Let's suppose the 32 key values, k_i where i is in {1...32}, chosen at random from the range {0...26} are

22 23 **8** 8 **3** 13 **14** 15 **24** 22 **5** 9 **8** 18 **25** 16 **10** 7 **21** 1 **2** 4 **23** 1 **12** 11 **4** 14 **4** 23 **15** 6

Call this sequence of keys the cipher key K. (To obtain these 32 keys you could use all the hearts and diamonds from a pack of cards and a joker because this gives 27 cards. Shuffle the pack then take the top card, write down its corresponding number: the joker is 0, hearts are 1...13, diamonds are 14...26 with Ace 1 or 14, Jack 11 or 24, etc, Put the card back and shuffle the pack again, repeat the process until you have 32 randomly chosen numbers.)

Questions

14 Why is it unnecessary for this cipher to choose numbers greater than 26?

Background

The use of a truly random key, as long as the plaintext, is an essential part of the one-time pad algorithm. The one-time pad algorithm itself is mathematically secure. Thus the codebreaker cannot retrieve the plaintext by examining the ciphertext. The best that the codebreaker can do is to try to retrieve the key. If the random values for the one-time key are not truly random but generated by a deterministic mechanism or algorithm then there is a possibility of predicting the key. Thus, selecting a good random number generator is the most important part of the system. To see one way of manually generating a truly random key using ten-sided dice visit http://users.telenet.be/d.rijmenants/en/onetimepad.htm

The plaintext codes p_i where i is in {1...32} are

2 11 **14** 2 **10** 26 **19** 14 **22** 4 **17** 26 **20** 18 **20** 0 **11** 26 **19** 8 **12** 4 **26** 19 **14** 13 **8** 6 **7** 19 **26** 9

The ciphertext codes [$c_i = (p_i + k_i) \bmod 27$ where i is in {1...32}]

are

24 22 **22** 10 **1** 12 **6** 2 **19** 26 **15** 7 **1** 9 **18** 16 **21** 6 **13** 9 **14** 8 **22** 20 **26** 24 **12** 20 **11** 15 **14** 15

The ciphertext is

YGWKLMGCT FGBJSQVGNJOIWU YMULPOP

The tendency of applying random shifts is to flatten the distribution. Analysis reveals that applying random shifts to a large number of plaintext messages leads to the following two powerful properties possessed by ciphertexts

1. The shifts do not fall into a repetitive pattern, e.g. E → H every time is avoided
2. The ciphertext distribution is flattened and has a uniform frequency distribution

Achieving a uniform frequency distribution as in Figure 5.6.8.13 will mean that there is no frequency differential and therefore no leak of information about the plaintext message that an attacker or eavesdropper could exploit to guess the plaintext.

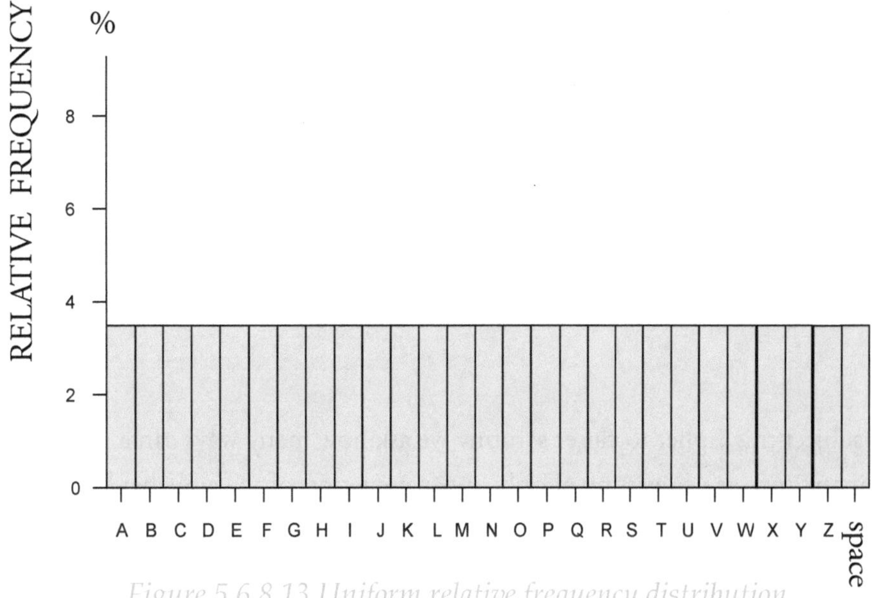

Figure 5.6.8.13 Uniform relative frequency distribution

Task

3 Watch the Khan Academy polyalphabetic video and try the tool to see how a non-uniform plaintext distribution can be flattened as described in this section.
https://www.khanacademy.org/computing/computer-science/cryptography/crypt/v/polyalphabetic-cipher

Questions

15 Suppose Alice and Bob communicate messages to each other which have been encrypted using the Caesar cipher and a previously agreed secret key. Now suppose that Eve intercepts the ciphertext and that she happens to know or suspect that Alice starts all her messages to Bob with the characters "DEAR BOB". The corresponding ciphertext is GHDUCERE. Alice and Bob make no secret of the fact that they use the Caesar cipher believing that keeping the key secret is sufficient to maintain the security of their messages. The encryption equation that Alice and Bob use is

ciphertext_character = (plaintext_character + key) mod 27

Explain how Eve using the plaintext and ciphertext could recover the secret key used by Alice and Bob.

16 Alice and Bob decide to use a new key for each character, generated randomly, and apply the stream of random keys using the Caesar cipher to future messages. Explain why this could offer greater security over the scheme described in Q15 even though Eve continues to intercept the ciphertext and Alice continues to start messages with "DEAR BOB".

To subject this cipher to closer scrutiny we ask how many ways can a particular plaintext message consisting of only uppercase letters of the alphabet be encrypted by a shift cipher which chooses key values randomly? Well consider that for the first character, there are 26 different possible key values, for the second character, 26 different possible values again and so on. If plaintext messages of length 32 characters are encrypted then a key will consist of 32 key values. The total number of keys of length 32 is therefore

$$26 \times 26 \times 26 \times \ldots\ldots \times 26 \times 26 = 26^{32} \approx 2 \times 10^{45}$$

Key principle

One-time pad:
Plain text of a message is 'mixed' with random text taken from a one-time pad resulting in cipher text which is truly random. The same one-time pad is used to 'unmix' the random text from the cipher text, which results in the original plain text.

One only has to guarantee that the one-time pad is safe, that it comprises truly random numbers, that there are only two copies of it, and that both copies are destroyed immediately after use to prevent it being used again (the one-time property), for it to be used to send a message safely without the risk of being deciphered by an attacker or eavesdropper.

Background

The "red phone" used in the 1980s for secure communication between the USA and the USSR was based on a one-time pad. The random key sequences or pads were delivered by courier.

The total number of possible ciphertexts corresponding to any particular 32 character plaintext message is thus 2×10^{45} one for each possible key consisting of 32 key values.

If each of these possible ciphertexts is written on a separate piece of paper then the entire stack would be

$$2 \times 10^{45} \times 5 \times 10^{-5} \text{ metres high} = 1 \times 10^{40} \text{ metres}$$

taking the thickness of a piece of paper to be 5×10^{-5} metres.

By comparison the Milky Way galaxy is estimated to be 9.5×10^{20} metres across. If the key values were generated randomly then each ciphertext will be equally likely.

The decryption cipher is

$$p_i = (c_i - k_i) \bmod 27$$

Likewise a particular ciphertext could have come from any one of 2×10^{45} possible plaintext messages. The chance of an attacker guessing which one correctly is therefore vanishingly small. It is impossible therefore for an attacker or eavesdropper to break this encryption scheme because the ciphertext yields no possible information about the plaintext (except its length).

This is the strongest possible method of encryption. It is known as the one-time pad because when first used the key was written on a sheet of paper or pad and used only once - *Figure 5.6.8.14*.

Summarising, the one-time pad method is based on the principle that the plain text of a message is 'mixed' with truly random text taken from a one-time pad. Because the resulting cipher text is still truly random it can safely be sent without the risk of being deciphered by an attacker or eavesdropper.

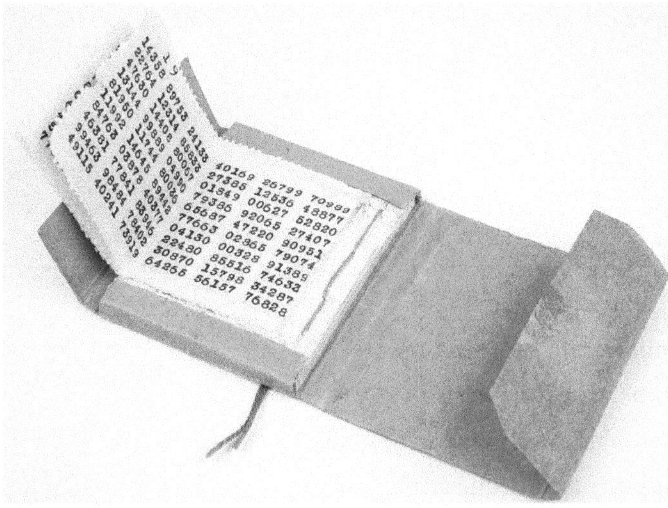

Figure 5.6.8.14 A one-time pad reproduced with kind permission of Paul Reuvers, Crypto Museum (www.cryptomuseum.com)

At the receiving end, the same one-time pad is used to 'unmix' the random text from the cipher text, which results in the original plain text. One only has to guarantee that the one-time pad is safe, that it comprises truly random numbers, that there are only two copies of it, and that both copies are destroyed immediately after use to prevent it being used again (the one-time property) on another plaintext message.

Task

4 Watch the Khan Academy one-time pad video https://www.khanacademy.org/computing/computer-science/cryptography/crypt/v/one-time-pad

5 The Venona project was a counter-intelligence program initiated by the United States Army Signal Intelligence Service (a forerunner of the National Security Agency) that lasted from 1943 to 1980. The program attempted to decrypt messages sent by Soviet Union intelligence agencies, including its foreign intelligence service and military intelligence services. The project produced some of the most important breakthroughs for western counter-intelligence in this period, including the discovery of the Cambridge spy ring and the exposure of Soviet espionage targeting the Manhattan Project. The NSA declassified the program in 1995. It can be read about in a NSA document at https://www.nsa.gov/about/_files/cryptologic_heritage/publications/coldwar/venona_story.pdf

Background

Hardware random number generators have been built into some processor systems or made possible in some operating system. E.g. Raspberry Pi includes a hardware-based random number generator that can generate cryptographic quality random numbers.
In Unix-like operating systems /dev/random is a special file that serves as a blocking pseudorandom number generator:

.dev>more –f random

Randomness

Randomness means lack of pattern or predictability of events. Randomness abounds in the physical world and in man-made devices such as electrical circuits as fluctuations of an unpredictable nature which we call noise. Electrical storms, the microwave background left over from the Big Bang and other events induce random currents of electricity in aerials connected to radio receivers and televisions that cause the hissing noise that we hear in their loudspeakers. This atmospheric noise can be captured, sampled and digitised to provide a source of truly random bits. Such a service is provided by https://www.random.org.
Another source is https://www.fourmilab.ch/hotbits/secure_generate.html which uses the unpredictable nature of radioactive decay to generate truly random bits.

A random number is one that is drawn from a set of possible values, each of which is equally probable, i.e., a uniform distribution, e.g. the throw of a six-sided die. When discussing a sequence of random numbers, each number drawn must be statistically independent of the others, i.e. knowledge of an arbitrarily long sequence of numbers is of no use whatsoever in predicting the next number to be generated. Each possible arbitrarily long sequence is thus equally likely.

Key principle

Randomness:
Randomness means lack of pattern or predictability of events.

Background

RandomX package for Java has an option to get random bits from hotbits.
http://www.fourmilab.ch/hotbits/source/randomX/randomX.html

Pseudorandom

Pseudorandomness is an important concept in cryptography.

Informally pseudorandom means:

cannot be distinguished from uniform i.e. random.

The cryptographic definition of pseudorandom however is

a distribution is pseudorandom if it passes all efficient statistical tests.

This definition has been arrived at by considering the need to resist an attack from an adversary who is trying to obtain information from ciphertexts about the corresponding plaintext messages.

Key point

Pseudorandom numbers:
Pseudorandom numbers are generated deterministically and can only approximate a truly random distribution because numbers calculated by a computer through a deterministic process, cannot, by definition, be random.

Generating large numbers of truly random numbers is extremely difficult so people have turned to the computer and algorithms programmed into the computer to generate pseudorandom numbers from an initial seed. These pseudorandom numbers are generated deterministically and can only approximate a truly random distribution because numbers calculated by a computer through a deterministic process, cannot, by definition, be random. Given knowledge of the algorithm used to create the numbers and the seed, it is possible to predict all the numbers returned by subsequent calls to the algorithm, whereas with genuinely random numbers, knowledge of one number or an arbitrarily long sequence of numbers is of no use whatsoever in predicting the next number to be generated. Therefore, computer-generated "random" numbers are more properly referred to as pseudorandom numbers, and pseudorandom sequences of such numbers. Pseudorandom generated sequences eventually repeat with the periodicity determined by the seed and the algorithm used. Pseudorandom generated sequences are also reproducible, i.e. for a given algorithm, starting from the same seed generates the same sequence.

Pseudorandom number generators (PRNGs)

Key point

Pseudorandom number generators:
A pseudorandom number generator is an efficient, deterministic algorithm that expands a short, uniform seed into a longer, pseudorandom output in polynomial time. The seed may be chosen from the small number of truly random numbers that are available but doesn't have to be.

A pseudorandom number generator is an efficient, deterministic algorithm that expands a short, uniform seed into a longer, pseudorandom output in polynomial time. It is useful whenever

1. It would be difficult to communicate a long sequence of numbers needed in a symmetric key cipher instead the seed is communicated
2. A large number of random numbers are required and access to truly random numbers is restricted to a much smaller number

The seed may be chosen from the small number of truly random numbers that are available but doesn't have to be.

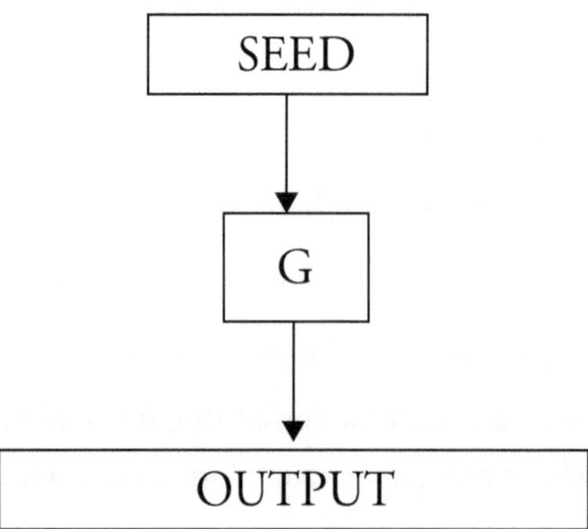

Figure 5.6.8.15 A pseudorandom number generator, G, producing a longer stream of "random" bits from a shorter length seed of true random bits

Care must be taken when relying on pseudorandom number generators for cryptographic purposes because they are deterministic. However, a class of improved random number generators, termed cryptographically secure pseudorandom number generators (CSPRNG) exist that rely on truly random seeds external to the software.

Background

Security experts have long suspected the National Security Agency (NSA) has been introducing weaknesses into CSPRNG standard 800-90 that they can exploit in ciphers that use this standard; this being confirmed for the first time by one of the top secret documents leaked to the Guardian by Edward Snowden.

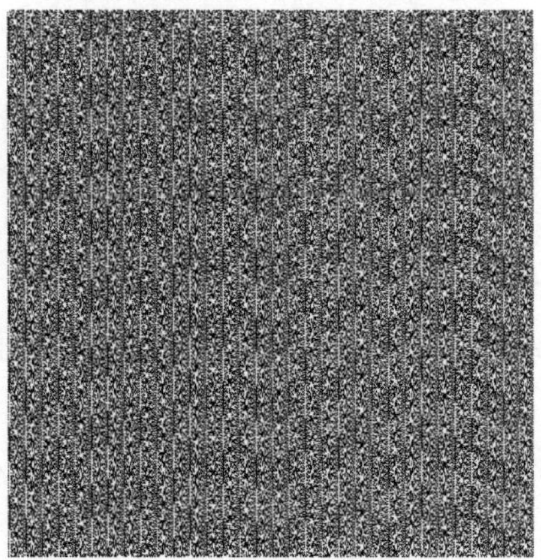

Figure 5.6.8.16 (a) Image generated from random numbers generated by the PHP rand() function on Microsoft Windows.

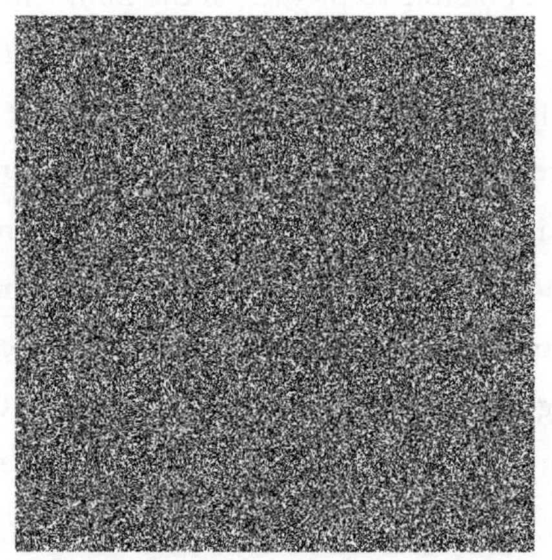

Figure 5.6.8.16 (b) reproduced with permission of RANDOM.ORG – image generated from random numbers obtained from atmospheric noise.

The image in *Figure 5.6.8.16(a)* (reproduced using a PHP script with kind permission of Bo Allen, http://boallen.com) exhibits patterns because the pseudorandom number generator, the programming language PHP's rand() function, is deterministic with a relatively short periodicity whereas the bitmap in *Figure 5.6.8.16(b)* does not because it relies on truly random numbers.

Task

6. Download the test program at http://www.fourmilab.ch/random/ Use it to test sequences of bytes/bits for their randomness. Run this program on data generated by a high-quality pseudorandom sequence generator. You should find it generates data that are indistinguishable from a sequence of bytes chosen at random. Indistinguishable, but not genuinely random.

7. Watch the video on pseudorandom number generators at https://www.khanacademy.org/computing/computer-science/cryptography/crypt/v/random-vs-pseudorandom-number-generators

Background

The Vernam cipher was exploited in the design of a high security teleprinter cipher machine that the Lorenz company made for the German Army High Command to enable them to communicate by radio in complete secrecy during WW2.
These transmissions were broken by Bill Tutte. The process of decrypting Lorentz machine ciphertexts was later automated using a refinement suggested by Max Newman and some clever engineering by Tommy Flowers who designed and built Colussus, the world's first stored program computer to decrypt Lorentz encrypted messages. Colussus reduced the time taken from weeks to hours. Colussus came online just in time to decrypt messages which gave vital information to Eisenhower and Montgomery prior to D-Day - http://www.codesandciphers.org.uk/lorenz/colossus.htm

The Vernam cipher

The Vernam Cipher is named after Gilbert Sandford Vernam (1890-1960) who, in 1917, invented the stream cipher and later co-invented the one-time pad (OTP). His patent US1310719 was filed in 1918 and is, according to the National Security Agency (NSA), perhaps one of the most important in the history of cryptography.

At the time of the invention, Vernam was working at AT & T Bell Labs in the USA. Messages were then sent by telegraph, a system that used pulses of electrical current to encode characters according to the Baudot code. The characters were entered into and read from the system using a teleprinter.

Figure 5.6.8.17 Gilbert Vernam

Vernam proposed a teleprinter cipher in which a previously prepared key, kept on paper tape, was combined character by character with the plaintext message to produce the ciphertext. To decrypt the ciphertext, the same key would be again combined character by character, producing the plaintext.

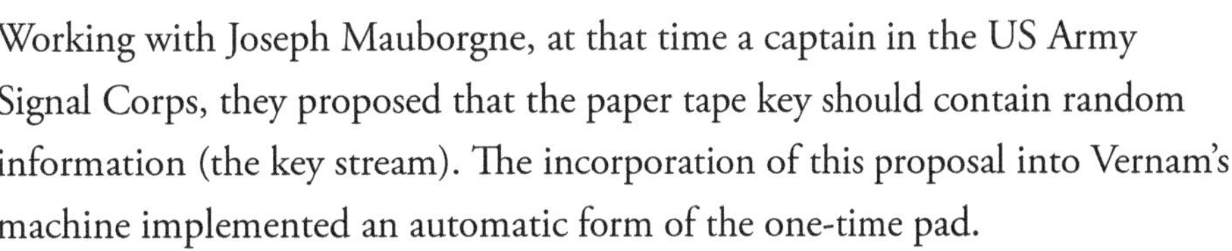

Working with Joseph Mauborgne, at that time a captain in the US Army Signal Corps, they proposed that the paper tape key should contain random information (the key stream). The incorporation of this proposal into Vernam's machine implemented an automatic form of the one-time pad.

Task

8. Watch AT & T Labs' video of the Vernam cipher http://techchannel.att.com/play-video.cfm/2009/10/12/From-the-Labs:-Encryption1

9. Read about the details of the Vernam cipher machine by visiting the website http://www.cryptomuseum.com/crypto/vernam.htm

The Vernam cipher relies on the bit-wise eXclusive-OR (XOR) Boolean function. This is symbolised by ⊕ and is represented by the following truth table, Table 5.6.8.3, where 1 represents true and 0 represents false

INPUT		OUTPUT
A	B	A ⊕ B
0	0	0
0	1	1
1	1	1
1	0	0

Table 5.6.8.3 Exclusive-Or truth table

A very useful property of the exclusive-or operation is that it is possible to recover an input given the output and the other input. For example, if the inputs A and B are 0 and 1 respectively, then A ⊕ B = 1. If we exclusive-or this output 1 with, say, input B which was 1, 1 ⊕ 1 = 0, we recover input A which was 0. It works for all inputs.

Therefore the same key stream can be used both to encrypt plaintext to ciphertext and to decrypt ciphertext to yield the original plaintext:

Plaintext ⊕ Key = Ciphertext

and:

Ciphertext ⊕ Key = Plaintext

If the key stream is truly random, and used only once, this is effectively a one-time pad.

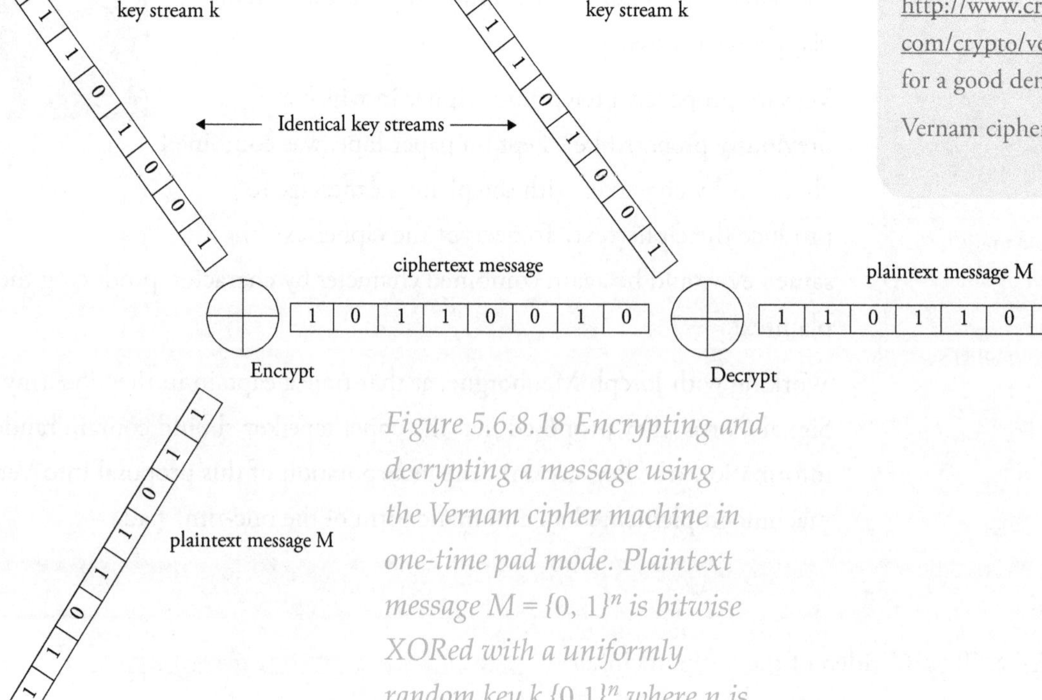

Figure 5.6.8.18 Encrypting and decrypting a message using the Vernam cipher machine in one-time pad mode. Plaintext message M = {0, 1}^{n} is bitwise XORed with a uniformly random key k {0,1}^{n} where n is the number of bits to encrypt the message.

Key principle

Vernam cipher:
Encrypts and decrypts a message using a one-time pad approach in which the plaintext message M = {0, 1}^{n} is bitwise XORed with a uniformly random key k {0,1}^{n} where n is the number of bits to encrypt the message.

Background

The eXclusive-OR function is an example of an involution. An involution is a function

$$f : X \rightarrow X$$

That, when applied twice, brings one back to the starting point

$$f(f(x)) = x$$

Information

Visit the cryptomuseum at http://www.cryptomuseum.com/crypto/vernam.htm for a good demonstration of the Vernam cipher.

Background

RC4 is an example of a Vernam cipher. It has been and still is used in popular protocols such as Transport Layer Security (TLS) (to protect Internet traffic) and WEP (to secure wireless networks) although it is now considered insecure.

Substituting pseudorandom data generated by a cryptographically secure pseudorandom number generator is a common and effective construction for a stream cipher.

RC4 has been a very widely used software stream cipher. RC4 is an example of a Vernam cipher. It has been and still is used in popular protocols such as Transport Layer Security (TLS) (to protect Internet traffic) and WEP (to secure wireless networks) although it is now considered insecure.

WEP relies on a short secret key that is shared between a mobile station (e.g. a laptop with a wireless Ethernet card) and an access point (i.e. a base station).

The short secret key is expanded into an infinite pseudorandom key stream which is XORed with the message packets before they are transmitted.

Programming task

3 RC4 is a stream cipher used in WEP. The infinite pseudorandom key stream for RC4 is generated from a secret key using the following two algorithms. Code these in your preferred language and run the test below on secret key = AQACS and plaintext = Computer Science

Key-scheduling algorithm

```
for i from 0 to 255
  S[i] := i
endfor
j := 0
for i from 0 to 255
  j := (j + S[i] + key[i mod keylength]) mod 256
  swap values of S[i] and S[j]
endfor
```

PseudoRandom Number Generator

```
i := 0
j := 0
while PseudoRandom Numbers required:
  i := (i + 1) mod 256
  j := (j + S[i]) mod 256
  swap values of S[i] and S[j]
  PSRNumber := S[(S[i] + S[j]) mod 256]
  output PSRNumber
endwhile
```

Test

The keys and plaintext are ASCII, the keystream and ciphertext are expressed below in hexadecimal but stored as bytes.

Key: AQACS

Keystream: F163D4497F1C801DCB4E3C...

Plaintext: Computer Science

Ciphertext: B20CB9390A68E56FEB1D5FC4720A7BD7

Task

10 Attacks on RC4 have shown that it is possible to distinguish its output from a random sequence. Why does this make RC4 insecure? Use a search engine to research an RC4 attack.

Key principle

Perfect secrecy:
Perfect secrecy means an eavesdropper would not, by gaining knowledge of the ciphertext but not of the key, be able to improve their guess of the plaintext even if given unlimited computing power. Such cryptosystems are considered cryptoanalytically unbreakable and information-theoretically secure meaning they will not be vulnerable to future developments in computer power such as quantum computing.
The term perfect security is given to such systems.

RC4 is still installed on some operating systems. For example, running the *openssl ciphers* command on an Apple Mac running Mac OS X 10.8 reveals that the SSL(Secure Sockets Layer) cipher RC4 (128 bit) is being used for encryption on this machine because it has not been deselected:

```
$ openssl ciphers -tls1 -v RC4-SHA

RC4-SHA SSLv3 Kx=RSA Au=RSA Enc=RC4(128) Mac=SHA1
```

Perfect secrecy

Claude Shannon, at Bell Labs, proved that the one-time pad is unbreakable, and that it is the only cryptosystem that achieves perfect secrecy. He published his proof in a research paper in 1949. In it he defined a mathematical model of what it means for a cryptosystem to be secure. Essentially, any unbreakable system must have the same characteristics as the one-time pad:

Claude Shannon (Getty Image library)

The key

1. must be truly random
2. must be as long as the plaintext message
3. must never be reused in whole or part
4. and must be kept secret.

Points 1 and 2 mean that the number of possible keys must be at least as large as the number of possible messages of a given length.

Task

11 Watch the video on Perfect Secrecy from Khan Academy - www.khanacademy.org/computing/computer-science/cryptography/crypt/v/perfect-secrecy

Perfect secrecy means an eavesdropper would not, by gaining knowledge of the ciphertext but not of the key, be able to improve their guess of the plaintext even if given unlimited computing power.

Key point

Unconditional or Perfect Security (Perfect secrecy)

Regardless of any prior information the attacker has about the plaintext, the ciphertext leaks no additional information about the plaintext in a ciphertext-only attack.

Such cryptosystems are considered cryptoanalytically unbreakable and information-theoretically secure meaning they will not be vulnerable to future developments in computer power such as quantum computing.

The one-time pad is an example of an information-theoretically secure cryptosystem. These systems have been used for the most sensitive governmental communications, such as diplomatic cables and high-level military communications.

What if the plaintext was a sequence of bits that represented an image? If we apply a bitwise exclusive-or to this image using a sequence of randomly generated bits for the key, we get an image that contains no information about the original image because each ciphertext bit is just as likely to be a 0 as a 1 - *Figure 5.6.8.19(a)* and *Figure 5.6.8.19 (b)*.

The original image can only be recovered by using the same key, i.e. the exact sequence of randomly generated bits that produced the ciphertext.

Applying the "wrong" key will result in recovering a different image.

Information

Figure 6.8.19(a) Claude Elwood Shannon was an American mathematician, electronic engineer, and cryptographer famous for having founded information theory with a landmark paper that he published in 1948.

Shannon was also the first person to show how the logical algebra of 19th-century mathematician George Boole could be implemented using electronic circuits of relays and switches in which open or closed switches could represent. "true" and "false" and "0" and "1". Furthermore he showed how the use of electronic logic gates could be used to make decisions and to carry out arithmetic.

Figure 5.6.8.19(a) Plaintext image to be encrypted using a one-time pad.
(Getty Image Library)

Figure 5.6.8.19(b) One-time pad ciphertext image of (a).

Task

12 Try the reversible XOR demonstration at https://www.khanacademy.org/computer-programming/reversible-xor-demo/5580322717564928

How XOR and a random key achieves perfect secrecy

Let's suppose that Alice needs to send a private message to Bob and therefore encrypts the message with a secret key known only to her and Bob. Furthermore before encrypting the message, the letters of the plaintext message are replaced by their equivalent ASCII values expressed in binary. We would then have the problem of encrypting 0s and 1s. For the sake of argument, let's just focus on one bit of the message, call it p, and encrypt this obtaining a one-bit ciphertext, c.

Next, Alice chooses the key, k, at random and uniformly (with no bias) from the set of symbols {☺, 😑, ☹}. These symbols have equal likelihood, ⅓, of being chosen by Alice, i.e. ⅓ of the time Alice chooses ☺, ⅓ of the time 😑 and ⅓ of the time ☹. The chosen secret key is known only to Alice and Bob.

When Alice needs to send the message she uses the chosen key to encrypt her plaintext message bit p obtaining ciphertext, c according to the following table, *Table 5.6.8.4*.

p	k	c
0	☺	0
0	😑	1
0	☹	1
1	☺	1
1	😑	0
1	☹	0

Table 5.6.8.4 Look up table for encrypting p into c using key k

Let's suppose that Alice has chosen ☺ for k. The values in *Table 5.6.8.4* have been carefully chosen so that no two rows have the same k-value and c-value, so on receipt of c, Bob will be able to decrypt c.

Unfortunately, this encryption scheme leaks information to Eve, an eavesdropper who wishes to learn something about the plaintext so that she can read what Bob is able to read.

Here is the method that Eve uses:

Suppose plaintext message bit p = 1,

Then if the key was ☺, the ciphertext c = 1

But if it was 😑 or ☹ then c = 0

However, one of 😑 or ☹ are twice as likely as ☺ to have been chosen

Therefore, for p = 1, c = 0 is twice as likely as c = 1.

Suppose, plaintext message bit p = 0,

Then if the key was ☺, the ciphertext c = 0

But if it was 😐 or ☹ then $c = 1$

However, one of 😐 or ☹ are twice as likely as ☺ to have been chosen

Therefore, for $p = 0$, $c = 1$ is twice as likely as $c = 0$.

Although having knowledge of c doesn't allow Eve to determine the value of p with certainty, it does allow her to revise her estimate of the chance that $p = 0$ or $p = 1$, as follows:

If before seeing c, Eve believed that $p = 0$ and $p = 1$ were equally likely, then if she sees that $c = 1$ she can infer that $p = 0$ is twice as likely as $p = 1$. On the other hand, if she sees $c = 0$ then she can infer that $p = 1$ is twice as likely as $p = 0$ - Table 5.6.8.5.

Value of c seen by Eve	Probability p = 1	Probability p = 0
not seen	½	½
0	⅔	⅓
1	⅓	⅔

Table 5.6.8.5 How probability changes when Eve gets sight of value of c

The solution is to remove ☹ as a possible value for k. Encryption then takes place using the values in Table 5.6.8.6.

Alice randomly chooses the key, k, from the set of symbols {☺, 😐}. These symbols have equal likelihood, ½, of being chosen, i.e. ½ of the time Alice will choose ☺, ½ of the time 😐. The chosen secret key is known only to Alice and Bob.

p	k	c
0	☺	0
0	😐	1
1	☺	1
1	😐	0

Table 5.6.8.6 Look up table for encrypting p into c using key k

Why does this new cryptosystem thwart Eve's attempt to learn something about the plaintext by examining the ciphertext?

Suppose $p = 0$,

Then if the key was ☺, $c = 0$

But if it was 😐 then $c = 1$

Since ☺ is equally likely as 😐 to have been chosen

$c = 1$ is as equally likely to occur as $c = 0$.

Suppose, $p = 1$,

Then if the key was ☺, $c = 1$

But if it was 😐 then $c = 0$

Since ☺ is equally likely as 😐 to have been chosen

$c = 0$ is as equally likely to occur as $c = 1$.

If before seeing c Eve believed that $p = 0$ and $p = 1$ were equally likely, then seeing $c = 1$ or seeing $c = 0$ cannot alter that belief because $c = 1$ and $c = 0$ are equally likely whichever value of key k is chosen.

For this encryption scheme, the probability distribution of the output does not depend upon whether 0 or 1 is being encrypted, so knowing the output gives Eve no information about which is being encrypted. We say that the scheme achieves perfect secrecy or perfect security.

Key principle

Perfect security:
When the probability distribution of the output, the ciphertext, for the encryption system does not depend upon whether 0 or 1 is being encrypted we say that the scheme achieves perfect secrecy or perfect security because the output will leak no information about the input, the plaintext.

Background

GF(2) is covered in A Level Computer Science for AQA Unit 1 in section 2.8.1. GF is short for Galois Field and is applied to arithmetic in which there are a limited number of elements, i.e. a finite field; all operations performed in the finite field result in an element within that field. GF(2) means that there are just two elements.

Encrypting long messages

If we replace ☺ with 0 and ☹ with 1, the encryption *Table 5.6.8.6* becomes the modulo 2 addition table for GF(2), *Table 5.6.8.7*.

p	k	c
0	0	0
0	1	1
1	0	1
1	1	0

Table 5.6.8.7 Look up table for encrypting p into c using key k

The exclusive-or operator $\oplus$ can be used to implement this table and encrypt plaintext p using key k to produce ciphertext c as follows

$$c = k \oplus p$$

Similarly, the exclusive-or operator can be used to decrypt ciphertext c using key k to produce plaintext p as follows

$$p = k \oplus c$$

Key point

VERY IMPORTANTLY by using XOR and choosing the key randomly, the XOR operator has a 50% chance of outputting a 0 or a 1.

To encrypt a long message, we first represent it as a string of n bits. Next, Alice and Bob should agree an equally long sequence of key bits, $k_1, \ldots, k_n$ chosen randomly. Now once Alice has produced the plaintext $p_1, \ldots, p_n$, she obtains the ciphertext $c_1, \ldots, c_n$, one bit at a time as follows:

$$c_1 = k_1 \oplus p_1$$

$$c_2 = k_2 \oplus p_2$$

•

•

•

$$c_n = k_n \oplus p_n$$

The previous section argued that each bit c_i of ciphertext tells Eve nothing about the corresponding bit p_i of plaintext and nothing about any of the other bits of plaintext. From this we can draw the conclusion that the cryptosystem has **perfect secrecy** or **security**.

Questions

A 3-symbol message, AQA is encrypted as follows. Each symbol is represented by a number between 0 and 26 (A ↦ 0, B ↦ 1, ..., Z ↦ 25, space ↦ 26). Each number is represented by a five-bit binary sequence (0 ↦ 00000, 1 ↦ 00001, ..., 26 ↦ 11010). Finally, the resulting sequence of 15 bits is encrypted using the key consisting of 15 randomly chosen bits 110000000101110 (obtained from random.org) and modulo 2 addition.

Compute the ciphertext.

Computational security

Limitations of the one-time pad

The success of the one-time pad is that it achieves perfect secrecy. However the following limitations have prevented more widespread use:

- The key is as long as the message
- Only secure if each key is used to encrypt a single message (i.e. key not used more than once)

This means that the parties wishing to communicate in secret, e.g. Washington, DC and Moscow, Russia via the "red phone" must share keys of total length equal to the total length of all messages that they might ever send.

If the same key k is used twice, e.g

$$c_1 = k \oplus m_1$$
$$c_2 = k \oplus m_2$$

the attacker can compute

$$c_1 \oplus c_2 = (k \oplus m_1) \oplus (k \oplus m_2) = m_1 \oplus m_2$$

This leaks information about m_1 and m_2 because it reveals where these differ: the characteristics of the ASCII coding scheme can be exploited to identify some letters and frequency analysis can be brought to bear as well.

Information

The "red phone" used in the 1980s for secure communication between the USA and the USSR was based on a one-time pad. The random key sequences or pads were delivered by courier.

Questions

Study the ASCII code table and note that letters all begin with 01 and the space character begins with 00. Also note that XOR of two letters gives 00... and XOR of a letter and a space gives 01... It is easy to identify XOR of letter and space. If the identified XORed letters and spaces are XORed with space's ASCII code, the plaintext letter is recovered. The following two ciphertexts were intercepted. It is suspected that the same random key has been used to produce these. Assuming 8-bit ASCII, can you recover any letters of the plaintext messages?

c_1 = 010100001010110011001000111110111101000011101110
c_2 = 010000011010010011011101100100111101110011110011

(The key that was used so that you can check your answer:
000100011111110110001001110110111001001110111101)

Computational secrecy

In practice it is more convenient to allow the leak of information with a tiny probability to eavesdroppers with bounded computational resources, i.e. not unlimited. This means relaxing perfect secrecy by

- Allowing security to fail with tiny probability
- Only considering "efficient" attackers

To set this in perspective we need to consider what is meant by a tiny probability and "efficient" attackers.

Let's say we allow security to fail with probability 2^{-60} or 1 in 10^{18} times.

This is of the order of probability that a person will be struck by lightning in the next year.

Now consider a brute-force search of the key space.

Assuming for argument's sake that one key can be tested per clock cycle of the CPU (2014 commodity PC CPU):

- Desktop computer ≈ 2^{57} keys per year
- Supercomputer ≈ 2^{80} keys per year
- Supercomputer since Big Bang ≈ 2^{112} keys

The meaning of "efficient" attackers is attackers who can try 2^{112} keys.

Well, if we choose a key space of 2^{128}, i.e. keys of length 128 bits then we should meet the requirement for secrecy.

This kind of secrecy is called **computational secrecy**. It relies on allowing

1. security to fail but with a probability negligible in n where n is a measure of the challenge of breaking the system, e.g. factoring a given integer n
2. restricting attention to attackers running in time polynomial in n

The notion of computational secrecy leads to the classification of an encryption method as being **computational secure** if it safe to assume that no known attack can break it in a practical amount of time.

However, this is very different from a proof of security. Thus in theory, every cryptographic algorithm except for the Vernam cipher (one-time pad) can be broken, given enough ciphertext and time.

Key principle

Computational secrecy:
Computational secrecy relies on allowing

1. security to fail but with a probability negligible in n where n is a measure of the challenge of breaking the system, e.g. factoring a given integer n
2. restricting attention to attackers running in time polynomial in n

Key principle

Computational security:
An encryption method is computational secure if it safe to assume that no known attack can break it in a practical amount of time.

Information

IBM Quantum computer:
IBM makes quantum computer available to members of the public, 4th May 2016 - www-03.ibm.com/press/us/en/pressrelease/49661.wss
See www.research.ibm.com/quantum/

Task

Research why quantum computing might be a threat to ciphers that rely on computational security and not information-theoretical security.

Task

14 Look at the Kryptos transcript available from www.elonka.com/kryptos/. Can you decrypt the four ciphertexts? Don't worry if you can't – see www.wired.com/2013/07/nsa-cracked-kryptos-before-cia

In this chapter you have covered:

- What is meant by encryption and its definition
- Caesar cipher and applied it to encrypt a plaintext message and to decrypt a ciphertext
- The limitations of the Caesar cipher
- Vernam cipher or one-time pad and applied it to encrypt a plaintext message and to decrypt a ciphertext
- Why Vernam cipher is considered as a cipher with perfect security
- Comparison of Vernam cipher with ciphers that depend on computational security

6 Fundamentals of computer systems

6.1 Hardware and software

Learning objectives:

- *Understand the relationship between hardware and software and be able to define the terms:*
  - *hardware*
  - *software*
- *Explain what is meant by:*
  - *system software*
  - *application software*
- *Understand the need for, and attributes of, different types of software*
- *Understand the need for, and functions of the following software:*
  - *operating systems (OSs)*
  - *utility programs*
  - *libraries*
  - *translators (compiler, assembler, interpreter)*
- *Understand the role of the operating system*

Key concept

Hardware:
The hardware of a computer is the physical components, electronic and electrical, that it is assembled from. It is the platform on which software executes.

6.1.1 Relationship between hardware and software

What is hardware?

The hardware of a computer is the **physical components, electronic and electrical**, that it is assembled from. It is the **platform on which software executes**.

What is software?

Software consists of **sequences of instructions** called programs which can be **understood and executed by the hardware** in its digital electronic circuits or a virtual machine equivalent.

Questions

1. What is meant by hardware?
2. What is meant by software?

6.1.2 Classification of software

Computer software may be classified as follows:

1. The **system programs** (or system software), which control the operation of the computer itself, e.g. the operating system
2. The **application programs** (or application software), which solve problems for their users, e.g. constructing a letter using word processing software for printing and sending to someone.

What is system software?

A computer system uses a layer or layers of software to enable users to operate the computer without having to be familiar with its internal workings. This layer or layers is called systems software and includes the operating system and other forms of systems software.

What is application software?

Applications software is an application program or programs designed to support user-oriented tasks which would need to be carried out even if computers did not exist. For example, communicating in written form, placing orders for goods, looking up information.

Key concept

Software:
Consists of sequences of instructions called programs which can be understood and executed by the hardware in its digital electronic circuits or a virtual machine equivalent.

Key concept

System software:
A layer or layers of software which enables users to operate the computer without having to be familiar with its internal workings.

Key concept

Application software:
Application software is an application program or programs designed to support user-oriented tasks which would need to be carried out even if computers did not exist.

Key concept

Different types of software:

1. General purpose
2. Special purpose
3. Bespoke

Questions

 Describe the classification of computer software.

The need for and attributes of different types of software

Application software cannot execute unless it has been first translated into the language of the computer, machine code. or a form that is executable by a computer.

It needs to be loaded into main memory and it needs to obtain input from input devices such as keyboards and to write output to output devices such as printers and it may need to communicate with other computers.

Application software may need to store information permanently and to subsequently access stored information. The stored information should be backed up so, if necessary, it may be restored from a back-up copy. These services are provided by the operating system and utility software without which it would not be possible to run application software.

Application software may be classified as

- General purpose application software: software that is appropriate for many application areas is described as general-purpose application software. For example, word processing can be applied in writing-up project work, in personal correspondence, writing memos, writing a book, creating standard business letters. The software is relatively cheap because its development costs are spread among all the purchasers of the software, which in the case of popular application software will be a large number. It is likely to be very reliable because it has been produced by an experienced team of programmers and tested on a large customer base.
- Special purpose applications software: special purpose application software is used for a particular application. For example, a dentist might use application software written specifically to record and process dental treatments, a task that every dentist needs to do. A business might use an accounting package for its accounts of sales. It is likely to be very reliable because it has been produced by an experienced team of programmers and tested on a large but specialised customer base.
- Bespoke software: when no general purpose or special purpose software exists that could do the job, software must be written from scratch to solve the specific problem or to support the required task. This software is called bespoke (tailor-made) software. For example, a teacher interested in finding out how frequently his students logged on to the college's computer network and for how long, wrote a program

using the programming language C to handle this task because no application program existed which could do this job.

Questions

4 Describe the classification of application software?

5 Why is system software needed in addition to application software?

6.1.3 System software

Systems software can be classified as follows:

- **Operating system software:** an operating system is a program or suite of programs which controls the entire operation of a computer
- **Utility programs:** a utility program is a systems program designed to perform a common place task, for example, formatting and partitioning a disk or checking a disk for viruses. Some utility programs are supplied with the operating system, others can be installed at a later time.
- **Library programs:** a program library is a collection of compiled routines that other programs can link to and use. Linking may be done at compile-time when building an executable or at run-time. Run-time library programs are loaded on demand and shared by different software applications. Loaded run-time libraries remain resident in memory until the last executing application is closed. In the Microsoft Windows operating system, the run-time libraries are called dynamic linked libraries or dlls.
- **Compilers, assemblers, interpreters:** these are computer language translators.
    - Compiler: a compiler translates a high-level language program into a computer's machine code or some other low-level language. Machine code is a language that the hardware of a computer can understand and execute. It consists of executable binary codes.
    - Assembler: an assembler translates a program written in assembly language into machine code. Assembly language is a symbolic form of machine code. The symbolic form consists of mnemonics such as ADD and SUB that denote the machine operation to be performed. An assembler simply substitutes the corresponding executable binary code for the mnemonics.
    - Interpreter: translates and executes a high-level language or intermediate-code program one statement at a time. It provides a way of executing programs not in the machine code of the computer.

Key concept

System software classification:

1. Operating systems
2. Utility programs
3. Library programs
4. Translators
    1. Compilers
    2. Assemblers
    3. Interpreters.

Information

Intermediate code:

This is a language which lies between a high-level language (HLL) and machine code. It is closer to machine code than an HLL. It supports operations for a fictitious machine. Compilers consist of several stages, one of which is intermediate-code generation. It is a much simpler task to write an interpreter for a new machine designed with a different instruction set than it is to write a compiler. Any program in intermediate-code form, including a compiler, can be "executed" by interpreting its intermediate-code form with the interpreter written for the new machine.
Examples of intermediate-code are p-code and bytecode.

Questions

6 What are the functions of each of the following software:

(a) operating systems (b) utility programs (c) libraries (d) translators?

7 Name **three** different types of utility program.

6.1.4 Role of an operating system

The most fundamental of all the system programs is the operating system.

An operating system has two major roles:

- **Hide the complexities of the hardware** from the user so that the user is presented with a machine which is much easier to use.
- **Manage the hardware resources** to give an orderly and controlled allocation of the processors, memories and input/output (I/O) devices among the various programs competing for them, and manage data storage.

Key concept

Role of an operating system:
1. To hide the complexities of the hardware from the user.
2. Manage the hardware resources.

Questions

8 What is the role of the operating system?

In this chapter you have covered:

- The relationship between hardware and software and be able to define the terms:
  - hardware
  - software
- What is meant by:
  - system software
  - application software
- The need for, and attributes of, different types of software
- The need for, and functions of the following software:
  - operating systems (OSs)
  - utility programs
  - libraries
  - translators (compiler, assembler, interpreter)
- The role of the operating system

6.2 Classification of programming languages

Learning objectives:

- *Show awareness of the development of types of programming languages and their classification into low- and high-level languages*
- *Know that the low-level languages are considered to be:*
  - *machine code*
  - *assembly language*
- *Know that high-level languages include imperative high-level language*
- *Describe machine-code language and assembly language*
- *Understand the advantages and disadvantages of machine-code and assembly language programming compared with high-level language programming*
- *Explain the term 'imperative high-level language' and its relationship to low-level languages.*

Information

EDSAC film:

http://www.tnmoc.org/special-projects/edsac/edsac-history

Maurice Wilkes' 1976 commentary on the 1951 film about how EDSAC was used in practice.

6.2.1 Classification of programming languages

Low-level programming languages

Low-level programming languages are classified as

- machine code
- assembly language.

EDSAC and machine code

On May 6th, 1949, EDSAC ran its first program which printed a table of squares for integers in the range 0 to 99. The programme (sic) took two minutes to run. The program of order codes had been punched on paper tape as 5-bit binary codes (see *Figure 5.3.3* in *Chapter 5.5*). The order codes represented arithmetic and logical orders, shifts, jumps, data transfer orders, input and output orders and stop orders. The word "order" was literally an order for EDSAC to do something. These order codes were the first programming language, a low-level language known as **machine code** that was interpreted directly by the hardware of EDSAC. Two examples of these order codes are shown in *Table 6.2.1.1* where each 5-bit order code is expressed as a single letter. The single letter order codes were typed on a machine that punched the corresponding 5-bit code directly onto paper tape (see Information panel opposite for the 1951 film on how EDSAC was used in practice). Addresses were also expressed in decimal and then translated into binary.

Order code	Address	Description
A	n	Add the content of location n to the accumulator.
S	n	Subtract the content of location n from the accumulator.

Table 6.2.1.1 Examples of EDSAC order codes

Figure 6.2.1.1 shows a snippet of an EDSAC order code program. Each character represents a 5-bit code

```
T123SE84SPSPSP10000SP1000SP100SP10SP1S
QS#SA40S!S&S@SO43SO33SPSA46S
T65ST129SA35ST34SE61ST48SA47ST65SA33SA40S
```

Figure 6.2.1.1 EDSAC order code

Key concept

Machine code:
Machine code is a language consisting of bit patterns/ binary codes that a machine can interpret, i.e. executable binary codes.

Key concept

Machine code instruction:
A machine code instruction is an operation which a machine is capable of carrying out.

Key concept

Low-level programming language:
The direct relationship with the hardware gives machine code instructions their low-level classification.

What is machine code?

Machine code is a language consisting of bit patterns/binary codes that a machine can interpret, i.e. execute. For this reason, machine code is referred to as executable binary codes. For example, the EDSAC order code program instruction

0010100000010101

means "transfer the content of the accumulator to storage location 21."

A machine code instruction is an operation which a machine is capable of carrying out. This direct relationship with the hardware gives machine code instructions their low-level classification. Therefore, higher-level operations for which there is no direct machine counterpart have to be broken down into a sequence of machine code instructions.

What is a machine code program?

A machine code language program is a program consisting of executable binary codes.

Questions

1. What is machine code?
2. What is a machine code instruction?
3. Why is machine code classified as a low-level programming language?

Assembly language

Writing programs directly in machine code is challenging. The EDSAC programmers wrote their programs using letters for the operation to be performed and addresses in decimal using the digit characters '0'..'9'.

The hardware on which they typed these letters and digit characters was wired to punch paper tape with the 5-bit equivalent of each.

We would call the form of the program shown in *Figure 6.2.1.1* which uses letters, an assembly language program. In assembly language, a (symbolic) name is assigned to each operation/instruction code. The operation/ instruction code name is called a mnemonic or memory jogger. The operation code mnemonic should describe in some way what the instruction does, e.g. LDR means LoaD a Register, ADD means add - see *Table 6.2.1.2.* The address field &1234 is expressed in hexadecimal (& is used to indicate this).

Assembly language	Description
LDR R_d, &1234	LDR means LoaD a Register with content of a memory location or word, R_d is the symbolic name for the register, &1234 is the memory location's address expressed in hexadecimal.
ADD R_d, R_n, R_m	ADD means add content of registers R_n and R_m, store result in register R_d.
STR R_d, &4321	STR means STore the content of the specified Register in a memory location or word.

Table 6.2.1.2 Some assembly language instructions

There is a ONE-to-ONE mapping between an assembly language instruction and its equivalent machine code language instruction.

For example,

LDR R_d, &1234 might be assembled to 000000 0001 01001000110100

The one-to-one mapping makes translating instruction mnemonics into the binary of machine code a simple task that can be assigned to a computer. The translator is called an assembler.

Questions

4. What is assembly language code?
5. What is the mapping between assembly language instructions and machine code?
6. What language translator is required to translate assembly language into machine code?

High-level languages

As the 1951 EDSAC film showed, a problem had to be recast by hand into a form that could use the machine code language of EDSAC. Wouldn't it be much better if the problem could be expressed in a programming language much closer to the problem space, leaving the task of translating to machine code to the computer? This thought led to the development in the 1950s of high-level languages, some of which are still used. For example, Fortran (1957) was designed for numerical applications and is still used by mathematicians, scientists and engineers, today.

High-level languages are closer to English than they are to the machine. This means that the mapping from a high-level language statement to machine code will be a one-to-many mapping because each high-level language statement will need to be broken down into several machine code operations. For example, the assignment statement

```
x ← y + z
```

when translated could become in the assembly language form of machine code

LDR R_0, &1234

LDR R_1, &1235

ADD R_2, R_0, R_1

STR R_2, &1236

Questions

7. What is meant by the term *high-level programming language*?
8. What is the mapping between high-level language statements and machine code?

Key concept

Assembly language:
Assembly language is the symbolic form of machine code. Each operation/instruction code of machine code is assigned a symbolic name or mnemonic describing what the instruction does, e.g. ADD.
There is a ONE-to-ONE mapping between an assembly language instruction and its equivalent machine code language instruction.

Information

GNU Fortran:
GNU Fortran is the primary open source version of the Fortran compiler widely used both in and out of academia. It is one of the Fortran compilers available for the Raspberry Pi.

Key concept

High-level programming language:
High-level programming languages are problem-oriented and therefore closer to English than they are to the machine. This means that the mapping from a high-level language statement to machine code will be a one-to-many mapping because each high-level language statement will need to be broken down into several machine code operations.

Information

High-level language classification:

Imperative:
- Procedural
- Object-oriented

Declarative:
- Logic
- Functional

Information

Imperative languages with support for functional programming:
Several imperative languages such as Delphi, Visual Basic, C#, Python and Javascript now have versions of the language with support for functional programming, a non-imperative style of programming.

Imperative high-level languages (HLL)

The word "imperative" is derived from the Latin word imperare meaning "to command". High-level languages that are classified as imperative do just that. They consist of a sequence of commands for actions such as *assign*, *add*, *write*, *read* which a programmer has written to solve some problem or accomplish some task. Table 6.2.1.3 shows a snippet of program code for an imperative high-level language. Procedural and Object-Oriented Programming languages are classified as imperative high-level languages, e.g. Pascal, Delphi, Basic, C, C++, Java, C#, Python and Javascript.

Imperative program	Description
`y := 6;`	assign 6 to y
`z := 7;`	assign 7 to z
`x := y + z;`	add z to y and store result in x

Table 6.2.1.3 Imperative high-level program

Another important feature of imperative languages is that their commands change a program's state, e.g. Table 6.2.1.3 shows that the variable *y* has its state changed by the action of the assign command from whatever value it was before to 6.

Questions

9 Explain the term *imperative high-level language.*

Advantages of programming in machine code and assembly language compared with HLL programming

Information

Code optimisers of compilers:
The code optimisers built into compilers are less effective for machine code operations such as complex bit manipulation and floating-point arithmetic because these operations are not easily expressed in a high-level language.

High-level language programs are converted into machine code by a translator called a compiler. Most compilers attempt to optimise the machine code which is produced. The compiler scans the machine code to see if it contains any unnecessary code which it then attempts to remove or adapt. Fewer machine code instructions means the code will take up less memory (smaller footprint) as well as running more quickly when executed. However, the process is not perfect, for example, where floating-point operations are concerned. In embedded computer systems, where speed of execution is paramount or memory is at a premium, the compiled code can be examined by hand and sections that are not already optimised replaced by hand-coded assembly language code, which is then assembled into machine code.

For short sections of code which need to run quickly or take up little space, it may be better to code directly in assembly language. Some high-level programming languages allow assembly language code to be embedded (inline) in the HLL program to take advantage of the time and space efficiency of assembly language coding.

Assembly language and machine code programming allow direct access to registers and low-level operating system routines which is not generally possible with most high-level language programming languages.

Key fact

Adv. of programming in machine code and assembly language:

Hand-coded assembly language when assembled can

- achieve a smaller memory footprint in machine code than compiled high-level language code
- achieve better code optimisation than compiled high-level language code and therefore code that will run faster
- directly access registers and low-level operating system routines which is not possible with most high-level programming languages.

Questions

10 State **three** advantages of programming in assembly language compared with programming in a high-level language.

Disadvantages of programming in machine code and assembly language compared with HLL programming

Code written in assembly language or machine code is less readable than code written in a high-level language and therefore more difficult to understand and maintain, debug and write without making errors. Code written in assembly language or machine code uses the instruction set of a particular processor (processor family). It is therefore machine dependent and will only execute on processors that use this instruction set. High-level languages are machine independent. An HLL program is expressed in an English-like language which is turned into machine code by a compiler. As long as a compiler exists for a particular instruction set, the HLL program may be ported to and its compiled version run on a computer with a different instruction set processor from the one it was written on. HLL programs are easier to understand and therefore maintain than assembly language programs because they are written using statements that are close to English. They are less error-prone when writing for the same reason.

Key fact

Disadv. of programming in machine code and assembly language:

Code written in assembly language or machine code is less readable than code written in a high-level language and so more difficult to

- understand and maintain
- debug
- write without making errors

Code written in assembly language or machine code is machine dependent making it difficult to port to a different instruction set processor compared with code written using high-level languages which do port readily because they are not machine-oriented.

Questions

11 State **three** disadvantages of programming in assembly language compared with programming in a high-level language.

In this chapter you have covered:

- Classification of programming languages into low- and high-level languages
- Low-level languages classified as:
  - machine code
  - assembly language
- Imperative high-level language is a type of high-level language
- Machine-code language and assembly language
- The advantages and disadvantages of machine-code and assembly language programming compared with high-level language programming
- The meaning of the term 'imperative high-level language' and its relationship to low-level languages.

6.3 Types of program translator

Learning objectives:

- *Understand the role of each of the following:*
  - *assembler*
  - *compiler*
  - *interpreter*
- *Explain the differences between compilation and interpretation.*
- *Describe situations in which each would be appropriate*
- *Explain why an intermediate language such as bytecode is produced as the final output by some compilers and how it is subsequently used.*
- *Understand the difference between source code and object (executable) code*

6.3.1 Types of program translator

Types of program translator

There are three types of program translator:

- Assembler
- Compiler
- Interpreter

Role of an assembler

Programs written in assembly language have to be translated into machine code before they can be executed. This is done with an **assembler.**

Machine code is a language that the machine can execute, i.e. it is executable binary code (binary patterns for which machine operations are defined).

Assembly language is the mnemonic form of these executable binary codes. Thus there is a one-to-one correspondence between an assembly language statement and its machine code equivalent: one assembly language statement maps to one machine code statement. This is in contrast to a high level language statement which typically maps to several machine code statements.

Role of a compiler

A **compiler** is a program that reads a program (**the source code**) written in a high level programming language (the source language) and translates it into an equivalent program (**the object code**) in another language - the target language. As an important part of this translation process, the compiler reports the presence of errors in the source code program.

A compiler translates (compiles) a high level programming language source code program into a **separate and independently executable object code target language program**. The target language program or object code produced by the process could be

- Machine code of an actual machine (in which case the compiler is called a native language compiler)
- Intermediate code which can, if necessary, be interpreted by an interpreter, e.g. Java bytecode is an intermediate language produced by a Java compiler
- Executable code for execution by a virtual machine.

A compiler translates one high level language statement into several machine code or target language statements.

Key principle

Assembler:
An assembler translates assembly language into machine code.
One assembly language statement maps to one machine code statement.

> **Key principle**
>
> **Compiler:**
> A compiler translates a high level programming language source code program into a separate and independently executable object code target language program. Object code is typically machine code.
>
> A compiler translates one high level language statement into several machine code or target language statements.

A compiler only translates a high level language program (the whole of the program), it does not execute it.

The process that the compiler engages in is called compiling.

A compiler consists of several stages:

- Lexical analysis – splits the source into user-defined "words", e.g. variable identifiers and language-defined "words", e.g. While
- Syntax analysis – checks that statements are grammatically correct
- Semantic analysis – e.g. type checking, "A" + 3.142 is incorrect as you can't add a real to a string
- Intermediate code generation
- Code optimising
- Code generation

> **Key principle**
>
> **Interpreter:**
> An interpreter is a program that executes a high level programming language program, statement by statement, by recognising the statement type of a statement and then calling a pre-written procedure/function for the statement type, to execute the statement.

Role of an interpreter

An interpreter is a program that executes a high level programming language program, statement by statement, by recognising the statement type of a statement, e.g. `X = X + 1`, and then calling a pre-written procedure/function for the statement type, to execute the statement. Therefore, an interpreter does not, unlike a compiler, produce an independently executable target language equivalent of the source language program. The application of interpreter to a source code program is called interpreting.

The differences between compilation and interpretation

The major differences between the compilation and interpretation are:

- An interpreter both "translates" and executes whereas a compiler only translates.
- A compiler produces a separate independently executable form of the source code program whereas an interpreter does not.
- A compiler is not needed when target form of source program is executed whereas in the case of the interpreter, execution requires the source code form of the program together with the interpreter, i.e. the interpreter needs to be available on the machine where the program is being run.
- If an interpreter is used then only the source code form of program is needed to execute the program whereas, if a compiler is used then the object code form of program is needed in order to execute the program.
- Interpreters are usually easier to write than compilers.
- With the compiler approach, if an error is discovered while the program is executing the source form of program must be located. An editor and the source form of the program must be loaded. The error must be pin-pointed which is not always easy and then corrected.

> **Key principle**
>
> **Interpreter vs compiler:**
> An interpreter both "translates" and executes whereas a compiler only translates.

> **Key principle**
>
> **Interpreter vs compiler:**
> A compiler produces a separate independently executable form of the source code program whereas an interpreter does not.

The compiler must be loaded and a compilation carried out. The new target form of program must then be loaded and executed. With an interpreter, the execution is halted at the point where the error occurs. The interpreter gives precise details of location of error. The error is corrected with an editor which may be co-located with interpreter. If it isn't, an editor will have to be loaded. However, no time-consuming compilation is involved and execution can resume immediately.

Situations in which assemblers, compilers and interpreters would be appropriate

Assemblers

For time-critical sections of code where execution speed is important, e.g. interrupt service routines, assembly language still has a role to play because in the hands of a skilled programmer, assembly language code can be written that is highly optimised for speed. As an assembler simply translates one assembly language statement into one machine code statement, that optimisation is preserved. Compilers can optimise code but the binaries produced cannot be guaranteed to be fully optimised for the given hardware. In the pecking order of speed, interpreters come after compilers.

Assembly language is still used where direct access to hardware is required e.g. processor registers or I/O controller registers. This is the case when writing device drivers, e.g. a screen driver. In this instance an assembler would be required to translate the assembly language program into machine code.

Compilers and interpreters

It is considerably more productive to write programs in high-level languages than in assembly language. There are relatively few programmers who are skilled in writing assembly language programs compared with the number of programmers skilled in writing in one or more high-level programming languages.

Compiled code which has been compiled into machine code of the computer will execute a lot faster than its interpreted source code equivalent (i.e. interpreter + the source code equivalent of the compiled code).

The immediate feedback and ease of locating errors in source code give interpreters an advantage over compilers when developing programs. This advantage is particularly beneficial for novice programmers or when programs are being prototyped and the write, compile, debug, edit cycle can be too time consuming.

Compiling has an advantage over interpreting because it produces a separate executable which means that the source code program does not have to be distributed. There are plenty of situations where this is desirable such as when producing commercial software or where there is a requirement is to protect the algorithm or coding technique used.

Key principle

Interpreter vs compiler:
Where speed of execution and/or direct access to hardware is required, use assembly language and an assembler.

Key principle

Interpreter vs compiler:
Compiled code which has been compiled into machine code of the computer will execute a lot faster than its interpreted source code equivalent (i.e. interpreter + the source code equivalent of the compiled code).

Key principle

Interpreter vs compiler:
Where rapid debugging and immediate feedback on errors is required including pinpointing the location of both syntax and runtime errors, use an interpreter.

Key principle

Interpreter vs compiler:
Where a separate executable that can execute independently of its source code equivalent is required, use a compiler.

Key concept

Bytecode:
Bytecode is an intermediate language between machine code and high-level language source code.
It is produced by a compiler which has been designed to translate source code into object code for execution on a virtual machine based on a stack machine

Bytecode

Bytecode is an intermediate language between machine code and high-level language source code. Bytecode is produced by a compiler which has been designed to translate source code into object code for execution on a virtual machine based on a type of machine architecture called a stack machine. You will learn about an alternative type of machine architecture called a register machine in *Chapter 7.3.1*.

Compilers for stack machines are simpler and quicker to build than compilers for other machine architectures. For example, for a simple stack machine architecture, the compiled code for the statement `x ← x * y + z` would take, minus the comments, the form:

```
push x       /transfer a copy of local variable x to top of stack
push y       /transfer a copy of local variable y to top of stack
multiply     /multiply the top two items on the stack,replace with result
push z       /transfer a copy of local variable z to top of stack
add          /add the top two items on the stack,replace with result
pop x        /remove top item from stack and store in local variable
```

The stack operations `push` and `pop` are covered in Chapter 2.3.1 of the Unit 1 textbook and evaluating expressions using a stack covered in Chapter 3.3.1 of the same textbook. A compiler for this simple stack machine would output byte-long numeric codes, called opcodes, for the operations push, pop, multiply and add. These opcodes are known as bytecodes because they are one byte long and they form the instruction set of the stack machine.

The bytecode stream issued by the compiler for this example might be as follows `1a 1b 68 1c 60 3b`. This bytestream example uses bytecodes for the Java Virtual Machine which is a stack-based machine that is able to interpret Java bytecodes. *Table 6.3.1.1* shows the corresponding interpretation of these bytecodes.

Bytecode	Operation
1a	push first local variable onto stack
1b	push second local variable onto stack
68	pop top two items on stack, multiply them together, push result on stack
1c	push third local variable onto stack
60	pop top two items on stack, add them together, push result on stack
3b	pop top item on stack, store in first local variable

Table 6.3.1.1 Java bytecodes and their interpretation

To execute bytecode on a virtual machine requires that it be interpreted by the underlying real machine, i.e. the bytecode is executed in software running on the underlying real machine. This software is called an interpreter.

Writing a software interpreter to interpret bytecode is an easier task than writing an interpreter to interpret high-level language source code. All that a bytecode interpeter has to do is parse (identify) and directly execute the bytecodes, one at a time. This also makes the bytecode interpreter very portable, i.e. very easy to move onto a new machine with a different instruction set, and very compact.

Interpreting bytecode programs is also much faster than interpreting their high-level language source code program equivalents because the interpreter written to interpret bytecode has to perform much less work and is therefore simpler.

Bytecode targets a virtual machine not a real machine and so can run on any machine or operating system for which a bytecode interpreter has been written.

This means that the same object code can run on different platforms by simply creating an interpreter for the platform. A compiler that outputs bytecode thus produces object code that is portable.

However, bytecode may be further compiled into machine code for better performance. Some systems, called dynamic translators, or "just-in-time" (JIT) compilers, translate bytecode into machine language as necessary at runtime.

Questions

1 Explain the role of each of the following:
 (a) assembler
 (b) compiler
 (c) interpreter

2 State **three** differences between compilation and interpretation.

3 (a) Give two reasons why programs are still written in assembly language
 (b) What is the relationship between
  (i) assembly language statement and machine code
  (ii) high level programming language statement and machine code?

4 Given a choice, under what circumstances would it be preferable to use:
 (a) a compiler;
 (b) an interpreter?

Stretch & Challenge question

5 A particular computer has two compilers for a high level language HLL. The compilers are called HLL1 and HLL2. HLL1 compiles a program written in HLL into the machine code of this computer, whereas HLL2 compiles an HLL program into intermediate code, which can then be executed by an interpreter running on this computer, if one exists.

On purchase, compiler HLL2 was supplied in intermediate code form without an interpreter, the same intermediate code that is produced by HLL2, and HLL1 in source code program form.

(a) With only a means to write assembly language programs and to run an assembler on the computer at this stage, explain carefully what could be done to enable HLL2 to compile HLL programs for this computer.

(b) Explain carefully how HLL1 can now be executed.

(c) Explain carefully how the machine code form of HLL1 can now be produced on this computer.

In this chapter you have covered:

- The role of each of the following:
  - assembler
  - compiler
  - interpreter
- The differences between compilation and interpretation
- Situations in which each would be appropriate.
- Why an intermediate language such as bytecode is produced as the final output by some compilers and how it is subsequently used.
- The difference between source code and object (executable) code

6.4 Logic gates

Learning objectives

- *Construct truth tables for the following logic gates:*
  - *NOT*
  - *AND*
  - *OR*
  - *XOR*
  - *NAND*
  - *NOR*
- *Be familiar with drawing and interpreting logic gate circuit diagrams involving one or more of the above gates*
- *Complete a truth table for a given logic gate circuit*
- *Write a Boolean expression for a given logic gate circuit*
- *Draw an equivalent logic gate circuit for a given Boolean expression*

6.4.1 Logic gates

Boolean variables

In 1847 George Boole, an English mathematician, introduced a shorthand notation for a system of logic originally set forth by Aristotle. Aristotle's system dealt with statements considered either true or false. Here are two examples:

It is sunny today.

Today is Tuesday.

Quite clearly these two statements are either True or False. If today is Wednesday then the statement "Today is Tuesday" is False. *Table 6.4.1.1* shows the possible outcomes of examining the truth of each statement.

Statement	Outcome	
It is sunny today	False	True
Today is Tuesday	False	True

Table 6.4.1.1 Possible outcomes for truth of statements

Just as we might use an integer variable G to record the number of goats in a farmer's field so we can use variable X as shorthand for "It is sunny today", and Y for "Today is Tuesday". The values that G can be assigned are the natural or counting numbers. For X and Y, we have only two possible values, True or False, to assign. We call X and Y Boolean variables, after George Boole who introduced this form of algebra called Boolean algebra. *Table 6.4.1.2* shows the Boolean variable equivalent of *Table 6.4.1.1* for "It is sunny today" expressed as Boolean variable X. Boolean algebra deals with Boolean values that are typically labelled True/False (or 1/0, Yes/No, On/Off).

X (It is sunny today)	Meaning
False	It is not sunny today
True	It is sunny today

Table 6.4.1.2 Boolean variable representation of truth statements

Boolean algebra had very little practical use until digital electronics and digital computers were developed. As digital computers rely for their operation on using the binary number system, Boolean algebra can be applied usefully in the design of the electronic circuits of a digital computer. Using Boolean values 1 and 0 instead of True and False, True in *Table 6.4.1.2* becomes 1 and False becomes 0 as shown in *Table 6.4.1.3*. X = 1 now means that "It is true that it is sunny today" and X = 0 means "It is not true that it is sunny today".

X	Meaning
0	It is not sunny today
1	It is sunny today

Table 6.4.1.3 Boolean variable representation of truth statements using 0 in place of False and 1 in place of True

It is then a small step to use Boolean variables to represent the state of components such as switches and indicator lamps as follows:

- a switch can be either closed (1) or open (0) and
- an indicator lamp can be either on (1) or off (0).

Y	Meaning
0	Switch is not closed
1	Switch is closed

Table 6.4.1.4 Boolean variable representation for state of a switch Y

Z	Meaning
0	Lamp is not on
1	Lamp is on

Table 6.4.1.5 Boolean variable representation for state of an indicator lamp Z

Logical OR operation

Things become interesting when switches and lamps are combined together in circuits. *Figure 6.4.1.1* shows a simple circuit consisting of two switches wired in parallel, one indicator lamp and one battery.

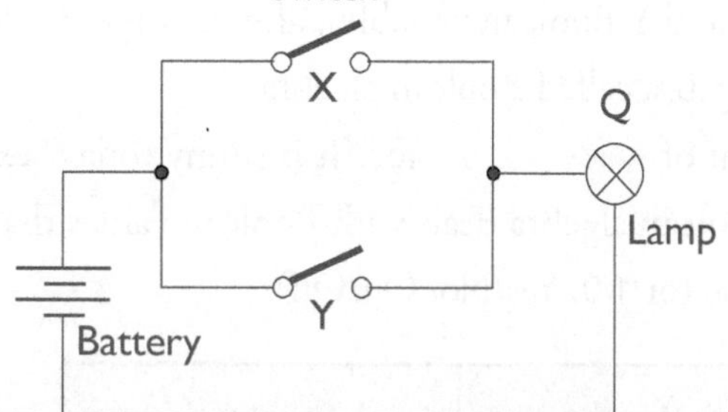

X	Y	Q
Open	Open	Off
Open	Closed	On
Closed	Open	On
Closed	Closed	On

X	Y	Q
0	0	0
0	1	1
1	0	1
1	1	1

Figure 6.4.1.1 OR logical operation: switch arrangement, switch state combinations and corresponding lamp state

The lamp is on if switch X is closed OR if switch Y is closed OR if both are closed, otherwise the lamp is off. The state of the switches can be expressed in the two Boolean variables, X and Y, as open or closed or using 0 for open and 1 for closed. The state of the lamp can also be expressed in a Boolean variable, Q, because the state has two possible values, off or on, which can be coded as 0 and 1, respectively.

Just as we can write the number equation for the total number of goats G, a farmer possesses,

$$G = X + Y$$

where X is the number in the first goat pen and Y is the number in the second, so we can write for the lamp circuit the Boolean equation

$$Q = X + Y$$

The operator "+" denotes the logical OR operation that behaves according to the tables in Figure 6.4.1.1, e.g. if X = 1 and Y = 1 then Q = 1, i.e. the lamp is on.

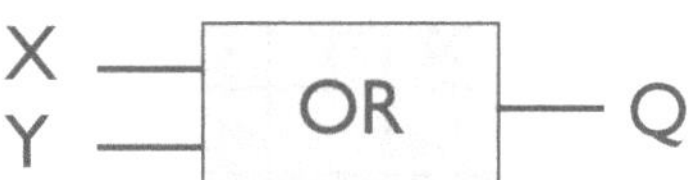

Figure 6.4.1.2 Logical OR operation: block diagram showing inputs X and Y and output Q

Logical OR Truth Table

If the logical operator "+" is represented by a rectangle labelled OR (Figure 6.4.1.2) then Boolean variables X and Y become its inputs and Q becomes its output. The inputs X and Y are transformed by the logical OR operation into Q.

X	Y	Q
0	0	0
0	1	1
1	0	1
1	1	1

Figure 6.4.1.3 Logical OR truth table

In fact, the logical OR operation defines a Boolean function OR because it operates on binary inputs and returns a single binary output (Figure 6.4.1.4).

Logical OR
Inputs: X, Y
Output: Q
Function: OR = X + Y

Figure 6.4.1.4 Logical OR function

Figure 6.4.1.2 is called a block diagram. A single block in a block diagram is sometimes called a black box even though it is not coloured black.

The black box approach is a convenient way of representing the logical OR operation with the details of how it is implemented abstracted away. We now define the logical OR operation by its truth table (Figure 6.4.1.3) not by the particular details of its implementation which could be, for example, electronic, magnetic, optical, biological, hydraulic, or pneumatic.

Key point

Boolean function:

A Boolean function is a function that operates on binary inputs and returns a single binary output.

Logical AND operation

Figure 6.4.1.5 shows a simple circuit consisting of two switches wired in series, one indicator lamp and one battery.

X	Y	Q
Open	Open	Off
Open	Closed	Off
Closed	Open	Off
Closed	Closed	On

X	Y	Q
0	0	0
0	1	0
1	0	0
1	1	1

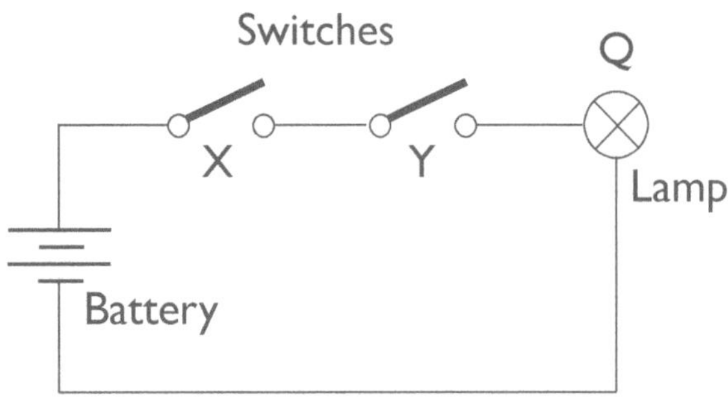

Figure 6.4.1.5 AND logical operation: switch arrangement, switch state combinations and corresponding lamp state

In this case, the lamp is only on if both switch X is closed AND switch Y is closed, otherwise the lamp is off. Again, the state of the switches can be expressed in the two Boolean variables, X and Y, as open or closed or using 0 for open and 1 for closed. The state of the lamp can also be expressed in a Boolean variable, Q, because the state has two possible values, off or on, which can be coded as 0 and 1 respectively.

We can write for the lamp circuit the Boolean equation

$$Q = X . Y$$

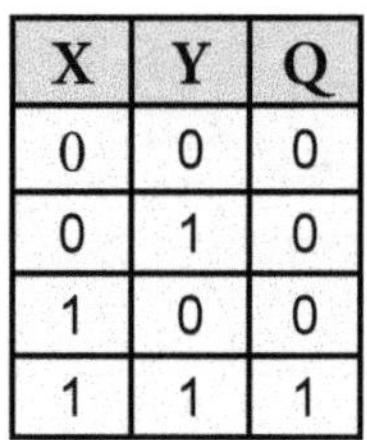

X	Y	Q
0	0	0
0	1	0
1	0	0
1	1	1

Figure 6.4.1.6 AND truth table

The operator "." denotes the logical AND operation that acts according to the truth table in *Figure 6.4.1.6*, e.g. if X = 1 and Y = 1 then Q = 1, i.e. the lamp is on.

Figure 6.4.1.7 Logical AND operation: block diagram

Figure 6.4.1.7 shows the block diagram representation of the logical AND operation with inputs X and Y transformed into output Q.

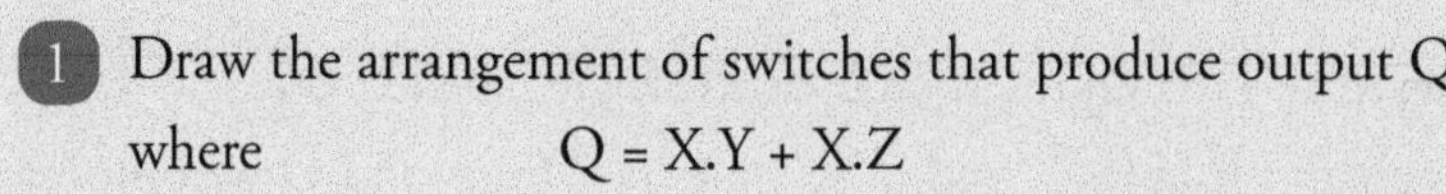

Questions

1. Draw the arrangement of switches that produce output Q where $Q = X.Y + X.Z$

Logical NOT operation

It is the convention to use Boolean value 1 for the active state, e.g. lamp on, Q = 1, and the Boolean value 0 for the inactive state, e.g. lamp off, Q = 0. Another way of expressing lamp off is NOT lamp on. This insight leads to

NOT lamp on = lamp off

Or, NOT 1 = 0

And, NOT lamp off = lamp on

Or, NOT 0 = 1

X	Q
0	1
1	0

Figure 6.4.1.9 NOT truth table

Figure 6.4.1.8 Logical NOT operation: block diagram

The NOT black box in *Figure 6.4.1.8* transforms input X into output Q using the logical NOT operation which inverts its input, 0 → 1, 1 → 0.

$$Q = \text{NOT } X$$

$$Q = \overline{X}$$

The line or bar placed over X is shorthand for NOT or the invert operation.

Logical NAND operation

If the output of the AND operation is inverted (*Figure 6.4.1.10*) then we have the NAND logical operation. Its Boolean equation is

$$Q = \overline{X\,.\,Y}$$

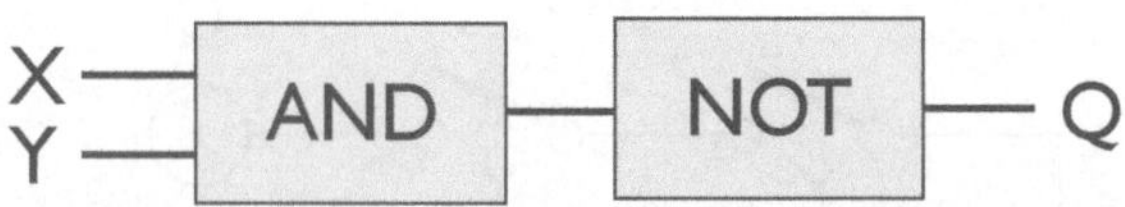

Figure 6.4.1.10 Logical NAND operation: constructed from an AND and a NOT, block diagram

Its truth table is *Figure 6.4.1.11*.

X	Y	Q
0	0	1
0	1	1
1	0	1
1	1	0

Figure 6.4.1.11 NAND truth table

Logical NOR operation

If the output of the OR operation is inverted (*Figure 6.4.1.12*) then we have the NOR logical operation. Its Boolean equation is

$$Q = \overline{X + Y}$$

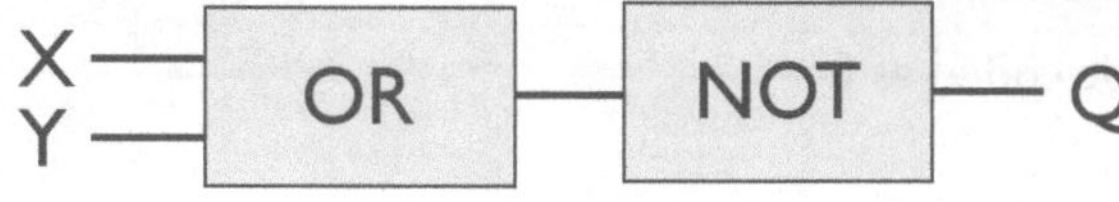

Figure 6.4.1.12 Logical NOR operation: constructed from an OR and a NOT, block diagram

Its truth table is *Figure 6.4.1.13*.

X	Y	Q
0	0	1
0	1	0
1	0	0
1	1	0

Figure 6.4.1.13 NOR truth table

Logical XOR operation

The truth table for the eXclusive-OR (XOR) operation (Figure 6.4.1.14) shows Q to be 1 if X is 1 and Y is 0 (Y not 1) or if X is 0 (X not 1) and Y is 1. Its Boolean equation is thus

$$Q = X.\overline{Y} + \overline{X}.Y$$

X	Y	Q
0	0	0
0	1	1
1	0	1
1	1	0

Figure 6.4.1.14 XOR truth table

It has its own symbol ⊕ so the Boolean equation is written as follows

$$Q = X \oplus Y$$

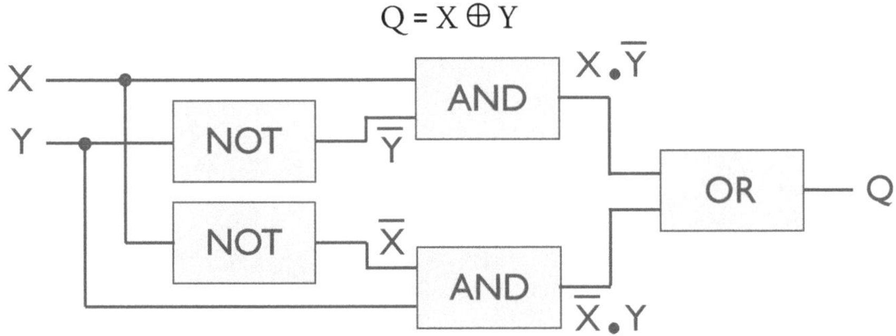

Figure 6.4.1.15 XOR logical operation: block diagram constructed from NOTs, ANDs and an OR

Key point

Logic gate:
A logic gate is a physical device that implements a Boolean function.

Questions

2 Q is only 1 if both X and Y are 1 and Z is 0 or if both Y and Z are 1 and X is 0 or if X, Y and Z are 1. Complete the truth table.

X	Y	Z	Q
0	0	0	
0	0	1	
0	1	0	
0	1	1	
1	0	0	
1	0	1	
1	1	0	
1	1	1	

3 Draw the block diagram using AND and OR operations that produces output Q where

$$Q = X.Y + X.Z$$

4 Draw the block diagram for logical operations that produce output Q where

$$Q = \overline{X.Y + X.Z}$$

Logic gates

The logical operations above are implemented in electronic circuits as logic gates. The circuit symbols for these logic gates are shown in Table 6.4.1.6.

Drawing and interpreting logic gate circuit diagrams

Logic gates may be connected together to perform a variety of logical operations. The output of one gate is used as the input to other gates.

For example, in Figure 6.4.1.16, Boolean variable, E, is the output of an AND gate and the input to an OR gate.

The full circuit uses Boolean variables, A, B, C, D, E, F, Q as follows

$$E = A.B$$
$$F = C.D$$
$$Q = E + F$$

therefore

$$Q = A.B + C.D$$

Logic gate symbol	Logical operation
	OR
	NOR
	AND
	NAND
	XOR
	NOT

Table 6.4.1.6 Logic gate symbols (ANSI/IEEE standard 91-1984)

Questions

5 What is the output of this logic gate circuit when its input is (a) 0 (b) 1?

6 What is the output of this logic gate circuit when its input is (a) 0 (b) 1?

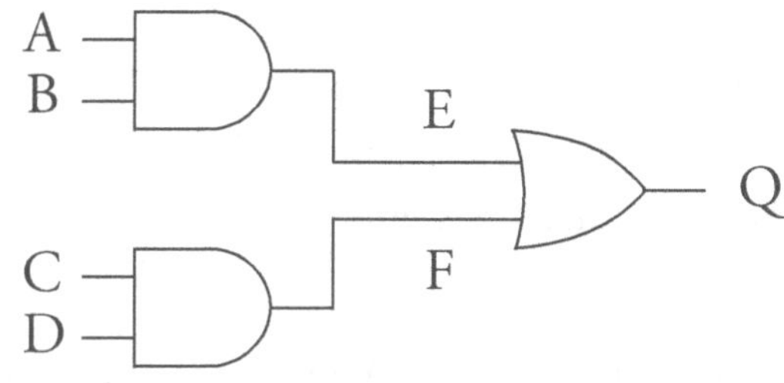

Figure 6.4.1.16 Three gates connected to perform a logical operation

Questions

7 What is the output, Q, of this logic gate circuit when its inputs A and B are (a) both 0 (b) both 1 (c) different from each other?

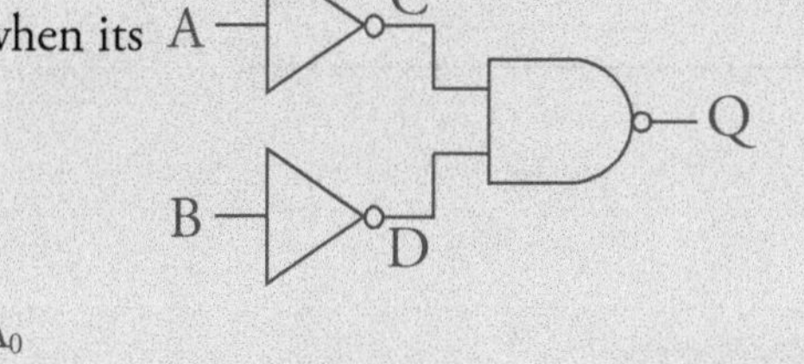

8 What is the output of this logic circuit when

(a) $A_0 = B_0$ and $A_1 = B_1$?

(b) $A_0 \neq B_0$ and $A_1 \neq B_1$?

(c) $A_0 \neq B_0$ and $A_1 = B_1$?

(d) $A_0 = B_0$ and $A_1 \neq B_1$?

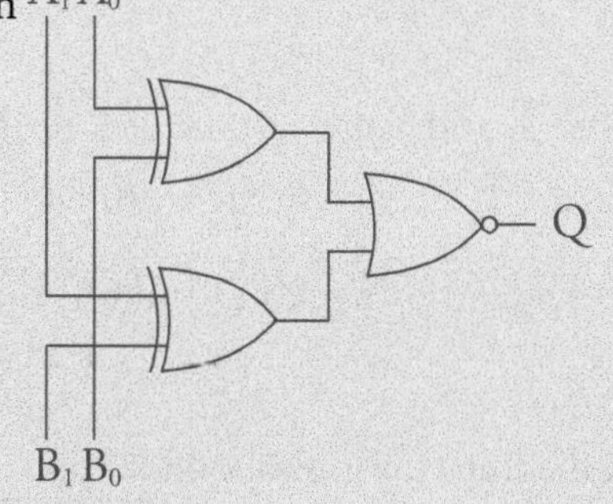

9 What is the purpose of the logic circuit in Q8?

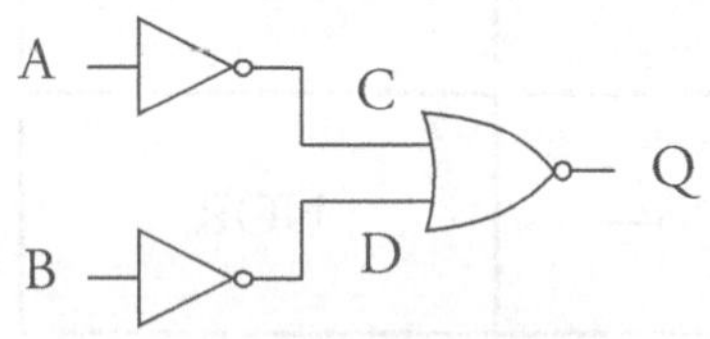

Figure 6.4.1.17 Three gates connected to perform a logical operation

Truth table equivalent of a logic gate circuit

A truth table can be used to analyse the behaviour of a logic gate circuit when inputs are applied to it. For the logic gate circuit shown in *Figure 6.4.1.17*, there are two inputs, A and B, and one output Q. The first two columns in *Table 6.4.1.7* contain all possible combinations of values for inputs A and B. Column C contains the values NOT A and column D the values NOT B. Q's column contains the values for C NORed with D, e.g. 1 NOR 1 → 0.

Figure 6.4.1.18 traces Boolean values through the three gates, for A = 1 and B = 0.

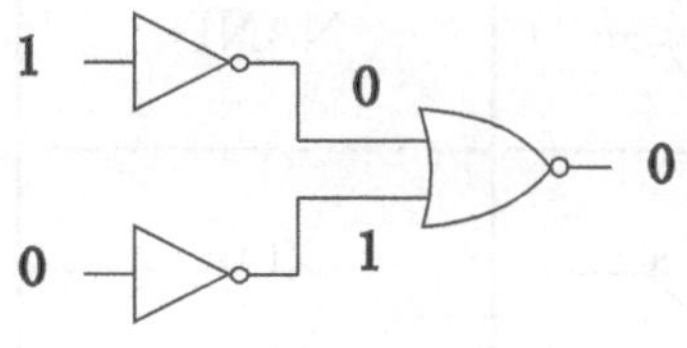

Figure 6.4.1.18 Tracing Boolean values through the three gates

A	B	C	D	Q
0	0	1	1	0
0	1	1	0	0
1	0	0	1	0
1	1	0	0	1

Table 6.4.1.7 Truth table for logic circuit shown in Figure 6.4.1.17

Information

Logic simulator:
A freeware logic simulator is available from http://www.cburch.com/logisim/

Questions

10 Complete the truth table for this logic gate circuit using Boolean variables A, B, C, D and Q.

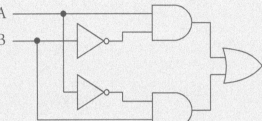

A	B	C	D	Q
0	0			
0	1			
1	0			
1	1			

11 Draw the truth table for this logic gate circuit using Boolean variables A, B and Q.

12 Draw the truth table for this logic gate circuit using Boolean variables A, B, C, D and Q. (Note: the table will have 16 rows for the values of the Boolean variables).

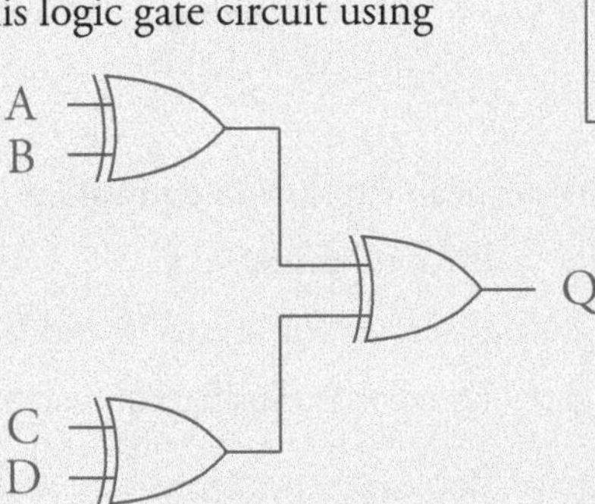

Questions

13 Complete the truth table for this logic circuit.

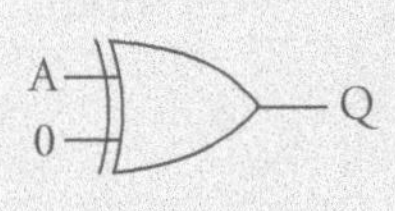

A	0	Q
0	0	
1	0	

14 Complete the truth table for this logic circuit.

A	1	Q
0	1	
1	1	

15 Complete the truth table for this logic gate circuit.

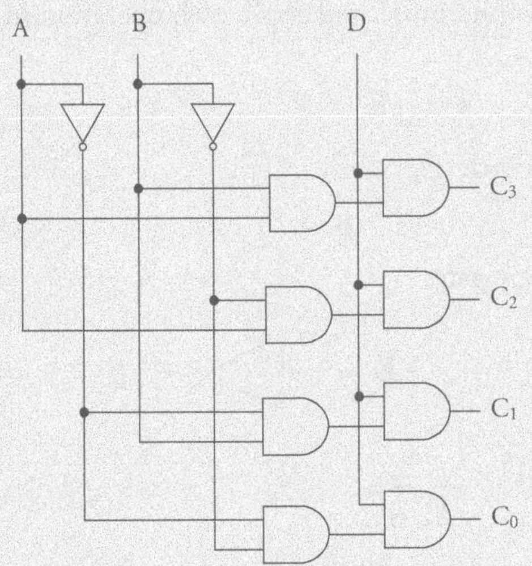

A	B	D	C_3	C_2	C_1	C_0
0	0	1				
0	1	1				
1	0	1				
1	1	1				
0	0	0				
0	1	0				
1	0	0				
1	1	0				

See Figure 6.4.1.32 for an example of how this circuit could be used.

Boolean expression equivalent of a logic gate circuit

The logic gate circuit in *Figure 6.4.1.19* may be expressed using Boolean variables, A, B, C, D and Q and the logical operators, NOT and NOR as follows

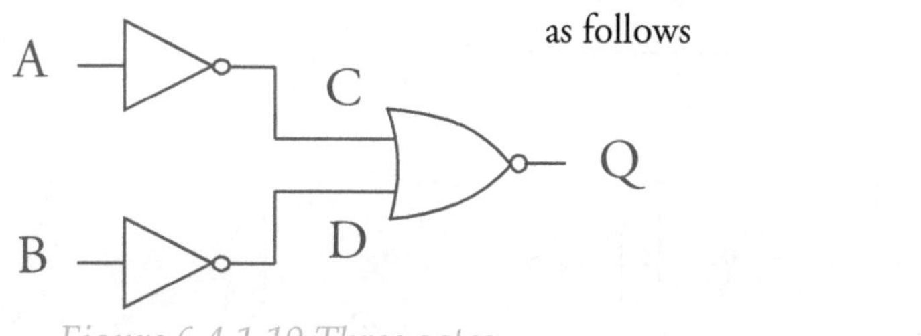

Figure 6.4.1.19 Three gates connected to perform a logical operation

$$C = \text{NOT } A = \overline{A}$$

$$D = \text{NOT } B = \overline{B}$$

$$Q = \overline{C + D}$$

therefore

$$Q = \overline{\overline{A} + \overline{B}}$$

$\overline{\overline{A} + \overline{B}}$ is the Boolean expression equivalent of the logic gate circuit shown in *Figure 6.4.1.19*. If we examine *Figure 6.4.1.6* carefully we see that the output from this logic gate circuit for inputs A and B is that of the truth table for an AND logic gate. Therefore, another equivalent Boolean expression is A . B.

Thus for the two Boolean expressions

$$A\,.\,B \text{ is equivalent to } \overline{\overline{A} + \overline{B}}$$

This means that we could replace the logic circuit in *Figure 6.4.1.19* by an AND gate with inputs A and B.

Logic gate circuit equivalent of a given Boolean expression

Consider the following Boolean expression

$$\overline{\overline{A}\,.\,\overline{B}}$$

To convert this into an equivalent logic gate circuit we must take each term in the expression, starting with the innermost, and apply each operation in turn. The innermost terms are

A and B

applying the NOT operation to each

$\overline{A}$ and $\overline{B}$

turning these into equivalent logic gates

A $\overline{A}$ B $\overline{B}$

applying the next operation AND

$$\overline{A}\,.\,\overline{B}$$

turning this Boolean expression into its equivalent logic gate circuit

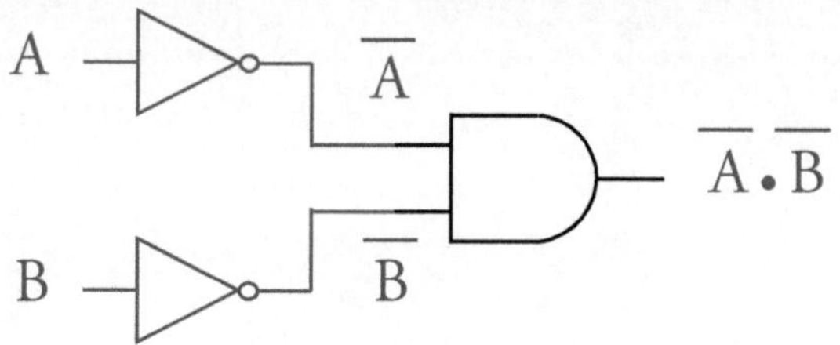

Finally applying the NOT operation to

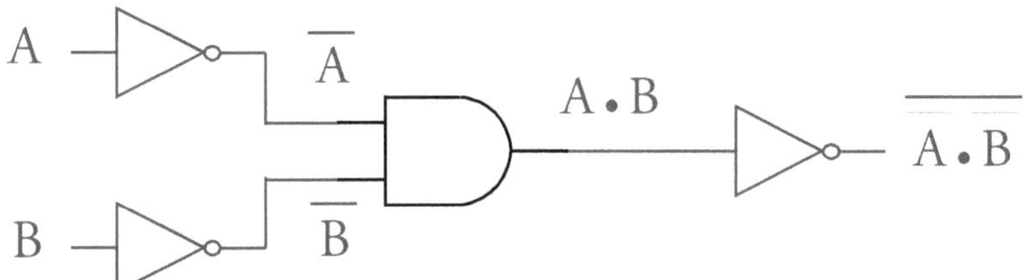

The number of gates can be reduced to three by replacing the AND-NOT combination by its logic gate equivalent NAND. The logic gate circuit becomes

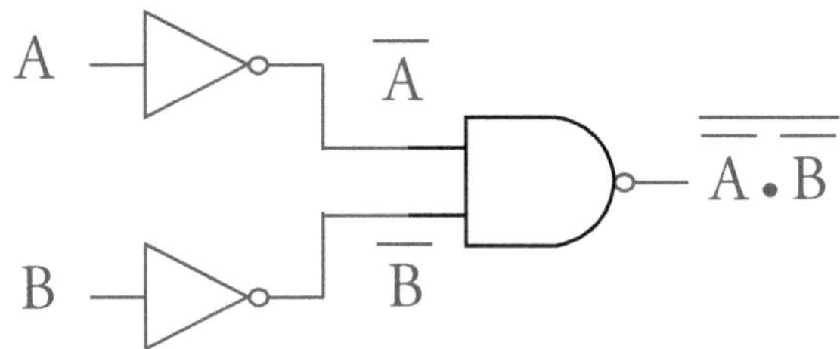

For more complicated Boolean expressions the same approach is used to arrive at the equivalent logic gate circuit, e.g.

$$\overline{\overline{A}\,.\,\overline{B}} + \overline{\overline{A}\,.\,B}$$

$\overline{\overline{A}\,.\,\overline{B}}$ is converted to its equivalent logic gate circuit W

$\overline{\overline{A}\,.\,B}$ is converted to its equivalent logic gate circuit Z

the output of these two circuits, W and Z is then ORed together, W + Z

If the order of evaluation needs to be controlled, brackets are used as the following example demonstrates

$$(\overline{A} + \overline{B})\,.\,(\overline{A} + B)$$

$(\overline{A} + \overline{B})$ is converted to its equivalent logic gate circuit W

$(\overline{A} + B)$ is converted to its equivalent logic gate circuit Z

the output of these two circuits, W and Z is then ANDed together, W . Z

Questions

16 Write an equivalent Boolean expression in terms of A, B, C and D for this logic gate circuit.

17 Write an equivalent Boolean expression in terms of A, B for this logic gate circuit.

In this chapter you have covered:

- Constructing truth tables for the following logic gates:
  - NOT
  - AND
  - OR
  - XOR
  - NAND
  - NOR
- Drawing and interpreting logic gate circuit diagrams involving one or more of the above graphs
- Completing a truth table for a given logic gate circuit
- Writing a Boolean expression for a given logic gate circuit
- Drawing an equivalent logic gate circuit for a given Boolean expression

6.5 Boolean algebra

Learning objectives:

- *Be familiar with the use of Boolean identities and De Morgan's laws to manipulate and simplify Boolean expressions*

6.5.1 Using Boolean algebra

Boolean algebra

In Boolean algebra as in the algebra you have studied in Maths, variables are combined into expressions with Boolean operators that obey certain laws (rules).

Boolean variables

The variables that we have used so far are known as Boolean variables because they are two-state variables whose states have the values 0 and 1. These are not the 0 and 1 of arithmetic but represent True and False.

Boolean operators

We need only consider **three** operators because all other operators can be expressed in terms of these. They are the

+	operator denoting Boolean addition
•	operator denoting Boolean multiplication
‾	operator denoting Boolean inversion

A	B	A • B
0	0	0
0	1	0
0	1	0
1	1	1

Table 6.5.1.1 Truth table for AND function

A	B	A + B
0	0	0
0	1	1
0	1	1
1	1	1

Table 6.5.1.2 Truth table for OR function

Boolean functions

We have encountered the Boolean AND function, the Boolean OR function and the Boolean NOT function in *Chapter 6.4.1* where they were implemented by logic gates with inputs, A and B, for AND and OR, and A for NOT. A and B are Boolean variables.

These Boolean functions and Boolean expressions containing Boolean operators are equivalent as shown below

AND(A, B) = A • B OR(A, B) = A + B and NOT(A) = $\overline{A}$

This means that Boolean algebra can be used to design logic gate circuits.

A	B	A • B	A + B	A • B + (A + B)
0	0	0	0	0
0	1	0	1	1
1	0	0	1	1
1	1	1	1	1

Table 6.5.1.3 Truth table for the two pairs of switches in parallel shown in Figure 6.5.1.1

Combining Boolean functions

We also learned in *Chapter 6.4.1* that we can combine Boolean functions. The functions AND and OR may be combined in exactly the same way that we can, for example, combine pairs of switches that can perform these functions.

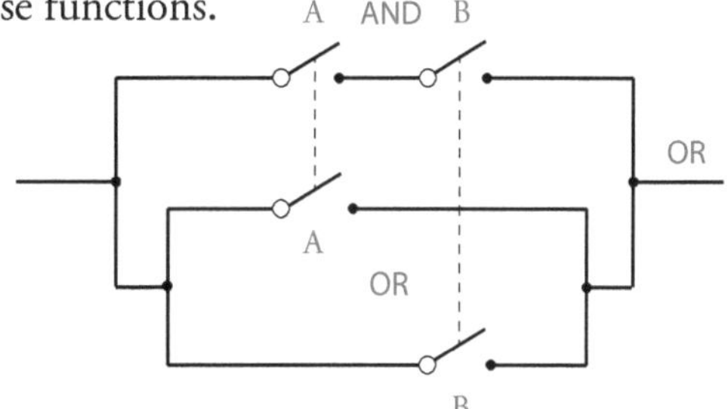

Figure 6.5.1.1 Pairs of switches connected in parallel

Table 6.5.1.3 shows the truth table for the combination of switches in *Figure 6.5.1.1.* The two switches labelled A are ganged together as shown by a dotted line, as are the two switches labelled B. This means that when the first switch A is open so is the second switch A and when the first switch A is closed so is the second A. Likewise for the two switches B.

Note that the A + B column of *Table 6.5.1.3* is exactly the same as the A • B + (A + B) column. Therefore, we can say that A • B + (A + B) is equivalent to A + B.

We draw the conclusion that the Boolean expression A • B + (A + B) can be simplified to A + B.

In general, many Boolean expressions may be simplified to Boolean expressions containing fewer terms. This is important if we are using Boolean algebra to design logic gate circuits because fewer terms means fewer gates.

Simplifying Boolean expressions

Boolean identities

In mathematics, an identity is a statement true for all possible values of its variable or variables. For example, the algebraic identity of A x 1 = A tells us that anything (A) multiplied by 1 equals the original "anything," no matter what value that "anything" (A) may be. Like ordinary algebra, Boolean algebra has its own unique identities based on the states 0 and 1 of Boolean variables as shown in *Figure 6.5.1.2*.

Did you know?

Simplifying Boolean expressions:
Inspecting truth tables is a useful way of identifying simplifications.

A + 0 = A

A	0	A + 0
0	0	0
1	0	1

A + 1 = 1

A	1	A + 1
0	1	1
1	1	1

A + A = A

A	A	A + A
0	0	0
1	1	1

$A + \overline{A} = 1$

A	$\overline{A}$	$A + \overline{A}$
0	1	0
1	0	1

0 • A = 0

0	A	0 • A
0	0	0
0	0	0

1 • A = A

1	A	1 • A
1	0	0
1	1	1

A • A = A

A	A	A • A
0	0	0
1	1	1

$A \cdot \overline{A} = 0$

A	$\overline{A}$	$A \cdot \overline{A}$
0	1	0
1	0	0

$\overline{\overline{A}} = A$

A	$\overline{A}$	$\overline{\overline{A}}$
0	1	0
1	0	1

Figure 6.5.1.2 Boolean identities and their truth tables

Laws of Boolean algebra

Commutative law

A + B = B + A

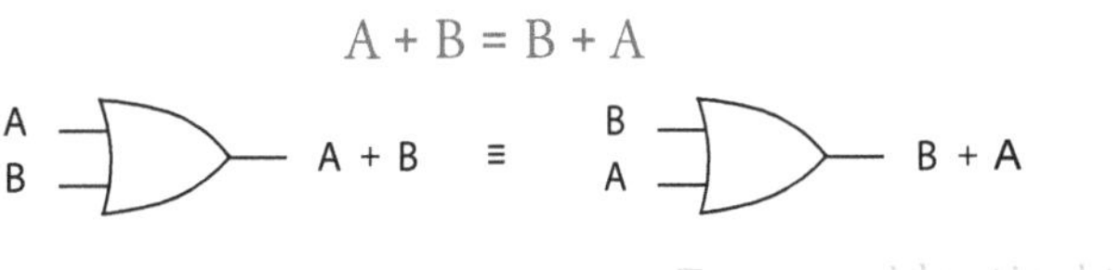

≡ means identical to

A • B = B • A

A • B ≡ B • A

Does it matter in which order inputs A and B are presented to an OR-gate or an AND-gate? The answer is no. Similarly, placing A to the left of the + operator or to the right doesn't matter, we still get the same answer. The same applies to the • operator. That is what is meant by saying that the + operator and the • operator are commutative.

Associative law

Does it matter whether the operator is applied to B and C first or to A and B first? The answer is no as long as it is the same operator. That is what is meant by saying that the + operator and the • operator obey the associative law.

A + (B + C) = (A + B) + C

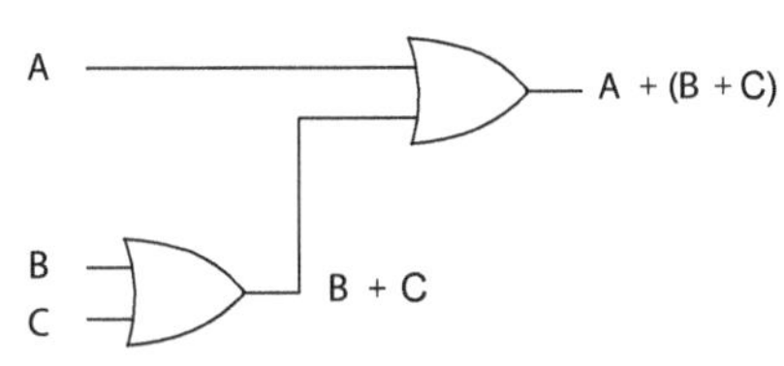

≡

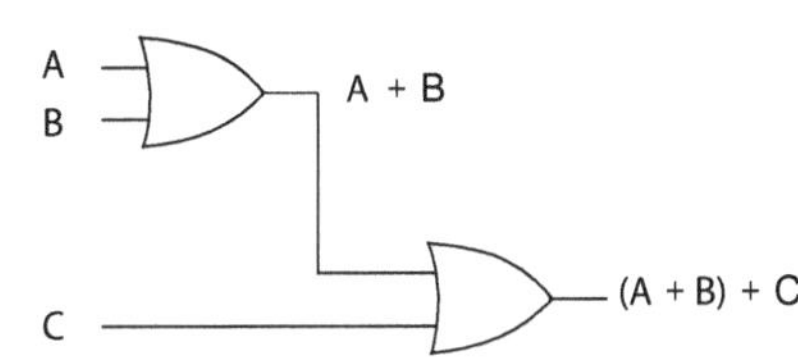

Take care because the associative law does not say that A + (B • C) has to be the same as (A + B) • C where the term in brackets is evaluated first. It is not. When written as A + B • C B • C is evaluated first because • has a higher precedence than +.

A • (B • C) = (A • B) • C

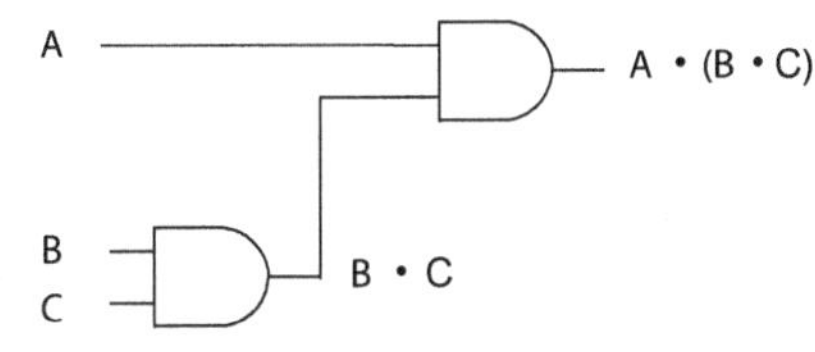

≡

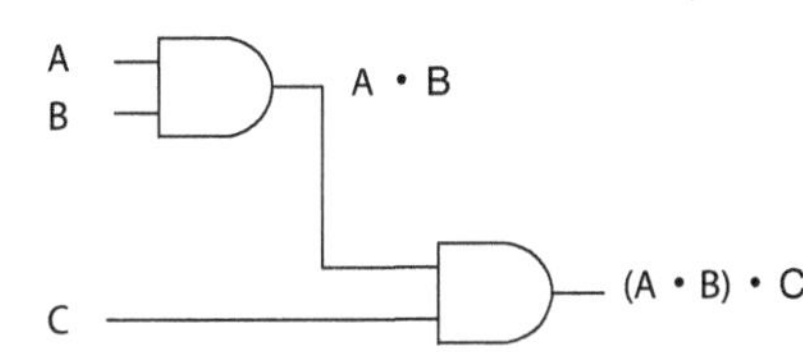

Distributive law

This law applies where a term or terms have been bracketed as follows

A *operator*1 (B *operator2* C) = A *operator1* B *operator2* A *operator1* C

operator1	operator2
•	+
+	•

Table 6.5.1.4 Operators for distributive law

where *operator1* may be • and *operator2* + or *operator1* may be + and *operator2* • as shown in *Table 6.5.1.4*.

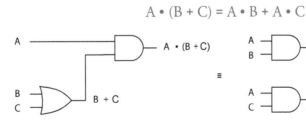

Note the use of brackets to define the order of evaluation. A • B + C is not the same as A • (B + C) because • has a higher order of precedence than + and is therefore evaluated before + unless brackets are used.

A • (B + C) = A • B + A • C

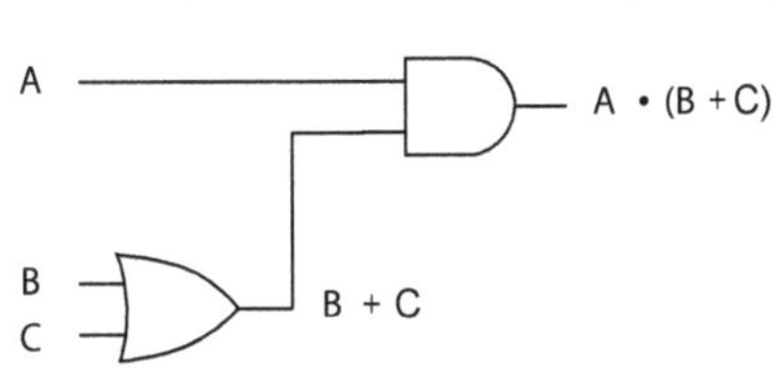

≡

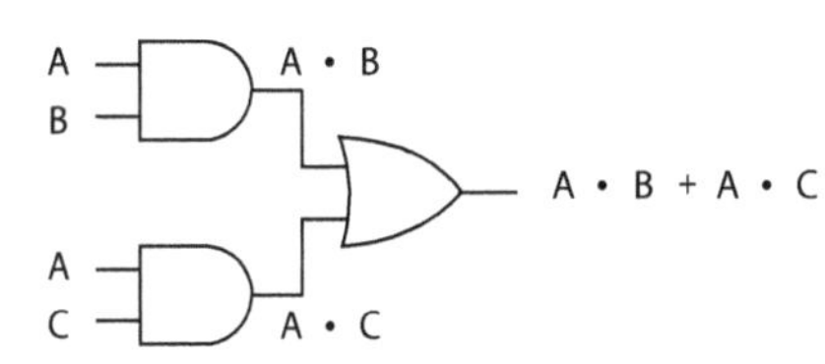

A + (B • C) = (A + B) • (A + C)

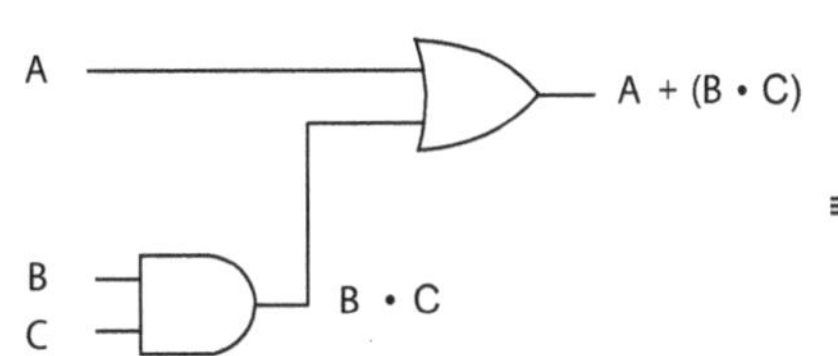

≡

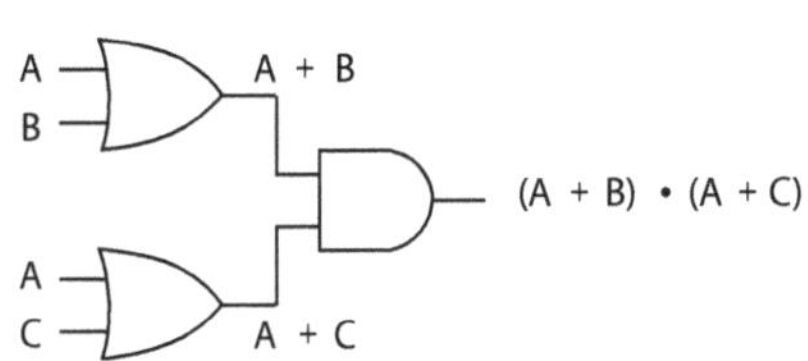

However, A + (B • C) = A + B • C because the brackets are redundant since • has higher precedence than +. Similarly, (A + B) • C is not the same as A + B • C because B • C is evaluated first in A + B • C whereas A + B is evaluated first in (A + B) • C and (A + B) • C = A • C + B • C.

Examples

Simplify A • A + B • 1

A • A + B • 1 = A + B • 1 using A • A = A

A + B • 1 = A + B using B • 1 = B

Simplify A • (B + 1)

A • (B + 1) = A • 1 using B + 1 = 1

A • 1 = A using A • 1 = A

Simplify B • A + B

B • A + B = B • (A + 1) using the distributive law

B • (A + 1) = B • 1 using A + 1 = 1

B • 1 = B using B • 1 = B

Simplify $A \cdot (\overline{A} + B)$

$A \cdot (\overline{A} + B) = A \cdot \overline{A} + A \cdot B$ using the distributive law

$A \cdot \overline{A} + A \cdot B = 0 + A \cdot B$ using $A \cdot \overline{A} = 0$

$0 + A \cdot B = A \cdot B$ using $0 + X = X$

The Boolean identities used in the examples and their truth tables are shown below

A • A = A

A	A	A • A
0	0	0
1	1	1

1 • A = A

1	A	1 • A
1	0	0
1	1	1

A + 1 = 1

A	1	A + 1
0	1	1
1	1	1

$A \cdot \overline{A} = 0$

A	$\overline{A}$	$A \cdot \overline{A}$
0	1	0
1	0	0

A + 0 = A

A	0	A + 0
0	0	0
1	0	1

Show that $(\overline{A} + \overline{B}) \cdot (A + B) = \overline{A} \cdot B + \overline{B} \cdot A$

$(\overline{A} + \overline{B}) \cdot (A + B) = \overline{A} \cdot A + \overline{A} \cdot B + \overline{B} \cdot A + \overline{B} \cdot B$ using distribution law

$\overline{A} \cdot A + \overline{A} \cdot B + \overline{B} \cdot A + \overline{B} \cdot B = 0 + \overline{A} \cdot B + \overline{B} \cdot A + 0$ using $\overline{A} \cdot A = 0$ and $\overline{B} \cdot B = 0$

$0 + \overline{A} \cdot B + \overline{B} \cdot A + 0 = \overline{A} \cdot B + \overline{B} \cdot A$ using $0 + X = X$ and $X + 0 = X$

Questions

Using Boolean algebra show that

1. $(\overline{A} + B) \cdot (A + \overline{B}) = \overline{A} \cdot \overline{B} + B \cdot A$
2. $A(\overline{A} + B)(\overline{B} + C) = ABC$
3. Use a truth table for each question above to verify that the identities are true.

Information

Writing A • B as AB:
We can omit the • operator and write the Boolean variables one after another, e.g. A • B as AB.

Key principle

Redundancy theorem:
In a sum of products Boolean expression, e.g. $A + A \bullet B$, a product such as $A \bullet B$ that contains all the factors of another product, $A \bullet 1$, is redundant.

Show that $A + A \bullet B = A$

$A + A \bullet B = A \bullet (1 + B)$ A is common factor

$A \bullet (1 + B) = A \bullet 1$ using $(1 + B) = 1$

$A \bullet 1 = A$ using $A \bullet 1 = A$

Distributive law for Boolean variables X, Y, Z:

$X + (Y \bullet Z) = (X + Y) \bullet (X + Z)$

Show that $B + A \bullet \overline{B} = A + B$

$B + A \bullet \overline{B} = (B + A) \bullet (B + \overline{B})$ using distributive law

$(B + A) \bullet (B + \overline{B}) = (B + A) \bullet 1$ using $B + \overline{B} = 1$

$(B + A) \bullet 1 = B + A$ using $X \bullet 1 = X$

$B + A = A + B$ using commutative law

Information

Product:
$A \bullet B$ is known as a product Boolean expression.

Sum:
$A + B$ is known as a sum Boolean expression.

Sum of products:
$A \bullet B + B \bullet C$ is known as a sum of products Boolean expression.

Product of sums:
$(A + B) \bullet (B + C)$ is known as a product of sums Boolean expression.

Simplify $A + A \bullet \overline{B}$

We could use the distributive law immediately but it is useful to be aware of other techniques:

$A + A \bullet \overline{B} = A \bullet 1 + A \bullet \overline{B}$ using $A \bullet 1 = A$

$A \bullet 1 + A \bullet \overline{B} = A \bullet (1 + \overline{B})$ using distributive law

$A \bullet (1 + \overline{B}) = A$ using $1 + \overline{B} = 1$

Questions

Using Boolean algebra show that

4. $\overline{A} + \overline{A} \bullet B = \overline{A}$

5. $A + \overline{A} \bullet B = A + B$

6. $A + \overline{A} \bullet B + \overline{B} \bullet C = A + B + C$

7. $A + \overline{A} \bullet C + B + D \bullet (\overline{B} \bullet \overline{C} + A \bullet \overline{C}) = A + B + C + D$
(HINT: Use the result proved in question 5)

Using Boolean algebra simplify the following

8. $A\overline{B}C + A\overline{B}\,\overline{C}$

9. $A \bullet (\overline{A} + B) + A \bullet \overline{B}$

10. $(\overline{A} \bullet \overline{B} + \overline{A} \bullet B) \bullet A \bullet B + A \bullet \overline{B}$

11. Show that $(\overline{A} + B) \bullet (A + \overline{B}) = \overline{A} \bullet \overline{B} + B \bullet A$

De Morgan's laws

De Morgan's laws expressed in a form that is useful for designing logic circuits are as follows

$$A + B = (\overline{\overline{A} \bullet \overline{B}})$$

$$A \bullet B = (\overline{\overline{A} + \overline{B}})$$

Table 6.5.1.4 demonstrates the equivalence of A + B and $(\overline{\overline{A} \bullet \overline{B}})$.

Table 6.5.1.5 demonstrates the equivalence of A • B and $(\overline{\overline{A} + \overline{B}})$.

$A + B = (\overline{\overline{A} \bullet \overline{B}})$

A	B	A + B	$\overline{A}$	$\overline{B}$	$(\overline{A} \bullet \overline{B})$	$(\overline{\overline{A} \bullet \overline{B}})$
0	0	0	1	1	1	0
0	1	1	1	0	0	1
1	0	1	0	1	0	1
1	1	1	0	0	0	1

Table 6.5.1.4 Truth table for A + B and $(\overline{\overline{A} \bullet \overline{B}})$

$A \bullet B = (\overline{\overline{A} + \overline{B}})$

A	B	A • B	$\overline{A}$	$\overline{B}$	$(\overline{A} + \overline{B})$	$(\overline{\overline{A} + \overline{B}})$
0	0	0	1	1	1	0
0	1	0	1	0	1	0
1	0	0	0	1	1	0
1	1	1	0	0	0	1

Table 6.5.1.5 Truth table for A • B and $(\overline{\overline{A} + \overline{B}})$

Examples

Show using Boolean algebra and De Morgan's laws that $\overline{A \bullet B} = \overline{A} + \overline{B}$

$\overline{A \bullet B} = \overline{\overline{\overline{A} + \overline{B}}}$ Using De Morgan's law $X \bullet Y = (\overline{\overline{X} + \overline{Y}})$

$\overline{\overline{\overline{A} + \overline{B}}} = \overline{A} + \overline{B}$ Using the Boolean identity $\overline{\overline{X}} = X$

Show using Boolean algebra and De Morgan's laws that $\overline{A + \overline{B}} = \overline{A} \bullet B$

$\overline{A + \overline{B}} = \overline{\overline{\overline{A} \bullet B}}$ Using De Morgan's law $X + Y = (\overline{\overline{X} \bullet \overline{Y}})$

$\overline{\overline{\overline{A} \bullet B}} = \overline{A} \bullet B$ Using the Boolean identity $\overline{\overline{X}} = X$

Information

Propositional logic form of De Morgan's laws:

1. $\neg(A \vee B) = (\neg A \wedge \neg B)$

2. $\neg(A \wedge B) = (\neg A \vee \neg B)$

where V means OR, Λ means AND, ¬ means NOT.

Using + and • in place of V and Λ respectively, and ‾ in place of ¬, De Morgan's laws become

1. $(\overline{A + B}) = (\overline{A} \cdot \overline{B})$

2. $(\overline{A \cdot B}) = (\overline{A} + \overline{B})$

Key point

Cancelling NOTs:
Care should be exercised when cancelling NOTs. The following examples illustrate when you may cancel and when you may not:

$(\overline{\overline{A + B}}) = (A + B)$ cancellation possible

$(\overline{\overline{A}} + \overline{\overline{B}}) = (A + B)$ cancellation possible

$(\overline{\overline{A} \cdot \overline{B}}) = (\overline{\overline{A} \cdot \overline{B}})$ cancellation not possible

$(\overline{\overline{\overline{A} \cdot \overline{B}}}) = (\overline{A} \cdot \overline{B})$ cancellation possible

Show using Boolean algebra and De Morgan's laws that $A \bullet \overline{B} + \overline{A} \bullet B = (A + B) \bullet (\overline{A} + \overline{B})$

$A \bullet \overline{B} + \overline{A} \bullet B = \overline{(\overline{A} + B)} + \overline{(A + \overline{B})}$	Using De Morgan's law $X \bullet Y = \overline{(\overline{X} + \overline{Y})}$
$= \overline{(\overline{A} + B) \bullet (A + \overline{B})}$	Using De Morgan's law $X + Y = \overline{(\overline{X} \bullet \overline{Y})}$ and $\overline{\overline{X}} = X$
$= \overline{\overline{A} \bullet A + \overline{A} \bullet \overline{B} + B \bullet A + B \bullet \overline{B}}$	Multiplying out the bracketed terms
$= \overline{0 + \overline{A} \bullet \overline{B} + B \bullet A + 0}$	Using the Boolean identities $\overline{A} \bullet A = 0$ and $B \bullet \overline{B} = 0$
$= \overline{\overline{A} \bullet \overline{B} + B \bullet A}$	Using the Boolean identity $0 + X = X$
$= \overline{(\overline{A} \bullet \overline{B})} \bullet \overline{(B \bullet A)}$	Using De Morgan's law $X + Y = \overline{(\overline{X} \bullet \overline{Y})}$ and $\overline{\overline{X}} = X$
$= (A + B) \bullet (\overline{B} + \overline{A})$	Using De Morgan's law $X \bullet Y = \overline{(\overline{X} + \overline{Y})}$ and $\overline{\overline{X}} = X$

Show using Boolean algebra and De Morgan's laws that $\overline{(\overline{A} + B)} + \overline{(A + \overline{B})} = \overline{(A \bullet B)} \bullet \overline{(\overline{A} \bullet \overline{B})}$

Let $\overline{(\overline{A} + B)} + \overline{(A + \overline{B})} = \overline{X} + \overline{Y}$	Where $X = (\overline{A} + B)$ and $Y = (A + \overline{B})$
$\overline{X} + \overline{Y} = \overline{X \bullet Y}$	Using De Morgan's law $C + D = \overline{(\overline{C} \bullet \overline{D})}$
$\overline{(X \bullet Y)} = \overline{(\overline{A} + B) \bullet (A + \overline{B})}$	Substituting for X and Y
$\overline{(\overline{A} + B) \bullet (A + \overline{B})} = \overline{\overline{A} \bullet A + \overline{A} \bullet \overline{B} + B \bullet A + B \bullet \overline{B}}$	Multiplying out the bracketed terms
$= \overline{0 + \overline{A} \bullet \overline{B} + B \bullet A + 0}$	Using $\overline{A} \bullet A = 0$ and $B \bullet \overline{B} = 0$
$= \overline{\overline{A} \bullet \overline{B} + B \bullet A}$	Using $0 + X = X$ and $X + 0 = X$
$= \overline{(\overline{A} \bullet \overline{B})} \bullet \overline{(B \bullet A)}$	Using De Morgan's law $C \bullet D = \overline{(\overline{C} + \overline{D})}$
$= \overline{(B \bullet A)} \bullet \overline{(\overline{A} \bullet \overline{B})}$	By commutative law
$= \overline{(A \bullet B)} \bullet \overline{(\overline{A} \bullet \overline{B})}$	By commutative law

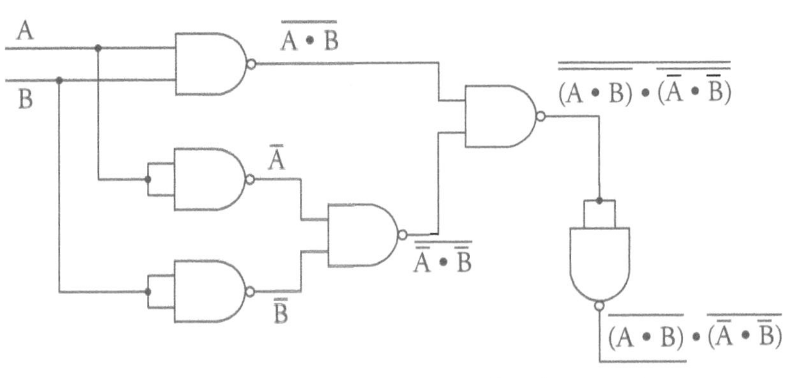

Figure 6.5.1.3 NAND gate implementation

The original Boolean expression has been transformed into one that can be implemented just with NAND gates as shown in Figure 6.5.1.3.

Questions

Using Boolean algebra and De Morgan's laws show for questions 12 to 15 that

12 $\overline{\overline{A} \cdot \overline{B} + A \cdot B} = \overline{\overline{(A + B)} + \overline{(\overline{A} + \overline{B})}}$

13 $\overline{(\overline{A} + B)} + \overline{(A + \overline{B})} = \overline{\overline{A} \cdot \overline{B} + B \cdot A}$

14 $\overline{A \cdot B} + A = 1$

15 $\overline{\overline{A \cdot \overline{B}} \cdot \overline{\overline{A} \cdot \overline{B}}} = \overline{B}$

16 Simplify the following:

(a) $\overline{\overline{A} + \overline{B} + (A \cdot \overline{B})}$ (b) $\overline{A} \cdot \overline{(\overline{A} + \overline{B})}$ (c) $\overline{A} \cdot B \cdot C + \overline{A} \cdot B$

(d) $\overline{\overline{A} + \overline{(A \cdot B)}}$ (e) $\overline{(A \cdot B)} + \overline{(A \cdot \overline{B})}$

17 An electronic control circuit is used to switch off an industrial process when certain parameters, indicated by two-state electronic signals W, X, Y and Z, reach critical values. The process must be stopped if either W and X or W, Y and Z become critical at the same time. Write a Boolean expression for these parameters that when evaluated will output 1 to switch off the process and 0 otherwise.

18 The Boolean expression for EXCLUSIVE-OR is $A \cdot \overline{B} + \overline{A} \cdot B$.

(a) Convert this expression into a form that could be implemented with NAND logic gates each with two inputs.
Draw the NAND logic gate circuit for this expression.

(b) Convert this expression into a form that could be implemented with NOR gates each with two inputs.
Draw the NOR logic gate circuit for this expression.

19 For a process to proceed the following Boolean expression must be true $W \cdot (X + Y \cdot Z)$.

(a) Convert this expression into a form that could be implemented with NAND logic gates each with two inputs.
Draw the NAND logic gate circuit for this expression.

(b) Convert this expression into a form that could be implemented with NOR gates each with two inputs.
Draw the NOR logic gate circuit for this expression.

20 A security light outside a house is controlled by two switches, which can be turned on or off from inside the house, and a light level sensor.
The switches are named A and B. The light level sensor is named C. The security light is labelled L.
If the light level is low (i.e. it is night time) the output of the sensor is on otherwise it is off.

- If both switches A and B are off then the light L is always off.
- If switch A is on the light L is always on.
- If switch B is on and switch A is off then:
  - the light L turns on if the light level is low
  - the light L turns off if the light level is not low.

Write a Boolean expression to represent the logic of the security light system.

Information

Dual-in-line package (DIP) Digital Integrated Circuits(ICs or chips):

Logic gates are available as integrated circuits. An integrated circuit (IC) containing four NAND logic gates each with two inputs is shown below in both schematic form and as an actual IC.

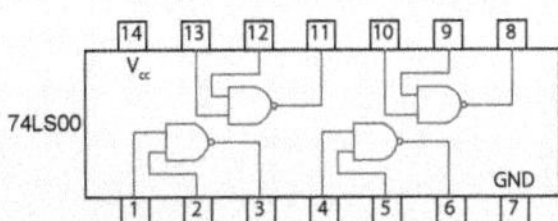

Questions

21 A second sensor is added to the system in Q20. This sensor is a movement detector. This second sensor is named M. The output of M is on if it senses movement otherwise it is off.

- If switch B is on and switch A is off then:
  - the light L turns on if the light level is low and movement is detected
  - the light L turns off after one minute if movement is not detected.

Write a Boolean expression to represent the logic of the security light system.

Information

NAND logic gate:

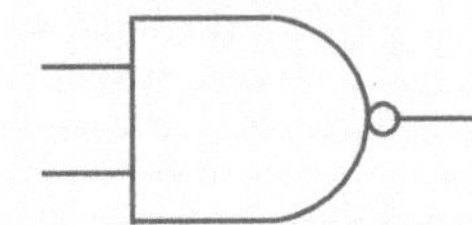

Information

NAND logic gate wired as a NOT gate:

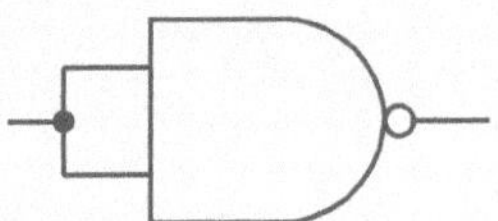

Did you know

Gate universality of NAND and NOR:

NAND and NOR gates possess the property of universality. This means, that a circuit consisting only of NAND gates or a circuit consisting only of NOR gates is able to perform the operation of any other gate type. The ability of a single gate type to be able to replicate the operation of any other gate type is one enjoyed only by NAND and NOR. NAND gates are preferred to NOR because

- NAND cheaper to fabricate than NOR
- NAND has a lower propagation delay than NOR.

Universality of NAND gates

Any logic circuit can be implemented using only NAND gates.

$$\text{NAND (A, B)} = \overline{(A \bullet B)}$$

$$\text{NOT(A)} = \text{NAND (A, A)} = \overline{A \bullet A} = \overline{A}$$

$$\text{AND (A, B)} = \text{NOT(NAND (A, B))} = \overline{\overline{(A \bullet B)}}$$

$$\text{OR (A, B)} = \text{NAND (NOT(A), NOT(B))} = \overline{(\overline{A} \bullet \overline{B})}$$

$$\text{NOR (A, B)} = \text{NOT (OR (A, B))} = \text{NOT (NAND (NOT(A), NOT(B)))} = \overline{\overline{(\overline{A} \bullet \overline{B})}}$$

Universality of NOR gates

Any logic circuit can be implemented using only NOR gates.

$$\text{NOR (A, B)} = \overline{(A + B)}$$

$$\text{NOT(A)} = \text{NOR(A, A)} = \overline{A + A} = \overline{A}$$

$$\text{OR (A, B)} = \text{NOT(NOR (A, B))} = \overline{\overline{(A + B)}}$$

$$\text{AND (A, B)} = \text{NOR (NOT(A), NOT(B))} = \overline{(\overline{A} + \overline{B})}$$

$$\text{NAND (A, B)} = \text{NOT (NOR (NOT(A), NOT(B)))} = \overline{\overline{(\overline{A} + \overline{B})}}$$

In this chapter you have covered:

- Boolean expressions, e.g. $\overline{(\overline{A} \bullet \overline{B})}$
- De Morgan's laws in a form for designing logic gate circuits

  $A + B = \overline{(\overline{A} \bullet \overline{B})}$

  $A \bullet B = \overline{(\overline{A} + \overline{B})}$
- Boolean identities

  $A + 0 = A$ $\quad A + 1 = 1$ $\quad A + \overline{A} = 1$ $\quad A + A = A$

  $\overline{A} + 0 = \overline{A}$ $\quad \overline{A} + 1 = 1$ $\quad \overline{A} + \overline{A} = \overline{A}$

  $0 \bullet A = 0$ $\quad 1 \bullet A = A$ $\quad A \bullet \overline{A} = 0$ $\quad A \bullet A = A$

  $0 \bullet \overline{A} = 0$ $\quad 1 \bullet \overline{A} = \overline{A}$ $\quad \overline{A} \bullet \overline{A} = \overline{A}$

  $\overline{\overline{A}} = A$
- Distribution laws

  $A \bullet (B + C) = A \bullet B + A \bullet C$ $\qquad A + (B \bullet C) = (A + B) \bullet (A + C)$
- Using De Morgan's laws and Boolean identities to manipulate and simplify Boolean expressions

7.1 Internal hardware components of a computer

7.1.1 Internal hardware components of a computer

Learning objectives:

- *Have an understanding and knowledge of the basic internal components of a computer system*
- *Understand the role of the following components and how they relate to each other*
  - *processor*
  - *main memory*
  - *address bus*
  - *data bus*
  - *control bus*
  - *I/O controllers*
- *Understand the need for, and means of, communication between components. In particular understand the concept of a bus and how address, data and control buses are used*
- *Be able to explain the difference between von Neumann and Harvard architectures and describe where each is typically used*
- *Understand the concept of addressable memory*

Structure of a simple computer

The architecture of a simple (traditional) computer system consists of a set of independent components or subsystems which may be classified as either internal or external. The internal subsystems are:

- processor or Central Processing Unit (CPU)
- main memory (RAM)
- I/O controllers - input only, output only, both input and output
- buses

The external subsystems are on the periphery of the computer system and are known, therefore, as peripherals or peripheral devices - for example, the keyboard, visual display unit, printer, magnetic disk drive. The main processor or CPU exchanges data with a peripheral device through a part of an I/O controller called an I/O port. Peripheral devices are not connected directly to the CPU because the former often operate with signal levels, protocols and power requirements which are different from those used by a CPU. Therefore, peripherals are not under the direct control of the CPU. Figure 7.1.1 illustrates the structure of a simple (traditional) computer.

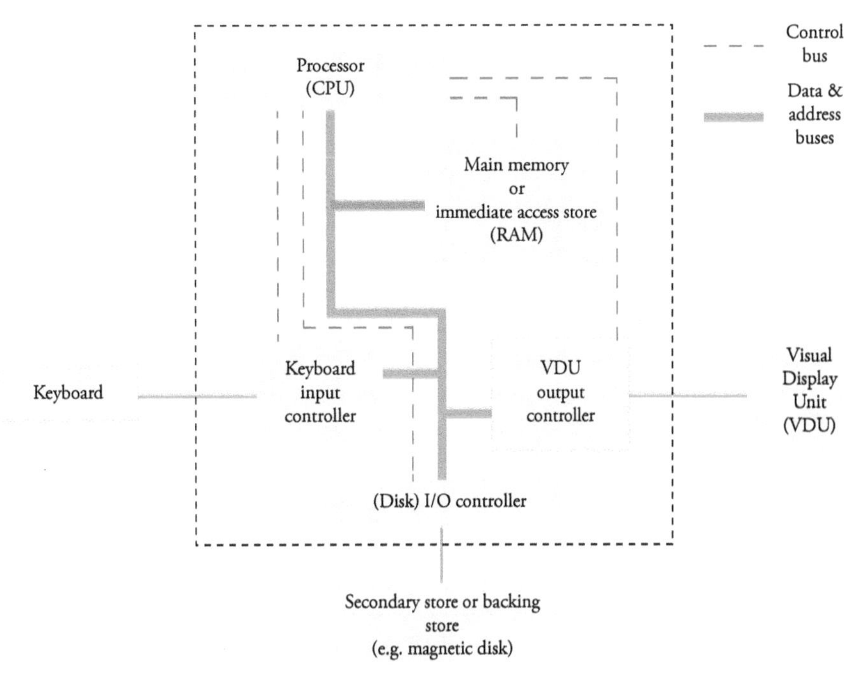

Figure 7.1.1 Block diagram of the simplified structure of a traditional (von Neumann) computer

Information

Processor (CPU):

The name processor was commonly used for the name of the central or general-purpose processor. Nowadays, CPU or Central Processing Unit refers to the general processor to distinguish it from other processors, e.g. Graphics Processing Unit (GPU). Originally, CPU meant processor + main memory.

Key concept

Peripheral:

A peripheral is a device that is connected to the computer system but which is not under the direct control of the processor. Instead the processor interacts with the peripheral indirectly via the peripheral's I/O controller which sits electrically between the peripheral and the system bus.

Key concept

System bus:

A bus that connects together processor, main memory and I/O controllers is called a system bus.

It consists of three dedicated buses:

1. data bus
2. address bus
3. control bus.

Information

Bus line:

The wires of a bus are often referred to as lines or bus lines because they resemble tram lines used by trams.

Key fact

Bus width:

The number of wires in a bus is referred to as the width of the bus.

Information

Bus masters:

In the traditional shared bus system, one device takes charge of the system bus at a time, e.g. the processor or the main memory. A device that is granted access to the system bus so that it can communicate with another device is called the master during the communication and the device receiving the communication the slave.

Questions

The components or subsystems of a traditional von Neumann computer system are classified as either internal or external.

(a) Name the four internal components

(b) Give **three** examples of an external component

The bus subsystem

Buses can be parallel buses, which carry data words in parallel on multiple wires, or serial buses, which carry data in bit-serial form (one bit after another) in one or more communication pathways or channels (channel = pair of wires or equivalent). A parallel bus is a set of parallel wires connecting two or more independent components of a computer; for example in *Figure 7.1.2* control, data and address buses are shown connecting the processor (CPU), memory and I/O controllers. A key characteristic of the parallel bus in this example is that it is a shared transmission medium, so that only one component can successfully transmit at any one time.

A bus that connects together processor (CPU), main memory and I/O controllers has traditionally been called a system bus. Typically such a bus consists of from 50 to 100 separate wires (conducting pathways). Each wire (line) conveys a single bit at a time. The number of wires is referred to as the width of the bus. Although there are different bus designs, on a traditional system bus the lines can be classified into three functional groups: data, address and control lines. The subsets of lines are known as the data, address and control buses, respectively.

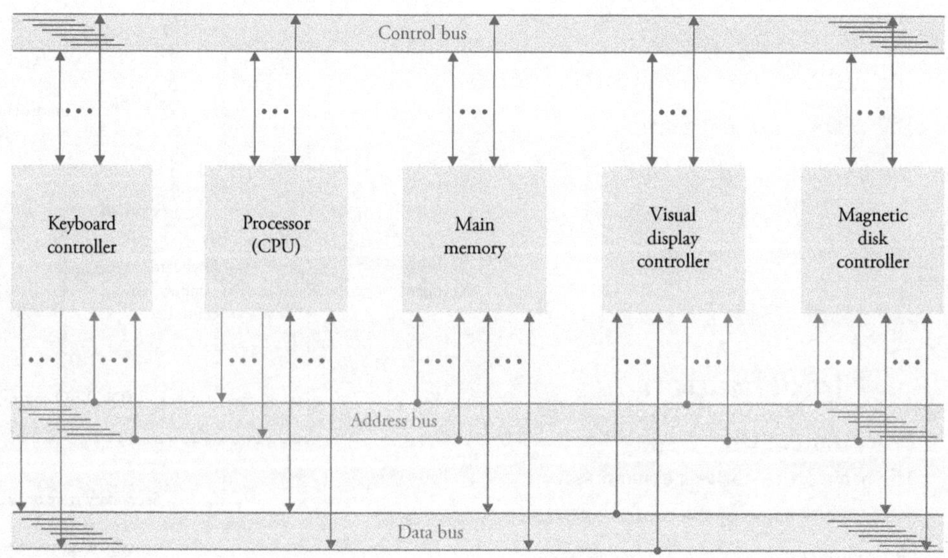

Figure 7.1.2 Internal components of a traditional shared bus computer system (von Neumann)

Questions

2 Distinguish between a parallel bus and a serial bus.

3 What is a parallel bus used for in the traditional von Neumann computer system and what name is given to this bus?

4 The system bus is subdivided into three functional groups of wires in the traditional von Neumann computer system. Name these groups.

5 What is meant by saying that this von Neumann system bus is a shared transmission medium?

Modern bus systems

The traditional computer system of von Neumann's design required that both processor (CPU) and main memory operate together at the same speed.

Modern general purpose processors operate at speeds much faster than main memory can operate. Thus the main processor or CPU in such a system will be held up waiting for a requested data word to be fetched from memory unless the CPU is decoupled from main memory in a way that allows it to do other tasks. *Figure 7.1.3* shows how the bus architecture is evolving to take account of this and differences in speed of operation of other devices that are connected to the computer system. *Figure 7.1.4* shows a printed circuit board (motherboard) for a relatively modern general purpose computer. In the latest processors and mother boards, the memory controller has been moved into the CPU and two separate buses are used, a memory bus and a packet-based (up to 32 bits) serial bus for peripherals.

Traditional (von Neumann) computer system data bus

The data bus, typically consisting of 8,16, 32, 64 separate lines, provides a bidirectional path for moving data and instructions between system components. The width of the data bus is a key factor in determining overall system performance. For example, if the data bus is 16 bits wide, and each instruction is 32 bits long, then the processor must access the main memory twice during each instruction cycle.

Questions

6 What is the purpose of the data bus and why is its width a factor in determining overall system performance?

Information

Serial bus:
Parallel buses suffer timing skew which limits their operating speed. and they only operate one-way at a time (half-duplex).
A serial bus does not suffer from timing skew and therefore can operate at a much higher rate than is possible with parallel buses. They can also operate in both directions simultaneously just by adding another serial channel. PCI Express, Serial ATA (SATA) and USB are all examples that support serial bus operation.

Address, data and control lines are replaced by address, data and control phases of the serial communication. which takes place in packets of bits.

The serial bus is now considered to be a point-to-point connection with one or more channels (pair of wires).

This has become an important mechanism for communicating between multiple cores and slices of main memory. One such system resembles the switching circuits of a telephone exchange which connects multiple pathways simultaneously to enable many independent calls to be made.

Key concept

Data bus:
The data bus provides a bidirectional path for moving data and instructions between system components.

Did you know?

The Spinnaker Human Brain project:
In this project 100000 to 1000000 simple microprocessors containing ARM processor cores and main memory are being connected together in a hexagonal grid to allow networks of many millions of neurons to be simulated in real time.
The communication between the microprocessors is based on an efficient multicast infrastructure inspired by neurobiology. It uses a packet-switched network to emulate the very high connectivity of biological systems.

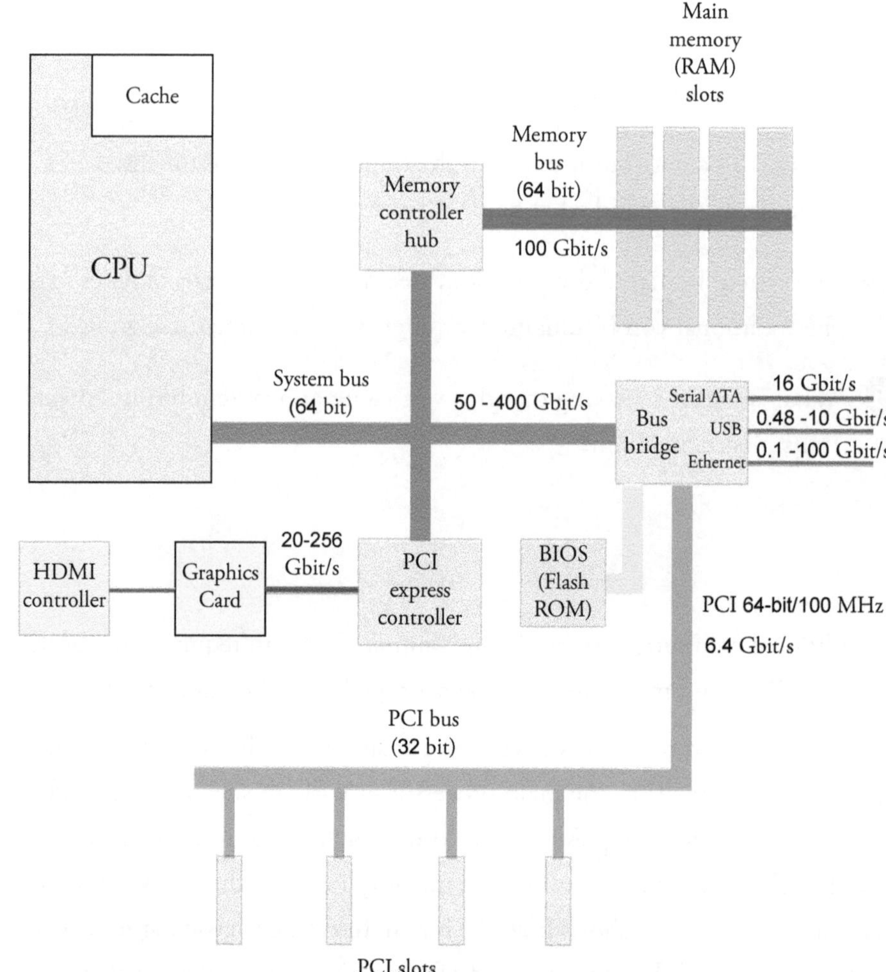

Figure 7.1.3 Block diagram of an I/O controller

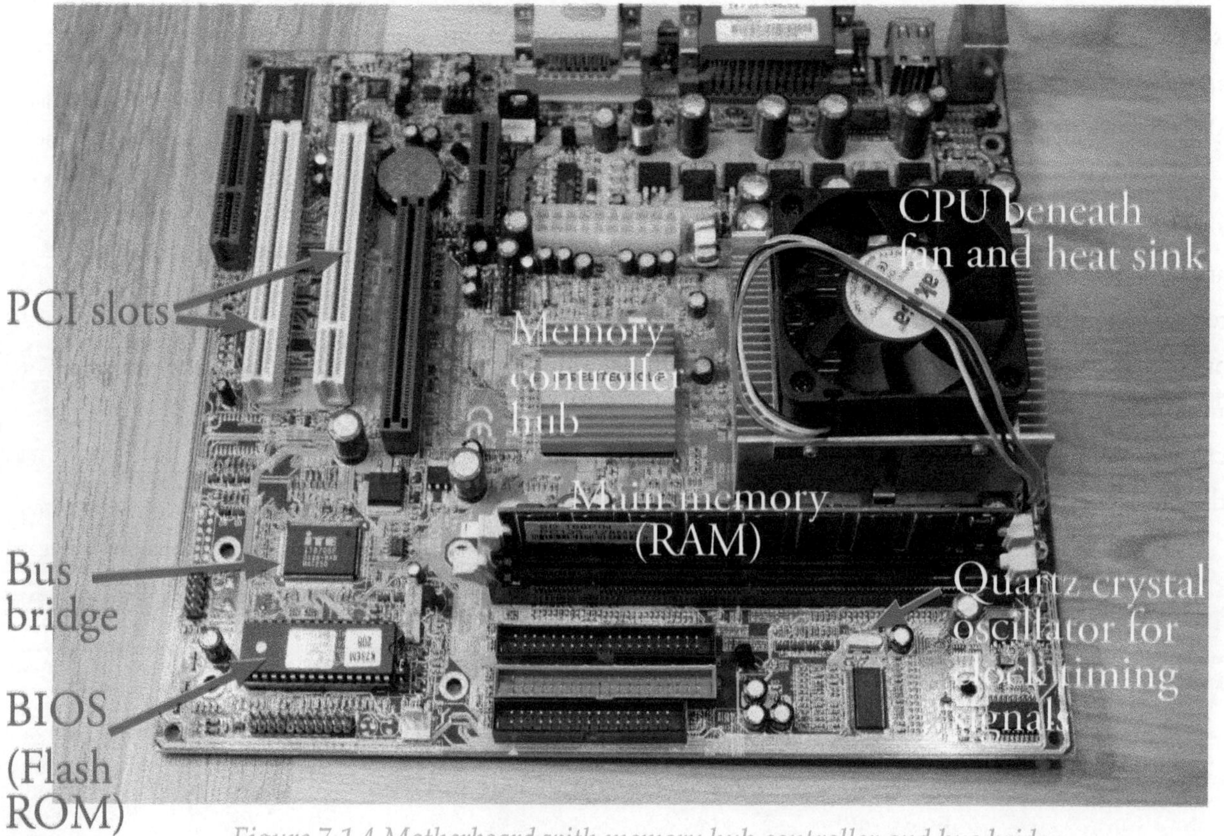

Figure 7.1.4 Motherboard with memory hub controller and bus bridge

Traditional (von Neumann) computer system control bus

The control bus is a bidirectional bus meaning that signals can be carried in both directions. The data and address buses are shared by all components of the system. Control lines must therefore be provided to ensure that access to and use of the data and address buses by the different components of the system does not lead to conflict. The purpose of the control bus is to transmit command, timing and specific status information between system components. Timing signals synchronise operations by indicating when information on the data, control and address buses is ready for consumption. Command signals specify operations to be performed. Specific status signals indicate the state of a data transfer request, or the status of a request by a system component to gain control of the system bus.

Key concept

Control bus:
The control bus is a bidirectional bus i.e. it carries signals between the processor and other system components and vice versa. The purpose of the control bus is to transmit command, timing and specific status information between system components.

Typical control lines include:

- Memory Write: causes data on the data bus to be written into the addressed location.
- Memory Read: causes data from the addressed location to be placed on the data bus.
- I/O Write: causes data on the data bus to be output to the addressed I/O port.
- I/O Read: causes data from the addressed I/O port to be placed on the data bus.
- Transfer ACK: indicates that data have been accepted from or placed on the data bus.
- Bus Request: indicates that a component needs to gain control of the system bus.
- Bus Grant: indicates that a requesting component has been granted control of the system bus
- Interrupt request: indicates that an interrupt is pending.
- Interrupt ACK: acknowledges that the pending interrupt has been recognised.
- Clock: used to synchronise operations.
- Reset: initialises all components.

Questions

7 Using examples, explain the purpose of the control bus in the traditional von Neumann computer system.

Key concept

Address bus:
The address bus is used to select a specific memory location containing a word of data or an instruction. It does this by carrying the address of the desired location on its bus, e.g. 234_{10} or 11101010_2.

Key concept

Address space:
The range of memory addresses that the machine can address.

Traditional (von Neumann) computer system address bus

When the processor wishes to read a word (say 8, 16, 32 or 64 bits) of data or an instruction from memory, it first puts the address of the desired word on the address bus. The width of the address bus determines the maximum possible memory capacity of the system - its address space. For example, if the address bus consisted of only 8 lines, then the maximum address it could transmit would be (in binary) 11111111 or 255 - giving a maximum memory capacity of 256 (including address 0). A more realistic minimum bus width would be 20 lines, giving a memory capacity of 2^{20}, i.e. an address space of 1048576 addressable memory locations (words). The address bus is also used to address I/O ports during input/output operations.

No of address lines, m	Maximum no of addressable locations	Maximum no of addressable locations expressed as a power of two, 2^m
1	2	2^1
2	4	2^2
3	8	2^3
4	16	2^4
8	256	2^8
16	65536	2^{16}
20	1048576	2^{20}
24	16777216	2^{24}

Table 7.1.1: Relationship between number of address lines m and maximum number of addressable memory locations

Questions

8. The address space of a particular computer system is 2^{20}. What does this mean?

9. The address bus of a traditional computer system consists of 16 lines. What is the total number of memory locations that theoretically can be addressed by this address bus?

Main memory

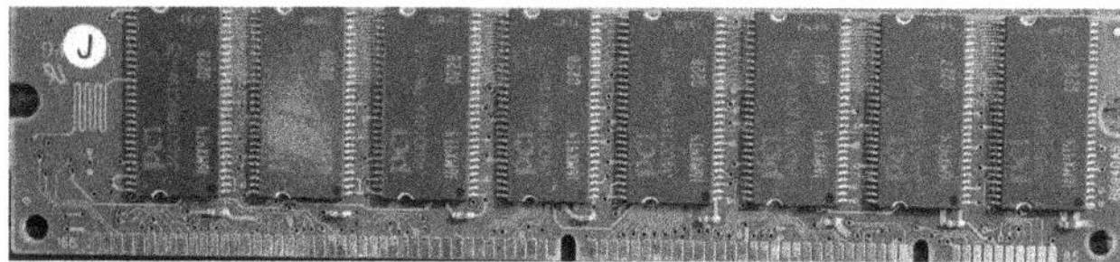

Figure 7.1.5 Main memory RAM chips

Main memory consists of a contiguous block of read/write, randomly accessible storage locations constructed from semiconductor technology - Figure 7.1.5. It is a store for addressable words, one word per location, with each word composed of the same number of binary digits - Figure 7.1.6

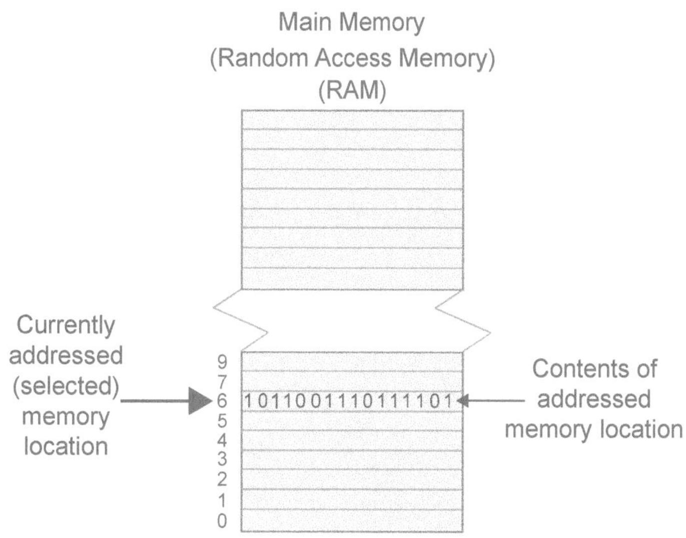

Figure 7.1.6 Main memory

Each location is

- capable of "remembering" what was written to it
- able to change its contents to another bit pattern when a write request is received if the memory is read/write
- assigned a unique integer address by which it may be located
- capable of providing a copy of its contents when a read request is received.

The semiconductor technology used in read/write main memory means

- that the main memory is volatile, i.e. the contents of each storage location is lost when the power is removed.
- the contents of main memory are not restored when powered up again but instead each location consists of a random pattern of bits.

Storage locations may be visited (selected) one after another in any order noncontiguously, starting from anywhere in the memory. The time taken to access any particular storage location is the same.

These two facts have led to main memory being labelled Random Access Memory or RAM.

Information

von Neumann architecture:
Memory contains addressable words each composed of the same number of binary digits; addresses consist of integers running consecutively through the memory, 0, 1, 2, ...

Questions

10 How is main memory organised?

11 What is meant by volatile memory?

12 What is meant by random access in the context of main memory?

I/O Controllers

Peripheral devices cannot be connected directly to the processor. Each peripheral operates in a different way and it would not be sensible to design processors to directly control every possible peripheral. Otherwise, the invention of a new type of peripheral would require the processor to be redesigned. Instead, the processor controls and communicates with a peripheral device through an I/O or device controller.

Key concept

I/O controller:
An I/O controller is a board of electronics that enables the processor to control and communicate with a peripheral device through an I/O port.

Information

Hardware interface:
An interface is a standardised form of connection defining such things as signals, number of connecting pins/sockets and voltage levels that appear on these pins/sockets.

Key concept

I/O port:
An I/O port is a set of registers (and block of storage cells in a block transfer device) located in an I/O controller connected to the system bus. An I/O port provides a standard interface through which a processor connected to the system bus can control and communicate with the peripheral device attached to the I/O controller.

Information

Memory-mapped peripherals:
The registers and block of storage locations of an I/O controller can use the same address space as main memory. In this case, memory addresses that would have been used for main memory are allocated to I/O controllers. The peripherals attached to these I/O controllers are then said to be memory-mapped.

Information

Direct Memory Access (DMA):
Block transfer devices such as magnetic disks can take charge of the system bus to transfer a disk block directly to main memory bypassing the processor entirely. This is called Direct Memory Access.

The controller is a board of electronics consisting of three parts:

- An interface that allows connection of the controller to the system or I/O bus.
- A set of data, command, address and status registers (for block transfer devices the data register will be replaced by a block of storage locations).
- An interface that enables connection of the controller to the cable connecting the device to the computer.

An I/O controller presents a standard interface to the system bus so that the peripheral device appears to the processor as just a set of registers mapped onto the address space of the machine and which can be referenced by machine instructions - see *Figure 7.1.7*. This set of registers (and for block transfer devices, block of storage locations) is known as an **I/O port**.

I/O controllers are available which can operate both input and output transfers of bits, e.g. magnetic disk controller. Other controllers operate in one direction only, either as an input controller, e.g., keyboard controller or as an output controller, e.g., VDU controller.

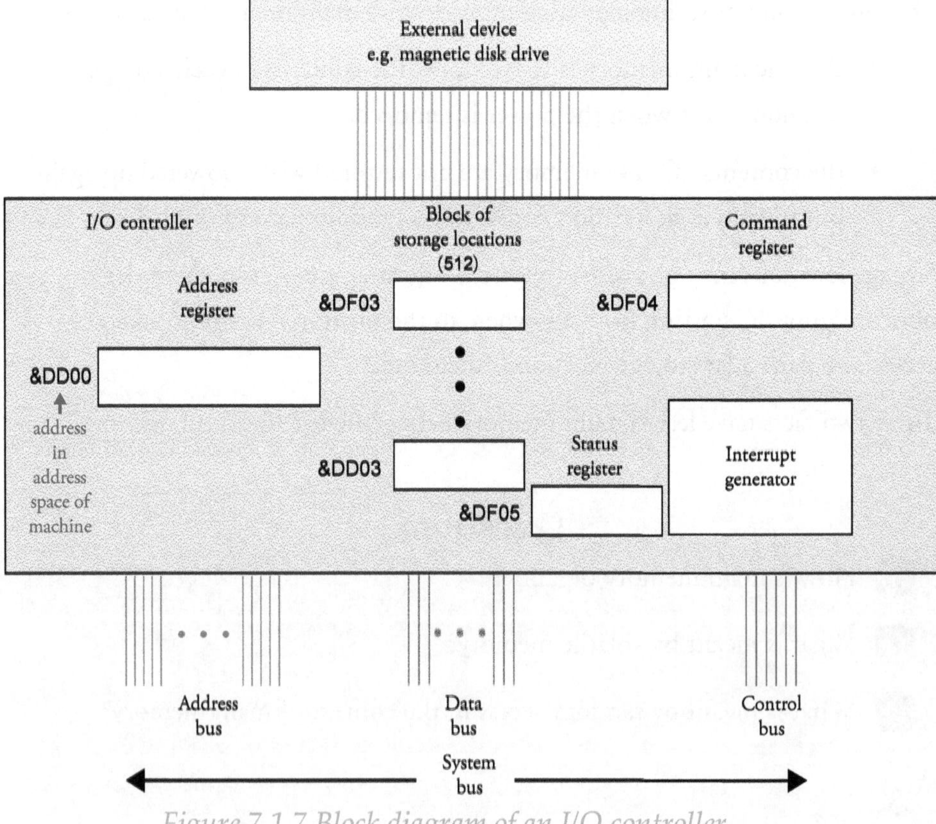

Figure 7.1.7 Block diagram of an I/O controller

Questions

13 What is an I/O controller?

14 Why is a processor not connected directly to external devices?

15 What is an I/O port?

Processor (CPU)

The processor (CPU) executes machine instructions that have been fetched along the data bus from main memory locations. The processor selects a memory location by placing the address of the location on the address bus. The data processed by machine instructions is also fetched along the data bus from main memory and the results of processing returned the same way. The control bus is used by the processor to assert actions, e.g. read from memory, write to memory, and to allow devices such as the keyboard controller to grab the attention of the processor via the interrupt mechanism when a key is pressed.

Von Neumann and Harvard architectures

General-purpose processors are designed to work well in a variety of contexts. In the von Neumann architecture, programs and data share the same memory which the processor communicates with over a shared bus called the system bus - Figure 7.1.8. As John von Neumann was working at Princeton university at the time this architecture is also known as the Princeton architecture.

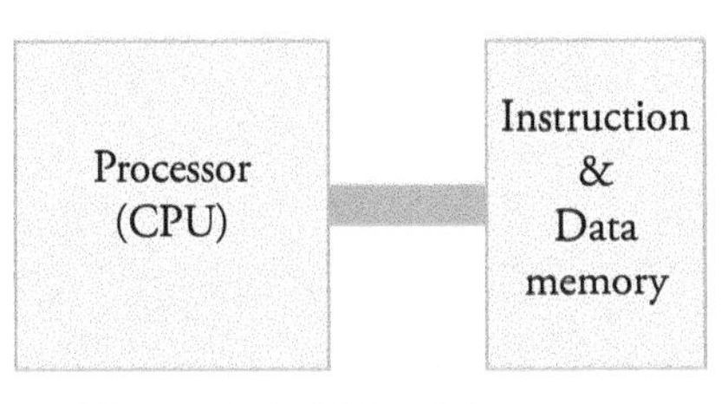

Figure 7.1.8 Von Neumann architecture

The Harvard architecture is often used in the design of processors where the context in which the processor is required to work is restricted or dedicated to a particular task, e.g. sampling and recording data from sensors. Such processors are used in embedded systems e.g., traction control systems in automobiles. In the Harvard architecture, program and data are allocated separate memories as shown in Figure 7.1.9. The processor is connected to both memories by separate buses so that each memory can be accessed simultaneously. The benefit of having a separate data memory is that data access is possible at a consistent bandwidth (same bit rate) which is particularly important for sampled-data systems.

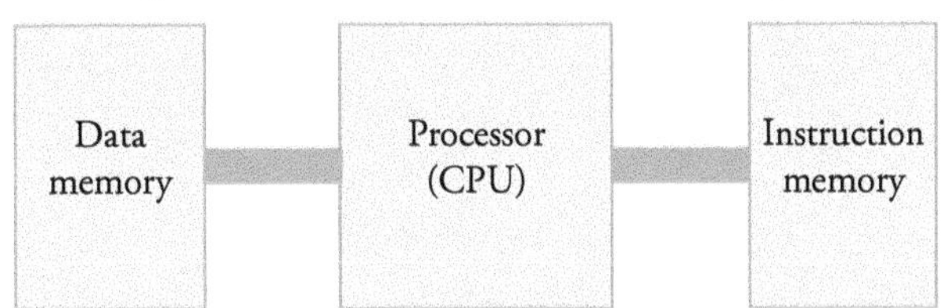

Figure 7.1.9 Harvard architecture

The Raspberry Pi computer is based on the Harvard architecture.

The instruction sets of Harvard architecture processors can be different from that of general purpose von Neumann processors because Harvard processors need to support the context in which they will be used, e.g. graphics processing.

In graphics processing, algorithms perform identical operations on each section of the screen. For this type of processing, a processor that can multiply and

Did you know?

Sales of processors for embedded applications, e.g., mobile phones, far exceed the sale of processors for general purpose computing.

accumulate a block of data in a single instruction is very useful. Processors that perform this kind of specialised processing are called **Digital Signal Processors** (DSP). They are usually based on the Harvard architecture because they need to perform single instruction multiple data processing and accumulate results in an accumulator register.

Questions

16 What is the major difference between the von Neumann computer architecture and the Harvard architecture?

17 Where is each typically used?

In this chapter you have covered:

- The basic internal components of a traditional computer system
  - processor
  - main memory
  - address bus
  - data bus
  - control bus
  - I/O controllers
- The concept of a bus, parallel and serial and how address, data and control buses are used
- The difference between von Neumann and Harvard architectures and where each is typically used
- The concept of addressable memory

7.2 The stored program concept

Learning objectives:

- *Be able to describe the stored program concept*

7.2.1 The meaning of the stored program concept

The **stored program concept** was proposed by John von Neumann and Alan Turing in separate publications in 1945. They proposed that both the program and the data on which it performed processing and calculations should be stored in memory together.

Figure 7.2.1.1 Plaque located at University of Manchester commemorating the creators of the first stored program computer

Specifically,

- The program to be executed is resident in an electronic memory directly accessible to the processor
- Instructions are fetched one at a time (serially) from this memory and executed in a processor
- Data is resident in an electronic memory directly accessible to the processor which can change it if instructed to by the executing program.

Information

EDSAC and SSEM:
The University of Manchester's Small-Scale Experimental Machine (SSEM) is generally recognized as the world's first electronic computer that ran a stored program—an event that occurred on 21st June 1948.
However, the EDSAC (designed and built at Cambridge university) is considered the first complete and fully operational electronic digital stored program computer. It ran its first program on 6th May 1949.

Figure 7.2.1.2 ENIAC computer being reprogrammed by changing the wiring (U.S. Army photo, http://ftp.arl.army.mil/~mike/comphist/)

The stored program model in which program and data reside together in main memory when the program is being executed became known as a **von Neumann computer**.

The world's first stored program electronic computer was designed and built at the university of Manchester.

The stored program concept enables computers to perform any type of computation, without requiring the user to physically alter or reconfigure the hardware.

In contrast, to program the forerunners of the von Neumann computer and to change the data, the programmer had to manually plug in cables and set switches. This was quite tedious and time consuming. Figure 7.2.1.2 shows two programmers changing the program and data by literally

Key concept

Stored program concept:
Both the program and the data on which it performs processing and calculations are stored in memory together.
Specifically,

1. The program to be executed is resident in a memory directly accessible to the processor
2. Instructions are fetched one at a time (serially) from this memory and executed by the processor
3. Data is resident in a memory directly accessible to the processor which can change it, if instructed to by the executing program.

Information

Harvard architecture:
Another stored program computer is the Harvard architecture computer, a rival architecture to the von Neumann architecture that came from Princeton university.
In the Harvard architecture, the program resides in one memory and data in a separate memory which is also directly accessible by the processor. Nevertheless a Harvard architecture computer is also a stored program computer.

Key principle

Program code and data are the same:
Program code and data can be treated as if they are the same when they occupy the same memory.
The memory is interpreted as an instruction when the next instruction pointer references it, and as data when an instruction references it.

rewiring the ENIAC computer, a non-stored program computer. This simple but fundamental idea of the stored program computer has been incorporated into all modern digital computers.

Program code and data are the same

The stored program concept, as embodied in the von Neumann computer, of having the program and data share the same memory means that the computer can modify its data or the program itself while it is executing.

Figure 7.2.1.3 shows the basic architecture of a von Neumann computer.

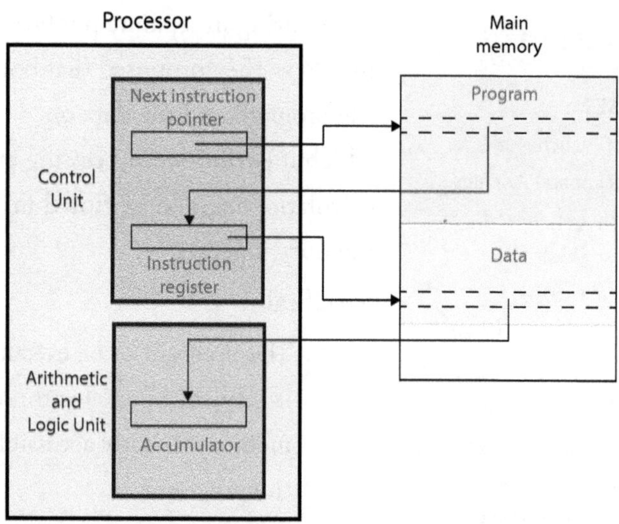

Figure 7.2.1.3 Stored program von Neumann computer basic architecture

Program code and data can be treated as if they are the same when they occupy the same memory. The memory is interpreted as an instruction when the next instruction pointer references it, and as data when an instruction references it.

Treating program code as data is useful when, for example, a program needs to be downloaded from a remote location because it can be treated as data and downloaded in the same way that an email can be.

Programs such as compilers also treat other programs as data when they read them. However, treating programs as data also has a downside. Computer viruses are programs too which get treated as data when being downloaded but as programs when the host computer is tricked into executing them.

Questions

1. What is meant by the *stored program concept*?
2. Explain what is meant by program code and data can be treated as the same thing in a von Neumann stored program computer.
3. State **one** advantage and **one** disadvantage of being able to do this.

Task

1. Explore the university of Manchester's site on the world's first stored program computer at

   http://curation.cs.manchester.ac.uk/digital60/www.digital60.org/birth/index.html

In this chapter you have covered:

- the stored program concept
- why program code and data can be treated as the same thing in a von Neumann stored program computer.

7.3 Structure and role of the processor and its components

Learning objectives:

- *Explain the role and operation of a processor and its major components:*
  - *arithmetic and logic unit*
  - *control unit*
  - *clock*
  - *general purpose registers*
  - *dedicated registers, including:*
    - *program counter*
    - *current instruction register*
    - *memory address register*
    - *memory buffer register*
    - *status register*

7.3.1 The processor and its components

Processor

A simplified block diagram of a traditional processor is shown in *Figure 7.3.1.1*.

A typical processor or Central Processing Unit (CPU) consists of the following components:

- Control Unit, which fetches instructions from memory, decodes and executes them one at a time
- Arithmetic and Logic Unit (ALU) which performs arithmetic and logical operations on data supplied in registers, storing the result in a register. It can perform, for example, addition and subtraction, fixed and floating point arithmetic, Boolean logic operations such as AND, OR, XOR and a range of shift operations.
- Registers: general purpose, e.g. $Register_A$, and special purpose or dedicated registers, e.g. **Current Instruction Register (CIR)**, **Program Counter (PC)**, **Memory Buffer Register (MBR)**, **Memory Address Register (MAR)**, **Status Register**.
- System clock, which generates a continuous sequence of clock pulses to step the control unit through its operation.

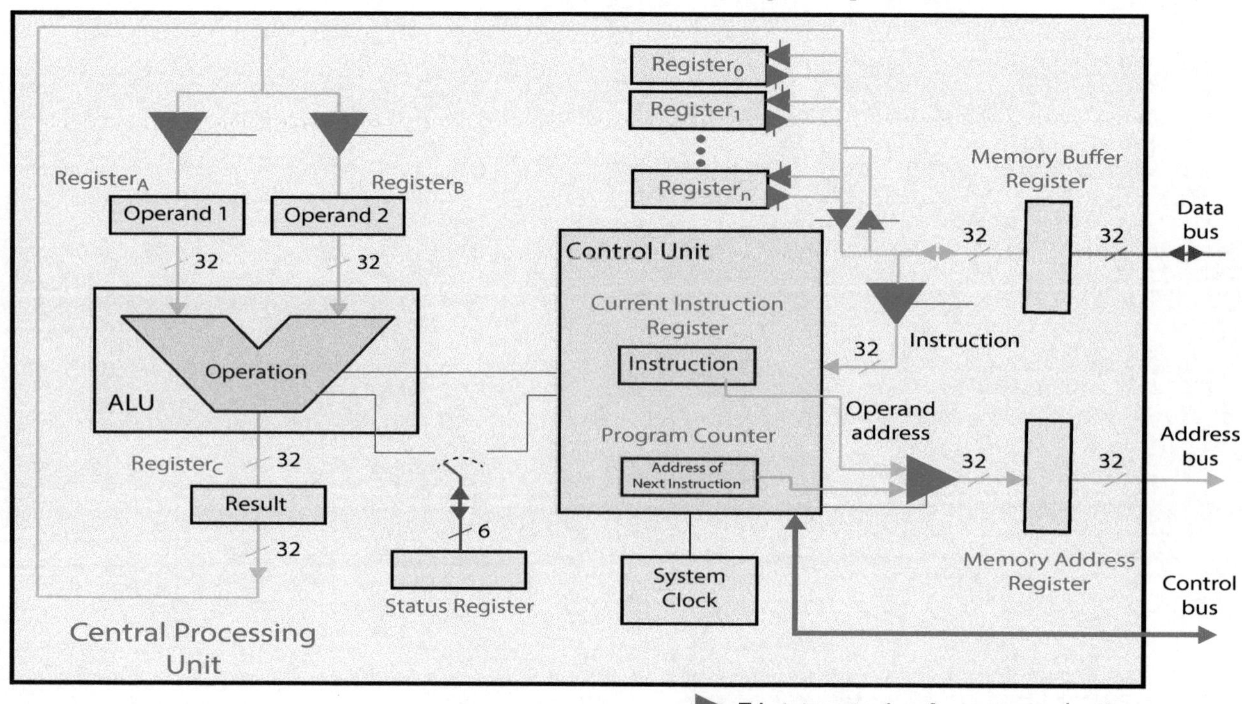

Figure 7.3.1.1 Simplified internal structure of a processor/central processing unit

Key fact

Processor (CPU):
The processor or central processing unit (CPU) consists of the following components:

- Control unit
- Arithmetic and Logic Unit (ALU)
- General purpose registers
- Dedicated or special purpose registers
- system clock

Key principle

Memory:
A memory is a set of words, each with an address and a content:

- The addresses are values of a fixed size, called the address length
- The contents are values of another fixed size, called the word length
- A load operation is used to obtain the content of a memory word
- A store operation changes the content of a memory word.

Key principle

Processor and memory:
A processor interacts with memory in 3 ways:

- by fetching instructions
- by loading a memory word into a processor register
- by changing the content of a memory word by a store operation.

Key fact

Processor word length:
The size of the registers in the processor defines the size of the processor, e.g. a 32-bit processor has registers that are 32 bits long. The length of a register is known as the word length of the processor.
This word length is also usually the size of the memory word transferred in a load operation.

The processor or central processing unit is connected to main memory by the system bus.

Questions

1 General purpose registers are one major component of a traditional processor. Name and describe the **four other** major components.

Processor operation with main memory

A memory is a set of words, each with an address and a content:

- The addresses are values of a fixed size, the address length
- The contents are values of another fixed size, the word length
- A load operation is used to obtain the content of a memory word
- A store operation changes the content of a memory word.

In a von Neuman computer both program and data reside in the same memory. This memory is called main memory.

A processor interacts with this memory in 3 ways:

- by fetching instructions
- by loading a memory word into a processor register
- by changing the content of a memory word by a store operation.

The size of the registers in the processor defines the size of the processor, e.g. a 32-bit processor has registers that are 32 bits long. The length of a register is known as the word length of the processor. This word length is also usually the size of the memory word transferred in a load operation.

In *Figure 7.3.1.1* the registers have a word length of 32 bits. Each is connected to a bus inside the processor which is also 32 bits wide shown as /32 in the figure.

Questions

2 State **three** ways that a processor interacts with memory.

Control Unit

The control unit of the processor shown in *Figure 7.3.1.1* controls fetching, loading and storing operations.

It fetches an instruction into the Current Instruction Register via the Memory Buffer Register and the data bus by

- reading the contents of the Program Counter to obtain the memory address of the memory word containing the instruction

- placing this memory address in the Memory Address Register connected to the address bus so that the addressed memory word can be selected and transferred across the data bus into the Memory Buffer Register
- transferring the instruction fetched from memory from the Memory Buffer Register into the Current Instruction Register

The control unit also

- decodes the instruction to determine if it is a load, store, arithmetic operation, or logic operation
- executes the instruction by
    - using the instruction's operand fields as addresses to use in load or store operations, if required, or
    - loading a memory word into a register, or
    - changing a word of memory in a store operation, or
    - controlling an arithmetic operation, e.g., ADD, or a logical operation, e.g., AND, in the Arithmetic and Logic Unit (ALU) using as operands the instruction's operand fields.

Key principle

Control unit:
Controls fetching, loading and storing operations.

Key principle

Control unit:
- Fetches an instruction from memory and places it in the Current Instruction Register.
- Decodes the instruction to determine if it is one of load, store, arithmetic operation, or logic operation
- Executes the instruction.

Questions

3 State the purpose of a processor's control unit.

4 Describe in detail the operation of a processor's control unit when executing a stored program, instruction by instruction. You should state the name and describe the role of each register in this process.

System clock

The system clock or clock is a unit inside the processor that provides regular clock pulses that the control unit uses to sequence its operations.

The clock signal is a 1-bit signal that oscillates between a "1" and a "0" with a certain frequency as shown in *Figure 7.3.1.2*. The change from "0" to "1" is called the positive edge, and the change from "1" to "0" the negative edge.

The time taken to go from one positive edge to the next is known as the clock period, and represents one clock cycle. The number of clock cycles that fit one second is called the clock frequency or clock speed.

Key fact

System clock:
The system clock is a unit inside the processor that provides regular clock pulses that the control unit uses to sequence its operations.

$$\text{Clock period} = \frac{1}{\text{Clock frequency}}$$

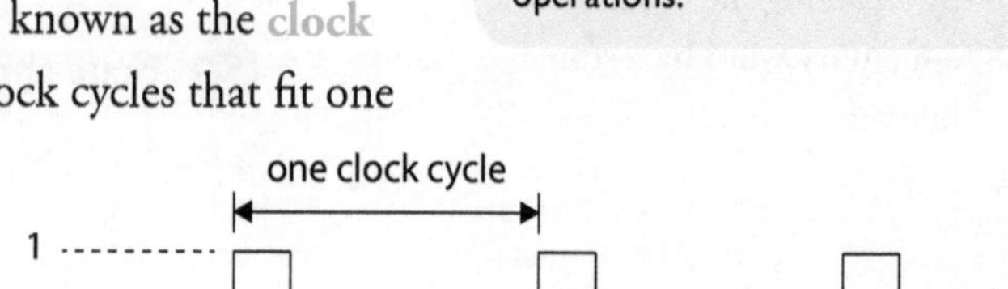

Figure 7.3.1.2 Clock signal

Table 7.3.1.1 shows some examples of clock speed/frequency for both current processors/CPUs and a very popular processor from the 1980s.

Information

Instructions per second:
The number of instructions fetched and executed per second is given by

$$\text{Instructions per second} = \frac{\text{Clock frequency}}{\text{no of cycles per instruction}}$$

Clock frequency	Clock period/cycle	CPU
4GHz	0.25 nanoseconds	AMD 6300
900MHz	1.1 nanoseconds	ARM Cortex-A7 (Raspberry Pi 2)
1 MHz	1 microsecond	Motorola 6502 (BBC Model B computer)

Table 7.3.1.1 Clock speeds for some processors/CPUs

The number of clock cycles an instruction takes to be fetched and executed varies from processor to processor. A very simple design might use one clock cycle to fetch an instruction from memory and another clock cycle to execute the instruction as shown in *Figure 7.3.1.3*.

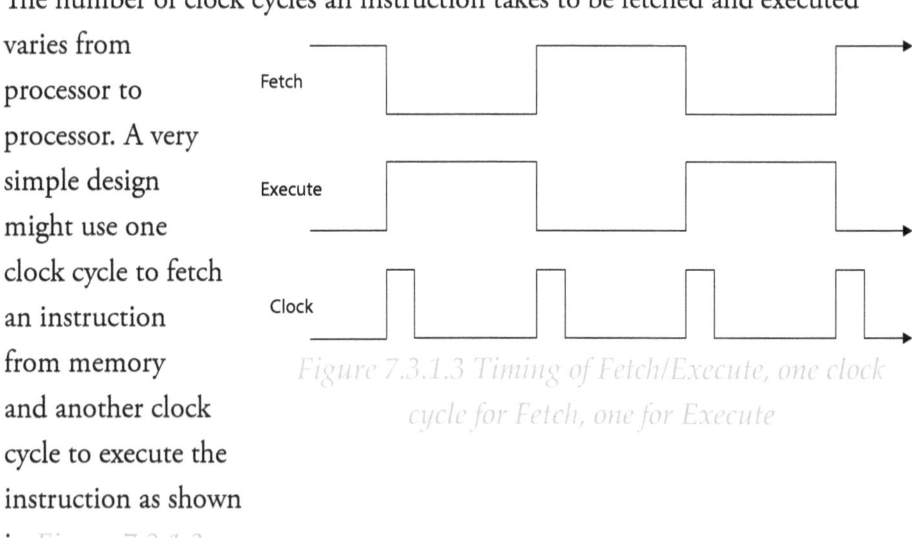

Figure 7.3.1.3 Timing of Fetch/Execute, one clock cycle for Fetch, one for Execute

Information

Quartz crystal oscillator:
The processor is usually connected to an external quartz crystal oscillator which provides a very stable and regular timing signal.
The clock unit in the processor uses this timing signal to derive all the timing signals that are needed by the control unit to synchronise operations within the processor.

A fetch phase occurs when the Fetch signal is 1 and the Execute signal is 0. An Execute phase occurs when the Execute signal is 1 and the Fetch signal is 0. Both Fetch and Execute signals are derived from the (master) clock signal and are therefore synchronised by this signal.

The number of instructions fetched and executed per second is given by

$$\text{Instructions per second} = \frac{\text{Clock frequency}}{\text{no of cycles per instruction}}$$

If the clock frequency for the 2-cycle processor design is 1 GHz then the number of instructions fetched and executed per second is

$$\text{Instructions per second} = \frac{1\text{GHz}}{2}$$

i.e. 500 million instructions per second.

Questions

5. What is the purpose of a processor's system clock?
6. What is meant clock speed?
7. With the aid of a diagram, explain how the control unit could use the system clock when an instruction in memory is executed in two clock cycles.
8. The clock frequency at which a particular processor is operated is 2GHz. The number of clock cycles per instruction is 2.
   How many instructions can be executed per second in this processor?

Registers

Registers are memory locations internal to the processor that support fast access as well as rapid manipulation of their contents because they are made from the fastest memory technology.

Moving data between the ALU and registers and between registers is facilitated by dedicated pathways within the processor that the control unit can open or close relatively quickly.

However, the memory technology used and the dedicated pathways make implementing registers expensive and so the processor will have only a limited number, typically 32 but the number can range from 4 to 256. This is in contrast to memory locations in main memory which are made from much slower but cheaper technology and which are accessed over a shared pathway, the system bus. The cheap technology and shared bus make it possible to have a very large number of main memory locations, e.g. 1000 0000 0000 locations, but access is much slower than the speed the processor operates at.

Questions

 9 What are processor registers?

 10 Processor registers and main memory are located in separate areas of a traditional computer system. State **four** other differences between processor registers and main memory.

General purpose registers

General purpose registers are registers that can be used by the programmer to store data, as needed. Each register will be capable of storing a memory word of a fixed size and will have a unique address known to the control unit. For example, if there are 16 general purpose registers then their addresses will be 0, 1, 2, 3, ..., 14, 15 (0, 1, 2, ..., E, F in hexadecimal).

Dedicated or special-purpose registers

Some registers are designed to be used by the control unit in a specific way, e.g. the Program Counter (PC) stores a memory address which is the address of the next instruction to be fetched and executed. The control unit sets this address to ensure it points to the next instruction. The control unit increments this address during a Fetch. It also changes this address if the current instruction is a branch instruction or a subroutine call instruction or an interrupt service routing call.

The following special-purpose registers are dedicated as follows:

- Memory Buffer Register (MBR): Connected to the data bus and contains a word to be stored in memory, or a word copied from memory. This is also called the Memory Data Register (MDR)

Key concept

Registers:
Registers are memory locations internal to the processor that support fast access to and manipulation of their contents because they are made from the fastest memory technology.

Key concept

General purpose registers:
General purpose registers are registers that can be used by the programmer to store data, as needed.

Key concept

Special purpose or dedicated registers:
These are registers that are used by the control unit in a specific or dedicated way, e.g. Program Counter.

Key concept

Program Counter (PC):
Points to the next instruction to be fetched and executed.

Key concept

Memory Buffer Register (MBR):
Connected to the data bus and contains a word to be stored in memory, or a word copied from memory.
This is also called the Memory Data Register (MDR).

Key concept

Memory Address Register (MAR):
Connected to the address bus so that the memory address it contains can appear on this bus and be used at the memory end of this bus to select a particular memory word.

Key concept

Current Instruction Register (CIR):
When an instruction is fetched from memory it is stored in this register while the control unit decodes and executes it.

Key concept

Status Register:
This register stores single bit condition codes each of which indicates the outcome of arithmetic and logical operations carried out in the ALU, e.g. Zero bit or flag is set to 1 if the result of the last arithmetic operation is zero otherwise it is set to 0.
The status register also has single bits to control the operation of the control unit, e.g. Interrupt Enable/Disable bit.

- Memory Address Register (MAR): Connected to the address bus so that the memory address it contains can appear on this bus and be used at the memory end of this bus to select a particular memory word
- Instruction Register (IR) or Current Instruction Register (CIR): When an instruction is fetched from memory it is stored in this register while the control unit decodes and executes it.
- Status register: This register stores single bit condition codes each of which indicates the outcome of arithmetic and logical operations carried out in the ALU - for example, an arithmetic operation may produce any of the following a positive, negative, zero result, a carry, overflow and the corresponding condition codes are set (made 1). Sometimes the name flag is used for a single bit condition code, i.e. a flag is set. These condition codes may subsequently be tested by the control unit when it is executing a conditional branch operation. The possible condition codes are
  - Sign: Contains the sign bit of the result of the last arithmetic operation
  - Zero: Set when the result is zero
  - Carry: Set if an operation resulted in a carry (addition) into or borrow (subtraction) out of a high-order bit. Used for multi-word arithmetic operations
  - Equal: Set if a logical compare result is equality. (Alternatively the zero flag may be used)
  - Overflow: Used to indicate arithmetic overflow.

  The status register will also have single bits to control the operation of the control unit:

  - Interrupt Enable/Disable: Used to enable or disable interrupts
  - Supervisor: Indicates whether the processor is executing in supervisor or user mode. Certain privileged instructions can be executed only in supervisor mode, e.g. disabling interrupts, and certain areas of memory can be accessed only in supervisor mode.

Questions

11 What is meant by general purpose register?

12 What is meant by a dedicated or special purpose register?

13 State the role of each of the following:

(a) Program Counter (b) Memory Buffer Register (c) Memory Address Register
(d) Current Instruction Register (e) Status Register.

Questions

14 Name **four** condition code flags and **two** control flags present in a typical status register.

Arithmetic and Logic Unit (ALU)

Figure 7.3.1.4 shows the ALU performing the arithmetic operation 3 + (- 5) producing the result -2.

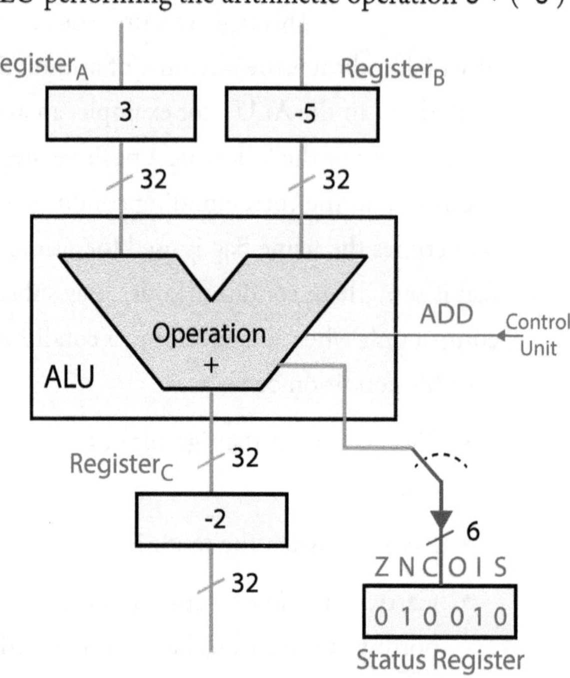

Figure 7.3.1.4 ALU performing an ADD operation

The Negative flag condition code (N) in the status register is set to 1 because the result is negative. The Zero flag (Z), Carry flag (C), Overflow flag (O) are set to 0. The Interrupt Enable flag is 1 therefore enabling interrupts. The Supervisor mode flag (S) is 0, therefore the processor is in User mode. The Supervisor flag is set to 1 when the operating system needs to use the processor, otherwise it is 0 when a user is executing a program in the processor.

The Arithmetic and Logic Unit (ALU) performs arithmetic and logical operations on data supplied in registers, storing the result in a register as shown in *Figure 7.3.1.4*. It can perform, for example, addition and subtraction, fixed and floating point arithmetic, Boolean logic operations such as AND, OR, XOR and a range of shift operations.

Questions

15 What is the purpose of the Arithmetic and Logic Unit?

16 Describe, with the aid of a diagram, the role of registers in the execution of arithmetic operation 4 + (-4) in the Arithmetic and Logic Unit.

Tasks

1 Explore the operation of a processor using a simulator such as ASMTutor or Visual X-Toy.

Key concept

Arithmetic and Logic Unit (ALU):
The Arithmetic and Logic Unit (ALU) performs arithmetic and logical operations on the data.

Key concept

Negative flag:
The Negative flag condition code is the Sign condition code.

Information

ASM Tutor:
Available from Educational Computing Services Ltd - www.educational-computing.co.uk

Visual X - Toy:
Available for Princeton university. http://introcs.cs.princeton.edu/xtoy/

In this chapter you have covered:

- The role and operation of a processor and its major components:
  - arithmetic and logic unit
  - control unit
  - clock
  - general purpose registers
  - dedicated registers,
    including:
    - program counter
    - current instruction register
    - memory address register
    - memory buffer register
    - status register

7.3 Structure and role of the processor and its components

7.3.2 The Fetch-Execute cycle and the role of the registers within it

Learning objectives:

- *Explain how the Fetch-Execute cycle is used to execute machine code programs including the stages in the cycle (fetch, decode, execute) and details of the registers used.*

Key concept

Machine code program:
A program consisting of machine code instructions.

Key principle

Fetch-Execute cycle:
A processor executes each machine code instruction by breaking its execution into a three-step sequence:
1. Fetch
2. Decode
3. Execute

Key fact

Registers always involved in the Fetch-Execute cycle:
- Program Counter (PC)
- Memory Address Register(MAR)
- Memory Buffer Register (MBR)
- Current Instruction Register (CIR)

Fetch-Execute cycle

A machine code program is made up of machine code instructions which are fetched from main memory, one at a time, and executed in the processor/CPU.

In Chapter 7.3.1, we learned that a processor executes each machine code instruction by breaking its execution into a three-step sequence with the execution synchronised by the system clock and controlled by the control unit.

This sequence of three steps is called the **Fetch-Execute cycle** or **instruction cycle**.

The first step is a fetch operation, the second a decode operation and the third step is execution.

These steps may be further broken down as follows:

(Fetch phase)

1. The address of the next instruction to be executed (held in the PC) is copied to the MAR which is connected to the address bus.
2. The instruction held at that address is fetched from memory along the data bus and placed in the MBR.
3. Simultaneously with step 2, the contents of the PC are incremented by 1 to point to the next instruction to be fetched.
4. The contents of the MBR are copied to the CIR. This frees up the MBR for the execute phase.

(Decode phase)

5. The instruction held in the CIR is decoded.

(Execute phase)

6. The instruction is executed. The sequence of micro-operations in the execute phase depends on the particular instruction being executed.

In register transfer notation, the Fetch-Execute cycle is described as follows:

MAR ← [PC]

MBR ← $[\text{Memory}]_{\text{addessed}}$;   PC ← [PC] + 1

CIR ← [MBR]

[CIR] opcode part decoded and executed

where [ ] means contents of and ← means assign.

This cycle repeats until the execution of the machine code program terminates. Machine interrupts to the processor, if enabled, are ignored until the current Fetch-Execute cycle is completed.

Chapter 7.3.3 covers the meaning of the term opcode. Essentially it is the part of an instruction which specifies the type of operation to be carried out, e.g., ADD, SUBTRACT, AND, etc.

The operation specified by the opcode is applied to the operands part of the instruction, i.e. the part which isn't the opcode.

The word field is used to mean a part of an instruction, e.g. an operand field. In the case of multiple operands, there is more than one operand field.

The execution step of the Fetch-Execute cycle will know from the opcode if an operand field is a datum for immediate use or an address of a memory word containing a datum. If the operand is an address, the execution step will fetch this datum.

Questions

1. Name the **four** registers that are always used in the Fetch-Execute cycle.
2. Using both register transfer notation and prose, explain how the Fetch-Execute cycle is used to execute machine code programs.

In this chapter you have covered:

- *How the Fetch-Execute cycle executes machine code programs, instruction by instruction, in a repeating cycle consisting of three steps:*
  - *Fetch*
  - *Decode*
  - *Execute*
- The registers that are always involved are
  - Program Counter (PC)
  - Memory Address Register (MAR)
  - Memory Buffer Register (MBR)
  - Current Instruction Register (CIR)
- These registers are used together with main memory in the Fetch-Execute cycle as shown here:

MAR ← [PC]

MBR ← $[\text{Memory}]_{\text{addressed}}$; PC ← [PC] + 1

CIR ← [MBR]

[CIR] opcode part decoded and executed

where [ ] means contents of and ← means assign.

Information

The PC is shown as being incremented by 1 in step 3 on the previous page. This assumes that every instruction is one memory word in length and therefore occupies one memory address. If this is not the case then the PC is incremented by the amount necessary for the PC to point to the next instruction to be fetched and executed.

Information

Branch instructions and effect on PC:
Branch instructions can change the contents of the PC when executed, e.g. Branch on zero <memory address> checks to see if the Zero flag in the status register is set. If it is, the contents of the PC will be replaced by the value of <memory address>. This value is the address of an instruction which the PC will now point to.

Information

Role of ALU:
The execution of an arithmetic or logical instruction will involve the ALU. The status register is updated during the execution to reflect the outcome of the arithmetic or logical operation.

Information

Role of other registers:
The execution of an instruction may involve one or more general purpose registers as well as the status register.

Learning objectives:

- *Understand the term 'processor instruction set' and know that an instruction set is processor specific*
- *Know that instructions consist of an opcode and one or more operands (value, memory address or register)*

Information

Risc simulator:

A Risc simulator designed by Peter Higginson is available from

www.peterhigginson.co.uk/RISC/

7.3.3 The processor instruction set

Processor instruction set

Format of instructions

The language of instruction for a digital computer is machine code; instructions consisting of sequences of binary digits which a machine can recognise and interpret. Machine code instructions are interpreted (executed) in a digital computer's processor (CPU) which must be designed so that it can understand and execute valid instructions. To understand why, consider instead a processor designed to understand certain three letter instruction words.

Table 7.3.3.1 shows examples of possible valid and invalid instructions formed from letters of the alphabet.

Valid instruction	Invalid instruction
ADD	DAD
SUB	BUS
MUL	ULM
DIV	VID

Table 7.3.3.1 3-letter valid and invalid English instruction words

Note that the instructions are of the same fixed length and only some particular combinations of letters are valid.

If these examples of valid combinations of letters correspond to the arithmetic operations, ADD, SUBTRACT, MULTIPLY, and DIVIDE then we need to include operand fields, R, B and C in each instruction so that an instruction such as ADD has something to add and somewhere to store the result. The instruction ADD R 3 4 adds together the values 3 and 4 and stores the result in R. We call ADD the **operation** and, R, B and C the **operands**. *Table 7.3.3.2* shows the new structure of two valid instructions

Valid instruction	Action
ADD R B C	Add C to B store result in R
SUB R B C	Subtract C from B store result in R

Table 7.3.3.2 Operation and two operands

Questions

1. What will be stored in R if the instruction is
(a) ADD R 3 4 (b) SUB R 4 3 (c) MUL R 4 3

Similar design constraints apply when designing the set of instructions (instruction set) that a processor (CPU) is capable of recognising as valid and then executing, i.e. instructions belonging to its instruction set. The processor or CPU will have access to registers, to memory, to an Arithmetic and Logic Unit and will also be able to make transfers of data to I/O devices such as magnetic disks.

The basic machine operations that a processor executes can be categorised as follows:

- Data processing: Arithmetic, logic and shift instructions
- Data transfers: Register and memory instructions
- I/O transfers: I/O instructions
- Control: Test, branch and halt instructions

Data processing instructions

The processor might support the instructions shown in column 1, Table 7.3.3.3, which also shows their abbreviated form in brackets, e.g. SUB.

Data transfer instructions

The processor might support the instructions shown in column 2, Table 7.3.3.3.

Control instructions

The processor might support the instructions shown in column 3, Table 7.3.3.3.

Data processing	Data transfers	Control
ADD	LOAD (LDR)	COMPARE (CMP)
SUBTRACT (SUB)		
Bitwise logical AND		Unconditional branch (B)
Bitwise logical OR (ORR)	STORE (STR)	
Bitwise logical EOR (EOR)		Conditional branch (B)
Bitwise logical NOT(MVN)	MOVE (MOV)	
Logical Shift Left (LSL)		HALT (HALT)
Logical Shift Right (LSR)		

Table 7.3.3.3 Some examples of basic machine operations

I/O transfer instructions

Instructions for this are not shown but I/O transfers could be done using the given data transfer instructions if the registers and data locations in the I/O controllers for each peripheral are mapped into the addressable memory space by allocating main memory addresses to these in the same way as locations in RAM are mapped into the addressable memory space.

Operands

The next choice is how many operands? ARM processors are very popular and successful processors. ARM is the market leader (2015) for processors in smartphones and tablets and an ARM processor is the main processor in the Raspberry Pi and in the Parallela platform. ARM is a three-register architecture, meaning that a single machine code instruction can reference up to three registers. For example, the ADD instruction can specify two registers from which to read the values to be added and a third register, the destination register to store the calculated sum.

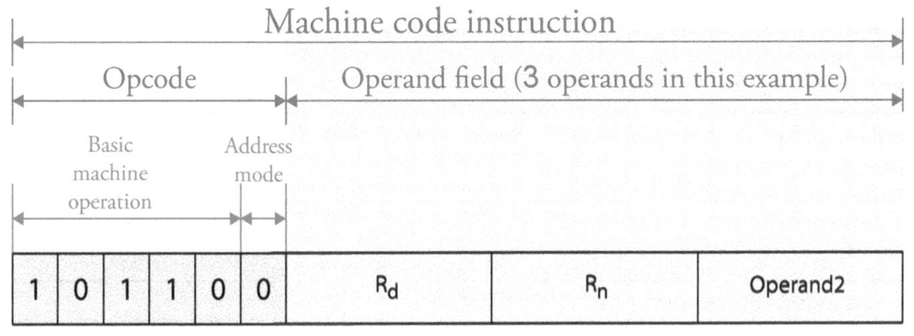

Figure 7.3.3.1 Structure of a machine code instruction with an example

Figure 7.3.3.1 shows that the structure of a machine code instruction is divided into an opcode field and an operand field. Register R_d is the destination register, register R_n contains the first input to the operation and Operand2, the second. Operand2 could be an actual value, 6, or it could be another register, R_m, containing the value to be used. The Address mode bit is used to select which is the case, e.g. 0 for value, 1 for value contained in specified register. The combined code for the basic machine operation and this address mode bit is known as the opcode or operation code field of the machine code instruction. The ARM processor has 16 programmer-accessible registers, R_0 through R_{15}. R_{15} is the Program Counter and R_{14} the link register (used to store the PC contents when a subroutine is called). Usually, another register is used for the Stack Pointer. Therefore, R_d, R_n and R_m can be any of the remaining thirteen registers, R_0 through R_{12}, e.g. R_1, R_2 and R_3, respectively.

With six bits allocated to the opcode field of the machine code instruction shown in *Figure 7.3.3.1* and every other instruction, there are a possible 2^6 different opcodes, one for each 6-bit pattern. *Table 7.3.3.4* shows how the number of possible opcodes varies with the number of bits reserved for the opcode field of a machine code instruction (remember: **opcode field size is fixed at the design stage of a processor**).

No of bits, n in opcode field	No of possible opcodes 2^n	No of possible opcodes
4	2^4	16
5	2^5	32
6	2^6	64

Table 7.3.3.4 No of possible opcodes for a given no of opcode field bits

Opcode	Machine code instruction format	Description
000000	LDR R_d, <memory ref>	Load the value stored in the memory location specified by <memory ref> into register R_d.
000010	STR R_d, <memory ref>	Store the value that is in register R_d into the memory location specified by <memory ref>.
000100 000101	ADD R_d, R_n, <operand2>	Add the value specified in <operand2> to the value in register R_n and store the result in register R_d. 000100 for when operand2 is a value, 000101 for when operand2 is another register, R_m. The same interpretation applies to the other two opcode instructions.
000110 000111	SUB R_d, R_n, <operand2>	Subtract the value specified by <operand2> from the value in register R_n and store the result in register R_d. For interpretation of why two opcodes, see ADD for why two opcodes.
001000 001001	MOV R_d, <operand2>	Copy the value specified by <operand2> into register R_d. For interpretation see ADD.
001010 001011	CMP R_n, <operand2>	Compare the value stored in register R_n with the value specified by <operand2>. See ADD
001100	B <label>	Always branch to the instruction at position <label> in the program.
011101 011110 011111 100000	B <condition> <label>	Conditionally branch to the instruction at position <label> in the program if the last comparison met the criteria specified by the <condition>. Possible values for <condition> and their meaning are: EQ: Equal to NE: Not equal to GT: Greater than LT: Less than.
010010 010011	AND R_d, R_n, <operand2>	Perform a bitwise logical AND operation between the value in register R_n and the value specified by <operand2> and store the result in register R_d. See ADD for why two opcodes.
010100 010101	ORR R_d, R_n, <operand2>	Perform a bitwise logical OR operation between the value in register R_n and the value specified by <operand2> and store the result in register R_d. See ADD for why two opcodes.
010110 010111	EOR R_d, R_n, <operand2>	Perform a bitwise logical eXclusive OR (XOR) operation between the value in register R_n and the value specified by <operand2> and store the result in register R_d. See ADD for why two opcodes.
011000 011001	MVN R_d, <operand2>	Perform a bitwise logical NOT operation on the value specified by <operand2> and store the result in register R_d. See ADD for why there are two opcodes.
011010 011011	LSL R_d, R_n, <operand2>	Logically shift left the value stored in register R_n by the number of bits specified by <operand2> and store the result in register R_d. See ADD for why there are two opcodes.
111100 111101	LSR R_d, R_n, <operand2>	Logically shift right the value stored in register R_n by the number of bits specified by <operand2> and store the result in register R_d. See ADD for why there are two opcodes.
111110	HALT	Stops the execution of the program.

Table 7.3.3.5 6-bit opcodes mapped to machine operations. Reproduced with permission of AQA. Currently only in specimen papers and has therefore not been through the complete rigorous question paper process and is liable to change. Please consult AQA's website for the most recent version of the specification.

Table 7.3.3.5 shows a possible mapping of some 6-bit opcodes (5 bits for basic machine operation, 1 bit for address mode) to machine operations for an imaginary processor.

Instruction set

The simple operations referenced in Table 7.3.3.5 may be combined together in sequences to perform quite complicated tasks.

The set of 28 bit patterns (strings of bits) shown in the opcode column of Table 7.3.3.5 represent these operations for a given processor and are known as the **processor instruction set**. Note that if Table 7.3.3.5 shows all the operations that a processor has been designed to understand and interpret then four bit patterns do not correspond to any defined machine operations because for a 6-bit opcode field, there are 32 possible bit patterns but only 28 are used to define opcodes. We therefore use the following definition of instruction set:

The set of bit patterns for which machine operations have been defined.

An instruction set is processor specific

An instruction set is specific to a particular processor for the following reasons:

- The machine operations that a processor is designed to perform varies in number and type from processor to processor, e.g. from the ARM® Cortex®-A7 CPU used in the Raspberry Pi 2 to the Intel® Core™ i7 CPU used in laptops and PCs.
- The number of bits allocated to the opcode field can also vary from processor to processor as well as how they are mapped to the operations that the processor supports. Therefore, machine code programs written for the ARM Cortex-A7 CPU will not run on an Intel Core i7 CPU.
- The number of possible operands, their type and the number of bits reserved for each may also vary from processor to processor.
- The design of a processor's control unit instruction decoder circuits reflects the structure of the machine code instructions and will not therefore be able to decode instructions designed for a different processor.

Structure of machine code instructions

We have learned that a machine code instruction is divided into an opcode part and an operand part as shown again in Figure 7.3.3.2.

Opcode	Operand(s)

Figure 7.3.3.2 Format of a machine code instruction

The machine code instruction with format MOV R_d, <operand2> has two possible opcodes which in binary are 001000 and 001001.

- opcode 001000 moves the value that is <operand2> into the register R_d, e.g., 001000 0000 0100 1111.This instruction is broken down as shown in Figure 7.3.3.3. The destination register is R_0 (binary code 0000) and <operand2> is replaced by the value $0100\ 1111_2$ (79_{10}).

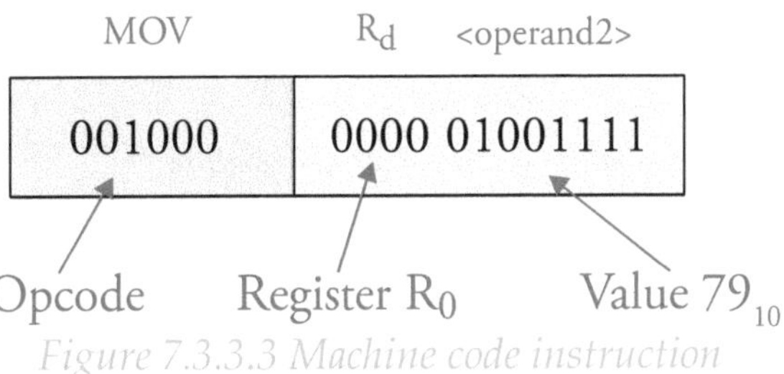

Figure 7.3.3.3 Machine code instruction

Key concept

Processor instruction set:
The set of bit patterns for which machine operations have been defined.

Information

ARM:
ARM processor technology is controlled by ARM Holdings. ARM stands for Advanced RISC Machine and RISC stands for Reduced Instruction Set Computer. RISC is a design philosophy in which the instruction set is deliberately designed as a small set of very simple instructions.
It does mean that a machine code program will consist of a large number of these simple instructions but execution of simple instructions is very fast.

The simplicity of the instructions simplifies the design of the control unit. In particular, the instruction decoder circuits. This turns out to have the advantage of lowering processor power consumption. Low power consumption is particularly desirable in portable devices such as smartphones and other embedded systems. This accounts for why ARM processors dominate the mobile, tablet, System On a Chip (SOC) and embedded systems markets. Considerably more ARM CPUs than Intel CPUs are sold.

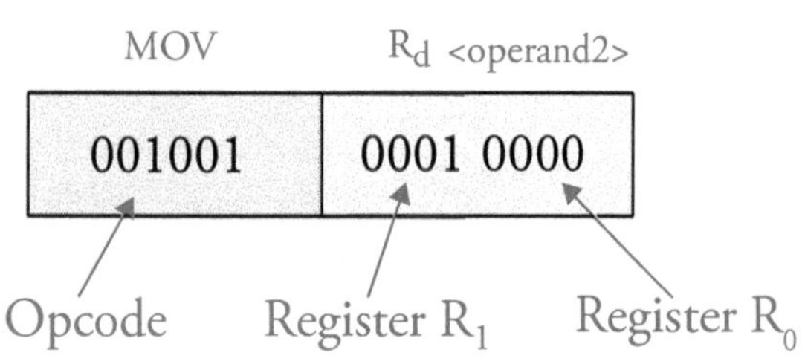

Figure 7.3.3.4 Machine code instruction

- opcode 001001 moves the value stored in the register specified by <operand2> into the register R_d, e.g., 001001 0001 0000.

This instruction is broken down as shown in *Figure 7.3.3.4*. The destination register is R_1 (binary code 0001) and <operand2> is replaced by register R_0 (binary code 0000). If when the processor executes this instruction the value 45_{10} is stored in register R_0 then at the end of the execution register R_1 will also contain 45_{10}.

Information

ARM processor architecture:

ARM is a load-store architecture. This means that before data can be processed, a LOAD instruction must be executed to load data from memory into registers. Similarly, after data has been processed, a STORE instruction must be executed to store the data in memory. Arithmetic and logic instructions cannot work directly with values in main memory.

Information

Possible binary codes for registers:

Register	Binary code for register
R_0	0000
R_1	0001
R_2	0010
R_3	0011
R_4	0100
R_5	0101
R_6	0110
R_7	0111
R_8	1000
R_9	1001
R_{10}	1010
R_{11}	1011
R_{12}	1100

The structure that has been used to illustrate machine code is a simplified one. It is not a good idea to design an instruction set that doesn't map to the word length of a memory word which is typically a multiple of eight. The word length of registers is usually a multiple of eight too, e.g. 32 bits. The unit of transfer between processor and main memory for load and store operations is usually the same as the word length of registers, e.g., 32 bits if registers are 32 bits. Bits of a memory word that are not needed for a particular machine code instruction are ignored by the instruction decoder.

The machine code instruction with format LOAD R_d, <memory ref> has a single opcode which is 000000 in binary. R_d is the destination register and <memory ref> is replaced by the memory address of a memory word stored in main memory. This instruction is broken down as shown in *Figure 7.3.3.5*. For example, 000000 0011 0100 1111 copies the memory word whose memory address is 0100 1111 into register R_3 (binary code 0011).

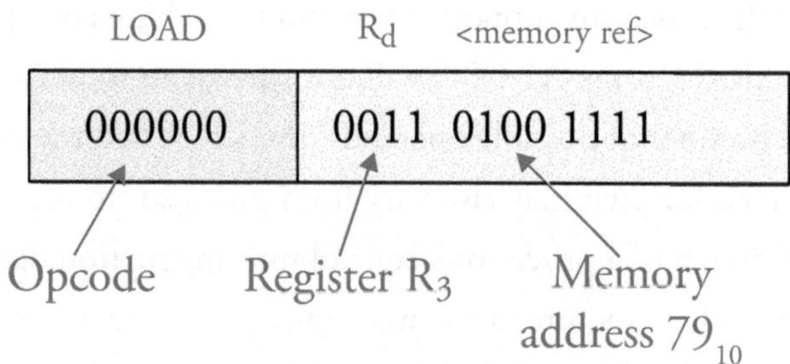

Figure 7.3.3.5 Machine code instruction

Key concept

Structure of a machine code instruction:

A machine code instruction consists of an opcode and one or more operands of type: value, memory address or register.

Questions

2. Eight bits are reserved for the opcode field of a particular processor's instruction set.
   (a) What is the total number of codes that could be used as opcodes for this processor?
   (b) Why might only some of these 8-bit codes be valid?
   (c) The 8-bit opcode is subdivided into two parts. What are the two parts?

Questions

3 What is meant by *processor instruction set*?

4 Explain using LOAD, STORE, ADD that machine code instructions consist of an opcode and one or more operands which may be value, memory address or register.

5 What is meant by saying that an instruction set is processor specific?

Task

1 You are required to design an instruction set for a processor based on a two register architecture in which the destination register is always the register called the accumulator. The processor must be able to add and subtract. The only instructions allowed to interact directly with main memory are load and store. The first input to an arithmetic operation is always read from the accumulator. The second input is read from one of fifteen other registers. Values may be set up in all sixteen registers either by a load instruction or by a move instruction. The second operand of a move instruction is always a value. The processor's instruction set must support four control instructions:

1. branch on zero
2. branch on negative
3. branch unconditionally
4. Halt

Branch instruction 1 tests the zero flag and branch instruction 2, the negative flag of the status register. All three branches use a single operand which is a value (positive or negative) to add to the current value of the program counter. The status register and program counter are separate from the sixteen registers also used by the instruction set.
Registers have a word length of 16 bits as does main memory.
Main memory consists of 256 memory words.
Some instructions may not use all 16 bits. The processor will use those bits which define the instruction.

In this chapter you have covered:

- The meaning of 'processor instruction set' and that an instruction set is processor specific
- The structure of machine code instructions which is an opcode and one or more operands (value, memory address or register)

7.3 Structure and role of the processor and its components

■ *Learning objectives:*

- *Understand and apply immediate and direct addressing modes*

Information

0x:
0x indicates a hexadecimal number, e.g. 0x3F.

	R0
before	?
after	0xFF

Figure 7.3.4.1 register R0 before and after execution of instruction MOV R0,#0xFF

Key concept

Immediate addressing:
The operand is the datum.

Key concept

Direct addressing:
The operand is the address of the datum.

7.3.4 Addressing modes

Immediate addressing

When the addressing mode is immediate addressing the operand is the datum.

For example, the MOV operation copies the value specified by <operand2> into register R_d.

```
MOV Rd,<operand2>
```

If R_d is register R0 and <operand2> is 0xFF in hexadecimal (255 in decimal) then the assembly language instruction is as follows

```
MOV R0,#0xFF
```

The # in front of 0xFF indicates that the mode of addressing is immediate addressing. The contents of register R0 will be the binary equivalent of hexadecimal value FF after this instruction is executed - *Figure 7.3.4.1*.

Questions

1. Register R0 contains the datum 43_{10}, register R1 the datum 56_{10}. What will register R0 contain after each of the following assembly language instructions have been executed?
Express your answer in decimal.
(a) MOV R0,#0x5E
(b) ADD R0,R1,#0x5E

Direct addressing

When the addressing mode is direct addressing the operand is the address in memory where the datum can be found.

For example, the LDR operation loads the value stored in the memory location specified by <memory ref> into register R_d.

```
LDR Rd,<memory ref>
```

If R_d is register R0 and <memory ref> is in hexadecimal 0xFCC0 (64704 in decimal) then the assembly language instruction is as follows

```
LDR R0,0xFCC0
```

Note that in this instruction there is no #. The absence of the # symbol indicates that this is direct addressing.

The operand 0xFCC0 is the main memory address of a memory location containing the datum to be used when this instruction is executed. The contents of register R0 will therefore be 0x4D (we can omit the leading 00) after this instruction is executed because memory location with address 0xFCC0 contains the datum 0x4D - Figure 7.3.4.2.

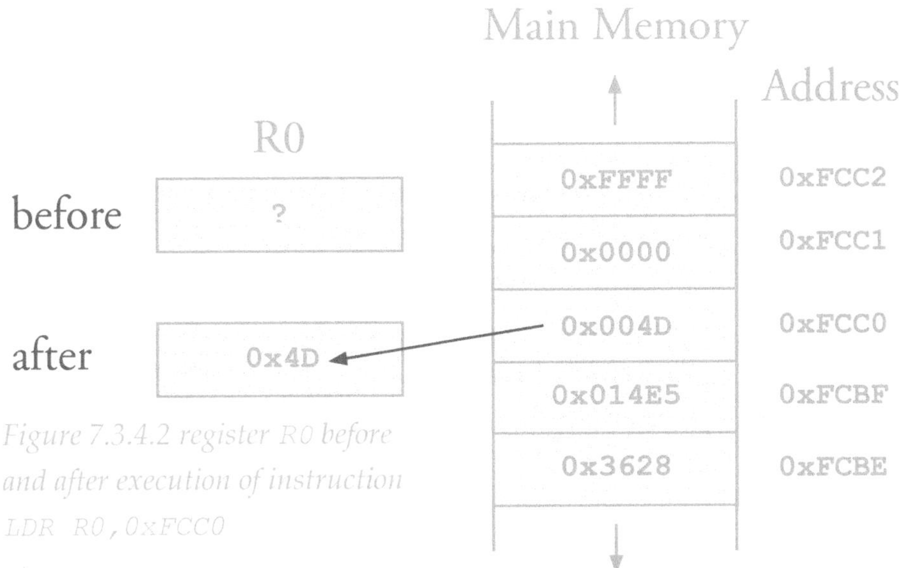

Figure 7.3.4.2 register R0 before and after execution of instruction `LDR R0,0xFCC0`

Questions

2 Register R0 contains the datum 43_{10}, main memory contents are as shown in Figure 7.3.4.2. What will register R0 contain after the following assembly language instruction has been executed?
Express your answer in decimal.

```
LDR R0,0xFCC0
```

3 In the assembly language instruction STR R_d, <memory ref>, the STR operation stores the value that is in register R_d in a memory location specified by <memory ref>. Register R0 contains the datum 43_{10}, register R1 the datum 56_{10}, main memory contents are as shown in Figure 7.3.4.2. What will the memory locations 0xFCC1 and 0xFCC2 contain after the following two instructions have been executed? Express your answers in decimal.

```
STR R0,0xFCC1
STR R1,0xFCC2
```

4 Main memory contents are as shown in Figure 7.3.4.2 What will be stored in register R1 after the following instructions are executed? Express your answer in decimal.

```
LDR R0,0xFCC0
ADD R1,R0,#0xFCC0
```

In this chapter you have covered:

- Immediate addressing: the operand is the datum
- Direct addressing: the operand is the address of the datum

7.3.5 Machine-code and assembly language operations

Learning objectives:

- *Understand and apply the basic machine-code operations of*
  - *load*
  - *add*
  - *subtract*
  - *store*
  - *branching (conditional and unconditional)*
  - *compare*
  - *logical bitwise operators (AND, OR, NOT, XOR)*
  - *logical*
    - *shift right*
    - *shift left*
  - *halt*
- *Use the basic machine-code operations above when machine-code instructions are expressed in mnemonic form- assembly language, using immediate and direct addressing*

Key concept

Load-store architecture:
No direct manipulation of memory contents. A value in memory that needs to be processed must be loaded into the processor (core) first, processed and then stored back in memory.

Information

See Table 7.3.3.5 in Chapter 7.3.3 for AQA instruction set.

Load-Store architecture

In a load-store architecture the only instructions that work directly with memory are load and store instructions or their equivalent. A value in memory that needs to be processed must be loaded into the processor (core) first, processed and then stored back in memory.

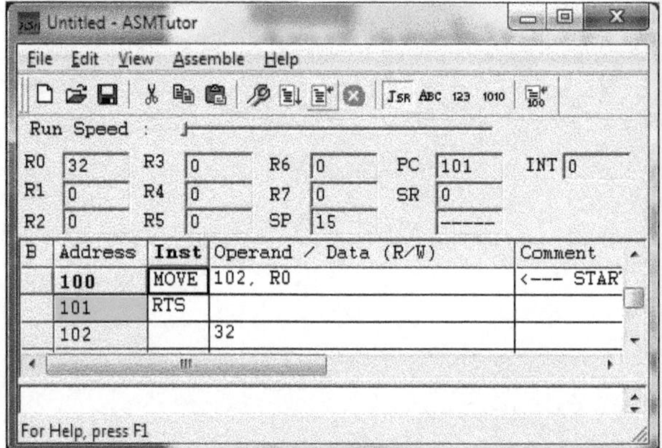

Figure 7.3.5.1 ASMTutor after executing the machine code equivalent of MOVE 102, R0

Load

A load register operation is used to transfer a copy of a datum from a specified location, e.g. main memory location 102, to a symbolically named register, e.g. R0.

For example using direct addressing, LDR R0, 102 transfers the contents of memory location with address 102 into register R0. In some instruction sets, the mnemonic MOV or MOVE is used instead of the mnemonic LDR, and the order of the operands can be reversed. The simulator ASMTutor shown in *Figure 7.3.5.1* is one that uses MOVE instead of LDR for a load operation. It also reverses the order of the operands.

Figure 7.3.5.1 shows an example of an assembly language program which transfers a copy of the datum 32 from memory location 102 to register R0. The assembly language program ends with RTS (ReTurn from Subroutine) because ASMTutor expects the last instruction to be RTS in order to work correctly. Note that memory location with address 102 in this example contains 32.

Figure 7.3.5.2 shows the register state just before the machine code equivalent of MOVE 102, R0 is executed.

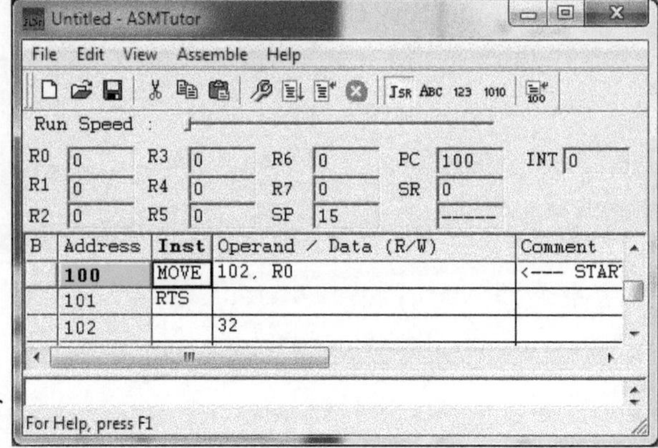

Figure 7.3.5.2 ASMTutor just before executing the machine code equivalent of MOVE 102, R0

Figure 7.3.5.3 shows the result when memory location 102 contains 64.

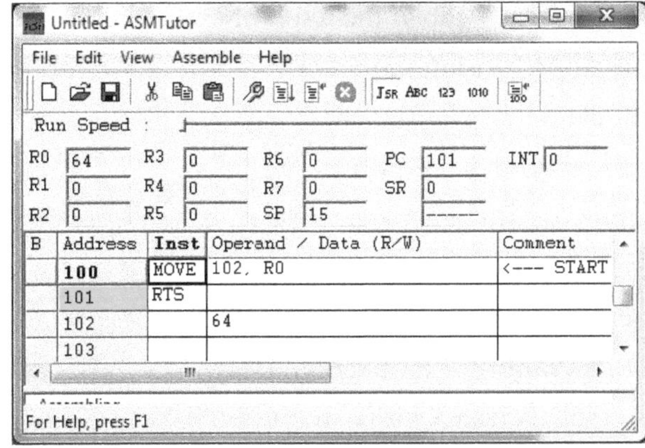

Figure 7.3.5.3 Just after with 102 containing 64

Memory address (in decimal)	Main memory contents (in decimal)
102	21
103	42
104	84

Figure 7.3.5.4

Questions

1. The assembly language instruction LDR R0, 102 transfers a copy of the contents of memory location 102 to register R0. Figure 7.3.5.4 shows the contents of memory locations 102, 103 and 104.
What does register R0 contain after the following instructions, expressed in assembly language, are executed in machine code?
(a) LDR R0, 102 (b) LDR R0, 103 (c) LDR R0, 104

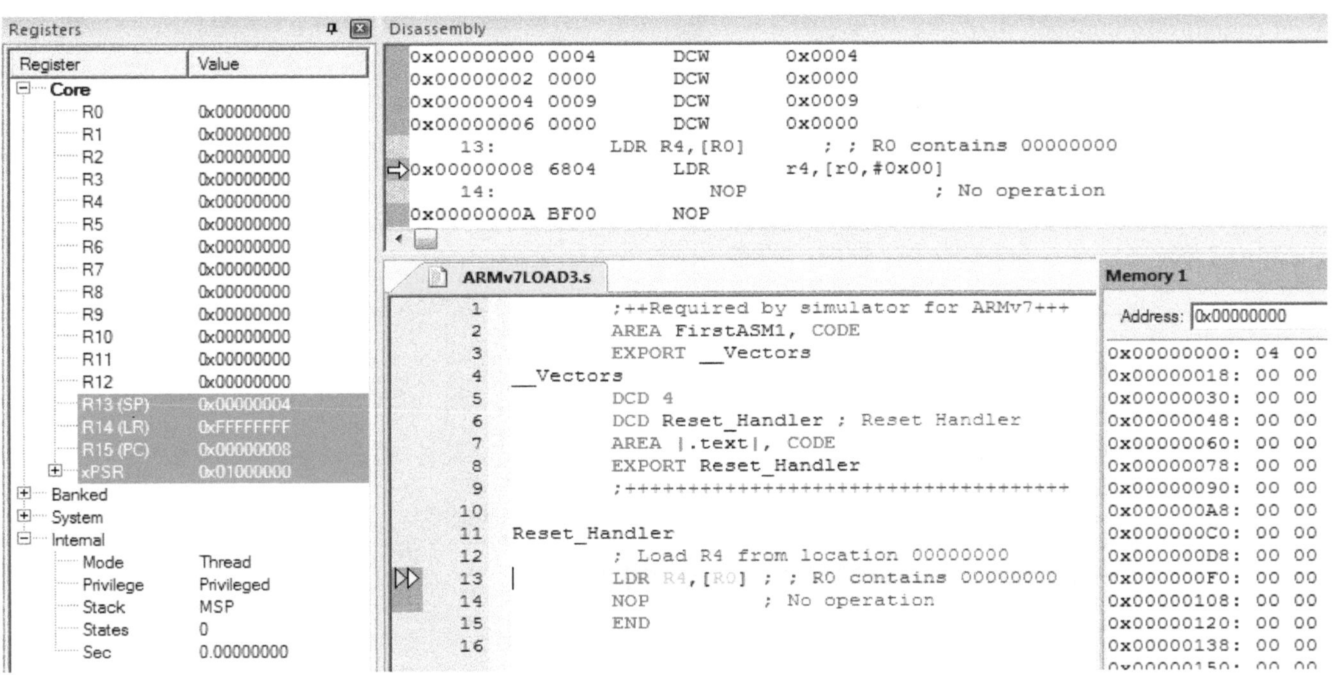

Figure 7.3.5.5 ARM® μVision® V 5.17 Debugger in single-step mode

Information

ARM μVision may be downloaded from https://www.keil.com/download/product/
The evaluation mode is free.
To configure for Thumb-2 instruction set, select Project/Options for Target.../Asm and tick Thumb Mode.

Figure 7.3.5.5 shows a screenshot of the ARM μVision simulator in debugger mode single-stepping through an assembly language program written for an ARM Cortex processor. ARM instruction sets use LDR but the reference to a memory location is not direct. Instead, the memory reference must be obtained from a register. This example uses register R0.
[R0] means contents of register R0. LDR R4, [R0] loads register R4 with the contents of memory location 0x00000000 as this is the memory address stored in register R0. The notation 0x indicates a hexadecimal number.

Figure 7.3.5.6 shows the result of executing the instruction **LDR R4, [R0]**.

The ARM *μ*Vision simulator simulates the execution of instructions for the Cortex™-M family of ARM microcontrollers. These microcontrollers implement the **ARMv7** instruction set. In order for this simulator to function, every assembly language program must start with the preamble shown in *Figures 7.3.5.5, 7.3.5.6*. The user chooses the identifier in **AREA FirstASM1, CODE**, i.e. **FirstASM1**, but the rest of the preamble must conform to that given.

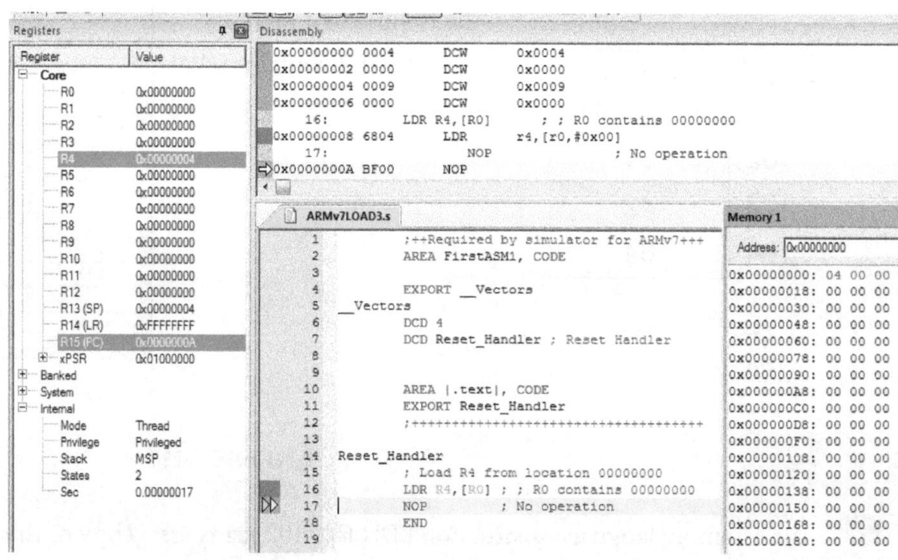

Figure 7.3.5.6 ARM® μVision® V 5.17 Debugger in single-step more

STORE

A store operation, STR, transfers a copy of the contents of a register to a specified memory location,

e.g. **STR R4, 0x20000000**

If **R4** contains **0x00000065** then execution of the machine code equivalent of this instruction will change the contents of memory location, address **0x20000000**, to the value **0x65**.

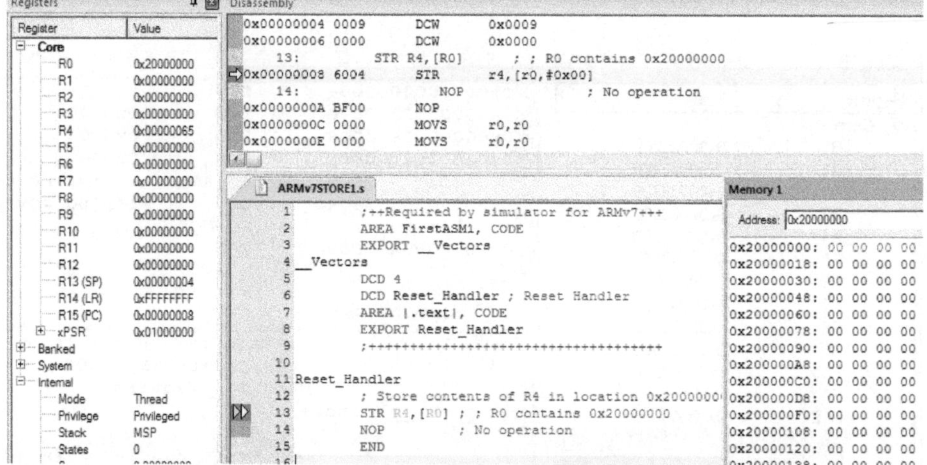

Figure 7.3.5.7 ARM® μVision® V 5.17 Debugger in single-step more

Figure 7.3.5.7 shows register **R4** preset with value **0x00000065**, register **R0** preset with value **0x20000000**, and memory location **0x2000000** initialised to **0x00000000**. The next instruction to be executed is **STR R4, [R0]** which is equivalent to

STR R4, #0x20000000

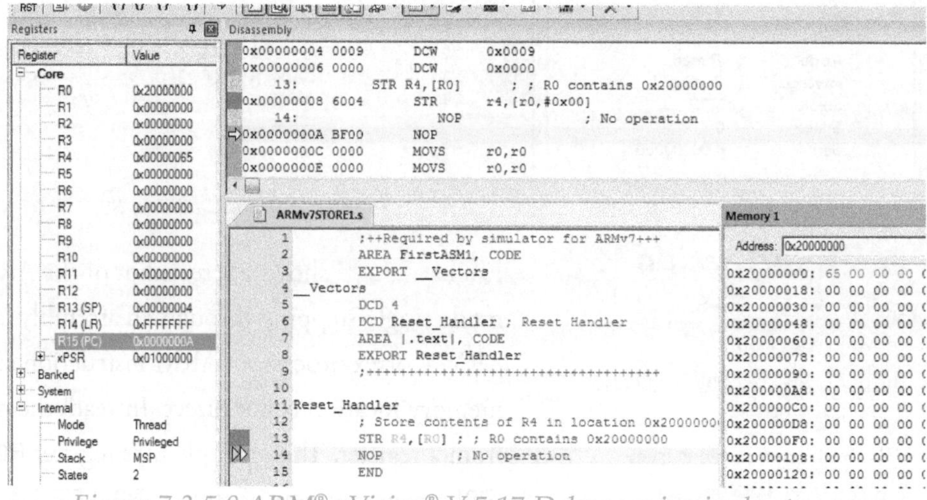

Figure 7.3.5.8 ARM® μVision® V 5.17 Debugger in single-step more

Figure 7.3.5.8 shows memory location **0x20000000**'s contents with value **0x65**, the result of executing **STR R4, [R0]**.

The ARM *μ*Vision simulator is configured so that **0x20000000** is the first available location that a program may write to.

Questions

2 The assembly language instruction STR R0, 102 transfers a copy of the contents of register R0 to memory location with decimal address 102. What are the contents of memory location 102 after this instruction is executed in machine code when the value in R0 is decimal 67?

MOVE

A MOVE operation copies a value from source to destination. The source could be a register, an immediate value (or a memory location but not in the case of ARM processors). The destination could be another register (or a memory location but not in the case of ARM processors).

For example, the ARM processor instruction set has a MOV instruction (MOVS in ARMv7 to update status register as well). MOV R_d, <operand2> copies the value specified by <operand2> into register R_d. For example, MOV R2, #36 copies the value 36 into the register R2. # indicates immediate addressing.

MOV R1, R2 copies the value in register R2 into register R1. Figure 7.3.5.9 shows an assembly language program, MOV.s, prepared in Notepad++ and then loaded into ArmSim# version 1.9.1 for assembling and executing one instruction at a time. Register contents are shown in the window on the left. Note how registers R2 and R3 are changed by the two different MOV operations. The hash symbol # before the decimal value 36 indicates immediate addressing, i.e. the operand is the value to be used. As with ASMTutor, the last instruction must be an instruction that enables ArmSim# to function correctly. This instruction is SWI 0x11.

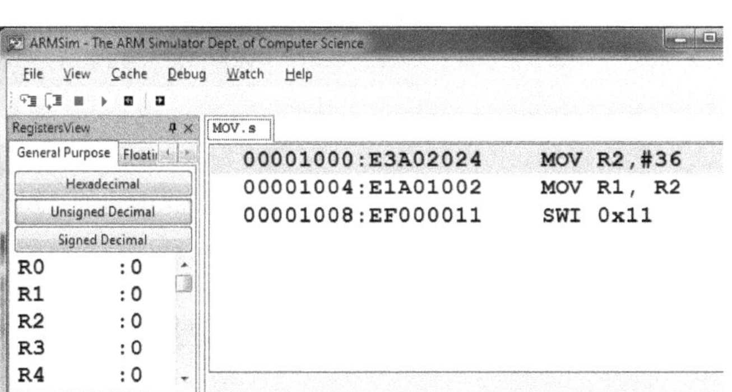

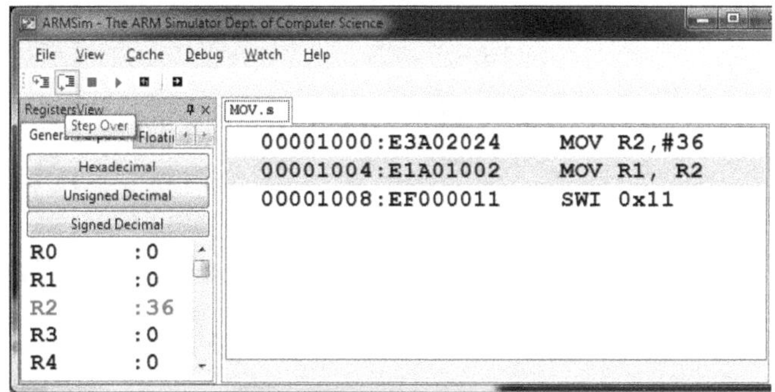

Figure 7.3.5.9 Single stepping through execution of machine code equivalent of assembly language program containing MOV R_d, <operand2> for an immediate operand and a register operand

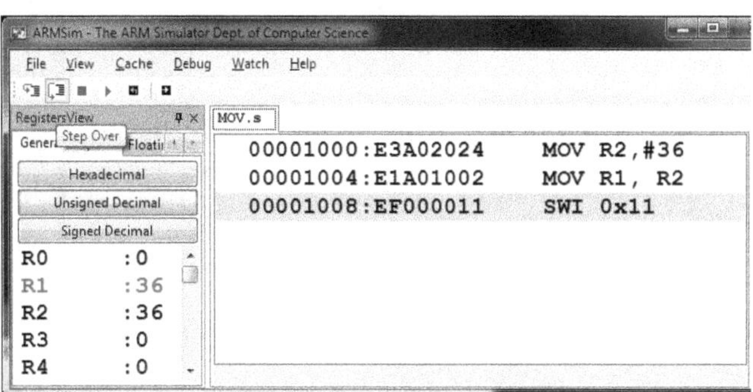

ArmSim simulates ARMv5 instruction set architecture.

It can be downloaded from http://armsim.cs.uvic.ca/DownloadARMSimSharp.html

Questions

3 The assembly language instruction MOV R0, R1 transfers a copy of the contents of register R1 to register R0. What does register R0 contain after the following instructions, expressed in assembly language, are executed in machine code?

(a) MOV R0, #78 (b) MOV R1, #25 followed by MOV R0, R1

ADD

An add operation ADD R_d, R_n, <operand2> is used to add the value specified in <operand2> and the value in register R_n, storing the result in register R_d. <operand2> may be an immediate value or a register.

For example, ADD R2, R3, #1 when executed in machine code adds 1 to the contents of register R3 before storing the result in register R2.

Figure 7.3.5.10 shows ArmSim# stepping through program ADD1.s one instruction at a time. This program assigns 24 to R3 and 36 to R2. It adds 1 to a copy of the 24 stored in R3 then stores the result 25 in R2.

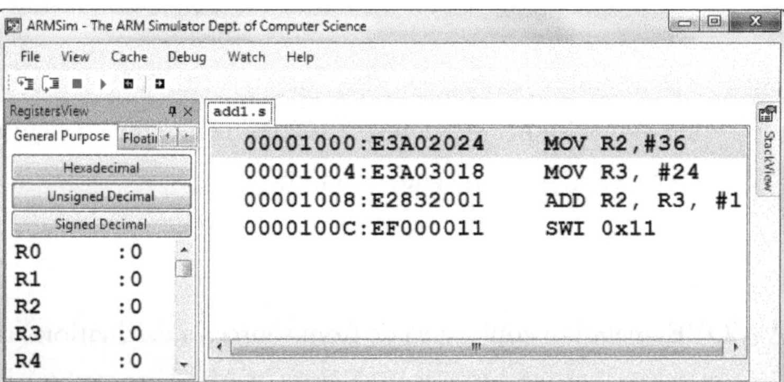

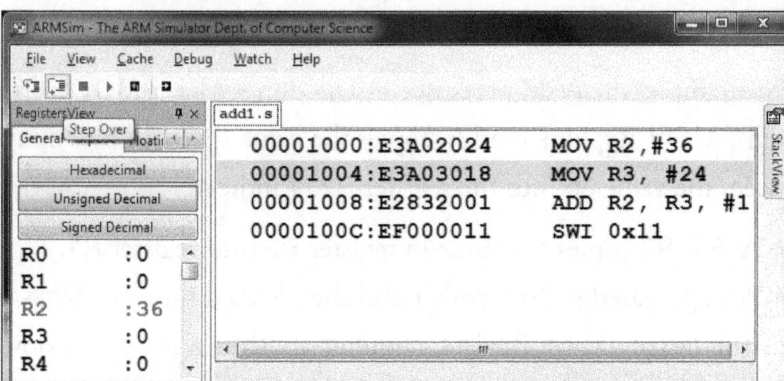

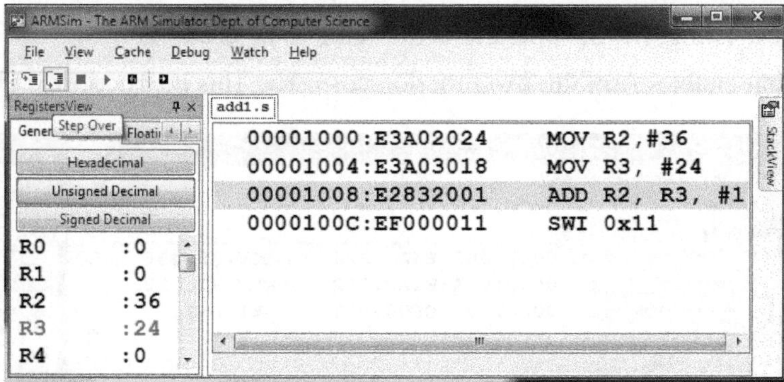

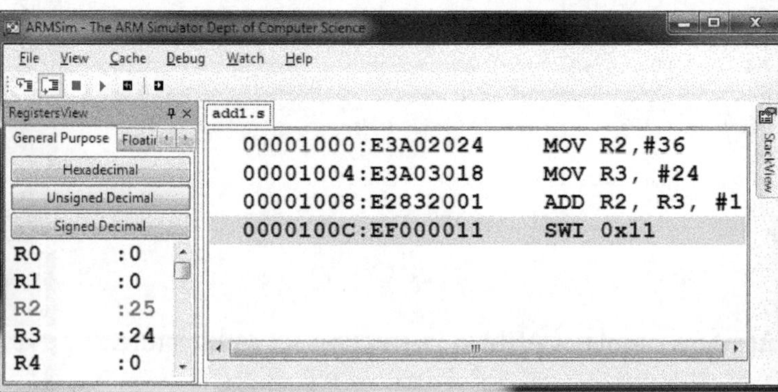

Figure 7.3.5.10 Before and after state of registers R2, R3 for execution of ADD R2, R3, #1

Task

1 Using a text editor such as Notepad++, create the file ADD32.s with the following contents:

```
MOV R4, #25
MOV R5, #43
ADD R5, R4, #32
SWI 0x11
```

Load ADD32.s into ArmSim# and single step through the instructions. Observe how registers R4 and R5 change.

Task

2 Using a text editor such as Notepad++, create the file ADD.s with the following contents:

```
MOV R4, #25
MOV R5, #43
MOV R3, #1
ADD R5, R4, R3
SWI 0x11
```

Load ADD.s into ArmSim# and single step through the instructions. Observe how registers R3, R4 and R5 change.

Questions

4 Write an assembly language program that stores the result of adding the contents of registers R1, R2, R3 in R0. The program will need to initialise R1 with decimal 5, R2 with decimal 3 and R3 with decimal 6.

SUBTRACT

A subtract operation SUB R_d, R_n, <operand2> is used to subtract the value specified in <operand2> from the value in register R_n before storing the result in register R_d. <operand2> may be an immediate value or a register.

For example, SUB R2, R3, #1 when executed in machine code subtracts 1 from the contents of register R3 before storing the result in register R2.

Figure 7.3.5.11 shows the before and after contents of the registers R2 and R3.

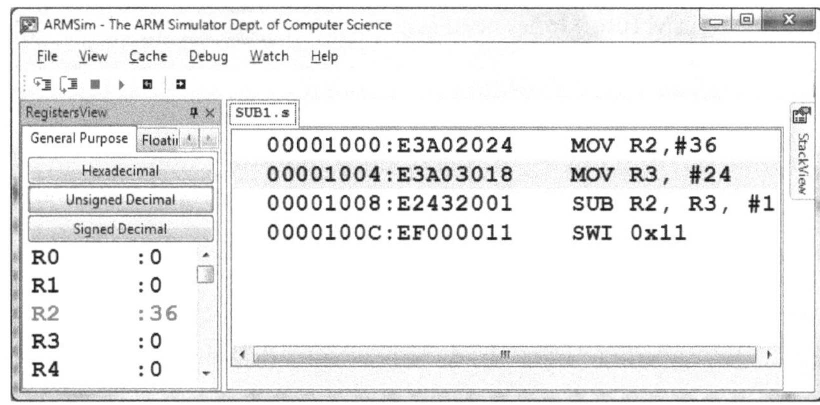

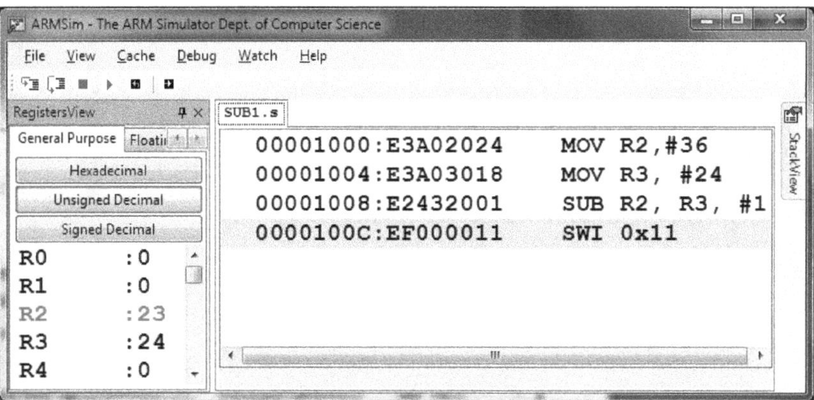

Figure 7.3.5.11 Before and after state of registers R2, R3 for execution of SUB R2, R3, #1

Task

3 Using a text editor such as Notepad++, create the file SUB5.s with the following contents:

```
MOV R4, #25
MOV R5, #43
SUB R5, R4, #5
SWI 0x11
```

Load SUB5.s into ArmSim# and single step through the instructions. Observe how registers R4 and R5 change.

Questions

5 Write an assembly language program that stores the result of subtracting the contents of register R1 from R2 in R0. The program will need to initialise R1 with decimal 5 and R2 with decimal 13.

Status register

The status register contains flags called condition codes which are set or reset to reflect the outcome of the last machine operation, e.g. if the result of an arithmetic operation was zero then the zero flag is set. A flag is a single bit code that can be set (binary 1) or reset (binary 0). A status register consists of at least four condition codes:

- Zero flag - set if the result of the last machine operation stores zero in the results register
- Negative flag - set if the result of the last machine operation stores a negative value in the results register
- Carry flag - set if the result of an *unsigned operation* overflows the result register or as a result sometimes of performing two's complement signed arithmetic.
- Overflow flag - set if the result of a *signed operation* overflows the result register.

Moving zero into a register can set the Z(ero) flag as will an arithmetic operation if the result is zero.

Moving a negative value into a register can set the N(egative) flag as will an arithmetic operation if the result is negative. A carry can be produced when a machine performs two's complement arithmetic or when it performs unsigned addition.

Figure 7.3.5.12 shows an assembly language program created in ASMTutor. It has been assembled so it can be executed. The first screenshot shows that the next instruction to be executed is MOVE #0, R0. The second screenshot shows the effect on the status register of executing this instruction. The zero flag has been set in the status register (indicated by a Z).

The third screenshot shows that the negative flag has been set in the status register as a result of the machine executing the instruction MOVE #-1, R1. Note the value stored in R1 is 65535_{10} or 1111111111111111_2 which is the two's complement representation for -1_{10}.

The fourth screenshot shows the effect on the status register of subtracting decimal 5 (register R2) from 0 (register R0). The negative flag is set because the result is negative.

Figure 7.3.5.13 shows that when the largest positive number 0111111111111111_2 ($7FFF_{16}$) is added to itself, overflow results and the overflow flag is set. The negative flag is also set because the result, 65534_{10}, that is stored in register R0 is interpreted as -2_{10} by the machine.

R0	0	R3	0	R6	0	PC	100
R1	0	R4	0	R7	0	SR	0
R2	0	R5	0	SP	15		-----

B	Address	Inst	Operand / Data (R/W)
	100	MOVE	#0, R0
	101	MOVE	#-1, R1
	102	MOVE	#5, R2
	103	SUB	R2, R0
	104	MOVE	#-1, R0

R0	0	R3	0	R6	0	PC	101
R1	0	R4	0	R7	0	SR	2
R2	0	R5	0	SP	15		--Z--

B	Address	Inst	Operand / Data (R/W)
	100	MOVE	#0, R0
	101	MOVE	#-1, R1
	102	MOVE	#5, R2
	103	SUB	R2, R0
	104	MOVE	#-1, R0

R0	0	R3	0	R6	0	PC	102
R1	65535	R4	0	R7	0	SR	1
R2	0	R5	0	SP	15		-N---

B	Address	Inst	Operand / Data (R/W)
	100	MOVE	#0, R0
	101	MOVE	#-1, R1
	102	MOVE	#5, R2
	103	SUB	R2, R0
	104	MOVE	#-1, R0

R0	65531	R3	0	R6	0	PC	104
R1	65535	R4	0	R7	0	SR	1
R2	5	R5	0	SP	15		-N---

B	Address	Inst	Operand / Data (R/W)
	100	MOVE	#0, R0
	101	MOVE	#-1, R1
	102	MOVE	#5, R2
	103	SUB	R2, R0
	104	MOVE	#-1, R0

Figure 7.3.5.12 Single-stepping an assembly language program in ASMTutor to show the effect on the status register

StatusRegisterb - ASMTutor

File Edit View Assemble Help

Run Speed :

R0	65534	R3	0	R6	0	PC	102	INT	0
R1	0	R4	0	R7	0	SR	5		
R2	0	R5	0	SP	15		-N-O-		

B	Address	Inst	Operand / Data (R/W)	Comment
	100	MOVE	#$7FFF, R0	<--- START
	101	ADD	#$7FFF, R0	
	102	RTS		

For Help, press F1

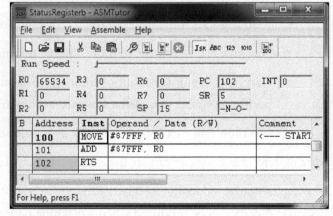

Figure 7.3.5.13 Shows the result of adding the most positive value $7FFF or $7FFF_{16}$ to itself

Questions

6. The format of the MOVE operation in an instruction set is MOV R_d, <operand2> which is interpreted as copy the value specified by <operand2> into register R_d. Assuming that MOV can set the condition codes.
Which, if any, status register condition codes are set when the machine code equivalents of the following are executed
(a) MOV R0, #-1 (b) MOV R1, #0
(c) MOV R2, #23?

7. The format of the SUBTRACT operation in an instruction set is SUB, R_d, R_n, <operand2> which is interpreted as subtract the value specified in <operand2> from the value in register R_n and store the result in register R_d. Register R0 stores decimal 7. Which status register condition codes are set, if any, when the machine code equivalents of the following are executed
(a) SUB R1, R0, #9 (b) SUB R1, R0, #7
(c) SUB R1, R0, #5?

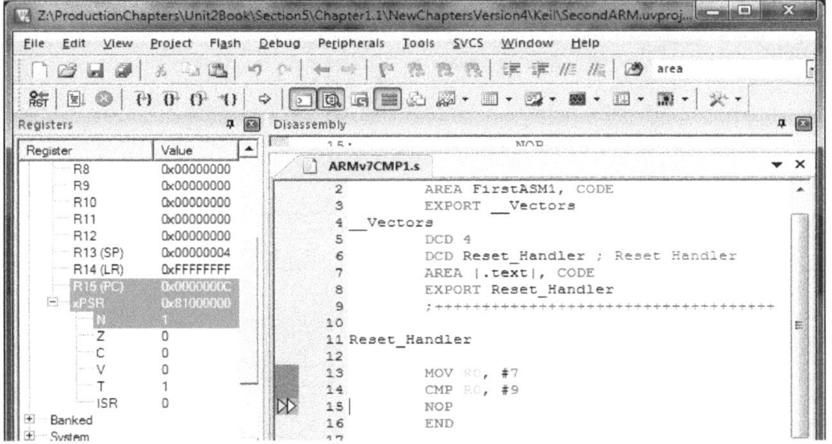

Figure 7.3.5.14 ARM µVision simulating the execution of CMP R0, #9

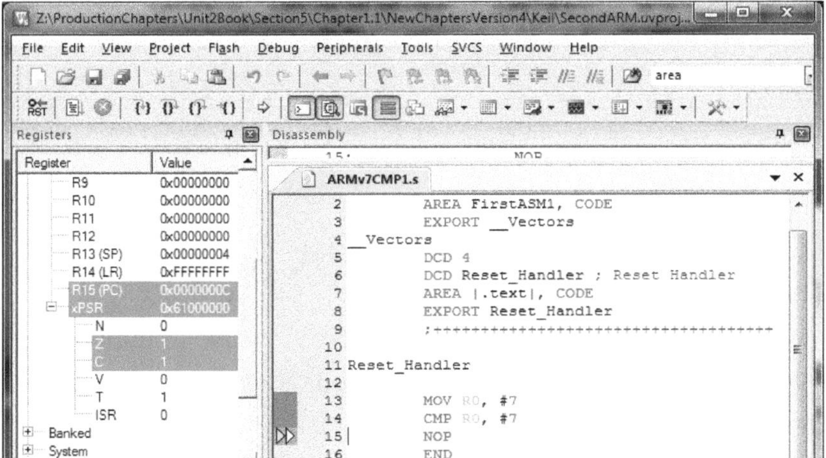

Figure 7.3.5.15 ARM µVision simulating the execution of CMP R0, #7

COMPARE

Compare instructions may be used to compare the contents of two registers or the contents of a register and an immediate value. For example, CMP R0, R1 compares the contents of registers R0 and R1. If the contents of these registers are equal, the zero flag in the status register is set. A compare operation performs a subtraction and uses the result to determine whether the two operand's values are equal or not. If unequal then the negative flag will be set if the subtraction result was negative. Figure 7.3.5.14 shows ARM µVision simulating the execution of CMP R0, #9 with decimal 7 stored in R0. The negative flag is set indicating that the operation [R0] - 9 has been performed by CMP. The notation [] means 'contents of'.

Figure 7.3.5.15 shows the result of CMP R0, #7 with decimal 7 stored in R0. Note that the zero flag is set. The carry flag is also set because two's complement arithmetic sometimes sets this flag.

Questions

8 What is the state of each condition code after the following comparison operations are executed in machine code? R0 contains the value decimal 9. Assume that CMP behaves as shown above.
(a) CMP R0, #15 (b) CMP R0, #7 (c) CMP R0, #9

Branching (conditional and unconditional)

Normally, a processor executes one instruction after another in a linear fashion. This means the next instruction to execute is found immediately following the current instruction. Branch instructions allow for a different order of execution. For example, the B loop instruction in Table 7.3.5.1 causes the previous instruction to be repeated indefinitely. The previous instruction is labelled loop so that the branch instruction can refer to it. The assembler will convert this symbolic label into a memory address when it translates the assembly language program into its machine code equivalent - object code column in Table 7.3.5.2.

Assembly language instructions or statements are divided into four fields separated by spaces or tabs as shown in Table 7.3.5.1.

Label field	Opcode field	Operand field(s)	Comment field
	MOV	R0, #1	; initialise counter to 1, R0 will hold a running count, R0 = 1
loop	ADD	R0, R0, #1	; increment counter by 1, R0 = R0 + 1
	B	loop	; repeat previous instruction
	END		; this is a pseudo-op that marks the end of the program to the assembler

AQA uses HALT

Table 7.3.5.1 ARM assembly language program showing how instructions are divided into four fields

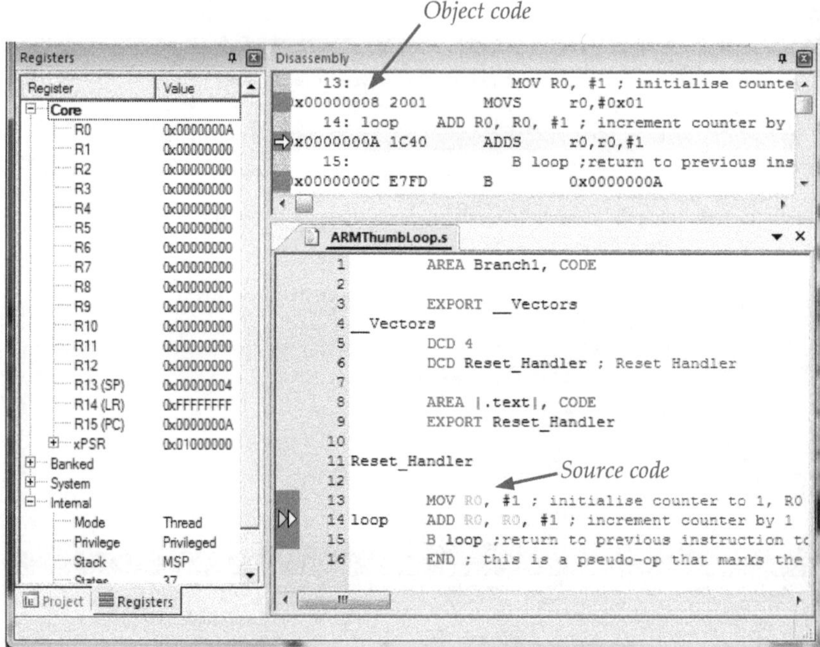

Figure 7.3.5.16 ARM µVision simulating the execution of a program that uses an unconditional branch instruction, B

The label field is optional and starts in the first column. It is used to identify the position in memory of the current instruction. It must be unique within the program. The opcode field expresses the processor command to execute. The operand field specifies where to find the data the command uses when it executes. ARM processor instructions have 0, 1, 2, 3 or 4 operands separated by commas. We will consider instructions that use only 0, 1, 2 or 3 operands.

The comment field is optional and is ignored by the assembler. It allows a programmer to write a few words describing the purpose of the instruction, e.g. 'increment counter by 1', to make it easier to understand. A semicolon (;) is used to separate the operand and comment fields.

Address	Object code	Label	Opcode	Operand
0x0000008	2001		MOV	R0, #1
0x000000A	1C40	loop	ADD	R0, R0, #1
0x000000C	E7FD		B	0x000000A

Table 7.3.5.2 ARM assembly language program showing both source and object code

The assembler translates assembly language source code into object code. Object code consists of the machine instructions executed by the processor. Table 7.3.5.2 shows ARM processor (Thumb-2 instruction set) object code alongside its equivalent assembly language source code. The first column shows the address in RAM of each machine code instruction, e.g. 0x00000008. The second column the opcode + operands, e.g. 1C40. The third, fourth and fifth columns show the corresponding assembly language source code. The comment field has been omitted. Figure 7.3.5.16 shows ARM µVision simulating this program. The loop label has been replaced in the instruction B loop by the memory address 0x000000A corresponding to label loop. In object code this is translated into the value to 'add' to the current address because ARM uses relative addressing[1]. The new address becomes the address of the next instruction to be fetched and executed. In this case FD in hexadecimal or -3 in decimal because two's complement coding is used for numbers.

Decimal	Hexadecimal	Object code byte
8	8	20
9	9	01
10	A	1C
11	B	40
12	C	E7
13	D	FD

Table 7.3.5.3 Memory map for ARM machine code program

Table 7.3.5.3 shows the memory map for the program's machine code. Note that 13_{10} is the address of byte value FD or -3_{10}. $13_{10} - 3_{10} = 10_{10} = A_{16}$. A_{16} is the address of instruction opcode 1C which is ADD in assembly language mnemonics.

Unconditional branch

The unconditional branch instruction B label always causes execution to branch (jump) to the instruction at the address indicated by label. Using direct addressing this would be for the example program

```
B 0x000000A
```

1 relative addressing not covered in AQA specification

Conditional branch

There is another kind of branch called a conditional branch. In this type of branch a condition must be true for branching of program execution to occur.

The instruction immediately before a conditional branch must be a COMPARE instruction. Execution of this instruction affects the condition code flags which conditional branch instructions examine before deciding whether or not to branch (SUBTRACT can be used instead of COMPARE, e.g. is an alternative to CMP R0, R1).

CMP R0, R1	Condition	Condition codes
R0 = R1	Equal	Zero flag set, Z = 1
R0 <> R1	Not Equal	Zero flag not set, Z = 0
R0 > R1	R0 Greater Than R1	Z = 0, N = 0
R0 < R1	R0 Less Than R1	Z= 0, N = 1

Table 7.3.5.4 Condition and condition codes for SUB and CMP

Table 7.3.5.5 shows the four conditional branch instructions, BEQ, BNE, BGT and BLT.

Instruction	Description	Condition codes
BEQ <label>	Branch if operands being compared are equal	Z = 1
BNE <label>	Branch if operands being compared are not equal	Z = 0
BGT<label>	Branch if first signed operand is greater than second signed operand	Z = 0, N = 0
BLT <label>	Branch if first signed operand is less than second signed operand	Z = 0, N = 1

Table 7.3.5.5 Conditional branch instructions

Figure 7.3.5.17 shows the simulation of conditional branch BEQ loop.

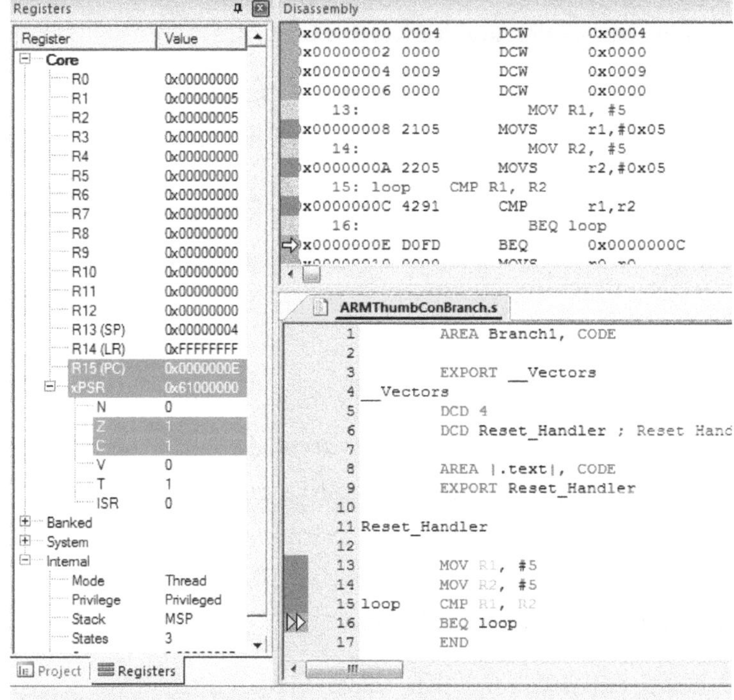

Figure 7.3.5.17 ARM µVision simulating the execution of a program that uses conditional branch instruction, BEQ

Questions

9 Explain what the following snippet of assembly language code does when its machine code equivalent is executed

```
        MOV R0, #12
        MOV R1, #6
loop    ADD R1, R1, #1
        CMP R1, R0
        BNE loop
        HALT    ; Stops the execution
```

Questions

10 Explain what the following snippets of assembly language code do when their machine code equivalent is executed

(a)
```
     MOV R0, #12
     MOV R1, #6
loop SUB R0, R0, #1
     CMP R0, R1
     BGT loop
     HALT   ; Stops the execution
```

(b)
```
     MOV R0, #12
     MOV R1, #6
loop ADD R1, R1, #1
     CMP R0, R1
     BLT loop
     HALT
```

11 What other conditional branch instruction would result in the code behaving in a similar way if used in place of BGT and BLT in (a) and (b)?

Logical bitwise operators

When designing digital logic gate circuits gates are used, such as AND, OR, NOT, which convert single bit input signals into single bit output signals.

For example, with the AND gate, if the inputs are 1 and 0 then the output is 0 because 1 AND 0 = 0.

Using AND, OR, NOT and XOR as operators in assembly language programs is slightly different. The inputs are typically 32-bit numbers and the output is a single 32-bit number. The inputs are transformed into the output by applying 32 logic operations, e.g. AND, at the same time in a bitwise fashion.

The format for ARM processors for the logical operations AND, OR and XOR is

Logical operation R_d, R_n, <operand2>

This means perform a bitwise logical operation between the value in register R_n and the value specified by <operand2> and store the result in register R_d. The symbolic opcode for the AND operation is AND; for the OR operation it is ORR and for XOR it is EOR.

The format for ARM processors for the logical operation NOT is

MVN R_d, <operand2>

This means perform a bitwise logical NOT operation on the value specified by <operand2> and store the result in register R_d.

AND

Figure 7.3.5.18 shows ARM μVision simulating 1111_2 AND 0001_2. The result is 0001_2 when AND R0, R0, R1 is executed in machine code. This instruction ANDs the contents of registers R0 and R1 and stores the result in R0, the register specified as the first operand.

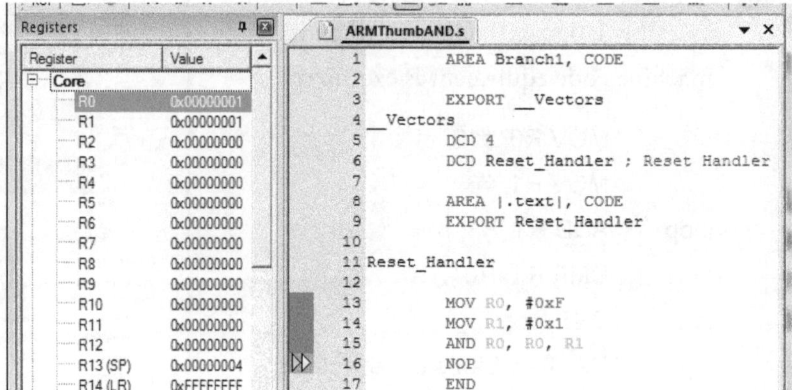

Figure 7.3.5.18 ARM μVision simulating the execution of a program that applies a bitwise AND operation to operands 0xF and 0x1 i.e. 1111_2 AND 0001_2

A mask operation is one that isolates bits to be tested. The logical AND can be used in this role. Suppose that we need to test the three least significant bits of a 32-bit word then we would choose the mask 0x00000007 because the last three bits are 111_2 (7_{16}) and the other bits are 0. If the bit pattern to be tested is stored in R0 then R1 will contain the state of the three least significant bits and zeroes everywhere else after executing

```
AND R1, R0, #0x7
```

To know if all three least significant bits are 1 then compare R1 with 0x7 as follows

```
CMP R1, #0x7
```

The zero flag will be set by CMP if they are.

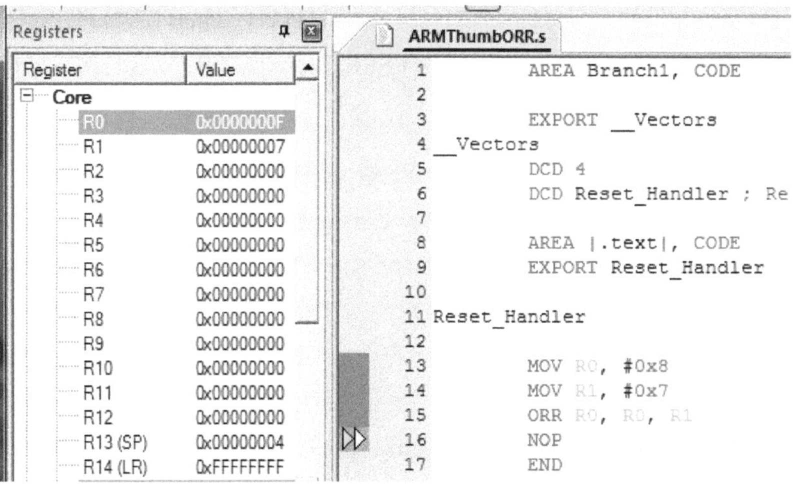

Figure 7.3.5.19 ARM µVision simulating the execution of a program that applies a bitwise OR operation to operands 0x8 and 0x7 i.e. 1000_2 OR 0111_2

OR

Figure 7.3.5.19 shows ARM µVision simulating 1000_2 OR 0111_2. The result is 1111_2 when ORR R0, R0, R1 is executed in machine code. This instruction ORs the contents of registers R0 and R1 and stores the result in R0, the register specified as the first operand.

XOR

XOR is the eXclusive-OR operation.

ARM names the operator for this operation EOR (Exclusive-OR)

Figure 7.3.5.20 shows ARM µVision simulating 1000_2 XOR 0111_2. The result is 1111_2 when EOR R0, R0, R1 is executed in machine code. This instruction Exclusive-ORs the contents of registers R0 and R1 and stores the result in R0, the register specified as the first operand.

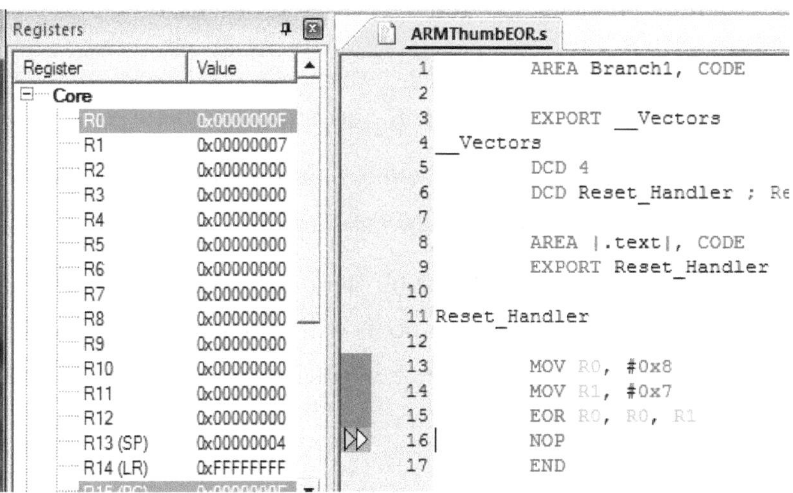

Figure 7.3.5.20 ARM µVision simulating the execution of a program that applies a bitwise XOR operation to operands 0x8 and 0x7 i.e. 1000_2 XOR 0111_2

NOT

To perform a bitwise logical NOT operation the instruction

MVN R_d, <operand2>

This instruction NOTs the value specified by <operand2> and stores the result in register R_d.

Figure 7.3.5.21 shows ARM µVision simulating NOT 0x00000000.

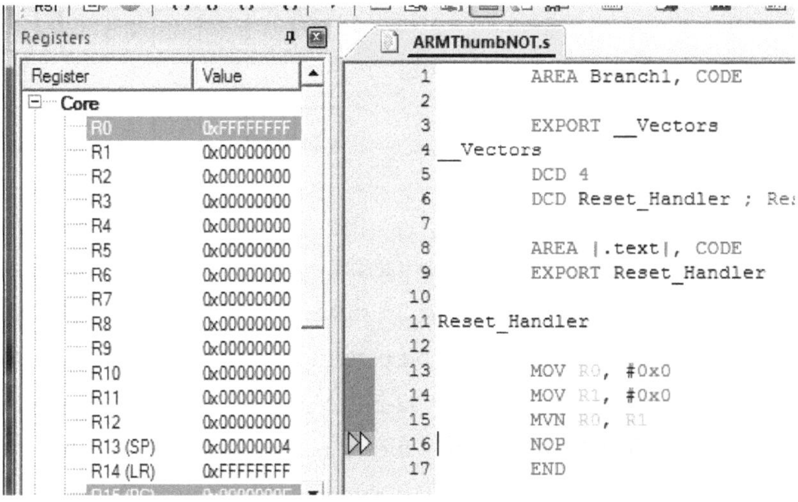

Figure 7.3.5.21 ARM µVision simulating the execution of a program that applies a bitwise NOT operation to operand 0x00000000, i.e. NOT $00000000000000000000000000000000_2$

The result is $11111111111111111111111111111111_2$ when MVN R0, R1 is executed in machine code. The result expressed in hexadecimal is FFFFFFFF. Note that R1 was assigned 0x0 in a MOV operation first.

Questions

12 What will the contents of register R0 be after the machine code equivalent of the following snippets of assembly language code are executed

(a)
```
MOV R0, #0xFF
EOR R0, R0, R0
HALT
```
(b)
```
MOV R0, #0xFF
MOV R1, #0x7
AND R0, R0, R1
HALT
```
(c)
```
MOV R0, #0x0
MOV R1, #0x7
ORR R0, R0, R1
HALT
```

13 A certain process may begin if bits 1, 3 and 5 of an 8-bit word are set. The state of the other bits may be ignored. Write the assembly language instructions to determine if the process may begin. You should assume that bit 1 is the least significant bit and that register R0 contains the 8-bit word.

14 Write an assembly language instruction using ORR to set bit 4 of register R0. Assume bits are numbered from the right 1...8 with bit 1 the least significant bit.

15 Write an assembly language instruction to isolate bits 1 and 3 of register R0 so that the state of each may be tested by other instructions. Assume bit numbering as in Q14.

16 "We use the logical OR to make bits become one, and we use the logical AND to make bits become zero." Explain using examples the meaning of this statement.

17 Register R0 contains a 32-bit word that represents the state of 32 pixels of a black and white image with colour depth one bit per pixel. Write a single assembly language instruction to invert the state of each pixel stored in R0. Write another instruction to restore the stored state.

Logical shift operations

A logical shift treats the bit pattern as being an unsigned pattern of bits. A shift operation takes two inputs, one the number of shifts to apply, *n*, and the other the bit pattern to be shifted by n bits. For example, the bit pattern in *Figure 7.3.5.22 (a)* when shifted by one bit to the left becomes the bit pattern shown in *Figure 7.3.5.22(b)*.

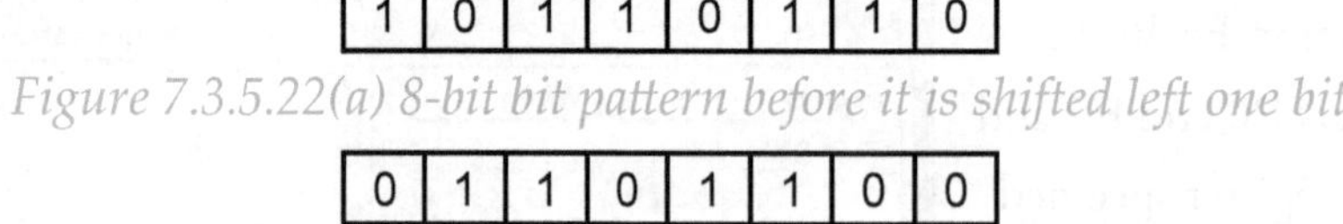

Figure 7.3.5.22(a) 8-bit bit pattern before it is shifted left one bit

Figure 7.3.5.22(b) 8-bit bit pattern after it has been shifted left one bit

Logical shift left operation

With a logical shift left the bit pattern is moved to the left with the least significant bit position replaced by a zero. The carry bit will contain the last bit shifted out. For the example in *Figure 7.3.5.22* the carry bit will contain 1 after shifting left one bit. The bit pattern in *Figure 7.3.5.22(a)* is unsigned decimal 178 or B2 in hexadecimal. In ARM assembly language, the 32-bit register R0 contains $B2_{16}$ after MOV R0, #0xB2 is executed. The ARM instruction LSL R1, R0, #1 shifts the bit pattern in R0 left one bit and stores the result 164_{16} or 356_{10} in R1. Notice that the value stored in R1 is double the value in R0. This is equivalent to multiplying by 2^1. If the shift operation is LSL R0, #2 and R0 contains 178_{10} or $B2_{16}$ then $2C8_{16}$ or 712_{10} will be stored in R1. This is equivalent to multiplying by 2^2.

Figure 7.3.5.23 shows the result of applying logical shift left to 0x1 eight times. The loop was stepped through eight times to change the pattern in R0 from 0x00000001 to 0x00000100. (Note these are hex numbers)

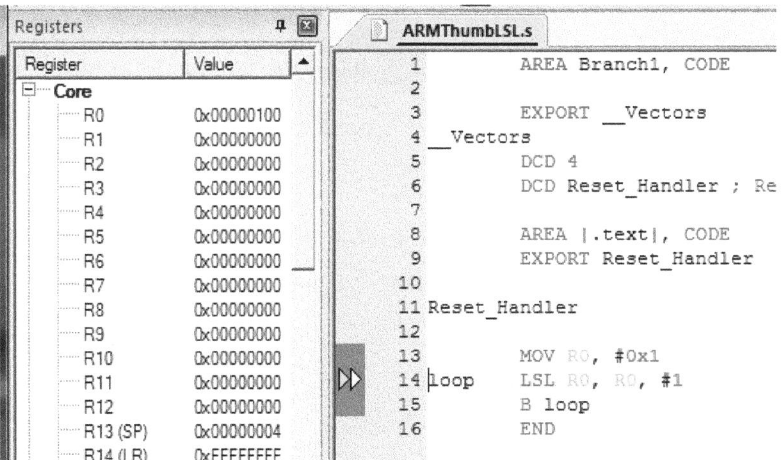

Figure 7.3.5.23 Logical Shift Left by one bit applied 8 times by single-stepping through loop eight times

Questions

18 Rewrite

```
loop    LSL R0, R0, #1
        B loop
        END
```

to obtain the bit pattern 0x00000100 from the bit pattern 0x00000001 stored in R0 without a loop.

Questions

19 The decimal number 4 is stored in register R0. Write an assembly language instruction that multiples this number by 2^4.

20 Using Figure 7.3.5.22 as a template, record the state of R0 after the following assembly language program is executed in machine code. Assume R0 is an 8-bit wide register. Include the carry bit in your answer.

```
MOV R0, #3
LSL R0, R0, #7
HALT
```

Logical shift right

With a **logical shift right** the bit pattern is moved to the right with the most significant bit position replaced by a zero. The carry bit will contain the last bit shifted out.

For the example in Figure 7.3.5.24 the carry bit will contain 0 after right shifting one bit. The bit pattern in Figure 7.3.5.24(a) is unsigned decimal 178 or B2 in hexadecimal. In ARM assembly language, the 32-bit register R0 contains $B2_{16}$ after MOV R0, #0xB2 is executed. The ARM instruction LSR R1, R0, #1 shifts the bit pattern in R0 right one bit and stores the result 59_{16} or 89_{10} in R1. Notice that the value stored in R1 is half that in R0. This is equivalent to dividing an unsigned number by 2^1. If the shift operation is LSR R1, R0, #2 and R0 contains 178_{10} or $B2_{16}$ then $2C_{16}$ or 44_{10} will be stored in R1. This is equivalent to unsigned integer division by 2^2, with the remainder 1 stored in the carry bit.

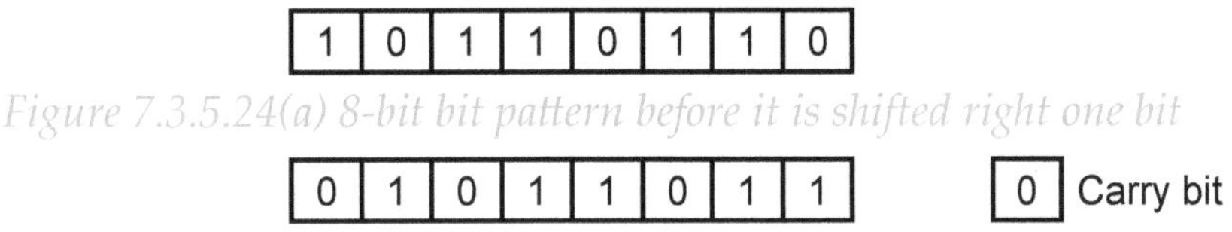

Figure 7.3.5.24(a) 8-bit bit pattern before it is shifted right one bit

Figure 7.3.5.24(b) 8-bit bit pattern after it is shifted right one bit

Questions

21 R0 contains 0x00000100. What does it contain after LSR R0, R0, #8 in machine code is executed?

22 The decimal number 64 is stored in register R0. Write an assembly language instruction that divides this number by 2^4. The result should be stored in register R1.

23 Using Figure 7.3.5.24 as a template, record the state of R0 after the following assembly language program is executed in machine code. Assume R0 is an 8-bit wide register. Include the carry bit in your answer.

```
MOV R0, #195
LSR R0, R0, #7
HALT
```

HALT

When a HALT instruction is encountered in an executing machine code program the execution of the program is stopped.

Questions

Use AQA's instruction set from Table 7.3.3.5 in Chapter 7.3.3 to answer these questions.

24 The high level language program statement "Sum := Sum + 100;" assigns to variable Sum the result of adding decimal number 100 to Sum. The symbol ":=" is the assignment operator. Write the equivalent assembly language instructions for this statement. Assume that memory location with address 0x1000 is used to store the current value of variable Sum.

25 Write the equivalent assembly language instructions for high level language statement

```
If Sum > 5 Then Sum := Sum + 1 Else Sum := Sum - 1;
```

Assume that memory location with address 0x1000 is used to store the current value of variable Sum.

26 Write the equivalent assembly language instructions for high level language statement

```
While Sum < 10 Do Sum := Sum + 1;
```

Assume that memory location with address 0x1000 is used to store the current value of variable Sum.

27 Write the equivalent assembly language instructions for high level language statement

```
Repeat Sum := Sum - 1 Until Sum = 0;
```

Assume that memory location with address 0x1000 is used to store the current value of variable Sum which is decimal 10.

28 Write the equivalent assembly language instructions for high level language statement

```
Sum := Sum * 8;
```

Assume that memory location with address 0x1000 is used to store the current value of variable Sum, an unsigned number.

29 Write the equivalent assembly language instructions for high level language statement

```
If (SwitchSettings BitWiseAND 4) = 1 Then Sum := 0 ;
```

Assume that memory location with address 0x1000 is used to store the current value of variable SwitchSettings, an unsigned number and memory location 0x1004 the current value of variable Sum.

30 Use an assembly language simulator to check your answers.

In this chapter you have covered:

- The basic machine-code operations of
  - load - LDR R_d, <memory ref>
  - add - ADD R_d, R_n, <operand2>
  - subtract - SUB R_d, R_n, <operand2>
  - store - STR R_d, <memory ref>
  - branching (conditional and unconditional)
    - B <label>
    - BEQ <label>
    - BNE <label>
    - BGT <label>
    - BLT <label>
  - compare - CMP R_n, <operand2>
  - logical bitwise operators
    - AND - AND R_d, R_n, <operand2>
    - OR - ORR R_d, R_n, <operand2>
    - NOT - MVN R_d, <operand2>
    - XOR - EOR R_d, R_n, <operand2>
  - logical
    - shift left - LSL R_d, R_n, <operand2>
    - shift right - LSR R_d, R_n, <operand2>
  - halt - HALT
- The use of the basic machine-code operations above when machine-code instructions are expressed in mnemonic form - assembly language, using immediate and direct addressing
- The instructions set of assembly language mnemonics identified by AQA to be used in questions - see *Table* 7.3.3.5 in *Chapter* 7.3.3. Question papers will supply the list of mnemonics and their description so that they do not need to be memorised.

7.3 Structure and role of the processor and its components

Learning objectives:

- *Explain the effect on processor performance of:*
  - *multiple cores*
  - *cache memory*
  - *clock speed*
  - *word length*
  - *address bus width*
  - *data bus width*

7.3.7 Factors affecting processor performance

How many instructions can be executed per second?

We have learned already about the basic computational model of CPU and memory from earlier chapters in Section 7. In this model, the program is fetched instruction by instruction from main memory and executed in the CPU. The executing program accesses data in main memory while it is executing. Figure 7.3.7.1 shows this basic model. The fetching, decoding and execution of an instruction is synchronised with the CPU's clock.

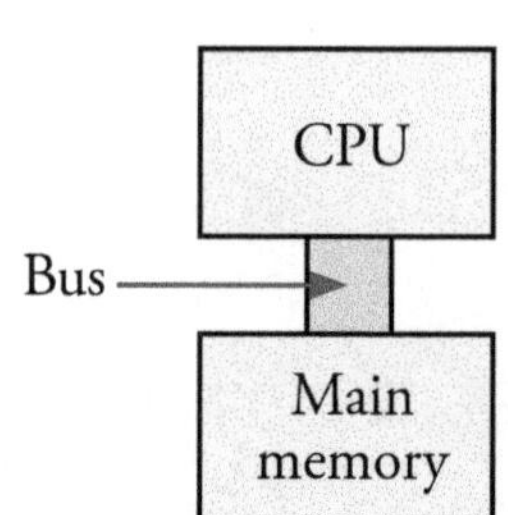

Figure 7.3.7.1 Basic computational model

The number of clock cycles ("ticks") of the CPU's clock it takes the CPU to execute an instruction varies from instruction to instruction with load instructions which load data from memory taking the most.

Suppose, *the average number of clock cycles per instruction* = 2

then *the average number of instructions executed per clock cycle* = $^1/_2$ = 0.5

If the CPU operates at a clock frequency of 800 MHz then there are 800 million clock cycles per second.

Using this, we calculate that

the average number of instructions executed per second is 0.5 x 800

= 400 million per second

Cycles per instruction (CPI)

Cycles per instruction (clock cycles per instruction) is one aspect of a processor's performance. When evaluating processor performance the average number of clock cycles per instruction is often used.

Information

No of clock cycles per instruction:
The number of clock cycles that an instruction takes to execute is determined by its complexity and the design of the control unit in the CPU. For a given Instruction Set Architecture (ISA), the same instruction may take longer to execute on one processor than another operating at the same clock frequency. The difference is in the design of the control unit.

Information

Average no of clock cycles per instruction:
The percentage of instructions that are load, store, integer arithmetic, branches varies from program to program so the average no of clock cycles per instruction will vary from program to program.

Questions

1. The performance of two processors with the same instruction set architecture but operating at different clock frequencies is assessed by measuring the average number of cycles per instruction (CPI) for various programs compiled by the same compiler and executed on each processor. Which processor do you think was the faster at executing these programs? Justify your answer.

   Processor 1: Clock frequency 5 GHz CPI = 3
   Processor 2: Clock frequency 3 GHz CPI = 1.5

Information

Listed below in order of popularity, as of 2015, are some of the most common ISAs (most popular first) :

- ARM
- IA-32 (Intel® x86)
- Intel® 64 (Intel® x86-64)
- IA-64 (Intel® Itanium®)

Information

Clock speed or rate:
Clock speed can be adjusted in the BIOS.

CPU time

CPU Time is the amount of time it takes the CPU to execute a particular program. CPU time is a function of the number of instructions in the program, the clock cycle time and average CPI:

CPU time = instruction count x CPI x clock cycle time

CPU time can be reduced by reducing any or all of the quantities on the right-hand side of the above equation.

Instruction count can be reduced by

- inspecting the compiled code and replacing sections of it with code that uses fewer instructions, written directly in assembly language by hand
- redesigning the compiler to produce fewer machine code instructions for a given program, i.e. better optimisation.

To reduce CPI and clock cycle time we must focus on the processor (CPU) itself.

Questions

2 What affects the amount of time it takes a CPU to execute a particular program?

Information

Tools for exploring the hardware of a computer system:
Speccy®: www.piriform.com/speccy
CPUID: www.cpuid.com / softwares/cpu-z.html

How can we improve processor performance?

CPI and clock cycle time are related to how the processor operates. To improve its performance we need to reduce the

- average CPI by redesigning the processor, using multiple cores, increasing memory bandwidth (number of bits transferred per second), or pre-fetching data and instructions and storing these in fast access memory (cache) located on processor chip.
- clock cycle time by clocking the processor at a higher rate.

Multiple cores

Arithmetic instructions are executed using the Arithmetic and Logic Unit (ALU). If the number of ALUs is increased from one to four then a single arithmetic instruction can use all four ALUs at the same time. For this to be possible,

1. The data must lend itself to being divided into four streams, one per ALU.
2. Four cores (ALU + Control Unit + Registers [+ Cache]) are required

This means that all the arithmetic instructions to which this applies for a given program can be executed in a quarter of the time. Single Instruction Multiple Data (SIMD) stream processing, as it is known, requires special control units to decode and execute instructions that are to be executed in parallel.

Data can also be pre-fetched at the same time the processors are busy decoding and executing arithmetic instructions. The pre-fetched data is stored in fast to

Key concept

Core:
A processing unit consisting of ALU + Control unit + Registers within a CPU.
A CPU or processor with just one core is called a single-core CPU.
A CPU with more than one core is called a multi-core CPU, e.g. a quad-core processor has four cores.

access memory on the processor chip so as not to hold up the processor.

Figure 7.3.7.2 shows a schematic for an ARM® Cortex®-A7 quad-core 32-bit processor based on ARM's licensed v7-A instruction set architecture (ISA). It has four CPUs or cores labelled 1, 2, 3 and 4. Each core has its own data cache as well as an instruction cache enabling instructions to be pre-fetched as well. SIMD operations for handling audio and video processing as well as graphics and gaming processing rely on a special control unit called the NEON Data Engine. Floating point operations take considerably longer than fixed point and integer operations (fixed point data can be treated and processed as integers). The A9 processor also includes a dedicated Floating Point Unit specially designed to allow the CPU to offload floating point operations to this unit.

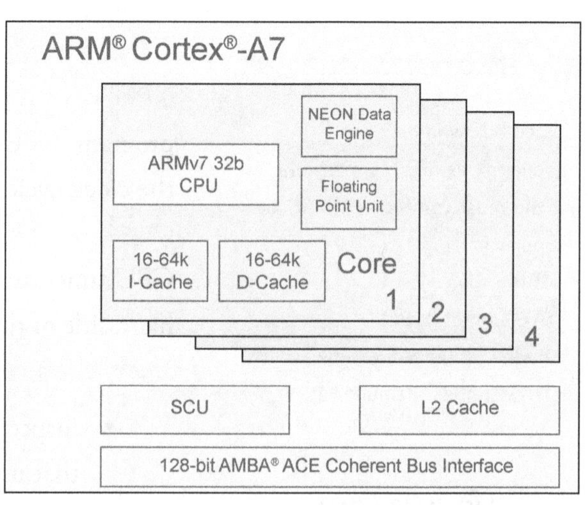

Figure 7.3.7.2 ARM® Cortex®-A7 quad-core processor

Figure 7.3.7.3 shows the Parallella computer platform which is an energy efficient, high performance, credit card sized computer based on the Epiphany multicore chips from Adapteva®. This desktop version cost £150 and is used for developing and implementing high performance, parallel processing. It uses a Zynq dual-core ARM A9 processor to launch and run programs which use the 16-core Epiphany coprocessor for parts of the program that can be executed in parallel. The Epiphany coprocessor is also available with 64 cores.The Parallela's Ethernet connection allows multiple units to be interconnected to make a cluster.

Gigabit Ethernet

Zynq dual-core ARM A9 processor with Field Programmable Gate Array (FPGA)

16-core Epiphany coprocessor

1GB SDRAM Memory

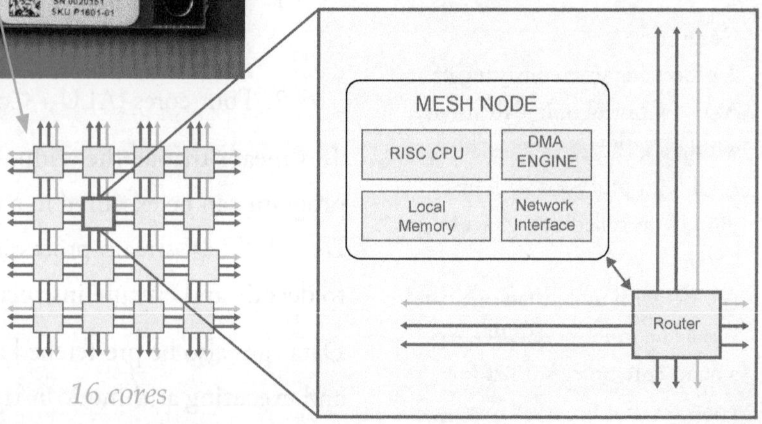

MESH NODE
RISC CPU
DMA ENGINE
Local Memory
Network Interface
Router

16 cores

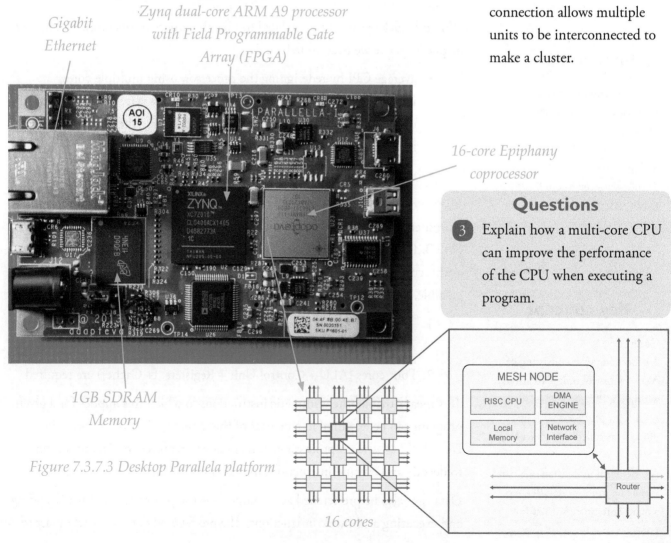

Figure 7.3.7.3 Desktop Parallela platform

Questions

3 Explain how a multi-core CPU can improve the performance of the CPU when executing a program.

Bus width effect on processor performance

Main memory or RAM is controlled by a circuit called a memory controller which is a part of the CPU. The memory controller is connected to main memory by a memory bus as shown in Figure 7.3.7.4.

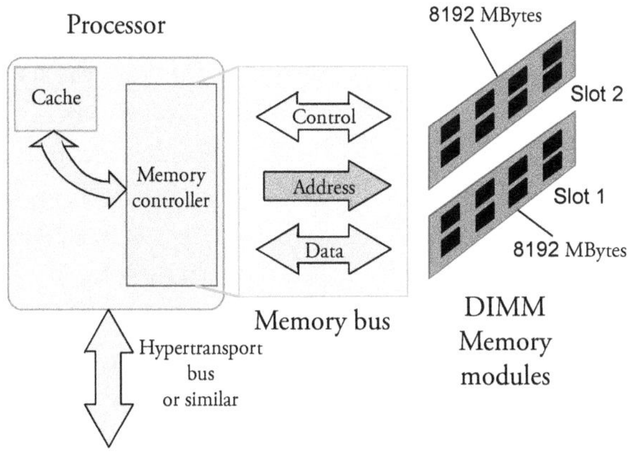

Figure 7.3.7.4 Memory bus

In modern computer systems every byte in memory has its own address. The data bus part of the memory bus is typically 64, 128, 192 or 256 bits wide on a modern general purpose Intel or AMD CPU. 64 bits means that when 64 bits are transferred along the data bus, these 64 bits have come from 8 memory addresses.

Modern computer systems use *synchronous dynamic random access memory* (SDRAM) that is dynamic random access memory (DRAM) synchronized with the system/memory bus.

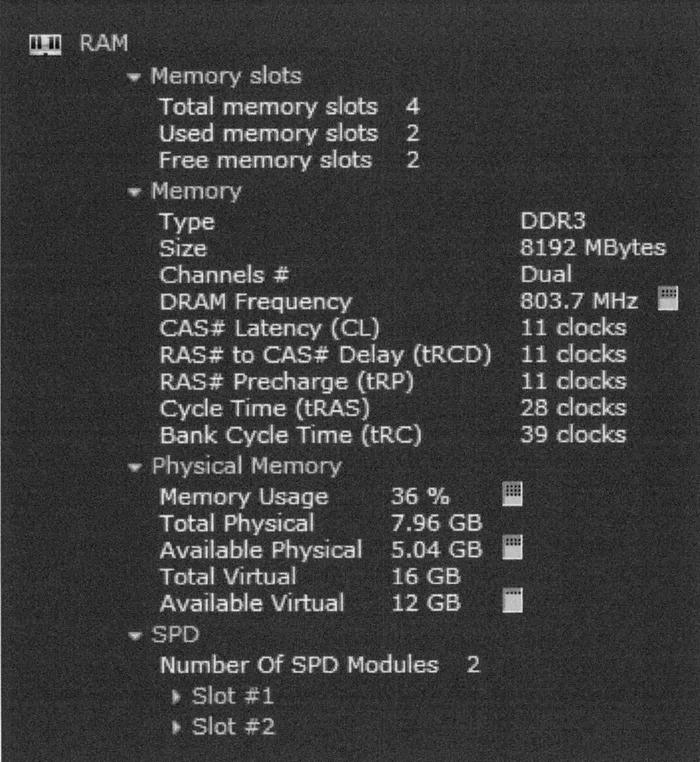

Figure 7.3.7.5 Details of RAM in author's computer

DDR3-1600 memory used in the computer on which this book was written stands for double data rate type three synchronous dynamic random-access memory. It is operated at a clock rate or clock speed of approximately 800MHz but because data is transferred on both the rising edge of the clock signal and the falling edge, twice as much data is transferred per clock cycle - Figure 7.3.7.5.

Each transfer consists of 64 bits, the width of the data bus (single channel). The **memory data bus must also operate at the same frequency as memory** because it has to be synchronised with the DDR memory.

A processor should take less time executing a program if more data can be transferred each time memory is accessed. **A wider data bus allows more data to be transferred in one go**. However, the speed at which the transfer takes place is also a factor. This is why both data bus width and memory bus clock rate must be taken into account.

Extension material: *Memory bandwidth and effect on processor performance*

Memory bandwidth is the rate at which data can be read from or stored in main memory by a processor. Memory bandwidth is usually expressed in units of bytes per second.

Memory bandwidth = memory clock rate x bits transferred per clock cycle / 8

For example, bits transferred per clock cycle = 64 bits x 2 x no of channels

(Multiple by 2 when Double Rate Dynamic RAM (DDR3) is used)

No of channels = 2, clock rate = 800MHz (8×10^6),

Memory bandwidth = $800 \times 10^6 \times 64 \times 2 \times 2/8 = 256 \times 10^8$ bytes per second = 25.6 Gigabytes per second

= 25.6 GB/s

This is a theoretical maximum because memory doesn't respond immediately to a read or write request. This is called latency, in particular, Column Access Strobe (CAS) latency - Figure 7.3.7.5. It is the delay time between the moment a memory controller tells the memory module to access a particular memory column on a RAM module, and the moment the data from the given location is available on the module's output pins. To overcome this latency, which can be as much as 11 clock cycles or more (see Figure 7.3.7.5), cache memory is employed.

Cache memory is faster to access than main memory because

(a) its technology is different from main memory technology

(b) the bus speed of the bus that accesses cache memory is much higher than the memory bus speed connecting main memory to the CPU.

Information

Bus width cannot be increased indefinitely because as more lines are added, it becomes more difficult to keep all the bits in step. A problem known as skew.
The solution is to reduce the number of bus lines to 32 or less but compensate by clocking these lines at a much higher rate. The bus interfaces at either end take care of aggregating bits into the required size, e.g. 128, before passing these on. The Hypertransport bus is one way that this is done. This is a packet based serial bus.
Just as USB has largely replaced the Centronics parallel communication interface, so Hypertransport and similar systems are replacing the traditional physical parallel computer bus.

Questions

4 Describe the effect on memory bandwidth of increasing
(a) the width of the data bus from 64 bits to 128 bits
(b) the clock rate that memory uses from 666.6MHz to 800MHz.

5 Explain why the transfer speed of bits along the data bus is not the only factor that determines the time taken to transfer data between processor and main memory.

The effect of cache on processor performance

CPU cache is memory on the CPU chip used by the central processing unit (CPU) of a computer to reduce the average time to access data from main memory.

The cache is a small amount of fast but expensive memory which stores copies of the data from frequently used main memory locations, data to be written to main memory and pre-fetched instructions.

When the processor attempts to read a word of main memory, a check is made first to determine if the word is in the cache. If it is, a copy of the word is transferred to the processor. This is a much faster operation than accessing main memory. If not, a block of main memory, consisting of a fixed number of words, is transferred into the cache and then a copy of the referenced word is transferred to the processor.

Similarly, when the processor needs to write to main memory it will write to the cache instead which is a much faster operation than writing directly to main memory.

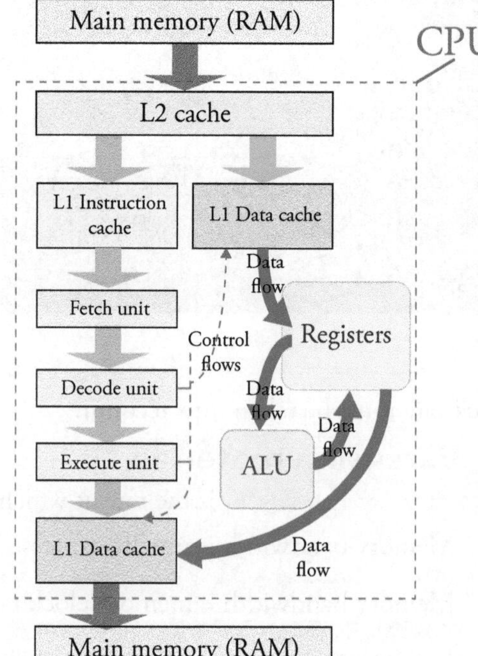

Figure 7.3.7.6 Cache hierarchy and role in Fetch-Execute cycle

Figure 7.3.7.6 shows the cache hierarchy and its role in the Fetch-Execute cycle. L1 cache has near zero latency but only a limited amount is provided because it is expensive. The L2 memory cache is cheaper to make than

Cores	6
Threads	6
Name	AMD FX-6300
Code Name	Vishera
Package	Socket AM3+ (942)
Technology	32nm
Specification	AMD FX-6300 Six-Core Processor
Family	F
Extended Family	15
Model	2
Extended Model	2
Stepping	0
Revision	OR-C0
Instructions	MMX (+), SSE, SSE2, SSE3, SSSE3,
Virtualization	Supported, Disabled
Hyperthreading	Not supported
Fan Speed	2129 RPM
Bus Speed	200.9 MHz
Rated Bus Speed	2411.0 MHz
Stock Core Speed	3500 MHz
Stock Bus Speed	200 MHz
Average Temperature	15 °C
Caches	
L1 Data Cache Size	6 x 16 KBytes
L1 Instructions Cache Size	3 x 64 KBytes
L2 Unified Cache Size	3 x 2048 KBytes
L3 Unified Cache Size	8192 KBytes

Figure 7.3.7.7 Cache present in AMD® FX-6300 CPU

L1 cache but is slower to respond than the L1 cache, and therefore it has some latency but still much less than main memory. Some systems use an additional layer of cache between main memory and L2 cache called L3 cache with latency greater than L2 cache but still less than main memory. More L3 cache is provided than L1 and L2 cache because it is cheaper than these.

Figure 7.3.7.7 shows the L1, L2 and L3 caches incorporated into AMD's FX-6300 CPU and their memory sizes. Note that there are two L1 caches, one for data and one for instructions.

Key concept

Cache memory:
A small amount of faster memory than main memory, that stores copies of the data from frequently used main memory locations, data to be written to main memory and pre-fetched instructions. L1 and L2 cache are usually located on the CPU chip. Slower L3 cache is often located on the motherboard.
The cache memory approach relies for its effectiveness on the fact that when a block of data is fetched into the cache to satisfy a single memory reference, it is likely that future references will be to other words in the block.

Questions

6 Explain how cache memory may be used to improve the performance of a processor.

The effect of word length on processor performance

The instruction set architecture of a processor is designed to work with registers of a given word length (number of bits). In a 32-bit processor, the registers are 32 bits in length, in a 64-bit processor, 64 bits. A machine code instruction will manipulate 32 bits at a time in a 32-bit processor and the unit of transfer between processor and main memory will also be 32 bits. In each case, 32 bits are presented for manipulation or transfer in 32-bit long registers.

If we need to work with 64 bits but are restricted to using a 32-bit processor then we have to use more 32-bit machine code instructions to accomplish the same task than would be the case if we could use 64-bit machine code instructions. A program compiled for a 32-bit machine is thus likely to have more instructions to execute than the same program compiled for a 64-bit processor other things being equal. More instructions to execute means more CPU time.

Questions

7 Explain the effect on processor performance of processor word length.

The effect of address bus width on processor performance

The language of digital computers is binary. Addresses of memory words are no different and are also expressed at the machine level in binary. Addresses can and are treated as data to be manipulated. The address bus width tends therefore to mirror the word length of the processor and therefore its registers. Although 8-bit processors have tended to be different by using an address bus width of 16 lines. More address lines means **more bytes can be addressed**. *Table 7.3.7.1* shows how the number of bytes that a processor can address increases with word length of processor. At present 64-bit processors are designed with a lower figure for the width of the address bus of 48 bits as 18,446,744,073,709,551,616 bytes is of the order of petabytes for 64-bit wide address bus. Memory of this capacity would cost a lot of money!

Processor	No of bytes that can be addressed
8-bit	256
16-bit	65,536
32-bit	4,294,967,296
64-bit	18,446,744,073,709,551,616

Table 7.3.7.1 Effect on no of bytes that can be addressed when address bus width is increased

Questions

8. Explain the effect on processor performance of address bus width.

Summary

To improve the performance of a processor timewise, CPU time needs to be reduced so that programs take less time to execute. CPU time is defined as follows: **CPU time = instruction count x CPI x clock cycle time**

To reduce CPU time the following need to be reduced

1. Instruction count
   - influenced by the design of the compiler or whether sections of code have been rewritten in assembly language to use fewer instructions.
2. CPI (cycles per instruction) and clock cycle time
   - influenced by the design of the processor and its operation.

CPI can be reduced by

- increasing the word length of the processor
- redesigning its control unit to take less time decoding and executing instructions
- using multiple cores
- increasing memory bandwidth (number of bits transferred per second)
  - by increasing the width of the data bus for a given clock rate
  - by clocking the memory bus at a higher rate for a given width of data bus
- pre-fetching data and instructions and storing these in fast access memory (cache) located on processor chip.

Clock cycle time can be reduced by increasing the clock speed and clocking the processor at a higher rate.

To improve the performance of a processor regarding the number of memory words it can address, the width of the address bus needs to be increased.

In this chapter you have covered:

- Explanations of the effect on processor performance of:
  - multiple cores
  - cache memory
  - clock speed
  - word length
  - address bus width
  - data bus width

7.4 External hardware devices

Learning objectives:

- *Know the main characteristics, purposes and suitability of the devices and understand their principles of operation*
  - *barcode reader*
  - *digital camera*
  - *laser printer*
  - *RFID*

Information

Barcode symbols:
A combination of several bars that make up an individual character or digit is often called a symbol. The set of symbols available for a specific barcode standard is referred to as its symbology. All these different symbologies can be read with a laser beam.

Key concept

One-dimensional barcode:
Barcodes are said to have one dimension if there's a single line (such as a line traced by a scanner's laser) that can cross all lines of the symbol.

Did you know?

Universal Product Code (UPC):
The first-ever product carrying a UPC code in its packaging was scanned June 26th 1974. It was a 10-pack of chewing gum, now on display at Smithsonian Institution's National Museum of American History in Washington, D.C.

7.4.1 Input and output devices

Barcode reader

A barcode reader, or barcode scanner, is an electronic device for reading barcodes printed on items such as cans, packaging, and the covers of books or magazines. A barcode is a sequence of white and black bars (*Figure 7.4.1.1*) that encodes information such as a product identifier. The product identifier is usually printed in human-readable form beneath the barcode.

Figure 7.4.1.1 Barcode encoding the characters 978-0-9927536-2-7

A barcode reader consists of a light source (low-powered laser diode), a lens, photoelectric detectors (photodiodes) and decoder circuitry to analyse the barcode's image data and generate character codes. The scanner uses the light source to illuminate the black and white bands. More light is reflected from a white band than from a dark band. The pattern of reflection is converted from optical form to electrical form by photoelectric detectors in the barcode reader. The electrical form of the reflection data is analysed and the barcode is decoded into character form. The path of a red laser beam as it moves over the barcode is shown in *Figure 7.4.1.2*. The relative time the beam spends scanning dark bars and light spaces which encode a character is measured and a lookup table is then used to translate this time into the corresponding character.

Figure 7.4.1.2 Laser beam scan of barcode

The scanner outputs the character codes, e.g. ASCII codes, as a sequence of binary digits for processing by a computer.

The line of the laser beam shown in *Figure 7.4.1.2* is the reason why barcodes that are scanned in this way are known as one-dimensional barcodes.

A major advantage of one-dimensional barcodes is that they can be decoded very reliably even when the items tagged with such barcodes are moving at high speed. They are also relatively cheap to use because the technology has been around for 40 years and the necessary components of laser diode and decoding electronics have benefited from high volume of use which has led to economies of scale in their manufacture.

Information

QR code:

Refers to a single member of the family of 2D barcodes 2D barcodes are machine-readable codes that use markings forming a two-dimensional grid. The example below is a QR code that represents the text Unit 2 CS.

A CCD camera is used to "see" the squares that make up a 2D barcode.

Figure 7.4.1.3 CCD SONY ICX493AQA 10.14 Mpixels APS-C 1.8" (23.98 x 16.41mm) sensor side

Information

The GS1 organization (www.gs1.org) maintains the standards related to the Global Trade Item Number (GTIN). There are several symbologies that belong to this family, all of them representing a product code and all using the same kind of barcode symbols:

UPC-A - The first product barcode (12 digits) now refered to as GTIN-12.

EAN-13 - European barcode (13 digits) now refered to GTIN-13.

Questions

1. What is a barcode?
2. Explain the operation of a barcode reader designed to read one-dimensional barcodes.
3. Why is the information encoded in barcode form also printed in human-readable form beneath the barcode?
4. The automated luggage handling system at Heathrow airport reads barcodes on labels attached to passengers' luggage to route the luggage to the correct conveyor belt among 30 miles of conveyors. The barcodes encode flight and passenger information. Why are barcodes suitable for this application?

Digital camera

Light reflected from objects is focussed by the lens of a digital camera onto a two-dimensional array of light-sensitive cells (photosensors) to form an analogue image. Each cell or site accumulates an electric charge proportional to the brightness of the illumination and as the latter varies in a continuous manner so does charge accumulation. Both are analogue quantities.

To process the analogue image digitally, the magnitude of the charge in each photosensor is sensed and converted into digital format by an analogue to digital converter (ADC).

The two-dimensional array (matrix) of photosensors and associated electronics to perform analogue to digital conversion is one of two types:

- Charge-Coupled Device (CCD)
- Complementary Metal-Oxide Semiconductor (CMOS)

Both are fabricated from metal oxide semiconductors with photodiodes used as photosensors. A single chip may contain millions of photodiodes laid out in rows and columns forming a matrix.

Information

Digital single-lens reflex cameras:

These use an aspect ratio of 3:2. Aspect ratio is the ratio of the width of the image to its height. The Canon EOS 600D (released February 2011) uses an APS-C CMOS sensor consisting of a sensor array of dimensions 5184 x 3456 pixels.

Figure 7.4.1.4(a) illustrates with a 6 x 6 matrix how coloured images can be sensed in a CCD-type camera sensor.

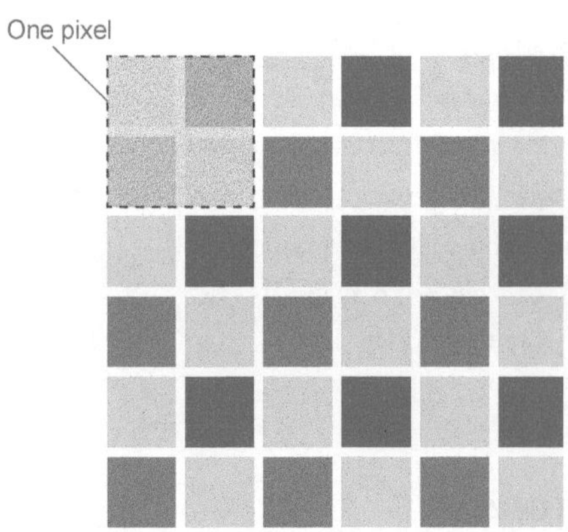

Figure 7.4.1.4(a) CCD-type Bayer filter sensor matrix for capturing coloured images

Red, green and blue filters cover the photodiodes. Each pixel is composed of one red, one blue and two green filtered photodiodes reflecting the fact that the human eye is more sensitive to green light. This filter arrangement is known as a Bayer filter mosaic.

Each row of photodiodes shares an ADC which is located to the right of each row. The accumulated charges in a row are shifted rightwards one cell at a time, converted into an analogue voltage and then into a digitally equivalent voltage by the ADC.

With some additional processing to take into account the filters, the whole image is converted to an equivalent pixel-based digital one (see *Chapter 5.6.1.1*). This is called a raw format digital image, e.g. Canon cameras save a raw format image in a file with extension CR2.

CR2 files use a format based on the TIFF specification. These files are extremely high quality, and are the very best when it comes to editing. CR2 files can be converted into JPEG format once the need to adjust the RAW image file is no longer needed.

In a CMOS sensor, each site in the matrix contains a photodiode plus some transistors to do some of the pre-processing as well as to allow each photosite to be independently accessed. It does however mean a smaller photodiode.

Figure 7.4.1.4(b) CMOS-type sensor photodiodes overlaid onto a CCD-type sensor matrix for capturing coloured images

Figure 7.4.1.4(b) shows with a black square the area occupied by a photodiode at a photosite compared with the area occupied by a photodiode in the equivalent CCD sensor. The rest of a CMOS photosite is occupied by transistors. Light falling on these does not get captured which means the site is less sensitive to light. It also leads to images with more noise than with the equivalent CCD-produced image.

Information

Bayer filter:

A Bayer filter mosaic is a colour filter array for arranging RGB colour filters on a square grid of photosensors (U.S. Patent No. 3,971,065). developed by Kodak employee Bruce Bayer in 1976. Kodak produced the world's first digital camera but the company went bankrupt because it continued to prioritise its film manufacturing business.

Information

DCIM (Digital Camera IMages):

DCIM is the default directory structure for digital cameras. When you put a memory card into a camera, the camera immediately looks for a 'DCIM' folder. If it doesn't find such a folder, it creates one.
Similarly, some desktop image-editing programs are designed to look specifically for 'DCIM' folders on any media inserted into the PC.

Key fact

CCD vs CMOS:

CCDs consume as much as 100 times more power than an equivalent CMOS sensor.
CMOS sensors are cheaper to manufacture than CCD.
The quality of manufacture of CCD is higher than CMOS because CCD has been around for a lot longer (since 1975).
CCD sensors have greater light sensitivity and produce images which are less noisy. Noise produces grainy images.
CCD sensors have a greater resolution than CMOS sensors because their packing density is higher.

Key fact

Colour laser printer:
A colour laser printer uses four toners, Cyan, Magenta, Yellow, and Black.
Colour laser printers use the CMYK colour model, Cyan, Magenta, Yellow, and Key (Black), This is a subtractive colour model,

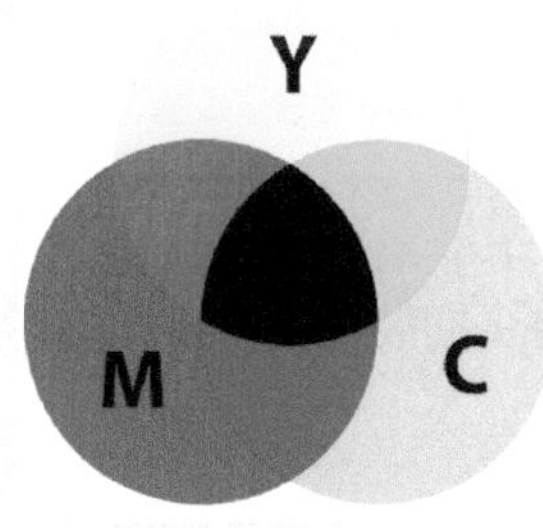

CMY "primaries" are combined at full strength, the resulting "secondary" mixtures are red, green, and blue. Mixing all three gives black. However, for a darker black the Key (Black) toner is used.

Key fact

Colour laser printer:
In a color laser printer, each of the four CMYK toner layers is stored as a separate bitmap.

Questions

5. Explain the operation of a digital camera capable of taking colour pictures.

6. State **one** situation where a digital camera with a CCD sensor would be used and **one** situation where a CMOS sensor would be used. Explain your choice in each case.

Laser printer

A laser printer prints a whole page at a time. It prints high-quality text and graphics on plain paper.

A page description language usually describes the page to be printed as lines, arcs and polygons. A processor in a monochrome laser printer generates a bitmap of the page in raster memory from the page description. A negative charge is applied to the photosensitive drum at the heart of the laser printer. One or more laser beams are directed onto the rotating drum's surface (*Figure 7.4.1.5*). The lasers are turned on or off at positions determined by the bitmap data stored in the raster memory. This causes the negative charge to be neutralised or reversed at positions corresponding to the black parts of the page to be printed.

Key fact

Monochrome laser printer:
A monochrome laser printer uses a single toner containing a black powder. It is only able to print text in black.
They are poor at printing greyscale images which has to be done by printing small dots and varying the spacing and arrangement of those dots. This is called dithering or halftoning.

The resulting pattern of charges on the drum's surface is an image of the page to be printed. The charged surface of the drum is exposed to toner, fine particles of dry plastic powder mixed with carbon black or colouring agents. The charged toner particles are given a negative charge so they attach to the uncharged or positively charged regions of the drum and not to the negatively charged regions. Darker areas are achieved by depositing thicker layers of toner. A higher voltage applied to the gap between toner cartridge and drum surface forces more toner onto the drum. The raster memory stores the greyscale data for each area of the page and this is used to set the appropriate voltage level.

Figure 7.4.1.5 Schematic of the operation of a laser printer
Reproduced with permission from Computer Desktop Encyclopedia, www.computerlanguage.com

By rolling and pressing the rotating drum over a sheet of paper, the toner is transferred onto the paper. Transfer may be assisted by using a positively charged transfer roller on the back of the paper to pull the toner from the surface of the drum to the paper. The paper is passed through heated rollers that squeeze the paper and fuse the toner to the paper.

Questions

7 Why is a laser printer described as a page printer?

8 Explain the operation of a monochrome laser printer.

9 What toners are used by a colour laser printer and why?

Key concept

Radio frequency identification (RFID):
Any method of identifying and tracking items using radio waves. Typically a reader (also called an interrogator) communicates with a transponder, which holds digital information in a microchip. Alternatively, a chipless RFID tag is used which just uses material to reflect back a portion of the radio waves beamed at them.

RFID

Radio frequency identification (RFID) uses radio frequencies (RF) to transmit data, a timing signal and radio frequency energy if necessary between a reader (*Figure 7.4.1.6(b)*) and an RFID device (transponder) as shown in *Figure 7.4.1.6(a)*.

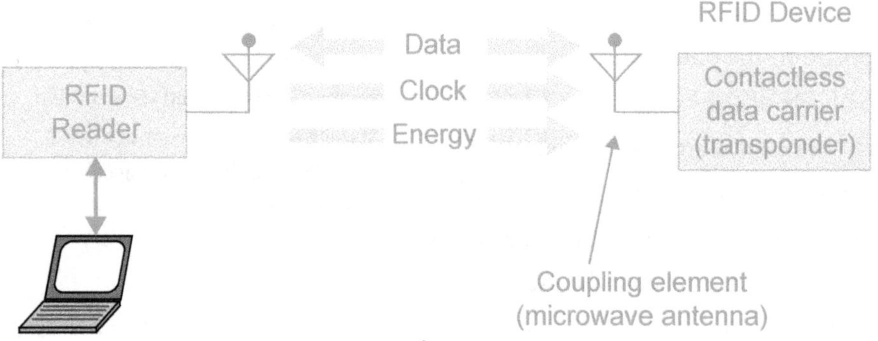

Figure 7.4.1.6(a) RFID reader and transponder

Information

RFID tag:
A microchip attached to an antenna which is packaged in a way that allows it to be applied to an object such as an item of clothing for sale. The tag picks up signals from and sends signals to a reader.
Tags come in many forms such as smart labels which have a barcode printed on them and tags simply embedded in plastic ready for attaching to an object.

Smart labels are manufactured to be fed through an RFID printer that both prints a bar code on the label and writes to its RFID microchip.

RFID devices do not need a physical electrical contact to transfer data. Nor do they need **visible** contact as they use radio waves to transfer data. This makes it possible to read many codes simultaneously from afar without the need to open boxes.

An RFID system has a transponder and a reader. The RFID transponder is located on the object to be identified. The reader, or interrogator, may be able to read data or to read and write data, but it is always called a reader.

The RFID transponder can be powered by RF energy from the reader if the transponder is a passive RFID device or it may use an internal battery if it is an active or semi-passive device.

The transponder has a small RF antenna and circuitry for transmitting and receiving data.

Figure 7.4.1.6(b) RFID reader

Active RFID tags can continuously broadcast their own signal which is useful when they are used to track the real-time location of an object but they are

Figure 7.4.1.7(a) RFID price smart tag

bulkier than passive RFID tags. Active tags provide a much longer read range than passive tags, but they are also much more expensive.

Passive RFID tags have applications including access control, smart labels, race timing, and more.

Passive RFID are much cheaper to make than active RFID tags as well as being much less bulky.

The data capacity of RFID transponders is normally a few bytes to several thousand bytes, but a transponder with a data capacity of just 1 bit can distinguish between transponder present and transponder not present.

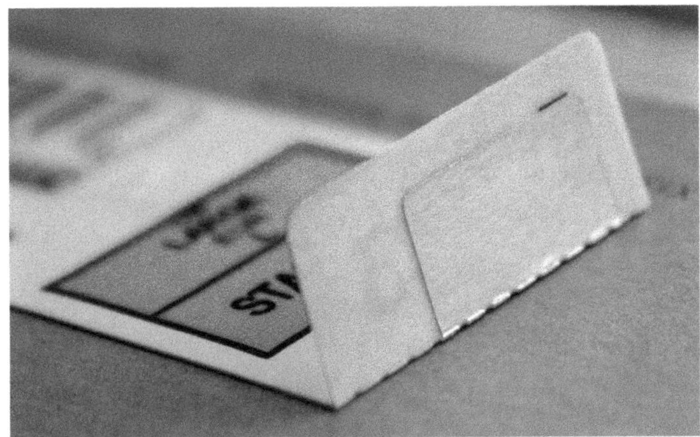

Figure 7.4.1.7(b) RFID price smart tag located on underside of price tag

Most 1-bit transponders are used in electronic article surveillance (EAS) systems to protect goods in shops and businesses. They are removed or deactivated at the till when the goods are paid for. A reader installed at the shop's exit raises an alarm if goods are removed before the transponder has been deactivated.

RFID smart cards, such as Transport for London's Oyster card, are used as tickets for journeys on public transport.

RFID devices are attached to products to respond with a unique code when interrogated. This means each item can be recognized individually instead of just recognising it as belonging to a particular product type. A part of the unique code could be used to identify the product type, e.g. 12345-1, 12345-2 where 12345 is product code for blue t-shirt, size small.

Key fact

RFID tag characteristics:
RFID tags can include a unique code, which makes every RFID label individual, meaning that each item can be recognized individually instead of just recognizing it as belonging to a particular product type.
RFID devices do not need a physical electrical contact to transfer data. Nor do they need **visible** contact as they use radio waves to transfer data. This makes it possible to read many codes simultaneously from afar without the need to open boxes.

Marks and Spencer uses such tags in its stores and warehouses for stock control purposes. For privacy reasons, this RFID tag is not read at the sales counter. If it were then the customer could be tracked when they leave the store by linking their identity, captured at the sales counter, to the unique serial number in the RFID tag attached to the purchased item.

However, the time staff spend stock checking is greatly reduced because RFID tags on store items can be read quickly with a handheld reader from a distance, using a barcode scanner would take considerably longer.

Figure 7.4.1.7(a) shows an item of clothing's price tag with an RFID transponder (Figure 7.4.1.7(b)) on its underside. The RFID transponder responds with the item's unique code or serial number when read by an RFID reader from as far away as 70cm.

They can be used as contactless security badges to give access to protected premises. Electronic immobilisers for cars use RFID; the ignition key is combined with a transponder. An RFID device placed under an animal's skin can be used for tracking and identification (one use is a cat flap which can be opened by cats with a recognised RFID tag, but not by other cats to stop these entering the house). RFID devices are put in the stomach of cattle and remain there for life.

Barcode scanning versus RFID scanning

RFID scanning allows many RFID tags to be read at a time even when the tags are hidden inside boxes or behind panels. Barcode scanning scans one item at a time and the barcode needs to be visible to the scanner.

When stocktaking it is important to avoid counting an item more than once. RFID tagging and scanning enables each item to be uniquely tagged and therefore uniquely identified when scanned. When combined with a timestamp it is very easy to avoid counting an item more than once in a stocktaking session. Barcodes do not usually identify an item uniquely but instead encode the product type of an item. Timestamping would be of little help in preventing an item being counted twice because items are not uniquely identified.

Questions

10 What is Radio Frequency Identification (RFID)?

11 What is an RFID tag?

12 Give **three** uses of RFID tags.

13 Give **two** advantages of RFID scanning over barcode scanning.

In this chapter you have covered:

- The main characteristics, purposes and suitability of the following devices and understand their principles of operation
  - barcode reader
  - digital camera
  - laser printer
  - RFID

7.4 External hardware devices

Learning objectives:

- *Explain the need for secondary storage within a computer system*
- *Know the main characteristics, purposes, suitability and understand the principles of operation of the following devices:*
  - *hard disk*
  - *optical disk*
  - *solid-state disk (SSD)*
- *Compare the capacity and speed of access of various media and make judgement about their suitability for different applications*

Did you know?

IBM obtained the technology for making magnetic disks from Manchester University where a one kilobyte magnetic disk had been made on a one metre-wide platter.

7.4.2 Secondary storage devices

Why do we need secondary storage?

The technology that primary storage (RAM) is built from and which supports read and write random access to individual words requires a continuous supply of electrical energy in order to work. Unfortunately, when the supply of electrical energy is removed the information stored in the memory words is lost. We say that read/write main memory is volatile (analogous to liquids which disappear by the process of evaporation). To retain information and programs after electrical power is removed requires a different form of storage, one which is non-volatile. There are three technologies with which such storage is built currently:

1. Magnetic
2. Optical
3. Solid-state

If we want to retain a program we have created in RAM, or some information we have written to RAM, then we must transfer both to a non-volatile secondary store. The commonest form of read/write secondary store is a magnetic hard disk encased in a magnetic hard disk drive (HDD) - Figure 7.4.2.1. A newer form of read/write secondary store that is now shipping in desktop PCs, laptops and tablets is a solid-state disk (SSD). Compact Disc (CD) and Digital Versatile Disc (DVD) storage are optical media that can be used for secondary storage. There are read only (CD-R, DVD-R), write once read many times (CD-R, DVD-R) and read/write versions (CD-RW, DVD-RW) of these.

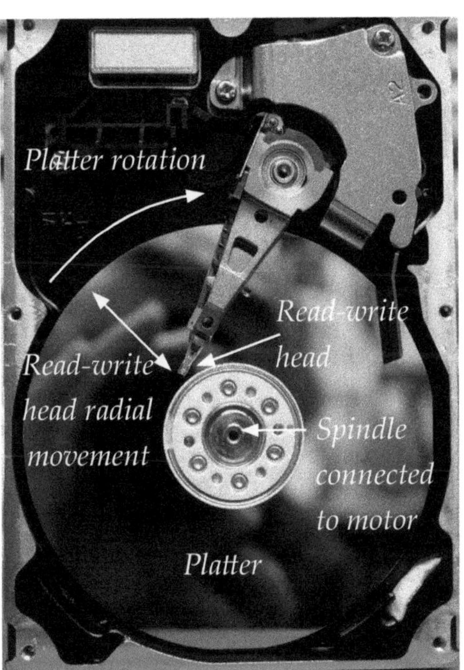

Figure 7.4.2.1 Hard disk drive with cover removed

Questions

1. Why is secondary storage needed?

Magnetic hard disk

IBM developed magnetic disk drives in the late 1950s. The disk drive allows rapid random (direct) access to large amounts of data. All disk drives use a thin circular platter made of non-ferrous metal or plastic which is rotated at up to 10,000 revolutions per minute beneath a read-write head that moves radially across the surface of the platter. Figure 7.4.2.1 shows a 20 GB hard disk drive with the cover removed. The platter and read-write head can be clearly seen as well as the photographer's reflection in the platter.

Key concept

Track:
One of the concentric rings on a platter of a hard disk.
Sector:
A subdivision of a track.
Disk block:
The smallest unit of transfer between a computer and a disk. A disk block is one sector of a track.

Did you know?

In 2015, the fastest rotation speeds of consumer disk drives was 10000 revolutions per minute.

Key point

Disk buffer:
Executing programs do not write directly to magnetic hard disks. Instead, they write to an area of main memory (RAM) called a disk buffer. Before a program can write to a file, it has first to open the file, if it exists, or create the file if it doesn't. This open/create action creates a disk buffer in main memory (RAM) which is then associated with the file. The program writes to this buffer. When the buffer becomes full or the program closes the corresponding file, the operating system writes the buffer to disk. The size of the buffer matches the size of a disk block or a multiple of this.
To read a file it must first be opened. This creates a disk buffer which receives a block at a time belonging to the file. The program that opened the file then reads from this buffer. When the buffer becomes empty, the operating system transfers the next disk block belonging to the file into this buffer.

The platter is coated with an emulsion of iron or cobalt oxide (or a cobalt-based alloy) particles that act as tiny magnets. Binary data is recorded by aligning these tiny magnets in one direction to represent a binary 0 and in the opposite direction to represent a binary 1. Binary data is recorded in concentric rings, or tracks, subdivided into sectors that hold a fixed number of bytes, such as 512. A hard disk can store and retrieve a large volume of data.

To read data stored on the hard disk, the read-write head moves to the desired track and waits for the relevant sector to pass beneath it. When data is transferred from the hard disk to the computer and vice versa, a whole sector of a track is read or written each time. A whole sector of a track is often called a **disk block** or a block. For this reason, a magnetic hard disk drive is known as a block-oriented storage device. The smallest unit of transfer is a block which is typically 512 bytes.

The top and bottom surfaces of a platter may be used to store data. A block address for a single-platter system is composed of a **surface address**, a **track address** and a **sector address**. Typically, the surfaces are numbered 0 and 1, the tracks 0 to 7,000 and the sectors 0 to 63. *Figure 7.4.2.2* shows a schematic for one surface of a magnetic hard disk.

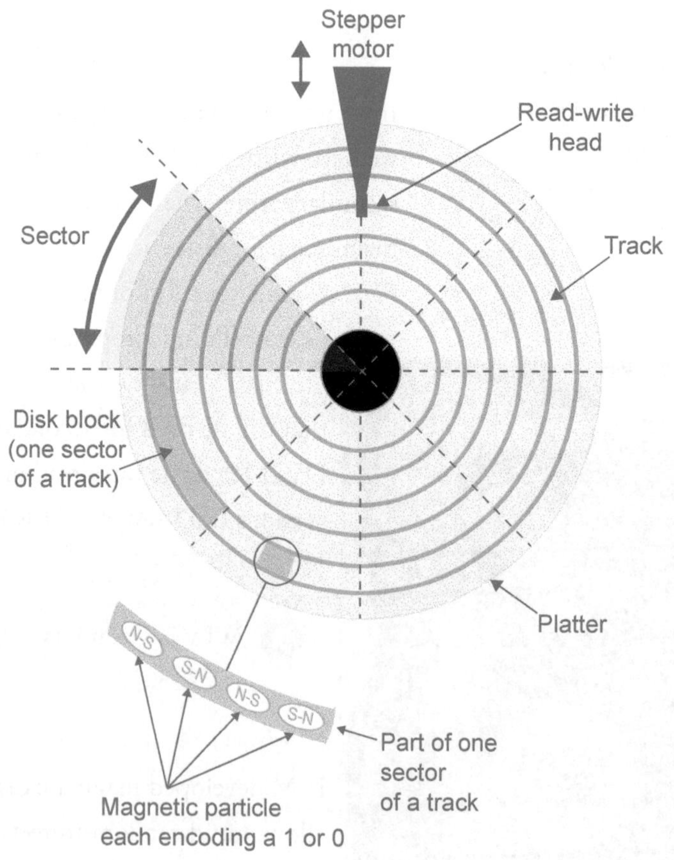

Figure 7.4.2.2 Hard disk platter showing concentric tracks and sectors

Modern hard disks for a PC system are sealed units, called Winchester disks, containing several platters mounted on a common spindle. The platters are sealed inside an assembly which allows the disk to operate with minimal risk of damage from contaminants. The read-write heads are built into the assembly with one head per surface. The greater the number of platters, the greater the storage capacity.

Questions

2. Why is a magnetic disk drive known as a block-oriented storage device?
3. In the context of a magnetic disk, what is (a) a track, (b) a sector, (c) a disk block and (d) disk block address?
4. Explain the principle of operation of a magnetic disk drive.
5. What effect do you think that having smaller platters and faster rotation speeds will have on the time taken to read a disk block?

Key concept

Access time:
Access time for a magnetic hard disk is the time interval between the moment the command is given to transfer data from disk to main memory and the moment this transfer is completed.
It is made up of three components:

1. seek time
2. rotational delay
3. data transfer time

Seek time:
The time it takes for the read/write heads to align on the desired track.

Rotational delay:
The time taken for the desired sector to come under the read/write head. On average, this is the time taken for half a revolution of the disk platters. This average is called the latency of the disk.

Data transfer time:
The total time taken to read the disk block and transfer it into main memory

Optical disc

An optical disc is a flat, usually circular disc which encodes binary data (bits) in a special reflective layer. In one form of optical disc, binary data is encoded in the form of pits (binary value of 0 due to lack of reflection when read) and lands (binary value of 1 due to a reflection when read) on a reflective material, usually metallic, on one of its flat surfaces as shown in *Figure 7.4.2.3*.

CD-ROM

The success of compact discs (CDs) for storing audio led to a new format, CD Read-Only Memory (CD-ROM). Introduced early in 1985, this format was initially used to publish encyclopedias, reference works, professional directories and other large databases. CD-ROMs were ideal for this because they had (for the time) a high storage capacity of 600–700 million bytes, offered fast data access and were portable, rugged and read-only. Today, CD-ROMs are also used for software distribution.

The data is written on the discs using disc-mastering machinery that impresses pits (physical depressions) into a continuous spiral track. The silvery data surface contains pits in a single track 3.5 miles (5.6 km) long. The disc spins at 200-500 revolutions per minute depending on which part of the track is being read.

A data bit is read by focusing a laser beam onto a point in the reflective metal layer where the pits are impressed (*Figure 7.4.2.3*).

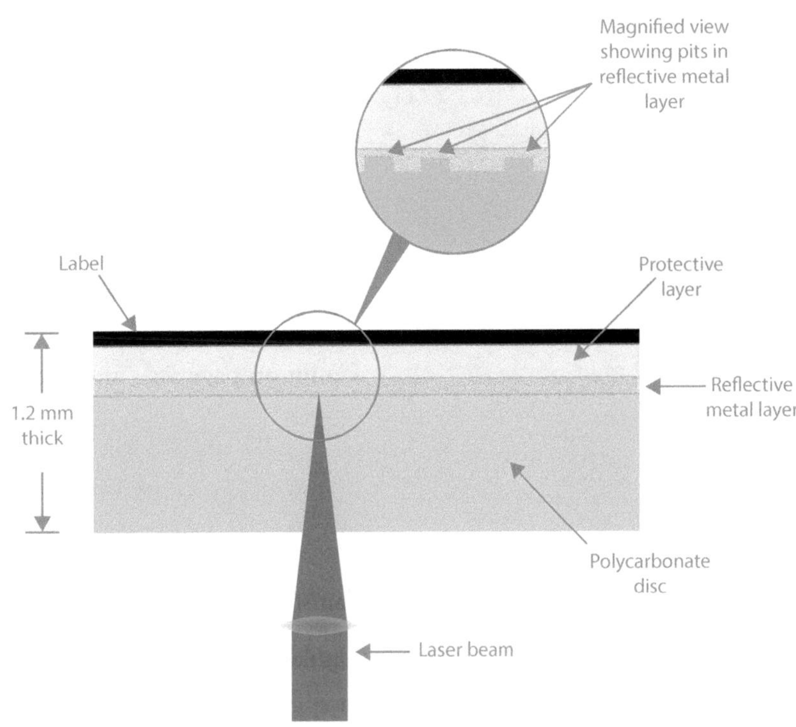

Figure 7.4.2.3 CD-ROM cross-section through its layers

Key fact

Optical disc:

An optical disc is a flat, usually circular disc which encodes binary data (bits) in a special reflective layer. In one form of optical disc, binary data is encoded in the form of pits (binary value of 0 due to lack of reflection when read) and lands (binary value of 1 due to a reflection when read) on a reflective material, usually metallic, on one of its flat surfaces.

Did you know?

CD-R:

Write Once, Read Many (WORM) times optical disc.

CD-R can record about 650 - 900 MiB of data

CD-RW:

CD-ReWritable disc that can be read and written to over and over again.

DVD-ROM:

Digital versatile disc or digital video disc (DVD) is an optical standard offering much greater storage capacity than CDs. Storage capacity of a single-layer DVD-ROM is 4.3 GiB (4.7 GB).

DVD-R:

DVD-R is a WORM format similar to CD-R.

DVD-RW:

The DVD-RW format provides a rewritable optical disc with a typical capacity of 4.3 GiB (4.7 GB).

DVD+RW:

A competing rewritable format to DVR-RW.

DVD-RAM:

DVD-RAM is a rewritable format that has built-in error control and a defect management system, so it is considered to be better than the other DVD technologies for tasks such as data storage, backup and archiving.

Blu-ray disc:

A Blu-ray disc (BD) is a high-density optical disc capable of storing 23.3 GiB (25 GB) in a single-layer which is considerably more than a DVD can store.

More laser light is reflected from the unpitted surface than from the pitted surface. This is detected by a photodiode that outputs an equivalent electrical signal. After some conditioning, the result is a digital signal representing a single data bit. This data bit encodes the amount of reflection as 0 or 1.

Did you know?

Blue-ray disc:

A Blu-ray disc (BD) is a high-density optical disc capable of storing 23.3 GiB (25 GB) in a single-layer which is considerably more than a DVD can store.

Questions

6. What is an optical disc?
7. Explain how information is recorded and then read from a CD-ROM.

Solid-state disk (SSD)

The solid-state disk (SSD) in a solid-state disk drive (*Figure 7.4.2.4*) operates by trapping electrons in a wafer of semiconducting material. These electrons and their electric charge remain trapped even when electric power is removed, i.e. SSD is non-volatile storage. Binary 0 is represented by trapped electrons and binary 1 by absence of trapped electrons.

The sites (floating gate transistors) where these electrons are trapped are organized in a grid. The entire grid layout is referred to as a **block**, while the individual **rows** that make up the grid are called a **page**.

Figure 7.4.2.4 Solid-state disk drive
©D-Kuru/Wikimedia Commons

Common page sizes are 2KiB, 4KiB, 8KiB, or 16KiB, with 128 to 256 pages per block. Block sizes are typically between 256KiB and 4MiB. For example, the Samsung™ SSD 840 EVO has blocks of size 2MiB, and each block contains 256 pages of 8 KiB each. The Samsung SSD 840 EVO comprises 8 NAND flash chips, each of capacity 64 GiB. Each Samsung flash chip contains 32 blocks.

Unlike magnetic disk drives, solid-state drives contain no moving parts or spinning disks. The absence of moving parts means that solid state disk drives can operate at speeds far above those of a typical hard disk drive.

Access time for a typical hard drive is on average 10-15 milliseconds whereas access time for an SSD drive is 25-100 microseconds (access time for RAM is typically 40 -100 nanoseconds).

The technology used is NAND flash memory which is a type of EEPROM (Electrically Erasable Programmable Read Only Memory). A solid-state disk is a block-oriented storage device which has to erase a block first in order to rewrite it because unlike magnetic hard disk drives, NAND flash memory can't overwrite existing data. Erasing a block in the SDD means "untrapping" electrons.

The solid-state disk drive requires an onboard controller which consists of an embedded microprocessor with RAM buffer to perform reading and writing to the solid state disk (Figure 7.4.2.5). The controller is a very important factor in determining the speed of the SSD drive.

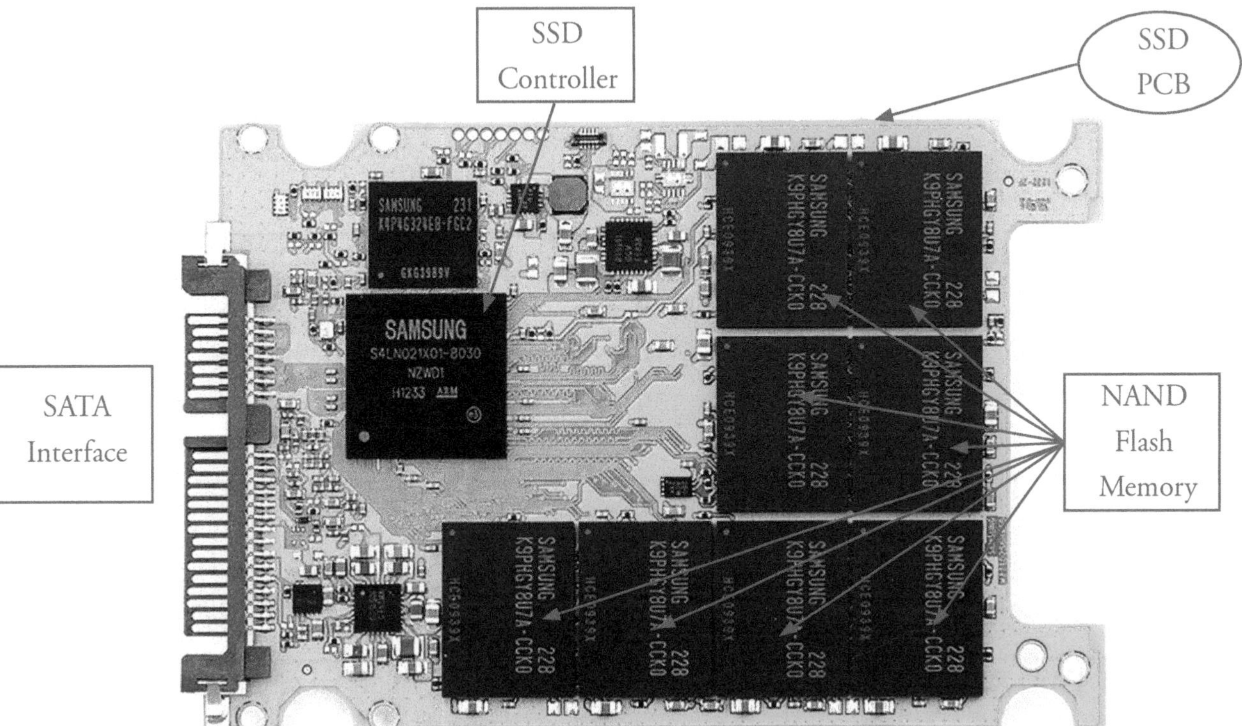

Figure 7.4.2.5 SSD drive printed circuit board (PCB) showing the controller and the NAND flash memory chips (image reproduced with kind permission of StorageReview.com).

To alter the contents of a particular memory location of SSD storage, an entire block must be constructed containing the new information and written to SSD. The controller arranges for this new block to be written to a different area of SSD. The reason for this is that SSD blocks can be programmed for only a limited amount of time before they become unreliable. This is known as write-endurance. It is measured in number of program erase (P/E) cycles. To lessen this effect, a controller uses a technique called wear-levelling, which effectively makes sure that all the drive's memory chips are used, cell by cell, before the first cell is written on again.

Information

SSD vs other flash-based devices:

SSDs are much faster than any of the other flash-based portable drives, e.g. USB memory stick.

SSD secondary storage is increasingly being used in laptops, tablets and is an option now for desktop PCs. The attraction is lower power consumption and faster booting of the operating system.

Questions

8. Explain the operation of a solid-state disk drive.

9. Give **four** reasons why a solid-state disk drive might be preferred to a magnetic disk drive.

Capacity and speed of access

Hard disk drive manufacturers specify disk capacity using the SI prefixes mega (10^6), giga (10^9), and tera (10^{12}), abbreviated to M, G and T, respectively. Byte is abbreviated to B. CD and DVD capacities are quoted in a similar fashion.

In the case of both magnetic hard disks and solid-state disks speed of access is determined by whether access is random or sequential. Sequential operations access locations on the storage device in a contiguous manner and are generally associated with large data transfer sizes, e.g., 128 KiB. Random operations access locations on the storage device in a non-contiguous manner and are generally associated with small data transfer sizes, e.g. 4 KiB. *Table 7.4.2.1* quotes read and write speeds for random operations for these devices using a unit, IOPS (Input/output Operations Per Second). For a magnetic hard disk drive (HDD), the random IOPS is primarily dependent upon the HDD's random seek time. For a solid-state disk drive, the random IOPS is primarily dependent upon its internal controller and memory interface speed.

Information

IOPS (Input/Output Operations Per Second): This is the unit for random access. Random access is the ability to access (read/write) data at an arbitrary location, in a non-contiguous manner. It is a unit used for storage devices such as hard disk and solid-state disks.

Storage medium	Capacity	Read speed	Write speed
Magnetic hard disk	20 GB to 10 TB (SI units: powers of 10, G = 10^9, T = 10^{12})	Random I/O operations: 75 -200 IOPS	Random I/O operations: 75 - 200 IOPS
CD-ROM, CD-R, CD-RW	650 - 900 MiB	CD-ROM 150 KiB/s (1x) to 6,750–10,800 KiB/s (72x)	CD-R 1.76 MiB/s (12x) CD-RW 1.46 MiB/s (10x)
DVD-ROM, DVD-R, DVD±RW, DVD-RAM	single layer: 4.3 GiB dual layer: 8.5 GiB	1,353 KiB/s (1x) to 21,648 KiB/s (16x)	1,353 KiB/s (1x) to 21,648 KiB/s (16x)
Blu-ray Disc (BD-ROM) Blu-ray Disc Recordable (BD-R) Blu-ray Disc Recordable (BD-RE)	single layer: 23.3 GiB dual layer: 46.6 GiB XL x3 layer: 93.2 GiB XL x4 layer: 119.2 GiB	4.3 MiB/s (1x) to 68.66 MiB/s (16x)	BD-R / BD-RE 50 MiB/s (12x)
Solid-state disk	128 MB to 4 GB	Random I/O operations: 150,000 IOPS	Random I/O operations: 80,000 IOPS

Table 7.4.2.1 Capacities and speed of access for various storage media

Information

CD drives:

1x means 150 KiB/s

DVD drives:

1x means 1,353 KiB/s

Storage medium	Applications
Magnetic hard disk	Online storage of programs and data files
CD-ROM	Distributing software
CD-R	Distributing software, storing photographs, backing up data, archiving data
CD-RW	Backing up data, transferring files
DVD-ROM	Distributing software or videos
DVD-R	Distributing software or videos, storing photographs, backing up data, archiving data
DVD±RW	Backing up data, transferring files
DVD-RAM	Backing up data
Blu-ray	Distributing high definition videos and video games
Solid-state disk	Online storage of programs and data files

Table 7.4.2.2 Storage media and typical applications to which they can be put

Did you know?

Backing up data means taking a copy of data and storing it somewhere safe, e.g. in a fireproof safe or off-site. Archiving data means removing it from the online storage medium, usually to free up space. Data qualifies for archiving if it has not been accessed recently and will not be accessed regularly in the future. Programs and data may be backed up and archived.

Questions

10 State what applications each of the following might be used for:
(a) magnetic hard disk drive (b) CD-ROM (c) DVD-R
(d) DVD-RAM (e) blu-ray disc.

11 What storage medium would be most suitable for distributing a 5 GiB file in each of the following cases:
(a) a single individual requiring read-only access
(b) a single individual who will need write access
(c) a large number of people requiring read-only access?

In this chapter you have covered:

- the need for secondary storage within a computer system
- the main characteristics, purposes, suitability and the principles of operation of the following devices:
  - hard disk
  - optical disk
  - solid-state disk (SSD)
- the capacity and speed of access of various media and their suitability for different applications

8 Consequences of uses of computing

8.1 Individual (moral), social (ethical), legal and cultural issues and opportunities

Learning objectives:

- *Show awareness of current individual (moral), social(ethical), legal and cultural issues and opportunities and risks of computing*
- *Understand that:*
  - *developments in computer science and the digital technologies have dramatically altered the shape of communications and information flows in societies, enabling massive transformations in the capacities to*
    - *monitor behaviour*
    - *amass and analyse personal information*
    - *distribute, publish, communicate and disseminate personal information*
  - *computer scientists and software engineers therefore have power, as well as the responsibilities that go with it, in the algorithms that they devise and the code that they deploy*
  - *software and their algorithms embed moral and cultural values*

8.1 Introduction

When we talk about the morality of human actions we are referring to whether the actions are right or wrong. **A moral action is one that is right. An immoral action is one that is wrong.** Morality is primarily about making correct choices between right and wrong or between good behaviour and bad behaviour.

When an individual reaches a conclusion or decision as to the morally right course of action they often draw on a framework or set of principles to help their reasoning, e.g. our actions should do no harm. The **framework or set of principles** is called an **ethical theory** or just, **ethics**. When applied to particular cases, the framework can provide clear choices. This can be helpful because often there isn't one right answer for a situation that requires a person to act morally - there may be several right answers, or just some least worst answers - and the individual must take responsibility and choose between them.

When a person 'thinks ethically' they are giving some thought to human action that has moral consequences for someone beyond themselves and their own desires and self-interest. When new possibilities for human action arise as is the case with computer technology, human beings face new ethical questions, i.e. questions requiring new ethics with which to reason.

Case study

The case of the Crown versus Dudley and Stephens in 1884 established a precedent, throughout the common law world, that necessity is not a defence to a charge of murder. The sailing ship Mignonette foundered in a storm on July 5th 1884 whilst on route to Southampton from Sydney. The crew of four, Tom Dudley, the captain, Edwin Stephens, Edmund Brooks and Richard Parker, aged 17, the cabin boy, took to a lifeboat. On the nineteenth day of their ordeal, Dudley suggested drawing lots to determine who would die so that the others might live. Brooks refused and so no lots were drawn. By this time, Parker, who had drunk sea water, appeared to be dying. On the next day and still with no ship in sight that could rescue them, Dudley took out a penknife and whilst saying a prayer over him, stabbed Parker in the jugular vein. For four days, the three men fed on the body and blood of Parker.

...continued on next page

Learning objectives:

- *Understand that:*
  - *the issue of scale, for software the whole world over, creates potential for individual computer scientists and software engineers to produce great good, but with it comes the ability to cause great harm*
- *Be able to discuss the challenges facing legislators in the digital age*

Case study continued

After their rescue on July 29th and arrest after returning to England Dudley and Stephens went to trial and Brooks turned state's witness. Defending killing Parker before his natural death they argued that his blood would be better preserved for them to drink. They freely confessed to killing and consuming Parker but claimed they had done so out of necessity. Parker was an orphan without dependents whilst Dudley and Stephens had families that depended upon them.

At the time maritime law was not clear cut on such cases and in such circumstances the custom of the sea applied as practised by the officers and crew of ships and boats in the open sea.

Questions for discussion

1. Suppose you were the judge at their trial. Putting aside the question of maritime law and assuming that you were making a moral judgement, how would you rule and what argument would you use to justify your ruling?

   (The actual ruling is available from https://en.wikipedia.org/wiki/R_v_Dudley_and_Stephens)

The case of the Crown versus Dudley and Stephens in 1884 was important for two reasons. Firstly, it established a precedent, throughout the common law world, that necessity is not a defence to a charge of murder. Secondly and more importantly, it highlighted that morality is more than a matter of cost-benefit analysis and calculating consequences but has more to do with the proper way for human beings to treat one another. Morality implies certain moral duties and human rights so fundamental that they rise above a matter of simply calculating consequences.

Questions for discussion

2. Suppose you were asked to draw up a list of fundamental moral duties and human rights. What would be on your list? You could use a search engine to research the general consensus on these but try yourself or discuss the question with others first. Bear in mind that your generation, the digital native one, may disagree with what you find on the World Wide Web which could reflect what has been framed by an older generation labelled digital immigrants.

The Global Information Society and a new Digital Ethics

Society is shaped by the technology at its disposal:

"The handmill gives you society with the feudal lord; the steam-mill the society with the industrial capitalist." Karl Marx

The information society that we live in today has been shaped by the information and communication technologies of the global networking of the digital computer.

"The digital computer and networking give you the Global Information Society"

Whilst previous societies have evolved relatively slowly, the Global Information Society has burst into existence in a relatively short period of time by comparison. Berkeley's School of Information Management and Systems estimated that humanity had accumulated approximately 12 exabytes of data in the course of its entire history before the advent of the desktop digital computer. Since then there has been an explosion in data. For example, in just one year, 2002, more than 5 exabytes of data were produced and recorded. According to IDC, in 2013 the digital universe contained some 4.4 zettabytes, a thousand-fold increase on 2002, roughly. Whilst bringing enormous benefits and opportunities, the information revolution's enormous growth rate has posed a conceptual, ethical and cultural challenge of how to put in place a viable philosophy and ethics of information.

The European Data Protection Supervisor (EDPS), an independent institution of the EU, published a report in 2015 entitled

"Towards a New Digital Ethics"

(https://secure.edps.europa.eu/EDPSWEB/webdav/site/mySite/shared/Documents/Consultation/Opinions/2015/15-09-11_Data_Ethics_EN.pdf)

At its core is the protection of human dignity:

"An ethical framework needs to underpin the building blocks of this digital ecosystem. The EDPS considers that better respect for, and the safeguarding of, human dignity could be the counterweight to the pervasive surveillance and asymmetry of power which now confronts the individual. It should be at the heart of a new digital ethics."

Asymmetry of power and pervasive surveillance

Asymmetry of power

Coded algorithms automate operations or actions according to a logic that differs little from that which humans have applied for centuries. Replacing the human brain by a digital computer enables more consistency, greater speed of calculation and more control. However, it adds an additional dimension that is not possible with a human agent: computers do not only carry out actions using information in the form of programmed instructions but they can also produce information that coded algorithms can capture and report.

Key principles

Protection of personal data:
EU Charter of Fundamental Rights Article 1 defines the right of an individual to protection of their personal data via data protection principles the following principles -necessity, proportionality, fairness, data minimisation, purpose limitation, consent and transparency.
These apply to data processing in its entirety, to collection as well as to use.

Key concept

Personal data:
Data about any living person.

Task

Data Protection Act

1. Look at the eight principles of the Data Protection Act 1998 at https://ico.org.uk/for-organisations/guide-to-data-protection/ and see if you can match these to the EU Charter principles.
2. Look at Regulation (EU) 2016/679 which applies to all 28 EU countries from 25 May 2018 and Directive (EU) 2016/680 which requires member states to enact legislation by 6 May 2018.

Key concept

Asymmetry of power:
Computers do not only carry out actions using information in the form of programmed instructions but they can also produce information that coded algorithms can capture and report. However, whilst you have some control over the former in that you have initiated the action, e.g. a search, you seemingly have much less control over the latter.

Key concept

Machine learning:
Machine learning is the science of getting computers to act without being explicitly programmed. This approach enables patterns in and links between data to be discovered autonomously once the machine has been "trained" on a large enough dataset. Examples are speech recognition and language translation software, and self-driving cars.

Key concept

Information:
Data is how information is represented.

Key concept

Knowledge:
Knowledge is usable information.

Key concept

Pervasive surveillance:
Capturing of small data from individuals' online actions and utterances as they go about their daily lives. These data flows have been labelled 'data exhaust'.

"Information Technology alone has this capacity to both automate and reflect information (informate)" - Professor Shoshana Zuboff. However, whilst you have some control over the former in that you have initiated the action, e.g. a search, you seemingly have much less control over the latter (e.g. collecting, storing and associating with you information about what you are searching for) and certainly many people do not perceive that the latter is happening behind the scenes. This is what is meant by asymmetry of power.

Visiting a particular website results in your visit being logged, tracked with cookies and then combined with information already held about you to send you personalised advertisements. You can see what is happening behind the scenes using packet capture software such as Wireshark. For example, visiting the New York Times' website results in the communication of information to the following other sites (as of October 2015):

https://www.doubleclickbygoogle.com/

http://www.conversantmedia.com/

http://www.facebook.com

Pervasive surveillance

The logic in automation is the logic of action, i.e. do this followed by do that, whereas the logic of information reflection is the logic of accumulation.
The latter has given rise to huge datasets labelled Big Data (see *Chapter 11.1*) and the impetus to analyse large datasets using machine learning techniques. Contributing to this Big Data phenomena in a major way is the capturing of small data from individuals' online actions and utterances as they go about their daily lives. Nothing is too trivial or unimportant for this data harvesting, from Facebook 'likes' and clicks on links, to smartphone location data.
Such data (representation of information) is aggregated, analysed, packaged and sold.
These data flows have been labelled 'data exhaust' because they are the byproduct of users' actions as they go about their daily business interacting with computer systems. Google and Facebook are among the largest and most successful Big Data companies because they sweep up this data exhaust. In 2015, Google's search engine was the most visited engine and Facebook the most visited social media site.
Although Google started out with no intention of offering advertisers space on their search results' Web pages, they eventually gave in to the need to generate revenue via an advertising model rather than a fees-for-service one because the latter might have impacted on the expansion of their user base. This advertising approach depended upon the acquisition of personal data as the raw material that after analysis and application of machine learning would sell and target advertising through a unique auction model reliant upon the accumulation of huge quantities of personal data to make it work with increasing precision and success.

Google's business is thus the auction business and its customers are advertisers. AdWords, Google's algorithmic auction method for selling online advertising, analyses massive amounts of data to determine which advertisers get which one of eleven sponsored links on each search results page (http://archive.wired.com/culture/culturereviews/magazine/17-06/nep_googlenomics?currentPage=all).

Information

What They Know, is an in-depth investigative series by the Wall Street Journal. It found that one of the fastest growing Internet business models is of data-gatherers engaged in intensive surveillance of people visiting websites in order to sell data about, and predictions of, their interests and activities, in real time.
http://juliaangwin.com/the-what-they-know-series/

Case study

In 2009 Google published a research paper in the prestigious scientific journal Nature that described a method to track influenza-like illness in a population by analyzing large numbers of Google search queries. The researchers reported that they could accurately estimate the current level of weekly influenza activity in each region of the United States, with a reporting lag of about one day.
(http://static.googleusercontent.com/media/research.google.com/en//archive/papers/detecting-influenza-epidemics.pdf)
"This seems like a really clever way of using data that is created unintentionally by the users of Google to see patterns in the world that would otherwise be invisible," said Thomas W. Malone, a professor at the Sloan School of Management at MIT.
Shortly after its publication, H1N1, a new strain of a particularly virulent strain of flu hit the United States. In order to track and contain the outbreak before it became pandemic, the Centers for Disease Control and Prevention (CDC) requested that doctors inform them of new flu cases. Unfortunately, this reporting at best involved a two-week lag, too long to enable effective control of the outbreak.

Information

Using Big Data to track population movements in an Ebola infected country
http://www.pri.org/stories/2014-10-24/how-big-data-could-help-stop-spread-ebola

Questions for discussion

3. "What companies know about me from my behavior online cannot hurt me. In fact, it is more likely to benefit me."
4. "What information I give out about myself is a fair tradeoff for benefits that I receive."
5. "Surrendering personal data for perceived benefits is not a square deal because I cannot control all the ways that my personal data will be used."
6. "I am powerless to stop my personal data being used for purposes that I am unaware of because the services that I use for free in exchange for surrendering my data are an integral part of my life."
7. "I am just amazed at all the innovative services, e.g. Google translate, DropBox, GoogleDocs, Apps or education, YouTube, etc, that I can get for free by interacting online. It doesn't bother me that my personal data and activities online can be used by the data scientists and data mining experts to create the weird and wonderful algorithms behind all these services."
8. Google's use of user-generated data to support public health efforts in significant ways is a benefit to society and therefore outweighs the concerns raised by two privacy organisations that Google could be compelled by court order to release sensitive user-specific information - the Electronic Privacy Information Center (https://www.epic.org) and the US Patient Privacy Rights organisation (https://patientprivacyrights.org).

Case study - adapted with permission from Forbes.com

The chief data scientist, Andrew Pole, of a US retail chain, Target, successfully figured out how to answer the question, "If we wanted to know if a customer is pregnant, even if she didn't want us to know, is it possible? ", by analysing data that the company collected on customers' spending habits.

As Pole's computers crawled through the collected personal data, he was able to identify about 25 products that, when analyzed together, allowed him to assign each shopper a "pregnancy prediction" score. More importantly, he could also estimate her due date to within a small window, so Target could send coupons timed to very specific stages of her pregnancy. The sending of such coupons did result in an unexpected outcome when a Target store was visited by an angry man to complain that Target was sending his teenage daughter coupons for baby clothes and cribs even though she was certainly not pregnant and was still at high school.

The manager was bemused and could only apologise profusely and then again a few days later by phone.

On the phone, though, the father was somewhat apologetic. "I had a talk with my daughter," he said. "It turns out there's been some activities in my house I haven't been completely aware of. She's due in August. I owe you an apology."

Target changed their mailing policy to mask the fact that they knew a lot more about their customers than their customers realised. So they started mixing coupons for other things with the baby item coupons so that the pregnant woman did not think that she had been spied on.

Key principle

Linking of information:
Two pieces of information about a person might individually be harmless but less so if linked.

For example:

1. Tony Blair is a former British Prime Minister
2. Tony Blair has a home in London

Google's street view map of Tony Blair's London home is now blurred. Google are required now to offer to blur properties visible in Street View after a European court ruling in favour of people's 'right to be forgotten'.

1. Dick Cheney was US Secretary of Defense during Operation Desert Storm, the 1991 invasion of Iraq
2. Dick Cheney has been fitted with a heart pacemaker, recently.

The pacemaker was specially adapted for Dick Cheney so that it would be resistant to hacking and disruption. This must be very reassuring to the rest of the population which has to make do with pacemakers that are vulnerable to hacking.

Questions for discussion

Revisit questions 3 to 6 shown again below, to see if you would respond in the same way after reading the case study above.

3. "What companies know about me from my behaviour online cannot hurt me. In fact, it is more likely to benefit me."

4. "What information I give out about myself is a fair tradeoff for benefits that I receive."

5. "Surrendering personal data for perceived benefits is not a square deal because I cannot control all the ways that my personal data will be used."

6. "I am powerless to stop my personal data being used for purposes that I am unaware of because the services that I use for free in exchange for surrendering my data are an integral part of my life."

The issue of scale

Google is the pioneer of hyperscale, the ability at relatively low cost to scale processing quickly across thousands of commodity computers housed in data centres. Other hyperscale businesses such as Facebook, Twitter, Alibaba, Baidu, Amazon, and Yahoo also possess this ability. Smaller firms without hyperscale revenues can leverage some of these capabilities by using a cloud facility such as Amazon's Elastic Cloud facility.

Having this hyperscale ability enables many results to be extracted from individuals' personal data that would have remained unknown but for the scaling of the processing it makes possible, as well as the support for massive datasets of personal information it grants. The extracted information can be of benefit to society but it also has the potential for misuse if the processing is used for social or economic discrimination, unsolicited advertising, or reputational damage.

This hyperscale ability also provides the capacity for sharing information amongst individuals on a global scale through social media sites, tweets, online blogs, etc., from which individuals derive much benefit of a social nature. All of this has been made possible by coded algorithms devised and deployed by computer scientists and software engineers. However, the free access and facilities provided by Internet companies to enable this sharing comes at a cost which may be difficult for the individual to assess or for that matter for anyone to know how the information surrendered freely will be used in the future.

"The Web means the end of forgetting" Jeffrey Rosen

YouTube demonstrates that people's eccentric behaviour can be distributed around the world without their knowledge or control as they may not know their behaviour was captured in a video or that the video has been uploaded to YouTube. Whilst access to lots of information is made possible by the hyperscale reach provided through the Internet, it also provides access to aspects of people's lives that were formally private. Sometimes people do knowingly give away or surrender their privacy, but it is also the case that sometimes they are innocent victims because of circumstances beyond their control. It is very difficult to protect privacy in such cases.

Questions for discussion

Topic: Practical obscurity

Practical obscurity is an important factor in the preservation of privacy. If the representation of information does not permit it to be easily queried, e.g. the information is on paper in a filing cabinet, then the extraction of important knowledge (usable information) is made more difficult.

9 Why does the ability to collect and process data on a mammoth scale in the way achieved by Google and other hyperscale companies reduce practical obscurity?

Information

Hyperscale computing:
In computing, hyperscale is the ability of an architecture to scale appropriately and quickly in a cost-effective manner as increased demand is added to the system. Hyperscale computing is necessary in order to build a robust and scalable cloud, big data, map reduce, or distributed storage system and is often associated with the infrastructure required to run large distributed sites such as Facebook, Google, Microsoft Azure or Amazon AWS.

Key fact

Memories for life:
The ability to record memories, and store them indefinitely in digital form in virtually unlimited quantities has been dubbed the phenomenon of memories for life. Photographs and documents featuring you may turn up in other people's memory banks. "The Spy in the Coffee Machine" © Kieron O'Hara and Nigel Shadbolt 2008, reproduced with permission of the publishers Oneworld Publications.

Information

The Web means the end of forgetting:
New York Times article by Jeffrey Rosen
http://www.nytimes.com/2010/07/25/magazine/25privacy-t2.html?pagewanted=all&_r=0

Key concept

Cookie:

A cookie is the standard way that a website uses to track its visitors to the site. They are little pieces of data harmless in themselves that are used to inform a website that a particular visitor to the website has returned. This is generally seen as a positive thing.
A benefit is that cookies allow e-commerce sites to maintain a virtual shopping basket for the visitor between visits.
However, some cookies collect data across many websites, creating 'behavioural profiles' of people. These profiles can then be used to decide what content or adverts to show you. This use of cookies for targeting in particular is what recent changes in UK law were designed to address by requiring websites to inform and obtain consent from visitors for the use of cookies. The law's aim is to give web users more control over their online privacy.

Task

Cookie Law:

Find out about Cookie law which was adopted by all EU countries in May 2011 and required an update in the UK to the Privacy and Electronic Communications Regulations.

The challenges facing legislators in the digital age

There is a general feeling that a person's privacy has shrunk in the global information society. There are something like five hundred companies that are able to track every move you make on the Internet, mining the raw material of the Web and selling it to marketers.

"Personal data are purchased, aggregated, analyzed, packaged, and sold by data brokers who operate, in the US at least, in secrecy – outside of statutory consumer protections and without consumers' knowledge, consent, or rights of privacy and due process" (*U.S. Committee on Commerce, Science, and Transportation, 2013*).

The law often places constraints on what computer scientists and software engineers are allowed to do, but equally the nature of software, data, and information, and the degree and scale of control over software available to this group constrain what the lawyers and legislators can achieve when local laws run up against the global Internet.

"In today's digital environment, adherence to the law is not enough; we have to consider the ethical dimension of data processing."

(*Towards a New Digital Ethics*)

This is the case whether the right under scrutiny is any one of copyright, trademark, privacy, or freedom of expression. Can a law made in one country be successfully applied to the global Internet whose content, algorithms and access embed value judgments from different cultures, societies and legal systems?

Case study

Guardian article: Right to be forgotten: Swiss cheese Internet, or database of ruin?

Read this Guardian article by Julia Powles at http://www.theguardian.com/technology/2015/aug/01/right-to-be-forgotten-google-swiss-cheese-internet-database-of-ruin

Questions for discussion

10 Do you think that one country should have the authority to control what content someone in another country can access on the Internet? Justify your opinion.

11 In respect of the Internet, should the reach of the law for each of the following apply (i) globally or (ii) locally with each country deciding what law to apply

(a) copyright (b) trademark (c) privacy (d) freedom of expression

Software and their algorithms embed moral and cultural values

Any artifact that interacts with human beings and that is able to change the dynamics of social processes is not value free.

Social processes are the ways in which individuals and groups interact, adjust and re-adjust and establish relationships and patterns of behaviour.

To be value free means to be without bias or to use criteria that do not reflect prejudice or cultural attitudes.

Cultural attitudes reflect the culture of a society and are expressed through the ideas, customs, and social behaviour that are held to define the society. British culture, for example, means to act fairly and justly; respect for the right of free expression; respect for the rule of law and the democratic process; respect for a free press (free from Government control); the right to protest in an orderly manner; and much more. Other cultures place a different emphasis on free speech, etc.

Email was the first killer application built on top of the Internet. It changed a major social process dramatically, i.e. the way that we communicate, but if you were not digitally connected then you could not use it. Although this is less true today there are sectors of the world's population who are unable to communicate via email because they do not have access to the necessary resources.

Background

In Egypt on January 25th, 2011 a Facebook page was posted calling for a day of protest after an incident in which a 28 year-old man was dragged from an Internet cafe and beaten to death by Egyptian police officers. When a large number of people signed up for the protest on Facebook the Egyptian government shut down Egypt's Internet and cellular phone service. Three weeks later, on February 11th, Egyptian President Hosni Mubarak was driven from office after 30 years in power.

Background

The built-environment:
The environment that consists of buildings, roads and railways.

Case study

The architecture of a place functions as a form of regulation; it constrains the behaviour of those who interact with it, often without them even realizing it. Build a bridge so low that buses cannot pass under it then it is possible to exclude people from travelling to what lies beyond the bridge, if economic circumstances mean that buses are their only means of travel. If these circumstances are associated with lack of education and therefore employment opportunities then it becomes a form of segregation, all the more worse if the lack of education opportunities and employment are linked to ethnicity.

The architecture of a place is the way it is because of how the built-environment was designed. The design is not value free if it has been based on criteria which are subjective, i.e. not objective. If the design was objective then the object of connecting one side of the bridge to the other would have applied equally to both buses and cars.

Questions for discussion

12 Think of **two** other ways in which the design of the architecture of the built-environment constrains access to certain social groups?

13 Generally speaking, securing privacy by controlling access is an inalienable right. After all privacy is a human right. What is morally wrong then with applying design to public places in a way that affects some peoples' access but protects other peoples' right to privacy?

14 Can you imagine a situation where the designers set out with the intention of creating fair access but are prevented from doing so by circumstances beyond their control?

Background

The algorithms of the Internet allow data about people to be collected in the following ways:

- Volunteered data – created and explicitly shared by individuals, e.g. social network profiles.
- Observed data – captured by recording the actions of individuals, e.g. location data when using cell phones.
- Inferred data – data about individuals based on analysis of volunteered or observed information, e.g., credit scores.

Information

Cloud service providers:
Amazon Web Services - https://aws.amazon.com
Google Cloud - https://cloud.google.com
Microsoft Azure: https://azure.microsoft.com

From your discussions you may have concluded that the architecture of the built-environment can be said to embed moral and cultural values, i.e. it is not value free.

This is also true of the Internet, the World Wide Web and other applications built on top of the Internet such as social media because each of these has been designed. Each has a particular architecture shaped by its designers in its hardware, software, and its algorithms, none of which can be value free because design decisions are always taken which inevitably embed moral and cultural values. Thus the design and operation of the Internet, the World Wide Web and other applications that rely on the Internet must also raise questions of justice, fairness and democracy.

This matters even more because there are major differences between the built environment and the architecture of the Internet, World Wide Web and these other applications.

- The first is one of scale, the Internet's reach is global whereas that of public space is local.
- Secondly, the Internet, World Wide Web and other Internet-based applications embody not only the logic of action, i.e. automation, but also the logic of information reflection or accumulation which facilitates a form of control.
- Thirdly, the distinction between hardware and software is blurred because cloud computing effectively delivers physical hardware packaged as software i.e. a virtual machine running the operating system of your choice and virtual storage such as DropBox. Users can gain access in minutes to virtualised, scalable hardware resources (e.g., Amazon's Elastic Cloud) which obviates the need to purchase the equivalent physical hardware. As there is no physical hardware to dismantle, terminating or halting such a provision also takes only minutes.

Cloud computing also decouples the physical possession of data from their ownership. It means dealing now with the issues of ownership of virtual assets and access to those virtual assets, i.e. the right to ownership and the right to usage. For example, if your personal data is aggregated and subjected to machine learning algorithms that derive new information about you, who owns this new information and who has the right to access this information?

Case study

There are a number of large gateways into China through which Internet access for Chinese citizens is controlled. The Chinese telecom companies that control these gateways are required by the Chinese government to configure their routers to use DNS servers that screen and filter out content that the Chinese government objects to because, according to Western opinion, of a fear of losing control to forces other than the Chinese government. While the primary purpose of routers is to direct or route Internet traffic to its correct destination, they can also be configured in this way to block content and thereby prevent information from getting to its destination. Routers can also be configured to block access to websites by their URL, e.g. Twitter.com and forbidden web page content by inspecting the packets of information, any content that mentions Tiananmen Square. The router, DNS server, and the software they use become a censor in these circumstances.

Questions for discussion

15 (a) Do you think that the world at large has an inalienable right to influence public opinion in China?
(b) What would be your motives if you do believe this?

16 What should be the limits of freedom of expression on social media sites?

17 Is it wrong for a search engine to return a list of web pages according to a profile that they have built up about you? Why?

18 Should governments make policies to govern access to certain web sites?

Information

Example:
URL to use to explore how China controls its citizens access to the Internet:
http://www.howtogeek.com/162092/htg-explains-how-the-great-firewall-of-china-works/

Task

Read
(1)
http://www.wired.com/2015/07/hackers-remotely-kill-jeep-highway/
(2)
http://www.theguardian.com/technology/2014/jun/29/facebook-users-emotions-news-feeds

Software can produce great good but with it comes the ability to cause great harm

It is not always enough to encrypt communications over the Internet because the packets that carry the encrypted communication also carry tracking data in plaintext form, i.e. the source and destination IP addresses, e.g. your computer's IP address and the IP address of the website that you are visiting. These IP addresses must be machine readable for the Internet to function and route packets successfully. Internet Service Providers can sell this tracking data to marketers and in some countries are required to keep and reveal this information to the authorities on demand. The packets can also be examined in transit by packet sniffing software snooping in on the communication.

Preserving privacy means not only hiding the content of messages, but also hiding who is talking to whom. The Tor project and the Tor software that it developed has made this tracking much more difficult as well as providing encryption of the content of messages. As a software tool for anonymous and confidential communication, it has been used successfully by journalists to

Background

How Tor works:
https://www.torproject.org/about/overview

communicate more safely with whistleblowers and dissidents. It has proved to be an effective tool to circumvent censorship of the Internet in countries such as China and Iran and as a building block for other software designed to protect privacy.

However, the Tor software has also been used to hide criminal activity and other undesirable activities. A question mark also hangs over whether Tor is secure against monitoring by governments as it was originally developed, built and financed by the US military which released it for general use in 2004, ostensibly to improve the cover of its spies overseas by masking their Internet activities amongst the activities of a diverse group of people to whom the Tor software was now available. If it is not secure against government monitoring, it might be difficult to know because the authorities would be careful about revealing their hand.

Background

Deep Web DVD:
Now available to purchase from www.amazon.com,
URL: http://www.amazon.com/Deep-Web-Directors-Keanu-Reeves/dp/B017WUEJ52

Information

Banning use of free or shared WiFi and Tor:
In December 2015 in the wake of the Paris attacks, it was reported that France's law enforcement authorities were proposing new legislation to forbid the use of free or shared WiFi during a state of emergency. They were also proposing that anonymous browsers like Tor should be blocked in general.

Background

Bitcoin:
Bitcoin is a decentralized digital currency or virtual currency. It uses peer-to-peer technology to operate with no central authority or banks.

Case study

The Dark Web is the World Wide Web content that exists on underground networks which use the public Internet but which require specific software such as Tor for access. The Dark Web forms part of the Deep Web, the part of the Web not indexed by search engines. In the Deep Web there are several online shopping sites that specialise in connecting sellers of illicit goods with willing buyers.

The online black market Silk Road launched in February 2011 used the anonymising tool Tor to protect the identities of buyers, sellers and the site's administrators. Payment was made in Bitcoin, allowing buyers a relatively high amount of protection. Ross William Ulbricht, its creator, was arrested in October 2013. On May 29, 2015, Ulbricht was handed five sentences to be served concurrently, including two for life imprisonment, without the possibility of parole. He was also ordered to forfeit $183 million obtained from his criminal activities that he held in Bitcoins, beyond the reach of the authorities until he was forced to hand over the encryption keys. In a letter to Judge Forrest before his sentencing, Ulbricht stated that his actions through Silk Road were committed through libertarian idealism and that "Silk Road was supposed to be about giving people the freedom to make their own choices" and admitted that he made a "terrible mistake" that "ruined his life".

Watch the film Deep Web by Alex Winter, if you can, which explores how the designers of the Deep Web and Bitcoin are at the centre of a battle for control of how the Internet may be used and its effect on our digital rights.

Questions for discussion

19 In 2014 Google launched a service in response to a European Court ruling to allow Europeans to ask for personal data to be removed from online search results.
(a) Why might removal of personal data from search engine results not be sufficient to comply with the right to be forgotten?
(b) If on the grounds of freedom of speech it is a human right to be able to access information, why might forcing people to conduct searches with engines that are able to access the Deep Web be undesirable?

20 "Software such as Tor should be banned because although it can be used for morally sound purposes it can also be used for criminal and immoral acts." Do you agree or disagree with this statement and why?

Questions

1 What is meant by personalised search results?

2 What is meant by personalised advertisements?

3 Some search engines return search results to fit the profile of the person making the query. State **two** dangers to individuals and society of providing such personalised search.

4 Social media and search engine companies collect personal data from users to make their services more useful to users. Explain why it can be beneficial for the user to give up personal data in this way and why it might not.

5 Software can produce great good but with it comes the ability to cause great harm. Using at least one example, explain the meaning of this statement.

6 Software and their algorithms embed moral and cultural values. Using at least one example, explain the meaning of this statement.

7 Why do legislators face difficulty enacting legislation where the Internet is concerned?

8 Developments in computer science and digital technology have dramatically altered the shape of information flows in society. The labels *asymmetry of power* and *pervasive surveillance* have been applied to these flows. What is the meaning of each of these labels?

9 Processes involving humans communicating with machines have been replaced by machine processes, i.e. machine to machine communication with machines making decisions and taking actions according to the code (automated algorithms) that they are programmed with. Machines in these cases could be embedded computers or nodes in a network such as the Internet, for example. Describe **two** examples of applications where machine to machine communication is relied on substantially.
Software engineers and computer scientists have responsibilities in the algorithms that they devise and the code that they deploy. What precautions should be observed by computer scientists and software engineers in the development of the two applications that you have described?

In this chapter you have covered:

- What it means for a person to act morally
- How ethics, a set of principles that applies to a society, can inform a person's reasoning when making moral judgements
- How the nature of software, data, and information and its global scale make it difficult to legislate for on the scale of the Internet especially when it crosses cultural divides, i.e. encounters a different culture
- Equally how the nature of software, data, and information and its global scale creates opportunities through social media, email, blogging, etc. for people to express themselves freely, to share information and ideas freely, and to associate freely
- The manner in which
  - developments in computer science and the digital technologies have dramatically altered the shape of communications and information flows in societies, giving rise to an asymmetry of power and pervasive surveillance
  - software is designed so cannot be value free and therefore will inevitably embed moral and cultural values. This places responsibilities on computer scientists and software engineers to act morally and ethically
- That the ability of computer scientists and software engineers to scale software and processing quickly for marginal cost offered creates the potential for great good through access to information whilst software can also be misused to cause great harm
- The difficulty of applying law made in one country to the global Internet whose content, algorithms and access embed value judgments from different cultures, societies and legal systems, e.g. online privacy versus freedom of speech

9 Fundamentals of communication and networking

9.1 Communication

Learning objectives:

- *Define serial and parallel transmission methods and discuss the advantages of serial over parallel transmission*
- *Define and compare synchronous and asynchronous data transmission*
- *Describe the purpose of start and stop bits in asynchronous data transmission*

Key principle

Serial data transmission:
In serial data transmission, single bits (binary digits) are sent one after another along a single wire.

Information

In Figure 9.1.1.1 the current travels along a single wire loop. The moving electric charge picks up electrical energy in the battery and delivers this energy to the lamp bulb.

9.1.1 Communication methods

Serial data transmission

In serial data transmission, **single bits (binary digits) are sent one after another along a single wire** by varying the voltage on the wire. *Figure 9.1.1.1* shows a simple electrical circuit for sending single bits coded as 0 volts and 5 volts. When the switch is in position A the lamp bulb is connected to 5 volts. When the switch is in position B the lamp bulb is connected to 0 volts. We need to decide what the signal lamp on and the signal lamp off represent.

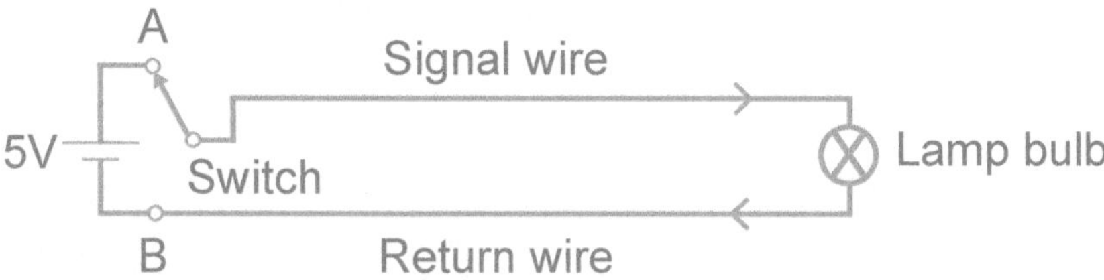

Figure 9.1.1.1 Simple circuit for sending binary digits serially

If single bits are being sent along the wire, then we have one of two possible binary digit values to represent at any moment, 0 or 1. We may choose to let the state *lamp on* represent binary digit 1 and the state *lamp off* represent binary digit 0. In which case, the equivalent signals travelling along the signal wire represent binary digit 1 by 5 volts and binary digit 0 by 0 volts. The binary digits represent data and the voltages 0 volts and 5 volts their signal equivalent. *Figure 9.1.1.2* shows the transmission of a sequence of data bits using signals of 0 volts and 5 volts.

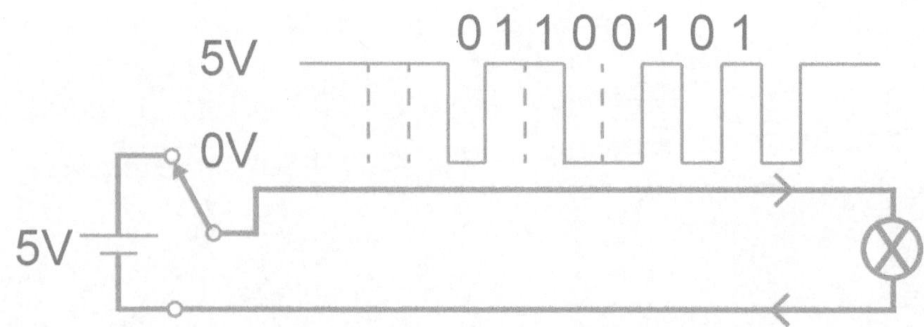

Figure 9.1.1.2 Serial data transmission of a sequence of data bits sent as electrical signals

Questions

1. What is serial data transmission?

Key principle

Parallel data transmission:
In parallel data transmission, bits are sent down several wires simultaneously. The connecting cable consists of many wires and is called a parallel bus.

Parallel data transmission

In parallel data transmission, bits are sent down several wires simultaneously. The connecting cable consists of many wires.

Figure 9.1.1.3 shows two parallel interfaces connected by a parallel connection that uses eight data wires labelled 0 to 7, one ground (GND) wire, one clock signal (CLK) wire. The clock signal wire is set to 5 volts or 0 volts. The data wires are set to 5 volts or 0 volts.

The receiver reads the data bits in one go by sampling the voltage on each data wire when it receives the clock signal pulse ⎍ on the clock wire.

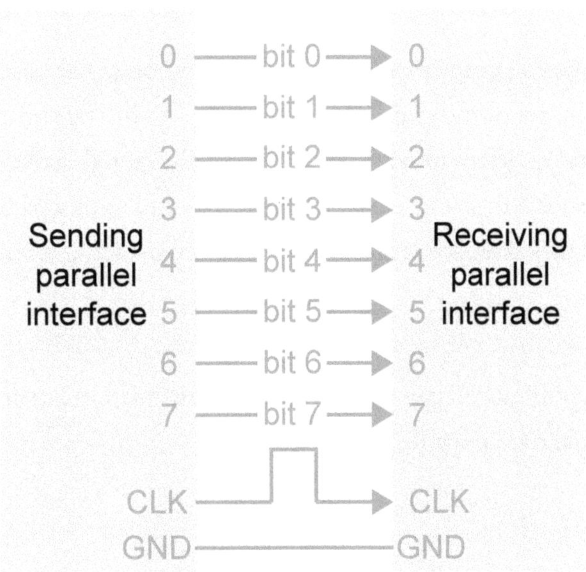

Figure 9.1.1.3 Parallel data transmission along an 8-bit data bus, controlled by a clock pulse to signal the arrival of 8 data bits

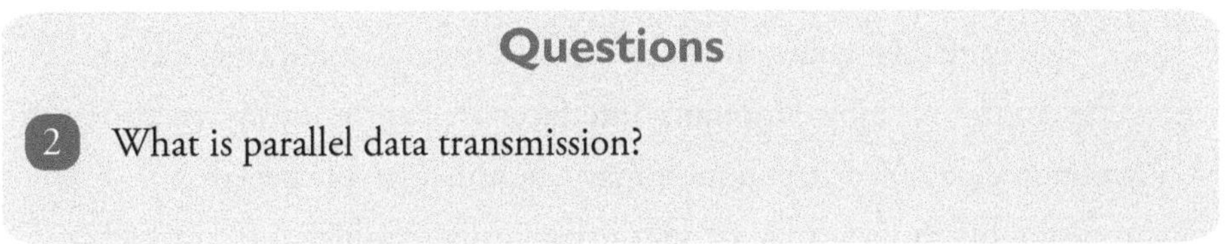

Questions

2 What is parallel data transmission?

Key fact

Parallel vs serial data transmission:
Parallel data transmission has a limited data rate and distance at which it can be reliably operated compared with serial.

Advantages of serial over parallel

Parallel data transmission has a limited data rate and distance at which it can be reliably operated compared with serial. The limited data rate and distance of parallel data transmission are caused by skew and crosstalk.

Skew is the phenomenon where the bits travel at slightly different speeds down each wire in a parallel bus. This includes the clock signal as well. The reading of the data on the data lines is synchronised with the clock signal. If data and clock signal get out of step to such a degree that the data lines are sampled before the clock signal has appeared or after it has disappeared then data will not be read correctly. A higher clock rate means narrower clock pulses and shorter time intervals between pulses. The consequence is a narrower sampling time window which means less tolerance of skew. The longer the parallel bus the more data bits on each wire can get out of step with each other and the clock signal.

Crosstalk is induced signals in adjacent wires of a parallel bus caused when a signal on one or more wires varies rapidly. The longer a wire and the more rapid the variation in voltage in adjacent wires the greater the effect.

Serial data transmission doesn't suffer from skew because it doesn't use a separate clock signal and crosstalk is minimised because there are fewer wires in close proximity and techniques can be applied relatively cheaply to guard against crosstalk. It is also considerably cheaper over long distances than parallel would be, simply because fewer wires are used.

A parallel interface is simpler to design than a serial one. The parallel interface just requires a buffer of the same width as the data to be transmitted or received. A serial interface must perform a parallel to serial conversion and vice versa and so is a little more complicated to design than a parallel interface. However, a parallel interface requires more pins than a serial one.

Questions

3 State **two** disadvantages of parallel data transmission when compared with serial data transmission.

Synchronous and asynchronous data transmission

Serial interfaces are divided into two groups: synchronous or asynchronous.

Synchronous serial data transmission is a form of serial communication in which the communicating endpoints' interfaces are continuously synchronized by a common clock. Synchronisation may take the form of special synchronising bit patterns that are sent periodically or which are attached to a block of data. It may also take the form of a special clock line as shown in *Figure 9.1.1.4* which is an I2C interface.

In the Inter-Integrated Circuit (I2C, pronounced I-two-C) synchronous serial interface, used by microcontroller-based systems such as the Raspberry Pi, the clock signal requires its own wire and so adds to the total number of wires that connect the communicating devices.

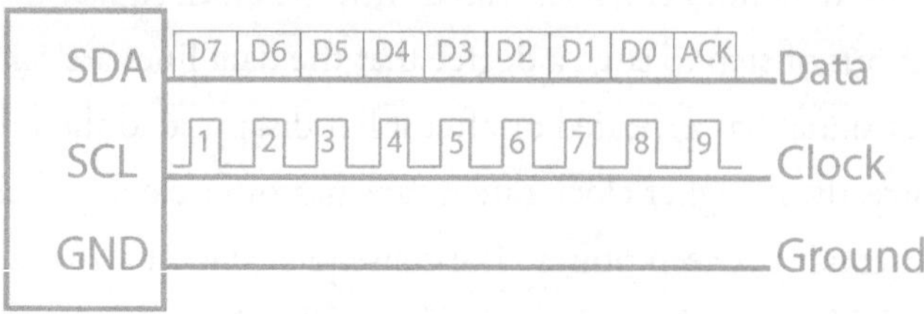

Figure 9.1.1.4 Synchronous serial data transmission for an I2C interface

Key fact

Serial interfaces:
Serial interfaces are divided into two groups: synchronous or asynchronous.

Key concept

Synchronous serial data transmission:
Synchronous serial data transmission is a form of serial communication in which the communicating endpoints' interfaces are continuously synchronized by a common clock.

Figure 9.1.1.4 shows the three pin and three wire interface for I2C. The data bits D7 to D0 are individually clocked into the receiving interface by 8 clock pulses. The receiving I2C interface places an acknowledgement bit onto the data wire on receipt of the 9th clock pulse.

Whatever the type of synchronous serial interface, a clock signal is associated with its data line(s) and this clock signal is used by all the devices connected to the serial bus to synchronise all data transfers.

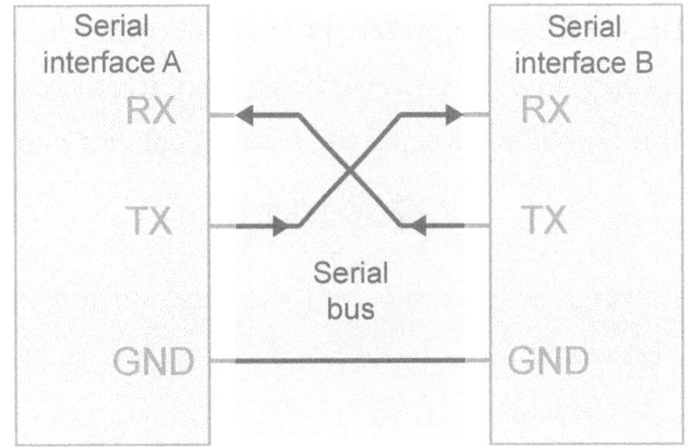

Figure 9.1.1.5 Asynchronous serial data transmission between two interfaces supporting transmit (TX) and receive (RX) in both directions simultaneously

Another example of a synchronous interface used by embedded microcontroller systems is the Serial Peripheral Interface bus (SPI).

Synchronous serial communication is used in telecommunication systems which the Internet relies upon. These are time-division systems which continuously send frames of bits between nodes. The nodes are kept in sync by synchronisation frames which are sent periodically and which distribute the common clock signal derived from an atomic clock. This enables very high data transfer rates not achievable with asynchronous data transfer.

Asynchronous means that data is transferred without support from an external clock signal. No clock wire is required so reducing the number of wires by one and the number of connecting pins in each interface by one as well.

Figure 9.1.1.5 shows a serial interface A connected to another serial interface B by a serial bus consisting of three wires, one to transmit from interface A to interface B and one to transmit from interface B to interface A. Both interfaces share a common ground wire.

Asynchronous serial data transmission sends 7 or 8 data bits at a time and an optional parity bit framed by start and stop bits in the RS232/RS422 protocol as shown in Figure 9.1.1.6. These 7 or 8 bits often represent character data from the ASCII character data set.

Information

Serial ports:

Desktop PCs used to have at least one serial port called the COM port but the advent of USB meant manufacturers stopped supplying PCs with serial ports. They are absent from tablets and smart phones where the space for ports is limited. However, the demise of serial ports is greatly exaggerated. Serial ports are everywhere, in everything from industrial automation systems to scientific instrumentation and in Internet of Things (IoT) devices. The Arduino has at least one TTL serial port for transmitting and receiving serial data.

Key concept

Asynchronous data transmission:

Asynchronous means that data is transferred without support from an external clock signal. No clock wire is required.

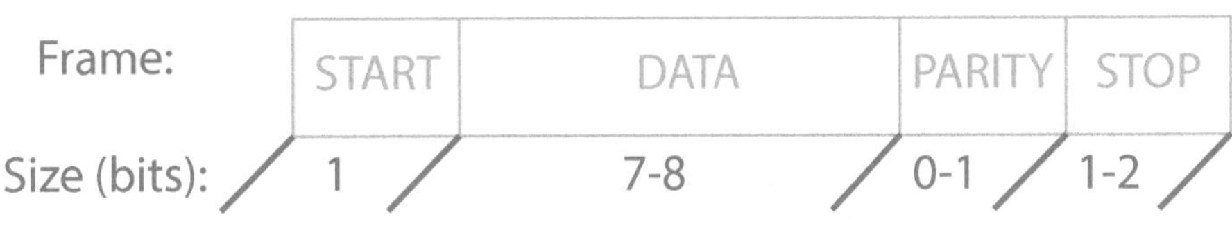

Figure 9.1.1.6 Asynchronous serial data transmission frame

The serial interface is usually a part of an integrated circuit called a UART (Universal Asynchronous Receiver Transmitter) that buffers a serially received data byte before placing it on an internal 8-bit bus as shown in *Figure 9.1.1.7*.
The UART buffers a byte from the 8-bit data bus before clocking it out onto the serial TX wire framed in start and stop bits. The UART performs serial to parallel conversion and vice versa. If the parity bit system is being used, it also generates a parity bit as well as checking the received data for parity errors.

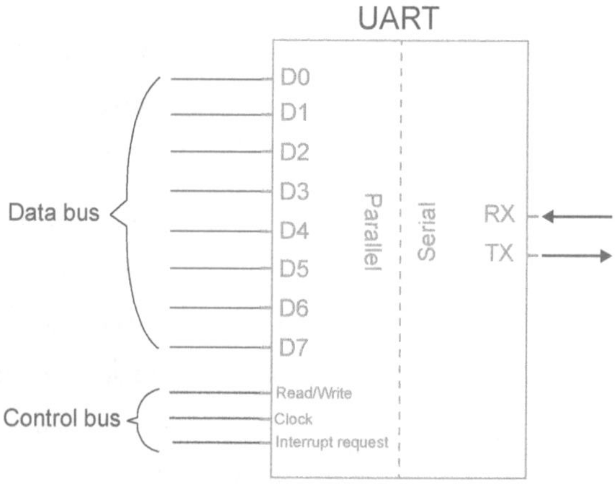

Figure 9.1.1.7 UART

Questions

4 Define the following modes of data transmission
(a) synchronous
(b) asynchronous

Information

Ethernet and USB:
These are serial data transmission protocols that both encode timing information in the communication symbols, i.e. the bit patterns or codes that they use. This coding therefore delivers both a clock signal and data, so both can be classified as synchronous.

Comparison of synchronous and asynchronous data transmission

RS232/RS422 asynchronous serial data transmission is relatively cheap because it requires less hardware than synchronous serial data transmission and is appropriate in situations where messages are generated at irregular intervals, for example from embedded systems used in scientific instruments as initiation of a transfer is relatively quick. However, two in nine or ten bits are control bits thus a significant proportion of the data transmission conveys no information.

Synchronous data transmissions requires the distribution of a stable clock signal. In parallel synchronous data transmission this limits the distance and clock speed. This can also limit serial synchronous data transmission if a separate clock wire is used. However, in time-division multiplexed synchronous serial data transmission, this is less of a problem because all clocks are kept in synchronisation with a master clock by periodically sending synchronising frames and thus doing away with the need for a separate clock wire. High speed data transmission is achievable with this method.

Questions

5 Compare synchronous and asynchronous data transmission.

The purpose of start and stop bits

In asynchronous serial data communication such as RS232 the data are words of a certain word length, for example, a byte, each word is delimited by start and stop bits as shown in *Figure 9.1.1.6*. In asynchronous serial data transmission the transmitter and receiver are not kept synchronised between transmissions. Instead, the receiver is synchronised with the transmitter only at

Key concept

Start and stop bits:
The start bit signals the arrival of data at the receiver. This enables the receiver to sample the data correctly by generating clock pulses synchronised to the bits in the received data. Effectively, transmitter and receiver clocks are synchronised by the arrival of a start bit.

Both transmitter clock and receiver clock must have been set up previously to "tick" at the same rate when running. Other parameters must agree in both transmitter and receiver interface such as the number of data bits that will be sent, the number of stop bits and whether parity is used or not and if so, what parity, even or odd. These parameters are set up once before either interface is used.

the time of transmission. This allows data to be transmitted intermittently such as when typing characters on a keyboard.

Start bit

The arrival of data at the receiver is signalled by a special bit called a **start bit**. As the arrival of data cannot be predicted by the receiver, the transmission is called **asynchronous**.

The start bit is used to wake up the receiver. The receiver's clock is set ticking by the start bit. The clock is just a circuit that is designed to generate a preset number of pulses at fixed intervals which are used to sample the data bits as they arrive one after another. The signal changes in the serial data transmission take place at regular time intervals so the receiver must operate a timing device **set at the same rate as the transmitter**, so the received bits can be read at the same regular time intervals.

The transmitter also operates a timing device, a clock, that is set at a rate determined by the baud rate (see *Chapter 9.1.2*). Again this can be as simple a circuit to generate a preset number of pulses at fixed intervals of time.

It is important that the receiver reads each bit during the time that it is not changing, i.e. in the time interval between when changes can take place. This is why the receiver's timing device needs to be brought in step or synchronism with the transmission's timing.

Figure 9.1.1.8 shows two computers, A and B, with a TTL serial connection between their serial ports. TTL is Transistor-Transistor Logic and is a logic that operates between 0 volts and 5 or 3.3 volts. TTL relies on circuits built from bipolar transistors to achieve switching and maintain logic states.

For the link from computer A to computer B, the data wire is kept at the voltage level corresponding to a binary digit 1 when not sending – the **idle state**. A data transmission is started by changing the voltage level to the level for binary digit 0. This is the **start bit**. The transmitter (TX) then follows the start bit with 7 or 8 data bits depending on how the serial port has been configured. The least significant data bit (LSB) is sent first and

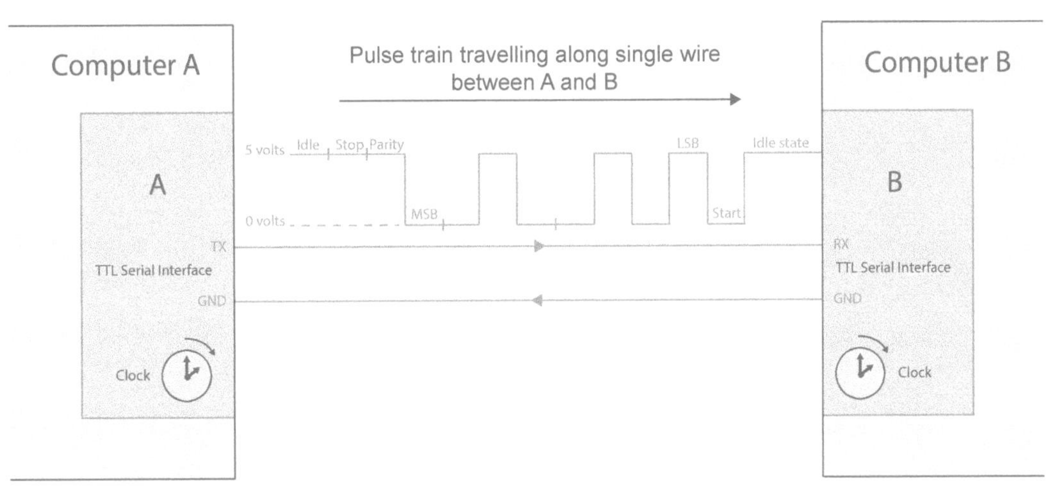

Figure 9.1.1.8 Asynchronous serial data transmission between the TTL serial interface of two computers, A and B

the most significant data bit (MSB) last. If parity is enabled, the last data bit is followed by a parity bit.

Stop bit

Finally, the transmitter attaches a **stop bit**. The voltage level chosen for the stop bit is the level for binary digit 1. The time interval for the stop bit allows the receiver (RX) to deal with the received bits, i.e. transfer them into the RAM of the computer, before receiving and processing the next serial frame as shown in *Figure 9.1.1.9*. Two stop bits are used if the receiver needs more time to deal with the received bits.

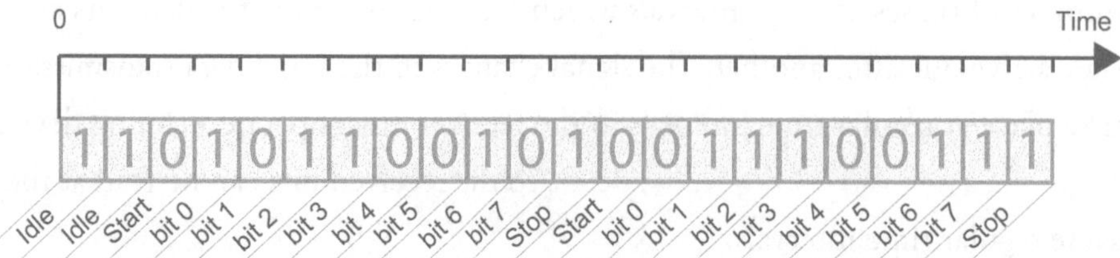

Figure 9.1.1.9 Asynchronous serial data transmission frame showing transmission of two bytes without parity

Questions

6 Describe the purpose of start and stop bits in asynchronous data transmission.

In this chapter you have covered:

- Serial and parallel transmission methods and the advantages of serial over parallel transmission
- Synchronous and asynchronous data transmission and how they compare with each other
- The purpose of start and stop bits in asynchronous data transmission

9.1 Communication

Learning objectives:

- *Define:*
  - *baud rate*
  - *bit rate*
  - *bandwidth*
  - *latency*
  - *protocol*
- *Differentiate between baud rate and bit rate*
- *Understand the relationship between bit rate and bandwidth*

Key concept

Baud rate: The maximum rate at which signals on a wire or line may change.

1 baud: One signal change per second.

9.1.2 Communication basics

Baud rate

The **baud rate sets the maximum frequency at which signals may change**. To understand the meaning of baud rate consider the following simplified switching system shown in *Figure 9.1.2.1*. Switch A operates at the baud rate. For example if the baud rate is 1 baud then the switch remains connected to one of the four electrical voltages for one second. At the end of each second, the switch can switch the connection to any one of the four possible voltages. The changeover happens in a time period very much smaller than one second (theoretically, it happens instantaneously). Thus, the output signal that appears on the signal wire may change every one second but no quicker. If the baud rate is 10 baud then the switch can change position every tenth of a second.

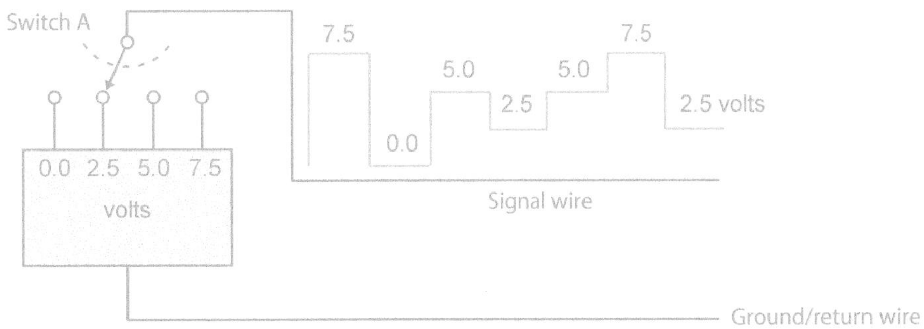

Figure 9.1.2.1 Simplified switching system illustrating baud rate

For example, a computer's serial port may be set to send at 1 baud, the signal sent out by the computer can change only at the end of each elapsed second.

Table 9.1.2.1 shows the rates of signal change for some baud rates.

Baud rate	Time between signal changes (s)	Rate of signal changes (changes per second)
1	1	1
2	0.5	2
4	0.25	4
1000	0.001	1000
10000	0.0001	10000

Table 9.1.2.1 Relationship between baud rate and rate of signal changes

Questions

1. How often may switch A change if the baud rate is 100 baud?
2. How many times a second can the switch change if the baud rate is 1000 baud?

Key concept

Bit rate: The number of bits transmitted per second.

Key fact

bit rate = baud rate x the no of bits per signal (voltage)

Bit rate

Bit rate is measured in bits per second. It is the number of bits transmitted per second. The bit rate is the same as the baud rate when one bit is sent between consecutive signal changes. However, it is possible to send more than one bit between signal changes if more than two voltage levels are used to encode bits. If the voltages 0 volts, 2.5 volts, 5 volts and 7.5 volts are used, then the decimal numbers in Table 9.1.2.2 can be encoded.

Signal level (volts)	Decimal number	Binary number
0	0	00
2.5	1	01
5	2	10
7.5	3	11

Table 9.1.2.2 Linking signal levels and number of bits they encode

Figure 9.1.2.2 shows how two bits of data can be encoded per time slot on a 1 baud line, giving a bit rate of 2 bits per second.

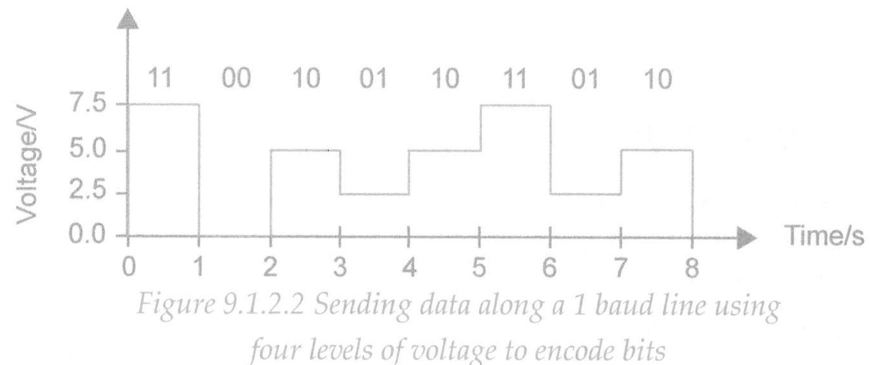

Figure 9.1.2.2 Sending data along a 1 baud line using four levels of voltage to encode bits

From this we may conclude that the relationship between but rate and baud rate is

bit rate = baud rate x the no of bits per signal (voltage)

Questions

3 What is meant by (a) baud rate (b) bit rate?

4 Explain the difference between baud rate and bit rate.

5 The following voltage levels expressed in volts are chosen to encode bits:

-6.0, -4.5, -3.0, -1.5, +1.5, +3.0, +4.5, +6.0

How many bits represent these voltages?

6 For the voltages given in question 5 write down one possible set of corresponding bit patterns (an example of a bit pattern is 01).

7 If the baud rate of the line is 900 baud what is the bit rate for the voltage levels given in question 5?

Bandwidth

Bandwidth is a measure of how fast the data may be transmitted over the transmission medium. The greater the bandwidth, the greater the rate at which data can be sent.

The bandwidth of a transmission medium, e.g. copper wire, is the range of signal frequencies that it may transmit from one end of the wire to the other without significant reduction in strength. Bandwidth is measured in hertz (Hz), e.g. 500Hz. The hertz is a unit of frequency equal to one cycle per second. Figures 9.1.2.3 and 9.1.2.4 show the effect of the transmission medium on two different frequencies.

> **Key concept**
>
> **Bandwidth:**
> The bandwidth of a transmission medium, e.g. copper wire, is the range of signal frequencies that it may transmit from one end of the communication link to the other without significant reduction in strength of the signal.

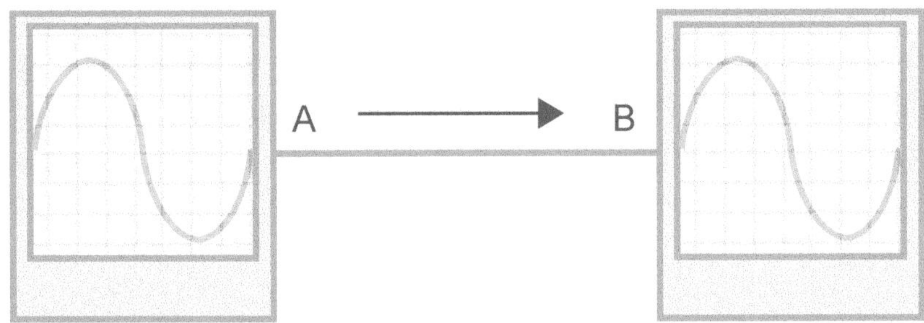

Figure 9.1.2.3 Low-frequency signal injected onto wire at A arrives at B with its strength relatively undiminished

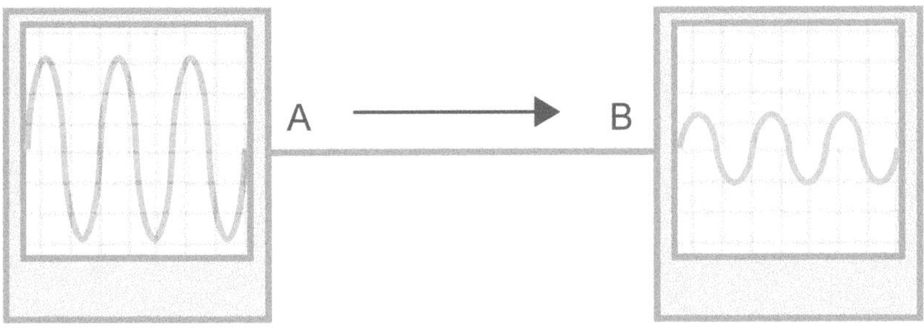

Figure 9.1.2.4 Higher-frequency signal injected onto wire at A arrives at B with its strength diminished significantly

Although a given signal may contain frequencies over a very broad range, any medium used to transmit the signal will be able to accommodate only a limited band of frequencies. This limits the bit rate that can be carried on the transmission medium. Figure 9.1.2.5 shows the effect of a 500 Hz bandwidth signal channel, e.g. a copper wire, on a transmission with bit rate of 2000 bits per second.

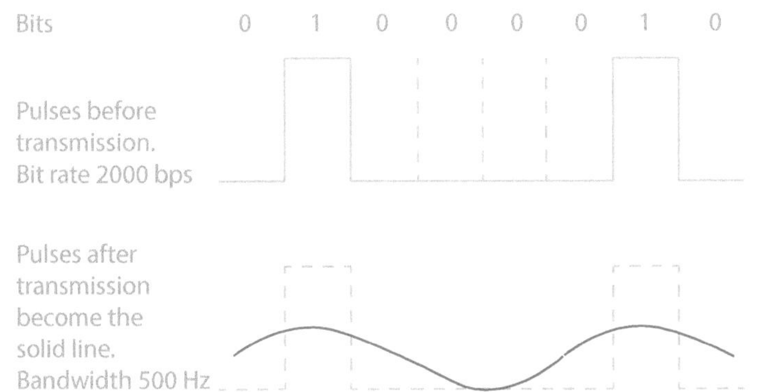

Figure 9.1.2.5 A 2000 bps transmission over a 500 Hz signal channel

Questions

 8 What is meant by bandwidth?

Key concept

Latency:
Latency is the time delay that can occur between the moment something (an action) is initiated and the moment its first effect begins.

Latency

Latency is the time delay that can occur between the moment something (an action) is initiated and the moment its first effect begins. In a wide area network involving satellites, significant time delay occurs because of the physical distance between the ground stations and the geostationary satellite.

Requesting and receiving a web page can involve a considerable time delay, even though the bit rate of the uplink and downlink to the satellite is high, i.e. the bandwidth is large. The speed of microwaves is 3×10^8 m/s. With a round-trip distance of over 143,200 km, the propagation time delay is approximately 0.4 s.

Questions

 9 What is latency in the context of communications?

Key concept

Communication protocol:
A set of pre-agreed signals, codes and rules to be used for data and information exchange between computers, or a computer and a peripheral device such as a printer, that ensure that the communication is successful.

Information

Handshaking protocol:
The sending and receiving devices exchange signals to establish that the receiving device is connected and ready to receive. Then the sending device coordinates the sending of the data, informing the receiver that it is sending. Finally, the receiver indicates it has received the data and is ready to receive again.

Protocol

A communication protocol is a set of pre-agreed signals, codes and rules used to ensure successful communication between computers or a computer and a peripheral device such as a printer.

A protocol will govern such things as:

- Physical connections – e.g. RS423 serial
- Data format – packet/frame size
- Error detection and correction
- Cabling – Cat 5, Optical fibre
- Speed – baud rate, bit rate
- Flow control
- How data is to be sent

C	→	Are you ready?	→	P
C	←	Yes I am	←	P
C	→	Here it is (Start bit)	→	P
C	←	Busy	←	P
C	→	That's it (Stop bit)	→	P
C	←	I'm ready again	←	P

Table 9.1.2.3 Handshaking protocol: computer = C, printer = P

For example, serial data communication, uses a handshaking protocol to control the flow of data. In a handshaking protocol, the sending device checks first to see if the receiving device is present. If it is present, the sending device then enquires if the receiving device is ready to receive. The sending device waits for a response which indicates that the receiving device is ready to receive. On receipt of this signal, the sending device coordinates the sending of the data and informs the receiver that it is sending the data. The sender then waits for the receiver to become ready to receive more data.

Questions

10 What is a communications protocol?

Understand the relationship between bit rate and bandwidth

There is a direct relationship between bit rate and bandwidth. The greater the bandwidth of the transmission system, the higher the bit rate that can be transmitted over that system. If the data rate of the digital signal is W bits per second (bps) then a very good representation can be achieved with a bandwidth of 2W Hz.

Key principle

Bit rate and bandwidth:
The greater the bandwidth of the transmission system, the higher the bit rate that can be transmitted over that system.

For example, Figure 9.1.2.6 shows a 4 x 5 chequered board of black and white squares. Suppose that the information contained within this board of which squares are black and which white is sent as a bit stream row by row, starting from the top left square. The bits and the corresponding stream of voltage pulses are also shown in the figure. The fundamental frequency with which the pulses alternate between 5 volts and 0 volts is $W/_2$ Hz where W is the bit rate in bits per second. We know from section 5.6 that a square wave is made of harmonics of the fundamental frequency, *f*. Therefore, the bandwidth of the communication channel must allow at least the first harmonic which is 3*f* to travel without significant reduction in amplitude. A bandwidth of four times the fundamental frequency, *f*, should therefore be adequate,

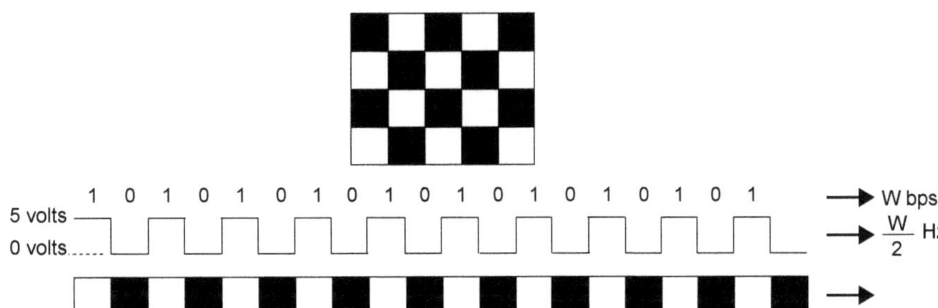

Figure 9.1.2.6 A chequered pattern being encoded in bits and sent serially as a bit stream at W bps

i.e. 4 x $W/_2$ = 2W Hz.

Questions

11 What is the relationship between bandwidth and bit rate?

In this chapter you have covered:

- Definitions for
  - baud rate
  - bit rate
  - bandwidth
  - latency
  - protocol
- The difference between baud rate and bit rate
- The relationship between bit rate and bandwidth

9.2 Networking

Learning objectives:

- *Understand*
  - *physical star topology*
  - *logical bus network topology*
- *Differentiate between both*
- *Explain their operation*
- *Compare each (advantages and disadvantages)*

9.2.1 Network topology

Topology

The way computers are cabled together or linked to form a network is very important. The term **topology** is used to describe the layout of a network. When the computers that are linked are in close proximity, e.g. in a single building, the network is called a **local area network**.

The topology in *Figure 9.2.1.1(a)* is a mesh and that in *Figure 9.2.1.1(b)* is a bus.

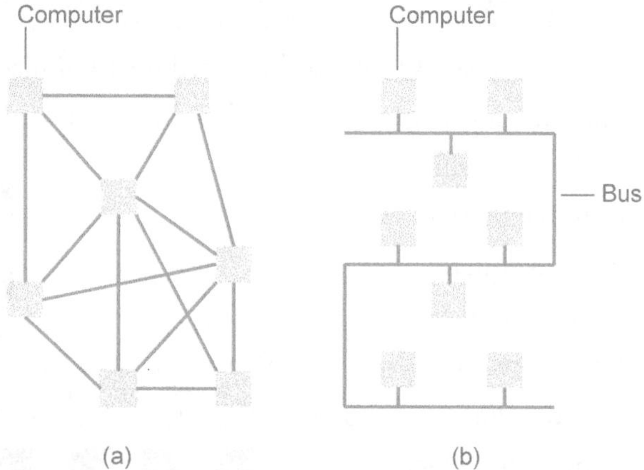

Figure 9.2.1.1 Two different network layouts

Key concept

Network topology:
The shape, layout, configuration or structure of the connections that connect devices to the network.

Star topology

The most common physical network topology is the star which is shown in outline in *Figure 9.2.1.2*. The centre of the star is either a network switch or a central computer.

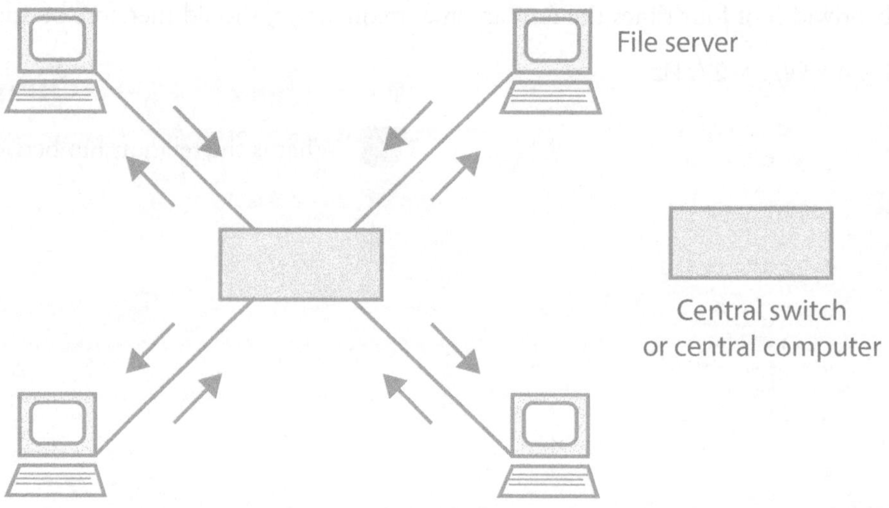

Figure 9.2.1.2 Star network topology

Key concept

Local Area Network (LAN):
Linked computers in close proximity or in a small geographical area.

Key fact

MAC address:
A MAC address is a 48-bit address expressed in hexadecimal and separated into 6 bytes, e.g. 00-02-22-C9-54-13.
It is the physical or hardware address of the network adapter and is designed to be unique.

Did you know?

Ethernet uses CSMA/CD (Carrier Sense Multiple Access/ Collision Detection). Ethernet is a very popular bus system and generally refers to a standard published in 1982 by Digital Equipment Corporation, Intel Corporation and Xerox Corporation.
It is the predominant form of local area technology used with TCP/IP today. It operates at three speeds:
10 Mbps (standard Ethernet), 100 Mbps (fast Ethernet) and 1000 Mbps (gigabit Ethernet).
It uses 48-bit addresses. Data to be transmitted is broken into variable sized packets called frames (Figure 9.2.1.4).

A computer communicates on the network through a network interface card or network adapter. A network adapter plugs into the motherboard of a computer and into a network cable. Network adapters perform all the functions required to communicate on a network. They convert data between the form stored in the computer and the form transmitted or received on the cable (Figure 9.2.1.3).

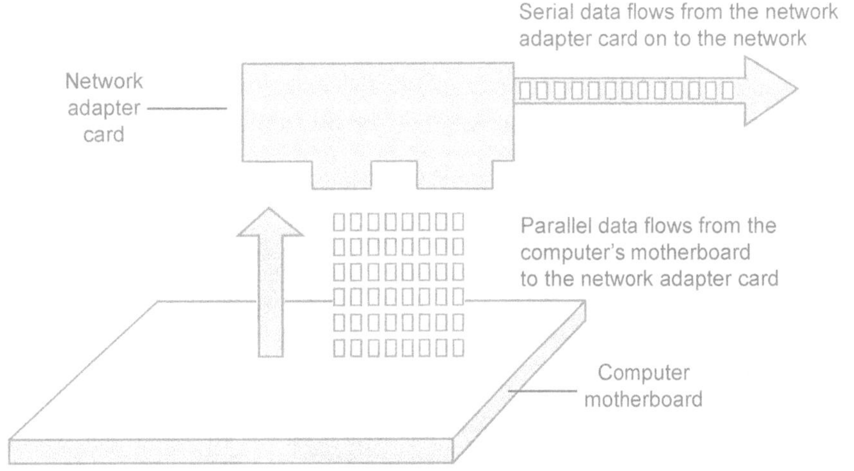

Figure 9.2.1.3 Network adapter

A network adapter receives data to be transmitted from the motherboard of a computer into an area of memory called a buffer. The data in the buffer is then passed through some electronics that calculates a checksum value for the block of data (CRC) and adds address information, which indicates the address of the destination card and its own address, which indicates where the data is from; each network adapter card is assigned a permanent unique address at the time of manufacture. The block is now known as a **frame**.

Ethernet bus protocol uses the frame structure shown in Figure 9.2.1.4.

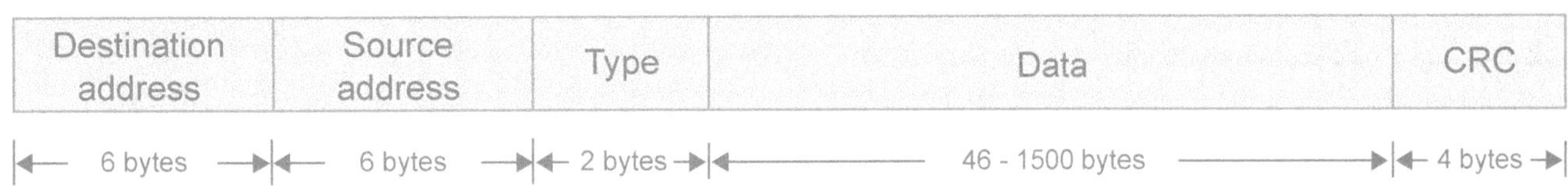

Figure 9.2.1.4 Ethernet frame

Did you know?

The MAC address is written to EEPROM (Electrically Erasable Programmable Read Only Memory) on the network adapter. This means that it is possible with the right software to alter a card's MAC address. Why might a person want to do this?

The network adapter then transmits the frame one bit at a time onto the network cable. The address information is sent first, followed by the data and then the checksum. In the Ethernet protocol, each network card is assigned a unique address called its **MAC address**. MAC stands for Media Access Control. A MAC address is a 48-bit address normally expressed in hexadecimal and separated into 6 bytes, e.g. 00-02-22-C9-54-13. Part of the MAC address identifies the manufacturer. Each network card manufacturer has been allocated a block of MAC addresses to assign to their cards.

Figure 9.2.1.5 shows how three computers connected via T-pieces to a bus can send Ethernet frames to each other.

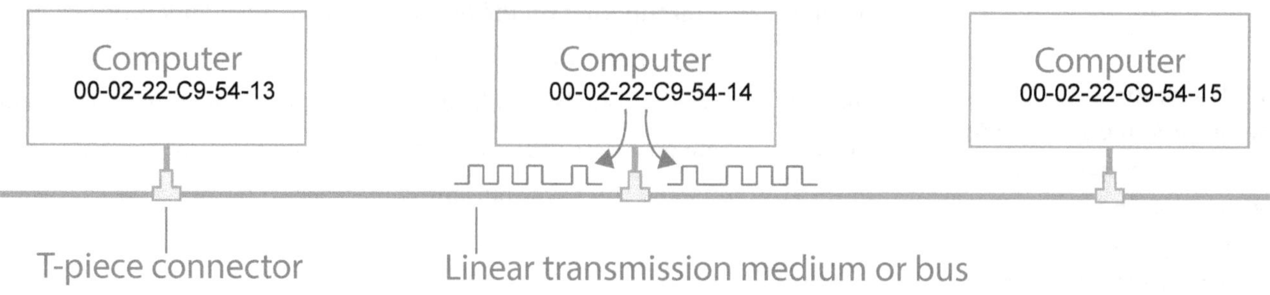

Figure 9.2.1.5 Bus network topology

Figure 9.2.1.6 shows a physical bus network that uses the transmission medium of coaxial cable to interconnect network adapters and their computers. Since the bus transmission medium is a shared medium only one computer can send at a time. However, because it is a shared medium, every network adapter is able to "see" each transmitted Ethernet frame. Each network adapter checks Ethernet frames to see if the destination address field contains the adapter's MAC address. If it does it buffers the frame and reads the data. Collisions can occur when two adapters try to send at the same time. Each will stop transmitting and delay sending again for a random time period. If collisions occur too frequently the speed of communication over the network is reduced.

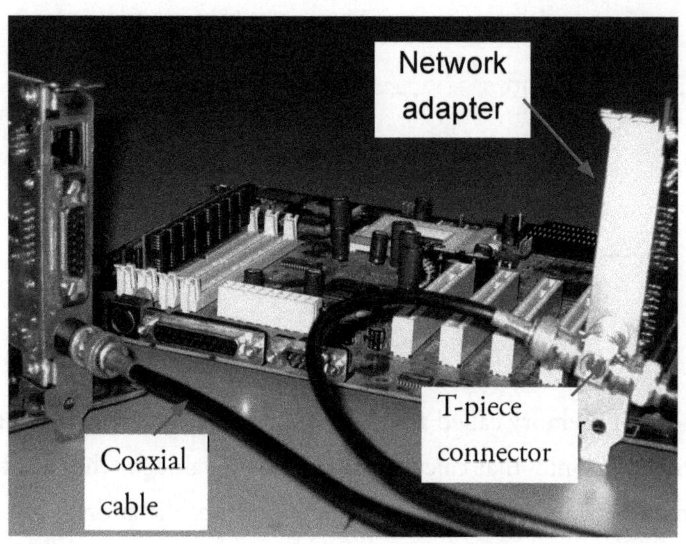

Figure 9.2.1.6 Physical bus network using coaxial cable to interconnect network adapters

Switched Ethernet

The solution to the collision problem is to restrict the communication channel to just each pair of sending and receiving computers, at a time. To cope with more than one computer sending at the same time, the transmissions are buffered and then sent in turn to the corresponding receiving computer. A fast switch is required to make the temporary bus connection between each pair of sending and receiving computers. This is what an Ethernet switch is designed to do.

In switched Ethernet the LAN is wired in star topology with the nodes (computers or workstations) connected to a central switch (*Figure 9.2.1.7*).

Even though the physical layout or topology is a star, **the LAN still behaves as a bus**. We say that the network physically wired in a star topology can behave **logically as a bus network** by using a bus protocol and appropriate

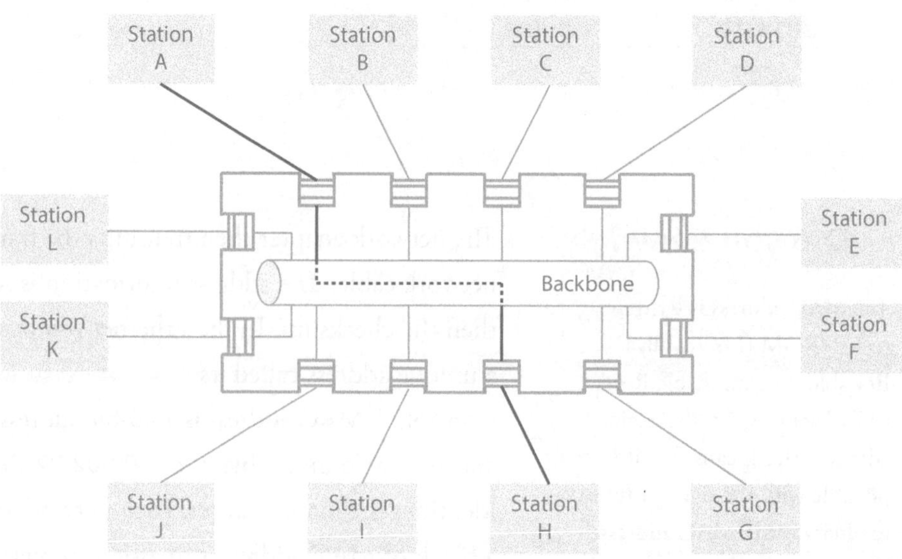

Figure 9.2.1.7 Central switch details and computers or workstations connected in a star configuration to this central switch

physical switching. The central switch queues frames until each frame can be placed onto the backbone. The switch ensures that collisions do not occur. For example, if computer A launches an Ethernet frame for computer H, the switch creates a **temporary exclusive connection** from computer A to computer H. If computer B simultaneously launches an Ethernet frame for computer D, the switch will buffer the frame until the backbone becomes free. Switched Ethernet eliminates collisions, so its performance is superior to Ethernet LANs based on multidrop coaxial cable.

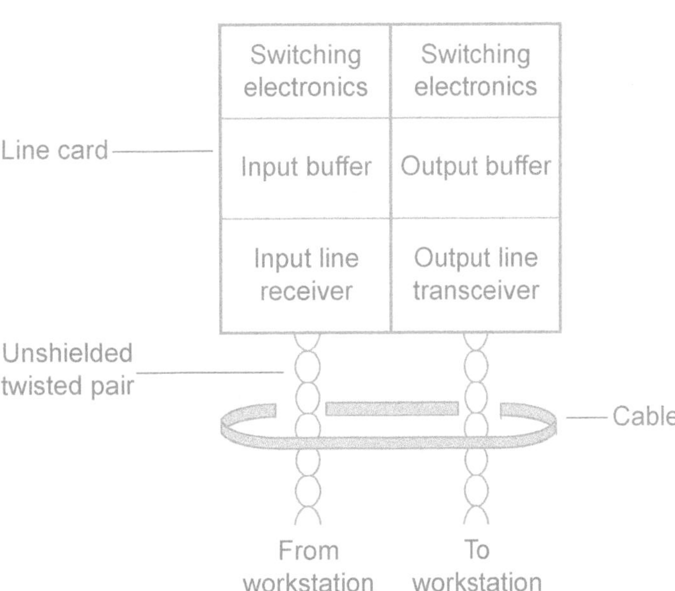

Figure 9.2.1.8 A line card connected to a cable containing two unshielded twisted pairs

In switched Ethernet a separate cable is run from a central switch to each workstation. If there are *n* workstations, there are *n* separate cables. At the switch end, a cable is connected to a line card. Therefore, for *n* cables there are *n* line cards. *Figure 9.2.1.8* shows a cable connected to a line card. *Figure 9.2.1.9* shows a network cable plugged into the Ethernet switch and a cutaway of two twisted pairs emerging from CAT5 cable terminated by an RJ45 connector. To enable bidirectional data transfer, the cable consists of two independent pairs of wires. One pair of wires forms the input circuit and the other the output circuit. The wires in each pair are twisted together, hence the name **twisted pair**.

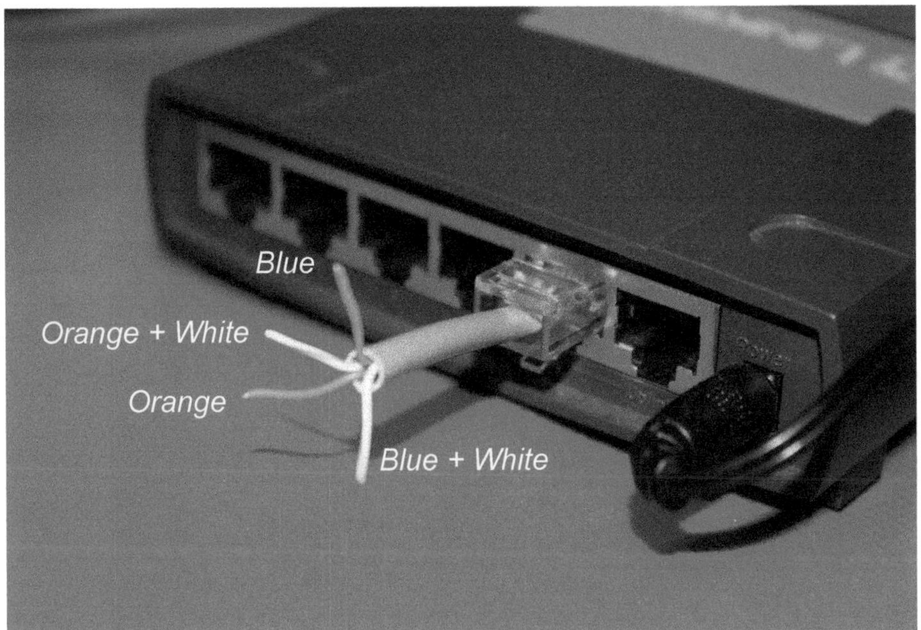

Figure 9.2.1.9 Cat 5 network cable showing two twisted pairs: Orange + White & Orange, Blue + White & Blue

A workstation may be a workstation computer, a server, a dumb terminal or some other device. A workstation transmits a packet of data to the line card along the input pair. The packet is stored in the input buffer of the line card. The switching electronics reads the destination address contained in the packet then routes the packet along a backbone in the switch to the line card connected to the destination. A backbone is a high-speed bus.

Figure 9.2.1.10 shows a 10/100 Mbps Ethernet network adapter that connects to the PCI bus of a computer.

Figure 9.2.1.10 10/100 Mbps Ethernet network adapter that plugs connects to the PCI bus of a computer

Questions

1. In the context of networking, what is a topology?
2. Draw a diagram that illustrates the essentials of a bus network.
3. Draw a diagram that illustrates the essentials of a star network.
4. Explain how a network wired in star topology can behave logically as a bus network.
5. What is a network adapter?
6. What is a MAC address?
7. Explain the collision problem in the context of a bus network.
8. How does switched Ethernet overcome the collision problem?

Comparing bus and star networks

Bus and star topologies appear very similar in the way that they are physically wired using the current switch-based hardware. Even thin-client systems, which can be considered to resemble a traditional star network, use an Ethernet bus switch to connect a central server to nodes.

In a traditional star network, each link from node to central computer is an independent link. Each link is therefore secure from eavesdropping by other nodes.

If a link to a node goes down, the other links and nodes are unaffected. However, if the central computer / central switch goes down, the whole network will fail.

In a true star-based network, the speed of each link to the central computer should remain high, because the links are not shared. Traffic between nodes in a switch-based bus network will not be adversely affected if a node goes down, unless the traffic involves the broken node or the node is a domain server that validates users when they attempt to log in. Unplugging a network cable in a switch-based bus network will not affect the rest of the network. In a coaxial cable bus network, a break in the cable stops the whole network from working. All connected nodes are able to read the frames travelling on the coaxial cable bus network. Therefore coaxial cable bus networks are not secure against eavesdropping. The frames in a coaxial cable Ethernet bus network can collide when multiple nodes send at the same time, causing a noticeable slowdown. Although collisions between frames in switch-based Ethernet bus networks cannot occur, performance can be affected when traffic volumes are high, because the buffers in the switches suffer overflow.

A wireless network is a broadcast network, so it is less secure than a cabled switch-based Ethernet network unless wireless encryption is enabled. In a wireless network without encryption, it is possible to eavesdrop on traffic intended for other computers. A wireless network can also suffer congestion because the channels are shared.

Questions

9 Discuss the advantages and disadvantages of operating a logical bus network topology wired as a physical star topology. You may wish to make reference in your answer to a physical bus topology and a traditional star topology.

In this chapter you have covered:

- The operation of
  - physical star topology
  - logical bus network topology
- Differences between both
- The advantages and disadvantages of each

9.2 Networking

Learning objectives:

- *Explain the following and describe situations where they might be used*
  - *peer-to-peer networking*
  - *client-server networking*

Key concept

Peer-to-peer network:
A network in which there is minimal or no reliance on dedicated servers. All computers are equal, and are called peers. Each peer may act as both a client and server.

9.2.2 Types of networking between hosts

Peer-to-peer networking

In a peer-to-peer (P2P) network there is minimal or no reliance on dedicated servers.

All computers are equal hence the name peer.

Each computer can communicate with any other computer on the network to which it has been granted access rights.

Each peer computer acts as a client when initiating requests to another computer(s) for resources and as a server when satisfying requests from another computer(s).

Figure 9.2.2.1 shows a wired peer-to-peer local area network and the possible communication paths between peers.

.

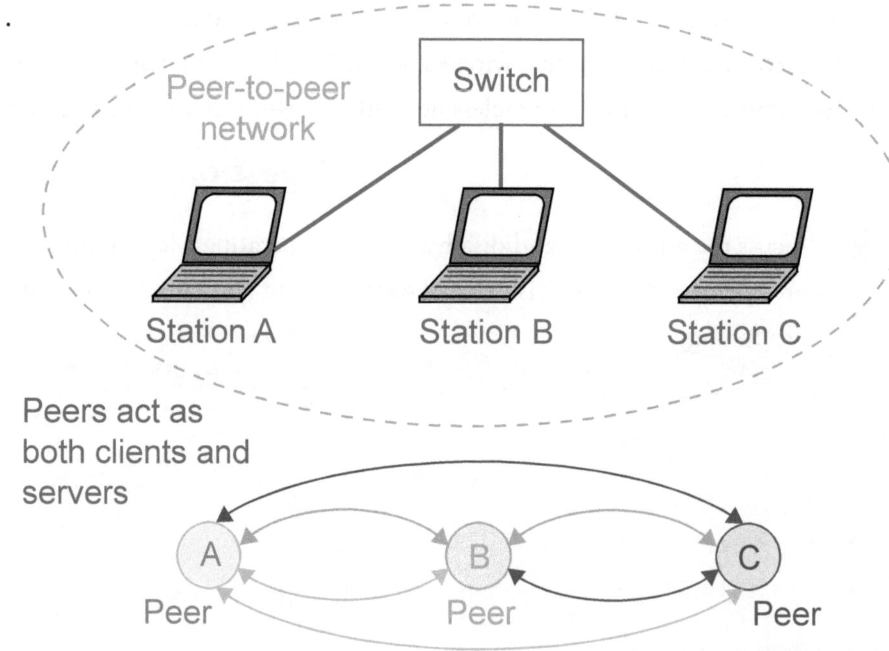

Figure 9.2.2.1 Peer-to-peer wired local area network

There is no central control and normally there is no administrator responsible for the entire network. The user at each computer acts as a user and an administrator, determining what data, disk space and peripherals on their computer get shared on the network.

Security control is limited because it has to be set on the computer to which it applies. The computer user typically sets the computer's security and they may choose to have none. It is possible to give password protection to a resource on the computer, e.g. a directory, but there is no central login process where a user's access level is protected by a single password. A user logged in at one peer computer is able to use resources on any other peer computer if the resources are unprotected by passwords or if the user knows the relevant password. Peer-to-peer networks can be as small as two computers or as large as thousands of computers.

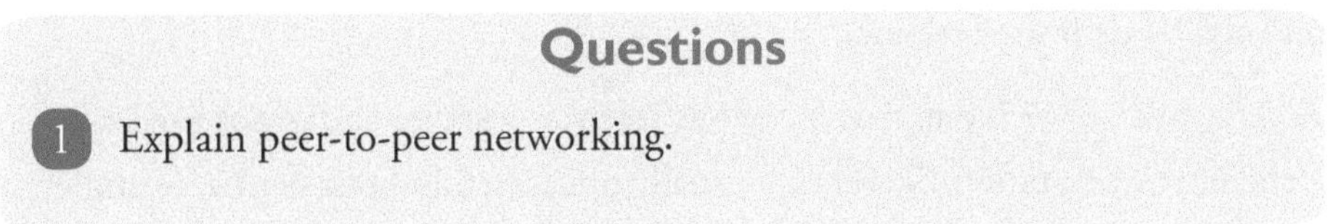

Peer-to-peer local area networks

A peer-to-peer local area network (LAN) is a good choice for environments where:

- there are fewer than 10 users
- the users are all located in the same area and the computers will be located at user desks
- security is not a major concern, so users may act as their own administrators to plan their own security
- the organisation and the network will have limited growth over the foreseeable future.

For Windows 7 desktop operating system, the maximum number of peers permitted in a peer-to-peer local area network is 20 as revealed by the command NET CONFIG SERVER as shown in Figure 9.2.2.2.

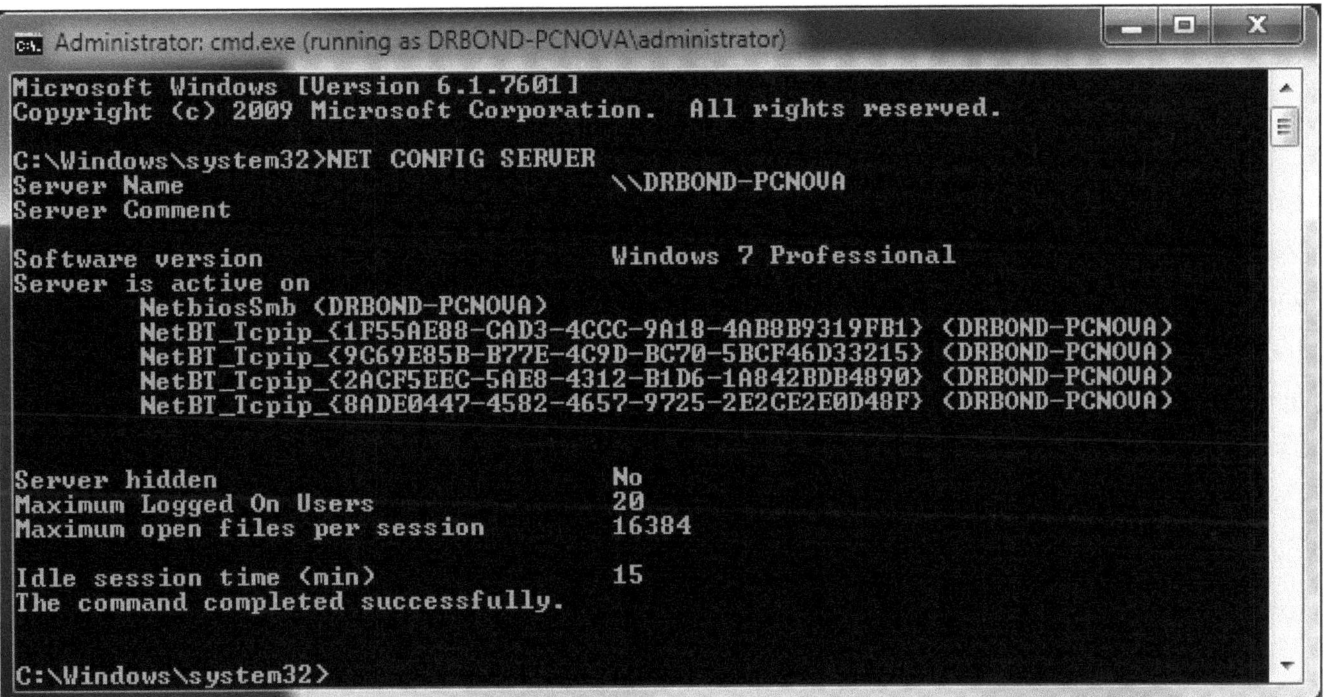

Figure 9.2.2.2 NET CONFIG SERVER command run in Windows 7 console

Questions

2 Describe the circumstances when peer-to-peer is an appropriate choice for local area networks.

Server-based network

A peer-to-peer local area network, with computers acting as both client and server, is seldom adequate for a system with more than 10 users. Therefore, most networks use dedicated servers. A server-based local area network is a client-server network in which resources, security, administration and other functions are provided by dedicated servers. Clients request services that are satisfied by dedicated servers.

A dedicated server is one that functions solely as a server and is not used as a client or workstation. Servers are usually optimised in both hardware and operating system to quickly service requests from network clients and to ensure the security of files and directories. Larger networks with a higher volume of traffic employ more than one server.

Clients use servers for services such as file storage and printing in a local area network. Client computers are usually less powerful than server computers. A server can also authenticate users attempting to log on at client workstations; it stores the client users' IDs and passwords for this purpose. Typically, school networks are server-based networks (thick-client networks): a central domain controller stores user accounts and a central file server stores users' work and some applications that users download into the client machines they work at.

Information

Hosts in networks:
A host is a computer or device that is accessible over a network.

Key concept

Server-based network:
A server-based local area network is a client-server network in which resources, security, administration and other functions are provided by dedicated servers. Clients request services that are satisfied by dedicated servers.

Questions

3 Explain how a server-based local area network differs from a peer-to-peer local area network and why it is considered a client-server network.

Client-server and peer-to-peer networking architectures

Web browsing and sending email are client applications that rely on an underlying network architecture to interact with the corresponding server applications, a web server and an email server, respectively.

Both clients and servers are software applications. They conform to one of two particular application architectures used in modern networking:

1. the client-server architecture
2. the peer-to-peer (P2P) architecture

Web servers and email servers are examples of server-based systems.

Client-server networking architecture

In a client-server architecture, there is an always-on host, called the server, which services requests from many other hosts, called clients. A classic example is the web application for which an always-on web server services requests

Key concept

Client-server architecture:
In a client-server architecture, there is an always-on host, called the server, which services requests from many other hosts, called clients. For example, when a web server receives a request from a client host for a web page, it responds by sending the requested web page to the client host.

from browsers running on client hosts. When a web server receives a request from a client host for a web page, it responds by sending the requested web page to the client host.

In the client-server architecture, clients do not directly communicate with each other. For example, two web browsers do not directly communicate. This is very different from the peer-to-peer architecture where peers can communicate with each other because peers can act as both client and server (Figure 9.2.2.1).

Another characteristic of the client-server architecture is that a server has a fixed, well-known address in TCP/IP networks, called an IP address. A client can always contact the server by sending a packet to the server's IP address and get a response because the server is always on.

Search engines such as Google and Bing employ more than one server (hundreds of thousands, in fact) in order to meet demand. However, to the client these servers appear as a single machine, a virtual server.

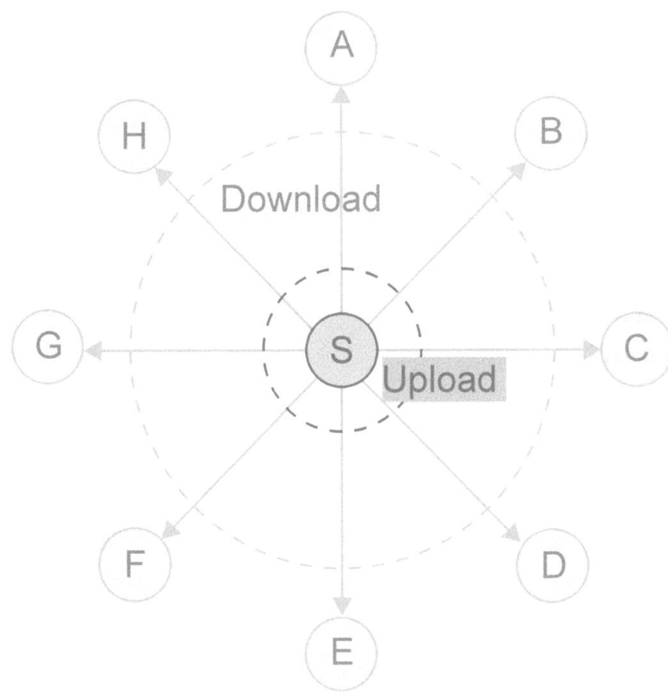

Figure 9.2.2.3 Client-server architecture

Questions

4 What is meant by client-server architecture and describe a situation where it is used?

Figure 9.2.2.3 shows a server, S, connected to eight clients, A to H. The server may be capable of uploading (transferring to clients) at a rate of, say, 5000 KiB/s whilst each client may be capable of downloading at a rate of, say, 500 KiB/s, i.e. a ratio of ten to one. If the server application running at the server is an FTP server delivering eight copies of a file to an FTP client application running at each of the eight clients then the server is more than capable of serving each client at their download rate of 500 KiB/s. Therefore, a file of size 500 KiB (500 x 1024 bytes) will take one second to download to all eight clients. Figure 9.2.2.4 shows an FTP client downloading a file from an FTP server.

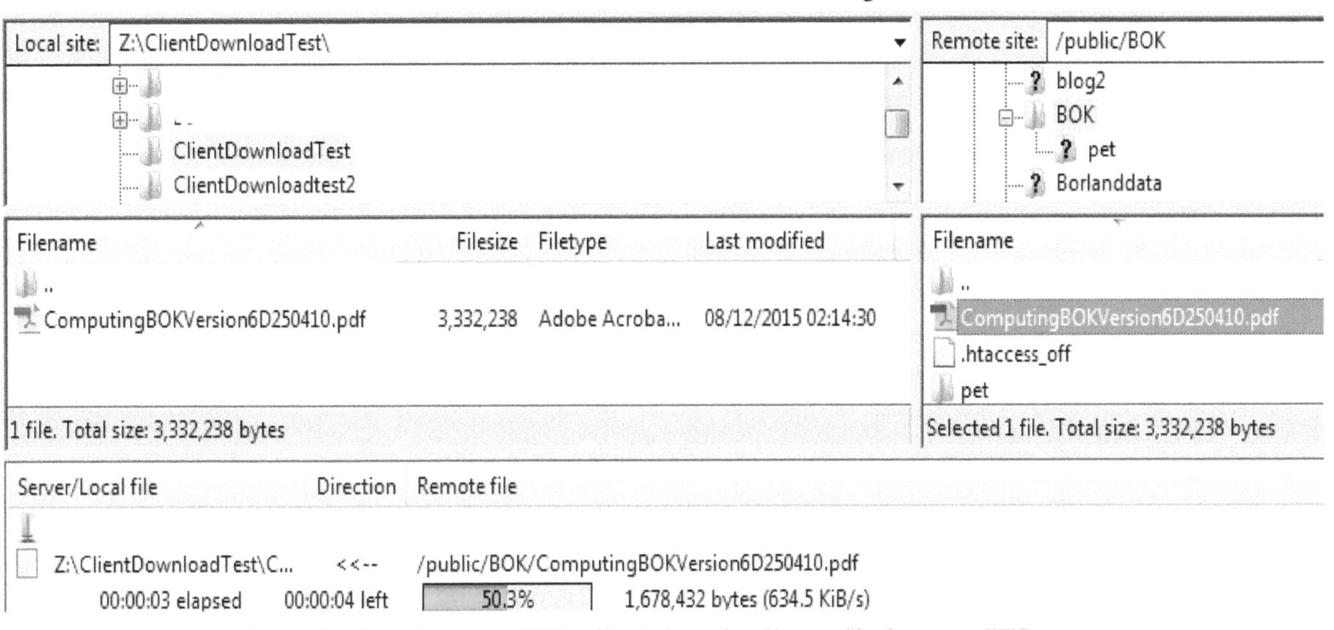

Figure 9.2.2.4 shows an FTP client downloading a file from an FTP server

Increasing the number of clients to twenty reduces the download rate because the server's upload rate of 5000 KiB/s is now shared by 20 clients. This means a maximum download rate of $5000/_{20}$ KiB/s per client = 250 KiB/s. This is less than the client's maximum of 500 KiB/s.

One solution is to add another server so that the demand from twenty clients is shared now between two servers. This should restore the download rate to 500 KiB/s assuming that each client is able to operate at a download speed of 500 KiB/s.

Peer-to-peer networking architecture

The client-server model works well for many applications. However, if many clients are downloading very large files from a server, then download speeds diminish unless more servers are added. It would be better if uploads could be shared amongst both servers and clients. This would lighten the load on servers and reduce the amount of server bandwidth that clients have to pay for. In fact, web hosting could be eliminated altogether. Client hosts not only download a file, but can upload what they have obtained to others as well. Client hosts are perfectly capable of doing both at the same time. They are then called peers rather than clients. *Figure 9.2.2.5* shows how separate parts of a file are uploaded to three peers which in turn upload what they have to their peers. Peer distribution can start whilst each peer is still downloading their part of the file from the server. The server doesn't have to be a dedicated server but can be another peer that happens to have the file that other peers want to download.

> **Key concept**
>
> **Peer-to-peer architecture:**
> In a peer-to-peer architecture, client hosts not only download a file, but can upload what they have obtained to others as well. Client hosts are capable of doing both at the same time. They are then called peers rather than clients.

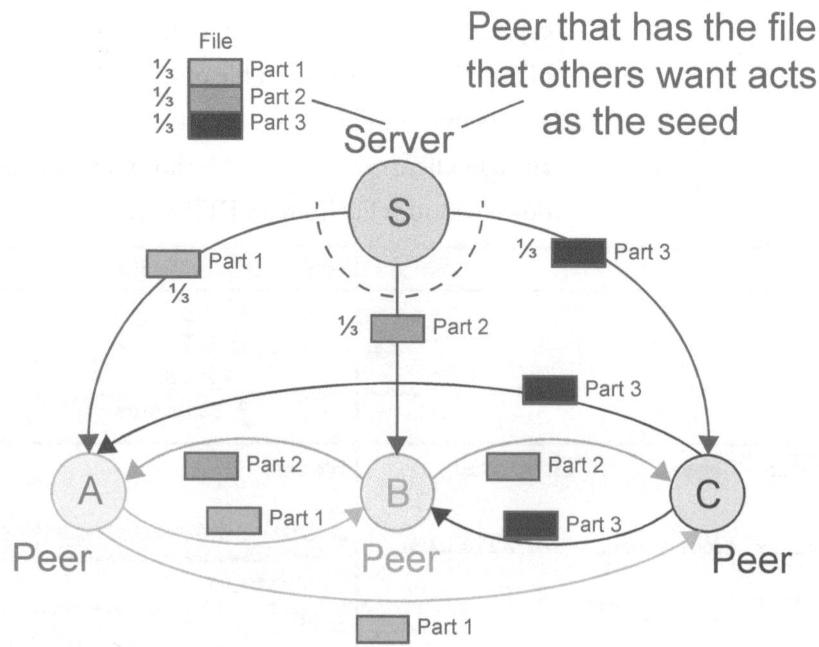

Figure 9.2.2.5 shows peers uploading and downloading files using FTP

BitTorrent came up with a protocol for distributing large files in this way. BitTorrent doesn't overload servers that provide the download since it relies on peers contributing upload capacity. The result is that large files can be received faster than would be the case in a client-server architecture where downloads rely on just a central server.

Decentralized P2P networks have several advantages over traditional client-server networks. P2P networks scale well because they don't rely on costly centralized resources. Scaling doesn't lead to a deterioration in download speed because P2P networks use the processing and networking power of the end-users' machines which grows in direct proportion to the network itself.

The costs associated with a large, centralized infrastructure are virtually eliminated because the processing power and bandwidth reside in the peers within the network.

Did you know?

Jaan Tallinn was one of the co-founders and authors of Skype. Read an interview with Jaan at http://affairstoday.co.uk/interview-jaan-tallinn-skype/

Investigation

1. Peer-to-peer (P2P) architecture became widely used and popularized by file-sharing applications such as Napster and Kazaa. Research the history of Napster and Kazaa.
2. Skype originally relied on a form of P2P architecture. Research the history of Skype and why its P2P supernodes were replaced with Linux boxes hosted by Microsoft.

Questions

5. Explain what is meant by peer-to-peer architecture and describe a situation where it is used?

In this chapter you have covered:

- peer-to-peer networking
- client-server networking
- situations where they might be used

9.2 Networking

Learning objectives:

- *Explain the purpose of WiFi*
- *Be familiar with the components required for wireless networking*
- *Be familiar with how wireless networks are secured*
- *Explain the wireless protocol Carrier Sensing Multiple Access with Collision Avoidance (CSMA/CA) with and without Request to Send/ Clear to Send (RTS/CTS)*
- *Be familiar with the purpose of Service Set Identifier (SSID)*

Key concept

WiFi LAN or WLAN:
A wireless local area network that is based on international standards laid down by the organisation known as the IEEE.
It is used to enable devices to connect to a local area network wirelessly.

Information

802.11 mobile and portable devices:
A requirement of the 802.11 standard is to handle mobile as well as portable wireless stations. A portable station is one that is moved from location to location, but that is only used while at a fixed location. Mobile stations actually access the LAN while in motion.

9.2.3 Wireless networking

The purpose of WiFi

WiFi was invented to provide a wireless connection between computing devices and to enable these devices to connect to the Internet via a bridge between a wireless LAN and a wired LAN known as an **access point**.

WiFi or Wi-Fi® is officially called IEEE 802.11, because of the naming scheme that the IEEE (Institute of Electrical and Electronic Engineers) uses to name their standards. The 802 part means a Local Area Network (LAN) as wireless is short-range, and the .11 part is for wireless.

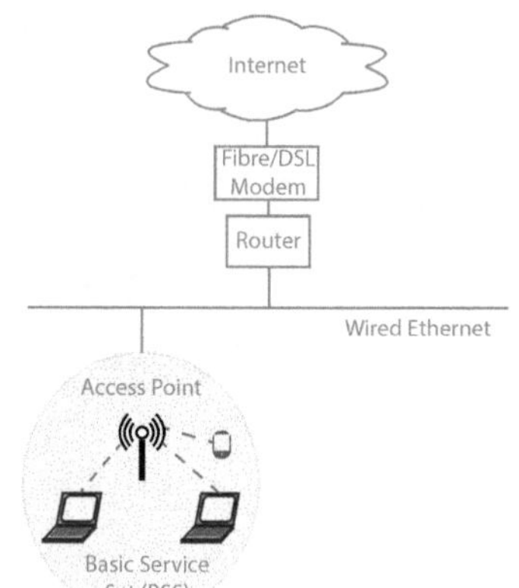

Figure 9.2.3.1 Wireless Access Point connection to Internet

Figure 9.2.3.1 shows WiFi providing wireless connections to computing devices such as laptops, tablets and smartphones that are close to an access point. The access point is also connected to a wired local area network (Ethernet) which in turn provides wired access to the Internet via a router and modem (Digital Subscriber Line (DSL) or optical fibre).

Wireless networking uses radio waves from the electromagnetic spectrum in two bands of frequencies centred around 2.4 and 5 GHz. Very importantly, these two bands of frequencies do not require licensing to use them unlike the mobile phone network spectrum which uses expensive licensed frequencies.

Table 9.2.3.1 shows the standards as they have evolved over the years from 802.11 to 802.11ac. Maximum speeds are very rarely achieved for reasons that will be given later.

802.11 Standard	Year	Frequency (GHz)	Maximum speed (Mbps)
-	1997	2.4	2
b	1999	2.4	11
a	1999	5	54
g	2003	2.4	54
n	2009	2.4 & 2.5	150
ac	2013	2.4 & 5	Typical 800 (theoretical1.3 Gbps)

Table 9.2.3.1 WiFi standards

Questions

1. What is the purpose of WiFi?

2. In a wired network, data travels between wired devices by electrical means. What is the equivalent means by which data travels in a wireless network?

Key concept

Frame/packet:
A frame or packet is a unit of transfer consisting of data, addresses and control information.

Components for wireless networking

Wireless networks typically consist of the following major physical components:

- Stations: computing devices with wireless network interfaces
- Access Points (APs): provide the wireless-to-wired bridging function in which wireless frames are converted to wired frames - usually Ethernet frames (a frame is a unit of transfer consisting of data, addresses and control information; sometimes called a packet); access points are also used to control access to a wireless network by authenticating users or devices that wish to join the network
- Wireless medium: to move frames from station to station, the 802.11 standard uses a wireless medium consisting of two frequency bands, 2.5 GHz and 5 GHz, each divided into channels
- Distributing system: used to connect several access points to form a large coverage area of the same LAN, e.g. a hotel with WiFi access in rooms. The APs are often connected by a wired Ethernet backbone.

Information

Wireless propagation characteristics:
Propagation characteristics are dynamic (not static) and unpredictable.

In WiFi, devices (stations) belong to what is called a Basic Service Set (BSS) which is simply a group of stations that communicate with each other wirelessly in an area (green shading) defined by the propagation characteristics of the wireless medium and called the basic service area (Figure 9.3.2.2).

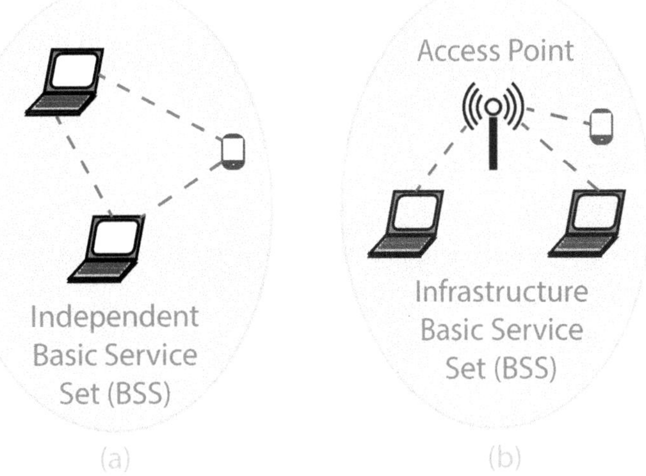

Figure 9.2.3.2 (a) independent BSS (b) infrastructure BSS

BSSs are of two types:

- Independent BSS: stations communicate with each other directly and therefore must be within direct communication range. Independent BSSs are used to create short-lived networks, e.g. for a meeting in a conference room. This type of BSS network is commonly known as an ad hoc network because of its limited duration, small size and focused purpose.
- Infrastructure BSS: infrastructure BSSs always use at least one access point and access points are used for all communications including communication between stations. Two hops are therefore used to send frames.

Information

BSSID address:
A BSSID address is used to identify a wireless LAN. Stations in the same area may be assigned to a Basic Service Set (BSS) to form a LAN. The LAN is then identified by its BSSID.
In infrastructure networks, the BSSID is the MAC address used by the wireless interface in the access point. It is a 48-bit identifier for the BSS.

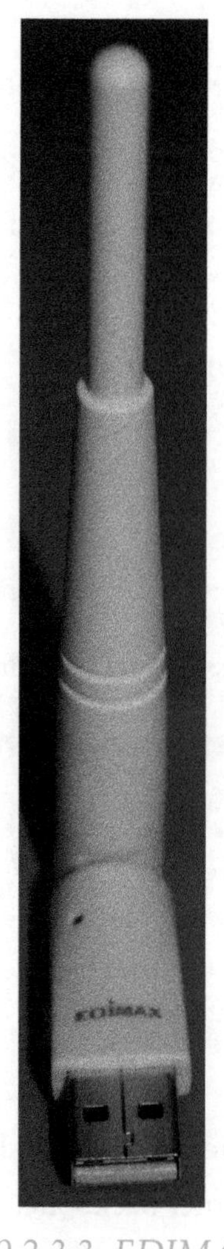

Figure 9.2.3.3 EDIMAX® USB port wireless adapter 802.11b/g

The originating station transfers the frame to the access point (first hop) which then relays it to the destination station (second hop). This lifts the restriction that stations must be in range of each other. They only have to be in range of an access point belonging to the BSS. Secondly, access points can buffer frames so that stations which are battery-powered can be powered down until they need to transmit and receive frames, e.g. wireless sensors.

The stations must have the capability to send and receive over a WiFi connection. Figure 9.2.3.3 shows an EDIMAX® **wireless network adapter** that plugs into a USB port of a computer. This particular adapter has MAC address 001F1FCD5D7A.

All adapters, wireless or wired have a unique MAC address so that they can be identified.

The tall slim tubular structure is its antenna through which it radiates and receives radio waves on specific frequencies designated by the IEEE.

A wireless network adapter is also known as a **wireless interface**.

Desktop computers can have a wireless network adapter installed on their motherboard in a PCI slot and tablets and smartphones use a built-in wireless network adapter.

Within each BSS, stations communicate directly with an **Access Point (AP)**, similar to a mobile phone network base station. The Access Point acts as a bridge between a wireless and a wired local area network. When a device searches for WiFi connectivity, it sends messages to discover which APs are in its transmission range.

This results in a list of names such as shown in Figure 9.3.2.4: *educational-computing* and *Kevin Bond's Guest Network*. These are user-friendly names, commonly known as **Service Set Identifiers / Identities (SSIDs)**, used to identify a service set to users of the wireless network.

The user-friendly name, or SSID, maps to the BSSID which is the MAC address equivalent. It is the BSSID that is sent in wireless frames to identify the access point.

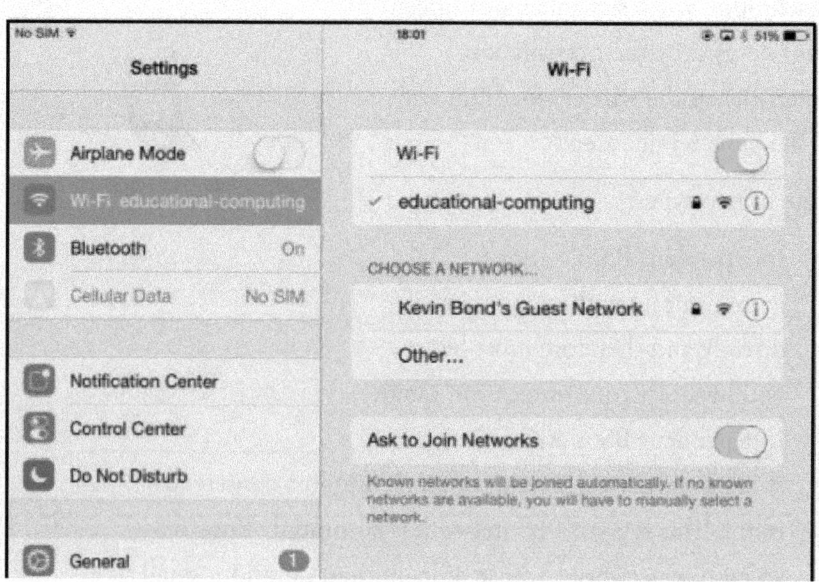

Figure 9.2.3.4 IPad WiFi settings screen showing two APs

Key concept

SSID:
A user-friendly network name, e.g. *educational-computing*, commonly known as a Service Set Identity/Identifier/ Identification (SSID). It is used to identify a **Basic Service Set (LAN)** to users of a wireless network.

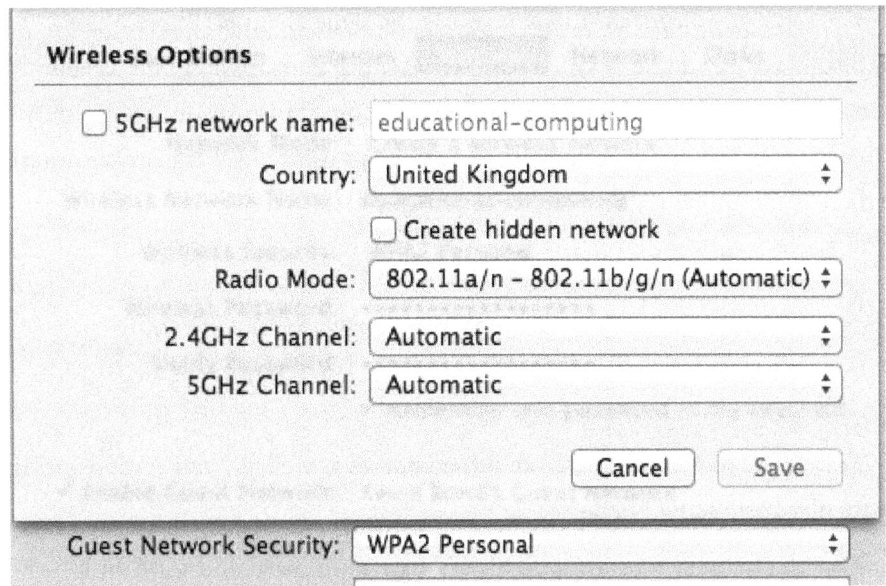

Figure 9.2.3.5 Wireless radio frequency options for wireless network with SSID educational-computing

Information

Beacon frames:
In an infrastructure network, the access point is responsible for transmitting beacon frames at regular intervals. Wireless stations in range receive these beacon frames and use them to find and identify a network. The reception area for beacon frames defines the basic service area. All communication in an infrastructure network is done through an access point, so stations on the network must be close enough to the access point to receive beacon frames.

Figure 9.2.3.5 shows the settings for an AP with SSID *educational-computing*. The AP automatically chooses either 2.4 GHz or 5 GHz depending on which currently provides the better transmission, and then within the chosen band a particular channel[1].

Questions

3. Name and describe **four** major physical components that may be found in a wireless network.

4. What is the purpose of an SSID?

Carrier Sense Multiple Access with Collision Avoidance (CSMA/CA)

Channel selection

Each access point (AP) operates on a given frequency channel, e.g. channel 36. Both the 2.4 GHz and the 5 GHz frequency bands are divided into a number of such channels, each with a predetermined width. *Figure 9.2.3.6* shows that the channels for the 5 GHz band are 20 MHz wide. For example, channel 36 is centred on the frequency 5180 GHz and it covers the range 5170 to 5190 GHz.

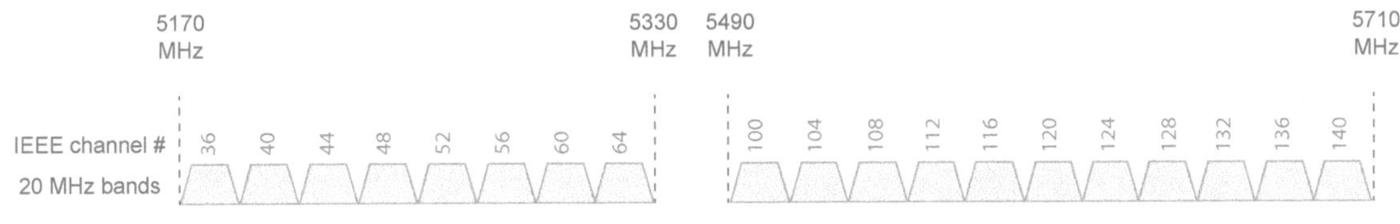

Figure 9.2.3.6 Operating channel bands and frequencies for 5 GHz wireless transmission in Europe

In order for a station to communicate with its access point, it selects the channel that its AP is using. This means that all the stations in the same basic

1 Explained in the next section.

service set, e.g. *educational-computing*, use the same channel. Therein lies a problem, as more stations join a basic service, the transmission rate usually goes down which is one reason why the maximum transmission rate is rarely achieved. The AP will actually tell the stations to use a lower transmission rate if there is too much traffic from too many devices.

Did you know?

The late Steve Jobs, former CEO of Apple had difficulty connecting via WiFi at the conference in 2010 that launched the iPhone 4 smartphone. Too many people in the auditorium were already using the WiFi channel Steve needed for his demonstration. Steve had to ask all the delegates to disconnect their WiFi to enable him to connect.

Questions

5 What is meant by channel selection in wireless networking?

Interference

WiFi is prone to interference from other sources as well as from stations using a particular basic service because

- the frequency bands used by WiFi are unlicensed and so WiFi is not the sole user of the spectrum. The spectrum is used by lots of other equipment over which the basic service set has no control, e.g. microwave ovens used to heat and cook food in the kitchen
- its maximum transmit power is restricted to a very low level because it is unlicensed
- it is typically used indoors where there are lots of objects to block the signal or reflect and echo a transmitted signal into the path of another

Noise

The circuits used in WiFi generate unwanted electrical noise (random electrical fluctuations) which can mask signals of too low power.

Collisions

When two stations, A and B are transmitting at similar times their frames will collide if they are within interference range of each other which is the case when they both use the same access point (*Figure 9.2.3.7*). The outcome is determined by the signal-to-interference + noise ratio (SINR) of each.

Figure 9.2.3.8 shows the overlap of two frames one from A and one from B. The greater the overlap with another frame, the higher the chance that neither frame will be properly decoded at the receiver.

Information

Signal to Interference + Noise Ratio (SINR):

Radio wave communication relies on differentiating a signal from background noise and interference. If the signal power level falls below the noise + interference power level, it becomes more difficult to extract the signal. The ratio of signal power level to noise + interference power level is a measure of how easy or difficult it is to extract a signal

$$\text{SINR} = \frac{\text{Signal power}}{\text{Interference + Noise power}}$$

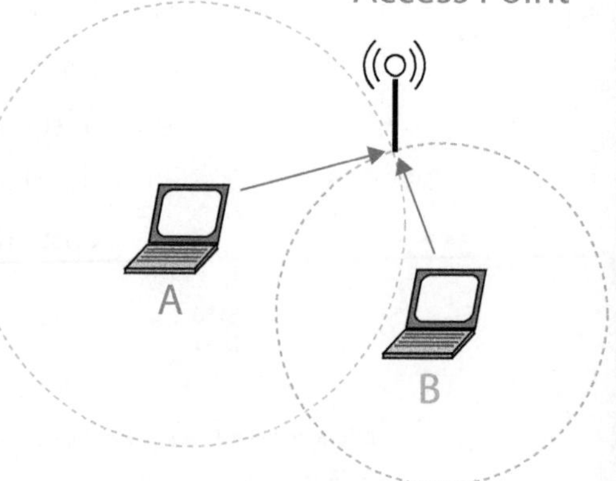

Figure 9.2.3.7 shows the energy of two frames spreading through the air and crossing at the access point

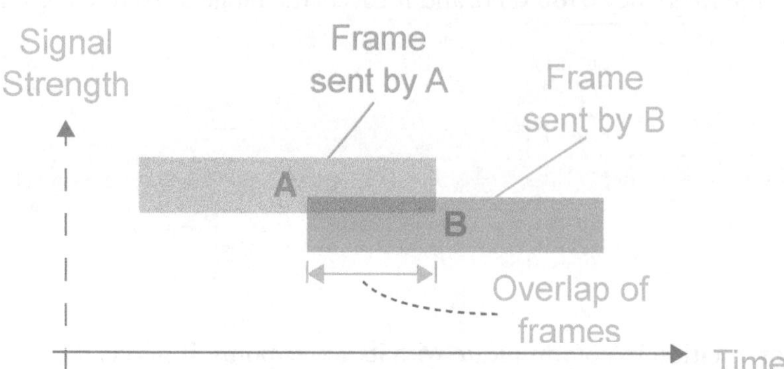

Figure 9.2.3.8 Two frames overlapping in time. A is a stronger signal than B

Questions

6. What is meant by a collision in wireless networking?

Key concept

Collision:
A collision occurs when two transmitters are within interference range of each other, and they send at similar times. What actually collides are frames, one from each transmitter. The result is that neither frame will be properly decoded at the receiver. A frame is a unit of digital data transmission.

Collision avoidance

The approach in wireless networking to this problem is to try to avoid collisions in the first place by requiring WiFi-enabled devices to be aware of whether other devices are currently transmitting, i.e. sensing other device's transmissions. A device can transmit only if others are not. It is a bit like a crossroads controlled by Give Way signs. You can proceed across the crossroads as long as you can see that your intended path is clear of other traffic (Figure 9.2.3.9). If two road users arrive at the crossroads at the same time, each can sense that it is not safe for both to proceed if it will result in crossing each other's path. Instead, each delays their movement until they can interpret what the other's intentions are. The delay is a random amount of time whilst some form of mutual coordination for a safe crossing is achieved.

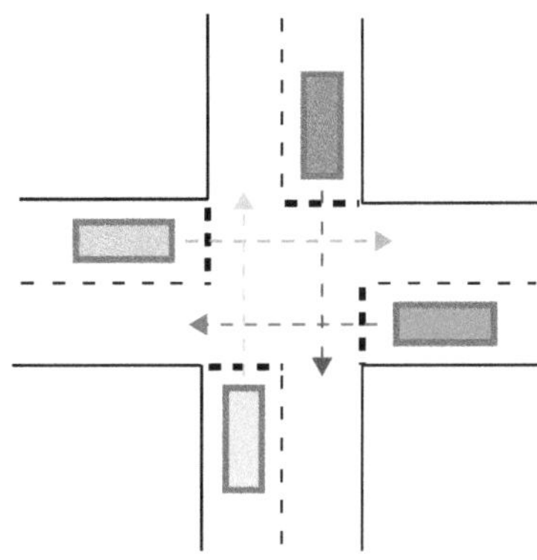

Figure 9.2.3.9 Crossroads

Multiple access

The WiFi channel through which the WiFi signals travel is a shared medium, shared between devices on this channel, e.g. channel 36. For this reason, we say it is multi-access or a multiple access medium. Access must be coordinated and controlled.

Carrier Sense Multiple Access/Collision Avoidance (CSMA/CA) explained

The CSMA/CA protocol was designed to allow a station to send as long as no other station is sending. It is called Carrier Sense Multiple Access (CSMA) because each station tries to sense the presence of others on the shared medium. It is called Collision Avoidance (CA) because each station tries to avoid a collision by not sending when another station is sending.

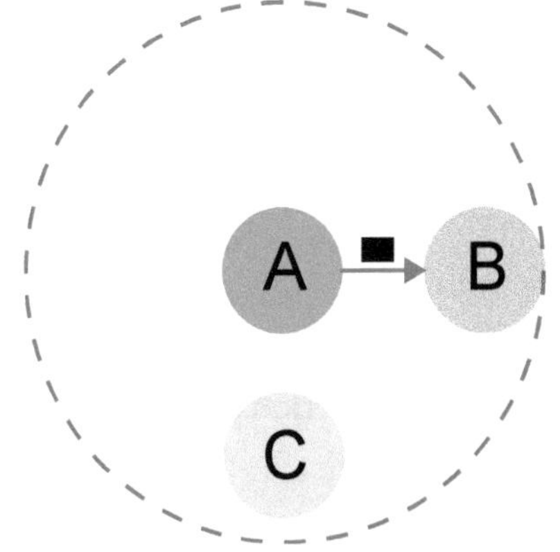

Figure 9.2.3.10 Station A transmitting to station B but with the transmission also reaching station C

Figure 9.2.3.10 shows station A transmitting a frame to station B. The dotted red circle with A at its centre shows the reach of A's transmission. Station C is within this reach and so is able to sense that A is currently transmitting. If station C was also transmitting at the same time to, say a station D, but with enough signal strength to also reach station B, then B might not be able to decode the transmission from A because both transmissions interfere with each other in the receiver B's electronics.

The CSMA/CA protocol requires that the receiving station, for whom the transmission is intended, sends back an acknowledgement (ACK) signal to the sending station on successfully receiving and decoding the transmission (Figure 9.2.3.11). This is how the sending station knows that its transmission got through. If an acknowledgement is not received then the sending station will know that a collision has occurred and its transmission did not get through.

The situation shown in *Figure 9.2.3.12* can arise when two stations, A and C that wish to transmit cannot detect the transmissions of each other because they are not within each other's wireless reach. Station A may start transmitting but the out-of-range C cannot sense this and so starts transmitting as well. C's transmission to D reaches B at about the same time that A's does. A collision arises at B between A's transmission and C's which results in neither transmission being decoded by B. B will therefore not send an ACK to A. The use of an acknowledgement signal enables stations to detect a collision and to take remedial action which consists of sending the frame again after a delay of an appropriate amount of time.

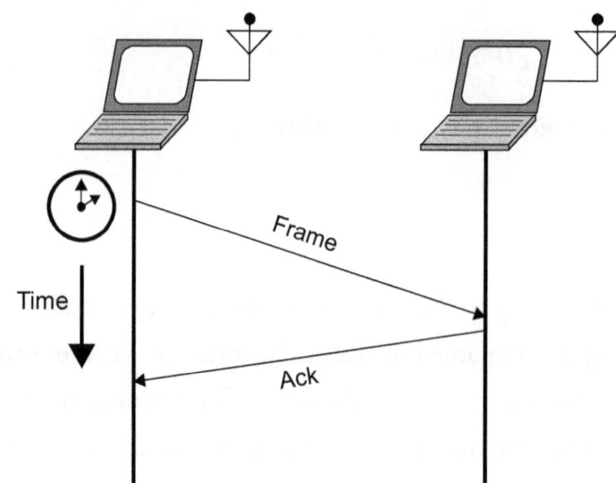

Figure 9.2.3.11 Timing for the sending of a frame, its processing at the receiver, and the sending of an acknowledgement signal to the sender

Key point

Acknowledgement (ACK):

The ACK signal is the only mechanism of indicating that a transmission was successful.

If an acknowledgement doesn't arrive, the sender is to conclude that the transmission is lost followed by the re-sending of the frame.

Error recovery is thus the responsibility of the sending station.

We have simplified the scenario to make a point. In an infrastructure BSS where everything goes through an access point, B could be an access point shared by A, C and D. A may in fact be sending to C via B and C could be sending, via B, to D.

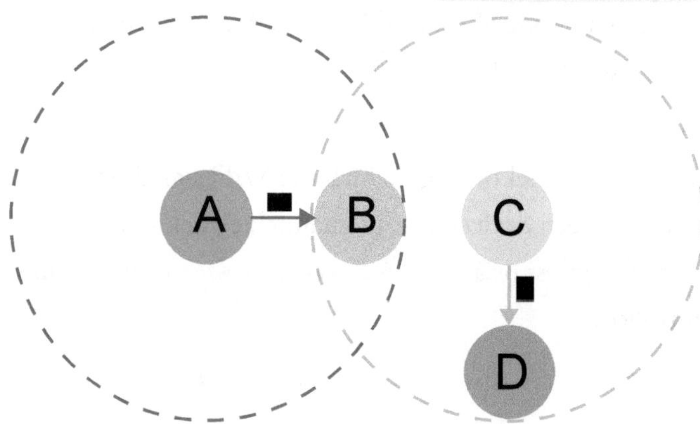

Figure 9.2.3.12 Station A transmitting to station B and station C transmitting to D at a similar time with neither A nor C able to sense the other

Before sending, a station has to observe a wait and listen period. If during this period the station does not detect any transmissions, it can start transmitting at the end of the period as shown for station A in *Figure 9.2.3.13*.

If a station that wants to send senses that the channel is busy at any time during the wait and listen period, then the station does not transmit. C starts its *wait & listen* period just after A's. It senses during this period that A starts sending. It waits a frame + ACK + a little bit more before starting another *wait & listen* period.

It is still possible that a collision can occur even though a sending station

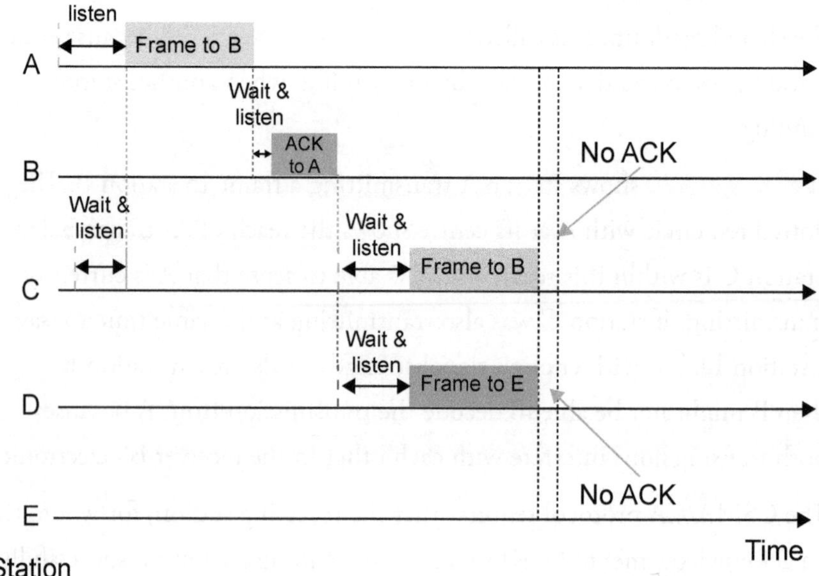

Figure 9.2.3.13 Shows the timing for the sending of frames by A C, D and an ACK from B to A, a collision occurs between frames from C and D which is detected by both not receiving the corresponding ACK

waited and found the channel idle before sending. Another station might have begun sending at the same time because it began its waiting period at the same time and also concluded that the channel was idle. This is shown in Figure 9.2.3.14 where both C and D start sending at the same time and cause a collision. However, neither receives an acknowledgement signal within the expected window of time and so both conclude that an error has occurred.

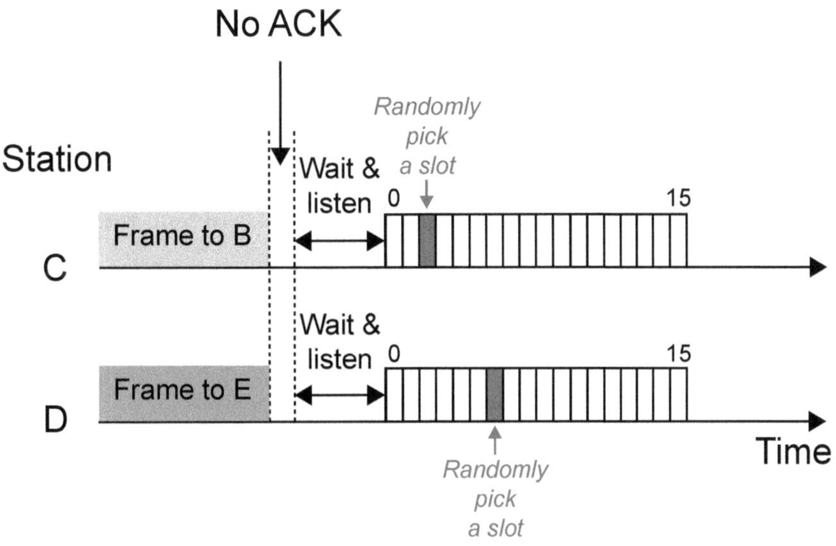

Figure 9.2.3.14 Shows stations C and D in addition to a wait & listen period backing off a randomly determined number of time slots between 0 and 15 after concluding by receiving no ACK that that a collision has occurred

If both resend at the same time the same result ensues.

The solution in this circumstance is for stations C and D to employ a contention window of say size 15. Such a window is divided into 15 equal-sized time slots. Stations C and D then each choose one of the time slots at random, e.g. C might choose slot 3 and D slot 7 (there remains a small chance that they could choose the same slot). C will now listen for the wait & listen period + 3 time slots; D will now listen for the wait & listen period + 7 time slots. If one or the other finds the channel idle after its wait then each can send.

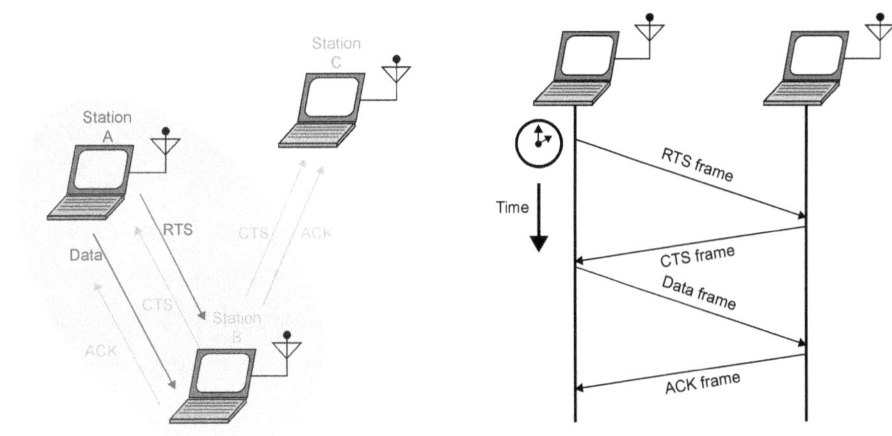

Figure 9.2.3.15 Using RTS and CTS to reserve channel for one station to send to another collision-free

To prevent collisions 802.11 allows a station to use Request To Send (RTS) and Clear To Send(CTS) signals to obtain exclusive use of the channel for sending. This is necessary if many collisions are occurring such as when there are many hidden stations. Too many collisions reduces transmission speed. The sending station sends an RTS frame to the target station. The target station responds by transmitting a CTS frame. The sending station now sends the data frame to the target. The target responds by returning an ACK frame.

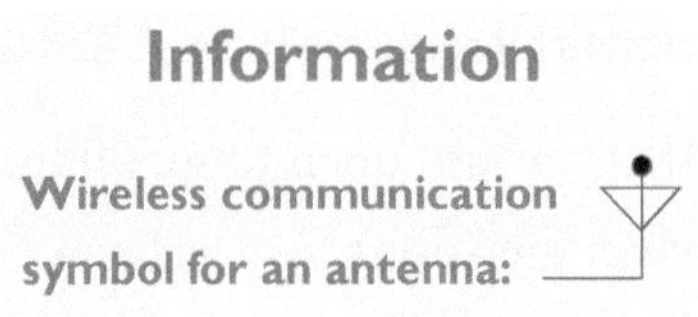

Figure 9.2.3.15 shows the RTS frame, CTS frame, data frame and ACK frame forming a single atomic transaction between sending and receiving stations.

If the target station receives an RTS it responds with a CTS.

The RTS silences stations within its range and the CTS silences stations within its range. In this way collisions that result from the hidden station problem shown in *Figure 9.2.3.12* are avoided.

In *Figure 9.2.3.15* station A is able to reach station B but not station C whilst station B is able to reach both. Station A sends an RTS to station B, B responds with a CTS which reaches both A and C. C now avoids sending until it receives an indication that the transaction between A and B is over. This is the ACK signal. Meanwhile A receives the CTS signal and proceeds to send the data frame. A finishes sending and then waits for the ACK signal from B.

Questions

7 What is meant by multiple access in wireless networking?

8 Explain the CSMA/CA protocol used in wireless networking.

9 What is the hidden node problem in wireless networking?

10 What is the purpose of RTS and CTS in CSMA/CA wireless networking?

11 RTS and CTS add extra time to a data transmission between two stations. Under what circumstance would they be used?

Securing wireless networks

WPA/WPA2

Wi-Fi Protected Access (WPA) and Wi-Fi Protected Access II (WPA2) are two security protocols developed by the Wi-Fi Alliance to secure wireless computer networks. WPA was a backwards-compatible temporary measure adopted before WPA2's development was complete. WPA/WPA2 replaced WEP which is easily broken because it is a stream cipher which exclusive-ORs the data stream with a fixed key stream (see RC4 *Chapter 5.6.10*).

User's data sent between two devices, e.g. a wireless station and an access point needs to be private to those two devices, i.e. kept confidential by securing against unauthorised access. Unfortunately, radio transmissions over a wireless network are easily intercepted and read by third parties unless encrypted.

They are also open to spoofing, i.e. purporting to originate from a genuine user when they don't. Message authentication lets communicating partners who share a secret key verify that a received message originates with the party who claims to have sent it.

Messages can also be easily intercepted and altered in transit by a third party. Message integrity checks allow such alterations to be detected.

Key concept

Security:
Security means protecting against unauthorised access, alteration or deletion.

Key concept

Authentication:
Proving that the user is who they say they are.

Key principle

Access control WPA/WPA2:
To join a WPA/WPA2-secured personal wireless network, a user (client) has to successfully negotiate an authentication stage which checks that the client knows a pre-shared secret key (PSK).

Key principle

Pre-shared secret key (PSK):
In WPA/WPA2 personal, the access point and stations that are allowed to join the wireless network share a secret key called the Pairwise Master Key (PMK). This is a 256-bit key (32 bytes).

Key principle

Generating the PMK:
In WPA/WPA2 personal, the 256-bit Pairwise Master Key (PMK) is generated from a passphrase/password known to the user and the SSID. The passphrase is a plaintext string.

Access control and authentication

To join a WPA/WPA2-secured personal wireless network, a user (client) has to successfully negotiate an authentication stage which checks that the client knows a pre-shared secret key (PSK). This checking is based on a message authentication code (Message Integrity and Authentication Code or MIAC, abbreviated further to MIC) generated from the pre-shared secret key. The checking is done at the access point. The access point is responsible for controlling access to the wireless network.

Pre-shared secret key

In WPA/WPA2 personal, the access point and stations that are allowed to join the wireless network share a secret key called the Pairwise Master Key (PMK). This is a 256-bit key (32 bytes). Fortunately, users/clients don't have to remember this key. Instead, clients share a passphrase/password consisting of up to 133 ASCII characters which is set up on the access point for a specific SSID. The PMK is generated by combining the SSID and this passphrase. To join a known SSID network, a user enters the passphrase for this specific SSID at their wireless station. The wireless station now has everything it needs to calculate its own copy of the PMK for this SSID network. For example, if the passphrase/password is LetMeIn and the SSID is MyWirelessNetwork then the generated PMK could be c4f9 400d 1cc7 cc3c 6b68 5b12 13a8 20dc

Pairwise Transient Key (PTK)

The PMK is never transmitted to avoid an unauthorised third party obtaining a copy.

How is it possible then for both access point and station to demonstrate that they possess the same pairwise master key (PMK) without sending each their copy of the PMK?

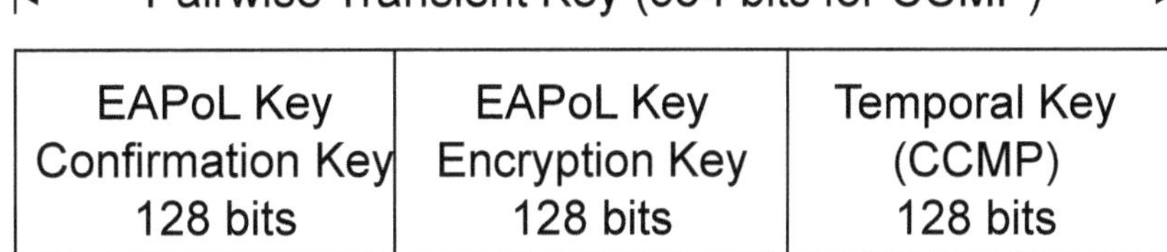

Figure 9.2.3.16 Pairwise Transient Key for Counter Mode with CBC-MAC Protocol (CCMP)

The solution is for both wireless station and access point to use a Pairwise Transient Key (PTK) derived from the PMK and to demonstrate to each other knowledge of this PTK.

Extension material beyond AS level

Knowledge is demonstrated using the Key Confirmation Key to produce a message authentication code which the station sends to the access point. If more than one wireless station has joined the network then each station-access point pairing will have its own PTK.

The Pairwise Transient Key is a collection of other keys as shown in Figure 9.2.3.16:

- Key Confirmation Key (KCK) – used to prove possession of the PMK
- Key Encryption Key (KEK) – used to encrypt the Group Transient Key (GTK)
- Temporal Key (TK) – used to secure data traffic once connection is established
- The PTK temporal key is used to secure unicast (communication between a single sender and a single receiver over a network) data transmissions.

The Group Transient Key is used to secure multicast/broadcast transmissions.

The pairwise transient key CCMP uses CCM, a provably secure cipher based on an AES block encryption algorithm.

The particular algorithm used by the transmissions shown in Figures 9.2.3.17-21 is the 128-bit AES block cipher one, a very secure cipher.

Questions

12 What are WPA and WPA2?

13 State and explain **three** reasons why wireless networks need to be secured.

Information (This material is not required for AS level)

Four-way handshake

Communications begin with an unauthenticated supplicant (client device, e.g. station 1) attempting to connect with an authenticator (802.11 access point). The client sends an Extensible Authentication Protocol (EAP)-start message. This begins a series of message exchanges called a **four-way handshake** to authenticate the client. *Figure 9.2.3.17* shows a simplified version of this exchange.

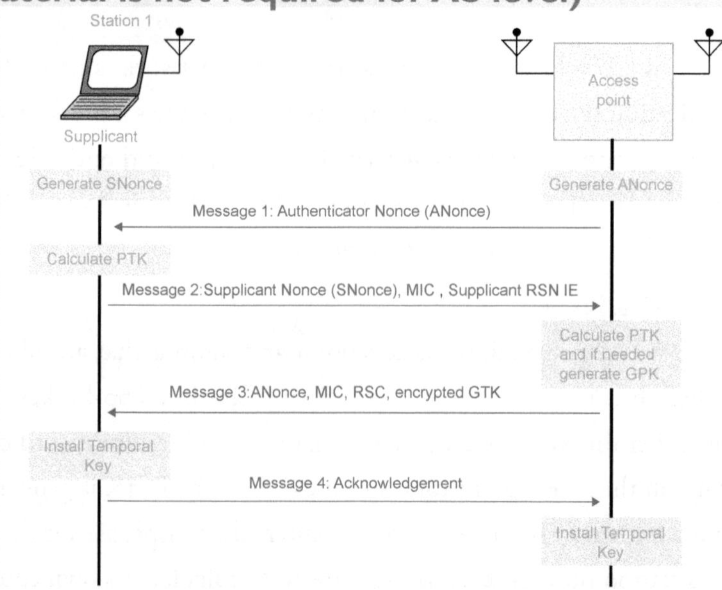

Figure 9.2.3.17 The Pairwise Transient Key (PTK) is computed at the station and the access point it is connecting to so that each has a copy

Message 1:

The authenticator sends an unencrypted message to the supplicant which contains the authenticator-generated random number ANonce (*Figure 9.2.3.18*).

Nonces are random numbers which are used once (**N**umber **ONCE**).

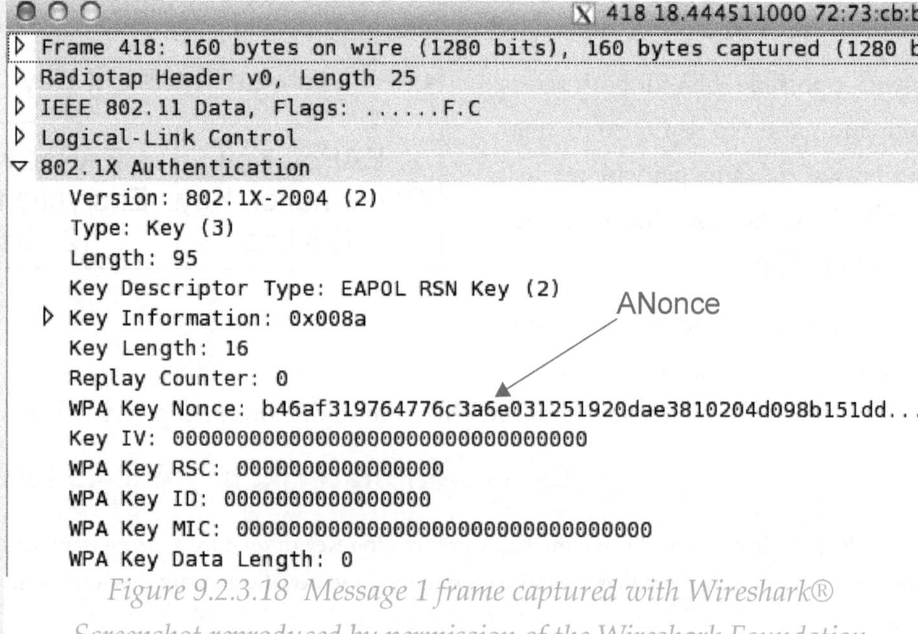

```
418 18.444511000 72:73:cb:b7
▷ Frame 418: 160 bytes on wire (1280 bits), 160 bytes captured (1280 bi
▷ Radiotap Header v0, Length 25
▷ IEEE 802.11 Data, Flags: ......F.C
▷ Logical-Link Control
▽ 802.1X Authentication
    Version: 802.1X-2004 (2)
    Type: Key (3)
    Length: 95
    Key Descriptor Type: EAPOL RSN Key (2)
  ▷ Key Information: 0x008a
    Key Length: 16
    Replay Counter: 0
    WPA Key Nonce: b46af319764776c3a6e031251920dae3810204d098b151dd...
    Key IV: 00000000000000000000000000000000
    WPA Key RSC: 0000000000000000
    WPA Key ID: 0000000000000000
    WPA Key MIC: 00000000000000000000000000000000
    WPA Key Data Length: 0
```


Figure 9.2.3.18 Message 1 frame captured with Wireshark®

Message 2:

The supplicant knows its own PMK, the value of ANonce sent to it, its own MAC address, the supplicant's MAC address and its own nonce, SNonce which it generates.

It now has all it needs to generate its copy of the pairwise transient key (PTK) - see *Figure 9.2.3.21*. It responds to the authenticator by sending its SNonce in unencrypted form across the channel (*Figure 9.2.3.19*). The authenticator now has all it needs to calculate its copy of the PTK.

```
424 18.449397000 Apple_e8:e3:09 72:7:
▷ Frame 424: 180 bytes on wire (1440 bits), 180 bytes captured (1440 bits) on
▷ Radiotap Header v0, Length 25
▷ IEEE 802.11 QoS Data, Flags: .......T
▷ Logical-Link Control
▽ 802.1X Authentication
    Version: 802.1X-2001 (1)
    Type: Key (3)
    Length: 117
    Key Descriptor Type: EAPOL RSN Key (2)
  ▷ Key Information: 0x010a
    Key Length: 0
    Replay Counter: 0
    WPA Key Nonce: ff41683c4814e9322014da33e5fc60b04c9d1858e803bbe7...
    Key IV: 00000000000000000000000000000000
    WPA Key RSC: 0000000000000000
    WPA Key ID: 0000000000000000
    WPA Key MIC: 57673428683c62ad358d58dc0095c133
    WPA Key Data Length: 22
  ▷ WPA Key Data: 30140100000fac040100000fac040100000fac020000
```

SNonce

Message Authentication & Integrity Code (MIC) generated using the KCK key from PTK

Supplicant RSN Information Elements (IE)

Figure 9.2.3.19 Message 2 frame captured with Wireshark

Information

Message 2 includes a MIC. This is a message digest that has used the EAPoL Key Confirmation Key (KCK) from the supplicant's copy of the PTK. The authenticator now uses its copy of KCK and the received message to calculate the corresponding MIC. The two MICs, one received and the other calculated, are compared.

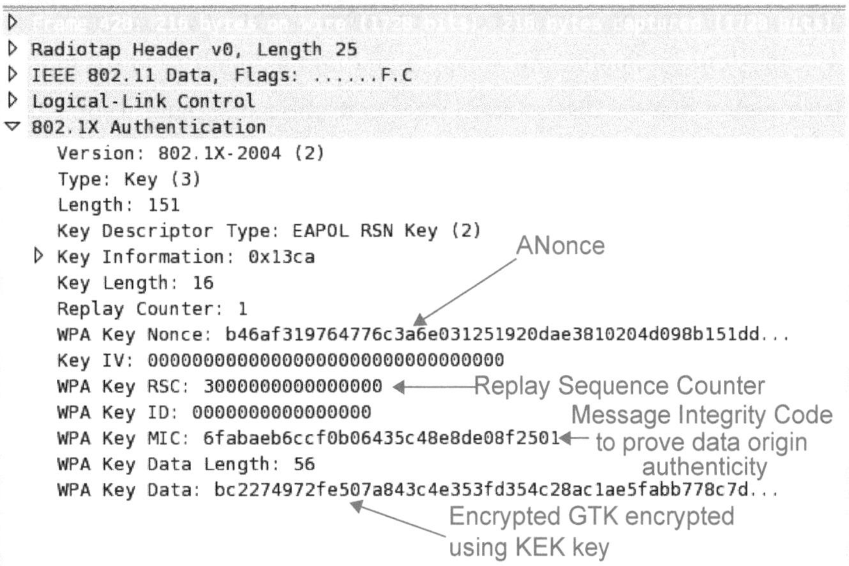
Radiotap Header v0, Length 25
IEEE 802.11 Data, Flags: ......F.C
Logical-Link Control
802.1X Authentication
Version: 802.1X-2004 (2)
Type: Key (3)
Length: 151
Key Descriptor Type: EAPOL RSN Key (2)
Key Information: 0x13ca
Key Length: 16
Replay Counter: 1
WPA Key Nonce: b46af319764776c3a6e031251920dae3810204d098b151dd...
Key IV: 00000000000000000000000000000000
WPA Key RSC: 3000000000000000
WPA Key ID: 0000000000000000
WPA Key MIC: 6fabaeb6ccf0b06435c48e8de08f2501
WPA Key Data Length: 56
WPA Key Data: bc2274972fe507a843c4e353fd354c28ac1ae5fabb778c7d...
ANonce
Replay Sequence Counter
Message Integrity Code to prove data origin authenticity
Encrypted GTK encrypted using KEK key

Figure 9.2.3.20 Message 3 frame captured with Wireshark

Message 3:

If the MICs agree, the authenticator sends an acknowledgment message to the supplicant confirming that it has been authenticated and is now allowed to join the network and to install the PTK data encryption key (*Figure 9.2.3.20*). The authenticator awaits confirmation from the supplicant that it has installed the data encryption key (temporal key) before it installs its copy. The same GTK is used for all stations.

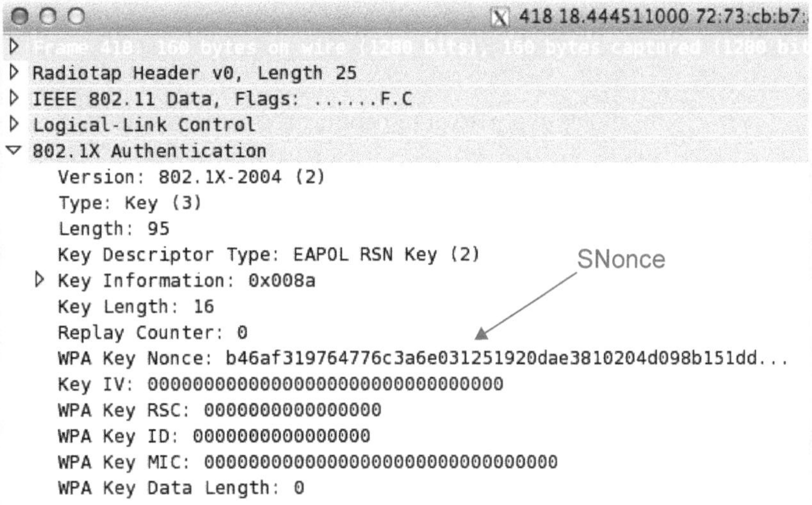
418 18.444511000 72:73:cb:b7:
Frame 418: 160 bytes on wire (1280 bits), 160 bytes captured (1280 bi
Radiotap Header v0, Length 25
IEEE 802.11 Data, Flags: ......F.C
Logical-Link Control
802.1X Authentication
Version: 802.1X-2004 (2)
Type: Key (3)
Length: 95
Key Descriptor Type: EAPOL RSN Key (2)
Key Information: 0x008a
Key Length: 16
Replay Counter: 0
WPA Key Nonce: b46af319764776c3a6e031251920dae3810204d098b151dd...
Key IV: 00000000000000000000000000000000
WPA Key RSC: 0000000000000000
WPA Key ID: 0000000000000000
WPA Key MIC: 00000000000000000000000000000000
WPA Key Data Length: 0
SNonce

Figure 9.2.3.21 Message 4 frame captured with Wireshark

Message 4:

The supplicant responds with an acknowledgement message (*Figure 9.2.3.21*) confirming to the authenticator that it has installed the temporal key (data encryption key) that should be used from now on to encrypt data transmissions as well as to generate the MIC to protect the integrity of the data as well as authenticate its origin. The authenticator now installs its copy of the temporal key.

Task

1. Download and install Wireshark from www.wireshark.org on a computer with a wireless interface. In Wireshark, select the wireless interface and enable monitor mode. Start capturing wireless frames whilst at the same time connecting to a wireless network access point. Stop the capture once you are connected. Set the filter in the main window filter to EAPoL so that you can see four messages similar to those above. Expand the Authentication part of the frame and examine messages 1 to 4 in turn as above. What you will see will depend on the wireless protocol that you have chosen and the cipher suite supported by your wireless interface. Clear the EAPoL filter and search for Beacon, Probe Request and Probe Response frames.

Extension material (Beyond AS level)

Figure 9.2.3.22 shows a block diagram of the computation of the PTK.

A random number generator at the access point generates the first nonce (ANonce) and another random number generator at the station generates the second Nonce (SNonce). ANonce is short for Authenticator Nonce and SNonce is short for Supplicant Nonce. A new and different ANonce and a new and different SNonce are generated when a station that has disassociated itself from the access point reconnects. This means that a new and different PTK is generated.

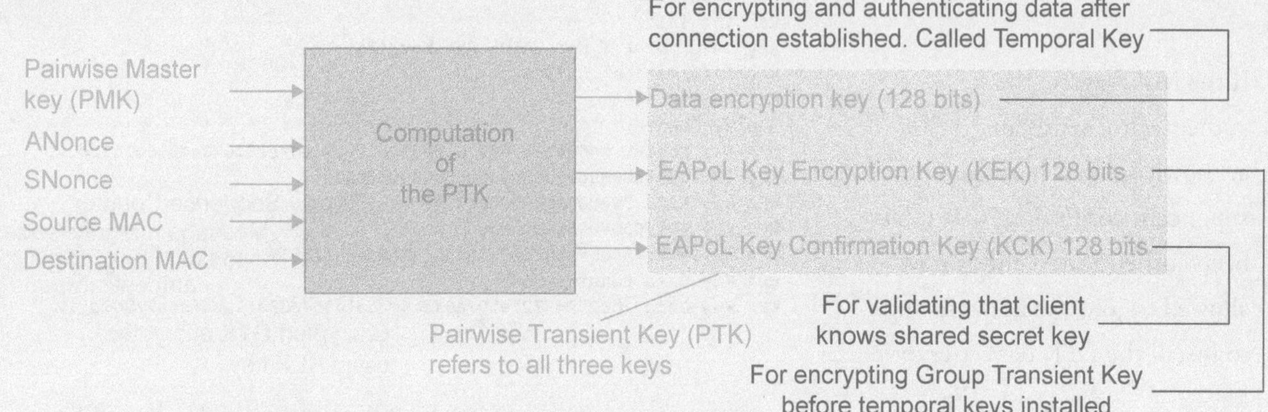

Figure 9.2.3.22 Computing the Pairwise Transient Key (PTK) takes place at the station and the access point it is connecting to so they both have a copy. EAPoL is Extensible Authentication Protocol over LAN

Figure 9.2.3.23 shows two networked connected stations each with a different paired temporal key (data encryption and MIC key).

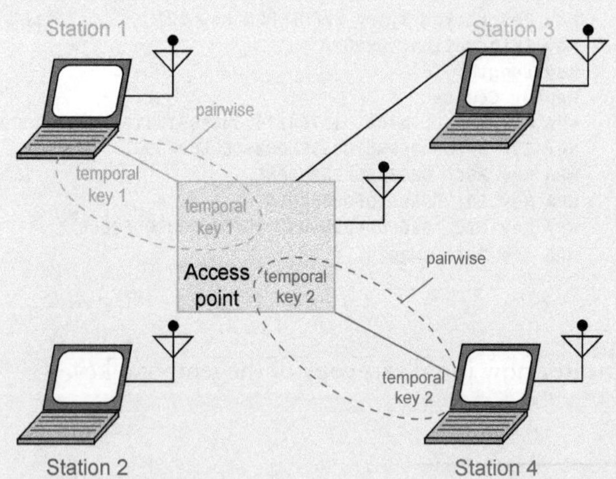

Figure 9.2.3.23 Station 1 and the access point are connected with a pair of keys, temporal key 1; station 4 and the access point are connected with a different pair of keys, temporal key 2.

Questions

14 Why is relying on PMK, source and destination addresses alone as input to the PTK computation not as secure as the method which includes two nonces?

Information

Man-in-the middle attack:
In cryptography and computer security, a man-in-the-middle attack is an attack where the attacker secretly relays and possibly alters the communication between two parties who believe they are directly communicating with each other.

Information

Replay attack:
In network security, a replay attack is a form of network attack in which a valid data transmission is maliciously or fraudulently repeated or delayed.
One way that replay attacks are defeated is to use the sequence number of packets. If stations and access points record the highest received sequence number then they can reject packets with lower sequence numbers which occur with replayed packets.

Key principle

Media Access Control (MAC) address white list filtering:
In MAC address white list filtering, the access point has an internal table of MAC addresses which it consults to decide whether to permit access to the network or not.

Key principle

SSID broadcast disabled protection:
Wireless stations require a knowledge of the SSID in order to join the network. If broadcast, the SSID appears in the network settings window of stations within range.
In this form of protection, an access point disables broadcasting its SSID to wireless stations. Thus, only clients who already know the pre-configured SSID can establish a connection, others will not be able to (without a bit of extra effort).

Media Access Control (MAC) address white list filtering

A wireless network could not use any form of encryption for its packets but instead rely on filtering of packets. MAC address white list filtering is one such form of filtering. MAC addresses are 48-bit addresses uniquely assigned to each wireless network interface card. In MAC address white list filtering, the access point has an internal table of MAC addresses which it consults to decide whether to permit access to the network or not. If the supplicant's MAC address is on this list then it may join the wireless network controlled by this access point. If its MAC address is not on the list then the access point will reject any attempt that the supplicant makes to join the network. Whilst MAC address white list filtering gives a wireless network some additional protection, MAC filtering can be defeated by a spoofer who learns the MAC address of a valid wireless network interface card, i.e. one on the white list, by scanning wireless traffic and then replacing a validated one with their own MAC. Task 1 with Wireshark should have revealed that MAC addresses do not get encrypted when travelling over the air between computer and wireless access point. A MAC address is "glued" into a network card, but it is possible to command the operating system to change information about the MAC address in every data packet it sends out to the network. In this way a spoofer could gain access to the white list protected network.

SSID broadcast disabled protection

Access points have the option to disable broadcasting their SSID. This means that the SSID will not appear in the client's network settings window (see Figure 9.2.3.4). Clients who already know the pre-configured SSID can establish a connection, others will not be able to (without a bit of extra effort). Unfortunately, clients who already know the SSID cause the SSID to be revealed to snoopers when establishing a connection with the access point. Before the authentication stage begins, the client sends a Probe Request message and receives a Probe Response from the access point in return as shown in Figure 9.2.3.24. The (unencrypted) SSID is present in these packets, therefore reducing the effectiveness of disabling broadcasting of the SSID.

To discover the SSID, a snooper might first send a deauthentication message to the stations that are connected to force them to disconnect and reconnect. Reconnecting should cause Probe and Response Request messages to be broadcast which reveal the SSID.

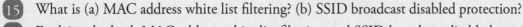

```
156 Probe Request, SN=0, FN=0, Flags=........, SSID=Kevin Bond's Guest Network
259 Probe Response, SN=1192, FN=0, Flags=........C, BI=100, SSID=Kevin Bond's Guest Network
```

Figure 9.2.3.24 Probe and Response Request frame/packets captured with Wireshark to reveal the SSID

Questions

15 What is (a) MAC address white list filtering? (b) SSID broadcast disabled protection?

16 Explain why both MAC address white list filtering and SSID broadcast disabled protection are insufficient alone to protect a wireless network.

In this chapter you have covered:

- The purpose of WiFi
- The components required for wireless networking
- How wireless networks are secured
- The wireless protocol Carrier Sensing Multiple Access with Collision Avoidance (CSMA/CA) with and without Request to Send/Clear to Send (RTS/CTS)
- The purpose of Service Set Identifier (SSID)

Index

Symbols

A

B

C

D

E

F

G

H

I

J

K

L

M

N

O

P

Q

R

S

T

U

V

W

X

Z

Lightning Source UK Ltd.
Milton Keynes UK
UKHW051151170919
349931UK00004B/8/P